T0192028

# Lecture Notes in Computer Science     13205

## Founding Editors

Gerhard Goos
  *Karlsruhe Institute of Technology, Karlsruhe, Germany*

Juris Hartmanis
  *Cornell University, Ithaca, NY, USA*

## Editorial Board Members

Elisa Bertino
  *Purdue University, West Lafayette, IN, USA*

Wen Gao
  *Peking University, Beijing, China*

Bernhard Steffen
  *TU Dortmund University, Dortmund, Germany*

Gerhard Woeginger
  *RWTH Aachen, Aachen, Germany*

Moti Yung
  *Columbia University, New York, NY, USA*

More information about this series at https://link.springer.com/bookseries/558

Tassadit Bouadi · Elisa Fromont ·
Eyke Hüllermeier (Eds.)

# Advances in Intelligent Data Analysis XX

20th International Symposium on Intelligent Data Analysis, IDA 2022
Rennes, France, April 20–22, 2022
Proceedings

 Springer

*Editors*
Tassadit Bouadi 🆔
University of Rennes
Rennes, France

Elisa Fromont 🆔
University of Rennes
Rennes, France

Eyke Hüllermeier 🆔
University of Munich, LMU
Munich, Germany

ISSN 0302-9743 ISSN 1611-3349 (electronic)
Lecture Notes in Computer Science
ISBN 978-3-031-01332-4 ISBN 978-3-031-01333-1 (eBook)
https://doi.org/10.1007/978-3-031-01333-1

© The Editor(s) (if applicable) and The Author(s), under exclusive license
to Springer Nature Switzerland AG 2022
This work is subject to copyright. All rights are reserved by the Publisher, whether the whole or part of the material is concerned, specifically the rights of translation, reprinting, reuse of illustrations, recitation, broadcasting, reproduction on microfilms or in any other physical way, and transmission or information storage and retrieval, electronic adaptation, computer software, or by similar or dissimilar methodology now known or hereafter developed.
The use of general descriptive names, registered names, trademarks, service marks, etc. in this publication does not imply, even in the absence of a specific statement, that such names are exempt from the relevant protective laws and regulations and therefore free for general use.
The publisher, the authors and the editors are safe to assume that the advice and information in this book are believed to be true and accurate at the date of publication. Neither the publisher nor the authors or the editors give a warranty, expressed or implied, with respect to the material contained herein or for any errors or omissions that may have been made. The publisher remains neutral with regard to jurisdictional claims in published maps and institutional affiliations.

This Springer imprint is published by the registered company Springer Nature Switzerland AG
The registered company address is: Gewerbestrasse 11, 6330 Cham, Switzerland

# Preface

We are delighted to introduce the proceedings of the 20th International Symposium on Intelligent Data Analysis (IDA 2022).

IDA is a worldwide scientific event that aims at exploiting new ideas and applications for intelligent data analysis. We were delighted that the community decided to have IDA 2022 in France, especially after being deprived of face-to-face relationships during the COVID-19 pandemic for almost two years.

IDA is traditionally limited to a small-scale, single-track meeting, allowing a fruitful discussion without parallel spreading of researchers, but with a research-oriented program that aims at being a forum for high quality, novel research in intelligent data analysis. This year, we again followed this tradition. The research program also included four invited speakers, namely Dominique Lavenier, Cynthia C. S. Liem, Michèle Sebag, and Julia Stoyanovich, one PhD track, and the well-renowned Frontier Prize. The event received 73 paper submissions, of which 31 (42%) were accepted for inclusion in the symposium after a round of blind reviewing, where we managed to collect at least three independent, high-quality reviews per paper. Papers were evaluated on the basis of common scientific criteria such as novelty, technical quality, scholarship, and significance, though always keeping in mind IDA's mission to promote potential breakthroughs and game-changing ideas over elaboration to the last detail. This volume contains the full papers accepted for presentation at the symposium meeting. The scientific program resulted from continuous collaboration between the general chair and the program co-chairs.

We would also like to acknowledge Albrecht Zimmermann for his helpful advice and publicity work, Jaakko Hollmén for choosing and delivering the Frontier Prize (sponsored by Knime), and Pance Panov for managing the PhD track. Throughout we had the unfaltering support of the local organizers and in particular Edith Blin, Nathalie Lacaux, and Gaëlle Tworkowski from Inria. The quality of IDA 2022 was only possible due to the tremendous efforts of the Program Committee—our sincere thanks for all the great work and patience to make these proceedings possible. Last but not least, we would like to sincerely thank all the authors who submitted their work to the symposium. We are convinced this volume of proceedings will allow you to remember the fruitful and everlasting event that was held in Rennes.

February 2022

Tassadit Bouadi
Elisa Fromont
Eyke Hüllermeier

# Organization

## General Chair

Elisa Fromont      Université de Rennes 1, France

## Program Co-chairs

Tassadit Bouadi      Université de Rennes 1, France
Eyke Hüllermeier      Ludwig-Maximilians-Universität München,
     Germany

## Program Committee

| | |
|---|---|
| Ehsan Aminian | Iran University of Science and Technology, Iran |
| José P. Amorim | University of Coimbra, Portugal |
| Thiago Andrade | INESC TEC, Portugal |
| Paulo Azevedo | University of Minho, Portugal |
| Michael Berthold | University of Konstanz, Germany |
| Adrien Bibal | Université catholique de Louvain, Belgium |
| Hendrik Blockeel | Katholieke Universiteit Leuven, Belgium |
| Jose Borges | University of Porto, Portugal |
| Henrik Boström | KTH Royal Institute of Technology, Sweden |
| Tassadit Bouadi | IRISA, Université Rennes 1, France |
| Paula Branco | University of Ottawa, Canada |
| Paula Brito | University of Porto, Portugal |
| Dariusz Brzezinski | Poznan University of Technology, Poland |
| Humberto Bustince | UPNA, Spain |
| Rui Camacho | University of Porto, Portugal |
| Ricardo Cardoso Pereira | University of Coimbra, Portugal |
| Paulo Cortez | University of Minho, Portugal |
| Bruno Cremilleux | Université de Caen Normandie, France |
| Sebastian Dalleiger | CISPA Helmholtz Center, Germany |
| Thi-Bich-Hanh Dao | University of Orleans, France |
| Claudia Camila Dias | University of Porto, Portugal |
| Wouter Duivesteijn | Eindhoven University of Technology, The Netherlands |
| Saso Dzeroski | Jozef Stefan Institute, Slovenia |
| Fazel Famili | University of Ottawa, Canada |

| | |
|---|---|
| Hadi Fanaee-T | Halmstad University, Sweden |
| Brígida Mónica Faria | Polytechnic of Porto, Portugal |
| Ad Feelders | Utrecht University, The Netherlands |
| Alberto Fernández | University of Granada, Spain |
| Sebastien Ferre | CNRS, IRISA, Université de Rennes 1, France |
| Carlos Ferreira | LIAAD-INESC Porto LA, Portugal |
| Cesar Ferri | Universitat Politècnica de València, Spain |
| Francoise Fessant | France Telecom R&D, France |
| Benoît Frénay | Université de Namur, Belgium |
| Elisa Fromont | Université de Rennes 1, France |
| Mikel Galar | Universidad Pública de Navarra, Spain |
| Esther Galbrun | University of Eastern FInland, Finland |
| Luis Galárraga | Inria, France |
| Romaric Gaudel | Ensai, CREST, Université de Rennes 1, France |
| Rui Gomes | University of Coimbra, Portugal |
| Tias Guns | Vrije Universiteit Brussel, Belgium |
| Thomas Guyet | Inria, France |
| Barbara Hammer | Bielefeld University, Germany |
| Pedro Henriques Abreu | University of Coimbra, Portugal |
| Martin Holena | Czech Academy of Sciences, Czech Republic |
| Jaakko Hollmén | Aalto University, Finland |
| Tomas Horvath | Eötvös Loránd University, Hungary |
| Frank Höppner | Ostfalia University of Applied Sciences, Germany |
| Baptiste Jeudy | Laboratoire Hubert Curien, France |
| Bo Kang | Ghent University, Belgium |
| Frank Klawonn | Ostfalia University of Applied Sciences, Germany |
| Arno Knobbe | Universiteit Leiden, The Netherlands |
| Bartosz Krawczyk | Virginia Commonwealth University, USA |
| Georg Krempl | Utrecht University, The Netherlands |
| Anne Laurent | LIRMM, Université de Montpellier, France |
| Nada Lavrač | Jozef Stefan Institute, Slovenia |
| Xiaohui Liu | Brunel University London, UK |
| João Mendes Moreira | INESC TEC, Portugal |
| Vera Migueis | University of Porto, Portugal |
| Ioanna Miliou | Stockholm University, Sweden |
| Alina Miron | Brunel University London, UK |
| Nuno Moniz | INESC TEC and University of Porto, Portugal |
| Mohamed Nadif | Université de Paris, France |
| Ana Nogueira | LIAAD, INESC TEC, Portugal |
| Andreas Nürnberger | Otto-von-Guericke-Universität Magdeburg, Germany |
| Rita P. Ribeiro | University of Porto, Portugal |

| Kaustubh Raosaheb Patil | Massachusetts Institute of Technology, USA |
| Ruggero G. Pensa | University of Turin, Italy |
| Pedro Pereira Rodrigues | University of Porto, Portugal |
| Marc Plantevit | LIRIS, Université Claude Bernard Lyon 1, France |
| Lubos Popelinsky | Masaryk University, Czech Republic |
| Filipe Portela | University of Minho, Portugal |
| Ronaldo Prati | Universidade Federal do ABC, Brazil |
| Jan Ramon | Inria, France |
| Luis Paulo Reis | APPIA and LIACC, University of Porto, Portugal |
| Solange Rezende | University of São Paulo, Brazil |
| German Rodriguez | CUD-ENM, Spain |
| Duncan D. Ruiz | Pontifical Catholic University of Rio Grande do Sul, Porto Alegre, Portugal |
| Miriam Santos | University of Coimbra, Portugal |
| Jörg Schlötterer | University of Duisburg-Essen, Germany |
| Roberta Siciliano | University of Naples Federico II, Italy |
| Arno Siebes | Utrecht University, The Netherlands |
| Paula Silva | University of Porto, Portugal |
| Arnaud Soulet | Université de Tours, France |
| Myra Spiliopoulou | Otto-von-Guericke-University Magdeburg, Germany |
| Jerzy Stefanowski | Poznan University of Technology, Poland |
| Stephen Swift | Brunel University London, UK |
| José A. Sáez | University of Salamanca, Spain |
| Shazia Tabassum | University of Porto, Portugal |
| Maguelonne Teisseire | Irstea, UMR Tetis, France |
| César Teixeira | University of Coimbra, Portugal |
| Sónia Teixeira | INESC TEC, Portugal |
| Alexandre Termier | Université de Rennes 1, France |
| Alicia Troncoso | Universidad Pablo de Olavide, Spain |
| Allan Tucker | Brunel University London, UK |
| Peter van der Putten | LIACS, Leiden University and Pegasystems, The Netherlands |
| Matthijs van Leeuwen | Leiden University, The Netherlands |
| Fabio Vandin | University of Padua, Italy |
| Cor Veenman | Netherlands Forensic Institute, The Netherlands |
| Bruno Veloso | Universidade Portucalense and LIAAD, INESC TEC, Portugal |
| João Vinagre | INESC TEC, Portugal |
| Veronica Vinciotti | University of Trento, Italy |
| David Weston | Birkbeck, University of London, UK |
| Paul Youssef | University of Duisburg-Essen, Germany |

Filip Zelezny                      Czech Technical University, Czech Republic
Leishi Zhang                       Canterbury Christ Church University, UK
Albrecht Zimmermann                Université Caen Normandie, France
Indre Zliobaite                    University of Helsinki, Finland

## Additional Reviewers

Ayats, Hugo
Breskvar, Martin
Guyomard, Victor
Kafando, Kafando
Kostovska, Ana
Melgar-García, Laura
Omidvarnia, Amir
Petković, Matej
Polley, Sayantan
Thiel, Marcus
Torres Maldonado, José Francisco
Troncoso García, Angela del Robledo

# Contents

# Multi-modal Ensembles of Regressor Chains for Multi-output Prediction

Ekaterina Antonenko[1,2(✉)] and Jesse Read[1]

[1] LIX, École Polytechnique, Institut Polytechnique de Paris, Palaiseau, France
ekaterina.antonenko@polytechnique.edu
[2] Digitalent lab (Moteur Intelligence Artificielle), Paris, France

**Abstract.** Multi-target regression is a predictive task involving multiple numerical outputs per instance. In the domain of multi-label classification there exist a large number of techniques that successfully model outputs together. Classifier Chains is one such example that is naturally extendable to the multi-target regression task (as Regressor Chains). However, although this method is straightforward to adapt to the regression setting, large improvements over independent models (as seen already in the multi-label classification context over the recent decade) have not as of yet been obtained from Regressor Chains. One of the reasons for this is the adoption of squared-error-based loss metrics which do not require consideration of joint-target modeling. In this paper, we consider cases where the predictive distribution can be multi-modal. Such a scenario, which easily manifests in real-world tasks involving uncertainty, motivates a different loss metric and, thereby, a different approach. We thus present a new method for multi-target regression: Multi-Modal Ensemble of Regressor Chains (mmERC), which performs competitively on datasets exhibiting a multi-modal distribution, both against independent regressors and state-of-the-art ensembles of regressor chains. We argue that such distributions are not sufficiently considered in the regression and particularly multi-target regression literature.

**Keywords:** Multi-target regression · Regressor chains · Multi-modal prediction

## 1 Introduction

Multi-target prediction refers to machine learning models predicting values for multiple variables for each test instance. Such techniques can be a solution to the nowadays extensively growing number of multi-output data science problems across academy and industry areas [18,19]. Multi-label classification, which refers to the multi-output case with binary variables, has made a significant progress in the previous decade. Within this area, Classifier Chains is a family of methods that have proved to have high predictive performance [3,15]. Compared to the naive approach with an independent classifier per label (known in the literature

© The Author(s), under exclusive license to Springer Nature Switzerland AG 2022
T. Bouadi et al. (Eds.): IDA 2022, LNCS 13205, pp. 1–13, 2022.
https://doi.org/10.1007/978-3-031-01333-1_1

as binary relevance), advanced methods such as Classifier Chains outperform w.r.t. most metrics. This has been widely attributed to their ability to extract and exploit the dependencies between the targets, as well as other factors linked to multi-target modeling [15,18].

Chaining methods can be adapted in a straightforward way to the regression context, however, their performance on regression tasks shows relatively few advantages compared to individual regression models.

There has been recent work attempting to unravel some of the explanations for Regressor Chains underperforming. It has been identified that Classifier Chains perform well with respect to the 0/1-loss, i.e., in the probabilistic sense, by seeking out a posterior *mode*. However, in the case of Regressor Chains, an almost-ubiquitous choice of loss metric is the mean squared error (MSE) or its variants; as also for regular regression problems. By definition, minimizing MSE is the same as maximizing the likelihood of a Gaussian distribution; it will thus correspondingly incur a posterior *mean-seeking* behaviour. This may be inadequate if the posterior is bi-modal or (more generally) multi-modal, as may be invoked by uncertainty under a multi-modal data distribution; a prediction may be placed between two modes not corresponding to the ground truth. This situation is illustrated in Fig. 1.

There are plentiful real-world examples of multi-modal outputs; e.g., in agriculture [17], evolution biology [6], and gene expression [12]. For instance, [6] considers a finch (*Geospiza fortis*) population that shows bi-modality in beak size, an important trait in this taxon, while [12] studies bi-modality in gene expression for certain pheromones, which allows a cell population to diversify its transcriptional response. In such cases, an estimate under MSE and under uncertainty can be inappropriate.

Naturally, this discussion of multi-modality relates to regression tasks in general, but it becomes particularly crucial in many multi-target regression problems due to the effect of error propagation [14] and the potential presence and complexity of modes.

This paper introduces a novel method, Multi-Modal Ensemble of Regressor Chains (mmERC), which combines an ensemble approach for Regressor Chains [16] and a novel mechanism designed to recognise the multi-modality and produce the predictions taking it into account. We argue that multi-modal scenarios are not widely studied in machine learning research (as opposed to statistics), while taking them into account can significantly boost power of machine learning methods. Our experimental results show the improvement of the performance of Regressor Chains with the novel technique. In particular, we show that mmERC can outperform independent regressors.

The rest of the paper is organized as follows. After summarizing background and related work in Sect. 2, we present our method in Sect. 3. We describe our implementation and the setup for comparison to independent regressors and standard Regressor Chains in Sect. 4. The results and their discussion are in Sect. 5. In Sect. 6, we draw the conclusions.

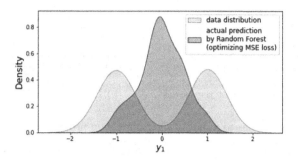

**Fig. 1.** A distribution of actual target labels vs predictions by Random Forest; both provided via a KDE estimate. Most predictions – when provided under uncertainty (inputs are poorly informative) – are in the space highly likely to be incorrect.

## 2    Background and Related Work

In a multi-target regression, we are given a dataset $\mathcal{D} = \{(\boldsymbol{x}^i, \boldsymbol{y}^i)\}_{i=1}^{N}$ of $N$ samples, each instance $\boldsymbol{x}^i = [x_1^i, ..., x_M^i]$ is associated with a vector $\boldsymbol{y}^i = [y_1^i, ..., y_L^i]$ of real numbers. One can build an independent model $h_j$ for each target $y_j$ and (for test instance $\boldsymbol{x}$) produce predictions

$$\hat{\boldsymbol{y}} = [\hat{y}_1, ..., \hat{y}_L] = [h_1(\boldsymbol{x}), ..., h_L(\boldsymbol{x})].$$

This approach is graphically represented in Fig. 2a. In the classification context, this approach is known as the *binary relevance* method and it has been widely improved upon by models which model targets together. For example, the method of Classifier Chains [15] arranges per-target (base) models in a chain, such that the prediction of one model becomes an additional feature for the subsequent models, obtaining predictions via:

$$\hat{\boldsymbol{y}} = [\hat{y}_1, ..., \hat{y}_L] = [h_1(\boldsymbol{x}), h_2(\boldsymbol{x}, \hat{y}_1), ..., h_L(\boldsymbol{x}, \hat{y}_1, ..., \hat{y}_{L-1})].$$

This approach is demonstrated in Fig. 2b. It is observed that performance of Regressor Chains can suffer from sensitivity to the chain order. Different approaches have been suggested to optimize chain order including evolutionary algorithms [11] and using correlation to build the best structure [9]. One of state-of-the-art solutions to overcome this issue is using an Ensemble of Regressor Chains (ERC) [16], where $n$ random chains are trained independently and then the final predictions are obtained as the means of the $n$ estimates for each target. The same mechanism is used, for example, in Random Forests [7], which output the average mean of a number of Decision Trees. However, we observe that while Ensembles of Regressor Chains work on average better than standard Regressor Chains, they may produce inadequate results in case of multi-modal distributions, and the improvement is neither as significant as in the classification scenario. This brings our interest to multi-modal regression.

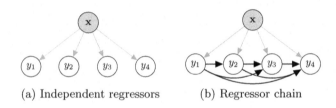

(a) Independent regressors        (b) Regressor chain

**Fig. 2.** Two approaches to a multi-target regression problem with $L = 4$ targets.

In taking a squared-error loss metric such as MSE, conventional regression models predict their estimated mean of the distribution. This approach may produce inadequate results if the data distribution is bi-modal or multi-modal (recall the example in Fig. 1) or whenever the mode is not close to the mean. Modal regression (e.g., [20]) is by definition more likely to capture a mode; values that are – in those settings – more likely to occur in practice. Multi-modal regression has been approached previous due to its properties of robustness to outliers and heavy tail distributions [4].

Mode estimation has been studied in the Bayesian statistics literature [1,2]. These methods suggest, in particular, optimizing the Uniform Cost Function (which we have denoted below in Eq. (2)), as an approximation of 0/1 loss. We recall that Classifier Chains are a natural choice if the 0/1-loss is to be used, yet this metric cannot be directly optimized in the regression context where an *exact match* is unlikely to be obtained on the continuous spectrum. In any case, these mentioned works do not consider the multi-target regression case. Multi-modality was considered in the context of multi-target regression in [14], but specifically to probabilistic models, therefore their study could not include methods such as decision trees; and results were not strong. In our experiments, decision trees show competitive performance both as independent methods and as base models for Regressor Chains.

## 3   Multi-modal Ensemble of Regressor Chains

We present our novel method based on Ensembles of Regressor Chains, which targets the Uniform Cost Function (UCF) in order to provide successful outputs in the context of multi-modal predictive distributions; in two mechanisms.

### 3.1   Mechanism 1: Base Estimator Training

Using UCF as a loss function promotes mode-seeking by entailing a uniform penalty when the correct mode is not found; unlike MSE which entails a quadratic penalty (compare under Fig. 3). We select correntropy [5]

$$\text{corr}(y^i, \hat{y}^i) = 1 - e^{-(y^i - \hat{y}^i)^2}, \quad i = 1, \dots, N \tag{1}$$

as a smooth approximation of UCF, allowing fine-grained threshold selection.

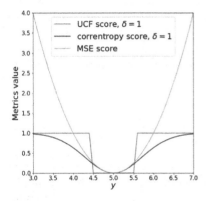

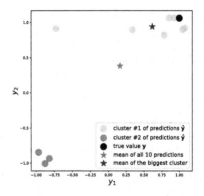

**Fig. 3.** Comparison of MSE, UCF, and correntropy errors; for single target estimate where true $y = 5$.

**Fig. 4.** mmERC, mechanism 2: average of the largest cluster gives the prediction closer to the ground truth.

---

**Algorithm 1.** mmERC: Training $h_j$ for target $y_j$ (done for $j = 1, \ldots, L$)

1: **procedure** FIT($h_j$, $\{x, y_j\}$)    ▷ Train Base Estimator $h_j$ for target $y_j$ on $\{x, y_j\}$
2:    $\tilde{h}_j \leftarrow$ clone of $h_j$
3:    fit $\tilde{h}_j$ on $\{(x, y_j)\}$    ▷ First training phase (full training set)
4:    $y_{pred} \leftarrow \tilde{h}_j(x)$    ▷ Prediction of $\tilde{h}_j$ on $x$
5:    $corr \leftarrow 1 - e^{-(y_j - y_{pred})^2}$    ▷ Correntropy; See Eq. 1
6:    $\{x', y_j'\} \subset \{x, y_j\}$    ▷ Top $s$-instances wrt (lowest) $corr$, $0 < s < 1$
7:    fit $h_j$ on $\{(x', y_j')\}$    ▷ Second training phase
8:    **return** $h_j$    ▷ Return the trained model

---

In the vein of regressor chains, we train one target (corresponding to one base estimator) at a time; $y_j | j = 1, \ldots, L$. However we propose a second step, in which we select a portion $0 < s < 1$ of instances $\{(x^i, y^i)\}$ with the lowest correntropy $corr(y^i - \hat{y}^i)$ and train a second regressor on this reduced dataset.

This process bears some resemblance to iteratively reweighted least squares or expectation maximization (EM) as mentioned in [20] for the context of single-target regression; however, here we only take a single step rather than an iterative EM-like procedure. The mechanism is summarized as pseudocode in Algorithm 1; where $s$ is a hyper-parameter.

### 3.2   Mechanism 2: Ensemble Mode Prediction

We train an ensemble of Regressor Chains, each with a random order. Most ensemble methods (e.g., Random Forests [7] and ERC [16]) use mean averaging to obtain the final predictions. But we would like to fit our models on datasets with a multi-modal distribution (and have them identify a mode).

Therefore, instead of averaging, we first apply K-means clustering [8] in order to identify modes, and then produce the mean of the largest cluster as an estimate of the mode of the predictive distributions. An example is given in Fig. 4. We select 10 Regressor Chains in ensemble as a standard trade-off between accuracy of prediction and computation time.

## 4   Experiments

### 4.1   Methods

Table 1 summarizes the methods used in the experiments; all of which as implemented in Scikit-Learn [13]. We experimented with different base estimators for multi-target methods (as indicated in the table). The implementation of our novel approach (Multi-Modal Ensemble of Regressor Chains; mmERC) is publicly available at https://github.com/ekaantonenko/mmERC.

**Table 1.** Regression methods compared in the experiments

|  | (Meta)Method | Base estimator |
|---|---|---|
| DT | Multi-output Decision Tree | |
| RF | Multi-output Random Forest | |
| IR (dt) | Independent Regressors | Decision Tree |
| IR (rf) | Independent Regressors | Random Forest |
| IR (svr) | Independent Regressors | Support Vector Regression |
| RC (dt) | Regressor Chain | Decision Tree |
| RC (rf) | Regressor Chain | Random Forest |
| RC (svr) | Regressor Chain | Support Vector Regression |
| ERC (dt) | Ensembles of Regressor Chains | Decision Tree |
| ERC (rf) | Ensembles of Regressor Chains | Random Forest |
| ERC (svr) | Ensembles of Regressor Chains | Support Vector Regression |
| mmERC (dt) | Multi-Modal Ensembles of Regressor Chains | Decision Tree |
| mmERC (rf) | Multi-Modal Ensembles of Regressor Chains | Random Forest |
| mmERC (svr) | Multi-Modal Ensembles of Regressor Chains | Support Vector Regression |

### 4.2   Evaluation

We used two evaluation metrics: average Relative Root Mean Squared Error (aRRMSE), which is common to use in multi-target regression;

$$\text{aRRMSE} = \frac{1}{L}\sum_{j=1}^{L}\sqrt{\frac{\sum_{i=1}^{N}(y_j^i - \hat{y}_j^i)^2}{\sum_{i=1}^{N}(y_j^i - \overline{y}_j)^2}},$$

(where $\bar{y}_j$ is the mean value of the $j$-th target in the training data); and UCF [2] – an analog of the 0/1 loss for regression problems within given neighbourhood $\delta$ of the true values:

$$\mathsf{UCF}(\delta) = \frac{1}{N} \sum_{i=1}^{N} \begin{cases} 0 \text{ if } \|\boldsymbol{y}^i - \hat{\boldsymbol{y}}^i\|_2 < \frac{\delta}{2}, \\ 1 \text{ otherwise,} \end{cases} \tag{2}$$

where $\delta$ is an adjustable parameter. For the experiments we take $\delta = 1.0$ for the targets scaled normally.

All the methods were evaluated using a 10-fold cross-validation.

### 4.3 Datasets

We evaluated our algorithm on 40 synthetic datasets and one real-world dataset.

We generate $40 = 8 \cdot 5$ synthetic datasets as pairwise combinations of 8 distributions for target variables $y_1, y_2$ and 5 distributions for a feature variable $x$. The distributions of target variables are Gaussian mixtures, forming a variety of shapes (Fig. 5). The feature variable $x$ is designed to provide little information about the targets and thus invoke high predictive uncertainty, so that the dependencies between the targets are even more useful for the model than the feature. Different distributions of $x$ reflect different degrees of uncertainty about which cluster the model should choose for a particular sample (Table 2).

A real-world dataset (432 instances) was taken from the R package *agricolae* [10] and refers to a native plant of the Peruvian Andes called *yacon* (Smallanthus sonchifolius). As targets, we consider two multi-modally distributed features from the dataset: *degrees brix* ( density or sugar concentration ) and *height* of the plant. We add feature $x \sim \mathcal{N}(0,1)$. The distributions of the targets are demonstrated in Fig. 6.

**Table 2.** Distributions of the feature $x$ in synthetic datasets

| | |
|---|---|
| A: | $\sim U(0,1)$ where $U$ stands for uniform distribution |
| B: | $\sim \{0,1\}$ (according to the cluster) |
| C: | $\{\sim U(0,1), \sim U(1,2)\}$ (according to the cluster) |
| D: | $\{\sim \mathcal{N}(0,1), \sim \mathcal{N}(1,1)\}$ (according to the cluster) |
| E: | $\sim \mathcal{N}(0,1)$ |

## 5 Results and Discussion

An initial investigation indicates that mmERCs achieves generally the best performance with a parameter value $s = 0.5$ in Algorithm 1, i.e. taking a half of the training dataset in the second training phase (see Fig. 7). The subsequent experiments in this paper were conducted with $s = 0.5$.

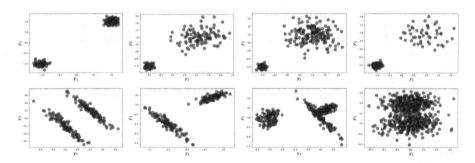

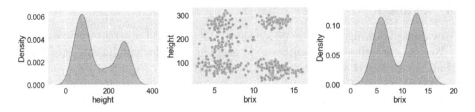

**Fig. 5.** Distributions of the targets $y_1, y_2$ in synthetic datasets

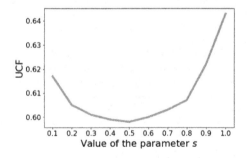

**Fig. 6.** Distributions of the targets in the *yacon* dataset.

**Fig. 7.** Averaged UCF for mmERC method, measured across all Synthetic datasets and grouped by value of the $s$ parameter, $s \in (0, 1]$

The experimental results for UCF metrics (Table 3a) show that our method, mmERC, on average outperforms the independent regressors as well as standard Regressor Chains with a sequential cascade order. This is already an important result not found in other Regressor Chains implementations. Moreover, our proposed mechanism to deal with multi-modal distributions improves Ensembles of Regressor Chains for all base estimators in most of the scenarios.

As expected, the results under aRRMSE are opposite (Table 3b). However, we show (Fig. 8) that mmERCs recognize clustered distributions better than ERCs both for Decision Trees and Random Forests as base estimators. The same situation is observed for the other datasets and other base estimators. We propose the following explanation: MSE-based metrics penalize choosing the

**Table 3.** Experimental results. For simplicity of presentation, we show results for synthetic datasets grouped and averaged by type of $x$ feature distribution as they reflect different degrees of uncertainty. This simplification does not affect average values of metrics and average ranks. The boldfaced numbers in the tables correspond to the best value per dataset. The results are rounded to 2 decimal points to display, so minor differences may be not seen in this representation.

| Regressor | A | B | C | D | E | Average | AvgRank |
|---|---|---|---|---|---|---|---|
| DT | 0.71 | 0.50 | 0.50 | 0.70 | 0.73 | 0.63 ± 0.01 | 7.9 |
| RF | 0.84 | 0.47 | 0.45 | 0.78 | 0.84 | 0.67 ± 0.04 | 10.2 |
| IR (dt) | 0.79 | 0.50 | 0.52 | 0.74 | 0.78 | 0.66 ± 0.02 | 11.1 |
| IR (rf) | 0.86 | 0.47 | 0.47 | 0.79 | 0.87 | 0.69 ± 0.04 | 11.0 |
| IR (svr) | 0.72 | **0.40** | 0.52 | 0.70 | 0.72 | 0.61 ± 0.02 | 6.0 |
| RC (dt) | 0.74 | 0.50 | 0.51 | 0.70 | 0.72 | 0.63 ± 0.01 | 8.6 |
| RC (rf) | 0.81 | 0.45 | 0.45 | 0.75 | 0.82 | 0.66 ± 0.03 | 8.8 |
| RC (svr) | 0.70 | **0.40** | 0.51 | 0.67 | 0.71 | 0.60 ± 0.02 | 4.2 |
| ERC (dt) | 0.78 | 0.50 | 0.49 | 0.72 | 0.76 | 0.65 ± 0.02 | 8.6 |
| ERC (rf) | 0.83 | 0.44 | **0.44** | 0.76 | 0.83 | 0.66 ± 0.04 | 8.6 |
| ERC (svr) | 0.71 | **0.40** | 0.50 | 0.67 | 0.72 | 0.60 ± 0.02 | 5.0 |
| mmERC (dt) | 0.72 | 0.50 | 0.51 | 0.69 | 0.71 | 0.63 ± 0.01 | 8.2 |
| mmERC (rf) | 0.69 | 0.43 | **0.44** | **0.63** | **0.67** | **0.57 ± 0.02** | **2.2** |
| mmERC (svr) | **0.69** | **0.40** | 0.52 | 0.67 | 0.68 | 0.59 ± 0.02 | 4.6 |

(a) UCF results for the synthetic datasets.

| DT | 1.46 | 0.64 | 0.67 | 1.38 | 1.48 | 1.13 ± 0.19 | 12.4 |
|---|---|---|---|---|---|---|---|
| RF | 1.17 | 0.55 | 0.55 | 1.11 | 1.17 | 0.91 ± 0.11 | 6.2 |
| IR (dt) | 1.47 | 0.64 | 0.69 | 1.38 | 1.47 | 1.13 ± 0.18 | 12.8 |
| IR (rf) | 1.17 | 0.55 | 0.55 | 1.11 | 1.17 | 0.91 ± 0.11 | 6.8 |
| IR (svr) | **1.10** | 0.46 | 0.60 | **1.02** | **1.10** | **0.86 ± 0.09** | 2.8 |
| RC (dt) | 1.46 | 0.64 | 0.69 | 1.40 | 1.47 | 1.13 ± 0.18 | 12.6 |
| RC (rf) | 1.29 | 0.53 | 0.54 | 1.21 | 1.30 | 0.97 ± 0.16 | 7.4 |
| RC (svr) | 1.13 | 0.46 | 0.60 | 1.05 | 1.12 | 0.87 ± 0.10 | 3.6 |
| ERC (dt) | 1.35 | 0.63 | 0.64 | 1.28 | 1.36 | 1.05 ± 0.14 | 10.0 |
| ERC (rf) | 1.17 | 0.51 | **0.52** | 1.09 | 1.17 | 0.90 ± 0.12 | 4.8 |
| ERC (svr) | 1.12 | **0.46** | 0.59 | 1.03 | 1.11 | **0.86 ± 0.10** | **2.6** |
| mmERC (dt) | 1.42 | 0.63 | 0.71 | 1.40 | 1.45 | 1.12 ± 0.17 | 12.2 |
| mmERC (rf) | 1.20 | 0.49 | 0.53 | 1.11 | 1.20 | 0.91 ± 0.13 | 5.8 |
| mmERC (svr) | 1.16 | 0.47 | 0.61 | 1.06 | 1.16 | 0.89 ± 0.11 | 5.0 |

(b) aRRMSE results for the synthetic datasets.

| DT | RF | IR (dt) | IR (rf) | IR (svr) | RC (dt) | RC (rf) | RC (svr) | ERC (dt) | ERC (rf) | ERC (svr) | mmERC (dt) | mmERC (rf) | mmERC (svr) |
|---|---|---|---|---|---|---|---|---|---|---|---|---|---|
| 0.92 | 0.94 | 0.92 | 0.94 | 0.91 | 0.92 | 0.94 | 0.92 | 0.92 | 0.94 | 0.94 | 0.89 | 0.89 | **0.83** |

(c) UCF results for the Yacon dataset.

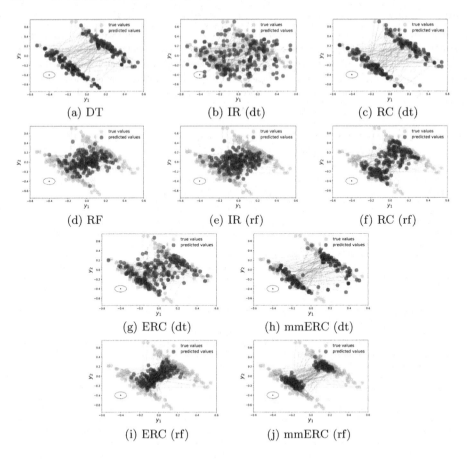

**Fig. 8.** Models based on DTs and RFs on one of synthetic datasets with a feature $x \sim \mathcal{N}(0, 1)$. Black lines connect pairwise true and predicted values. Black dashed ellipses represent size of $\delta$-neighborhood used in UCF metrics.

wrong cluster more than putting estimations in-between of actual clusters since the distance between prediction and the actual value is bigger in the former case. Thus, when a model recognizes a multi-modal distribution but fails to choose the right cluster for some points, it can perform worse under MSE-based metrics than models fitting to a single Gaussian distribution. We therefore argue that this standard choice of the aRRMSE metrics may be inappropriate in the case of multi-modal distributions and requires further investigation.

In general, Decision Trees and DT-based models recognize well clustered distributions, but in lack of informative features they assign clusters randomly. This can be seen on Random Forests (which are an average of a number of random Decision Trees) results: all models, based on Random Forests, put the predictions between the real clusters. Furthermore, Decision Trees are formed as sets of decision boundaries and thus are not smooth. Random Forests should be able to solve this issue, but, as we mentioned above, do not work well for recognising

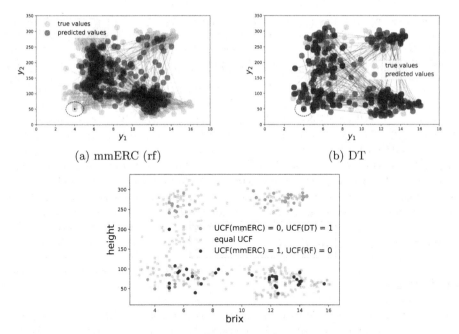

(a) mmERC (rf)                              (b) DT

(c) Comparison of mmERC (rf) and DT models on
*yacon* dataset. The mmERC (rf) method performs
better (w.r.t. UCF) on blue dots and worse on violet dots. On grey dots both methods have the same
UCF values.

**Fig. 9.** Performance of two models on *Yacon* dataset.

multi-modal nature. Our method, mmERC, improves the performance of Random Forests methods and outputs a smooth function at the same time.

In the *Yacon* dataset, we observe the best predictive performance under UCF
for the mmERC models (see Table 3c). Figure 9a and 9b illustrate performance
of the two models, mmERC (based on Random Forests) and Decision Trees.
Though graphically it seems that Decision Trees better mimic the clusters distribution, from the UCF comparison we imply that they assign these clusters
in a more random way. Figure 9c compares precision of predictions of these two
models per sample. It shows that our method is more precise on some of the
clusters. Though we have not observed a significant advantage of our method
on real-world datasets, we argue that it performs well on some datasets with
explicit multi-modality, particularly on some subsets of samples.

## 6    Conclusions and Future Work

In this work we have developed a new method, multi-modal Ensembles of
Regressor Chains (mmERC), for multi-target regression. As opposed to the

conventional approaches assuming a uni-modal predictive distribution approximating Gaussians, our approach is better able to capture the modes of the distribution.

In results mmERC achieves important performance improvement across the multi-modal distributed datasets, outperforming baseline and state-of-the-art improvements, which we modeled using the UCF metric. This is unlike the vast majority of multi-target (and standard single-target) regression approaches which target squared-error based metrics. Our study hints that this metric deserves further investigation.

In future work we will look at additional evaluation schemas, such as allowing multiple multi-output predictions (hypotheses) for a single instance. This would allow a greater chance of capturing the true mode, even when uncertainty is high. We will also work on adding more sophisticated structure of the chains in the ensembles in order to better exploit dependencies between the targets and achieve better predictive results.

# References

1. Bassett, R., Deride, J.: Maximum a posteriori estimators as a limit of Bayes estimators. Math. Program. **174**, 129–144 (2018). https://doi.org/10.1007/s10107-018-1241-0
2. Burger, M., Lucka, F.: Maximum a posteriori estimates in linear inverse problems with log-concave priors are proper Bayes estimators. Inverse Probl. **30**(11), 114004 (2014). https://doi.org/10.1088/0266-5611/30/11/114004
3. Dembczyński, K., Waegeman, W., Hüllermeier, E.: An analysis of chaining in multi-label classification. In: ECAI: European Conference of Artificial Intelligence, vol. 242, pp. 294–299. IOS Press (2012)
4. Feng, Y., Fan, J., Suykens, J.A.: A statistical learning approach to modal regression. J. Mach. Learn. Res. **21**(2), 1–35 (2020)
5. Fenga, Y., Huang, X., Shi, L., Yang, Y., Suykens, J.: Learning with the maximum correntropy criterion induced losses for regression. J. Mach. Learn. Res. **16**, 993–1034 (2015)
6. Hendry, A.P., Huber, S.K., León, L.F.D., Herrel, A., Podos, J.: Disruptive selection in a bimodal population of Darwin's finches. Proc. Roy. Soc. B: Biol. Sci. **276**(1657), 753–759 (2008). https://doi.org/10.1098/rspb.2008.1321
7. Ho, T.K.: Random decision forests. In: Proceedings of 3rd International Conference on Document Analysis and Recognition, vol. 1, pp. 278–282 (1995). https://doi.org/10.1109/ICDAR.1995.598994
8. Lloyd, S.: Least squares quantization in PCM. IEEE Trans. Inf. Theory **28**(2), 129–137 (1982). https://doi.org/10.1109/TIT.1982.1056489
9. Melki, G., Cano, A., Kecman, V., Ventura, S.: Multi-target support vector regression via correlation regressor chains. Inf. Sci. **415–416**, 53–69 (2017). https://doi.org/10.1016/j.ins.2017.06.017
10. de Mendiburu, F., de Mendiburu, M.: Package 'agricolae' (2019). https://cran.r-project.org/package=agricolae
11. Moyano, J.M., Gibaja, E.L., Ventura, S.: An evolutionary algorithm for optimizing the target ordering in ensemble of regressor chains. In: 2017 IEEE Congress on Evolutionary Computation (CEC), pp. 2015–2021. IEEE (2017)

12. Paliwal, S., Iglesias, P.A., Campbell, K., Hilioti, Z., Groisman, A., Levchenko, A.: MAPK-mediated bimodal gene expression and adaptive gradient sensing in yeast. Nature **446**(7131), 46–51 (2007). https://doi.org/10.1038/nature05561
13. Pedregosa, F., et al.: Scikit-learn: machine learning in Python. J. Mach. Learn. Res. **12**, 2825–2830 (2011)
14. Read, J., Martino, L.: Probabilistic regressor chains with Monte Carlo methods. Neurocomputing **413**, 471–486 (2020). https://doi.org/10.1016/j.neucom.2020.05.024
15. Read, J., Pfahringer, B., Holmes, G., Frank, E.: Classifier chains: a review and perspectives. J. Artif. Intell. Res. (JAIR) **70**, 683–718 (2021)
16. Spyromitros-Xioufis, E., Tsoumakas, G., Groves, W., Vlahavas, I.: Multi-target regression via input space expansion: treating targets as inputs. Mach. Learn. **104**(1), 55–98 (2016). https://doi.org/10.1007/s10994-016-5546-z
17. Vasconcelos, J.C.S., Cordeiro, G.M., Ortega, E.M.M.: Édila Maria de Rezende: a new regression model for bimodal data and applications in agriculture. J. Appl. Stat. **48**(2), 349–372 (2021). https://doi.org/10.1080/02664763.2020.1723503
18. Waegeman, W., Dembczyński, K., Hüllermeier, E.: Multi-target prediction: a unifying view on problems and methods. Data Min. Knowl. Disc. **33**(2), 293–324 (2018). https://doi.org/10.1007/s10618-018-0595-5
19. Xu, D., Shi, Y., Tsang, I.W., Ong, Y.S., Gong, C., Shen, X.: Survey on multi-output learning. EEE Trans. Neural Netw. Learn. Syst. **31**(7), 2409–2429 (2019)
20. Yao, W., Li, L.: A new regression model: modal linear regression. Scand. J. Stat. **41**(3), 656–671 (2014). https://doi.org/10.1111/sjos.12054

# A Two-Step Approach for Explainable Relation Extraction

Hugo Ayats[(⊠)], Peggy Cellier, and Sébastien Ferré

Univ Rennes, INSA, CNRS, IRISA, Campus de Beaulieu, 35042 Rennes, France
{hugo.ayats,peggy.cellier,sebastien.ferre}@irisa.fr

**Abstract.** Knowledge Graphs (KG) offer easy-to-process information. An important issue to build a KG from texts is the Relation Extraction (RE) task that identifies and labels relationships between entity mentions. In this paper, to address the RE problem, we propose to combine a deep learning approach for relation detection, and a symbolic method for relation classification. It allows to have at the same time the performance of deep learning methods and the interpretability of symbolic methods. This method has been evaluated and compared with state-of-the-art methods on TACRED, a relation extraction benchmark, and has shown interesting quantitative and qualitative results.

## 1 Introduction

Knowledge Graphs (KG) [10] have the advantage to offer easy-to-process information. However, most available information is still in the form of texts. A key problem is therefore the extraction of KGs from text, which amounts to identify named entities and relationships [16]. Relation Extraction (RE) [9] is the sub-problem of identifying and labelling relationships, assuming that the named entities have already been identified. Currently, the best scores on RE are achieved by deep learning methods, such as LUKE [22] or BERT [4]. While their scores have recently increased significantly (e.g., F1-score 72.7 for LUKE), the KGs that would result from their systematic application would still be noisy and incomplete to a large extent (e.g., 30% incorrect triples, and 25% missing triples for LUKE). Therefore, a completely automated process does not seem realistic if we aim at reliable and complete KGs and the RE task is too tedious to perform by hand only.

It seems necessary to introduce some human control in the extraction process while providing support for automation. Our idea is to base the automation on an increasing set of extraction rules, which are generated from previous examples and validated by humans. Human validation ensures the reliability of the extracted KG, and the generic aspect of rules supports the automation of the information extraction process. In this paper, we focus on the sub-task of generating extraction rules from *examples*, i.e. sentences in which relationships have already been identified and labelled. Unfortunately, deep learning methods only predict relationships at the instance level, they do not provide information that

© The Author(s), under exclusive license to Springer Nature Switzerland AG 2022
T. Bouadi et al. (Eds.): IDA 2022, LNCS 13205, pp. 14–25, 2022.
https://doi.org/10.1007/978-3-031-01333-1_2

can be leveraged into general and interpretable extraction rules. In previous work [1] a symbolic approach based on Concepts of Neighbours [5] was proposed to provide explainable predictions. Those explanations have the potential to be translated into extraction rules. However, it only solves the sub-problem of *relation classification*, i.e. when the relationships have already been detected and only remains to be labelled. Indeed, explanations can be found for the label of a relationship but hardly for the absence of a relationship as there are many ways for two entities not to be in relationship.

To address the RE problem, we propose to combine a deep learning approach for relation detection, and the symbolic approach based on Concepts of Neighbours for relation classification. It allows to have at the same time the performance of deep learning methods and the interpretability of symbolic methods. We conducted experiments showing that in terms of F1-score on the full RE task, our composite approach is comparable to deep learning approaches using the same kind of information from texts (i.e., syntactic structure, lexical semantics), namely GCN and C-GCN [23]. In contrast to deep learning methods, our approach generates explanations for each prediction, and convert them into extraction rules. Those extraction rules exhibit rich structures, mixing different levels of information from texts: lexical, syntactical, and semantic. In addition, they are generalizations of the current prediction, which makes them useful for the automation of future extractions.

## 2   Related Works

Most approaches addressing the Relation Extraction task use deep learning methods. Historically, convolutional neural networks [19] and LSTM [21] were used first, then were replaced by graph convolution networks methods [23], which allow to take into account the syntactic structure of sentences. Currently, the approaches that give the best results for the RE task use pre-trained language models such as BERT [4] and its variants [11,22]. However, the performance of those approaches (with an F-score between 70 and 75% on the TACRED benchmark [24]) are still too low to allow a full automation. In addition, those fully statistical approaches lack of explanations for their predictions, which limits the possibilities of introducing human control in the process to improve reliability.

Symbolic approaches have also been proposed for the RE task. Their performance are often lower than deep learning methods, but by definition they provide interpretable results that can be used in a process with human control. The first symbolic approaches use rules such as regular expressions [8] or syntactic patterns [7]. However, these rules are handcrafted and thus those approaches are time consuming and often devoted to a specific corpus. Some symbolic approaches automatically learn the linguistic rules. For instance [3] uses pattern mining techniques to automatically extract those rules. The method presented in [2] combines symbolic and machine learning techniques and proposes to learn patterns from a list of seed terms, i.e. pairs of entities known to be in some target relation. More recently, two symbolic approaches based on Formal

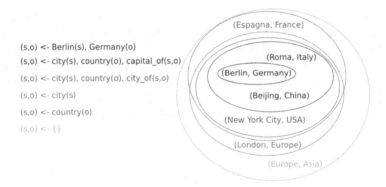

**Fig. 1.** Example of concepts of neighbours

Concept Analysis (FCA) have been proposed to populate a KG from texts [1,12]. The latter is based on Concepts of Neighbours, which have also been used for KG completion [6].

## 3    Relation Classification with Concepts of Neighbours

In this section, we describe the use of Concepts of Neighbours for the problem of explainable relation classification. Given a sentence (e.g., "Berlin became the capital of Germany in 1990"), two named entities in the sentence (e.g., "Berlin" and "Germany"), and the assumption that there is a relationship between the two entities, the problem is to predict the label of the relationship (e.g., "is the capital of"), and to provide interpretable explanations for the predicted label. The work presented in this section is developed in more details in [1].

### 3.1    Concepts of Neighbours

Concepts of Neighbours [5] is a graph mining method for entity-relation graphs that aims, for a given tuple of entities, to compute which are the most similar tuples of entities. It can be seen as a symbolic form of the k-nearest neighbours method, where numeric distances are replaced by common graph patterns. The bigger the common graph pattern between two tuples, the closer they are. For example, suppose that we want to find couple of entities similar to *(Berlin, Germany)* in a graph about geography. Concepts of Neighbours hierarchically clusters all couples of entities into *concepts* according to their similarity with *(Berlin, Germany)*. Figure 1 shows the set of concepts as a Venn diagram. Each concept is defined by its *intension*, which is a graph pattern with distinguished variables, and its *extension*, which is the set of couples matching the intension. It can be seen that *(Roma, Italy)* is a close neighbour as it shares the "capital of" relation, while *(New York, USA)* is a farther neighbour because New York is only a city of USA. The *proper extension* of a concept is defined as the subset

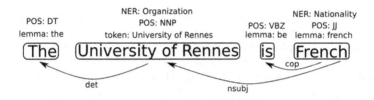

**Fig. 2.** Example of sentence modeling

of tuples of its extension that are not in the extension of more specific concepts. The *extensional distance* is defined as the size of its extension, and can be used as a numerical distance.

### 3.2 Application to Text

In order to apply Concepts of Neighbours to texts, we first need to model a text as an entity-relation graph. Figure 2 shows the modeling of the sentence "The University of Rennes is French". We rely on NLP tools and resources to extract syntactic and semantic information from text[1].

The graph representing each sentence is defined as follows. *Tokens* are used as entities, and are linked by the *dependency relations. Lemmas, named entity types* and *part-of-speech (POS) tags* are then added as entity labels.

From there we apply a few enhancements to the graph. First, some named entities extend over several tokens but have a syntactic and semantic unity: e.g. "University of Rennes" is split in three tokens. We decided to merge those tokens into a single entity in our graph representation, and to label it with the concatenation of tokens instead of using the lemmas, considering them as proper nouns. Second, we enrich the graph labelling following syntactic and semantic inferences. The objective is to help finding common graph patterns with Concepts of Neighbours. For instance, on the syntactic side, singular nouns have POS tag NN whereas plural nouns have POS tag NNS. To relax the singular/plural distinction, we infer POS tag NN for every entity that has POS tag NNS. On the semantic side, given an entity labelled with some lemma (e.g. "school"), we infer labels for the synonyms and hypernyms of the lemma (e.g., "educational institution")[2]. The Concepts of Neighbours method is capable of handling such inferences efficiently, without having to materialize them in the graph, by relying on a partial ordering over the entity and relation labels.

### 3.3 Application to Relation Classification

Given the graph modeling of a text, and the choice of a couple of named entities (*subject, object*), Concepts of Neighbours can compute a set a concepts of neighbours, each concept being associated with a set of neighbour couples (the proper

---

[1] We decided to use the *Stanford CoreNLP* toolkit [15].

[2] We used *WordNet* [18] to do so.

extension), and to an extensional distance. From there, a label of the relation from *subject* to *object* can be predicted by looking at the relationships holding for the neighbour couples of each concept $c$. Intuitively, the more neighbours in the proper extension of $c$ hold some relation $r$, and the smaller the extensional distance of $c$, then the stronger the prediction for relation $r$ is. This is formalized as the confidence of the rule $R_{r,c} : P_c \to r(s,o)$, where $(s,o) \leftarrow P_c$ is the intension of concept $c$.

$$conf(R_{r,c}) = \frac{|\{(s,o) \mid r(s,o)\} \cap ext(c)|}{ext\_dist(c)}$$

To aggregate the rules from all concepts to all relations and to get a ranking of predicted relations, we use *Maximum Confidence* [17], which was applied with success for link prediction [6,17]. Informally, the predicted relation is the relation which has the higher maximal confidence. In case of equality, the predicted relation is the one with the higher second maximal confidence, and so on.

In practice, the generic prediction method presented above is specialized to the settings of relation extraction benchmarks like TACRED. First, neighbours are only searched among the couples of entities that are annotated by a relation that is compatible with the entity types, according to the RECENT paradigm [13]. Second, we apply the pruning strategy proposed in [23], where only tokens that are at a maximal distance $k$ of the path between the subject and object are kept in the representation of a sentence.

## 4   A Two-Step Approach for Relation Extraction

The method presented in the previous section works by similarity, classifying test examples among the different relations according to similar training examples. If it works for deciding *which* relation exists between a subject and an object, it does not work for knowing *if* a relation exists. Indeed, there is no reason for a negative example (*i.e.* an example with no relation) to look like other negative examples. Therefore, this method can perform *relation classification* but cannot perform *relation detection*. However, those two steps are necessary to perform proper relation extraction.

The idea is to combine two methods, one for relation detection only, and the method presented in the above section for relation classification. Figure 3 presents how such a system works: the method for relation detection discriminates the positive examples from the negative examples, and our neighbours-based method classifies the positive examples among the compatible relation types. Such a two-step approach has already been exploited with promising results [14].

### 4.1   Relation Detection with Deep Learning

As there is no efficient symbolic or fully explainable method for relation detection that we know of, we decided to favor performance and therefore to use a state-of-the-art deep learning approach. Moreover, there is not much need to explain the

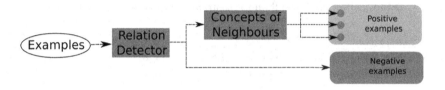

**Fig. 3.** Two-step relation classification process

non-existence of a relation, and an explanation for a type of relation is also an explanation for the existence of a relation. Today, the state-of-the-art in relation extraction is dominated by pre-trained language models such as BERT [4] and its variants. One of those variants, LUKE [22], has the particularity to handle both single words and multi-word entities, and has shown impressive results on diverse NLP tasks, including relation extraction. We decided to use this model as a relation detector.

We consider several configurations of LUKE for relation detection. The first one, called *luke-base*, simply consists in reusing the fully trained model for relation extraction and post-process the output in order to merge all the positive predictions into one class. A second configuration, called *luke-detect* consists in specializing LUKE for relation detection. We remove LUKE's last classification layer, and replace it by two layers: a fully connected layer of size $n$ and an output neuron with a *sigmoid* activation function. Then the model is fine-tuned in order for it to predict 1 on the positive examples and 0 on the negative examples.

## 4.2   Explainability

The main asset of this two-step method is its explainability: for a given prediction, if this prediction is not *no_relation*, the method is able to provide an explanation. This limitation to positive prediction may seem odd, but this can be understood by the fact that if it is easy to imagine how to explain why there is a relation between two examples (by giving other annotated examples looking like the given example), it is more complicated to explain why a given example has no relation between its subject and its object, as negative examples do not have to look like other negative examples.

For a given example annotated as positive, the raw explanation that can be given is the whole set of Concepts of Neighbours of this example. However, whereas it is a complete explanation, it is hardly readable for a non-expert. However, among this set of concepts, only a few ones are used to make a prediction: the ones that have an intension which was used to create a rule of maximum confidence. Therefore, by displaying those intensions and the examples matching it, we obtain a short and readable explanation (only a few graph patterns and the related sentences).

**Table 1.** Precision, recall and F-score for relation detection methods

| Approach | P | R | F1 |
|---|---|---|---|
| luke-base | 74.8 | 79.9 | **77.3** |
| luke-reprod | **76.8** | 75.2 | 76.0 |
| luke-redetect | 73.1 | **80.1** | 76.4 |

## 5   Experiments and Results

In this section, we present the different experiments made with our relation extraction system and the subsequent results. Those experiments can be divided in three parts: 1) the LUKE-based Relation Detection module, 2) the Concepts of Neighbours-based Relation Classification module, and 3) the whole system.

All experiments were made on the TACRED dataset [24], one of the most used dataset for Relation Extraction. This dataset is made of 106,264 examples, split into a training corpus (68,124 examples), a development corpus (22,631 examples) and a test corpus (15,509 examples). Each example of this dataset is a sentence with two entity mentions (a subject and an object), each mention being typed among 23 possible types, and annotated with a relation type among 41 effective classes plus a *no_relation* class representing the absence of relation between the subject and the object. For greater accuracy compared to random pairs of entity mentions occurring in real-world sentences, 79.5% of the examples are in the *no_relation* class.

### 5.1   Relation Detection

We evaluate the different configurations of LUKE [22] presented in Sect. 4.1, in order to choose the best one for relation detection.

*Experiment Design.* As presented in Sect. 4.1, several configuration of LUKE were tested. In addition to *luke-base* and *luke-detect*, a third configuration, called *luke-reprod* has been tested. Theoretically equivalent to *luke-base*, it consists into reproducing the fine-tuning on TACRED to see if this fine-tuning is reproducible, and to have another comparison point for *luke-redetect*. Concerning *luke-detect*, several values have been tested for the size of the hidden layer, and best results have been obtained with $n = 400$. The implementation is freely accessible[3], and the experiments were run using a Tesla V100 GPU.

*Results.* Table 1 shows the performance for the three detailed configurations. It can be read that, contrary to our expectations, *luke-reprod* does not reproduce the results from *luke-base*, by having an F-score inferior by 1.3 points. LUKE's implementation being in Python, this is probably due to a problem in dependency versioning. However, even if the reproduction was a failure, we can

---

[3] See https://gitlab.inria.fr/hayats/luke-redect.

observe that *luke-detect*'s F-score is superior by 0.4 points to *luke-reprod*'s one. Therefore, it can be hoped that if we were able to reproduce perfectly *luke-base*, *luke-detect* would have a better F-score.

It is interesting to point out that if *luke-base* has an overall better F-score, *luke-reprod* outperforms its precision and *luke-redetect* outperforms its recall. However, having a lower recall means having more false-negative examples, which means missing some examples expressing a relation, which we want to avoid, while having a lower precision means trying to classify a relation on examples that express none, which is also problematic. This is why we prefer F-score over precision or recall, and therefore we use *luke-base* as a relation detection module in the following experiments.

## 5.2   Relation Classification

We now evaluate our Concepts of Neighbours-based module individually on the Relation Classification task.

*Experiment Design.* These experiments are made on the positive examples of TACRED, *i.e.* the examples that have an annotation other than *no_relation*. As our method does not have any use of a development corpus, we merge this corpus with the training one. We finally obtain a dataset composed of 18,446 training examples and 3,325 test examples. The quality measure usually used on TACRED is the micro-averaged F-score. However, as there is no negative class on this task, this measure does not make sense, and therefore we use accuracy.

In these experiments, as we work on a subset of TACRED we cannot compare this approach directly to other existing methods. Therefore, we compare our approach to a basic baseline in the RECENT paradigm. This baseline simply predicts, for given subject and object types, the relation type that appears the most among the training examples with the same subject and object types.

As the algorithm for the computation of Concepts of Neighbours is *anytime*, we have to choose a timeout for our experiments. In order to see how the timeout influences the classification task, several timeouts were tested between 10 and 1200 seconds. Concerning the dependency tree pruning, several values of $k$ were tested, and the best results have been obtained with $k = 1$. Our approach was implemented in Java[4] and uses *ConceptualKNN*[5] for the computation of Concepts of Neighbours, which is based on Apache Jena[6], a Java library for the semantic web.

*Results.* Table 2 presents the accuracy for the baseline and for our approach. First it can be observed that the baseline has an accuracy of 80.4%, which is particularly high, which means that the dataset leaves little space for progress. Then, it can be read that for any timeout, the proposed approach has a better accuracy than the baseline, surpassing it by 2.2 points for a timeout of over 300 s.

---

[4] Accessible here: https://gitlab.inria.fr/hayats/conceptualknn-relex.
[5] https://gitlab.inria.fr/hayats/jena-conceptsofneighbours.
[6] https://jena.apache.org/.

**Table 2.** Accuracy for relation classification, compared to the baseline.

| Timeout (s) | 10 | 20 | 30 | 60 | 120 | 300 | 600 | 1200 |
|---|---|---|---|---|---|---|---|---|
| Ours | 82.0 | 82.1 | 82.7 | 82.9 | 83.4 | **83.6** | 83.6 | **83.6** |
| Baseline | 80.4 | | | | | | | |

**Table 3.** F-score for several Relation Extraction methods on TACRED

| Method | F1 score |
|---|---|
| LUKE [22] | **72.7** |
| BERT-LSTM-Base [20] | 67.8 |
| *Ours* | *66.9* |
| C-GCN [23] | 66.4 |
| GCN [23] | 64.0 |

In addition, this table clearly shows a saturation phenomenon: there is an important gain when timeout gets from 10 s to 120 s, gain that is far smaller from 120 s to 1200 s. It can be intuited that this comes from the fact that most concepts are computed before 120 s, and only a few concepts are added after 120 s. This also can be seen in the proportion of examples for which the full set of Concepts of Neighbours is computed: of less than 30% for a timeout of 10 s, it rises to over 80% for a timeout of 120 s and to over 99% for a timeout of over 600 s. This shows that despite the anytime algorithm, most of the prediction is made on the real set of Concepts of Neighbours, and not an approximation.

### 5.3   Relation Extraction

Now that we have shown that our Concepts of Neighbours-based method is a valid approach for relation classification and that we have chosen a deep learning relation detection module, both can be assembled to form a full relation extraction method. In this subsection we present the experimental process to evaluate this method, as well as both quantitative and qualitative results.

*Experiment Design.* We evaluate our two-step approach on the full TACRED dataset in order to compare it to previous approaches. To do so, according to the structure presented in Fig. 3, we process the test examples of TACRED with *luke-base*, and obtain examples classified as positive or negative. Then, each example classified as positive is processed by our Concept-of-Neighbours module for relation classification.

*Quantitative Results.* Table 3 compares our method with previous Relation Extraction methods. It shows that although our method is not competitive with pre-trained language models such as BERT or LUKE, it outperforms approaches based on graph convolution networks. Indeed, our method beats by 2.9 F-score points the basic graph convolution network (GCN) and by 0.5 points the contextualized graph convolution network (C-GCN). This is interesting because our

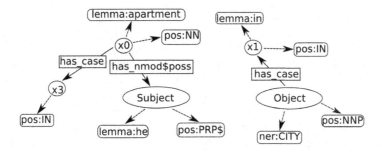

**Fig. 4.** Example of rule body

method and those two methods are conceptually close: both are based on the representation of sentences as a graph, both use the pruned dependency tree of the sentences, and both add to this modeling a semantic layer (a word embedding for GCN and C-GCN, WordNet for our approach). The difference between those approaches is that ours aims to provide explanations for the examples classified as positive.

*Qualitative Results.* As mentioned above, the main advantage of our approach is its explainability. Let us take for example the sentence *"Sollecito has said he was at **his** own apartment in **Perugia**, working at his computer."* luke-base predicts that there is a relation between the subject (*his*) and the object (*Perugia*). As the subject is a person and the object a city, there are only three compatible relations: *per:cities_of_residence, per:city_of_death* or *per:city_of_birth*. After computation of the Concepts of Neighbours, we observe that the relation *per:city_of_residence* is predicted, as six rules of confidence 1 predict it, while only one rule each predicts the other two compatible relations. Figure 4 shows the body of one of those rules. It can be read as:

- The subject has lemma *he* and is the possessor of an apartment;
- The object is the name of a city in which there is something.

Even if this pattern is too specific to form a general rule, it can be infered that, knowing there is a relation between the subject and the object, we can be pretty sure that any sentence following this pattern has the relation *per:cities_of_residence* between its subject and its object. To complete this explanation, we can look at the training examples matching this rule. In our case, there is one sentence matching it: *"Wilbert Gibson walked from **his** apartment to the grocery store earlier this week – that's what people do in **New York City** – and thought this must be what it's like to be a celebrity."* We can see that this sentence effectively expresses the relation *per:cities_of_residence*, but quite implicitly. Therefore, this is interesting to see that this kind of pattern can be captured and exploited by our approach.

In practice, we observe that the rules of maximum confidence have systematically a confidence equal to 1. This is due to the fact that Concepts of Neighbours compute rules specific enough to match a few cases, and therefore to have a low extensional distance. After reviewing the explanations for ten randomly chosen correct predictions, we can observe that 56% of the 172 graph patterns seem reliable. Most of those reliable explanations are considered as such because of a lemma or a synset appearing in the graph pattern (for example the word *daughter* to characterize the relation *per:children*). In addition, we observe that the reliability of the explanations depends on the relation type. For example it can be pointed out that for an example predicting the relation *per:top_member/employee*, most of the explanations are invalid. This is caused by the fact that there is a great variety of words or formulations expressing this relation, and therefore the same one is rarely used several times. In addition, it appears that most of graph patterns are disconnected, but, as we could hope, most of the connected ones are valid.

## 6    Conclusion

In this article, we presented a new method for relation extraction. The core idea of this method is to combine an explainable and symbolic approach for relation classification with a deep learning method for relation detection. More precisely, we present a FCA-based approach that has shown promising results on relation classification, and we couple it with a state-of-the-art pre-trained language model fine-tuned for relation detection. Experiments have shown that this two-step approach gives promising results. In addition, this new method explains each positive prediction with interpretable rules.

In the future, work has to be made on the FCA-based relation classifier, on the modeling, by adding sequentiality for example, as well as on the concepts of neighbours, in order to use more expressive and flexible patterns. There is also work to do on the explainability, on how to display those explanations in order to make them easily readable, in order to allow for interaction with the user.

## References

1. Ayats, H., Cellier, P., Ferré, S.: Extracting relations in texts with concepts of neighbours. In: Braud, A., Buzmakov, A., Hanika, T., Le Ber, F. (eds.) ICFCA 2021. LNCS (LNAI), vol. 12733, pp. 155–171. Springer, Cham (2021). https://doi.org/10.1007/978-3-030-77867-5_10
2. Ben Abacha, A., Zweigenbaum, P.: Automatic extraction of semantic relations between medical entities: a rule based approach. J. Biomed. Semant. **2**, 1–11 (2011)
3. Cellier, P., et al.: Sequential pattern mining for discovering gene interactions and their contextual information from biomedical texts. J. Biomed. Semant. **6**, 27 (2015)
4. Devlin, J., Chang, M.W., Lee, K., Toutanova, K.: BERT: Pre-training of Deep Bidirectional Transformers for Language Understanding. NAACL-HLT (2019)
5. Ferré, S.: Concepts de plus proches voisins dans des graphes de connaissances. In: Ingénierie des Connaissances (IC) (2017)
6. Ferré, S.: Application of concepts of neighbours to knowledge graph completion. Data Sci. **4**(1), 1–28 (2021)

7. Fundel, K., Küffner, R., Zimmer, R.: RelEx - relation extraction using dependency parse trees. Bioinformatics **23**(3), 365–371 (2007)
8. Giuliano, C., Lavelli, A., Romano, L.: Exploiting shallow linguistic information for relation extraction from biomedical literature. In: Conference European Chapter of the Association for Computational Linguistics, pp. 401–408 (2006)
9. Grishman, R.: Twenty-five years of information extraction. Nat. Lang. Eng. **25**, 677–692 (2019)
10. Gutierrez, C., Sequeda, J.F.: Knowledge graphs. Commun. ACM **64**(3), 96–104 (2021)
11. Joshi, M., Chen, D., Liu, Y., Weld, D.S., Zettlemoyer, L., Levy, O.: SpanBERT: improving pre-training by representing and predicting spans. Trans. Assoc. Comput. Linguist. **8**, 64–77 (2020)
12. Leeuwenberg, A., Buzmakov, A., Toussaint, Y., Napoli, A.: Exploring pattern structures of syntactic trees for relation extraction. In: Baixeries, J., Sacarea, C., Ojeda-Aciego, M. (eds.) ICFCA 2015. LNCS (LNAI), vol. 9113, pp. 153–168. Springer, Cham (2015). https://doi.org/10.1007/978-3-319-19545-2_10
13. Lyu, S., Chen, H.: Relation Classification with Entity Type Restriction, May 2021. http://arxiv.org/abs/2105.08393
14. Mallart, C., Le Nouy, M., Gravier, G., Sébillot, P.: Active learning for interactive relation extraction in a french newspaper's articles. In: Recent Advances in Natural Language Processing - Deep Learning for Natural Language Processing Methods and Applications (2021)
15. Manning, C.D., Surdeanu, M., Bauer, J., Finkel, J., Bethard, S.J., McClosky, D.: The Stanford CoreNLP Natural Language Processing Toolkit. In: Annual Meeting of the Association for Computational Linguistics: System Demonstrations (2014)
16. Martinez-Rodriguez, J.L., Hogan, A., Lopez-Arevalo, I.: Information extraction meets the semantic web: a survey. Semant. Web **11**(2), 255–335 (2020)
17. Meilicke, C., Chekol, M.W., Ruffinelli, D., Stuckenschmidt, H.: Anytime bottom-up rule learning for knowledge graph completion. In: International Joint Conference Artificial Intelligence, pp. 3137–3143 (2019)
18. Miller, G.A.: WordNet: An Electronic Lexical Database. MIT Press, Cambridge (1998)
19. Nguyen, T.H., Grishman, R.: Relation extraction: perspective from convolutional neural networks. In: Workshop Vector Space Modeling for Natural Language Processing, pp. 39–48 (2015)
20. Shi, P., Lin, J.: Simple BERT Models for Relation Extraction and Semantic Role Labeling, April 2019. arXiv: 1904.05255
21. Xu, Y., Mou, L., Li, G., Chen, Y., Peng, H., Jin, Z.: Classifying relations via LSTM networks along shortest dependency paths. In: Conference on Empirical Methods in Natural Language Processing. Association for Computational Linguistics (2015)
22. Yamada, I., Asai, A., Shindo, H., Takeda, H., Matsumoto, Y.: LUKE: deep contextualized entity representations with entity-aware self-attention. In: Conference on Empirical Methods in Natural Language Processing (EMNLP) (2020)
23. Zhang, Y., Qi, P., Manning, C.D.: Graph convolution over pruned dependency trees improves relation extraction. In: Conference on Empirical Methods in Natural Language Processing, pp. 2205–2215 (2018)
24. Zhang, Y., Zhong, V., Chen, D., Angeli, G., Manning, C.D.: Position-aware attention and supervised data improve slot filling. In: Conference on Empirical Methods in Natural Language Processing, pp. 35–45 (2017)

# Towards Automation of Topic Taxonomy Construction

Yann Dauxais[1][✉], Urchade Zaratiana[1,2], Matthieu Laneuville[3],
Simon David Hernandez[1], Pierre Holat[1,2], and Charlie Grosman[1]

[1] FI Group, 14 Terrasse Bellini, 92800 Puteaux, France
{yann.dauxais,urchade.zaratiana,simon.hernandez,
pierre.holat,charlie.grosman}@fi-group.com
[2] LIPN, Université Sorbonne Paris Nord - CNRS, UMR 7030, Villetaneuse, France
[3] SURF B.V., P.O. Box 19035, 3501 DA Utrecht, The Netherlands

**Abstract.** The automation of taxonomy construction has increased in popularity recently. Such an interest for the domain has been motivated by the large number of new scientific papers published each year that implies a growing difficulty in following the new topics of the different scientific domains and their importance in the topic hierarchy. In this paper, we propose a way to automatically construct topic taxonomies from millions of scientific article abstracts and ways to automatically evaluate this construction. While, to our knowledge, other approaches rely on pipelines of models and human evaluation to validate them, we chose to rely on simple models that are easier to evaluate automatically and, thus, promote the improvement of our models thanks to a large number of iterations. The contribution of this paper is threefold: 1) the proposition of a new method to construct taxonomies from a large set of scientific papers, 2) a method to precompile taxonomy information into matrices that will be quickly queried, and 3) an objective method to automatically evaluate the constructed taxonomies without requiring human evaluation.

**Keywords:** Topic taxonomy construction · Knowledge extraction · Automatic evaluation · Text mining

## 1 Introduction

The number of scientific articles published by the research community is growing rapidly. It has become nearly impossible to navigate through the scientific literature without limiting oneself to a very specific topic in the literature, or a subset of conferences, journals and authors. Search platforms like Google Scholar[1], Microsoft Academic[2] or Semantic Scholar[3] are specialized in exploring the scientific literature but topic keywords or author names are still the main entry point.

---

[1] https://scholar.google.com.
[2] https://academic.microsoft.com.
[3] https://www.semanticscholar.org.

© The Author(s), under exclusive license to Springer Nature Switzerland AG 2022
T. Bouadi et al. (Eds.): IDA 2022, LNCS 13205, pp. 26–38, 2022.
https://doi.org/10.1007/978-3-031-01333-1_3

This creates the risk of introducing biases towards the most visible research papers.

In the same way as scientific articles, new topic keywords appear frequently and their usage change through time. It is especially true in a fast-growing domain like neural networks. This makes any systematic literature review, related-work analysis and state-of-the-art documentation a more and more tedious and time-consuming task for academic as well as corporate researchers, peer-reviewers, experts, and scientific advisors. This issue is widely recognized and approaches emerged to help with topic discovery [6,17]. Among them, topic taxonomy construction methods [5,9,10,12,14,18,19] are promising approaches allowing the user to navigate in a graph of topics from a known topic to the new topics to discover.

The most recent approaches focus on pipelines in which it is potentially difficult to assert the effectiveness of each component, and their validation rely solely on human evaluation. This is inevitable due to the lack of gold standard taxonomies to compare against, but it has several flaws that make it difficult to really assess the whole taxonomy generation. First of all, the evaluation is difficult to reproduce as the humans selected for the evaluations are different from a method to another and, as the appreciation of a taxonomy can be subjective, the reasons why an evaluator preferred the results of a method from another are unknown. Secondly, it is not possible to ask a user to evaluate the entire generated taxonomy and small subsets have to be chosen to be evaluated. These chosen subsets are potentially not representative of the whole taxonomy, in terms of quality or affinity with the evaluators, but also subjectively selected and different from the evaluation of an approach to another. A good example of these problems is the evaluation of TaxoGen [19] and NetTaxo [9] that are two methods sharing authors but that seemed to be evaluated by different people and on different topics. It becomes then difficult to compare these approaches even if their evaluations were produced in similar environments. Thus, the automation of taxonomy construction is hampered by the lack of automation of its evaluation.

To tackle the difficulties of reproducible and automatable evaluations, we propose to use a general scientific classification system constructed by human experts. This approach would allow us to automatically determine the need for specific components in any taxonomy construction pipelines. We use the 2012 ACM Computing Classification System[4] that is already used to sort computer science papers and the classification[5] used by the European Commission to categorize research projects. Such a comparison allows us to independently evaluate the topic generation from different papers and the taxonomy generation as we attempt to reconstruct the dataset classification using the same topics. We discuss the pros and cons of this approach but, nonetheless, the use of these datasets is a step towards the creation of a gold standard for topic taxonomy construc-

---

[4] https://www.acm.org/publications/class-2012.
[5] https://ec.europa.eu/research/participants/data/call/trees/portal_keyword_tree.
json.

tion. The closest work attempting to propose an automatic evaluation [3] is, however, limited to a specific domain of topics constructing its taxonomies using a contrastive set of documents containing all the documents not belonging to the targeted domain. Furthermore, their evaluation, while automatic, is based on a score that is a trade-off between a term frequency measure which is already used in their topic extraction method and the depth of the taxonomy, making their results difficult to interpret.

Our contribution in this paper is, thus, threefold: 1) we propose a new efficient way to construct taxonomies from a huge set of scientific papers that favors its evaluation, 2) we propose a method to precompile taxonomy information into matrices for efficient querying, and 3) we introduce an objective method to automatically assess the constructed taxonomies without requiring human evaluation and, thus, favor iterations. The following sections are organized as follows: Section 2 presents the data structure and the taxonomy construction based on it, Sect. 3 presents the visualization concepts to help users navigate the constructed taxonomies and, Sect. 4 presents different results of our evaluation and a comparison with TaxoGen, an approach from the state-of-the-art. To conclude, we will discuss our results in Sect. 5 and present different perspectives we want to explore after this work.

## 2   Method

In this paper, we present an approach of taxonomy construction based on three levels of publicly available information and one additional level of generated information. Such a choice is motivated by the willingness to use as much information as possible from the scientific papers, in a homogeneous format and in an easy reproducible way. The structure of the data is as follows:

- Document nodes representing a corpus $\mathcal{D}$ and associated to the whole articles and their metadata.
- Author nodes representing the authors of the documents and gathered as the author set $\mathcal{A}$.
- Field of study nodes that represent the field of study of the venue or journal in which the document has been published from the set $\mathcal{F}$.
- Topic nodes that are terms generated or extracted from the documents and gathered in the topic set $\mathcal{T}$.

Every type of node that is not a document is represented by a sparse **co-occurrence matrix** $\mathcal{O}$ in which $\mathcal{O}_{i,j}$ is true if and only if the node $i$ occurs in the paper $j$. In the following sections, we denote $\mathcal{O}_\mathcal{A}$, $\mathcal{O}_\mathcal{T}$, and $\mathcal{O}_\mathcal{F}$ the matrices $\mathcal{O}$ representing the authors, topics, and fields of study, respectively. Such a representation allows us to store all the data in memory and apply matrix operations on the different types of nodes to compute the matrices that we will use to construct our taxonomies quickly. As an extension, we denote $\mathcal{O}_{\mathcal{X},\mathcal{Y}}$ the co-occurrence matrix of the nodes $\mathcal{X}$ and $\mathcal{Y}$ where $\mathcal{O}_{\mathcal{X},\mathcal{Y}} = (\mathcal{O}_\mathcal{Y}{}^T.\mathcal{O}_\mathcal{X})^b$ where the result matrix is binarized.

*Example 1.* Let *neural network* (that will be abbreviated *nn*) and *lstm* be two example topics from $\mathcal{T}$ and *Sofia* be an author from $\mathcal{A}$. The number of documents of $\mathcal{D}$ containing an occurrence of *neural network* is $|\mathcal{O}_{\mathcal{T}nn}|$, the number of documents of $\mathcal{D}$ containing an occurrence of *lstm* is $|\mathcal{O}_{\mathcal{T}lstm}|$ and the number documents of $\mathcal{D}$ containing an occurrence of *Sofia* is $|\mathcal{O}_{\mathcal{A}Sofia}|$. The number of documents containing *lstm* and authored by *Sofia* is then $|\mathcal{O}_{\mathcal{T},\mathcal{A}lstm,Sofia}|$ and the number of documents containing *neural network* and authored by *Sofia* is $|\mathcal{O}_{\mathcal{T},\mathcal{A}nn,Sofia}|$.

## 2.1 Topic Generation

In this section, we present our approach to automatically generate useful topics from scientific articles. Instead of using traditional topic extraction approaches, which rely on hand-crafted features and heuristics [2,11,16] (such as Tf-idf weight, PageRank or part-of-speech models), we use a state-of-the-art scientific topic generator based on the transformer architecture [13] proposed by Meng et al. [7]. In fact, the main drawback of traditional topic extraction is that it can only extract topics that appear in the source text, whereas neural network-based architectures are more flexible, i.e. they can generate diverse, coherent and high-quality topics based only on the semantic content of the input document (not necessarily using the exact words that appear in the source text). More precisely, the model of [7] is based on an encoder-decoder transformer architecture and is trained to conditionally generate a set of keyphrases/topics from an input scientific text (concatenation of the title and abstract). Model learning is performed by teacher forcing and inference by a beam search algorithm. For a detailed description of the model, please refer to the original paper [7].

## 2.2 Taxonomy Construction

From the occurrence matrices, we defined two types of computed matrices that are used for the construction. **Subsumption matrices** represent the subsumption of nodes regarding their co-occurrences in the documents. We denote $\mathcal{S}_{\mathcal{X},\mathcal{Y}}$ the subsumption matrix for the nodes $\mathcal{X}$ with respect to the nodes $\mathcal{Y}$ where the subsumption of $\mathcal{X}_i$ by $\mathcal{X}_j$ is $\mathcal{S}_{\mathcal{X},\mathcal{Y}_{i,j}} = \dfrac{|\mathcal{O}_{\mathcal{X},\mathcal{Y}_i} \cap \mathcal{O}_{\mathcal{X},\mathcal{Y}_j}|}{|\mathcal{X}_i|}$, i.e., $\mathcal{S}_{\mathcal{X},\mathcal{Y}_{i,j}} = 1$ if all nodes $\mathcal{Y}$ co-occurring with the node $\mathcal{X}_i$ co-occur with the node $\mathcal{X}_j$ and $\mathcal{S}_{\mathcal{X}_{i,j}} = 0$ if it does not exist a node from $\mathcal{Y}$ co-occurring with $\mathcal{X}_i$ that co-occurs with $\mathcal{X}_j$. Such a matrix can simply be computed as $\mathcal{S}_{\mathcal{X},\mathcal{Y}} = \mathcal{O}_{\mathcal{X},\mathcal{Y}}^T.\mathcal{O}_{\mathcal{X},\mathcal{Y}}/diag(\mathcal{O}_{\mathcal{X},\mathcal{Y}})$ where $diag(\mathcal{O}_{\mathcal{X}})$ is the diagonal of the occurrence matrix. Similarly to the occurrence matrix, we denote $\mathcal{S}_{\mathcal{X}} = \mathcal{S}_{\mathcal{X},\mathcal{D}}$.

*Example 2.* Based on our previous example, $\mathcal{S}_{\mathcal{T}lstm,nn}$ represents the fraction of documents containing *lstm* that also contain *neural network* while $\mathcal{S}_{\mathcal{T}nn,lstm}$ represents the fraction of documents containing *neural network* that also contain *lstm*. As *lstm* is a subtopic of *neural network*, $\mathcal{S}_{\mathcal{T}lstm,nn}$ should be close to 1 as a document describing an lstm approach is very likely to refer to neural networks.

On the contrary, $\mathcal{S}_{\mathcal{T}nn,lstm}$ should be much smaller because a paper describing a neural network approach should not necessarily refer to LSTMs. In a similar way, $\mathcal{S}_{\mathcal{T},\mathcal{A}lstm,nn}$ and $\mathcal{S}_{\mathcal{T},\mathcal{A}nn,lstm}$ are the fraction of authors that have written at least one paper about LSTMs that have also written a paper about neural networks and the fraction of authors that have written at least one paper about neural networks that have also written a paper about LSTMs, respectively.

**Similarity matrices** represent the similarity between two nodes of the same type based on direction of the vector of co-occurrences with another type, i.e., the cosine similarity between these two vectors. We denote $\mathcal{C}_{\mathcal{X},\mathcal{Y}} = \widehat{\mathcal{O}_{\mathcal{X},\mathcal{Y}}}^{T} . \widehat{\mathcal{O}_{\mathcal{X},\mathcal{Y}}}$ the similarity matrix between the nodes from $\mathcal{X}$ regarding to their co-occurrences with the node from $\mathcal{Y}$ where $\widehat{\mathcal{O}_{\mathcal{X},\mathcal{Y}}}$ denotes the normalized matrix obtained from $\mathcal{O}_{\mathcal{X},\mathcal{Y}}$, i.e., the sum of the vectors representing the nodes from $\mathcal{Y}$ equals to 1.

To build a taxonomy from these sets of matrices, we chose to compile all the matrices relative to the topics as a weighted sum of matrices. We denote $\mathcal{W}$ the result matrix where $\mathcal{W} = \sum_{\mathcal{Z}\in\{\mathcal{S},\mathcal{C}\},\mathcal{Y}\in\{\mathcal{A},\mathcal{D},\mathcal{T},\mathcal{F}\}} w_{\mathcal{Z},\mathcal{Y}}.\mathcal{Z}_{\mathcal{S},\mathcal{Y}}$ and $w_{\mathcal{Z},\mathcal{Y}}$ is used to weight the importance of $\mathcal{Z}_{\mathcal{S},\mathcal{Y}}$ in this sum. The taxonomy is then simply constructed by using a maximum spanning tree algorithm on $\mathcal{W}$. As the similarity matrices are asymmetric matrices, the result of this computation is an undirected graph. To obtain a proper taxonomy in which the relationship between the parents and children are clear, we propose two different methods to reorient the undirected result. The first method is to simply use the subsumption matrices used to create the taxonomy. Indeed, if the subsumption of a topic $i$ by a topic $j$ is greater than the subsumption of the same topic $j$ by the topic $i$, this matrix suggests that the topic $j$ is the parent of $i$. The second method is to designate a root in the taxonomy and to propagate the relationships from it.

## 3   Visualization

Because the main goal of our approach is to allow the exploration of a scientific topic taxonomy by a user to help with topic discovery, the visualization of the constructed taxonomies is a crucial point. Indeed, it enables us to experiment and observe different use cases, from free topic exploration to related-work analysis in actual research studies to technology scouting in an open innovation context, etc. Furthermore and in a similar way to the other approaches of the state-of-the-art, visualizing our results allows us to qualitatively evaluate them and discover problems in parts of the taxonomy in which we have enough knowledge.

**Visualize from an Entry Point.** Our tool allows us to select a topic as an entry point and explore the taxonomy around it. As the computation of a new taxonomy is nearly instantaneous, we manage to construct subtaxonomies based on the topics that are the closest to the entry point. Such a behavior allows to detect topics that are distant from each other in the global taxonomy but quite close in a specific context, as for example, "network" which is used in diverse scientific fields but is a direct parent of "neural network" in a subtaxonomy where the entry point is "lstm". To choose which topics should be in the subtaxonomy, we use simple thresholds on the matrices presented in the previous section. For example, we can choose the topics that occur in more than 5% of the documents containing the entry point topic and the topics for which the entry point topic occurs in more than 5% of the documents in which they occur. Also thanks to the taxonomy computation speed, the user may easily use simple cursors to adjust these parameters and show the right amount of topics they desire. Figure 1 represents a fraction of the subtaxonomy we computed for the entry point "lstm" with the previous parameters. Leaves under "lstm" are mainly applications where its parents start from "paper" to stop at "recurrent neural network". Sibling branches are also interesting to understand the context of the topic. In such a case, topic taxonomy construction allows the user to quickly order the information as a small graph containing all the interesting topics relative to a topic familiar to them or at least in which the user may want to dive.

**Visualize from the Root.** The second option of our tool is to visualize the whole taxonomy from the root. The user sees a small graph centered on "paper" the root and its children such as "design", "application", "algorithm" or "time". Then, they can expand the node of their interest to show its children and, after several iterations of expansion, discover topics of interest. Such a method allows the user to guide themselves into the taxonomy without being flooded by the large number of its topics and alleviate the computation load of the visualization client.

## 4   Evaluation and Experiments

### 4.1   Datasets

To proceed with the evaluation of our taxonomy construction method, we chose two public scientific corpora to compare with: 1) The 2012 ACM Computing Classification System[6] is a subject classification used by computer scientists for ACM publications. In the following sections, we refer to it as **ACM**. This classification contains 2299 nodes representing topics with unique names and 2390 edges linking them. Such a difference between the number of nodes and edges, while the classification is a tree, is due to nodes such as "Visualization" that are shared by several branches. And 2) the classification[7] used by the European Commission to categorize research projects. In the following sections, we refer to it as **Europa**. This classification contains 3546 nodes and 3559 edges linking them.

To build the taxonomies presented in the previous section, we used the S2ORC[8] (Semantic Scholar Open Research Corpus) from which, in a first part,

---

[6] https://cran.r-project.org/web/classifications/ACM-2012.html.
[7] https://ec.europa.eu/research/participants/data/call/trees/portal_keyword_tree. json.
[8] https://github.com/allenai/s2orc.

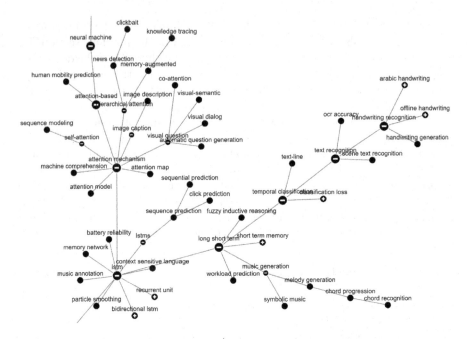

**Fig. 1.** Representation of a taxonomy related to the topic "lstm" generated using our prototype.

we generated the topics and in a second part we computed the occurrences of the topics, authors and venues in the 76 million documents containing an abstract in their metadata. Data and code are available on GitHub[9].

## 4.2   Evaluation Measures

Different measures have been used to evaluate our taxonomies and determine which part of the handmade taxonomies we wanted to keep or not. To our knowledge, this is different to the state-of-the-art as recent approaches focus on human evaluation of small result quality to validate their whole model. This further justifies our approach based on several automated evaluation iterations.

- **Common edges** (#*edges*): This is the number of common edges between the original and extracted taxonomies. Such a measure does not take into account the direction of the edges but only evaluates the direct relationships in the constructed taxonomy.
- **Average distance** (*avg*): To complete the common edges measure, the average distance between two nodes linked by an edge in the original taxonomy and computed in the constructed one has been used to evaluate both the differences of depth and the distance failure that can be generated.

---

[9] https://github.com/ydauxais/TATTC.

**Table 1.** On top, the 5 best results obtained while optimizing common edges for ACM ordered then by directed paths. On bottom, the 5 best results obtained while optimizing directed paths for ACM ordered then by common edges.

| $wc_{T,\mathcal{A}}$ | $ws_{T,\mathcal{A}}$ | $wc_{T,\mathcal{F}}$ | $ws_{T,\mathcal{F}}$ | $wc_T$ | $ws_T$ | #edges | #paths | avg | $\overline{avg}$ |
|---|---|---|---|---|---|---|---|---|---|
| 57.60 | 13.01 | 10.01 | 0.79 | 46.76 | 100.00 | **195** | **276** | **8.12** | **2.27** |
| 67.50 | 12.17 | 11.62 | 0.71 | 45.41 | 99.87 | **195** | 274 | 8.15 | 2.32 |
| 66.58 | 15.62 | 10.95 | −1.52 | 47.56 | 99.76 | **195** | 271 | 8.14 | 2.30 |
| 58.25 | 14.51 | 10.56 | −1.41 | 41.26 | 92.98 | **195** | 269 | 8.30 | 2.32 |
| 62.91 | 9.72 | 9.95 | 0.02 | 41.64 | 94.18 | **195** | 266 | 8.23 | 2.31 |
| 92.33 | 65.27 | 6.26 | 22.63 | 28.16 | 62.29 | **152** | **467** | 11.16 | 7.11 |
| 89.38 | 63.20 | 4.27 | 18.81 | 22.65 | 46.37 | 149 | 466 | 11.08 | 7.16 |
| 93.74 | 66.54 | 4.42 | 20.11 | 24.77 | 34.64 | 148 | 466 | 11.02 | **7.07** |
| 99.93 | 71.73 | 2.63 | 21.14 | 26.35 | −11.46 | 144 | 466 | **10.87** | 7.14 |
| 94.09 | 71.79 | 5.74 | 23.59 | 31.52 | 53.18 | **152** | 465 | 11.01 | 7.08 |

- **Directed paths** (*#paths*): As the common edges measure does not take into account the direction of the edges, this measure is useful to evaluate if a parent and a child in the original taxonomy have the same relationship of predecessor/successor in the constructed one.
- **Average distance of directed paths** ($\overline{avg}$): Similar to the precedent measure of average distance, we computed the average distance of the paths that are well oriented between a parent and its child in the original taxonomy.

### 4.3 Results

**Taxonomy Evaluation and Iterations.** We initially ran some naive taxonomy computation based on the topic subsumption matrix and the author similarity matrix and observed that ACM and Europa contain both nodes of the type "X and Y" that are parents of the nodes "X" and "Y". As these nodes are redundant, we decided to remove them and directly attach the children to the first remaining ancestor. Based on this choice, we obtained two new taxonomies containing 1999 nodes and 2830 nodes for ACM and Europa, respectively.

Through a random search of 10000 trials optimizing the common edges and another optimizing the directed paths for weights in the range [−100, 100], we obtained the 5 best results for each represented in Table 1 on ACM and the 5 best results for each represented in Table 2 on Europa. We can observe from these results that the method is very stable and does not depend on a heavy fine-tuning to obtain the best results, in terms of common edges or directed paths. Field similarity and subsumption matrices are often less used than the others, the weight of the subsumption one is even optimized to be close to 0 which means it is not really useful to obtain such results. It does not mean it could not be useful but as matrices carry redundant information between them, the optimization process does not need it.

**Table 2.** On top, the 5 best results obtained while optimizing common edges for Europa ordered then by directed paths. On bottom, the 5 best results obtained while optimizing directed paths for Europa ordered then by common edges.

| $wc_{T,\mathcal{A}}$ | $ws_{\mathcal{S}_T,\mathcal{A}}$ | $wc_{T,\mathcal{F}}$ | $ws_{\mathcal{S}_T,\mathcal{F}}$ | $wc_T$ | $ws_{\mathcal{S}_T}$ | #edges | #paths | avg | $\overline{avg}$ |
|---|---|---|---|---|---|---|---|---|---|
| −7.20 | 71.15 | 37.78 | −2.55 | 86.81 | 83.37 | **179** | **230** | **7.09** | 2.20 |
| −8.87 | 68.31 | 36.07 | −2.73 | 82.72 | 94.59 | **179** | **230** | 7.16 | 2.21 |
| −33.88 | 70.35 | 33.22 | −1.44 | 86.33 | 87.76 | **179** | 229 | 7.12 | **2.17** |
| −16.41 | 69.17 | 36.26 | −2.29 | 83.12 | 93.20 | **179** | 229 | 7.13 | 2.21 |
| −17.32 | 58.52 | 33.39 | −2.58 | 76.10 | 96.27 | **179** | 229 | 7.12 | 2.21 |
| 0.96 | 76.54 | 5.64 | 6.31 | 21.91 | 59.60 | **161** | **273** | **9.14** | **3.40** |
| 4.79 | 80.92 | 4.03 | 6.02 | 19.04 | 54.68 | **161** | 272 | 9.71 | 3.53 |
| 14.25 | 91.71 | 6.79 | 1.26 | 11.83 | 67.20 | 158 | 272 | 10.05 | 3.50 |
| 14.71 | 99.84 | 9.36 | 1.45 | 13.55 | 69.45 | 150 | 272 | 9.92 | 3.58 |
| 6.07 | 82.07 | 0.46 | 1.64 | 4.80 | 64.10 | 147 | 274 | 11.70 | 4.30 |

**Evaluation of the Classification Reconstruction.** It is worth noticing that 1639 and 1496 pairs of nodes sharing an edge in ACM and Europa, respectively, was found in the documents and, thus, these numbers are the ceilings for the number of common edges and directed paths. Thus, the optimization of the common edges for ACM obtained a score of 11.90% of common edges and 16.84% of directed paths while the optimization of the directed edges for the same classification obtained a score of 9.27% of common edges and 28.49% of directed paths. For the Europa classification, these scores are 11.97% of common edges and 15.37% of directed paths while optimizing common edges and 10.76% of common edges and 18.25% of directed paths while optimizing the directed paths. The low average distance for directed paths is also a good point to validate our directed path results. Indeed, a bad way to optimize the directed paths measure without taking into account the quality of the taxonomy is to create a single path containing every topic. Such an optimization would lead to an increase of the average distance between the nodes of the directed paths. As the average distance between the nodes are low, our method only reorganize some topics to have a stronger relationship than being just siblings. For example, it is the case with the ACM classification where every technology topics are children of the "technologies" topic but our method find that the topic "AJAX" can be the child of the topic "javascript" which is also true. In this example, we lose a common edge for a directed edge that belongs to a valid alternative classification.

To evaluate the reusability of the optimized parameter sets and the level of over-tuning these results implied, we computed the results for a classification using the best parameters obtained for the other. As a result we obtained 168 common edges and 188 directed paths using the best parameters for ACM optimizing the common edges on Europa which represent a loss of 0.74% common edges and 2.81% of directed paths; 158 common edges and 196 directed paths using the best parameters for ACM optimizing the directed paths on Europa which represent a loss of 0.20% common edges and 5.15% of directed paths; 176 common edges and 252 directed paths using the best parameters for Europa optimizing the common edges on ACM which represent a loss of 1.16% common edges and 1.46% of directed paths; finally, 151 common edges and 217 directed paths using the best parameters for Europa optimizing the directed paths on ACM which represent a loss close to 0% common edges and 15.25% of directed paths. It shows that the optimized parameter sets obtained through the optimization of the common edges provide stable results from a classification to another. The highest loss obtained on the parameter set relative to the directed paths are potentially due to a difference in construction between the ACM and Europa classification. For example, the ACM classification contains a node whose children are technologies and another whose children are authors while the Europa classification is more homogeneous and refers to scientific project domains. A good approach to improve the stability of the results between different classification is to use L1-regularization through the optimization process. However, we discovered that the regularization worked better while considering the common edges and directed paths together which implies to add weights to leverage the importance of both measures. As an example, for our purpose, we found that using a score of $4\#edges + \#paths - L1$ produced the best results but it probably depends of which results are expected.

**Comparison with the State of the Art.** We focused on TaxoGen [19] as a comparison for our state-of-the-art evaluation. Such a method is a good comparison as it focuses on a pipeline of heavier methods than ours like clustering and rely on human evaluation. Some other approaches could also have been suitable such as NetTaxo [9] as it is more recent and builds on TaxoGen but its implementation is not available at this time and it would be difficult to reproduce the assumptions made to obtain the same results. The TaxoGen approach requires two main inputs to extract a taxonomy: a map between the topics and their embeddings and the documents represented by the topics occurring in them.

The original approach computes the embeddings of the topics using a Word2Vec [8] model trained on their data, however, since pre-trained language models such as BERT [4] or SciBERT [1] have become the de facto method for computing text embedding, we decided to encode the topics using Phrase-BERT [15], a variant of BERT which has been optimized for phrase-level embedding. More specifically, their code recompute the embeddings of the topics with Word2Vec for the inner levels and we decided to modify it as little as possible which makes the use of these new embeddings interesting only for the first level of topics. The occurrences of the topics in the documents were already calculated for our approach and TaxoGen simply requires a different formatting of the $\mathcal{O}_T$ matrix. Such a similarity allows us to directly compare the two approaches on the same topics and their occurrences which helped us with their evaluation.

Running TaxoGen is not as simple as our approach because it requires some hyperparameters which require an intuition of the best results to be optimized.

**Table 3.** Comparison results between our method and TaxoGen for the topic taxonomy constructions based on the ACM and Europa classification topics. Size refers here to the number of pairs of nodes sharing an edge that are also in the constructed taxonomy.

| | Dataset | Size | #edges | #paths | avg | $\overline{\text{avg}}$ | #clusters |
|---|---|---|---|---|---|---|---|
| Ours | ACM | 1639 | **195** | 276 | 8.12 | **2.27** | |
| | | | 152 | **467** | 11.16 | 7.11 | |
| | Europa | 1496 | **179** | 230 | 7.09 | 2.20 | |
| | | | 161 | **273** | 9.14 | 3.40 | |
| Random (Ours) | ACM | 1639 | 1.6 | 2.4 | 31.27 | 3.1 | |
| | | | ±0.49 | ±0.80 | ±4.06 | ±0.58 | |
| | Europa | 1496 | 1.6 | 4.2 | 32.62 | 3.03 | |
| | | | ±0.80 | ±2.04 | ±2.48 | ±0.69 | |
| TaxoGen | ACM | 1461 | 79.8 | 136.8 | **4.39** | 2.31 | 116.8 |
| | | ±116.12 | ±28.69 | ±20.41 | ±0.30 | ±0.16 | ±20.41 |
| | Europa | 1283.2 | 128 | 96.4 | **2.95** | 2.17 | 350.2 |
| | | ±4.45 | ±36.92 | ±17.12 | ±0.47 | ±0.22 | ±84.92 |
| Random (TaxoGen) | ACM | 1461 | 21.35 | 25.45 | 4.85 | 1.61 | 10.45 |
| | | ±116.12 | ±5.57 | ±16.97 | ±0.23 | ±0.16 | ±3.47 |
| | Europa | 1283.2 | 18.68 | 19.4 | 4.90 | 1.55 | 8.6 |
| | | ±4.45 | ±4.00 | ±7.33 | ±0.11 | ±0.24 | ±3.74 |

The most important parameters for this comparison are the maximum number of branches a node can have, which is represented by the number of clusters to compute and the maximal depth of the taxonomy. We decided to use the default parameters of their implementation to compute the ACM and Europa taxonomies that are 5 clusters and a depth of 3. It theoretically leads to 155 nodes different from the root and most topics will be grouped with other topics in the same cluster. Thus, we adapted our measures to represent the different relationships of the topics with the addition of this cluster level.

The results presented by Table 3 for TaxoGen were obtained on a 5-cross-validation for each classification. We computed taxonomies for fewer edges shared with the ACM and Europa classifications as we did not succeed to complete the run with TaxoGen, the actual implementation tending to crash while clustering rare topics. Nevertheless, the numbers of topics handled by both approaches are similar and that will allow us to compare them.

To evaluate the gap in complexity between the construction of a hierarchy of clusters and the construction of a complete taxonomy, we also compared the random generations of taxonomies containing as many topics as ours and hierarchies of 155 clusters with a depth of 3 under the root and where parent clusters have 5 children. To generate the first random taxonomy, we generated a matrix of random weights between the nodes and applied the minimum spanning tree algorithm as usual. For the other one, we randomly split the topics in the hierarchy of clusters. The results, presented by Table 3 capture the difference in difficulty between both tasks. This difference is emphasized by the interest of the clusters to improve the measures but not the quality of the taxonomy. Indeed, ACM and Europa topics are meant to represent themselves and merging them into clusters implies losing a lot of information. Extracted clusters also contain lots of errors, grouping unrelated topics which is partially due to the rigid parameters forcing the maximal child number and the maximal depth of the taxonomy. Finally, even with these differences in difficulty and information representation, our approach is able to compete with the results of TaxoGen, generating more common and directed paths and even compete with the count of cluster edges as common and directed paths on ACM. It is worth noticing that it had been impossible to optimize the hyperparameters of TaxoGen as we did for our approach as a TaxoGen run takes several hours to be computed while our method can run thousands of iterations in the same time.

## 5    Conclusion and Perspectives

In this paper, we proposed a new efficient way to automatically construct topic taxonomies from millions of documents and a way to automatically evaluate them through the comparison with human-constructed scientific classifications. Thanks to this evaluation, we showed that our taxonomy construction competes with state-of-the-art approaches and can outperform TaxoGen, especially in terms of possible iterations. Specifically, we based our taxonomy construction on a public open research corpus containing more than 76 million documents and more than 46 million authors. It is designed in a way that allows us to query it nearly instantaneously to build taxonomy based preference parameters.

In future work, our method could be improved by adding new levels of information, as for example, the venues and journals of the documents which should lead to an improvement over just the field of study, and, moreover, enable a generalization of the combination of the subsumption and similarity matrices. Indeed, the weighted sum was the easiest way to combine them but other approaches could help us to find better combinations, as for example if the weights are more relative to the topics or their frequencies than the matrices themselves. Finally, the improvement of the measures to compare different approaches and the use of different datasets will pave the way to a gold standard for topic taxonomy construction. Indeed, we consider that contributions in this domain will help the scientific community explore knowledge related to their work, bring a better understanding of the most recent discoveries and emerging concepts, and accelerate innovation processes in businesses and administrations.

## References

1. Beltagy, I., Lo, K., Cohan, A.: Scibert: a pretrained language model for scientific text. arXiv (2019)

2. Bougouin, A., Boudin, F., Daille, B.: TopicRank: graph-based topic ranking for keyphrase extraction. In: IJCNLP, pp. 543–551 (2013)
3. De Knijff, J., Frasincar, F., Hogenboom, F.: Domain taxonomy learning from text: the subsumption method versus hierarchical clustering. Data Knowl. Eng. **83**, 54–69 (2013)
4. Devlin, J., Chang, M.W., Lee, K., Toutanova, K.: Bert: pre-training of deep bidirectional transformers for language understanding. arXiv (2018)
5. Huang, J., Xie, Y., Meng, Y., Zhang, Y., Han, J.: Corel: seed-guided topical taxonomy construction by concept learning and relation transferring. In: KDD, pp. 1928–1936 (2020)
6. Jayabharathy, J., Kanmani, S., Parveen, A.A.: Document clustering and topic discovery based on semantic similarity in scientific literature. In: International Conference on Communication Software and Networks, pp. 425–429. IEEE (2011)
7. Meng, R., Yuan, X., Wang, T., Zhao, S., Trischler, A., He, D.: An empirical study on neural keyphrase generation (2021)
8. Mikolov, T., Chen, K., Corrado, G., Dean, J.: Efficient estimation of word representations in vector space. arXiv (2013)
9. Shang, J., Zhang, X., Liu, L., Li, S., Han, J.: Nettaxo: automated topic taxonomy construction from text-rich network. In: WWW, pp. 1908–1919 (2020)
10. Shen, Z., Ma, H., Wang, K.: A web-scale system for scientific knowledge exploration. In: System Demonstrations, pp. 87–92 (2018)
11. Song, M., Song, I.Y., Hu, X.: Kpspotter: a flexible information gain-based keyphrase extraction system. In: International Workshop on Web Information and Data Management, pp. 50–53 (2003)
12. Tang, J., Zhang, J., Yao, L., Li, J., Zhang, L., Su, Z.: Arnetminer: extraction and mining of academic social networks. In: KDD, pp. 990–998 (2008)
13. Vaswani, A., et al.: Attention is all you need. In: NeurIPS, pp. 6000–6010 (2017)
14. Wang, K., Shen, Z., Huang, C., Wu, C.H., Dong, Y., Kanakia, A.: Microsoft academic graph: when experts are not enough. Quant. Sci. Stud. **1**(1), 396–413 (2020)
15. Wang, S., Thompson, L., Iyyer, M.: Phrase-bert: improved phrase embeddings from bert with an application to corpus exploration (2021)
16. Witten, I.H., Paynter, G.W., Frank, E., Gutwin, C., Nevill-Manning, C.G.: Kea: practical automatic keyphrase extraction. In: Conference on Digital Libraries, pp. 254–255 (1999)
17. Yan, X., Guo, J., Lan, Y., Xu, J., Cheng, X.: A probabilistic model for bursty topic discovery in microblogs. In: AAAI (2015)
18. Yu, Y., Li, Y., Shen, J., Feng, H., Sun, J., Zhang, C.: Steam: self-supervised taxonomy expansion with mini-paths. In: KDD, pp. 1026–1035 (2020)
19. Zhang, C., et al.: Taxogen: unsupervised topic taxonomy construction by adaptive term embedding and clustering. In: KDD, pp. 2701–2709 (2018)

# A Fault Detection Framework Based on LSTM Autoencoder: A Case Study for Volvo Bus Data Set

Narjes Davari[1(✉)], Sepideh Pashami[2,7], Bruno Veloso[1,4,5],
Sławomir Nowaczyk[2], Yuantao Fan[2], Pedro Mota Pereira[6],
Rita P. Ribeiro[1,3], and João Gama[1,4]

[1] INESC TEC, Porto, Portugal
davari2002@gmail.com
[2] Center for Applied Intelligent Systems Research, Halmstad University,
Halmstad, Sweden
[3] Faculty of Sciences, University of Porto, Porto, Portugal
[4] School of Economics, University of Porto, Porto, Portugal
[5] University Portucalense, Porto, Portugal
[6] Metro of Porto, Porto, Portugal
[7] RISE Research Institute of Sweden, Kista, Sweden

**Abstract.** This study applies a data-driven anomaly detection framework based on a Long Short-Term Memory (LSTM) autoencoder network for several subsystems of a public transport bus. The proposed framework efficiently detects abnormal data, significantly reducing the false alarm rate compared to available alternatives. Using historical repair records, we demonstrate how detection of abnormal sequences in the signals can be used for predicting equipment failures. The deviations from normal operation patterns are detected by analysing the data collected from several on-board sensors (e.g., wet tank air pressure, engine speed, engine load) installed on the bus. The performance of LSTM autoencoder (LSTM-AE) is compared against the multi-layer autoencoder (mlAE) network in the same anomaly detection framework. The experimental results show that the performance indicators of the LSTM-AE network, in terms of F1 Score, Recall, and Precision, are better than those of the mlAE network.

**Keywords:** Fault detection · Outliers · Time series · LSTM · Autoencoder

## 1 Introduction

In many industries, maintenance is a significant part of the operation. As an example, a key parameter for bus operators is vehicle downtime, namely whenever a vehicle is needed but not available [17]. Analysing the time buses from a

This work was supported by the CHIST-ERA grant CHIST-ERA-19-XAI-012, project CHIST-ERA/0004/2019 funded by FCT - Fundação para a Ciência e Tecnologia and project 2020-00767 funded by Swedish Research Council.

© The Author(s), under exclusive license to Springer Nature Switzerland AG 2022
T. Bouadi et al. (Eds.): IDA 2022, LNCS 13205, pp. 39–52, 2022.
https://doi.org/10.1007/978-3-031-01333-1_4

particular fleet spend in a workshop (or on the way there) is vital for understanding the efficiency of operations, especially for follow-up on any improvements. An essential next step is to develop systems that can automatically detect faults, i.e., analyse the data on-board vehicles and identify anomalous behaviour. A fault prevents the bus from operating. One of the reasons for the surprisingly large amount of (costly) time buses spend at workshops is the waiting time – even though there is no work being done on it. The bus operator cannot optimally plan their operation since much of this waiting time is insufficient planning. Unexpected failures typically lead to long waiting times. The framework proposed in this paper aims to support the automotive industry in more efficient planning.

Anomalies are good indicators of malfunctions in a system. In the era of big data, considerable research efforts focus on designing online algorithms capable of detecting anomalies from streaming data. To detect anomalies in a given system, it is necessary to define a "normal system behaviour". However, when the volumes of data and the complexity of systems are continuously growing, it becomes infeasible for human experts to build an exhaustive definition of each system's normal behaviour. Moreover, the definition of normal is dynamic, as sensors generate data that is subject to change over time due to external conditions (i.e., normal data samples are drawn from a non-stationary distribution). In a real-world application domain, we monitor one bus operating in typical conditions in Sweden. We are particularly interested in detecting deviations that identify faults during a bus's operation. In this paper, we implement a fault detection framework based on deep learning (DL) to detect failures of bus air system. Our goal is to identify abnormal behaviours in the data stream obtained from sensors installed in the system while the bus is in operation. The objective is to predict if a failure evolves using unsupervised methods based on deep learning.

The remainder of the paper is structured as follows: an overview of the related work in the context of anomaly detection is provided in Sect. 2. Section 3 discusses the problem description. In Sect. 4 we present fault detection methodology and proposed failure detection framework. The case study, pre-processing and data cleaning, feature generation, and anomaly detection are discussed in Sect. 5. Section 6 contains experimental results obtained by the LSTM autoencoder (LSTM-AE) and multi-layer autoencoder (mlAE), and finally, the concluding remarks are provided in Sect. 7.

## 2   Related Work

The current industrial solution for vehicle on-board fault detection and diagnostic systems, e.g., [15], still rely heavily on domain knowledge from a human expert and is essentially based on either building a pattern recognition classifier or a reference model. This paradigm requires domain experts such as field engineers to drive the development, i.e., modelling the physical process involved, determining potential faults or risky events, conducting controlled experiments, and collecting relevant data for analysis. Relevant reviews can be found in [6–8,18]. While this paradigm has proven effective for predefined faults by domain experts, unexpected faults occurred post-deployment in the field not covered by the system, which is developed prior to the deployment.

An alternative approach is to monitor systems on-board vehicles and autonomously captured key characteristics of the operation (in model space) for anomalous event detection: the reference system representation is learned with unsupervised models (e.g., LSTM or AE networks) on data stream coming from machines working under normal conditions. In contrast, an abnormal machine would yield a deviation in the model space and a higher reconstruction error. Similar concepts are studied in, e.g., [3,10].

Deep learning methods have been employed for many different real-world applications. Fan et al. [5] utilised echo state network to capture air system dynamics and perform conformal anomaly detection with learned features for detecting compressor faults. Munir et al. [13] presented a DL approach to detect a range of anomalies (point anomalies, contextual anomalies and discords) in time series data. Michau et al. [12] used AE network for unsupervised feature parameter learning and integrated it with a one-class classifier that is only trained with samples of healthy conditions for fault detection. Davari et al. [4] proposed a data-driven predictive maintenance framework for the air production unit system of a train by deep learning based on a sparse AE network that efficiently detects abnormal data and considerably reduces the false alarm rate.

The anomaly detection techniques for time series sequence based on DL algorithms augmented with LSTMs are used in several studies (e.g., [9,19]). Chauhan et al. [1] applied recurrent neural network (RNN) and LSTM to detect anomalies in ECG signals. Nguyen et al. [14] proposed a LSTM based method for forecasting multivariate time series data and an LSTM AE combined with a one-class support vector machine algorithm for detecting anomalies in sales. Maleki et al. [11] introduced a probability criterion based on the central limit theorem to evaluate the likelihood of a data point that is drawn from an unknown probability distribution for the goal of data labelling. Then, normal data is passed to train an LSTM autoencoder that distinguishes anomalies when the reconstruction error exceeds a threshold.

This paper proposes a framework based on LSTM autoencoder to address the challenges and limitations of anomaly detection. The contribution of this study is a multivariate time series anomaly detection method based on LSTM autoencoder with the application to data from a Volvo bus in regular operation.

## 3   Problem Description

*Data Description.* The data used in this study were collected from buses operated in traffic around a city on the west coast of Sweden. Four vehicles were year model 2009, one was 2008, and the remaining was produced in 2007. On-board data collection took place from August 2011 until the end of 2017, in regular operation, where each bus was driven approximately 100 000 km per year.

Data from the J1587 diagnostic bus and two CAN buses (the vehicle and the powertrain CANs) were sampled once per second, collecting approximately one hundred sensor and control signal values. An in-house developed system called the Volvo Analysis and Communication Tool (VACT) was used in the study; it uses a telematics gateway for communication and can wirelessly receive new sampling configurations.

In addition, we have analysed an off-board database containing Vehicle Service Record (VSR) information. Each entry in this database contains information about repair and maintenance services done on the vehicles, including date, mileage and unique part identifiers. There are, unfortunately, frequent quality issues with the data since the VSR is primarily manually entered by maintenance personnel. Given that the primary purpose is accounting and invoicing, the detailed information about the repairs, especially the degree of component deterioration and root cause analysis, is less than perfect. This data was partly curated using vehicle GPS data and bus operator's internal operation notebooks.

*Fault Detection.* The key to reducing downtime is building a system capable of detecting early symptoms of wear and faults. If the operator and workshop personnel become alerted before they become real problems or failures, i.e., before they take the bus out of commission, they can be handled much more efficiently. Optimally, one could solve these problems during the next planned maintenance visit. In our study, we have noticed that vehicles would spend, on average, almost 1.5 months per year in workshops. Early discovery of faults and improved diagnostics is expected to decrease the waiting time, incorrect repairs significantly, and other similar issues, conservatively reducing the total downtime by 50% or more.

In this study, we aim to detect periods of abnormal vehicle operation, i.e., quantify the "strangeness" of sensor data, compared to what is expected. Many current approaches for equipment monitoring require (semi-)manual creation of some model of what is expected. On the other hand, our goal is to automatically monitor a wide range of complex equipment with many possible faults. This goal requires autonomously constructed knowledge from the data, with very little reliance on human experts. In particular, one cannot assume that a list of all possible faults can be provided for training.

## 4    Fault Detection Methodology

This experimental fault detection framework aims to predict and detect faults by cleaning and extracting time series data features in an optimal sliding time window and feeding them into a deep LSTM-AE network that performs a classification task.

*LSTM Encoder-Decoder.* An autoencoder is an unsupervised neural network (NN) trained to reconstruct the inputted time-series data as its output. The encoder learns to compress a high-dimensional input to a low-dimensional latent space, and the decoder then attempts to reconstruct the output with minimal error faithfully. The general form of multivariate time-series at the sliding time window $i$ can be expressed as $\mathbf{X}^{(i)} = \mathbf{X}_1^{(i)}, \mathbf{X}_2^{(i)}, \ldots, \mathbf{X}_j^{(i)}, \ldots, \mathbf{X}_m^{(i)}$ of length $m$, where $m$ is the number of time series variables (number of sensors) and $\mathbf{X}_j^{(i)}$ is an observation vector of readings from $j^{th}$ sensor at the sliding time window $i$.

The difference between the input vector $\mathbf{X}^{(i)}$ and the reconstructed vector $\hat{\mathbf{X}}^{(i)}$ is called the reconstruction error $\mathbf{e}_r^{(i)}$. The trained network tries to minimise the reconstruction error as its objective function. A common metric for this error is Mean Squared Error (MSE): $\mathbf{e}_r^{(i)} = \left\| \mathbf{X}^{(i)} - \hat{\mathbf{X}}^{(i)} \right\|^2$ which measures the proximity of the reconstructed input to the original input.

The trained LSTM Encoder-Decoder model reconstructs the normal multivariate time series. The reconstruction errors of the training data are then compared to test data, i.e., an anomaly score for each dataset in a sliding time window is calculated, and identifies whether it follows the normal distribution of the time series. The higher the anomaly score, the more likely is it that the given data time window should be considered an anomaly.

Figure 1 illustrates the steps of the LSTM-AE network for a time-series data consisting of $n$ sliding time windows, in which $\mathbf{h}_i^E$ and $\mathbf{h}_i^D$ are the hidden state of the encoder and decoder, respectively, at the sliding time windows $i = 1, \ldots, n$.

The LSTM encoder learns an input time series and generates an encoded state while the LSTM decoder produces the reconstructed data at the sliding time window $i$ by applying the hidden decoding state at sliding time window $i$ and the predicted time series at the sliding time window $(i-1)$. In order to reconstruct the time series, the encoder and decoder parts are jointly trained.

In order to obtain the hidden state of the encoder at sliding time window $i$, $\mathbf{X}^{(i)}$ at sliding time window $i$ and the hidden state of the encoder at sliding time window $(i-1)$, ( $\mathbf{h}_{i-1}^E$) are used. The hidden state of the encoder at the end of the input sequence, $\mathbf{h}_n^E$, is used as the initial state of the decoder, $\mathbf{h}_n^E = \mathbf{h}_n^D$. The decoder uses hidden state $\mathbf{h}_i^D$ and the predicted value of time series at sliding time window $i$, (i.e., $\hat{\mathbf{X}}^{(i)}$) to produce the next hidden state.

*The Proposed Framework.* The time-series dataset includes normal and abnormal observations. We split the normal data into two sets: training and validation. The training dataset is used to learn the LSTM-AE network, while the validation dataset is used for an early stop in the autoencoder training (i.e., when the validation loss does not improve and the generalisation error begins to degrade). The root mean square of reconstruction error for the training dataset ($RMSE_r^{train}$) is used to estimate a threshold value (through a Boxplot analysis) for labelling test data. The training dataset is assumed to have normal behaviour, so as we can consider, the $RMSE_r^{train}$ follows a normal distribution. However, if there are some outliers in the training dataset, the distribution will be asymmetric; i.e., the methods work based on normality assumption may not be useful. Boxplot is useful as a consistent method to display the distribution of

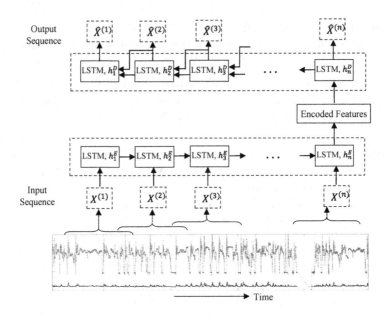

**Fig. 1.** An LSTM-AE network for a sequence with length $n$

the dataset. Extreme observations can be easily ignored, thus, it can be used to set the threshold of $RMSE$ of test data ($RMSE_r^{test}$).

Next, the test data that contain normal and abnormal samples is employed to validate the network performance. If $RMSE_r^{test}$ is larger than the threshold value, then the data is considered as an anomalous observation; otherwise, it is a normal one. In this paper, the anomalies are detected as a classification problem, where the classification labels "0" and "1" indicate normal and anomaly observations, respectively. The maximum and minimum values of the Boxplot are obtained from $1.5 * IQR$ above the third quartile ($Q_3$) and $1.5 * IQR$ below the first quartile ($Q_1$), respectively; where $IQR$ is the interquartile range, i.e. the difference between the upper and the lower quartiles. The interval $[Q1 + 1.5 * IQR, Q3 + 1.5 * IQR]$ contains 99.3% of data. Therefore, points outside this interval are considered as an anomaly [16].

Finally, the above output is post-processed using a low-pass filter through which the sudden variations are removed, decreasing the number of false alarms [16]. The flow chart of the framework is shown in Fig. 2.

## 5    Case Study

A data-driven fault detection framework is developed that issues an alert whenever one of the key components in a specific bus exhibits an abnormal behaviour. The focus of the study is on the readings from ten sensors (e.g., wet tank air pressure, engine speed, engine load) installed on the bus by which real-time data

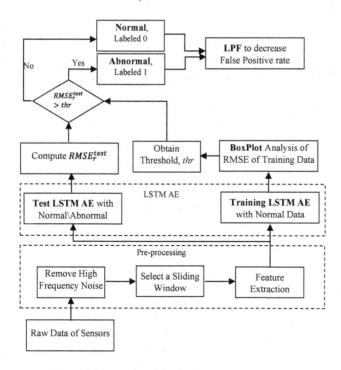

**Fig. 2.** Flow chart of fault detection framework.

was logged at 1 Hz frequency by an on-board embedded device. The anomaly detection framework performs data pre-processing, learns a network to combine several sensors readings, and identifies anomalies in sensor readings that can be symptoms of imminent faults. In order to evaluate the performance of the proposed framework, we compare the alarms raised by the framework against bus repair records.

***Analysis and Cleaning of the Input Data.*** To reduce the influence of noisy data and outliers, we remove the high-frequency noises through a low pass filter (LPF) in pre-processing stage of data [2]. It encourages training data distribution to be close to the Gaussian distribution. In other words, the goal is to reconstruct the noisy data so that its distribution becomes similar to the normal distribution. Figure 3 shows the measured data of "engine speed" sensor during a short duration. The blue curve shows the raw data before filtering, and the data after filtering is shown in red. It is visible that the variations of raw data over time are very noisy, which can be further smoothed by the LPF.

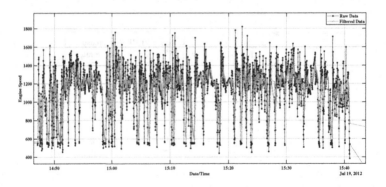

**Fig. 3.** The raw and filtered data of engine speed over time (Color figure online)

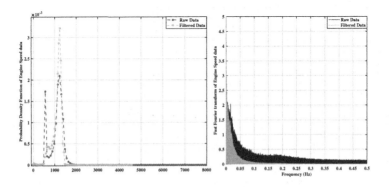

**Fig. 4.** The Probability Density Function - PDF (left) the Fast Fourier Transformation - FFT (right) for raw and filtered engine speed data. (Color figure online)

Fast Fourier Transform (FFT) of the raw and filtered data on the frequency domain is shown in the right part of Fig. 4. It shows that the raw data with frequencies less than 0.1 Hz have higher FFT values while the data with frequencies higher than 0.1 Hz have almost similar low FFT values indicating the specification of white noise. Figure 4 left shows the Probability Density Function (PDF) for the raw and the filtered engine speed data. The PDF of raw data (blue curve) shows a sideband peak around the main peak, which can be removed through filtering (red curve).

***Feature Extraction.*** After cleaning, the raw data must be parsed to extract relevant information that could allow us to detect suspicious behaviours. Although the autoencoder reduces the dimension of multivariate data points to improve the network's performance, raw data with a large learning dimension cannot be

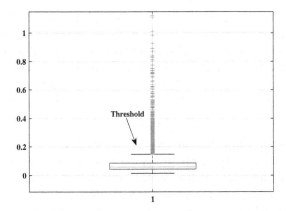

**Fig. 5.** The Boxplot analysis of the $RMSE$ of training dataset.

directly applied. Therefore, statistical values of the multivariate time series in an selected sliding time window are used as input into the network. These statistical values (features) for $j^{th}$ sensor include mean, $x_j^{(1)}$, standard deviation, $x_j^{(2)}$, skewness, $x_j^{(3)}$, kurtosis, $x_j^{(4)}$, quantiles, $\{x_j^{(5)}, \ldots, x_j^{(8)}\}$, and deciles $\{x_j^{(9)}, .., x_j^{(18)}\}$, approximating the original raw data. Thus, through the pre-processing, for each sensor in a sliding time window 18 statistical features are computed; i.e., the dimension of the input to the network is 180 for 10 sensors. This conversion reduces the dimensionality and better expresses the characteristics of the data.

**Anomaly Detection.** As mentioned earlier in Sect. 4, through the Boxplot analysis, the distribution of all $RMSE_r^{train}$ is obtained, and its maximum value is set as a threshold ($thr$) with which normal and abnormal data in the test dataset are labelled as 0 and 1, respectively. Alternatively, the $RMSE$ could be computed using a separate validation dataset, however, we found it does not make a significant difference. Figure 5 shows the Boxplot of all $RMSE_r^{train}$. Note that $thr$ is calculated for the training dataset to identify abnormal behaviours of the test dataset, i.e., if $RMSE_r^{test} > thr$ then the respective sliding time window is detected as an anomaly.

## 6   Experimental Results

This section presents and discusses the experimental results of the case study introduced in Sect. 5. We consider two different downtimes of the bus: unplanned and planned interruptions. The former occurs when one of the bus systems fails; i.e., the vehicle may be inoperable and towed to the workshop for repair, while the latter happens when the workshop personnel determines that a system is not functioning satisfactorily and decides to repair or replace it. A failure report provided by the company (see Table 3) describe repair information, particularly the date and operations performed and some comments. These off-board data makes it possible to evaluate true and false, positive and negative, alarms raised by the proposed anomaly detection framework. In order to evaluate the performance of the proposed solution, we report the following metrics: Recall, Precision, and F1 Score (%).

***Impact of Size of Sliding Window.*** Here, we evaluate the impacts of different sizes (ranges from a smaller window size 1 min to a larger window size of 10 min) of the sliding time window on the performance of the proposed framework. Note that the sliding time window with the same size is applied for the training and test datasets. Table 1 shows the metrics for the framework using $W_1$, $W_2$,..., $W_{10}$, i.e., sliding time windows with length 1 min, 2 min, ..., 10 min, respectively. The results shown (in bold) indicate that the sliding time window of size 4 min ($W_4$) leads to the largest value of $TP$ and the lowest value of $FP$. Generally speaking, the value of $TP$ decreases with increasing the sliding time window length but the $FP$s increases alongside.

**Table 1.** Effect of sliding time window size in performance of LSTM-AE

| Metrics | W1 | W2 | W3 | W4 | W5 | W6 | W7 | W8 | W9 | W10 |
|---|---|---|---|---|---|---|---|---|---|---|
| $TP$ | 14 | 17 | 18 | **22** | 19 | 16 | 14 | 12 | 11 | 12 |
| $FP$ | 5 | 4 | 4 | **3** | 4 | 6 | 6 | 4 | 7 | 8 |
| $FN$ | 12 | 9 | 8 | **4** | 7 | 10 | 12 | 14 | 15 | 14 |
| Recall (%) | 53.8 | 65.4 | 69.2 | **84.6** | 73.1 | 61.5 | 53.8 | 46.1 | 42.3 | 46.1 |
| Precision (%) | 73.7 | 80.9 | 81.8 | **88.0** | 82.6 | 72.7 | 70.0 | 75.0 | 61.1 | 60.0 |
| F1 Score (%) | 62.7 | 72.3 | 75.1 | **86.2** | 77.5 | 66.6 | 60.8 | 57.1 | 49.9 | 52.1 |

***Comparison of LSTM-AE and mlAE.*** For evaluation purposes, we experimentally studied and tuned different LSTM-AE settings, and then the performance of the LSTM-AE was compared versus the mlAE. Since the network topology needs to be consistent with the experimental settings, we explored several structures for the network and selected the one that leads to optimal performance in the learning and prediction stages. The parameters are summarised in Table 2.

**Table 2.** Parameters of the LSTM-AE and mlAE.

| Parameter | LSTM-AE | mlAE |
|---|---|---|
| Nodes in input layer | 160 | 160 |
| Neurons in the 1st hidden layer | 120 | 100 |
| Neurons in the 2nd hidden layer | 60 | 50 |
| Neurons in the 3rd hidden layer | 30 | 25 |
| Neurons in the Bottleneck layer | 15 | – |
| Dropout | 20% | – |
| Learning rate | 1e−3 | 1e−3 |
| Batch size | 100 | 50 |
| Number of epochs | 300 | 300 |

Figure 6 illustrates the estimated normal data and anomalies, over time, for the LSTM-AE and the mlAE. The $x$ and $y$ axes, respectively, represent date/time and the value of $RMSE_r$, changes between one (anomaly) and zero (normal). The areas highlighted in pink and light green rectangles, respectively, show the unplanned and the planned failures reported by the company (see Table 3, columns *"Mode"*, *"Start time"* and *"End time"*). Since detecting a specific anomaly is not sufficient to conclude a persistent failure, the network generates an alarm when a sequence of anomalies is predicted at least for two hours. The predicted alarms by the proposed framework are reported under the *"Failure alarm"* column in Table 3.

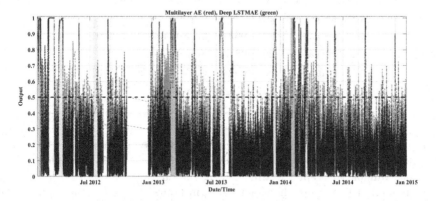

**Fig. 6.** The output of LPF over-time for the LSTM-AE (green) and mlAE (red); data above 0.5 (empirically set) are predicted as anomalies. The pink and light green rectangles indicate the unplanned and planned failures reported by the company. (Color figure online)

**Table 3.** Failures reported by the company and start time of failure alarm.

| Nr. | Mode | Start time | End time | Failure alarm |
|-----|------|-----------|----------|---------------|
| #1 | planned | 2012-02-02 | 2012-02-09 | 2012-02-01 |
| #2 | planned | 2012-03-01 | 2012-03-02 | 2012-02-29 |
| #3 | unplanned | 2012-03-05 | 2012-03-05 | 2012-03-03 |
| #4 | unplanned | 2012-03-16 | 2012-03-19 | 2012-03-14 |
| #5 | unplanned | 2012-04-01 | 2012-04-13 | 2012-03-31 |
| #6 | planned | 2012-05-29 | 2012-05-29 | 2012-05-29 |
| #7 | unplanned | 2012-07-10 | 2012-07-23 | 2012-07-10 |
| #8 | planned | 2012-08-21 | 2012-08-23 | 2012-08-21 |
| #9 | unplanned | 2012-10-08 | 2012-10-08 | 2012-10-08 |
| #10 | planned | 2012-12-27 | 2012-12-28 | 2012-12-25 |
| #11 | planned | 2013-02-19 | 2013-03-06 | 2013-02-19 |
| #12 | unplanned | 2013-04-23 | 2013-04-24 | 2013-04-22 |
| #13 | unplanned | 2013-04-29 | 2013-04-29 | – |
| #14 | unplanned | 2013-07-11 | 2013-07-19 | 2013-07-11 |
| #15 | planned | 2013-08-12 | 2013-08-16 | 2013-08-12 |
| #16 | unplanned | 2013-12-11 | 2013-12-19 | 2013-12-10 |
| #17 | planned | 2014-01-09 | 2014-01-09 | 2014-01-09 |
| #18 | planned | 2014-01-31 | 2014-02-11 | 2014-01-31 |
| #19 | unplanned | 2014-02-23 | 2014-02-23 | 2014-02-22 |
| #20 | unplanned | 2014-03-13 | 2014-03-20 | 2014-03-12 |
| #21 | unplanned | 2014-04-14 | 2014-04-14 | 2014-04-13 |
| #22 | unplanned | 2014-04-20 | 2014-04-20 | – |
| #23 | unplanned | 2014-06-08 | 2014-06-08 | 2014-06-05 |
| #24 | unplanned | 2014-08-14 | 2014-08-15 | – |
| #25 | planned | 2014-09-03 | 2014-09-05 | 2014-09-03 |
| #26 | planned | 2014-11-28 | 2014-11-28 | – |

From the table, we observe that the predicted date for some of the failures is the same as the date reported for failure ("*Start date*") by the company. Since it is not available at a specific time during the day for the reported failures, it is not possible to compute the exact time (in hours) of the alarms prior to the failures. A detailed comparison between the performance of the two networks is reported in Table 4 where the LSTM-AE obtains a higher Recall, Precision, and F1 Score than those using mlAE.

Table 4. Performance comparison of LSTM-AE and mlAE

| Metric | Threshold = 0.5 | | Threshold = 0.7 | |
| --- | --- | --- | --- | --- |
| | Multi-layer AE | LSTM AE | Multi-layer AE | LSTM AE |
| $TP$ | 19 | 22 | 20 | 22 |
| $FP$ | 8 | 5 | 4 | 3 |
| $FN$ | 7 | 4 | 6 | 4 |
| $Recall(\%)$ | 73 | 84 | 76 | 84 |
| $Precision(\%)$ | 70 | 81 | 83 | 88 |
| $F1\ Score(\%)$ | 71 | 82 | 84 | 86 |

## 7   Conclusions

We propose a data-driven anomaly detection framework based on deep learning for multivariate time series. We compared two networks, the LSTM-AE and mlAE, which fuse the real-valued data from sensors installed in a bus, compress them and reconstruct to detect anomalies. Raw data are pre-processed to remove noisy data and outliers. Then, statistical parameters of the data are used as features to detect sequences of abnormal operation, since detecting a single instance of abnormal reading is not sufficient to make conclusions about a component failure. Results from analysing the data collected over a period of approximately three years shows that the LSTM-AE has performance superior over that of the mlAE.

Future work includes experiments on rule-based models to explain detected faults and empirically investigate larger datasets, for example from a fleet of vehicles.

## References

1. Chauhan, S., Vig, L.: Anomaly detection in ECG time signals via deep long short-term memory networks. In: 2015 IEEE International Conference on Data Science and Advanced Analytics (DSAA), pp. 1–7. IEEE (2015)
2. de Cheveigné, A., Arzounian, D.: Robust detrending, rereferencing, outlier detection, and inpainting for multichannel data. Neuroimage **172**, 903–912 (2018)
3. Choi, K., Yi, J., Park, C., Yoon, S.: Deep learning for anomaly detection in time-series data: review, analysis, and guidelines. IEEE Access **9**, 120043–120065 (2021). IEEE
4. Davari, N., Veloso, B., Ribeiro, R.P., Pereira, P.M., Gama, J.: Predictive maintenance based on anomaly detection using deep learning for air production unit in the railway industry. In: 2021 IEEE 8th International Conference on Data Science and Advanced Analytics (DSAA), pp. 1–10. IEEE (2021)
5. Fan, Y., Nowaczyk, S., Rögnvaldsson, T., Antonelo, E.A.: Predicting air compressor failures with echo state networks. In: Third European Conference of the Prognostics and Health Management Society 2016, Bilbao, Spain, 5–8 July 2016, pp. 568–578. PHM Society (2016)

6. Hines, J., Garvey, D., Seibert, R., Usynin, A.: Technical review of on-line monitoring techniques for performance assessment. Volume 2: Theoretical issues (NUREG/CR-6895, vol. 2) (2008)
7. Hines, J., Seibert, R.: Technical review of on-line monitoring techniques for performance assessment. Volume 1: State-of-the-art (NUREG/CR-6895) (2006)
8. Isermann, R.: Fault-Diagnosis Systems: An Introduction from Fault Detection to Fault Tolerance. Springer, Heidelberg (2006). https://doi.org/10.1007/3-540-30368-5
9. Lei, J., Liu, C., Jiang, D.: Fault diagnosis of wind turbine based on long short-term memory networks. Renew. Energy **133**, 422–432 (2019)
10. Lindemann, B., Maschler, B., Sahlab, N., Weyrich, M.: A survey on anomaly detection for technical systems using LSTM networks. Comput. Ind. **131**, 103498 (2021)
11. Maleki, S., Maleki, S., Jennings, N.R.: Unsupervised anomaly detection with LSTM autoencoders using statistical data-filtering. Appl. Soft Comput. **108**, 107443 (2021)
12. Michau, G., Hu, Y., Palmé, T., Fink, O.: Feature learning for fault detection in high-dimensional condition-monitoring signals (2018)
13. Munir, M., Siddiqui, S.A., Dengel, A., Ahmed, S.: Deepant: a deep learning approach for unsupervised anomaly detection in time series. IEEE Access **7**, 1991–2005 (2018)
14. Nguyen, H., Tran, K.P., Thomassey, S., Hamad, M.: Forecasting and anomaly detection approaches using LSTM and LSTM autoencoder techniques with the applications in supply chain management. Int. J. Inf. Manag. **57**, 102282 (2021)
15. Palai, D.: Vehicle level approach for optimization of on-board diagnostic strategies for fault management. SAE Int. J. Passeng. Cars-Electron. Electr. Syst. **6**(2013-01-0957), 261–275 (2013)
16. Ribeiro, R.P., Pereira, P., Gama, J.: Sequential anomalies: a study in the railway industry. Mach. Learn. **105**(1), 127–153 (2016)
17. Rognvaldsson, T., Nowaczyk, S., Byttner, S., Prytz, R., Svensson, M.: Self-monitoring for maintenance of vehicle fleets. Data Min. Knowl. Disc. **32**, 344–384 (2018)
18. Venkatasubramanian, V., Rengaswamy, R., Kavuri, S.N., Yin, K.: A review of process fault detection and diagnosis. Part I: quantitative model-based methods. Comput. Chem. Eng. **27**, 293–311 (2003)
19. Zhao, R., Yan, R., Wang, J., Mao, K.: Learning to monitor machine health with convolutional bi-directional LSTM networks. Sensors **17**(2), 273 (2017)

# Detection and Multi-label Classification of Bats

Lucile Dierckx[1,2](✉) ⓘ, Mélanie Beauvois[2], and Siegfried Nijssen[1,2] ⓘ

[1] TRAIL Institute, Louvain-la-Neuve, Belgium
[2] ICTEAM/INGI, UCLouvain, Louvain-la-Neuve, Belgium
{lucile.dierckx,siegfried.nijssen}@uclouvain.be

**Abstract.** As bats are an important indicator for the health of their habitat, projects in multiple countries monitor bat populations by collecting audio recordings of bat calls. Analysing these recordings is however a tedious task and there is a need for systems that accurately and efficiently detect and classify bat calls. While earlier studies focused on detection and classification separately, in this paper we propose a first approach that combines these two tasks. Moreover, we aim to build a multi-label classifier that is able to detect if multiple bat species are present in the same audio recording. One of the challenges we face is that the available data focuses either on detection or single-label classification, but not on the combined task of detection and multi-label classification. We propose to address this by a data augmentation approach, and demonstrate that the resulting approach achieves the objectives of being accurate and efficient.

**Keywords:** Acoustic event detection and classification · Multi-label classification · Acoustic bat monitoring

## 1 Introduction

Bats are mammals that are very sensitive to their environmental changes and are, therefore, often used as a bioindicator of the health of their habitat [8]. Nowadays, one out of three species in Europe suffers from a sharp population decline, which is, among others, due to the destruction of the bats' roosting and hunting sites, the poisoning of insects with chemicals and the collisions of bats with built infrastructures such as wind farms [15]. That is why various organisations monitor the evolution of bats' population and the different species present on given sites. Bats can be monitored using portable recorders that start to record when hearing sounds above a fixed frequency threshold. The obtained recordings then have to be analysed to identify the calls and the species that emitted them. This tedious task is very time-consuming and requires a good knowledge of bats.

As the number of available recordings constantly increases and not all study groups have a chiropterologist available, there is a clear need for an automated

© The Author(s), under exclusive license to Springer Nature Switzerland AG 2022
T. Bouadi et al. (Eds.): IDA 2022, LNCS 13205, pp. 53–65, 2022.
https://doi.org/10.1007/978-3-031-01333-1_5

analysis of these audio recordings. Some commercial products exist, such as SonoChiro, SonoBat and Kaleidoscope, but these are expensive and, as shown in [11,14], not highly accurate.

The motivation for our work is that there is a need for open software that meets the following challenges:

C1 It should be able to *detect* at which moments in audio signals a bat is present;
C2 It should be able to *classify* which types of bats are present at those moments;
C3 It should be able to perform *multi-label* classification, i.e., it should identify multiple bats in the scenarios in which more than one bat species emit calls simultaneously, which happens regularly in nature;
C4 It should perform its task *accurately*;
C5 It should perform its task with *low computational resources,* as the final goal is to analyse the recordings on the devices that collect the data.

Some research projects have already studied the analysis of bat recordings. In particular, Bat detective [9] studied the detection of bats; BatNet [5] studied the classification of bat calls. However, none of these projects meets all challenges C1–C5. The goal of this paper is to propose a first approach to meet all these challenges.

Meeting these challenges is not straightforward. A major concern is the lack of available data. We only have access to two different types of data:

**Detection data:** these are audio recordings in which labels are present to indicate when a bat call is present, but the bat species are not known;
**Classification data:** these are audio recordings for calls of individual bat species; however, there is no label to indicate the timing of the bat calls.

To complicate the situation further, these data sets are from different locations, where the distribution of bat species may be different.

In this paper, we propose to address these challenges by using a data augmentation approach, in which the existing data sources are used to create new multi-label training data. This data is subsequently used to train a machine learning model. This machine learning model is a combination of a Convolution Neural Network (CNN) and an XGBoost, for which we will show that, on the combination of detection and multi-label classification tasks, the overall performance on the different challenges is better than that of architectures used in earlier work.

The rest of the paper is structured as follows: Sect. 2 gives an overview of the related work on this topic. Section 3 presents the input data available, the data augmentation and the architecture of our proposed model. The datasets used, the evaluation methods, the models used for comparison and the different results obtained are presented in Sect. 4. Finally, Sect. 5 concludes this paper.

## 2 Related Work

The first methods developed to automatically classify bat calls are based on features that are also used when the classification is performed manually from

**Table 1.** Characteristics fulfilled by the presented related works

|  | C1: detect | C2: classify | C3: multi-label | C4: accuracy | C5: resources |
|---|---|---|---|---|---|
| Bat detective | Yes | No | No | Yes | Yes |
| Schwab et al. | No | Yes | No | Yes | No |
| Tabak et al. | No | Yes | No | Yes | No |
| Zualkernan et al. | No | Yes | No | Yes | Yes |
| Chen et al. | No | Yes | No | Yes | No |

the spectrograms of the recordings, such as the peak frequency, the duration and frequency band of each call [1,2,10]. The Bat detective project [9] then showed that it was possible to apply models like CNNs to obtain good performance in the audio monitoring of bats. More importantly, it showed that it was possible to use raw audio as input instead of the precomputed features. Bat detective's program detects the positions of bat calls in audio files and achieves an average precision of approximately 0.88 and a recall at 0.95 precision of about 0.75. To do so, it uses a simple CNN with three convolutional and two dense layers, which receives spectrograms as input and outputs, for each window, the probability that it contains a call.

Some other projects then focused on the classification of bat calls to their corresponding species using CNNs. A first example is the work of Schwab et al. [12] that classifies the calls of bats present in Germany. They first implemented a small algorithm that identifies the position of calls in recordings, but they do not evaluate this detection in terms of performance. They compared four algorithms on the classification task and obtained the best mean accuracy (0.96) when using a modified version of ResNet50 [7] that takes spectrograms as input. Instead of using classical full-spectrum recordings, Tabak et al. [14] use zero-crossing acoustic data to perform the classification of bat calls. The calls were detected by finding sequences of consecutive decreasing frequency, and the images of the generated spectrograms were used as input features. The model used is ResNet18 and has an average accuracy of 0.92 and an average F1-score of 0.91. Some other works tried to avoid the use of too deep and heavy networks like ResNets. Zualkernan et al. [17], for instance, developed a CNN that has only 220K parameters and has an average accuracy of 0.9751 and average F1-score of 0.9578. The network receives Mel-scaled filter banks as input features. Finally, Chen et al. [5] implemented a network called BatNet to recognise 36 tropical bat species. Their particularity is that they have a "weak" label for all calls, no matter the species, that are not strong enough and could be misidentified. BatNet is composed of twenty-two convolutional layers and eight shortcut connections. The input of BatNet consists of the spectral image of the audio files. BatNet was compared to ResNet_v2, VggNet [13] as well as to a CNN inspired by Bat detective, and BatNet has the best AUC and overall accuracy among all. To have a global view of the characteristics of the related works, we present in Table 1 an overview of which of our defined challenges are fulfilled by the different projects presented in this section.

All these papers mainly focus on the classification without performing or evaluating the detection step. Furthermore, they all have to discard from their training set the recordings where more than one species is present. Only Schwab et al. [12] provide circumstantial evidence that shows that for one of their recordings with two species present in it, their model gives a high probability for both species, but no specific evaluation is made on that topic. It is, however, important to be able to recognise calls in a multi-label context as it is common that, on the same observation site, more than one species is present and therefore, the different calls overlap in the recordings. That is why the model we propose in this paper focuses on making correct multi-label predictions in addition to the detection of bat calls.

To train models for detection and classification tasks, labelled training data is needed. Two types of labelled data can be distinguished in the aforementioned studies. The first type is audio recordings in which the time intervals during which a bat call is present are indicated; the second type is audio recordings for which it is indicated which bat type is present in that recording, without indicating the time interval of the calls. Hence, a challenge is that there is no single labelled data set that can be used to train a model for both detection and multi-label classification at the same time.

## 3    Approach

This section introduces the details of our contribution.

### 3.1    Input Data

All datasets consist of audio recordings; to turn these data into training data, a window is slid over these recordings and, for each window, a spectrogram is calculated following the approach of Bat detective [9].

The available data differs in the label information that is available for each audio recording. In detection datasets, a label is known for each window that indicates whether or not a bat call is present in that window. In classification datasets, there is no label for the time windows, but only one label per time series is given, indicating the bat type present in that time series.

### 3.2    Data Augmentation

To train a model that is capable of both detection and multi-label classification, we propose to use an approach of *data augmentation*, where we create new data in which each window is labelled with the bat species present in it; if no bat species is indicated, no bat is assumed to be present in that window.

The process to create such data is presented in Fig. 1. First, we train a Bat detective model on a detection dataset. Subsequently, we use this model to indicate windows at which a call is present in a classification dataset. Then, we label the windows with the species of bat of the audio recording; as a result, we have a

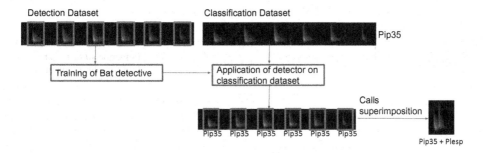

**Fig. 1.** Process to create the augmented multi-label dataset.

dataset with time series in which windows are labelled with the presence of individual bat species. Finally, a new dataset is created by artificially superimposing time series for different bat species on top of each other; this yields windows in which multiple bat species are present, and the identity of these species are known. On this new dataset, we propose to train a multi-label classifier, which for a given window predicts all species present in that window.

Note that the evaluation of the resulting model is complex, as we have no ground truth for the multi-label classifier. As we will discuss in more detail later, we propose to resolve this by evaluating our algorithm in 3 different ways: (1) by evaluating its performance on the augmented data; (2) by evaluating its performance as a detector on the original detection data; (3) by evaluating its performance as a classifier on the original classification data. The challenge is to find a model that performs well across these different metrics.

### 3.3 Proposed Architecture

One of the most common architectures used in detection and classification tasks is the simple CNN, as it is for instance the case for the Bat detective tool. However, this simple network limits the level of performance that can be reached in complex tasks due to the small number of layers that are used. A common method to overcome this limitation is to use very deep convolutional networks instead. Indeed, it is more and more common to use networks such as variations of ResNet to perform detection or classification tasks. Unfortunately, these models require a much higher amount of nodes and have a bigger computational complexity than the simple CNNs. In this paper, we propose to improve the performance of the simple CNN by separating the calculation of features from the classification algorithm and by using other efficient, but computationally lighter, nonlinear multi-label classifiers than deep neural networks.

The model we propose to fulfil these requirements is made of a simple CNN that computes new features, which are then given as input to XGBoost models that perform the classification for each of the classes in the multi-label context.

We train this model as follows. First, a CNN is trained in which the last layer consists of artificial neurons, one for each class. This model is trained as if it has

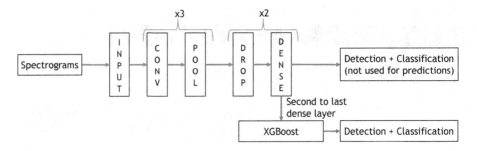

**Fig. 2.** The architecture of our proposed model, the CNN XGBoost, for the detection and multi-label classification of bat calls.

to perform detection and classification. Once it is fully trained, it is applied to the augmented training data; the output of the second to last dense layer on this training data will be used as an input dataset to train XGBoost models, which will then detect and classify. The resulting architecture is presented in a schematic way in Fig. 2.

To tackle the multi-label classification problem, the binary relevance [16] method was chosen to train the CNN, including the last fully connected layer.

Subsequently, one binary XGBoost model is trained for each separate class. These models predict a probability for each class.

Note however that these probabilities need to be thresholded in order to predict whether or not a specific type of bat is present in a window. We exploit this ability to pick thresholds to take into account the various requirements on our model. After all, our aim is not only to obtain good performance on the augmented data, but also on the original detection dataset. We take this requirement into account by choosing the thresholds such that the sum is optimised of the average multi-label classification F1-score on the augmented dataset and the detection F1-score on the detection dataset.

Our algorithm for optimising the thresholds works as follows, as inspired by [6]. We iterate over all the classes, and for each class separately, we vary the thresholds from 0 to 1 with steps of 0.01, while the thresholds of the other classes remain fixed; if our optimisation criterion improves, we accept the new threshold; we continue this process of iterating over the classes and the thresholds until no further improvement can be found.

## 4   Results

This section presents the detection dataset and the classification dataset used in our experiments, as well as how they were combined to be used in a detection and multi-label classification context. It also presents the evaluation methods and the models to which our architecture will be compared on the challenges C1–C5. It then analyses to which degree our proposed model answers to those challenges and verifies whether the latter indeed performs better than the architectures used in earlier works.

## 4.1   Datasets

The two datasets that we have at our disposal are a detection dataset, made available by Bat detective on their website[1], and a classification dataset, provided by Natagora, a Belgian association aiming at protecting nature and collecting various data samples in Wallonia and Brussels.

Bat detective's dataset is made of bat calls recorded from four different regions in Europe between 2005 and 2011, namely in Bulgaria, Romania, UK and Norfolk. The dataset is labelled with the starting position of each call but contains no information about the species that emitted the call. Therefore, these recordings are used to train the networks that are only used for detection.

Natagora's dataset is composed of bat calls recordings taken between 2012 and 2019 at various observation sites in Belgium. The dataset contains seven different groups of bat species that cover the twenty-four species of bat that can be found in Belgium. The seven groups of bat species are Barabar, Envsp, Myosp, Pip35, Pip50, Plesp and Rhisp. The labels provided indicate for each file which group of species can be heard in it. So each file is associated with a tag, but the exact timings of the calls in a given recording are not known.

To create the augmented multi-label dataset, we first needed a detection model. The detection model we used is the one proposed by Bat detective [9] and it was trained with their dataset. This detection model could then be used to find calls positions in the Natagora classification dataset. From that newly labelled dataset, calls were superimposed to generate multi-label samples.

To have a dataset representative of a real-life case, the same amount of files having superimposed calls and of files with no calls and a single group in it were taken for the multi-label dataset. In that way, the models learn to differentiate a call from background noise and to determine whether there is a single call or more than one at a given time of the recording. The total number of bat calls available is 94766. 8801 of them form the test set, used to compute the multi-label performance. The validation set is made of 8772 calls and the 77193 remaining ones form the training set. The validation set is used for thresholds optimisation while the training set is used for training and tuning the models.

## 4.2   Evaluation

As we do not have ground truths available for the multi-label classifiers, we evaluate our algorithms on three different aspects.

The first aspect is the evaluation of the model on the augmented data. This is done by computing the precision, recall and F1-score for the detection as well as for the classification of each class on the multi-label test set. A macro average of the classification metrics is also performed to have a global score of the classification performance while giving the same importance to each class.

To compute the different metrics in a multi-label fashion, $2 \times 2$ confusion matrices are used, one for each of the classes. To fill in the confusion matrices,

---

[1] http://visual.cs.ucl.ac.uk/pubs/batDetective/.

the choice was made to consider each class independently. In other words, to update the confusion matrix of a given class, we ignore all the calls and all the predictions that are not from that class and evaluate the remaining labels as one would do in a binary detection problem. The only difference is that a detected call is considered as correctly predicted if it overlaps with an actual call position, i.e. if they are less than ten milliseconds away from each other, and not only if the prediction and ground truth are in the same window.

The second aspect that needs to be evaluated is the performance of the model as a detector. This is done on the original detection dataset, as it is our only dataset in which the call positions are ground truths. The metrics used are the same as for the multi-label evaluation, but only the detection performance is considered as we cannot say if the classes predicted are correct or not.

Finally, the models are also evaluated as classifiers on the original classification data. The ground truths from that dataset are, for each recording, the type of bat present in it but not the exact timing of the calls. Therefore, we have to look at the class that is the most predicted for each file and we verify if this matches with the ground truth class for that file. Our metric here is thus the percentage of files that are labelled with the correct majority class.

### 4.3    Architectures for Comparison

To make sure that our new architecture is indeed better in terms of performance than a simple CNN and smaller in terms of size than a ResNet, we compare our approach with a number of other architectures. Our proposed model and all the following architectures can be found in the GitHub of our project on https://github.com/luciledierckx/batML. All the details about the models' parameters are also given there.

For calculating features, we consider ResNet50 as an alternative, as used in earlier work and adapted to receive a spectrogram as input [12], in addition to a simple CNN.

As our use of XGBoost models aims to improve the performance over a simple fully connected layer, we also compare with a basic neural network in which a fully connected layer is used for both detection and classification. In our experiments, we use data with seven bat species groups; these networks have eight output classes with one for the class "not a bat" and the seven others for the seven bat species groups. We will refer to these networks as CNN8 and ResNet8, based on the convolutional neural network used.

In addition to these architectures, two baseline alternatives are also evaluated. In these, the detection and classification tasks are separated into two different networks. The recordings are thus first fed to the detection network, and the windows that are predicted as containing a bat call are then given to the second network. The latter predicts which of the seven groups of species are present in the considered window.

The decision thresholds needed for the binary relevance method are tuned for all architecture independently, as these have different strengths and weaknesses in the detection and classification.

**Table 2.** Performance of the compared architectures on Norfolk detection dataset. The best value for each threshold type and metric is highlighted.

| Bat detective | | | ResNet8 | | | Double ResNet | | | ResNet XGBoost | | | CNN8 | | | Double CNN | | | CNN XGBoost | | |
|---|---|---|---|---|---|---|---|---|---|---|---|---|---|---|---|---|---|---|---|---|
| Pre | Re | F1 | Pre | Re | F1 | Pre | Re | F1 | Pre | Re | F1 | Pre | Re | F1 | Pre | Re | F1 | Pre | Re | F1 |
| a) Thresholds on Natagora | | | | | | | | | | | | | | | | | | | | |
| 82 | 86 | 84 | 55 | 76 | 64 | 63 | 87 | 73 | 67 | 81 | 73 | 60 | 85 | 71 | 64 | 88 | 74 | 73 | 77 | 75 |
| b) Thresholds on both Natagora and Norfolk | | | | | | | | | | | | | | | | | | | | |
| 82 | 86 | 84 | 72 | 78 | 75 | 68 | 88 | 77 | 74 | 80 | 77 | 75 | 83 | 79 | 79 | 85 | 82 | 77 | 82 | 79 |

Finally, all the networks' hyperparameters and architecture are tuned using the Hyperopt [3] library. The models were trained, tuned and tested on an i7-9800X CPU @ 3.80 GHz, 32 GB RAM and an RTX 2080 SUPER GPU.

### 4.4 Performance on the Different Challenges

To evaluate challenge C1, corresponding to the detection task, the tuned models were evaluated on the Norfolk test set. In the first experiment, the thresholds are only optimised on the augmented dataset. The results of this evaluation are presented in Table 2a, which also gives the results obtained by the Bat detective architecture when using the same evaluation method.

From Table 2a, we see that our CNN XGBoost model has the highest precision and F1-score, and is the most balanced for the detection, but remains nine percent lower than Bat detective for all metrics. This can be explained by the fact that, even though the species present in Belgium and Norfolk are the same [4], their occurrence frequency at the two places is different, and therefore, the thresholds for each class have to be adapted. This is why we decided to use half of the Norfolk dataset as a training set in order to optimise the thresholds not only on Natagora's validation set but also on the Norfolk training set, as described earlier. This is presented in Table 2b.

Table 2b shows that the performance improves with the new thresholds, although it does not reach the performance of Bat detective. While our network is not the best in terms of F1-score, overall its performance as a detector is reasonable; the important next question is whether this performance as a detector provides benefits as a classifier.

Concerning the classification challenge C2, the evaluation of the classification is done using the recordings from Natagora's dataset that contain a single species. The percentage of files labelled with the correct majority class is reported in Table 3 for both threshold types.

From Table 3 we observe that, no matter the type of threshold used, our CNN XGBoost model has the best classification performance. A noticeable aspect is that, for our proposed architecture, the number of correctly predicted files does not decrease with the new thresholds and is even a bit higher here. This shows

**Table 3.** Percentage of files for which the model predict the correct species. The model is considered as predicting the correct class for a file when it is the class predicted the most for that file. The best value for each threshold type is highlighted.

|  | ResNet8 | Double ResNet | ResNet XGBoost | CNN8 | Double CNN | CNN XGBoost |
|---|---|---|---|---|---|---|
| Thresholds on Natagora | 78 | 76 | 84 | 84 | 79 | 85 |
| Thresholds on both Natagora and Norfolk | 79 | 36 | 85 | 74 | 77 | 86 |

**Table 4.** Performance of the compared architectures for the detection task on the augmented data set. The best value for each threshold type and metric is highlighted.

| ResNet8 | | | Double ResNet | | | ResNet XGBoost | | | CNN8 | | | Double CNN | | | CNN XGBoost | | |
|---|---|---|---|---|---|---|---|---|---|---|---|---|---|---|---|---|---|
| Pre | Re | F1 | Pre | Re | F1 | Pre | Re | F1 | Pre | Re | F1 | Pre | Re | F1 | Pre | Re | F1 |
| a) Thresholds on Natagora | | | | | | | | | | | | | | | | | |
| 77 | 73 | 75 | 76 | 73 | 74 | 76 | 74 | 75 | 81 | 76 | 78 | 86 | 69 | 77 | 78 | 74 | 76 |
| b) Thresholds on both Natagora and Norfolk | | | | | | | | | | | | | | | | | |
| 81 | 67 | 73 | 78 | 74 | 76 | 82 | 67 | 74 | 85 | 65 | 74 | 90 | 60 | 72 | 83 | 68 | 75 |

that the model has a strong classification performance and is not too quickly disturbed by a change of distribution in the number of class samples.

Now that the basic cases of detection and classification have been assessed, the multi-label classification and detection, i.e., challenges C3 and C4, must be evaluated on the artificially created multi-label dataset. The performance of each architecture for the detection task is reported in Table 4 for the two different thresholds. The classification performance of the different models for each of the bat species groups and the macro average over the seven classes is presented in Table 5 for the new thresholds. The performance with the thresholds tuned on the augmented data only are not displayed but are higher for all models.

Looking at the detection performances from Table 4a, we see that the network the most fitted to detect the bat calls in the recordings is the CNN8 as it has the best F1-score and best recall. Our CNN XGBoost model has an F1-score of two percent less so its detection performance is not too low compared to the best architecture. It can also be noticed that, for the detection, the models using ResNet all have a lower F1-score than those using CNNs. And in a general manner, we see that all the models perform better in terms of precision than in terms of recall. That indicates that the models tend to miss some low quality, less obvious calls, and recognise more easily when a sound is not a bat call. When using the new thresholds, we can see in Table 4b that for most of the models, the F1-score only slightly decrease, but the gap between detection and recall gets

**Table 5.** Performance of the compared architectures for the classification of each species group as well as the macro average over all the classes with the thresholds optimised on both Natagora and Norfolk. The best F1-score for each class and for the macro-average is highlighted.

| | ResNet8 | | | Double ResNet | | | ResNet XGBoost | | | CNN8 | | | Double CNN | | | CNN XGBoost | | |
|---|---|---|---|---|---|---|---|---|---|---|---|---|---|---|---|---|---|---|
| | Pre | Re | F1 | Pre | Re | F1 | Pre | Re | F1 | Pre | Re | F1 | Pre | Re | F1 | Pre | Re | F1 |
| Barbar | 71 | 88 | 78 | 97 | 56 | 71 | 87 | 61 | 72 | 90 | 73 | 81 | 90 | 80 | 85 | 91 | 52 | 66 |
| Envsp | 89 | 87 | 88 | 88 | 51 | 64 | 88 | 93 | 90 | 92 | 81 | 86 | 94 | 82 | 87 | 91 | 92 | 91 |
| Myosp | 94 | 83 | 88 | 92 | 53 | 67 | 95 | 90 | 92 | 98 | 80 | 88 | 94 | 84 | 89 | 97 | 87 | 92 |
| Pip35 | 73 | 71 | 72 | 60 | 53 | 57 | 71 | 78 | 74 | 73 | 72 | 73 | 74 | 72 | 73 | 82 | 76 | 79 |
| Pip50 | 51 | 89 | 65 | 48 | 23 | 31 | 62 | 88 | 72 | 47 | 92 | 63 | 52 | 90 | 66 | 56 | 93 | 70 |
| Plesp | 87 | 70 | 78 | 85 | 43 | 57 | 81 | 70 | 75 | 95 | 67 | 79 | 93 | 63 | 75 | 82 | 68 | 75 |
| Rhisp | 87 | 83 | 85 | 10 | 100 | 19 | 92 | 81 | 86 | 86 | 86 | 86 | 93 | 73 | 82 | 95 | 84 | 89 |
| Avg | 79 | 81 | 79 | 69 | 54 | 52 | 82 | 80 | 80 | 83 | 79 | 79 | 84 | 78 | 80 | 85 | 79 | 80 |

**Table 6.** Computational resources of the different networks in terms of number of parameters for deep networks and longest paths in the decision trees for XGBoost.

| | ResNet8 | Double ResNet | ResNet XGBoost | CNN8 | Double CNN | CNN XGBoost |
|---|---|---|---|---|---|---|
| Size | 23 571 272 | 47 128 201 | 23 794 880 | 569 048 | 1 185 521 | 806 480 |

higher. In this case, it is the double ResNet model that performs best but our CNN XGBoost remains the second-best performing model.

In terms of average multi-label classification performance, it can be observed in Table 5 that with the Norfolk-optimized thresholds our CNN XGBoost model is one of the models having the best average F1-score. This model also has the best F1-score for most bat species groups. For the classes where it is not the best, it is always quite close to it, except for the Barbar class. In general, we observe that the networks using CNNs tend to perform better than the ones composed of ResNets.

The last challenge to evaluate is the challenge C5, concerning the computational resources used by the architectures to perform a prediction. The resources used by the models are presented in Table 6. For the neural networks, the number of parameters is used as a metric. For models based on XGBoost, in addition, the number of nodes visited to produce a prediction is estimated by summing up the depths of all the trees in the model.

From Table 6 we can conclude that the models using ResNet require much larger computational resources than the ones using simpler CNNs. Our CNN XGBoost model is heavier in terms of computational resources than the basic architecture made of a single CNN, but the difference is much smaller than with ResNet. We can therefore say that our model is light compared to others state of the art architectures.

From the evaluation of challenges C1–C5, we see that our proposed model is the best performing model for many of the evaluated challenges, even though not for all of them. However, in those cases, our CNN XGBoost architecture is always reasonably close to the best model. Therefore, we can say that among all the proposed models, it is the one that is the most well-balanced and is hence best fitted for the problem of multi-label detection and classification using detection and classification data solely.

## 5    Conclusion

We have addressed the need for an automated tool performing both detection and multi-label classification for bat calls in recordings as well as the challenge of the limited datasets available. We presented a data augmentation method and implemented a new architecture responding to that need. We showed that it has good detection and classification performance despite the fact of being trained on an augmented dataset. We then verified that our architecture delivered better performance than the state of the art models for multi-label acoustic bat monitoring tasks. Finally, we verified that the computational resources required by the model are reasonable. From these various evaluations, we concluded that our CNN XGBoost model was the one responding the best to the multiple challenges of the multi-label detection and classification. Future work includes implementing our model on a portable recording device, and studying its use on a more fine-grained bat classification tasks.

**Acknowledgements.** This work was supported by Service Public de Wallonie Recherche under grant n°2010235 - ARIAC by DIGITALWALLONIA4.AI.

We would like to express our gratitude to Natagora and the Plecotus team for the large amount of labelled bat call recordings they shared with us. We would also like to thank Bat detective for the data they have made available and their detection tool, used as starting point in this work. We thank Olivier Bonaventure for joining discussions on this project.

## References

1. Armitage, D.W., Ober, H.K.: A comparison of supervised learning techniques in the classification of bat echolocation calls. Eco. Inform. **5**, 465–473 (2010)
2. Barataud, M.: Acoustic ecology of European bats. Species Identification and Studies of Their Habitats and Foraging Behaviour. Biotope Editions (2015)
3. Bergstra, J., Yamins, D., Cox, D.: Making a science of model search: Hyperparameter optimization in hundreds of dimensions for vision architectures. In: Proceedings of the 30th International Conference on Machine Learning, pp. 115–123 (2013)
4. Border, J.A., Newson, S.E., White, D.C., Gillings, S.: Predicting the likely impact of urbanisation on bat populations using citizen science data, a case study for Norfolk, UK. Landsc. Urban Plan. **162**, 44–55 (2017). https://doi.org/10.1016/j.landurbplan.2017.02.005

5. Chen, X., Zhao, J., Chen, Y.H., Zhou, W., Hughes, A.C.: Automatic standardized processing and identification of tropical bat calls using deep learning approaches. Biol. Conserv. **241** (2020). https://doi.org/10.1016/j.biocon.2019.108269
6. Fan, R.E., Lin, C.J.: A study on threshold selection for multi-label classification (2007)
7. He, K., Zhang, X., Ren, S., Sun, J.: Deep residual learning for image recognition. In: 2016 IEEE Conference on Computer Vision and Pattern Recognition (CVPR), pp. 770–778 (2016). https://doi.org/10.1109/CVPR.2016.90
8. Jones, G., Jacobs, D., Kunz, T., Racey, P.: Carpe noctem: the importance of bats as bioindicators. Endanger. Spec. Res. **8**, 93–115 (2009). https://doi.org/10.3354/esr00182
9. Mac Aodha, O., et al.: Bat detective - deep learning tools for bat acoustic signal detection. PLOS Comput. Biol. (2018). https://doi.org/10.1371/journal.pcbi.1005995
10. Runkel, V., Gerding, G., Marckmann, U.: The Handbook of Acoustic Bat Detection. Pelagic Publishing (2021). https://doi.org/10.53061/XDDW7329
11. Rydell, J., Nyman, S., Eklöf, J., Jones, G., Russo, D.: Testing the performances of automated identification of bat echolocation calls: a request for prudence. Ecol. Ind. **78**, 416–420 (2017). https://doi.org/10.1016/j.ecolind.2017.03.023
12. Schwab, E., Pogrebnoj, S., Freund, M., Flossmann, F., Vogl, S., Frommolt, K.H.: Automated bat call classification using deep convolutional neural networks (2021)
13. Simonyan, K., Zisserman, A.: Very deep convolutional networks for large-scale image recognition. arXiv preprint arXiv:1409.1556 (2014)
14. Tabak, M., Murray, K., Lombardi, J., Bay, K.: Automated classification of bat echolocation call recordings with artificial intelligence (2021). https://doi.org/10.1101/2021.06.23.449619
15. Voigt, C.C., Kingston, T. (eds.): Bats in the Anthropocene: Conservation of Bats in a Changing World. Springer, Cham (2016). https://doi.org/10.1007/978-3-319-25220-9
16. Zhang, M.-L., Li, Y.-K., Liu, X.-Y., Geng, X.: Binary relevance for multi-label learning: an overview. Front. Comp. Sci. **12**, 191–202 (2018). https://doi.org/10.1007/s11704-017-7031-7
17. Zualkernan, I., Judas, J., Mahbub, T., Bhagwagar, A., Chand, P.: A tiny CNN architecture for identifying bat species from echolocation calls. In: 2020 IEEE/ITU International Conference on Artificial Intelligence for Good (AI4G), pp. 81–86 (2020). https://doi.org/10.1109/AI4G50087.2020.9311084

# End-to-End Mobile System for Diabetic Retinopathy Screening Based on Lightweight Deep Neural Network

Yaroub Elloumi[1,2,3(✉)], Nesrine Abroug[4], and Mohamed Hedi Bedoui[1]

[1] Medical Technology and Image Processing Laboratory, Faculty of Medicine, University of Monastir, Monastir, Tunisia
yaroub.elloumi@esiee.fr
[2] LIGM, Univ Gustave Eiffel, CNRS, ESIEE Paris, 77454 Marne-la-Vallée, France
[3] ISITCom Hammam-Sousse, University of Sousse, Sousse, Tunisia
[4] Department of Ophthalmology, Fattouma Bourguiba University Hospital, Faculty of Medicine, University of Monastir, Monastir, Tunisia

**Abstract.** Diabetic Retinopathy (DR) is the leading cause of visual impairment among working-aged adults. Screening and early diagnosis of DR is essential to avoid visual acuity reduction and blindness. However, a worldwide limited access to ophthalmologists may prevent an early diagnosis of this blinding condition. In this paper, we propose a novel method for screening DR from smartphone-captured fundus images. The main challenges are to perform higher accurate detection even with reduced quality of handheld captured fundus images and to provide the result into the smartphone used for acquisition. For such a need, we apply transfer learning to the lightweight deep neural network "NasnetMobile" which is used as a feature descriptor, while configuring a multi-layer perceptron classifier to deduce the DR disease, in order to take benefit from their lower complexity. A dataset composed of 440 fundus images is structured, where the acquisition and statement are performed by expert ophthalmologists. A cross-validation process is conducted where 95.91% accuracy, 94.44% sensitivity, 96.92% specificity and 95.71% precision in average are achieved. In addition, the whole processing flowchart is implemented into a mobile device, where the execution time is under one second whatever the fundus image is. Those performances allow deploying the proposed system in a clinical context.

**Keywords:** Diabetic retinopathy · Deep learning · Transfer Learning · Mobile-health

## 1 Introduction

Diabetic Retinopathy (DR) is an ocular disease registered for 30% of diabetes-affected patients [1]. Based on the world health organization report, 146 million suffer from DR [2]. Advanced stages of DR may lead to severe visual acuity impairment and blindness [3, 4], with 37 million blind persons worldwide. Therefore, DR screening is mandatory

© The Author(s), under exclusive license to Springer Nature Switzerland AG 2022
T. Bouadi et al. (Eds.): IDA 2022, LNCS 13205, pp. 66–77, 2022.
https://doi.org/10.1007/978-3-031-01333-1_6

for the early diagnosis and initiation of appropriate treatment to improve the visual outcome and to prevent blindness. Fundus examination is the main clinical approach to screen DR.

Actually, a heavy workload is requested from ophthalmologists, where a ratio of 50 per million persons worldwide is required to ensure early screening and timely management of DR. However, only 21 countries have verified the targeted ratio, where the actual global ratio is about 29 ophthalmologists per million persons [5, 6]. Consequently, in many countries, there is a lack of periodical DR screening, hence an important delay of DR diagnosis.

Recently, several optical lens-based devices have been proposed, which can be snapped into smartphones to capture fundus images. Those devices are distinguished by their low-cost and mobility, which are associated to the smartphone availability in terms of connectivity, data storage and processing [7–9]. The mobile devices ensure capturing fundus images with sufficient quality compared to those captured by conventional fundus cameras. However, blurs and noise are always deduced caused by the handheld aspect of the mobile capturing. Several clinical studies have been performed and have shown similar DR detection accuracy from smartphone-captured fundus images and conventional fundus cameras-captured images [10–12].

Previous studies have aimed to automatically screen DR from smartphone-captured fundus images [13–15]. Some work has addressed the problem of limited quality of fundus images, where the different limitations were highlighted in [16]. To outperform those problems, the methods have been based on intensive computational processing. In [17], DR detection was provided though a multiple instance for the AlexNet Deep Convolutional Neural Network (DCNN) architecture, while the method suggested in [16] used the ResNet50 neural network as a feature descriptor. Such processing could not be run into embedded or smartphone devices, due to the limited material resources.

Other methods have aimed to run DR screening into smartphones where the main contribution was based on suggesting low complexity processing. In [18, 19], features were extracted though linear computational complexity, where the DR stages were detected using the SVM classifier. Elsewhere, lightweight DCNNs were employed such as mobilenet-V2 and inception-V3, respectively used in [20–22]. However, these methods did not consider the decreased quality of smartphone-captured fundus images, where they were validated using database images acquired by classical conventional fundus cameras. Little work has addressed both challenges, hence failing to achieve higher performance, such as the one described in [14] where 62% precision was registered.

The originality of our work is to describe an automated method that (1) ensures higher performant DR screening from smartphone-based fundus photography and which (2) has a low complexity to be implemented into a smartphone associated with a mobile device. The whole hardware and software tool presents an end-to-end mobile system from fundus image acquisition to DR screening. For such a need, a preprocessing is performed to enhance the image quality. Then, the DCNN "Nasnet-Mobile" is used as a feature descriptor, which is characterized by its higher performance, lightweight processing and fast convergence even with a reduced database size. Then, the extracted features are provided to a Multi-Layer Perceptron (MLP) classifier with a single hidden layer, to deduce the DR disease. This work is a part of project leading to mobile computer-screening system for DR which we already developed in [10, 18, 19].

The suggested method is introduced in the rest of the paper. Section 2 describes the automated method for DR screening. The experimental evaluation of the detection performance and the execution time is presented in Sect. 3. The conclusion and some future work are detailed in Sect. 4.

## 2   Novel Method for DR Screening

### 2.1   Pre-processing and Data Processing

Basically, the dataset images must be resized to (224 × 224 × 3) to be provided to the NasNet-Mobile. Preprocessing aims to enhance the fundus image quality in order to promote DR screening. In fact, the handheld capture of fundus images leads to a blurred illustration of retinal components, especially the DR lesions characterized by a small size such as micro-aneurysms or hard exudates. Thus, the point spread function is applied to clearly model the retina [18], as shown in Fig. 1(b). The variability on the light source causes a non-balanced contrast of the smartphone-captured fundus images. To resolve this problem, the Contrast Limited Adaptive Histogram Equalization (CLAHE) approach [23] is applied, as illustrated in Fig. 1(c).

Thereafter, a data augmentation is applied in order to increase the dataset size and enhance the DL model robustness. For this purpose, all images are flipped and shifted horizontally and vertically, rotated with angle 30°, zoomed and contrast-adjusted with respect to the varied contrast of the smartphone-captured fundus images [24, 25].

### 2.2   Nasnet-Mobile Architecture

The Nas Network (NasNet) is a CNN architecture provided by the neural architecture search (Nas) framework [26]. It a research algorithm that designs an optimal convolutional architecture is for a given dataset, through a scalable method. The framework is based on a controller recurrent neural network (RNN) where networks are iteratively generated and trained using the provided dataset. Then, their accuracies are returned to the controller to enhance the next versions of architectures [27, 28]. The research leads to compose the network by convolutional layers called "normal cell" and "reduction

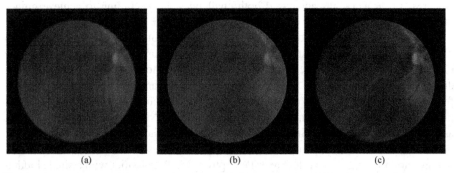

Fig. 1. Fundus images: (a) captured with Volk-inView, (b) after deblurring, (c) after contrast enhancement

cell" having identical structure with different weights. The first cell type generates a feature map preserving the same resolution than the input. the second one reduces the feature map size through a stride = 2. Using the "ImageNet" dataset that contains 1,000 categories [29], the Nas framework was provided an architecture where the selected cells are as modelled in Fig. 2. We note that Nas framework may provide a lightweight architecture called "NasNet-Mobile" made up of only four million parameters [28], which is able to perform an accurate classification [30].

## 2.3 Transfer Learning of Nasnet-Mobile Architecture

The available dataset is composed of few hundreds of smartphone-captured fundus images. To ensure reliable performance, the transfer learning method is endorsed [31], where the NasNet-Mobile model, initially trained with the "ImageNet" dataset that contains 1,000 categories [29, 32] is retrieved. The classification layer is interchanged by the four ones, as described in Fig. 2. The first layer consists of an Average Pooling where the input feature map is spatially partitioned into a grid of square blocks with side 2, and average over each blocks are stored in the output feature map. Then, a flatten is performed to align all features into a single row. The third layer applies a dropout function to prevent overfitting, with a threshold equal to 0.7. The last one is a dense layer with a ReLU function where the feature vector size is reduced to 32, while decreasing the error through back-propagation.

The model is finetuned in order to update the weights of neurons during training, where the chosen learning rate is 0.000005 [29, 33]. The optimal weight is stored after each epoch, to guarantee converging the model. Training is performed into 150 epochs, and the weights are updated following the "Adam" optimizer [34]. The "categorical-cross entropy" loss function is adopted, where the loss is based on the sum of all computed ratios. The main hyper parameters used for training are summarized in Table 1.

**Table 1.** Hyper parameters of training NasNet-Mobile model

| Parameter | Value |
| --- | --- |
| Optimizer | Adam optimizer |
| Learning rate | 0.000005 |
| Regularization | Dropout (0.7) |
| Mini-batch size | 2 |
| Epoch | 200 |
| Loss function | Binary cross-entropy |

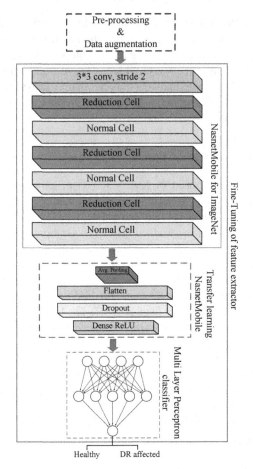

**Fig. 2.** Processing flowchart of the proposed DR screening method

## 2.4 MLP Configuration

The classifier must retrieve a feature map from the NasNet-Mobile deep learning model in order to ensure a performant classification, through low-complexity processing. Based on those constraints, the MLP classifier is chosen to ensure the classification of DR-affected fundus images. It is considered as a neural network where the weights are randomly predefined. Indeed, it is widely employed in medical classification problems. The MLP can be configured in terms of number of hidden layers and number of neurons inside. We choose a single hidden layer to reduce the computational complexity. After that, we perform an experimental study where the neuron number is varied. Then, training and testing processes are iteratively performed to evaluate the current MLP, as detailed in Table 2. Based on the experiment results, we deduce that a hidden layer with 10 neurons will allow achieving the best classification result.

**Table 2.** Performance classification in terms of neuron number of hidden layer

| Neuron number of hidden layer | 8 | 10 | 12 |
|---|---|---|---|
| Sens | 88.57 | 94.44 | 94.29 |
| Spec | 91.67 | 96.15 | 85.42 |
| Acc | 89.83 | 95.4.45 | 90.68 |
| Prec | 93.94 | 94.44 | 90.41 |

## 3 Experimental Results

### 3.1 Dataset

Patients' data were collected in the department of ophthalmology belonging to Fattouma Bourguiba University Hospital (Tunisia), between 2019–2020. Image acquisition was performed after preliminary eye examination and dilating pupil of patient eyes using mydriatic substance. Fundus images were captured using a Volk-InView dispositive, as shown in Fig. 3, allowing a field of view of 50°. Several clinical studies have attested the higher quality of fundus images captured by Volk-InView, compared to other optical lenses such as D-Eye, Retina Peek and Welch Allyn [16]. All anonymized captured images were evaluated by two independent masked retina specialists (NA and IK). Screening the DR lesions of retinal photographs using the "International Clinical Diabetic Retinopathy Classification Severity Score" was performed, where images were graded as non DR and DR.

The dispositive was snapped into an "Ipod Touch" device where the camera resolution was about 8 Mp. The dataset was composed of 440 images, where 260 were classified as healthy and 180 contained DR lesions. The image resolution was 892 * 892 pixels with 96 dpi, where some healthy and DR affected captured retina are shown in Table 3. It is easy to distinguish retinal components, such as the optic disk, the macula and DR lesions, even those having small sizes.

The evaluation is performed through a five-fold cross validation approach to guarantee a reliable evaluation, where the dataset is partitioned into 5 subsets. To overcome the problem of the reduced dataset size, four subsets representing 80% of fundus images are dedicated for training. The fifth subset is partitioned equitably between validation and testing sub-sets, as illustrated in Fig. 3.

| Val. Test | Training | Training | Training | Training |
|---|---|---|---|---|
| Training | Val. Test | Training | Training | Training |
| Training | Training | Val. Test | Training | Training |
| Training | Training | Training | Val. Test | Training |
| Training | Training | Training | Training | Val. Test |

**Fig. 3.** Dispatching of subsets for 5-fold cross validation

**Table 3.** Healthy and DR-affected fundus images

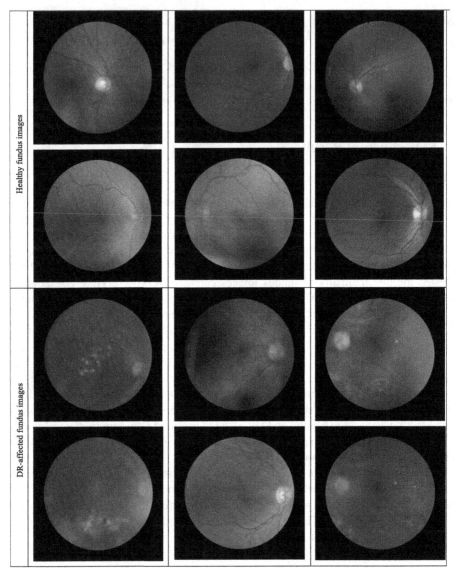

## 3.2  ML Implementation

The method is coded using the Python language. Preprocessing is performed using the OpenCV library, while NasNet-Mobile and MLP are implemented using the "Keras" API. The training and testing steps are executed on the cloud service "google Colab". The curve slopes of accuracy and loss for both training and validation are retrieved as depicted in Fig. 4. It is deduced that both accuracy (resp. loss) curves increase (resp. decrease) progressively to become almost constant.

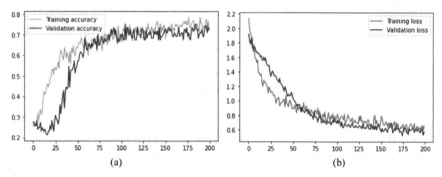

**Fig. 4.** Evaluation of training performance in terms of epochs: (a) Training and validation accuracy values; (b) Training and validation loss values

### 3.3 Evaluation Metrics

The performance of our method is evaluated through the Accuracy (Acc), Sensitivity (Sens), Specificity (Spec) and Precision (Prec) metrics, which are computed as indicated in Eqs. 1, 2, 3 and 4.

$$Sensitivity = \frac{TP}{TP + FN} \tag{1}$$

$$Specificity = \frac{TN}{TN + FP} \tag{2}$$

$$Accuracy = \frac{TP + TN}{TP + FP + TN + FN} \tag{3}$$

$$Prec = \frac{TP}{TP + FP} \tag{4}$$

where TP (True Positive) is the number of images classified correctly as DR-affected, TN (True Negative) is the number of images classified correctly as healthy, FP (False Positive) is the number of healthy images identified as DR, and FN (False Negative) is the number of DR-affected images classified as healthy.

### 3.4 Performance Evaluation of Proposed Method

This method is evaluated using all cross-datasets, where the performance metrics of each one are shown in Table 4. We deduce that our method carries out higher accuracy, which achieves 97.73%. Even with an equitable partition between healthy and DR-affected images, sensitivity and specificity have higher values whatever the cross dataset is.

**Table 4.** DR screening performances in terms of cross-datasets

|  | Acc (%) | Sens (%) | Spec (%) | Prec (%) |
|---|---|---|---|---|
| First cross-database | 97.73 | 94.44 | 100.00 | 100.00 |
| Second cross-database | 93.18 | 88.89 | 96.15 | 94.12 |
| Third cross-database | 95.45 | 94.44 | 96.15 | 94.44 |
| Fourth cross-database | 97.73 | 94.44 | 100.00 | 100.00 |
| Fifth cross-database | 95.45 | 100.00 | 92.31 | 90.00 |

The performances of cross-validation sets are illustrated through the box plots represented in Fig. 5. The reduced plot sizes justify the sustainability of the DR screening whatever the image set, either used for testing or for training. Consequently, it reflects the method robustness and confirms its capacity to be used as a mobile aided screening system for DR.

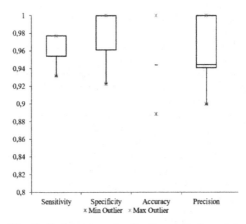

**Fig. 5.** Performance visualization using box plots

### 3.5 Execution Time Evaluation of the Mobile-Aided Screening System

The trained Nasnet-Mobile model associated to the MLP classifier must be updated to be suitable for smartphone uses. Therefore, the method is implemented as an android app through an Android Studio 4.2 and JAVA Development Kit (JDK) 15.0.2. Therefore, the "TFLiteConverter" class of the public "tf.lite" API is used to convert the trained "TensorFlow" model into a "TensorFlowLite" model. The NasNet-Mobile is converted into a FlatBuffer file (.tflite) and stored into a"TensorFlowLite" model to be called through the "TensorFlow Lite Android Support" library. The MLP classifier and the image enhancement processing are implemented using the predefined function of the "Open Source Computer Vision (OpenCV)" multiplatform library which is compiled by an Android Native Development Kit (NDK).

Thereafter, we evaluate the computational performance of DR screening when run in a mobile device as an app. For such a need, 10 images (partitioned equitably on healthy and DR-affected fundus images) are randomly selected from the dataset and tested through the app executed into a "Samsung Galaxy A31" smartphone having an octa-core processor ($2 \times 2$ GHz & $6 \times 1.95$ GHz) and 4 Go RAM. We deduce that all execution time is above one second, as depicted in Fig. 6. In addition, close values are registered where the average value is equal to 0.894 s. Accordingly, we deduce that the computational performance is adequate to promote using our system in clinical contexts.

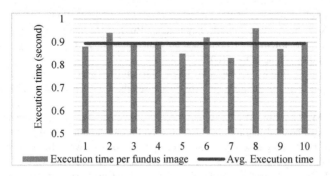

**Fig. 6.** Execution time of DR screening application in terms of fundus images

## 4 Conclusion

DR is a major cause of blindness worldwide. Our challenge consists in screening DR using a mobile CAD system, while ensuring all tasks from the fundus image acquisition to the decision generation. For such a requirement, we have proposed a preprocessing to enhance the image quality. Then, we have employed a lightweight DL architecture and a low complexity classifier to carry out higher performant DR screening. The experimentation has been proved respecting the clinical constraints in terms of screening performance and execution time.

In our future work, we aim to extend the dataset size by continuous collaboration with the expert ophthalmologist team. Afterwards, the provided system will be extended to ensure fundus image grading into DR severity. Otherwise, the system will be oriented to other ocular pathologies such as glaucoma, aged macular degeneration or hypertensive retinopathy. Furthermore, the lightweight processing principle can be carried out into other mobile-health domains [35].

**Funding.** This work was supported by the Campus-France PHC-UTIQUE (19G1408) Research program.

## References

1. Sabanayagam, C., et al.: Incidence and progression of diabetic retinopathy: a systematic review. Lancet Diab. Endocrinol. **7**, 140–149 (2019)

2. Pan, J., et al.: Characteristics of neovascularization in early stages of proliferative diabetic retinopathy by optical coherence tomography angiography. Am. J. Ophthalmol. **192**, 146–156 (2018)

3. Ting, D.S.W., Cheung, G.C.M., Wong, T.Y.: Diabetic retinopathy: global prevalence, major risk factors, screening practices and public health challenges: a review: global burden of diabetic eye diseases. Clin. Exp. Ophthalmol. **44**, 260–277 (2016)

4. Chalakkal, R.J., Abdulla, W.H., Hong, S.C.: Fundus retinal image analyses for screening and diagnosing diabetic retinopathy, macular edema, and glaucoma disorders. In: Diabetes and Fundus OCT, pp. 59–111. Elsevier (2020)

5. Resnikoff, S., et al.: Estimated number of ophthalmologists worldwide (International Council of Ophthalmology update): will we meet the needs? Br. J. Ophthalmol. **104**, 588–592 (2020)

6. Singh, J., Kabbara, S., Conway, M., Peyman, G., Ross, R.D.: Innovative diagnostic tools for ophthalmology in low-income countries. In: Nowinska, A. (ed.) Novel Diagnostic Methods in Ophthalmology. IntechOpen (2019)

7. Panwar, N., et al.: Fundus photography in the 21st century—a review of recent technological advances and their implications for worldwide healthcare. Telemed. e-Health **22**, 198–208 (2016)

8. Bolster, N.M., Giardini, M.E., Livingstone, I.A., Bastawrous, A.: How the smartphone is driving the eye-health imaging revolution. Expert Rev. Ophthalmol. **9**, 475–485 (2014)

9. Russo, A., et al.: Comparison of smartphone ophthalmoscopy with slit-lamp biomicroscopy for grading vertical cup-to-disc ratio. J. Glaucoma **25**, e777–e781 (2016)

10. Akil, M., Elloumi, Y.: Detection of retinal abnormalities using smartphone-captured fundus images: a survey. In: Kehtarnavaz, N., Carlsohn, M.F. (eds.) Real-Time Image Processing and Deep Learning 2019, vol. 21. SPIE (2019)

11. Prasanna, P., Jain, S., Bhagat, N., Madabhushi, A.: Decision support system for detection of diabetic retinopathy using smartphones. In: Proceedings of the ICTs for improving Patients Rehabilitation Research Techniques. IEEE (2013)

12. Monjur, M., et al.: Smartphone based fundus camera for the diagnosis of retinal diseases. Smart Health **19**, 100177 (2021)

13. Karakaya, M., Hacisoftaoglu, R.E.: Comparison of smartphone-based retinal imaging systems for diabetic retinopathy detection using deep learning. BMC Bioinf. **21**, 259 (2020)

14. Kashyap, N., Singh, D.K., Singh, G.K.: Mobile phone based diabetic retinopathy detection system using ANN-DWT. In: 2017 4th IEEE Uttar Pradesh Section International Conference on Electrical, Computer and Electronics (UPCON), pp. 463–467. IEEE (2017)

15. Kalpiyapan, V., Aimmanee, P., Makhanov, S., Wongsakittirak, S., Karnchanaran, N.: An automatic system to detect exudates in mobile-phone fundus images for DR pre-screening. In: 2018 Thirteenth International Conference on Knowledge, Information and Creativity Support Systems (KICSS), pp. 1–6. IEEE (2018)

16. Hacisoftaoglu, R.E., Karakaya, M., Sallam, A.B.: Deep learning frameworks for diabetic retinopathy detection with smartphone-based retinal imaging systems. Pattern Recogn. Lett. **135**, 409–417 (2020)

17. Mueller, S., et al.: Automated detection of diabetic retinopathy from smartphone fundus videos. In: Fu, H., Garvin, M.K., MacGillivray, T., Xu, Y., Zheng, Y. (eds.) OMIA 2020. LNCS, vol. 12069, pp. 83–92. Springer, Cham (2020). https://doi.org/10.1007/978-3-030-63419-3_9

18. Boukadida, R., Elloumi, Y., Akil, M., Bedoui, M.H.: Mobile-aided screening system for proliferative diabetic retinopathy. Int. J. Imaging Syst. Technol. **31**, 1638–1654 (2021)

19. Elloumi, Y., Ben Mbarek, M., Boukadida, R., Akil, M. & Bedoui, M. H. Fast and accurate mobile-aided screening system of moderate diabetic retinopathy. in *Thirteenth International Conference on Machine Vision* (eds. Osten, W., Zhou, J. & Nikolaev, D. P.) 93 (SPIE, 2021)

20. Suriyal, S., Druzgalski, C., Gautam, K.: Mobile assisted diabetic retinopathy detection using deep neural network. In: 2018 Global Medical Engineering Physics Exchanges/Pan American Health Care Exchanges (GMEPE/PAHCE), pp. 1–4. IEEE (2018)
21. Hagos, M.T., Kant, S.: Transfer learning based detection of diabetic retinopathy from small dataset. arXiv:1905.07203 [cs] (2019)
22. Majumder, S., Elloumi, Y., Akil, M., Kachouri, R., Kehtarnavaz, N.: A deep learning-based smartphone app for real-time detection of five stages of diabetic retinopathy. In: Kehtarnavaz, N., Carlsohn, M.F. (eds.) Real-Time Image Processing and Deep Learning 2020, vol. 5. SPIE (2020)
23. Chalakkal, R.J., Abdulla, W.: Automatic segmentation of retinal vasculature. In: 2017 IEEE International Conference on Acoustics, Speech and Signal Processing (ICASSP), pp. 886–890. IEEE (2017)
24. Blaiech, A.G., Mansour, A., Kerkeni, A., Bedoui, M.H., Ben Abdallah, A.: Impact of enhancement for coronary artery segmentation based on deep learning neural network. In: Morales, A., Fierrez, J., Sánchez, J.S., Ribeiro, B. (eds.) IbPRIA 2019. LNCS, vol. 11868, pp. 260–272. Springer, Cham (2019). https://doi.org/10.1007/978-3-030-31321-0_23
25. Elloumi, Y.: Mobile aided system of deep-learning based cataract grading from fundus images. In: Tucker, A., Henriques Abreu, P., Cardoso, J., Pereira Rodrigues, P., Riaño, D. (eds.) AIME 2021. LNCS (LNAI), vol. 12721, pp. 355–360. Springer, Cham (2021). https://doi.org/10.1007/978-3-030-77211-6_40
26. Gupta, A., Anjum, S., Katarya, R.: InstaCovNet-19: a deep learning classification model for the detection of COVID-19 patients using Chest X-ray. Appl. Soft Comput. 99, 106859 (2021)
27. Cogan, T., Cogan, M., Tamil, L.: MAPGI: Accurate identification of anatomical landmarks and diseased tissue in gastrointestinal tract using deep learning. Comput. Biol. Med. 111, 103351 (2019)
28. Bahri, A., Majelan, S.G., Mohammadi, S., Noori, M., Mohammadi, K.: Remote sensing image classification via improved cross-entropy loss and transfer learning strategy based on deep convolutional neural networks. IEEE Geosci. Remote Sens. Lett. 17, 1087–1091 (2020)
29. Li, F., et al.: Automatic detection of diabetic retinopathy in retinal fundus photographs based on deep learning algorithm. Trans. Vis. Sci. Tech. 8, 4 (2019)
30. Winoto, A.S., Kristianus, M., Premachandra, C.: Small and slim deep convolutional neural network for mobile device. IEEE Access 8, 125210–125222 (2020)
31. Bouden, A., Blaiech, A.G., Ben Khalifa, K., Ben Abdallah, A., Bedoui, M.H.: A novel deep learning model for COVID-19 detection from combined heterogeneous X-ray and CT chest images. In: Tucker, A., Henriques Abreu, P., Cardoso, J., Pereira Rodrigues, P., Riaño, D. (eds.) AIME 2021. LNCS (LNAI), vol. 12721, pp. 378–383. Springer, Cham (2021). https://doi.org/10.1007/978-3-030-77211-6_44
32. Elloumi, Y., Akil, M., Boudegga, H.: Ocular diseases diagnosis in fundus images using a deep learning: approaches, tools and performance evaluation. arXiv:1905.02544 [cs, eess] (2019)
33. Mateen, M., Wen, J., Nasrullah, N., Sun, S., Hayat, S.: Exudate detection for diabetic retinopathy using pretrained convolutional neural networks. Complexity 2020, 1–11 (2020)
34. Boudegga, H., et al.: Fast and efficient retinal blood vessel segmentation method based on deep learning network. Comput. Med. Imag. Graph. 90, 101902 (2021)
35. Khessiba, S., Blaiech, A.G., Ben Khalifa, K., Ben Abdallah, A., Bedoui, M.H.: Innovative deep learning models for EEG-based vigilance detection. Neural Comput. Appl. 33, 6921–6937 (2021)

# Efficient Bayesian Learning of Sparse Deep Artificial Neural Networks

Mohamed Fakhfakh[1,2]($\boxtimes$), Bassem Bouaziz[1], Lotfi Chaari[2], and Faiez Gargouri[1]

[1] MIRACL Laboratory, University of Sfax, Sfax, Tunisia
{bassem.bouaziz,faiez.gargouri}@isims.usf.tn
[2] University of Toulouse, INP, IRIT, Toulouse, France
{mohamed.fakhfakh,lotfi.chaari}@toulouse-inp.fr

**Abstract.** In supervised Machine Learning (ML), Artificial Neural Networks (ANN) are commonly utilized to analyze signals or images for a variety of applications. They are increasingly performing as a strong tool to establish the relationships among data and being successfully applied in science due to their generalization ability, noise and fault tolerance. One of the most difficult aspects of using the learning process is optimization of the network weights.

A gradient-based technique with a back-propagation strategy is commonly used for this optimization stage. Regularization is commonly employed for the benefit of efficiency. This optimization gets difficult when non-smooth regularizers are applied, especially to promote sparse networks. Due to differentiability difficulties, traditional gradient-based optimizers cannot be employed.

In this paper, we propose an MCMC-based optimization strategy within a Bayesian framework. An effective sampling strategy is designed using Hamiltonian dynamics. The suggested strategy appears to be effective in allowing ANNs with modest complexity levels to achieve high accuracy rates, as seen by promising findings.

**Keywords:** Artificial neural networks · Optimization · Deep learning · LSTM · MCMC · Hamiltonian dynamics

## 1 Introduction

Machine learning (ML) [1] is an artificial intelligence subfield (AI). It has expanded at an incredible rate, drawing a large number of academics interested in studying how a system may learn to do a task. In reality, an ML system does not follow instructions but instead learns from experience, such as making predictions or decisions based on data and continuously improving performance by reviewing new data. ML research achieved outstanding results on several complex cognitive tasks, including Computer Vision [2–5], Medical diagnoses [6–9], Signal Processing [10,11], recommendation systems [12], etc. Deep Learning

© The Author(s), under exclusive license to Springer Nature Switzerland AG 2022
T. Bouadi et al. (Eds.): IDA 2022, LNCS 13205, pp. 78–88, 2022.
https://doi.org/10.1007/978-3-031-01333-1_7

(DL) [13,14] architectures have proved their capacity to deal with progressively voluminous data during the previous two decades. Furthermore, it has gradually become the most extensively employed computational strategy in the field of machine learning, generating exceptional results on a variety of cognitive tasks, equal or even surpassing human performance in some cases. The capacity to learn from huge volumes of data is one of the benefits and challenges of deep learning.

In a similar vein, Convolutional neural networks (CNN) [2,15,16] are one of the state-of-art deep learning techniques. CNNs are designed to automatically and adaptively learn spatial hierarchies of features through backpropagation [17,18] by using multiple building blocks, such as convolution layers, pooling layers, and fully connected layers. However, training a CNN is a challenging task, especially for deep architecture involving a high number of parameters (model weights) to be estimated. Sophisticated optimization algorithms need therefore to be used. This is indeed the key step in order to fit a given architecture to learning data in order to minimize the error between ground truth and estimates.

Many optimization techniques have been presented in recent years [19]. The convexity and differentiability of the target loss function have a significant impact on the performance of the deployed algorithms. Hence, choosing an optimization strategy that seeks to find the global optima in the learning stage is generally challenging, especially when the number of parameters is large. A nonappropriate optimization technique may for instance lead the network to lie in a local minimum during training phase. Speeding up the optimization process is also a challenging issue for large databases.

In this context, Bayesian approaches have made significant progress in a number of areas over the years, and there are several practical benefits. The core concept is to use probabilities to represent all uncertainties throughout the model. One of the most significant benefits is the ability to incorporate prior information. Indeed, recent developments in Markov Chain Monte Carlo (MCMC) methods [20–24] facilitate the implementation of Bayesian analyses of complex data sets containing missing observations and handling multidimensional outcomes. The main goal of this paper is to highlight a Bayesian model for the minimization of the target cost function of a learning model through hyperparameters adjustment.

Specifically, we propose a Bayesian optimization method to minimise the target cost function and derive the optimal weights vector. Indeed, we demonstrate that using the proposed method leads to high accuracy results, which cannot be reached using competing.

The rest of this paper is organized as follows. The addressed problem is formulated in Sect. 2. The proposed efficient Bayesian optimization scheme is developed in Sect. 3 and validated in Sect. 4. Finally, conclusions and future work are drawn in Sect. 5.

## 2   Problem Formulation

It is well known that weights optimization is one of the key steps to design an efficient artificial neural network. For instance, if we consider a classification problem, the ANN weight vector $W$ is updated during the learning phase by minimizing an error between the ground truth and the labels estimated using the network. An iterative procedure is generally performed, and gradient-based optimization procedures are used. For the sake of efficiency, regularization can also be performed in order to have a more accurate weights configuration. In this sense, smooth regularizers such as the $\ell_2$ norm are used. In this case, gradient-based algorithms could still be used. However, if one aims at promoting sparse networks, sparse regularizations such as the $\ell_1$ norm should be used, which makes the use of gradient-based algorithms inefficient since the error to be minimized in this case is no longer differentiable.

In this paper, we propose a method to allow weights optimization under non-smooth regularizations. Let us denote by $x$ an input to be presented to the ANN. The estimated label will be denoted by $\widehat{y}(x, W)$ as a non-linear function of the input $x$ and the weights vector $W \in \mathbb{R}^N$, while the ground truth label will be denoted by $y$.

Using a quadratic error with an $\ell_1$ regularization with $M$ input data for the learning step, the weights vector can be estimated as:

$$
\begin{aligned}
\widehat{W} &= \arg\min_{W} \mathcal{L}(W) \\
&= \arg\min_{W} \sum_{m=1}^{M} \|\widehat{y}(x^m; W) - y^{(m)}\|_2^2 + \lambda \|W\|_1
\end{aligned}
\tag{1}
$$

where $\lambda$ is a regularization parameter balancing the solution between the data fidelity and regularization terms, and $M$ is the number of learning data.

Since the optimization problem in (1) is not differentiable, the use of gradient-based algorithms with back-propagation is not possible. In this case, the learning process is costly and very complicated.

In Sect. 3 we present a method to efficiently estimate the weights vector without increase of learning complexity. The optimization problem in (1) is formulated and solved in a Bayesian framework.

## 3   Bayesian Optimization

As stated above, the weights optimization problem is formulated in a Bayesian framework. In this sense, the problem parameters and hyperparameters are assumed to follow probability distributions. More specifically, a likelihood distribution is defined to model the link between the target weights vector and the data, while a prior distribution is defined to model the prior knowledge about the target weights.

## 3.1   Hierarchical Bayesian Model

According to the principle of minimizing the error between the reference label $y$ and the estimated one $\widehat{y}$, and assuming a quadratic error (first term in (1)), we define the likelihood distribution as

$$f(y; W, \sigma) \propto \prod_{m=1}^{M} \exp \left( -\frac{1}{2\sigma^2} \|\widehat{y}(x^m; W) - y^{(m)}\|^2 \right), \tag{2}$$

where $\sigma^2$ is a positive parameter to be set.

As regards the prior knowledge on the weights vector $W$, we propose the use of a Laplace distribution in order to promote the sparsity of the neural network:

$$f(W; \lambda) \propto \prod_{k=1}^{N} \exp \left( -\frac{\|W^{[k]}\|_1}{\lambda} \right), \tag{3}$$

where $\lambda$ is a hyperparameter to be fixed or estimated.

By adopting a Maximum A Posteriori (MAP) approach, we first need to express the posterior distribution. Based on the defined likelihood and prior, this posterior writes:

$$f(W; y, \sigma, \lambda) \propto f(y; W, \sigma) f(W; \lambda)$$

$$\propto \prod_{m=1}^{M} \exp \left( -\frac{1}{2\sigma^2} \|\widehat{y}(x^m; W) - y^{(m)}\|^2 \right) \prod_{k=1}^{N} \exp \left( -\frac{\|W^{[k]}\|_1}{\lambda} \right). \tag{4}$$

It is clear that this posterior is not straightforward to handle in order to derive a closed-form expression of the estimate $\widehat{W}$. For this reason, we resort to a stochastic sampling approach in order to numerically approximate the posterior, and hence to calculate an estimator for $\widehat{W}$. The following Section details the adopted sampling procedure.

## 3.2   Hamiltonian Sampling

Let us denote $\alpha = \dfrac{\lambda}{\sigma^2}$ and $\theta = \{\sigma^2, \lambda\}$. For a weight $W^k$ we define the following energy function

$$E_\theta^k(W^k) = \frac{\alpha}{2} \sum_{m=1}^{M} \|\widehat{y}(x^m; W) - y^{(m)}\|_2^2 + \|W^k\|_1. \tag{5}$$

The posterior in (4) can therefore be reformulated as

$$f(W; y, \theta) \propto \exp \left( -\sum_{k=1}^{N} E_\theta^k(W^k) \right). \tag{6}$$

To sample according to this exponential posterior, and since direct sampling is not possible due to the form of the energy function $E_\theta^k$, Hamiltonian sampling is adopted. Indeed, Hamiltonian dynamics [25] strategy has been widely used in the literature to sample from high dimensional vectors. However, sampling using Hamiltonian dynamics requires computing the gradient of the energy function, which is not possible in our case due to the $\ell_1$ term. To overcome this difficulty, we resort to a non-smooth Hamiltonian Monte Carlo (ns-HMC) strategy as proposed in [26]. More specifically, we use the plug and play procedure developed in [27]. Indeed, this strategy requires to calculate the proximity operator only at an initial point, and uses the shift property [28,29] to deduce the proximity operator during the iterative procedure [27, Algorithm 1].

As regards the proximity operator calculation, let us denote by $G_{\mathcal{L}}(W^k)$ the gradient of the quadratic term of the loss function $\mathcal{L}$ with respect to the weight $W^k$. Let us also denote by $\varphi(W^k) = \|W^k\|_1$. Following the standard definition of the proximity operator [28,29], we can write for a point $z$

$$\text{prox}_{E_\theta^k}(z) = p \Leftrightarrow z - p \in \partial E_\theta^k(p). \tag{7}$$

Straightforward calculations lead to the following expression of the proximity operator:

$$\text{prox}_{E_\theta^k}(z) = \text{prox}_\varphi \left( z - \frac{\alpha}{2} G_{\mathcal{L}}(W^k) \right). \tag{8}$$

Since $\text{prox}_\varphi$ is nothing but the soft thresholding operator [29], the proximity operator in (8) can be easily calculated once a single gradient step is applied (back-propagation) to calculate $G_{\mathcal{L}}(W^k)$.

The main steps of the proposed method are detailed in Algorithm 1.

---

**Algorithm 1:** Main steps of the proposed Bayesian optimization.

---

- Fix the hyperparameters $\lambda$ and $\sigma$;
- Initialize with some $W_0$;
- Perform one back-propagation step to provide an initialization for $G_{\mathcal{L}}(W_0)$;
- Compute $\text{prox}_{E_\theta}(W_0)$ according to (8);
- Use the Gibbs sampler in [27, Algorithm 1] until convergence;

---

After convergence, Algorithm 1 provides chains of coefficients sampled according to the target distribution of each $W^k$. These chains can be used to compute an MMSE (minimum mean square error) estimator (after discarding the samples corresponding to the burn-in period).

It is worth noting that hyperprior distributions can be put on $\lambda$ and $\sigma$ in order to integrate them in the hierarchical Bayesian model. These hyperparameters can therefore be estimated from the data at the expense of some additional complexity.

## 4 Experimental Validation

In order to validate the proposed method, two image classification experiments are conducted using two different datasets: COVID-19 dataset including Computed tomography (CT) images [30], and a standard dataset, namely, CIFAR-10 [31]. For the sake of comparison, two kinds of optimizers are used: *i)* MCMC-based method, precisely the standard Metropolis-Hastings (MH) algorithm and the random walk Metropolis Hastings (rw-MH) [32], and *ii)* the most popular optimization techniques used in DL. : Adam and Adagrad [33]. One of the key hyper-parameters to set in optimizers in order to train a neural network is the learning rate. This parameter scales the magnitude of the weight updates in order to minimize the network's loss function. In the experiments, the learning rate is equal to $10^{-3}$. In addition, the hyper-parameters $\beta_1$ and $\beta_2$ are equals to 0.9 and 0.999 respectively. They stand for the initial decay rates used when estimating the first and second moments of the gradient. As regards coding, we used python programming language with Keras and Tensorflow libraries on an Intel(R) Core(TM) i7-2720QM CPU 2.20 GHZ architecture with 16 Go memory. The same behavior with the computational time and accuracy which justify the effectiveness of our proposed MCMC method.

### 4.1 ConvNet Models

Two CNN architectures are used in this study. Like the LeNet model [34], the first one (CNN_1) includes three convolutional (Conv3 × 3-32, Conv3 × 3-64, Conv3 × 3-128), and two fully-connected (FC-64 and FC-softmax). The second one (CNN_2) has five convolutional (Conv3 × 3-32, Conv3 × 3-32, Conv3 × 3-64, Conv3 × 3-64, Conv3 × 3-128, Conv3 × 3-128) and three FC layers (FC-128,FC-64,FC-softmax) that are organized similarly to VGG-Net [35]. All of them involve convolutional layers with 3 × 3 Kernel filters in addition to 2 × 2 max-pooling, with stride size equal to 1. All layers in the different configurations used ReLU as an activation function except the output layer.

As deep neural networks can easily overfit when trained with small datasets, the used CNNs are extended with three regularizing techniques [33]:

- Batch Normalization: deals with the feature space distribution variability during the training. The input of the layer is normalized to be zero-mean with unitary variance. This step not only acts as a regularizer, but also allows faster training, higher learning rates, and less sensitivity to weights initialization.
- $\ell_1$ Regularization: $\ell_1$ regularization is the preferred choice when having a high number of features as it provides sparse solutions. In our case, the regularization parameter was set to $\lambda = 0.001$.
- Dropout : random disabling of neurons during training with rate $p$. Temporarily ignoring some activation forces the other neurons to learn a more robust representation of the input data while reducing the sensitivity of specific neurons. In our study, the dropout rate is set by cross validation to $p = 0.35$.

## 4.2   Experiment 1: Challenging Case

A challenging classification case is addressed in this experiment. The same CNNs are used for CT images classification to identify Covid-19 infections from other pneumonia. This task is challenging due to the *rich content of CT images* and *similarity between Covid-19 infection and other pneumonia*. The COVID-CT dataset contains 349 CT images positive for COVID-19 belonging to 216 patients and 397 CT images that are negative for COVID-19. The dataset is open-sourced to the public. We used 566 images for the train and 180 images for the test with size of 230 × 230.

The reported scores in Table 1 indicate that the proposed method clearly outperforms the competing optimizers in training both models to solve this challenging classification problem. Moreover, severe performance decrease is observed for some optimizers like Adagrad. This is mainly due to the challenging classification, which leads to a more complex learning process.

**Table 1.** Experiment 1: results for CT image classification using CNN_1 and CNN_2.

| Optimizers | CNN_1 | | | CNN_2 | | |
|---|---|---|---|---|---|---|
| | Comp. time (hrs) | Accuracy | Loss | Comp. time (hrs) | Accuracy | Loss |
| **ns-HMC** | **0.40** | **0.84** | **0.26** | **0.51** | **0.88** | **0.22** |
| MH | 1.19 | 0.73 | 0.36 | 1.54 | 0.76 | 0.33 |
| rw-MH | 0.59 | 0.76 | 0.34 | 1.58 | 0.77 | 0.31 |
| Adam | 0.58 | 0.70 | 0.43 | 1.35 | 0.73 | 0.36 |
| Adagrad | 0.55 | 0.66 | 0.44 | 1.43 | 0.68 | 0.41 |

In order to confirm this performance decrease, Figs. 1 and 2 shows loss and accuracy curves obtained using the competing optimizers, and this for CNN_1 and CNN_2, respectively. The displayed curves clearly indicate an overfitting effect for classical optimizers, in contrast to the proposed method.

## 4.3   Experiment 2: CIFAR-10 Image Classification

In this scenario, the learning performance using the competing optimization algorithms is evaluated using the standard *CIFAR-10* dataset. The CIFAR-10 dataset consists of 60000 32 × 32 colour images in 10 classes, with 6000 images per class. There are 50000 training images and 10000 test images. The dataset is divided into five training batches and one test batch, each with 10000 images. The test batch contains exactly 1000 randomly-selected images from each class. The training batches contain the remaining images in random order, but some training batches may contain more images from one class than another. Between them, the training batches contain exactly 5000 images from each class.

The reported scores in Table 2 indicate that the proposed method outperforms the competing optimizers in terms of learning precision, and hence classification performance. Furthermore, the competing optimizers do not perform

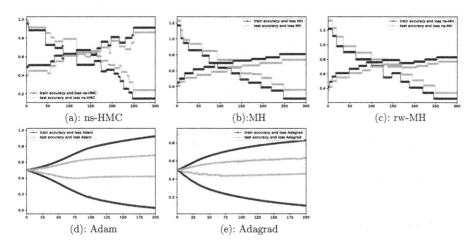

**Fig. 1.** Experiment 1: train and test curves using CNN_1.

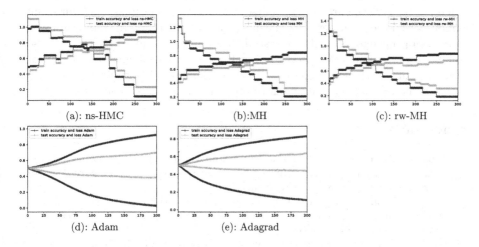

**Fig. 2.** Experiment 1: train and test curves using CNN_2.

well to learn both CNNs on the CIFAR-10 dataset. This confirms the ability of the proposed method to allow different networks reaching high accuracy levels, in contrast to standard optimizers, even when regularization is use. The gain in terms of computational time using the proposed method is more important on this experiment.

**Table 2.** Experiment 2: results for CIFAR-10 image classification using CNN_1 and CNN_2.

| Optimizers | CNN_1 | | | CNN_2 | | |
|---|---|---|---|---|---|---|
| | Comp. time (hrs) | Accuracy | Loss | Comp. time (hrs) | Accuracy | Loss |
| **ns-HMC** | **1.17** | **0.92** | **0.22** | **5.13** | **0.93** | **0.19** |
| MH | 2.77 | 0.86 | 0.35 | 12.43 | 0.87 | 0.33 |
| rw-MH | 3.06 | 0.88 | 0.33 | 13.29 | 0.88 | 0.31 |
| Adam | 2.60 | 0.90 | 0.46 | 7.40 | 0.92 | 0.32 |
| SGD | 2.73 | 0.88 | 0.71 | 7.54 | 0.89 | 0.56 |
| Adagrad | 2.78 | 0.75 | 0.81 | 7.22 | 0.78 | 0.64 |

## 5   Conclusion

In this paper, we proposed a new Bayesian optimization method for fitting weights for artificial neural networks. The suggested method uses Hamiltonian dynamics to solve the problem of sparse regularization optimization. Our results demonstrated the good performance of the proposed method in comparison with standard optimizers, as well as classical Bayesian ones. Moreover, the proposed technique allows simple networks to enjoy high accuracy and generalization properties. Future work will focus on testing our proposed optimizer with larger datasets, as well as proposing a distributed or parallel implementation.

## References

1. Alpaydin, E.: Introduction to Machine Learning. MIT press, Cambridge (2020)
2. Krizhevsky, A., Sutskever, I., Hinton, G.E.: Imagenet classification with deep convolutional neural networks. Adv. Neural Inf. Process. Syst. **25**, 1097–1105 (2012)
3. Lan, X., Zhang, S., Yuen, P.C., Chellappa, R.: Learning common and feature-specific patterns: a novel multiple-sparse-representation-based tracker. IEEE Trans. Image Process. **27**(4), 2022–2037 (2017)
4. Sainath, T.N., et al.: Deep convolutional neural networks for large-scale speech tasks. Neural Netw. **64**, 39–48 (2015)
5. Shao, R., Lan, X., Yuen, P.C.: Joint discriminative learning of deep dynamic textures for 3D mask face anti-spoofing. IEEE Trans. Inf. Forensics Secur. **14**(4), 923–938 (2018)
6. Kononenko, I.: Machine learning for medical diagnosis: history, state of the art and perspective. Artif. Intell. Med. **23**(1), 89–109 (2001)
7. Boudaya, A., et al.: EEG-based hypo-vigilance detection using convolutional neural network. In: Jmaiel, M., Mokhtari, M., Abdulrazak, B., Aloulou, H., Kallel, S. (eds.) ICOST 2020. LNCS, vol. 12157, pp. 69–78. Springer, Cham (2020). https://doi.org/10.1007/978-3-030-51517-1_6
8. Chaabene, S., Bouaziz, B., Boudaya, A., Hökelmann, A., Ammar, A., Chaari, L.: Convolutional neural network for drowsiness detection using EEG signals. Sensors **21**(5), 1734 (2021)
9. Safaei, A.A., Habibi-Asl, S.: Multidimensional indexing technique for medical images retrieval. Intell. Data Anal. **25**(6), 1629–1666 (2021)

10. Dong, Yu., Deng, L.: Deep learning and its applications to signal and information processing [exploratory dsp]. IEEE Signal Process. Mag. **28**(1), 145–154 (2010)
11. Zhang, X.-L., Ji, W.: Deep belief networks based voice activity detection. IEEE Trans. Audio Speech Lang. Process. **21**(4), 697–710 (2012)
12. Pazzani, M.J., Billsus, D.: Content-based recommendation systems. In: Brusilovsky, P., Kobsa, A., Nejdl, W. (eds.) The Adaptive Web. LNCS, vol. 4321, pp. 325–341. Springer, Heidelberg (2007). https://doi.org/10.1007/978-3-540-72079-9_10
13. Schmidhuber, J.: Deep learning in neural networks: an overview. Neural Netw. **61**, 85–117 (2015)
14. Zhang, Y.D., Morabito, F.C., Shen, D., Muhammad, K.: Advanced deep learning methods for biomedical information analysis: an editorial. Neural Netw. Off. J. Int. Neural Netw. Soc. **133**, 101–102 (2020)
15. Yamashita, R., Nishio, M., Do, R.K.G., Togashi, K.: Convolutional neural networks: an overview and application in radiology. Insights Imaging **9**(4), 611–629 (2018)
16. He, K., Zhang, X., Ren, S., Sun, J.: Deep residual learning for image recognition. In: Proceedings of the IEEE Conference on Computer Vision and Pattern Recognition, pp. 770–778 (2016)
17. Rumelhart, D.E., Hinton, G.E., Williams, R.J.: Learning representations by back-propagating errors. Nature **323**(6088), 533–536 (1986)
18. Leung, H., Haykin, S.: The complex backpropagation algorithm. IEEE Trans. Signal Process. **39**(9), 2101–2104 (1991)
19. Lin, T., Kong, L., Stich, S., Jaggi, M.: Extrapolation for large-batch training in deep learning. In: International Conference on Machine Learning, pp. 6094–6104. PMLR (2020)
20. Neal, R.M.: Probabilistic inference using Markov chain Monte Carlo methods. Department of Computer Science, University of Toronto Toronto, Ontario, Canada (1993)
21. Andrieu, C., Doucet, A., Holenstein, R.: Particle markov chain monte carlo methods. J. Royal Stat. Soc. Ser. B (Stat. Methodol.) **72**(3), 269–342 (2010)
22. Robert, C., Casella, G.: Monte Carlo Statistical Methods. Springer, Heidelberg (2013). https://doi.org/10.1007/978-1-4757-4145-2
23. Chaari, L., Batatia, H., Dobigeon, N., Tourneret, J.Y.: A hierarchical sparsity-smoothness bayesian model for l0+l1+l2 regularization. In: IEEE International Conference on Acoustics, Speech and Signal Processing (ICASSP), pp. 1901–1905 (2014)
24. Chaari, L.: A bayesian grouplet transform. Signal Image Video Process. **13**, 871–878 (2019)
25. Hanson. K.M.: Markov Chain Monte Carlo posterior sampling with the hamiltonian method. In: Medical Imaging 2001: Image Processing, vol. 4322, pp. 456–467. International Society for Optics and Photonics (2001)
26. Chaari, L., Tourneret, J.-Y., Chaux, C., Batatia, H.: A Hamiltonian Monte Carlo method for non-smooth energy sampling. IEEE Trans. Signal Process. **64**(21), 5585–5594 (2016)
27. Chaari, L., Tourneret, J.Y., Batatia, H.: A plug and play Bayesian algorithm for solving myope inverse problems. In: European Signal Processing Conference EUSIPCO, pp. 742–746 (2018)
28. Moreau, J.-J.: Proximité et dualité dans un espace hilbertien. Bull. de la Société mathématique de France **93**, 273–299 (1965)

29. Chaux, C., Combettes, P.L., Pesquet, J.Y., Wajs, V.R.: A variational formulation for frame-based inverse problems. Inverse Prob. **23**(4), 1495 (2007)
30. Angelov, P., Soares, E.A.: Sars-cov-2 ct-scan dataset: a large dataset of real patients ct scans for sars-cov-2 identification. medRxiv (2020)
31. Recht, B., Roelofs, R., Schmidt, L., Shankar, V.: Do cifar-10 classifiers generalize to cifar-10? arXiv preprint arXiv:1806.00451 (2018)
32. Lee, C.H., Xu, X., Eun, D.Y.: Beyond random walk and metropolis-hastings samplers: why you should not backtrack for unbiased graph sampling. ACM SIGMETRICS Perf. Eval. Rev. **40**(1), 319–330 (2012)
33. Sun, S., Cao, Z., Zhu, H., Zhao, J.: A survey of optimization methods from a machine learning perspective. IEEE Trans. Cybern. **50**(8), 3668–3681 (2019)
34. LeCun, Y., Bottou, L., Bengio, Y., Haffner, P.: Gradient-based learning applied to document recognition. Proc. IEEE **86**(11), 2278–2324 (1998)
35. Muhammad, U., Wang, W., Chattha, S.P., Ali, S.: Pre-trained vggnet architecture for remote-sensing image scene classification. In 24th International Conference on Pattern Recognition (ICPR), pp. 1622–1627 (2018)

# Tensor Completion Post-Correction

Hadi Fanaee-T[✉][ID]

Halmstad University, Halmstad, Sweden
`hadi.fanaee@hh.se`

**Abstract.** Many real-world tensors come with missing values. The task of estimation of such missing elements is called tensor completion (TC). It is a fundamental problem with a wide range of applications in data mining, machine learning, signal processing, and computer vision. In the last decade, several different algorithms have been developed, couple of them have shown high-quality performance in diverse domains. However, our investigation shows that even state-of-the-art TC algorithms sometimes make poor estimations for few cases that are not noticeable if we look at their overall performance. However, such wrong estimates might have a severe effect on some decisions. It becomes a crucial issue in applications where humans are involved. Making bad decisions based on such poor estimations can harm fairness. We propose the first algorithm for tensor completion post-correction, called TCPC, to identify some of such poor estimates from the output of any TC algorithm and refine them with more realistic estimations. Our initial experiments with five real-life tensor datasets show that TCPC is an effective post-correction method.

**Keywords:** Tensor completion · Missing value estimation · Post-correction

## 1 Introduction

A tensor is a multi-dimensional array to extend scalars, vectors, and matrices to higher orders. With this definition, scalars, vectors, and matrices can be considered zero-order, first-order, and second-order tensors.

Tensor completion deals with estimating the value of unobserved elements in a tensor, based on the relationship between the known and unknown parts. If there is no relationship between available and missing pieces, completion is not possible. However, in real-life datasets, this is typically not the case, and often there are various types of correlations and repetitions [1]. For vectors, estimation of missing elements is straightforward. Linear, spline, or polynomial interpolation are typically used. For the matrix data, the usual practice is to use a low-rank approximation for recovering the missing elements. For the tensors, there exist two major types of methods. The first group is based on trace norm minimization, and the second class is based on low-rank tensor decomposition techniques. This paper is not about a new method for TC, so we do not go into

© The Author(s), under exclusive license to Springer Nature Switzerland AG 2022
T. Bouadi et al. (Eds.): IDA 2022, LNCS 13205, pp. 89–101, 2022.
https://doi.org/10.1007/978-3-031-01333-1_8

more details on the algorithms and solutions for TC. Instead, we refer readers to a recent comprehensive survey on tensor completion algorithms [2].

Although state-of-the-art TC algorithms show promising performance in various domains and applications [2–4], our initial investigations show that even the best state-of-the-art methods sometimes suffer from very poor estimations in a few cases. Unfortunately, we cannot identify this problem when we look at the overall performance. However, such poor estimates might have a severe effect on some decisions. This issue becomes a critical challenge in applications where humans are involved. Making wrong decisions based on such poor estimations can harm fairness.

The current trend of solution development for tensor completion is more focused on the general performance of these methods. New methods are typically compared against previous techniques using global performance metrics such as Mean absolute error (MAE) or Root Mean Square Error (RMSE).

There is almost no research devoted to making partial corrections on the output of these algorithms. However, if we compare the individual estimation of some of these state-of-the-art TC algorithms with ground truth, we observe some peculiar estimations. For instance, we demonstrate the estimates of two popular TC algorithms in Table 1. We can see that there are poor estimations with 20 units of difference away from the ground truth. These cases are not that common. That is why they have less influence on the overall error. However, if we make no corrections on these cases, it may have severe consequences on the concerned subjects. For instance, if values are in a million-dollar, 20 units of difference translates to the same amount of revenue loss.

Given the above arguments, it is clear that post-correction of poor estimations may have commercial value or avoid potential losses in some applications. To solve this problem, we have to face this problem: How can we identify very poor estimation? In Table 1 we used ground truth to show the poor predictions, but in real-life problems, we know the indices of missing elements and nothing more. So, how can we even assess the quality of estimations without having ground truth values?

This research is an effort to answer these questions and provide a solution for post-correction of TC solutions. To the best of our knowledge, this is the first effort of this kind in the literature. We first introduce a novel data structure that converts tensors of any order to a regular feature matrix. Later, upon the new data structure, we develop our method to identify poorly estimated cases. Finally, we propose an approach for correcting poor estimations.

## 2   Method

In this section, we first describe our proposed method. Later, we provide an illustrative example and provide the time complexity analysis of the proposed method.

The general idea of the proposed method is to transform both observed elements and missing elements into a unified space so that we can perform a nearest neighbor search after we had the estimations by any TC algorithm. At first

**Table 1.** An example of poor estimations of two popular state-of-the-art tensor completion methods on a few elements and our method's corresponding correction (specified with Corrected column). Dataset: Peppers, Missing ratio: 70%

| Actual | HaLRTC | Corrected | Actual | t-SVD | Corrected |
|--------|--------|-----------|--------|-------|-----------|
| 4 | −18.5885436 | 0 | 0 | −29.292 | 0 |
| 212 | 238.3056218 | 229 | 212 | 268.4384 | 225 |
| 227 | 236.7395851 | 221 | 205 | 260.6259 | 225 |
| 2 | −17.12847877 | 3 | 0 | −30.3158 | 0 |
| 0 | −17.30172716 | 3 | 213 | 245.5625 | 218 |
| 223 | 232.7940263 | 224 | 211 | 258.441 | 230 |
| 188 | 179.365688 | 177 | 207 | 247.9978 | 220 |
| 216 | 228.3721368 | 220 | 0 | −28.9757 | 0 |

glance, it seems impossible to reach this objective since there is no information except indices of elements of missing values. We propose to solve this problem by performing normalization across the different combinations of modes, once before TC output and once after. With this approach, we will have a unified space before and after running the TC algorithm. We assume that if there is a very close nearest neighbor in the observed tensor for a missing element, the value of that nearest neighbor should be a better estimation than the original estimation by the TC algorithm. We will explain this idea in more detail in the following subsections.

## 2.1 Proposed Algorithm: TCPC

The proposed method is presented in Algorithm 1. The central part of this algorithm is calling a sub-procedure called Tensor2MetaFeature to transform the observed input tensor to a two-dimensional meta-feature matrix. This meta-feature matrix preserves the information of multi-way interactions across different mode permutations. We first describe this sub-procedure and then go into the rest.

The sub-procedure Tensor2MetaFeature is presented in Algorithm 2, where the algorithm receives the $N$th-order tensor $X$ and returns Meta-feature Matrix $M$ as an output. At line 2 of this algorithm we generate a $(\{1, .., N-1\})$-order permutations of modes' indices, which is basically all possible $\{1, .., N-1\}$ order combinations between modes. For instance, C is defined as $\{1, 2, 3, (1, 2), (1, 3), (2, 3)\}$ for a third-order tensor and $\{1, 2, 3, 4, (1, 2), (1, 3), (1, 4), (2, 3), (2, 4), (3, 4), (1, 2, 3), (1, 2, 4), (1, 3, 4), (2, 3, 4)\}$ for a fourth-order tensor.

At lines 6-17 we do multi-way normalization of the tensor elements. We use min-max normalization using the following formula:

$$X_n = \frac{X - min_c}{max_c - min_c} \tag{1}$$

Where $c$ refers to one of the generated above-explained permutations. If the normalized value becomes lower than zero or greater than one, we replace it with lower/upper limits. Also, if $min$ and $max$ are equal for some indices in a particular permutation, we replace the normalized value with a very tiny quantity to not become problematic in the nearest neighbor search.

The final meta-feature matrix $M$ will have six columns for a third-order tensor. The first three columns represent normalized tensor based on modes 1, 2, and 3, respectively. The following three columns correspond to normalized values for second-order combinations: $(1, 2)$, $(1, 3)$, and $(2, 3)$. For the fourth-order tensor, the number of columns will be 14. The first four columns are devoted to the first-order normalization, the following six columns represent second-order normalization, and the last four columns correspond to third-order normalization.

The rationale behind this approach is that we want to see how tensor elements look like if we view them from a specific mode or combination of modes. Thus, we create meta-features for each element of tensor, which later can be used for similarity search.

Now let's back to Algorithm 1. Once we generate tensor meta-feature $O$ on the observed tensor $Xo$ we fill the missing values using our tensor completion algorithm of interest. Then we recall Algorithm 2 again to re-estimate a new meta-feature matrix, this time with the completed tensor $Xc$ estimated by the TC algorithm. We already have the meta-feature matrix computed for each missing element, so we find their nearest neighbor in the original meta-feature matrix $O$. We assume that if two tensor elements have identical multi-way normalized vectors, they should have a similar value. So, based on this, we make corrections for those items with a neighbor with a very close distance to elements in the observed tensor. So, the primary assumption we use here is that if there is a very close neighbor for a missing element in the observed tensor, the nearest neighbor's value is more accurate than its estimation by the TC algorithm.

## 2.2   Illustrative Example

Figure 1 shows an illustrative example of the proposed method for a third-order tensor. In this fictional example, we have six missing elements. The whole procedure is composed of five steps specified in the figure with black circles and white fonts.

In STEP 1, we compute the Meta-feature matrix for the observed elements of the tensor using Algorithm 2. Since the example is for third-order tensor, all possible permutations of modes' indices (C in Algorithm 2) are $\{1, 2, 3, (1, 2), (1\ 3), (2, 3)\}$. For instance, element $(5, 6, 9)$ with value of 25 is transformed to six-dimensional vector of $(0.1702, 0.1817, 0.3083, 0.1665, 0.9021, 0.7246)$. The first three values of this vector is obtained by normalizing 25 by min-max normalization across the first, the second, and the third mode, i.e., $Xo(5, :, :)$, $Xo(:, 6, :)$ and $Xo(:, :, 9)$, respectively. The following three values of the vector are computed by normalizing 25 across second-order mode combinations, i.e., $Xo(5,$

6, :), Xo(5 ,:, 9), and Xo(:, 6, 9), respectively, where Xo represents the observed tensor.

In STEP 2, we estimate the missing values with our TC algorithm of interest and complete the tensor with the estimated values. Later, in STEP 3, we re-compute the meta-feature matrix via Algorithm 2, this time with the completed tensor Xc, and obtain the meta-features for missing elements. For example, the missed item (3, 4, 5) that got estimation of 16.42 by the TC algorithm obtains the six-dimensional meta-feature vector of (0.2166, 0.1800, 0.1651, 02833, 0.952, 0). This is obtained by min-max normalization of 16.42 over Xc(3, :, :), Xc(:, 4, :) and Xc(:, :, 5), Xc(3, 4, :), Xc(3, :, 5), and Xc(:, 4, 5).

In STEP 4, we find their nearest neighbor and the corresponding distance from the meta-feature matrix $O$ (meta-features for observed elements) for each missing element. For instance, in this fictional example, the nearest neighbor of the missing element (3, 4, 5) is (3, 1, 11) with a distance of 0. So, we compute the distance of the six-dimensional meta-feature vector of this element with all six-dimensional vectors in the observed meta-feature and find the lowest distance. Then we make corrections for those elements that have the nearest neighbor with a distance lower than $\epsilon$ (in the example $\epsilon = 0.0001$). By correction, we mean replacing the estimation obtained via TC algorithm with the value of the nearest neighbor from the observed tensor. For instance, since the neighbor of element (3, 4, 5) has a value of 10, we replace the estimation of 16.42 with 10. The idea is that if for any missing element there is a very close nearest neighbor in the meta-feature space, the value of the nearest neighbor is more reliable than the TC estimation, so by replacing it, we correct some of these poor estimations.

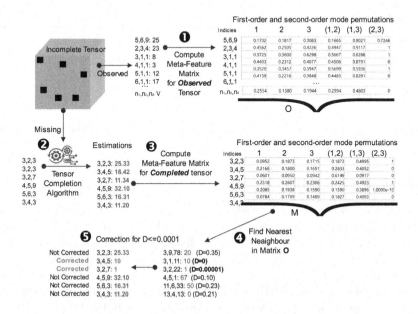

**Fig. 1.** Illustrative example of the proposed method for a third-order tensor

## 2.3   Time Complexity

Computing meta-feature matrix requires $O(2n\|C\|)$ (one time before TC and one time after). Since $\|C\|$ is a fixed value (e.g. for third-order tensor is equal to 6) the time complexity of this part is linear with the number of tensor elements. The time complexity of nearest neighbor search is $O(mn)$, where m is the number of missing elements and n is the number of observed elements. This is dominant part, which makes the total cost $O(mn)$. In the very large datasets, use of this post-processing approach is computationally justifiable if time complexity of the chosen TC algorithm is greater or equal to $O(mn)$. In any case the proposed method is competitive when $m << n$, which makes the solution linear with the number of observed tensor.

---

**Algorithm 1.** TCPC

---

    **Input tensor** $X$, **observed indices** $A$, **missing indices** $U$, $\epsilon$
    **Output: corrected completed tensor** $Xc$

1: $Xo \leftarrow X(A)$
2: $Xm \leftarrow X(U)$
3: $O \leftarrow Tensor2MetaFeature(Xo)$
4: $Xc \leftarrow TensorCompletion(Xo)$
5: $M \leftarrow Tensor2MetaFeature(Xc)$
6: $[NN, D] \leftarrow KNNSearh(O, M)$
7: **for** All $u$ in $U$ **do**
8:     **if** $D(u) < \epsilon$ **then**
9:         Replace $Xc(u)$ with $NN.value$
10:    **end if**
11: **end for**

---

# 3   Experimental Evaluation

In this section, we present the empirical evidence on the effectiveness of the proposed method.

## 3.1   Tensor Completion Algorithms

We test how the proposed method is effective in correcting estimations of 12 TC algorithms. See Table 2 for more details. Some of these methods are highly cited (See the third column in Table 2) and quite popular in the community. The code of *all* of these algorithms is publicly available in MATLAB package mctc4bmi (https://github.com/andrewssobral/mctc4bmi) and another GitHub repository (https://github.com/Kaimaoge/Tensor-decomposition-completion-and-recovery-papers-and-codes) or from the authors' websites.

---

**Algorithm 2.** Tensor2MetaFeature

---

**Input** $N$th-order tensor $X$

**Output:** $M$

1: $C \leftarrow (N-1)$-order permutations of modes' indices
2: % e.g., For 3rd-order tensor, C={1,2,3,(1,2),(1,3),(2,3)}
3: **for** $i = 1 : |C|$ **do**
4:    **for** each index combination $k$ in $C\{i\}$ **do**
5:       $id \leftarrow$ elements of $X$ satisfying $C\{i\}\{k\}$
6:       $mn = min(X(id)); mx = max(X(id))$
7:       **if** $(mx - mn) \neq 0$ **then**
8:          $M(id, i) = (X(id) - mn)/(mx - mn)$
9:          **if** $M(id, i) < 0$ **then**
10:            $M(id, i) = 0$
11:          **end if**
12:          **if** $M(id, i) > 1$ **then**
13:            $M(id, i) = 1$
14:          **end if**
15:       **else**
16:          $M(id, i) = 10^{-10}$
17:       **end if**
18:    **end for**
19: **end for**

---

**Table 2.** Tested tensor completion algorithms

| Name | P. Year | Cited | Type | Optimization |
|------|---------|-------|------|--------------|
| HaLRTC [5] | 2012 | 1225 | Tucker | ADMM |
| SPC [1] | 2016 | 146 | PARAFAC | Hierarchical ALS |
| BCPF [6] | 2015 | 300 | PARAFAC | Bayesian |
| NNFCP [7] | 2018 | 24 | PARAFAC | Nesterov's optim. grad. |
| T3C_WOPT [8] | 2017 | 21 | Tensor-Train | Weighted optimization |
| T3C_SGD [9] | 2019 | 21 | Tensor-Train | SGD |
| geomCG [10] | 2014 | 251 | Tucker | Riemannian optimization |
| ncpc [11] | 2013 | 815 | NN-PARAFAC | Block Coordinate descent |
| TenALS [12] | 2014 | 167 | PARAFAC | ALS |
| TMac [13] | 2013 | 215 | MatrixFactorization | Cyclic block minimization |
| tSVD [14] | 2014 | 377 | Tensor-SVD | ADMM |
| tTNN [15] | 2015 | 20 | Tensor-SVD | ADMM |

## 3.2   Datasets

We use five publicly available tensor datasets (See Table 3), which are widely used in tensor completion and decomposition problems. Our claim is not computational efficiency, so we intentionally did not choose large datasets for more efficient experimental evaluation. However, the selected datasets have an apparent tensor (multi-way) structure.

## 3.3   Evaluation Metric

We use Mean absolute error (MAE) for the evaluation of performance. MAE is a widely used metric in the TC literature. It is defined as:

$$\text{MAE} = \frac{\sum_{i=1}^{m} |Y_i - X_i|}{m}$$

Where $m$ is the number of missing elements and $Y_i$ represents the estimations for missing elements, and $X_i$ is a ground truth data.

**Table 3.** Datasets

| Dataset | Size | Type | Domain | Ref. |
|---------|------|------|--------|------|
| Peppers | (256, 256, 3) | Visual image | Computer vision | [16] |
| Amino | (5, 201, 61) | Fluorescence data | Chemometrics | [17] |
| Ribeira | (203, 268, 33) | Hyperspectral image | Computer vision | [18] |
| Sugar | (268, 571, 7) | Fluorescence data | Chemometrics | [19] |
| Tongue | (13, 10, 5) | Processed X-ray | Computer vision | [20] |

## 3.4   Experimental Configuration

We use default parameters in the software packages for running TC algorithms, except two parameters in optimization that are set equal for all methods for fair comparisons among them. These parameters are tol (lower band change tolerance for convergence detection) and the maximum number of iterations, which are set as $10^{-5}$ and 500, respectively. The only parameter of our method is $\epsilon$, which is the $\epsilon$ for one estimation get selected as a potential candidate for correction. In the first part of the experiment, we set this as $10^{-4}$, but we will present the performance of the proposed method on different TC algorithms on a broader range from 0 to 0.1 by an increment of 0.00002, in total 500 possible $\epsilon$ values.

Note that our method is not a new TC algorithm. We claim that our proposed method can improve some poor estimations of any TC algorithm. So, optimizing the hyper-parameter of TC algorithms is not relevant in our empirical evaluation. However, it can be good to see in what hyperparameter configuration our post-processing approach works better for each of these algorithms. However, due to the scale of required experiments, we do not perform this experiment for this report and postpone it for the journal version.

All five datasets are full tensors. So, we artificially remove 30% and 70% of elements to assess both conditions where missing elements are in minority and majority, respectively. We do this because some algorithms exhibit poor performance when the missing ratio is higher than the observed elements and vice versa. So, we should see how our TCPC method performs on both of these settings.

### 3.5    Evaluation of TCPC on Improvement of TC Estimation

To evaluate how TCPC is effective in correcting poor estimations, we apply it after we performed tensor completion via 12 TC algorithms on five datasets. The partial MAE result for $\epsilon = 10^{-4}$ is presented in Table 4 and Table 5 for two missing ratio configurations 30% and 70%, respectively. In the table, "N" represents the number of treated cases, "Original" represents the partial MAE for original estimations by TC algorithms, and "Corrected" corresponds to the partial MAE after applying TCPC.

As we can see, TCPC, in the majority of cases, has been able to effectively correct estimations for missing elements that had a very close nearest neighbor in the meta-feature space. However, it seems that its competitiveness may also depend on the TC algorithm and the dataset properties.

For instance, TCPC is more effective for some datasets such as Sugar, Peppers, and Ribeira. TCPC has been capable of post-correcting outputs of all 12 algorithms (except for Ribeira dataset on TenALS), both in terms of partial MAE measured and the number of corrections. This observation is important because most of the current application of TC is with image data.

TCPC also sounds more robust upon some TC algorithms such as TMac, HaLRTC, and tSVD and geomCG, ncpc, and tTNN. For instance, we can observe that TCPC has been effective in almost all datasets on both missing ratio settings with these algorithms. This is an interesting result because we can safely prescribe TCPC for highly popular methods such as HaLRTC and tSVD, irrespective of the dataset properties.

Comparing the results with 70% missing ratio versus 30% missing ratio also reveals that when missing elements are higher than the observed elements, TCPC sounds more valuable. This is also promising because we have highly sparse tensors in modern applications such as recommender systems and time-evolving networks.

### 3.6    Sensitivity of TCPC's Unique Parameter: $\epsilon$

As we can see in Algorithm 1 the unique parameter of the algorithm is $\epsilon$. Contrary to the parameter of many algorithms, $\epsilon$ is highly intuitive. Since each value in the meta-feature vector is a normalized value in the range of $[0, 1]$, a distance of $10^{-4}$ between two points can be shown and interpreted in this space for a

**Table 4.** Partial MAE for corrected elements - 30% missing ratio

| Dataset | HaLRTC | SPC | BCPF | NNFCP | T3C_WOPT | T3C_SGD | geomCG | ncpc | TenALS | TMac | tSVD | tTNN |
|---|---|---|---|---|---|---|---|---|---|---|---|---|
| Amino |  |  |  |  |  |  |  |  |  |  |  |  |
| N | 4 | 4 | 4 | 2 | 3 | 1 | 2 | 3 | 6 | 1 | 1 | 3 |
| Original | 2.07 | 5.01 | 5.40 | 6.36 | 3.98 | 49.73 | 8.85 | 5.45 | 537.67 | 8.73 | 36.04 | 2.06 |
| Corrected | 2.19 | 13.84 | 26.82 | 20.86 | 14.26 | 13.44 | 6.72 | 15.66 | 68.72 | 6.91 | 8.65 | 3.70 |
| Peppers |  |  |  |  |  |  |  |  |  |  |  |  |
| N | 2 | 5 | 2 | 6 | 2 | 1 | 3 | 2 | 2 | 2 | 4 | 4 |
| Original | 20.15 | 30.18 | 64.59 | 19.04 | 73.43 | 89.73 | 59.35 | 49.16 | 154.74 | 55.91 | 20.19 | 11.42 |
| Corrected | 5.5 | 7 | 4 | 1.66 | 9 | 84 | 15.66 | 19 | 8.5 | 4 | 4.5 | 1.5 |
| Ribeira |  |  |  |  |  |  |  |  |  |  |  |  |
| N | 274952 | 6 | 4 | 0 | 5 | 2 | 3 | 0 | 2 | 3 | 6 | 2 |
| Original | 0.33 | 0.02 | 0.16 | — | 0.19 | 0.17 | 0.19 | — | 0.48 | 0.10 | 0.06 | 0.04 |
| Corrected | 0.32 | 0.02 | 0.11 | — | 0.15 | 0.17 | 0.11 | — | 0.54 | 0.10 | 0.06 | 0.04 |
| Sugar |  |  |  |  |  |  |  |  |  |  |  |  |
| N | 4 | 5 | 4 | 1930 | 2 | 0 | 4 | 61 | 3 | 5 | 7 | 12 |
| Original | 24.19 | 40.96 | 148.22 | 0.80 | 5583.65 | — | 237.10 | 5.55 | 947.95 | 107.79 | 15.28 | 7.44 |
| Corrected | 1.04 | 0.87 | 12.46 | 0.45 | 500.10 | — | 10.30 | 0.18 | 1.61 | 8.60 | 1.11 | 0.89 |
| Tongue |  |  |  |  |  |  |  |  |  |  |  |  |
| N | 195 | 1 | 1 | 195 | 2 | 2 | 2 | 1 | 0 | 0 | 0 | 0 |
| Original | 1.55 | 0.03 | 0.30 | 1.55 | 1.57 | 0.27 | 9.04 | 0.16 | — | — | — | — |
| Corrected | 1.35 | 0.05 | 0.15 | 1.35 | 1.1 | 0.35 | 1.87 | 0.15 | — | — | — | — |

**Table 5.** Partial MAE for corrected elements - 70% missing ratio

| Dataset | HaLRTC | SPC | BCPF | NNFCP | T3C_WOPT | T3C_SGD | geomCG | ncpc | TenALS | TMac | tSVD | tTNN |
|---|---|---|---|---|---|---|---|---|---|---|---|---|
| Amino |  |  |  |  |  |  |  |  |  |  |  |  |
| N | 5 | 5 | 1 | 0 | 2 | 0 | 2 | 6 | 0 | 1 | 2 | 5 |
| Original | 4.29 | 3.54 | 9.72 | — | 21.67 | — | 11.68 | 0.04 | — | 1192.56 | 58.90 | 7.75 |
| Corrected | 5.20 | 4.75 | 6.68 | — | 17.06 | — | 6.72 | 0.04 | — | 707.36 | 9.29 | 5.23 |
| Peppers |  |  |  |  |  |  |  |  |  |  |  |  |
| N | 5 | 3 | 3 | 1 | 2 | 3 | 2 | 22 | 0 | 3 | 4 | 4 |
| Original | 19.37 | 38.00 | 61.57 | 129.42 | 72.35 | 63.81 | 75.88 | 9.61 | — | 57.02 | 42.91 | 25.21 |
| Corrected | 6 | 1.66 | 8.66 | 25 | 0 | 57.33 | 5.5 | 6.86 | — | 8 | 8.25 | 4 |
| Ribeira |  |  |  |  |  |  |  |  |  |  |  |  |
| N | 274952 | 6 | 4 | 0 | 5 | 2 | 3 | 0 | 2 | 3 | 6 | 2 |
| Original | 0.33 | 0.02 | 0.16 | — | 0.19 | 0.17 | 0.19 | — | 0.48 | 0.10 | 0.06 | 0.04 |
| Corrected | 0.32 | 0.02 | 0.11 | — | 0.15 | 0.17 | 0.11 | — | 0.54 | 0.10 | 0.06 | 0.04 |
| Sugar |  |  |  |  |  |  |  |  |  |  |  |  |
| N | 4 | 3 | 4 | 3231 | 3 | 1 | 4 | 85 | 4 | 2 | 4 | 5 |
| Original | 22.55 | 66.09 | 168.27 | 0.21 | 2836.53 | 2.40 | 247.59 | 7.33 | 1975.84 | 185.96 | 24.41 | 9.63 |
| Corrected | 0.83 | 0.89 | 15.98 | 0.09 | 266.89 | 1.61 | 11.15 | 0.18 | 5.49 | 15.44 | 1.33 | 1.79 |
| Tongue |  |  |  |  |  |  |  |  |  |  |  |  |
| N | 455 | 2 | 0 | 455 | 2 | 4 | 3 | 1 | 0 | 5 | 0 | 1 |
| Original | 1.60 | 0.13 | — | 1.60 | 13.86 | 1.88 | 42.35 | 5.35 | — | 2.99 | — | 0.12 |
| Corrected | 1.30 | 0.15 | — | 1.30 | 1.95 | 0.67 | 1.86 | 1.4 | — | 1.43 | — | 0.1 |

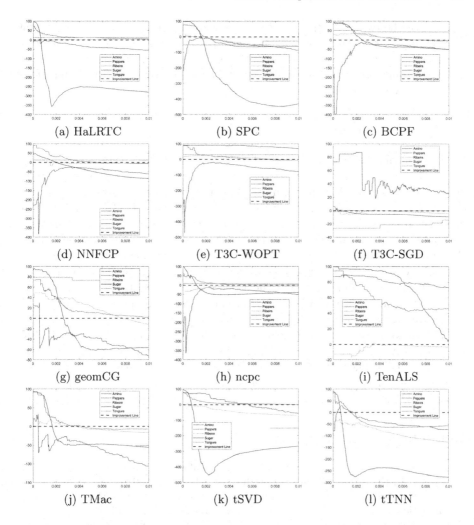

**Fig. 2.** Sensitivity: error improvement percentage (y) versus $\epsilon$ (x) on five datasets

six-dimensional vector. However, to have an idea that in what range TCPC has more value, we plot estimation error improvement by TCPC versus $\epsilon$ from 0.0000 to 0.10000 with an increment of 0.0002 (totally 500 possible value for $\epsilon$) applied upon each of TC algorithms on five datasets for two missing ratios.

The results are presented in Fig. 2, for missing ratio 30%. The plots show estimation error improvement in percentage in the x-axis versus $\epsilon$ in the y-axis. The improvement line is also specified with a dashed line for different datasets. The more above improvement line, the more effective TCPC is for different $\epsilon$ values.

The general observation is that by increasing $\epsilon$ more than 0.001, there will be a risk that TCPC is not effective anymore. The safest value is perhaps $10^{-4}$ that we used in the experiments. But, for some methods such as TenALS we might be able to set $\epsilon$ to larger numbers and make more corrections. For T3C-SGD we observe abnormal behavior that cannot be seen in other methods. For instance, for the Amino dataset, for any $\epsilon$ value, we have improvement, while for other datasets, any $\epsilon$ value does not give any improvement.

## 4  Conclusion and Future work

We propose the first procedure, called TCPC, for post-correction of tensor completion's outcome. This general procedure can partially correct poor estimations of any TC algorithm. We show empirical evidence on the effectiveness of TCPC on different datasets and two missing ratio conditions of 30% and 70%. We demonstrate that TCPC is effective upon state-of-the-art popular algorithms such as HaLRTC and t-SVD, but less effective on not very accurate methods. We also show that TCPC can be helpful for exact predictions of missing elements. According to our experiments, the current TC algorithms never make exact estimations. Thus, in the applications where exact estimation is required, TCPC upon an accurate TC algorithm can provide competitive results with some exact estimations.

The future work includes three main directions: 1) deeper evaluation of TCPC with more diverse data sets and configurations; 2) Further investigation on exact predictions is another exciting area to explore; and 3) investigation on the usefulness of tensor meta-feature on other problems such as clustering and anomaly detection [21].

## References

1. Yokota, T., Zhao, Q., Cichocki, A.: Smooth parafac decomposition for tensor completion. IEEE Trans. Signal Process. **64**(20), 5423–5436 (2016)
2. Song, Q., Ge, H., Caverlee, J., Hu, X.: Tensor completion algorithms in big data analytics. ACM Trans. Knowl. Disc. Data (TKDD) **13**(1), 1–48 (2019)
3. Sari, N.R.Y., Fanaee-T.H., Rahat, M.: A data-driven approach based on tensor completion for replacing "physical sensors" with "virtual sensors". In: 2021 IEEE 8th International Conference on Data Science and Advanced Analytics (DSAA), pp. 1–6. IEEE (2021)
4. Fernandes, S., Fanaee-T, H.., Gama, J.: The initialization and parameter setting problem in tensor decomposition-based link prediction. In: 2017 IEEE International Conference on Data Science and Advanced Analytics (DSAA), pp. 99–108. IEEE (2017)
5. Liu, J., Musialski, P., Wonka, P., Ye, J.: Tensor completion for estimating missing values in visual data. IEEE Trans. Pattern Anal. Mach. Intell. **35**(1), 208–220 (2012)
6. Zhao, Q., Zhang, L., Cichocki, A.: Bayesian CP factorization of incomplete tensors with automatic rank determination. IEEE Trans. Pattern Anal. Mach. Intell. **37**(9), 1751–1763 (2015)
7. Wu, Y., Tan, H., Li, Y., Zhang, J., Chen, X.: A fused CP factorization method for incomplete tensors. IEEE Trans. Neural Netw. Learn. Syst. **30**(3), 751–764 (2018)

8. Yuan, L., Zhao, Q., Cao, J.: Completion of high order tensor data with missing entries via tensor-train decomposition. In: International Conference on Neural Information Processing, pp. 222–229. Springer, Heidelberg (2017)

9. Yuan, L., Zhao, Q., Gui, L., Cao, J.: High-order tensor completion via gradient-based optimization under tensor train format. Signal Process. Image Commun. **73**, 53–61 (2019)

10. Kressner, D., Steinlechner, M., Vandereycken, B.: Low-rank tensor completion by riemannian optimization. BIT Numer. Math. **54**(2), 447–468 (2014)

11. Xu, Y., Yin, W.: A block coordinate descent method for regularized multiconvex optimization with applications to nonnegative tensor factorization and completion. SIAM J. Imag. Sci. **6**(3), 1758–1789 (2013)

12. Jain, P., Oh, S.: Provable tensor factorization with missing data. In: Ghahramani, Z., Welling, M., Cortes, C., Lawrence, N., Weinberger, K.Q. (eds.) Advances in Neural Information Processing Systems, vol. 27. Curran Associates Inc. (2014)

13. Xu, Y., Hao, R., Yin, W., Su, Z.: Parallel matrix factorization for low-rank tensor completion. ArXiv arXiv:1312.1254 (2013)

14. Zhang, Z., Ely, G., Aeron, S., Hao, N., Kilmer, M.: Novel methods for multilinear data completion and de-noising based on tensor-SVD. In: Proceedings of the IEEE Conference on Computer Vision and Pattern Recognition, pp. 3842–3849 (2014)

15. Hu, W., Tao, D., Zhang, W., Xie, Y., Yang, Y.: A new low-rank tensor model for video completion. arXiv preprint arXiv:1509.02027 (2015)

16. Chen, Y.-L., Hsu, C.-T., Liao, H.-Y.M.: Simultaneous tensor decomposition and completion using factor priors. IEEE Trans. Pattern Anal. Mach. Intell. **36**(3), 577–591 (2013)

17. Bro, R.: Parafac. tutorial and applications. Chemometr. Intell. Lab. Syst. **38**(2), 149–171 (1997)

18. Nimishakavi, M., Jawanpuria, P., Mishra, B.: A dual framework for low-rank tensor completion. In: Proceedings of the 32nd International Conference on Neural Information Processing Systems, pp. 5489–5500 (2018)

19. Bro, R.: Exploratory study of sugar production using fluorescence spectroscopy and multi-way analysis. Chemometr. Intell. Lab. Syst. **46**(2), 133–147 (1999)

20. Harshman, R., Ladefoged, P., Goldstein, L.: Factor analysis of tongue shapes. J. Acoust. Soc. Am. **62**(3), 693–707 (1977)

21. Fanaee-T, H., Gama, J.: Tensor-based anomaly detection: an interdisciplinary survey. Knowl.-Based Syst. **98**, 130–147 (2016)

# S-LIME: Reconciling Locality and Fidelity in Linear Explanations

Romaric Gaudel[1]([⊠]), Luis Galárraga[2], Julien Delaunay[2], Laurence Rozé[3], and Vaishnavi Bhargava[4]

[1] Univ. Rennes, Ensai, CNRS, CREST, Rennes, France
romaric.gaudel@ensai.fr
[2] Univ. Rennes, Inria, Irisa, Rennes, France
{luis.galarraga,julien.delaunay}@inria.fr
[3] Univ. Rennes, Insa, Inria, Irisa, Rennes, France
laurence.roze@insa-rennes.fr
[4] Inria/Irisa, Rennes, France

**Abstract.** The benefit of locality is one of the major premises of LIME, one of the most prominent methods to explain black-box machine learning models. This emphasis relies on the postulate that the more locally we look at the vicinity of an instance, the simpler the black-box model becomes, and the more accurately we can mimic it with a linear surrogate. As logical as this seems, our findings suggest that, with the current design of LIME, the surrogate model may degenerate when the explanation is too local, namely, when the bandwidth parameter $\sigma$ tends to zero. Based on this observation, the contribution of this paper is twofold. Firstly, we study the impact of both the bandwidth and the training vicinity on the fidelity and semantics of LIME explanations. Secondly, and based on our findings, we propose S-LIME, an extension of LIME that reconciles fidelity and locality.

**Keywords:** Explainable AI · Interpretability

## 1 Introduction

The pervasiveness of complex automatic decision-making nowadays has raised multiple concerns about the implications of AI for the values of fairness, trust, transparency, and privacy [2,4,13]. These concerns have propelled a plethora of work in explainable AI, a domain concerned with the design of models that can provide high-level comprehensive explanations for their answers. These models can be either explainable-by-design, or rely on external modules that compute explanations *a posteriori*. This need for post-hoc explainability is particularly compelling for sophisticated machine learning models, e.g., neural networks, whose logic is perceived as a black box by lay users.

One of the most prominent modules to compute post-hoc explanations for black-box supervised ML models is LIME [15]. This approach builds upon the notion of *local feature attribution* via a *linear surrogate*. Feature attribution means that the explanation quantifies the contribution of a set of features to the black box's answer. This allows users to build a ranking of the features that play the biggest role in the model's logic. We

© The Author(s), under exclusive license to Springer Nature Switzerland AG 2022
T. Bouadi et al. (Eds.): IDA 2022, LNCS 13205, pp. 102–114, 2022.
https://doi.org/10.1007/978-3-031-01333-1_9

say the explanation is local because it only holds for a *target instance* and its vicinity. By focusing on a region of the feature space, LIME reduces the complexity of the black box and can approximate it using a surrogate sparse linear function whose coefficients constitute the feature attribution scores of the explanation. To learn this surrogate, LIME constructs a training set by generating artificial instances – called neighbors – around the target instance, and labeling them using the black box. The neighbors may not lie in the original feature space, but rather on a *surrogate space* that is meaningful to humans, e.g., image segments instead of pixels for images. The neighbors are weighted using an exponential kernel that depends on the distance to the target and a *bandwidth* parameter $\sigma \in \mathbb{R}^+$. The weighting process controls the level of locality of the explanation: the smaller $\sigma$ is, the more local the explanation becomes as closer neighbors are weighted higher than farther ones. More locality also implies focusing on a smaller region where the black box is presumably easier to approximate.

As logical as this sounds, our experiments suggest that small values of $\sigma$ can yield unfaithful or even trivially empty explanations. This counter-intuitive result has thus motivated this work, which brings two contributions: (a) A study of the impact of the bandwidth and the training vicinity on the fidelity and semantics of LIME, namely the meaning of the feature attribution scores[1]; and (b) S-LIME, an extension of LIME that can solve the locality-fidelity paradox.

This paper is structured as follows. In Sect. 2 we introduce some background concepts and notations. We elaborate on our contributions in Sects. 3 and 4. Section 5 presents an experimental evaluation of S-LIME. In Sect. 6 we survey the state of the art. Section 7 concludes the paper.

## 2 Preliminaries

*Black Boxes and Linear Surrogates.* We assume our black box is a classification function $f : \mathbb{R}^d \rightarrow \mathbb{R}$ $(d \in \mathbb{Z}^+)$ that predicts the probability that a target instance $x \in \mathbb{R}^d$ belongs to a given class. We denote by $x[i]$ the $i$-th feature of $x$. Conversely, the explanation $g : \mathbb{R}^{\hat{d}} \rightarrow \mathbb{R}$ $(\hat{d} \in \mathbb{Z}^+)$ is a linear surrogate function that approximates $f$ in the locality of $x$, i.e., $g(\hat{x}) = \hat{\alpha}_0 + \sum_{1 \leq i \leq \hat{d}} \hat{\alpha}_i \hat{x}[i]$. Note that $g$ may be defined on a *surrogate space* different from $f$'s. This implies the existence of a conversion function $\eta_x : \mathbb{R}^{\hat{d}} \rightarrow \mathbb{R}^d$ from the surrogate to the original space.

*LIME.* In [15], the authors propose a model-agnostic method to compute local explanations for ML models in the form of sparse linear surrogates. LIME learns an explanation $g$ for a black box $f$ and an instance $x$ by solving the following minimization problem:

$$g = \underset{g \in \mathcal{G}: \, \|\hat{\alpha}\|_0 \leqslant k}{argmin} \quad \mathcal{L}_x(f, g) \tag{1}$$

In other words, the surrogate $g$ is chosen such that it minimizes the error $\mathcal{L}_x$ w.r.t. the answers of $f$ on a neighborhood $\mathcal{X}$ around a target instance $x$. To keep the explanation meaningful to humans, LIME restricts itself to surrogate functions $g$ with less than $k$

---

[1] By *semantics of LIME*, we mean the information carried by the feature attribution scores.

non-zero parameters, where $k$ is a user-configurable hyper-parameter set by default to 6. LIME does not assume access to the training data of the black box[2], therefore the neighbors $z \in \mathcal{X}$ take the form $z = \eta_x(\hat{z})$ where $\hat{z} \in \hat{\mathcal{X}} \subseteq \{0,1\}^d$ is a synthetic instance that lies on a binary space. This space is interpretated as the presence or absence of features of the target $x$, so that $x = \eta_x(\hat{x})$ with $\hat{x} = \mathbb{1}^d$. The neighbors in $\hat{\mathcal{X}}$ are obtained by toggling off bits in $x$'s binary representation $\hat{x}$. When a bit is set to zero in the surrogate space, the conversion function $\eta_x$ must map the resulting vector to the original space. For images, this can be achieved by replacing the toggled-off super-pixels with a baseline monochrome segment or with a patch from another image [16]. LIME weighs the neighbors in $\hat{\mathcal{X}}$ according to a kernel function $\pi_x^\sigma$ (based on a distance $D$ and a *bandwidth* hyper-parameter $\sigma \in \mathbb{R}^+$) on the surrogate space, that is,

$$\mathcal{L}_x(f,g) = \sum_{\hat{z} \in \hat{\mathcal{X}}} \pi_x^\sigma(\hat{z})(f(\eta_x(\hat{z})) - g(\hat{z}))^2, \quad \text{with } \pi_x^\sigma(\hat{z}) = \exp\left(-D(\hat{x},\hat{z})^2/\sigma^2\right).$$

The hyper-parameter $\sigma$ controls the locality of the explanation so that smaller values give more weight to the instances that lie close to $\hat{x}$, i.e., those instances with fewer toggled-off bits. LIME does not make any assumptions about the inner-workings of $f$, however the distance $D$ and the conversion functions $\eta_x$ depend on $f$'s original space, which at the same time depends on the instances' data type.

*Quality Metrics.* The quality of the local surrogate $g$ is evaluated in terms of its *fidelity*, which can be measured via the surrogate's adherence to the black box $f$ in the vicinity of $x$. Adherence is usually measured via the coefficient of determination $R^2$ [5, 17, 20]. The $R^2$ score measures the similarity between the predictions of both functions, compared to the variance of the black-box prediction. This coefficient lies in $(-\infty, 1]$, where $R^2 = 1$ means $g$ fits $f$ perfectly and $R^2 = 0$ (respectively $R^2 < 0$) implies that $g$ is as accurate as (resp. less accurate than) the best constant model.

When a gold standard set $F_f(x)$ of important features is available, we can also calculate fidelity as the agreement between the explanation and the gold standard. This can be quantified via metrics such as *recall* [15], *precision*, or *coverage* [8]. Assuming the surrogate and the original feature spaces are identical, if the explanation $g$ for the target instance $x$ reports features $F_g(x)$ as the most important, the recall and precision of $g$ are respectively $\frac{|F_f(x) \cap F_g(x)|}{|F_f(x)|}$ and $\frac{|F_f(x) \cap F_g(x)|}{|F_g(x)|}$. Coverage can be used for data types where segments, i.e., conglomerates of contiguous features, are more meaningful to humans than individual features. Examples are time series and images. For those cases, the coverage is the proportion of the gold standard regions that overlap with the regions reported by the surrogate. Further specialized metrics have been proposed to measure the fidelity of pixel attribution explanations for image classifiers [9].

## 3   Locality vs. Fidelity

In this section we study the impact of two important elements of LIME on the fidelity and semantics of explanations, namely the bandwidth $\sigma$ and the neighborhood $\hat{\mathcal{X}}$.

---

[2] The exception to this rule is its implementation for tabular data.

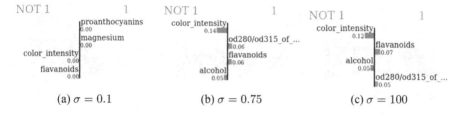

(a) $\sigma = 0.1$           (b) $\sigma = 0.75$           (c) $\sigma = 100$

**Fig. 1.** LIME explanations for three different bandwidths on the same instance of the wine dataset ($k = 4$).

### 3.1 The Paradox of Small Bandwidth

We illustrate the impact of $\sigma$ on the output of the tabular variant of LIME[3], which we use to explain a random forest classifier trained on the UCI wine dataset[4]. Tabular LIME sets $\sigma = 0.75$ with no further explanation. Changing $\sigma$ can, however, drastically change the resulting explanation as depicted in Fig. 1. In particular, LIME computes null attribution coefficients when $\sigma = 0.1$. Changing $\sigma$ from 0.75 to 100 rearranges the attribution ranking of the features.

To investigate the cause of this instability, we measure the adherence of the surrogate in $\hat{\mathcal{X}}$ as $\sigma$ varies for all the test instances of the dataset. We plot the results for two instances in Fig. 2a, where instance 2 is the example explained in Fig. 1.

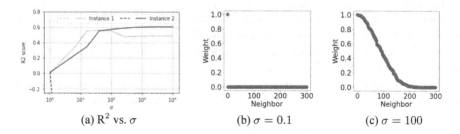

(a) $R^2$ vs. $\sigma$          (b) $\sigma = 0.1$          (c) $\sigma = 100$

**Fig. 2.** Left: Impact of the bandwidth $\sigma$ on the $R^2$ score of LIME for two instances of the wine dataset. Right: Distribution of the neighborhood weights for instance 2.

We recall that the $R^2$ score is calculated as $1 - v_r(g)/v(f)$, where $v_r(g)$ is the residual sum of squares of the surrogate $g$ and $v_r(f)$ is the total sum of squares of $f$'s answers. This means that the surrogate accounts for no more than 60% of the variability of the black box in $\hat{\mathcal{X}}$. The dashed regions of the curves indicate that the surrogate model has degenerated into a set of zero weights. This points out a counter-intuitive phenomenon: higher locality – achieved by making $\sigma$ small – yields poor explanations. We also observe that the $R^2$ may not increase monotonically with $\sigma$. Based on these

---

[3] The discretization is off, hence the classifier and the explanation operate in the same space.
[4] https://archive.ics.uci.edu/ml/datasets/wine.

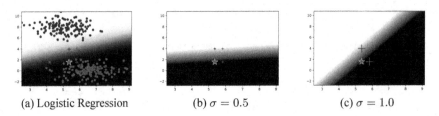

|(a) Logistic Regression | (b) $\sigma = 0.5$ | (c) $\sigma = 1.0$|

**Fig. 3.** Left: A logistic regression classifier and a neighborhood (denoted by + marks) generated on a 2D discrete surrogate space. Center and right: Two LIME explanations. The gradient of each of these functions at the target example (denoted by the * mark) is orthogonal to the border between white area and black area. The explanation in the middle captures the black box's gradient more faithfully. (Color figure online)

observations, we devise two research questions that drive our contribution: (i) Why do seem locality and fidelity in opposition?, and (ii) what makes a good LIME explanation?

### 3.2 Why do Seem Locality and Fidelity in Opposition?

We investigate the cause of this paradox by means of Figs. 2b and 2c that depict the distribution of weights for the neighbors of instance 2 for $\sigma = 0.1$ and $\sigma = 100$. In the first case, the LIME surrogate is a degenerated model that predicts a constant as hinted by Fig. 2a and its corresponding explanation in Fig. 1a. Figure 2b tells us that the bulk of the weights is concentrated on the target instance. Such a phenomenon leads to a trivial training set. Even though locality is defined in terms of the entire set of instances in $\hat{\mathcal{X}}$, almost all of them are dispensable because they do not have any influence when learning the surrogate. The situation is less skewed for $\sigma = 100$ (Fig. 2c), which yields the non-trivial explanation in Fig. 1c.

From this analysis we conclude that the selection of $\sigma$ and the construction of $\hat{\mathcal{X}}$ must go in hand. We thus propose a strategy to jointly select them in Sect. 4.

### 3.3 What Makes a Good LIME Explanation?

The human aspects of interpretability are beyond the scope of this paper; instead this study is concerned with the quality and meaningfulness of explanations from a mathematical point of view. As suggested by [6], LIME computes a scaled version of the gradient $\nabla f$ for linear black boxes $f$. The scaling arises because the surrogate is learned on a finite number of neighbors in a discrete space, and the scaling factor depends on $x$, $\sigma$, $\eta_x$, and $\hat{\mathcal{X}}$. We argue that in the absence of a reference instance (as in [12,18,19]), explanations based on instantaneous gradients are meaningful and desirable because their semantics are well-defined: the *surrogate gradient* $\hat{\nabla} f(x)$ is the contribution of each surrogate feature to $f$'s change rate at point $x$. That said, LIME does not always estimate $\hat{\nabla} f$ accurately as suggested by Fig. 3. The figures show that the weights associated to the neighbors may yield an estimation that differs largely from the black box's actual gradient in Fig. 3a.

---

**Algorithm 1.** S-LIME            applied to black-box function $f$ at target instance $x$

---

**Require:** Conversion function $\eta_x$, distribution $\nu_\sigma$ on the surrogate space
**Require:** Number $k$ of features in the explanation, number $n$ of local examples
1:  $\hat{\mathcal{X}} \leftarrow \left\{ \hat{z}^{(i)} : i = 1, \ldots, n \right\}$, where $\hat{z}^{(i)} \sim \nu_\sigma$ **for** $i = 1, \ldots, n$
2:  **return** $argmin_{g \in \mathcal{G}: \, \|\hat{\alpha}\|_0 \leqslant k} \sum_{\hat{z} \in \hat{\mathcal{X}}} \left( f(\eta_x(\hat{z})), g(\hat{z}) \right)^2$

---

## 4    S-LIME

To tackle the locality-fidelity paradox explained in Sect. 3.1, we introduce an extension of LIME, called S-LIME (*Smoothed LIME*), that we detailed in the following.

### 4.1    Generic Algorithm

LIME may compute degenerated explanations due to two main factors: (i) the discreteness of the surrogate space, and (ii) the fact that instance generation and weighting are decoupled. Indeed, LIME first generates a discrete neighborhood $\hat{\mathcal{X}}$ (independently of $\sigma$), and then weighs the instances in $\hat{\mathcal{X}}$ using $\pi_x^\sigma$. In the extreme cases when $\sigma$ tends to zero, the weighting is concentrated on $\hat{x}$.

To prevent this skewed concentration of weights, we control the locality of the explanation in a single step (see Algorithm 1). Hence, we define the neighbors in the continuous space $[0, 1]^{\hat{d}}$ and populate $\hat{\mathcal{X}}$ with examples $\hat{z}$ whose distance $D$ to $\hat{x}$ is of *the same magnitude* as $\sigma$. Concretely, the neighborhood $\hat{\mathcal{X}} = \{\hat{z}^{(1)}, \ldots, \hat{z}^{(n)}\}$ consists of $n$ equally-weighted instances drawn independently from a distribution $\nu_\sigma$. Such a design decision enables $g$ to approximate $\widehat{\nabla} f$ when $\sigma$ tends to zero, without hindering interpretability: $g$ still combines the contributions of the surrogate features linearly, and we can still confer an interpretable meaning to the neighbors as later explained in Sect. 4.4. Moreover, this allows controlling locality via the bandwidth of the neighborhood distribution, and not anymore through an a-posteriori weighting.

Note that S-LIME also requires the definition of new conversion functions $\eta_x$ as $\hat{\mathcal{X}}$ is now a subset of the continuous space $[0, 1]^{\hat{d}}$ instead of the discrete space $\{0, 1\}^{\hat{d}}$. In Sect. 4.4 we provide examples of proper distributions $\nu_\sigma$ and functions $\eta_x$ for images, time series, and tabular data.

### 4.2    S-LIME Subsumes LIME

**Lemma 1.** *Let $f$ be a function and $x$ a target instance. There is a distribution $\nu_\sigma$ over $[0, 1]^{\hat{d}}$ such that LIME and S-LIME are minimizing the same expected loss function.*

*Proof.* LIME outputs a function $g$ that minimizes the loss $\mathcal{L}_x(f, g)$ which is the residual sum of squares of the examples drawn from a distribution $\nu$. The expectation of this loss function w.r.t. to a random neighborhood is $\mathbb{E}_{\hat{z} \sim \nu} \left[ \pi_x^\sigma(\hat{z}) \left( f(\eta_x(\hat{z})) - g(\hat{z}) \right)^2 \right]$. Remark that $\nu$ is a distribution on the finite space $\{0, 1\}^{\hat{d}}$, then $\nu =$

$\sum_{\hat{z}\in\{0,1\}^d} w_\nu(\hat{z})\delta(\hat{z})$, where $\delta(\hat{z})$ is the Dirac distribution at point $\hat{z}$, and $w_\nu(\hat{z})$ is a positive real number.

Similarly, s-LIME returns the linear surrogate $g$ that minimizes a loss with expectation $\mathbb{E}_{\hat{z}\sim\nu_\sigma}\left[(f(\eta_x(\hat{z})) - g(\hat{z}))^2\right]$. Let $Z$ be $\sum_{\hat{z}\in\{0,1\}^d} \pi_x^\sigma(\hat{z})w_\nu(\hat{z})$. If we consider s-LIME with generating distribution $\nu_\sigma = 1/Z \sum_{\hat{z}\in\{0,1\}^d} \pi_x^\sigma(\hat{z})w_\nu(\hat{z})\delta(\hat{z})$, then

$$\mathbb{E}_{\hat{z}\sim\nu_\sigma}\left[(f(\eta_x(\hat{z})) - g(\hat{z}))^2\right] = \sum_{\hat{z}\in\{0,1\}^d} \frac{\pi_x^\sigma(\hat{z})w_\nu(\hat{z})}{Z} (f(\eta_x(\hat{z})) - g(\hat{z}))^2$$

$$= \frac{1}{Z}\mathbb{E}_{\hat{z}\sim\nu}\left[\pi_x^\sigma(\hat{z}) (f(\eta_x(\hat{z})) - g(\hat{z}))^2\right],$$

which concludes the proof.

*Remark 1.* It follows from Lemma 1 that s-LIME may be used as a placeholder for LIME. Still, the proposed distribution $\nu_\sigma$ is practical only when $d$ is small, or when $\nu_\sigma$ corresponds to a well-known distribution. Otherwise, storing the $2^d$ coefficients $\pi_x^\sigma(\hat{z})w_\nu(\hat{z})$ is unpractical. Anyway, we demonstrate in Sect. 5 that s-LIME with a continuous distribution is more faithful than LIME.

### 4.3  s-LIME and the Gradient of the Black-Box Function

Let us assume the surrogate function $f \circ \eta_x$ to be differentiable at $\hat{x}$. Let us also denote by $\hat{\alpha}$ the weights of the linear model returned by s-LIME when we drop the sparseness constraint. Then for any family of continuous distributions $\nu_\sigma$ on $[0, 1]^{\hat{d}}$, such that their mass concentrates on $\hat{x}$ when $\sigma$ tends to zero, $\hat{\alpha}$ tends to the gradient $\nabla f(x)$ of $f \circ \eta_x$ at point $\hat{x}$. An example of such family of distributions is the set $\{\mathcal{N}(\hat{x}, \sigma^2 I), \sigma \in \mathbb{R}^+\}$ of Gaussian distributions centered at $\hat{x}$ with variance $\sigma^2 I$, where $I$ is the identity matrix.

This property has two main implications. First, while LIME degenerates as $\sigma$ approaches zero, s-LIME remains well-defined for any value of $\sigma$. Secondly, we know what s-LIME is targeting when we look locally at $\hat{x}$: $\hat{\nabla} f(x)$.

*Remark 2.* There are settings for which surrogate gradients are meaningless: piece-wise constant functions such as random forests. In such a scenario, s-LIME outputs a zero gradient as soon as the bandwidth of the generating distribution is small enough. While the weights returned by s-LIME are mathematically consistent for such kinds of models, they are useless as they carry on information that is too local. If that is the case, users may pick a higher value for $\sigma$, or resort to a rule-based surrogate [16].

### 4.4  s-LIME Implementations

Let us now discuss examples of concrete distributions $\nu_\sigma$ and functions $\eta_x$. The generating distribution $\nu_\sigma$ is the same for image and time series datasets: the uniform distribution on $[1 - \sigma, 1]^{\hat{d}}$, with $\sigma \in (0, 1]$. As needed, this distribution concentrates around the surrogate target $\hat{x} = \mathbb{1}^{\hat{d}}$ when $\sigma$ tends to zero.

In regards to the conversion function $\eta_x$, we recall that for both images [15] and time series [8], LIME splits the original instance into $\hat{d}$ contiguous regions, namely super-pixels for images or fragments of fixed size for time series. Those regions define the features of the surrogate space. Given a neighbor $\hat{z} \in \hat{\mathcal{X}}$ and a surrogate feature $j$, we can project $\hat{z}$ back to the original space by interpolating the original features of the target $x$ with a baseline $x_0$, i.e., $\eta_x(\hat{z})[i] = (1 - \hat{z}[j])x_0 + \hat{z}[j]x[i]$ for all the original features $i$, i.e., pixels or time measures, covered by segment $j$. We set $x_0 = 0$ in our experiments, i.e., the interpolation is done w.r.t. a black image and a null time series.

Finally, for tabular data we consider one surrogate feature per original feature. Therefore, the generating distribution $\nu_\sigma$ is the centered multivariate Gaussian distribution with covariance $\sigma^2 I$, and the function $\eta_x(\hat{z}) = x + \hat{z}$.

*Remark 3.* The design of a proper distribution $\nu_\sigma$ and a proper function $\eta_x$ requires the black-box model to handle examples living in a continuous space. As a consequence, S-LIME cannot be defined for text data.

## 5   Experiments

We now show-case the impact of the bandwidth $\sigma$ on the fidelity of LIME and S-LIME explanations. We first detail our experimental setup and then elaborate on our findings.

### 5.1   Experimental Settings

*Datasets and Black Boxes.* We conduct our experiments on a variety of datasets, comprising Cifar10 [10] and MNIST [11] for image data, the FordA and StarlightCurves time series datasets from the *UEA & UCR Time Series Classification Repository*, and the Compas and Diabetes datasets from the *UCI Machine Learning Repository* for tabular data. We also consider a selection of black-box models, which may be smooth or piece-wise constant, simple or complex, interpretable or not.

*Protocol and Metrics.* For each combination of dataset, model, and explanation module, we compute the average value of the experimental metrics for different values of $\sigma$ on the test instances of the dataset. The experimental metrics were introduced in Sect. 2: the $R^2$ score for all models, and the precision/recall or the coverage for the interpretable models, i.e., those for which a ground truth is available. All these metrics take values either in $(-\infty, 1]$ or in $[0, 1]$, and higher values denote higher fidelity.

### 5.2   Impact of $\sigma$

To study the impact of $\sigma$ on the fidelity of the LIME and S-LIME explanations, we plot the surrogate's adherence on the StarlightCurves dataset for several black-box models all using 100 random shapelets as input features. The models include Learning Shapelets (LS) [7], RESNET [21], Fast Shapelets (FS) [14], and a sparse logistic regression (LR, with $L_1$-regularization to enforce at most 10 features). The results are depicted in Fig. 4. We set $k = 6$ for the number of features in explanations [15].

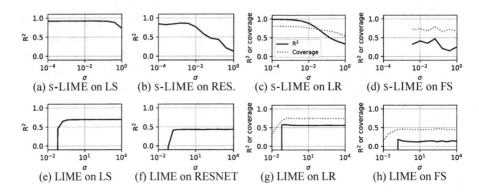

**Fig. 4.** $R^2$ and coverage vs. $\sigma$ on the StarlightCurves dataset. Each subplot corresponds to a couple (explainer, dataset). The plotted results are averaged on the instances of the test dataset. Recall that for S-LIME $\sigma$ is defined in $(0, 1]$.

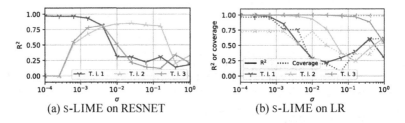

**Fig. 5.** $R^2$ and coverage vs. $\sigma$ on the StarlightCurves dataset. Each subplot corresponds to a couple (explainer, dataset). Each curve corresponds to one target instance.

We observe that very local S-LIME neighborhoods lead to higher adherence and coverage, except for FS. This translates into more faithful explanations as $\sigma$ approaches zero, where LIME cannot deliver proper explanations. In contrast, LIME achieves higher adherence and coverage for FS, because this model is a decision tree. Hence, the decision function is piece-wise constant and its gradient is zero almost every-where. When $\sigma$ is small enough, S-LIME recovers this gradient and returns an explanation with null coefficients, which has little practical value. That said, a wider locality can still yield a more informative explanation.

We also remark that, for complex models, the best value for $\sigma$ may depend on the target instance. This is corroborated by Fig. 5 that shows the disaggregated results for 3 instances on RESNET, a deep neural network. We can observe that the adherence is maximal when $\sigma$ is equal $10^{-4}$, $3 \times 10^{-3}$, and $2 \times 10^{-2}$ respectively. On the other hand, the same values of $\sigma$ are optimal for all examples on a simpler LR model.

Finally, we highlight that the coverage peaks when the adherence is maximal both at the instance (Fig. 5b) and dataset level (Figs. 4(cdgh)). This shows the pertinence of the $R^2$ score as metric to select the right level of locality.

**Table 1.** Best average recall and precision, or coverage (std. in parentheses) on different datasets and interpretable black-box classifiers.

| Data type | Dataset | Model | S-LIME | | LIME | |
|---|---|---|---|---|---|---|
| | | | Rec. or Cov. | Precision | Rec. or Cov. | Precision |
| Timeseries | FordA | LR on shapelets | **0.87** (0.15) | – (–) | 0.73 (0.17) | – (–) |
| | | Fast shapelets | **0.51** (0.30) | – (–) | **0.49** (0.27) | – (–) |
| | Starlight-curves | LR on shapelets | **0.81** (0.17) | – (–) | 0.75 (0.17) | – (–) |
| | | Fast shapelets | **0.68** (0.19) | – (–) | 0.45 (0.15) | – (–) |
| Tabular data | Diabetes | Logistic reg. | **1.00** (0.00) | **1.00** (0.00) | 0.88 (0.12) | 0.88 (0.12) |
| | | Dec. tree | **0.95** (0.13) | **0.81** (0.20) | 0.94 (0.14) | **0.80** (0.20) |
| | Compas | Logistic reg. | **1.00** (0.00) | **1.00** (0.00) | 0.52 (0.21) | 0.52 (0.21) |
| | | Dec. tree | **0.66** (0.33) | 0.25 (0.00) | **0.65** (0.33) | **0.33** (0.00) |

**Table 2.** Best average $R^2$ (std. in parentheses) on different datasets and black-box classifiers. MLP stands for a neural network with one hidden layer composed of 100 neurons and logistic sigmoid activation function. Column *Int.* indicates interpretable black-box models ($\checkmark$). FS, DT and RF are put aside as they are piecewise constant models.

| Data type | Model | Int. | k | S-LIME | LIME | k | S-LIME | LIME |
|---|---|---|---|---|---|---|---|---|
| Images | | | MNIST | | | Cifar10 | | |
| | Alexnet | | 10 | **0.80** (0.28) | 0.58 (0.20) | 10 | **0.84** (0.10) | 0.55 (0.25) |
| | VGG16 | | 10 | **0.56** (0.43) | **0.57** (0.21) | 10 | **0.69** (0.13) | 0.50 (0.27) |
| Timeseries | | | FordA | | | StarlightCurves | | |
| | Learning shapelets | | 6 | **0.84** (0.08) | 0.57 (0.15) | 6 | **0.92** (0.07) | 0.70 (0.07) |
| | RESNET | | 6 | **0.73** (0.20) | 0.10 (1.05) | 6 | **0.87** (0.15) | 0.44 (0.15) |
| | LR on shapelets | $\checkmark$ | 6 | **1.00** (0.01) | 0.56 (0.13) | 6 | **0.99** (0.02) | 0.58 (0.12) |
| | Fast shapelets | $\checkmark$ | 6 | 0.15 (0.18) | **0.19** (0.14) | 6 | **0.25** (0.13) | 0.19 (0.16) |
| Tabular data | | | Diabetes | | | Compas | | |
| | Logistic regression | $\checkmark$ | 4 | **1.00** (0.00) | **0.99** (0.01) | 11 | **1.00** (0.00) | 0.42 (0.23) |
| | MLP | | 4 | **0.97** (0.03) | 0.72 (0.13) | 6 | **0.79** (0.01) | 0.31 (0.16) |
| | Decision tree | $\checkmark$ | 3 | **0.46** (0.09) | **0.46** (0.10) | 3 | 0.34 (0.00) | **0.36** (0.00) |
| | Random forest | | 4 | **0.62** (0.03) | 0.58 (0.12) | 6 | **0.30** (0.01) | **0.30** (0.02) |

### 5.3 Fidelity Analysis

Tables 1 and 2 show the average scores obtained by S-LIME and LIME when $\sigma$ is selected to maximize the aggregated adherence ($R^2$ score) in the test instances of the experimental datasets. Table 1 shows recall, precision, and coverage for the interpretable models, whereas Table 2 provides the $R^2$ score for all models.

Firstly, we remark that S-LIME's explanations are strictly more faithful than LIME's except for piecewise constant models (FS, DT, and RF). That said, this does not prevent S-LIME from achieving higher adherence for such models on some datasets when we look at a larger vicinity.

Secondly, the $R^2$ score is a good proxy to predict the best neighborhood in terms of recall, precision, or coverage. This is a strong result from an application point of view. Practitioners are mostly interested by the features that are actually used by the black-box model. For cases where those actual features are unknown, the $R^2$ score enables the computation of faithful linear explanations that can identify the important features.

## 6    Related Work

*Feature-Attribution Explanations.* Methods such as DeepLIFT [18], Integrated Gradients (IG) [19], SHAP [12], or LIME [15] compute importance local attribution scores for the features of a black-box ML model. Among those, SHAP and LIME are model-agnostic and compute linear surrogates learned from artificial neighbors. Despite these similarities, the semantics of their explanations are different as confirmed by existing studies [1]. While LIME approximates – often coarsely – the instantaneous gradient of the black box w.r.t. the input features [6], SHAP computes – or rather approximates – the Shapley values [12], which quantify the feature contributions to the difference between the model's answer on a baseline instance and the target. The baseline depends on the use case, e.g., a single-color image (represented by the vector $0^d$ in the surrogate space). This makes SHAP and LIME complementary methods rather than competitors.

*LIME Extensions.* An important body of literature has studied the impact of the different components and parameters of LIME on the quality of the explanations. This has led to multiple extensions of the original LIME algorithm. As opposed to this work, some extensions [17, 20, 22] tackle the instability of LIME, i.e., the fact that two executions of the algorithm with the same input may not deliver the same explanation. This instability originates from the randomness in the different steps of the approach, e.g., sampling in the surrogate space, non-deterministic conversion functions, etc. On those grounds, the techniques to tackle instability are diverse. ALIME [17], for example, resorts to a denoising auto-encoder to create a surrogate space that characterizes the data manifold more accurately. DLIME [22], in contrast, applies hierarchical agglomerative clustering on the training instances to identify the closest neighbors of the target and use them to learn the surrogate. In another line of thought, the authors of OptiLIME [20] study the relationship between the bandwidth $\sigma$, the adherence, and the instability of LIME. Similar to our work, the authors highlight the importance of choosing the right $\sigma$ in a per-instance basis. Moreover, they show an inverse relationship between $\sigma$ and explanation instability. This observation constitutes the basis of a method to select the bandwidth $\sigma$ that yields the best trade-off between adherence and instability. We highlight that all these approaches have been proposed only for tabular data, and that none of them takes into account recall, precision, or coverage fidelity.

Other extensions of LIME have focused entirely on improving fidelity. ILIME [5] proposes the use of influence functions in order to up-weight the neighbors that play a higher role in the linear fit of the surrogate. QLIME-A [3] proposes to extend the local surrogate to report quadratic relationships for cases where a linear surrogate is still inaccurate. While quadratic functions do exhibit higher fit capabilities, their interpretability in general settings is debatable.

## 7    Conclusion

In this paper we have introduced S-LIME, an extension of LIME that reconciles locality and fidelity for linear explanations. We argue that LIME can produce degenerated explanations as locality – controlled through the bandwidth $\sigma$ – increases. We solve this paradox by means of a new neighbor generation process on a continuous surrogate space. Our experiments on image, time series, and tabular data suggest that this strategy can provide even more faithful linear explanations with gradient-compliant semantics that are not affected by high locality. As a future work, we envision to investigate the fidelity of S-LIME explanations with other generating distributions and conversion functions, as well as to study the impact on the stability of the explanations.

**Acknowledgements.** This research was partially supported by the Inria Project Lab "Hybrid Approaches for Interpretable AI" (HyAIAI), the project "Framework for Automatic Interpretability in Machine Learning" financed by the French National Research Agency (ANR JCJC FAbLe), and the network on the foundations of trustworthy AI, integrating learning, optimisation, and reasoning (TAILOR) financed by the EU's Horizon 2020 research and innovation program under agreement 952215.

# References

1. Amparore, E., Perotti, A., Bajardi, P.: To trust or not to trust an explanation: using LEAF to evaluate local linear XAI methods. PeerJ Comput. Sci. **7** (2021). https://doi.org/10.7717/peerj-cs.479
2. Bodria, F., Giannotti, F., Guidotti, R., Naretto, F., Pedreschi, D., Rinzivillo, S.: Benchmarking and Survey of Explanation Methods for Black Box Models. CoRR abs/2102.13076 (2021)
3. Bramhall, S., Horn, H., Tieu, M., Lohia, N.: QLIME-A: quadratic local interpretable model-agnostic explanation approach. SMU Data Sci. Rev. **3**, 4 (2020)
4. Doshi-Velez, F., et al.: Accountability of AI under the law: the role of explanation. CoRR abs/1711.01134 (2017). http://arxiv.org/abs/1711.01134
5. ElShawi, R., Sherif, Y., Al-Mallah, M., Sakr, S.: ILIME: local and global interpretable model-agnostic explainer of black-box decision. In: ADBIS (2019)
6. Garreau, D., von Luxburg, U.: Explaining the explainer: a first theoretical analysis of LIME. In: AISTATS (2020)
7. Grabocka, J., Schilling, N., Wistuba, M., Schmidt-Thieme, L.: Learning time-series shapelets. In: KDD (2014)
8. Guillemé, M., Masson, V., Rozé, L., Termier, A.: Agnostic local explanation for time series classification. In: ICTAI (2019)
9. Jia, Y., Frank, E., Pfahringer, B., Bifet, A., Lim, N.: Studying and exploiting the relationship between model accuracy and explanation quality. In: ECML/PKDD (2021)
10. Krizhevsky, A.: Learning Multiple Layers of Features from Tiny Images. Technical report, Canadian Institute for Advanced Research (2009)
11. LeCun, Y., Cortes, C.: MNIST Handwritten Digit Database (2010). http://yann.lecun.com/exdb/mnist/
12. Lundberg, S.M., Lee, S.: A unified approach to interpreting model predictions. In: NeurIPS (2017)
13. Merrer, E.L., Trédan, G.: The bouncer problem: challenges to remote explainability. CoRR abs/1910.01432 (2019). http://arxiv.org/abs/1910.01432
14. Rakthanmanon, T., Keogh, E.: Fast shapelets: a scalable algorithm for discovering time series shapelets. In: SDM (2013)
15. Ribeiro, M.T., Singh, S., Guestrin, C.: Why should I trust you?: explaining the predictions of any classifier. In: KDD (2016)

16. Ribeiro, M.T., Singh, S., Guestrin, C.: Anchors: high-precision model-agnostic explanations. In: AAAI (2018). https://www.aaai.org/ocs/index.php/AAAI/AAAI18/paper/view/16982
17. Shankaranarayana, S.M., Runje, D.: ALIME: autoencoder based approach for local interpretability. CoRR abs/1909.02437 (2019). http://arxiv.org/abs/1909.02437
18. Shrikumar, A., Greenside, P., Kundaje, A.: Learning important features through propagating activation differences. In: ICML (2017). http://proceedings.mlr.press/v70/shrikumar17a.html
19. Sundararajan, M., Taly, A., Yan, Q.: Axiomatic attribution for deep networks. CoRR abs/1703.01365 (2017)
20. Visani, G., Bagli, E., Chesani, F.: OptiLIME: optimized LIME explanations for diagnostic computer algorithms. In: AIMLAI@CIKM (2020). http://ceur-ws.org/Vol-2699/paper03.pdf
21. Wang, Z., Yan, W., Oates, T.: Time series classification from scratch with deep neural networks: a strong baseline. CoRR abs/1611.06455 (2016). http://arxiv.org/abs/1611.06455
22. Zafar, M.R., Khan, N.M.: DLIME: a deterministic local interpretable model-agnostic explanations approach for computer-aided diagnosis systems. CoRR abs/1906.10263 (2019). http://arxiv.org/abs/1906.10263

# Quantifying Changes in Predictions of Classification Models for Data Streams

Maciej Grzenda$^{(\boxtimes)}$ 

Faculty of Mathematics and Information Science, Warsaw University of Technology,
ul. Koszykowa 75, 00-662 Warszawa, Poland
M.Grzenda@mini.pw.edu.pl

**Abstract.** Evaluation methods for data stream classification have frequently been focused on how available data are used for learning a model and for its performance assessment, with major emphasis on the difference between predicted and true labels. More recently, growing interest in delayed labelling evaluation has resulted in the evaluation of multiple predictions made by an evolving model for an instance before its true label arrival. Still, under this setting predictions are also compared with true labels rather than changes in predictions focused on.

In this study, we aim to provide an intuitive evaluation framework to quantify changes in predictions made over time for the same input instances by evolving classification models. The primary motivation is to gain insight into the impact of the evolution of a classification model on the changes in decision boundaries, which may effectively re-assign the instances to other classes. The prediction change measures proposed in this study make it possible to reveal the scale of such changes. Furthermore, the notions of volatility of predictions and productive volatility are proposed and quantified. Results for a number of real and synthetic data streams show that similar accuracy of the models can be accompanied by significantly different volatility of predictions made by these models.

**Keywords:** Data stream · Classification · Delayed labels · Evaluation

## 1 Introduction

Stream mining methods [2,5,7] address the need for machine learning models operating on unbounded data. In particular, existing methods such as k Nearest Neighbours (kNN) have been adapted to a stream mining setting and novel methods have been proposed. In both cases, the primary assumption is that a model changes with time. One of the reasons for these changes is the growing availability of data, which may justify updates in the model. Furthermore, many data streams describe nonstationary processes. Hence, real concept drift [2,5] may occur i.e. the probability $p(y|\mathbf{x})$ that an instance $\mathbf{x}$ belongs to a class $y$ may change with time. Such changes are expected to be reflected by a classification model. This may happen with some latency, especially when ground truth labels

© The Author(s), under exclusive license to Springer Nature Switzerland AG 2022
T. Bouadi et al. (Eds.): IDA 2022, LNCS 13205, pp. 115–127, 2022.
https://doi.org/10.1007/978-3-031-01333-1_10

$y_i$ become available with some latency only compared to the corresponding $\mathbf{x}_i$ examples i.e. under a delayed labelling setting.

There has been much work on detecting concept drift and developing stream mining classifiers capable of adapting to it [1,2,7]. More recently, quantitative measures of concept drift have been proposed [11,12]. Importantly, changes in the performance measure calculated for a model can be caused by model changes resulting in changes in the classes assigned to the same input instances. However, another possible reason is the fact that the data distribution can change [11]. Not only real concept drift, but also virtual concept drift, i.e. a change only in $p(\mathbf{x})$, but not in $p(y|\mathbf{x})$ [5], may contribute to this phenomenon.

Importantly, even a constant value of a performance measure of a model does not mean that the model remains constant. As an example, it is possible that the growth in the number of instances of class $c_i$ wrongly mapped by a model to class $c_j, j \neq i$ is balanced by the growth in the number of instances correctly mapped by a model to class $c_i$. This raises the question of how many past predictions would be different if made by a more recent model, and how many of such new predictions actually improve on past predictions, which is what we actually would expect from an evolving model. Hence, we believe there is a need to quantify not only changes in data streams and in the performance of stream mining models, but also to quantify the way past predictions change. In particular, it is possible that even a model developed under a stationary setting and exhibiting stable accuracy of its predictions frequently changes its decision boundaries and predictions, even though such noisy changes yield no performance improvements.

Hence, we complement methods quantifying changes in evolving data streams and models by proposing a method for identifying changes in predictions made by online classifiers. With the *volatility* measure we propose to quantify the ratio of changes in classes predicted for individual instances by an evolving model over time. With the *productive volatility* measure the changes replacing previous wrong class predictions with correct predictions can be summarised. The primary contributions of this work are as follows:

- We propose how changes in predictions over time can be identified;
- We propose measures summarising how frequently an online model changes its past predictions and whether such changes are productive i.e. they eliminate previous errors in class assignment;
- We show with empirical experiments using reference data streams and methods that classifiers of similar accuracy may largely differ in how frequently they change their predictions for the same instances;
- We provide an open source implementation of the methods proposed in this study[1].

---

[1] The code and data sets repository are available at https://github.com/mgrzenda/PredictionVolatility. The code calculating the measures proposed in this study has been implemented as an extension of the Massive Online Analysis (MOA) [2] framework.

The remainder of this study is organised as follows. Section 2 consists of an overview of related works. Next, a proposal for tracking changes in predictions and calculating prediction change measures is made in Sect. 3. This is followed in Sect. 4 by the results of applying the methods proposed in this study to a number of real and synthetic data streams. Finally, conclusions and suggestions for future work summarise the study in Sect. 5.

## 2    Related Works

The fact that a data stream is by definition an unbounded sequence of instances has a major impact on the training and evaluation of classification models. The key aspects to consider are how to use stream instances for training and evaluating a model at the same time and what performance measures to calculate.

As far as the use of stream instances for model training and evaluation is concerned, an assumption of **immediate labelling** is frequently made, i.e. after instance $\mathbf{x}_i$, its true label $y_i$ is made available to a learner. In this approach, first a predicted label $\tilde{y}_i$ is generated and evaluated and next a model is updated with $(\mathbf{x}_i, y_i)$ before the arrival of the next example $\mathbf{x}_{i+1}$.

However, for many problems true labels are only available with some latency. Hence, an alternative approach allows **delayed labels** [5,9]. In a delayed labelling scenario, for many or all instances, a non-negligible period between receiving an instance and receiving its true label occurs. This results in **verification latency** [5,10] i.e. the prediction made at the time of receiving an instance can be compared with the true label of the instance only after some period. Hence, in [9] three categories of predictions, i.e. an **initial prediction** made at the time of receiving an instance, **periodic predictions** made next, but before true label arrival, and a **final prediction** polled from a model before updating the model using the true label, were proposed. Experiments performed in [8,9] for real and synthetic data streams show that the accuracy of initial and final predictions may be significantly different. What is common for immediate and delayed labelling settings is that the classification models are expected to evolve and the performance measures rely on the comparison of predicted vs. true labels [2,7–9].

Irrespective of whether immediate or delayed labelling is concerned, adapting a model to concept drift is one of the key challenges of stream mining [1,2,5]. One possible strategy is the use of a drift detection mechanism [1,11] to trigger model updates. Moreover, methods quantifying concept drift, and measures such as drift magnitude and duration [11] were proposed. Model updates may also follow from the growing availability of data in a stationary setting. As an example, the Hoeffding tree algorithm [6] is an example of an algorithm which includes no explicit drift detection mechanism. Still, it relies on the Hoeffding bound to build a decision tree and define how additional splits in the tree are introduced with time. Such splits defined by new tree branches are also added under a stationary setting. This effectively changes past predictions. These changes are expected to make a model better match the true decision boundaries and improve its performance in turn. Significantly, Webb et al. show in [11] that even in the seemingly simple case of pure covariate drift (also known as virtual concept drift) i.e. changes in $p(X)$ under constant $p(Y|X)$, not all Hoeffding tree models recover from such drift. Somewhat surprisingly, it was observed that the larger the magnitude of the drift, the more efficient the recovery and the lower the ultimate error of a Hoeffding tree [11].

Our study aims to complement the works on quantifying model performance and quantifying changes in data streams by providing an increased insight into changes in predictions for the same instances observed over time. We aim to develop techniques applicable to both static and evolving data streams i.e. streams in which different drifts occur. This is because in both cases, due to growing availability of data, models are expected to evolve as long as errors in predictions are observed. Importantly, even when no concept drift occurs models may change, yet such changes can be of a partly noisy nature and only partly improve model performance. In particular, in the case of delayed labelling, the issue of how many initial predictions were replaced with some other final predictions and whether this eliminated previous prediction errors is addressed.

## 3  Prediction Change Measures

### 3.1  Monitoring Prediction Changes

To address the challenges identified above, we propose an evaluation methodology for multiclass streaming classifiers. First of all, under the delayed labelling setting, a stream $\mathcal{S}_1, \mathcal{S}_2, \ldots$ can be defined as a stream of two categories of tuples. In line with [9], it includes unlabelled instances, which can be denoted by $\mathcal{S}_i = \{(\mathbf{x}_k, ?)\}$, while the arrival of the true label for this instance can be denoted by the arrival of $\mathcal{S}_j = \{(\mathbf{x}_k, y_k)\}, j > i$.

Let us observe that for any data stream for which no natural delay exists, such as data streams used under an immediate labelling setting, a comparison of prediction $h_t(\mathbf{x}_k)$ made by a model $h_t()$ available at the time $t(\mathbf{x}_k)$ of the arrival of instance $\{(\mathbf{x}_k, ?)\}$ with the prediction $h_{t+\Delta t}(\mathbf{x}_k)$ made by a more recent model $h_{t+\Delta t}()$ can be made. How many predictions change, i.e. $h_{t+\Delta t}(\mathbf{x}_k) \neq h_t(\mathbf{x}_k)$, is influenced by the number of other $(\mathbf{x}_i, y_i)$ instances made available to a learner in the period $(t(\mathbf{x}_k), t(\mathbf{x}_k) + \Delta t)$. Hence, for streams with no natural delay we propose to track the scale of prediction changes subject to a requested fixed label delay $D$. Next, let us observe that an immediate labelling task can be converted into a task in which the sequence of $\mathbf{x}_k$ examples is preserved, but each true label $y_k$ is made available to a learner with delay. First, the time of every instance is set to an instance index in this stream. Next, as proposed in [9], the labels from original instances $\mathcal{S}_a = \{(\mathbf{x}_k, y_k)\}$ are removed, i.e. every $\mathcal{S}_a$ is set to $\{(\mathbf{x}_k, ?)\}$, and labelled instances $\mathcal{S}_b = \{(\mathbf{x}_k, y_k)\}$ are added at $t(\mathcal{S}_b) = t(\mathcal{S}_a) + D$. In this way, a unified approach following a delayed labelling setting can be applied both to data streams for which natural delay exists and data streams typically used under an immediate labelling setting. In the latter case, the same label delay $D$

can be applied to all instances. Hence, without loss of generality we refer to a delayed labelling setting for all the data streams in the remainder in our study.

---

**Input:** $\mathcal{S}_1, \mathcal{S}_2, \ldots$ - data stream, $N$ - the size of prediction change window
**Data:** $P(k)$ - list of predictions for $\mathcal{S}_i = \{(\mathbf{x}_k, ?)\}$; $W$ - sliding prediction change window of $N$ recent tuples $(y_k^I, y_k^F, y_k^T)$ composed of initial predicted label, final predicted label and true label for $\mathbf{x}_k$, respectively; $h_i$ - the prediction model
**begin**
    $h_1 = InitModel()$; $W = InitWindow(N)$;
    **for** $i = 1, \ldots$ **do**
        `/* New unlabelled instance */`
        **if** $\mathcal{S}_i = \{(\mathbf{x}_k, ?)\}$ **then**
            `/* get and store initial prediction */`
            $P(k).y_I = h_i(\mathbf{x}_k)$;
        **else**
            `/* ` $\mathcal{S}_i = \{(\mathbf{x}_k, y_k)\}$`, i.e. true label arrived */`
            $y_F = h_i(\mathbf{x}_k)$;
            $\mathbf{v}_k = \big(P(k).y_I, y_F, y_k\big)$;
            $UpdateSlidingPredictionWindow(W, \mathbf{v}_k)$;
            $h_{i+1} = \text{train}(h_i, \{(\mathbf{x}_k, y_k)\})$;
        **end**
    **end**
**end**

**Algorithm 1:** Calculation of prediction change measures

---

Let us define *label change tuple* $\mathbf{v} \in \mathbb{C}^3$ to be a tuple used to record the change of initial prediction to final prediction, but also the true label of an instance, while $\mathbb{C} = \{c_1, \ldots, c_l\}$ denotes the set of possible classes. A tuple $\mathbf{v}_i = (y_i^I, y_i^F, y_i^T)$ is composed of initial prediction $y_i^I$ made for an instance $\mathbf{x}_i$, final prediction $y_i^F$ made for the instance, and the true label $y_i^T$ of the instance.

In Algorithm 1, we propose how label change tuples can be processed and prediction change measures calculated. The algorithm extends the delayed labelling evaluation algorithm proposed in [9]. As defined in Algorithm 1, every time a new unlabelled instance arrives, an initial prediction $y_I$ is made for this instance and recorded. When the true label for an instance arrives, the final prediction for the instance is made. Next, a new label change tuple $\mathbf{v}_k$ is created. Hence, one label change tuple is developed for every labelled instance. The tuple is inserted into the *prediction change window* $W$, which is a sliding window of at most $N$ most recent label change tuples. We rely on a standard sliding window maintaining the same size and moving over the stream as used to evaluate stream mining methods. Next, the classifier $h_i$ can be updated to yield model $h_{i+1}$. Let us note that this use of a sliding window is compliant with the standard mechanism of calculating measures such as accuracy over a sliding window present *inter alia* in MOA [2]. It serves the same purpose of aggregating measure values over a sliding window of a fixed size of $N$ instances. In particular, the size of $W$ can match the size of the sliding window used to calculate performance measures during the learning process and simplify the comparison of these measures with the measures proposed in this work.

To capture the changes in a model and its predictions over the entire latency period, i.e. the period between $t(\{(\mathbf{x}_k, ?)\})$ and $t(\{(\mathbf{x}_k, y_k)\})$, we will focus on summarising the difference between initial predictions and final predictions recorded in a prediction change window. In the case of data streams adopted from an immediate labelling setting, this means summarising the difference between predictions polled from an evolving model at time $t(\mathbf{x}_i)$ and $t(\mathbf{x}_i) + D$. Let us define the confusion matrices needed to calculate the volatility measures.

**Definition 1. Initial confusion matrix:** *Let* $\mathbf{C}_I(W)$ *denote a confusion matrix developed for initial predictions, i.e. a square* $l \times l$ *matrix. Every element* $c_{ij}^I$ *of the matrix denotes the total number of examples in* $W$ *of true class* $i$, *for which the initially predicted class was class* $j$. *More formally,* $\mathbf{C}_I(W)$ *is composed of* $c_{ij}^I = card(\{\mathbf{v} \in W : \mathbf{v}.y^T = i \wedge \mathbf{v}.y^I = j\})$.

**Definition 2. Final confusion matrix:** *Let* $\mathbf{C}_F(W)$ *denote the final confusion matrix, i.e. the confusion matrix developed for final predictions and composed of* $c_{ij}^F = card(\{\mathbf{v} \in W : \mathbf{v}.y^T = i \wedge \mathbf{v}.y^F = j\})$.

The two matrices provide the basis for calculating the *differential confusion matrix* summarising how the performance of a model for individual classes changes after the initial predictions are replaced with the final predictions.

**Definition 3. Differential confusion matrix:** *Let* $\mathbf{C}_D(W)$ *denote the differential* $l \times l$ *confusion matrix, the elements of which are defined as:* $c_{ij}^D = c_{ij}^F - c_{ij}^I$.

With the differential confusion matrix, questions such as whether a more recent model reduced the false positive rate can be answered. Let us note that $c_{ij}^F = c_{ij}^I$ does not mean that predictions made for individual examples have not changed.

## 3.2 Quantifying Prediction Changes

To provide insight into the way the predictions change during the latency period, let us define the *prediction transition matrix*.

**Definition 4. Prediction transition matrix:** *Let the prediction transition matrix* $\mathbf{C}_T(W)$ *be a square* $l \times l$ *matrix composed of elements revealing the number of instances for which the initial prediction of class* $i$ *was changed to the final prediction of class* $j$, *i.e. composed of:* $c_{ij}^T = card(\{\mathbf{v} \in W : \mathbf{v}.y^I = i \wedge \mathbf{v}.y^F = j\})$.

For many problems the number of transitions from initial to final predictions can be of interest. Examples include the number of cases in which the model changed the initial prediction for a client from paying back their loan to defaulting on the loan. However, substantial insight into the changes in models can also be provided by the overall ratio of prediction changes. Hence, let us propose the volatility measure.

**Definition 5. Volatility:** *Let the volatility measure $V(W)$ be the share of changed predictions among all predictions:*

$$V(W) = \frac{\sum_{i,j=1,...,l;i\neq j} c_{ij}^{\mathrm{T}}}{card(W)}$$

Volatility shows how many changes to initial predictions were made, i.e. the ratio of instances represented in $W$ for which the initial prediction was not the same as the final prediction. This raises the question of how many such new class assignments actually corrected initial prediction errors. Therefore, let us conclude with a proposal for *productive volatility*.

**Definition 6. Productive volatility (PV):** *Let the productive volatility measure $V_{\mathrm{P}}(W)$ be defined as follows:*

$$V_{\mathrm{P}}(W) = \frac{\sum_{i=1,...,l} c_{ii}^{\mathrm{D}}}{\sum_{i,j=1,...,l;i\neq j} c_{ij}^{\mathrm{T}}}, V(W) \neq 0$$

The numerator in $V_{\mathrm{P}}(W)$ formula quantifies the total number of changes in correct predictions i.e. it serves to aggregate the number of prediction changes causing changes in the number of instances of class $i$ for which correct prediction was made. The denominator serves to calculate the total number of changes in predictions i.e. the number of final predictions differing from initial predictions. It is interesting to note that $V_{\mathrm{P}}(W) \in [-1,1]$. In particular, $V_{\mathrm{P}}(W) = 1$ means that all observed changes in predictions were changes from initially wrong classes to correct i.e. true classes. On the other hand, $V_{\mathrm{P}}(W) = -1$ means that all changes in predictions caused by model evolution were changes from initial predictions of true classes to final predictions of incorrect classes. Therefore, by combining volatility and productive volatility we can understand for how many instances predictions changed and how many changes in predictions replaced a previously wrong prediction with the correct one. Finally, let us note that $W_N(m)$ will be used in the remainder of this study to refer to the window containing at most $N$ label change tuples after processing $m$ labelled instances.

## 4    Results

### 4.1    Reference Data Streams and Streaming Classifiers

To illustrate the use of the proposed measures, experiments with both real and synthetic data streams were performed. As our study concerns both immediate and delayed setting, we selected some of the most frequently used streaming classifiers of varied types applicable in both cases. These included Hoeffding tree (HT) [6], i.e. a decision tree learner, which incrementally grows a tree model based on newly arriving instances, but includes no mechanisms of replacing existing tree branches to respond to concept drift, and Hoeffding Adaptive Tree (HAT) [3], i.e. a method responding to concept drift by adapting an existing decision tree. The remaining methods were the streaming version of kNN, i.e. the kNN method applied to a sliding window of recent instances representing distance-based classifiers, Adaptive Random Forest (ARF) [7] representing ensemble models, and Naive Bayes (NB) classifier, i.e. an example of a probabilistic classifier. In addition, the No Change (NC) method using last known true label as the predicted label for the next instance, and the Majority Class (MC) method assigning a new instance the label most frequently observed until the instance arrived were included. In all cases, the standard implementation of the method available in MOA was used. By selecting the stream mining methods listed above we aim to investigate how predictions of models of different categories such as distance-based models and tree-based models change over time, rather than focus on just one model category e.g. ensemble models only.

The list of data streams used in our experiments is provided in Table 1. First of all, real data streams for which natural varied label delay exists were included. Secondly, to investigate the use of prediction change measures to reveal prediction changes over constant length periods, we used data streams for which no natural delay exists. We decided on the use of data streams considered in the recent evaluation of stream classification and regression methods under a delayed labelling setting [9]. Hence, while we provide a basic description of the data streams below, further details on these data streams can be found in [9]. Let us note that in the case of the latter group of streams, label delay $D$ can be set as needed in order to track how predictions change over a period of arbitrary length defined by delay value. The synthetic streams we used are non-stationary streams. As far as the real data streams listed in Table 1 are concerned, CovType represents a stationary problem, as no time notion exists for both the problem and the data describing it. However, as pointed out in [4] in the context of inter alia CovType, airlines and electricity data, a common assumption for these data streams is that it is not possible to unequivocally state when drift occurs or if there is any drift.

**Table 1.** Data streams used in the assessment of prediction volatility measures. $^*$ - see detailed discussion in Sect. 4

| Data | #labelled inst. | #attributes | Type | Stationary | Label delay $D$ |
|------|-----------------|-------------|------|------------|-----------------|
| Airlines | 7541 | 10 | real | $^*$ | varied |
| Electricity | 24957 | 149 | real | $^*$ | varied |
| CovType | 24500 | 54 | real | $^*$ | fixed, 1000 instances |
| Hyperplane | 24950 | 2 | synthetic | NO | fixed, 100 instances |
| LED | 20000 | 24 | synthetic | NO | fixed, 1000 instances |
| Agrawal | 10000 | 9 | synthetic | NO | fixed, 1000 instances |

## 4.2   Investigating Changes in Predictions for Hyperplane Data

Let us first apply the prediction change measures to the simple example of a synthetic hyperplane data stream. The stream was generated under a two-dimensional setting, in which the hyperplane separating instances of the two classes in $\mathbb{R}^2$ slowly rotates and gradually converges to its ultimate location. This illustrates the case of a simple concept drift setting. Figure 1 shows how the accuracy of selected stream mining models changes. Figure 1(a) provides the results for the initial stage of stream processing, during which significant gradual concept drift occurs. A major difference between the accuracy of initial and final predictions can be observed for most methods including ARF, which diminishes with time. Figure 1(b) shows that all methods except for MC achieve high accuracy with time, both for initial and final predictions.

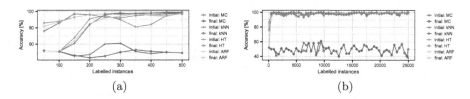

Fig. 1. The accuracy of stream mining methods for (a) the first instances and (b) entire stream. Hyperplane data

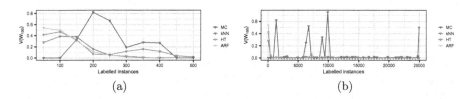

Fig. 2. The volatility of stream mining methods for (a) the first instances and (b) entire stream. Hyperplane data

Figure 2 shows the volatility of predictions made by individual models during the initial stage of stream processing and for the entire hyperplane stream. It follows from the figure that the volatility of predictions for all techniques except for MC decreases with time to a negligible level. It is only the MC method that periodically changes its predictions. This phenomenon can be explained by the fact that the majority class periodically changes, as the two classes have a similar share in the stream. Hence, every time this happens the entire instance space is reassigned to another class, which is reflected by high volatility.

### 4.3   Quantifying Prediction Changes for Airlines Data

Let us analyse the case of Airlines data, i.e. the task of predicting whether individual planes will land early, on time or late. In this case, the initial predictions are made by the model available at the time of flight departure. Final predictions are made with the models available at the time of actual arrival. Hence,

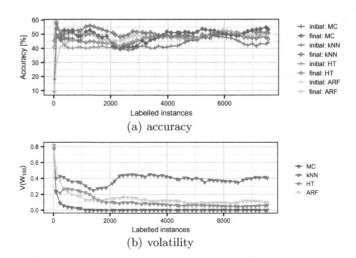

(a) accuracy

(b) volatility

**Fig. 3.** The accuracy and volatility of stream mining methods. Airlines data

**Table 2.** Median volatility and productive volatility. Results after processing all labelled instances, $N = 1000$. Note that when no prediction changes occur i.e. volatility equals 0 at some or all periods, productive volatility is not applicable (n.a.).

| Data | Volatility | | | | | | | Productive volatility | | | | | | |
|---|---|---|---|---|---|---|---|---|---|---|---|---|---|---|
| | NC | MC | NB | kNN | HT | HAT | ARF | NC | MC | NB | kNN | HT | HAT | ARF |
| Hyperplane | 0.50 | 0.00 | 0.00 | 0.00 | 0.00 | 0.00 | 0.00 | −0.02 | n.a. | n.a. | n.a. | n.a. | n.a. | n.a. |
| Airlines | 0.61 | 0.00 | 0.08 | 0.39 | 0.07 | 0.07 | 0.12 | 0.05 | n.a. | 0.08 | 0.16 | 0.16 | 0.17 | 0.10 |
| Agrawal | 0.50 | 0.00 | 0.11 | 0.40 | 0.22 | 0.22 | 0.23 | −0.03 | n.a. | 0.42 | 0.13 | 0.40 | 0.52 | 0.18 |
| Electricity | 0.51 | 0.00 | 0.03 | 0.35 | 0.12 | 0.17 | 0.39 | 0.69 | n.a. | n.a. | 0.24 | 0.32 | 0.37 | 0.30 |
| CovType | 0.77 | 0.00 | 0.04 | 0.52 | 0.24 | 0.29 | 0.56 | 0.52 | n.a. | n.a. | 0.63 | 0.59 | 0.54 | 0.70 |
| LED | 0.90 | 0.00 | 0.06 | 0.37 | 0.07 | 0.10 | 0.17 | 0.00 | n.a. | 0.50 | 0.03 | 0.33 | 0.36 | 0.22 |

the difference between an initial and a final prediction reflects the changes of the evolving model, possibly caused by concept drift, which occur over a relatively short time i.e. the time of the flight.

Let us start with an investigation of the accuracy of individual models provided in Fig. 3(a). It follows from the figure that after processing approx. 500 labelled instances, the accuracy of the different methods attains a similar level, after which different models reach their highest overall accuracy at different periods. Figure 3(b) reveals that in spite of similar accuracy, the volatility of predictions made with different techniques significantly varies. In particular, in spite of limited label delay approximately 40% of initial predictions made by kNN are not matched by final predictions. This shows that the decision boundary defined by a recent buffer of instances, which the kNN method relies on, frequently changes, and these changes mean than many instances are with time assigned to another class. The MC method yields the lowest volatility, which can be explained by the fact that one class dominates in the stream, which is unlike the case of hyperplane data. The volatility and PV results for Airlines data are provided in Table 2, which includes median values calculated based on raw values of these measures recorded every 100 instances.

The PV values reveal that for the Airlines data the share of successful prediction updates made while awaiting true labels, remains at a low level. Interestingly, the largest PV values are observed for HAT, i.e. a relatively high proportion of prediction changes made by HAT are correct. A similar improvement is observed for kNN and HT. However, in the case of HT and HAT prediction changes are very rare, i.e. the median proportion of changed predictions is at the level of 0.07 for the two techniques relying on Hoeffding trees. It turns out that adding new split(s) in a Hoeffding tree affected a lower number of predictions than the constant changes in the instance buffer used by kNN.

### 4.4  Summary of Results for Remaining Data Streams

Finally, let us summarise the volatility for the remaining data streams. First of all, the volatility values reported in Table 2 clearly show that little or no prediction changes occur when majority class is used, which is why productive volatility is not applicable in this case. Moreover, the instance-based classifier of kNN typically frequently reassigns instances to other classes while waiting for a true label, unless a nearly stationary setting of a hyperplane stream over a large number of instances is considered. This suggests the use of volatility combined with an instance-based classifier as a way to quantify model changes which may be due to concept drift. Furthermore, ARF models, i.e. ensemble models, produce high volatility of predictions as compared to NB, HT and HAT. The scale of prediction changes for ARF, reaching 56% for CovType data, can even be considered unexpectedly high. This is unlike the case of the single tree models, namely HT and HAT, which change their predictions far less frequently. Finally, NB is the classifier which changes its predictions least frequently, although its changes are typically productive, i.e. result in positive values of PV.

Moreover, let us observe that productive volatility for many techniques, even though it takes positive values, remains at a low level. An interesting finding is that except for CovType data, changes in predictions observed over time for kNN, HT, HAT yield median PV lower than 0.6. This shows that a major share of prediction updates over latency periods (Airlines and Electricity) and analysed label delay period (Agrawal and LED) are noisy updates not replacing past wrong predictions with the new correct predictions. Eliminating unnecessary model changes could be a way to increase the accuracy of predictions, including predictions made under an immediate labelling setting.

To sum up, let us note that there is a major difference between volatility and productive volatility values we expect under stationary and non-stationary streams. When no concept drift occurs, we expect volatility to gradually decrease as only minor model updates should occur in this case. Moreover, ideally model updates should result in high productive volatility i.e. high share of predictions for which wrong past predictions were replaced with correct predictions provided by a more recent model. When no concept drift occurs, volatility can be expected to be non-decreasing for growing label delay values, which is unlike in the case of e.g. recurring concept drifts. Moreover, lower delay values will help identify changes in predictions over shorter periods. Further investigation of this aspect is an interesting avenue for future research.

For non-stationary streams volatility is expected to be growing during and after concept drift periods. Ideally, the growth in volatility should be accompanied by high productive volatility. However, it is important to note that our results only partly match these expectations. In particular, high volatility is not necessarily matched by high productive volatility. This confirms that the use of the measures proposed in this work provides new insight into the model adaptation to concept drift and model updates under stationary data streams. Finally, let us note that a varied number of instances may be required for the model to adapt to a new concept for different subsets of an instance space. This makes the analysis of any performance measure calculated for a sliding window, including the measures proposed in this study and calculated over $W$ window, even more challenging for non-stationary streams. This is because setting one window size matching all streaming classifiers and concept drift types is not possible. Instead, a fixed-length window has to be used to reveal the volatility of predictions in spite of the fact that its length may not match unknown length of drift periods.

## 5 Summary

Most frequently, a more recent classification model is expected to yield performance improvements such as increased accuracy thanks to increased availability of the labelled data it relies on and possible adaptation to concept drift. However, our results show that model changes causing prediction updates frequently do not result in more accurate predictions. Interestingly, streaming classifiers vary in terms of how many initial predictions they change during latency periods and whether these changes are productive, i.e. replace incorrect predictions with predictions of true labels. Such varied volatility of predictions can also be observed when processing the same data stream with methods of similar accuracy. Hence, prediction volatility measures both quantify prediction changes and complement existing drift and model performance measures.

Needless to say, the instances for which predictions change with time are the instances affected by decision boundaries being moved in the process of model evolution. Hence, the instances for which volatility of predictions was observed can be considered instances close to these boundaries, i.e. with lower confidence of predictions. Furthermore, a method displaying high volatility of predictions can be considered less likely to be approved when high interpretability methods are expected.

Possible directions of future studies include extending the methods proposed in this work to quantifying changes in probabilities assigned to individual labels and quantifying changes in predictions for regression tasks. Furthermore, the PV measure can be used to assess individual stream mining methods in terms of the share of needed and unnecessary model updates they cause, which can be used to help develop new stream mining methods.

**Acknowledgements.** The project was funded by the POB Research Centre for Artificial Intelligence and Robotics of Warsaw University of Technology within the Excellence Initiative Program - Research University (ID-UB).

# References

1. Barros, R.S.M., Santos, S.G.T.C.: A large-scale comparison of concept drift detectors. Inf. Sci. **451–452**, 348–370 (2018). https://doi.org/10.1016/j.ins.2018.04.014
2. Bifet, A., Gavald, R., Holmes, G., Pfahringer, B.: Machine Learning for Data Streams: With Practical Examples in MOA. The MIT Press, Cambridge (2018)
3. Bifet, A., Gavaldà, R.: Adaptive learning from evolving data streams. In: Adams, N.M., Robardet, C., Siebes, A., Boulicaut, J.-F. (eds.) IDA 2009. LNCS, vol. 5772, pp. 249–260. Springer, Heidelberg (2009). https://doi.org/10.1007/978-3-642-03915-7_22
4. Brzezinski, D., Stefanowski, J.: Reacting to different types of concept drift: the accuracy updated ensemble algorithm. IEEE Trans. Neural Netw. Learn. Syst. **25**(1), 81–94 (2014). https://doi.org/10.1109/TNNLS.2013.2251352
5. Ditzler, G., Roveri, M., Alippi, C., Polikar, R.: Learning in nonstationary environments: a survey. IEEE Comput. Intell. Mag. **10**(4), 12–25 (2015)
6. Domingos, P., Hulten, G.: Mining high-speed data streams. In: 6th ACM SIGKDD International Conference on Knowledge Discovery and Data Mining, pp. 71–80. ACM (2000)
7. Gomes, H.M., et al.: Adaptive random forests for evolving data stream classification. Mach. Learn. **106**, 1469–1495 (2017). https://doi.org/10.1007/s10994-017-5642-8
8. Grzenda, M., Gomes, H.M., Bifet, A.: Performance measures for evolving predictions under delayed labelling classification. In: 2020 International Joint Conference on Neural Networks (IJCNN), pp. 1–8 (2020). https://doi.org/10.1109/IJCNN48605.2020.9207256
9. Grzenda, M., Gomes, H.M., Bifet, A.: Delayed labelling evaluation for data streams. Data Min. Knowl. Disc. **34**(5), 1237–1266 (2019). https://doi.org/10.1007/s10618-019-00654-y
10. Hofer, V., Krempl, G.: Drift mining in data: a framework for addressing drift in classification. Comput. Stat. Data Anal. **57**, 377–391 (2013). https://doi.org/10.1016/j.csda.2012.07.007
11. Webb, G.I., Hyde, R., Cao, H., Nguyen, H.L., Petitjean, F.: Characterizing concept drift. Data Min. Knowl. Disc. **30**(4), 964–994 (2016). https://doi.org/10.1007/s10618-015-0448-4
12. Webb, G.I., Lee, L.K., Goethals, B., Petitjean, F.: Analyzing concept drift and shift from sample data. Data Min. Knowl. Disc. **32**(5), 1179–1199 (2018). https://doi.org/10.1007/s10618-018-0554-1

# Impact of Dimensionality on Nowcasting Seasonal Influenza with Environmental Factors

Stefany Guarnizo[1,2] (ID), Ioanna Miliou[1(✉)] (ID), and Panagiotis Papapetrou[1] (ID)

[1] Stockholm University, Stockholm, Sweden
guarnizostefany@gmail.com, {ioanna.miliou,panagiotis}@dsv.su.se
[2] Karolinska Institute, Stockholm, Sweden

**Abstract.** Seasonal influenza is an infectious disease of multi-causal etiology and a major cause of mortality worldwide that has been associated with environmental factors. In the attempt to model and predict future outbreaks of seasonal influenza with multiple environmental factors, we face the challenge of increased dimensionality that makes the models more complex and unstable. In this paper, we propose a nowcasting and forecasting framework that compares the theoretical approaches of *Single Environmental Factor* and *Multiple Environmental Factors*. We introduce seven solutions to minimize the weaknesses associated with the increased dimensionality when predicting seasonal influenza activity level using multiple environmental factors as external proxies. Our work provides evidence that using dimensionality reduction techniques as a strategy to combine multiple datasets improves seasonal influenza forecasting without the penalization of increased dimensionality.

**Keywords:** Influenza · Nowcasting · Forecasting · Dimensionality reduction · Environmental factors

## 1 Introduction

Seasonal influenza is a public health event of multi-causal etiology, periodical recurrence, and one of the principal causes of morbidity and mortality worldwide [10]. Annually, the World Health Organization (WHO) estimates about 3 to 5 million cases of severe illness and about 290,000 to 650,000 respiratory deaths [27]. In the last years, we have seen a growing interest in generating real-time epidemic forecasts, and seasonal influenza forecasting approaches are leading the way in this front. The research on developing predictive models is based both on traditional surveillance systems, such as seasonal influenza incidence captured by the network of outpatient clinics [3,23], and digital data streams [17,24,29]. As the most prominent example, Google Flu Trends (GFT) was harnessing external data to provide forecasts of the level of influenza-like illness (ILI) incidence in the USA by employing search engine queries associated with flu-related keywords [8].

© The Author(s), under exclusive license to Springer Nature Switzerland AG 2022

T. Bouadi et al. (Eds.): IDA 2022, LNCS 13205, pp. 128–142, 2022.
https://doi.org/10.1007/978-3-031-01333-1_11

On the one hand, the availability of digital data streams facilitates the detection of potential outbreaks and provides immediate analysis and instant feedback for follow-ups. On the other hand, studies that make use of digital data ignore the multi-causal property of influenza. Recent associations between environmental factors with influenza [18,19,31] create an opportunity to deploy predictive models that respect the factors associated with the disease. As a result, the use of environmental variables as proxies for predicting future epidemics is a strategy to strengthen the surveillance systems at a population level.

Traditional epidemiological studies focus mainly on a single environmental factor [31]. As an example, seasonal influenza is principally associated with low temperatures, relative humidity [18,19], or high levels of particle matter in the atmosphere [20]. The benefit of such approaches is that they are easy to conduct. However, the challenge in working with environmental data is the spatiotemporal coexistence of independent variables that generate a risk factor in human health [11]. In the real world, dynamic changes in air pollutants and meteorological factors coexist simultaneously [6,30]. This means that human exposure to air pollutant contaminants or meteorological factors is dynamic and changeable over time. Thus, using a single environmental factor approach to predict seasonal influenza activity level is not realistic from the perspective of exposition risk [1]. In contrast, a multiple environmental factors approach would be more appropriate and more adequate to explain the multi-causality of influenza.

As a result, in this study, we introduce two theoretical approaches for predicting seasonal influenza activity level using exogenous factors:

- *Single Environmental Factor (SEF):* It is based on the single pollutant approach that studies the associations between a single pollutant and the disease [6] and chooses the pollutant with the highest correlation to the disease spread. Our study assumes a single environmental factor, such as an air pollutant or a weather variable, to be the predictor.
- *Multiple Environmental Factors (MEF):* It is based on the multi-pollutant approach, where the associations with influenza are measured using air pollution mixtures as a whole [6]. In our study, similarly to the SEF approach, we use multiple environmental factors (air pollutants and weather variables).

A key challenge of this conceptual transition from epidemiological models that consider seasonal influenza an isolated entity to models that capture the association between environmental factors and human health introduces an increase in dimensionality. Additionally, in the presence of multiple variables, data dimensionality and complexity increase, and the model becomes less stable [12].

A major limitation resulting from the increase in dimensionality when dealing with environmental data is *ecological bias* since the variables may overlap, potentialize, or annulate each other [22]. Therefore, current approaches suggest the use of machine learning classifiers to minimize such bias following a MEF approach [4]. Davalos et al. study several broad classes of statistical approaches that may decrease the adverse effect of ecological bias, specifically Additive Main Effects (AME), Effect Measure Modification (EMM), Unsupervised Dimension Reduction (UDR), Supervised Dimension Reduction (SDR), and Non-parametric methods [4].

This study focuses on the conceptual interrelation between single or multiple environmental factors and human health and explores the impact of dimensionality of exogenous variables (proxies) for the task of nowcasting and forecasting future seasonal influenza occurrence, with Norway as a use-case. More concretely, the aim is to assess the impact of the dimensionality of proxies for predicting seasonal influenza activity level from 1 to 4 weeks ahead. As proxies, we employ environmental factors, such as weather and air pollution. We propose three different problem instantiations: (i) *Baseline*, which only involves historical data of seasonal influenza activity level; (ii) *SEF*, that involves seasonal influenza activity level and one environmental variable (weather or air pollution) at a time; and (iii) *MEF*, that involves seasonal influenza activity level and all the environmental variables, with or without dimensionality reduction.

We use the seasonal variants of the ARIMA model, i.e., SARIMA and SARIMAX, to estimate the future influenza activity level. Typically, for diseases that show seasonality and their future behavior is highly correlated to their past behavior, statistical time series models are used to predict future outbreaks [2,9,21]. These models have two major advantages: (i) they are easily interpreted, and it is easy to understand the current state expressed as a function of the past states, and the influence of the exogenous variables; (ii) model selection can be performed over a time series in an automated fashion to maximize prediction accuracy.

This study aims to expand upon previous work from Zheng et al. [31] that examines the effects of single environmental factors on the incidence of influenza. In the presented work, we show quantitatively the value of incorporating multiple environmental factors in forecasting approaches as an adequate proxy that can explain the multi-causality of influenza.

Additionally, inspired by the work of Davalos et al. [4] we introduce dimensionality reduction techniques that permit the use of multiple data sources without the penalization of increased dimensionality. From the five statistical approaches introduced in Davalos' study we employ AME, SDR, and UDR, while EMM is disregarded since model uncertainty may introduce challenges when we have a large number of pollutants and interaction terms, especially in the presence of collinearity. Finally, we do not employ Non-parametric methods as they are difficult to construct and interpret.

## 2    Framework

### 2.1    Problem formulation

We propose a nowcasting and forecasting framework that provides estimates for influenza incidence using exogenous environmental variables by exploiting their dimensionality. This is a quasi-experimental study that compares the performance of predicting seasonal influenza activity level contrasting the theoretical approaches of *Single Environmental Factor* Vs. the *Multiple Environmental Factors*. In Fig. 1, we provide a diagrammatic illustration of the framework.

More formally, let $Y = \{y_i\}$ be the variable measuring the number of weekly influenza cases, with $y_i \in \mathbb{N}$ being the number of influenza cases in week $i$. Given the series of weekly influenza cases of up to week $t$, denoted as $Y_{[1:t]} = y_1, \ldots, y_t$,

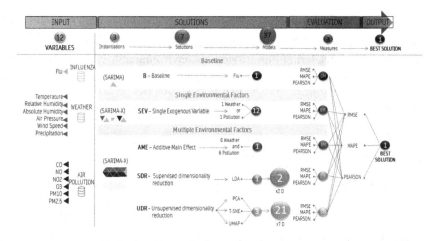

**Fig. 1.** Proposed approach workflow.

we are interested in estimating the influenza adoption trend at a weekly level for up to $k$ weeks ahead, i.e., $Y'_{[t+1:t+k]} = y'_{t+1}, \ldots, y'_{t+k}$. Additionally, we consider a set of $m$ exogenous time series variables $\mathcal{X} = \{X^1, \ldots, X^m\}$, with each $X^j \in \mathcal{X}$ corresponding to an environmental variable measured at a weekly level with $X^j_i$ denoting the value of $X^j$ in week $i$. Our problem can be defined as follows:

**Problem 1.** *Given* $Y_{[1:t]}$ *and* $\mathcal{X}_{[1:t]}$, *we want to predict* $Y'_{[t+1:t+k]}$ *using a seasonal statistical function* $f$ *and a mapping function* $g : \mathcal{X} \rightarrow \hat{\mathcal{X}}$, *that maps* $\mathcal{X}$ *to* $\hat{\mathcal{X}} = \{\hat{X}^1, \ldots, \hat{X}^{\hat{m}}\}$, *an* $\hat{m}$-*dimensional space, such that* $\hat{m} \leq m$.

$$Y'_{[t+1:t+k]} = f(Y_{[1:t]}, g(\mathcal{X}_{[1:t+k]})) ,$$

*Note that* $g$ *can also map to itself, in which case* $\hat{\mathcal{X}} = \mathcal{X}$.

### 2.2   Problem Instantiations and Solutions

We propose three problem instantiations alongside their solutions, varying the number of exogenous variables $m$, their dimensionality $\hat{m}$, and for different mapping functions $g(\cdot)$. In general, the release date of the influenza reports is delayed by one week. We consider $k \in \{1, 2, 3, 4\}$, distinguishing between hindcasting ($k = 1$): estimating the influenza activity level of a week that has already passed by, nowcasting ($k = 2$): predicting the influenza activity level during the present week and forecasting ($k > 2$): predicting the flu activity in the future weeks.

**Baseline.** This problem formulation assumes no exogenous variables, i.e., $\mathcal{X} = \emptyset$, and the solution is a linear combination of the previous instances of seasonal influenza activity level. The solution, i.e., *Baseline (B)*, is computed as follows:

$$y'_{t+k} = \alpha^k + \sum_{i=0}^{w-1} a^k_i y_{t-i}, \tag{1}$$

where $w$ is the model's window size, while $\alpha$ and $a_i$ are the regression coefficients.

**Single Environmental Factor.** This formulation extends the Baseline formulation by also considering one exogenous environmental variable (related to weather or air pollution) at a time, i.e., a single $X^j$ is chosen from $\mathcal{X}$. In total, this yields $m$ (e.g., in our case $m = 12$) models, one per environmental variable, and the solution, i.e., *Single Exogenous Variable (SEV)*, is computed as follows:

$$y'_{t+k} = \alpha^k + \sum_{i=0}^{w-1} a_i^k y_{t-i} + \sum_{i=0}^{w+k-1} b_i^k X_{t-i}^j, \tag{2}$$

where the exogenous variables iterate for $k$ additional time points since the up-to-date environmental data should be taken into account for each predicted week.

**Multiple Environmental Factors.** This formulation further extends SEV by including all exogenous environmental variables, either with or without applying dimensionality reduction. The solution is computed as follows:

$$y'_{t+k} = \alpha^k + \sum_{i=0}^{w-1} a_i^k y_{t-i} + \sum_{l=1}^{\hat{m}} \sum_{i=0}^{w+k-1} b_i^{kl} \hat{X}_{t-i}^l, \tag{3}$$

where $\hat{m}$ is the total number of exogenous variables.

We consider three cases for defining function $g$: (1) no dimensionality reduction is applied, i.e., g is a function that maps to itself, (2) we apply supervised dimensionality reduction, (3) we apply unsupervised dimensionality reduction.

*No Dimensionality Reduction:* In this case, no dimensionality reduction is applied, hence $\hat{m} = m$ and $\hat{\mathcal{X}} = \mathcal{X}$. The solution, i.e., *Additive main effects (AME)*, assumes that each exogenous environmental variable has an additive effect [4]. This solution involves seasonal influenza activity level and 12 environmental variables (6 weather and 6 air pollution variables) without treatment.

*Supervised Dimensionality Reduction (SDR):* In this case, the transformation of the set of environmental variables is considered dependent on the health outcome[4]. The solution, i.e., *Linear discriminant analysis (LDA)*, involves seasonal influenza activity level and 12 environmental variables with an SDR technique of up to 2 dimensions (1D, 2D), i.e., $\hat{m} \in \{1, 2\}$. Hence, we have two SDR-LDA models in total. The main objective of LDA is the projection of the normal vector in the linear discriminant hyperplane. It renders the distance between the classes as the largest and the distance within the classes as the smallest. Then, LDA makes a linear classification that attempts to model the difference between the labels, independent of the data dimensions [5]. The classifier is built using labels produced by the Symbolic Aggregate approXimation (SAX) algorithm [13]. SAX transforms a time series of length $h$ into the string of arbitrary length $\omega$, where $\omega << h$ typically, using an alphabet $A$ of size $s > 2$. In our case, $s = 5$.

*Unsupervised Dimensionality Reduction (UDR):* In this case, multiple environmental variables are transformed into a different set of variables independently of the health outcome of interest [4]. This solution involves seasonal influenza activity level and 12 variables with UDR techniques of up to 7 dimensions per technique, i.e., $\hat{m} \in [1,7]$. We propose 3 solutions for a total of 21 UDR models:

- *Principal component analysis (PCA)*: It is the process of computing the principal components to achieve the largest data variance in the dimensions of the projection. The principal component is the transformation of variables into the principal axis, which fixes the variance and co-variance distribution data and reorients the axis to make all the variables comparable [5].
- *t-Distributed stochastic neighbor embedding (TSNE)*: It transforms high dimensional Euclidean distances between data points into conditional probabilities that represent similarities, and then it uses Student's t distribution to compute the similarity between two points in the low-dimensional space [14].
- *Uniform manifold approximation and projection (UMAP)*: It builds a particular weighted k-neighbor graph using the nearest-neighbor descent algorithm, and it computes a low-dimensional projection mimicking the original fuzzy topology of data [15].

In order to solve the coefficients of the previous instantiations, we employ Auto Regression Integrated Moving Average (ARIMA). The process refers to the combination of Autoregressive (AR) and Moving Average (MA) that builds a composite model of the time series. An ARIMA model includes parameters to account for season and trend, and autoregressive and moving average terms to handle the autocorrelation embedded in the data. More concretely, ARIMA is defined by three non-seasonal parameters, $(p, d, q)$, where $p$ and $q$ correspond to the non-seasonal AR and MA processes, respectively, while $d$ is the amount of differencing applied to the original time series to stationarize it.

This study considers two variants of ARIMA, the seasonal variant SARIMA, which is used to solve for the coefficients of *Baseline*, and the seasonal variant with exogenous variables, i.e., SARIMAX, that is used to solve the other instantiations. Both variants include three seasonal parameters $(P, D, Q)$ in addition to the three non-seasonal parameters, where $P$ and $Q$ correspond to the seasonal AR and MA processes, respectively, while $D$ corresponds to seasonal differencing.

Finally, SARIMA and SARIMAX require stationary time series that show no fluctuation or periodicity over time. We use the Augmented Dickey-Fuller (ADF) test to verify the stationarity of the time series, and if needed, we apply multiple iterations of differencing until stationarization is achieved.

Overall, 37 models are deployed, and their performance is assessed in terms of Root Mean Square Error (RMSE), Mean Absolute Percentage Error (MAPE), and Pearson correlation. The best model of each solution is reported.

# 3   Empirical Evaluation

## 3.1   Data Description

**Influenza Data.** Seasonal influenza data are obtained from the World Health Organization (WHO) FluMart platform [28] that contains the reported cases through FluNet, a global web-based tool for influenza virological surveillance launched in 1997 [26]. The data of FluNet, e.g., the number of influenza viruses detected by subtype, are critical for tracking the movement of viruses globally and interpreting the epidemiological data. The data are provided remotely by National Influenza Centres of the Global Influenza Surveillance and Response System (GISRS) and other national influenza laboratories collaborating with GISRS or are uploaded from WHO regional databases. The data are publicly available at a country level and are updated weekly.

We focus our analysis on the country of Norway, and we obtain the number of total cases per week for 6 seasons. The data are collected from the 22nd week of 2013 to the 21st week of 2019 for the seasons of 2013/14, 2014/15, 2015/16, 2016/17, 2017/18, 2018/19. See Fig. 2a for a representation of the influenza cases per season. For our study, we normalize the data using the MinMax method for each season, ranging the values from 0 to 1. Then, we drop the weeks with a value smaller than 0.25 since the number of influenza cases for these weeks is either zero or not significant. See Fig. 2b for the weeks of each season that make part of the final data. We notice that the peak of each season is colored with a deeper violet color.

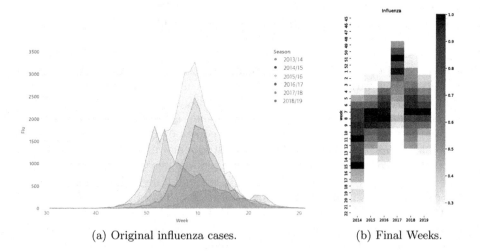

(a) Original influenza cases.                    (b) Final Weeks.

**Fig. 2.** Influenza cases before and after the filtering. In the left figure, we see the original influenza cases per season. In the right figure, we see the weeks of each season that make part of the final data after the filtering. (Color figure online)

**Weather Data.** Weather data are obtained from the API terminal of the Norwich Meteorological Institute [16]. We have 6 variables describing the weather conditions: temperature, relative humidity, absolute humidity, air pressure, wind speed, and precipitation. We collect data every 12 h for all the weather stations in the country. All data are averaged to one measurement per week to match the seasonal influenza dataset and normalized using the MinMax method for each season, ranging the values from 0 to 1.

**Air Pollution Data.** Air pollution data are obtained through web scraping from the European Environmental Agency [7]. We have 6 environmental variables regarding air pollution: CO, NO, NO2, O3, PM10, and PM2.5. Air Pollution data are collected every 12 h per monitoring station. All data are averaged to one measurement per week to match the seasonal influenza dataset and normalized using the MinMax method for each season, ranging the values from 0 to 1.

### 3.2   Dynamic Training and Hyperparameters

The environmental conditions change quickly in the real world, and a disease prediction model should respond quickly to such changes. Therefore, in this study, we borrow the idea of the rolling forecast scenario to perform a dynamic training of the models [25].

In order to generate each models' parameters and calculate the accuracy of the models, we split the data into training and test sets. Specifically, the training set spans 5 seasons, from the 4th week of 2014 to the 14th week of 2018 (see Fig. 2b for the final weeks). The test set is the last season of 2018/2019, from the 2nd to the 13th week of 2019, for a total of 13 time steps. In each step, we dynamically increase the training data to include the latest information. Through dynamic training, we can keep track of the changing situation at any time and quickly adjust the disease prevention and control points. The models that use the external variables employ historical influenza reports available until week $t - 1$ and the environmental data available until week $t$. Our models produce forecasts for 1 to 4 weeks ahead.

For LDA we set the range of the number of components as $n\_components \in [1, 2]$ while for PCA, TSNE and UMAP, we set $n\_components \in [1, 7]$. Additionally, for TSNE we set $perplexity = 40$, and method = 'exact'. The remaining hyperparameters are set to the default values.

### 3.3   Perfomance Indicators

Let $y_t$ denote the observed value of the influenza at time $t$, $y'_t$ the predicted value by the model at time $t$, $\bar{y}$ the mean or average of the values $y_t$ and similarly $\bar{y}'$ the mean or average of the values $y'_t$. We consider three performance indicators, which are described next.

*Root Mean Square Error (RMSE)*, a measure of predictive performance defined as the square root of the second sample moment of the differences between predicted values and true values. More concretely:

$$RMSE = \sqrt{\frac{1}{n} \sum_{i=1}^{n} (y_i' - y_i)^2}. \tag{4}$$

*Mean Absolute Percentage Error (MAPE)*, a measure of predictive performance defined as the ratio of the absolute difference between the predicted and true values over the true values. More concretely:

$$MAPE = (\frac{1}{n} \sum_{i=1}^{n} |\frac{y_i - y_i'}{y_i}|) \times 100. \tag{5}$$

*Pearson Correlation*, a measure of the linear dependence between two variables during a time period of length $n$, is defined as:

$$r = \frac{\sum_{i=1}^{n} (y_i - \bar{y})(y_i' - \bar{y}')}{\sqrt{\sum_{i=1}^{n} (y_i - \bar{y})^2} \sqrt{\sum_{i=1}^{n} (y_i' - \bar{y}')^2}}. \tag{6}$$

## 4   Results

In this study, our goal is to determine the impact of increased dimensionality to predict seasonal influenza activity level in Norway from 1 to 4 weeks in advance of the latest ground truth data released from the regular surveillance system. We use environmental factors, such as weather and air pollution, as proxies to improve our predictions. We propose 3 different problem instantiations for a total of 7 solutions: (i) Baseline - *B*, (ii) Single Environmental Factor - *SEV*, and (iii) Multiple Environmental Factors - *AME, LDA, PCA, TSNE, UMAP*.

In order to evaluate the performance of the different solutions, we consider the performance indicators (see Sect. 3.3) of the 1 to 4 weeks ahead forecast time series. In Table 1, we report these indicators for the best model of each solution for the four time horizons, as well as the overall performance. We evidently observe the added value of using the environmental factors over the simple baseline *B* that uses only historical influenza data. Forecasts obtained with *SEV*, using a single exogenous variable, are more accurate compared to the baseline approach, but in the case of *AME*, the inclusion of all the environmental variables increases the dimensionality and decreases the performance.

**Table 1.** Performance indicators for the best model in each solution.

| Weeks ahead | MAPE | | | | | RMSE | | | | | Pearson correlation | | | | |
|---|---|---|---|---|---|---|---|---|---|---|---|---|---|---|---|
| | 1 | 2 | 3 | 4 | All | 1 | 2 | 3 | 4 | All | 1 | 2 | 3 | 4 | All |
| B | 19.74 | 31.11 | 35.79 | 38.38 | 31.26 | 0.13 | 0.21 | 0.31 | 0.36 | 0.26 | 0.89 | 0.68 | 0.32 | 0.15 | 0.51 |
| SEV | **16.71** | 22.11 | 27.90 | 29.27 | 24.00 | 0.11 | 0.17 | 0.26 | 0.34 | 0.25 | **0.94** | **0.89** | 0.64 | 0.28 | 0.69 |
| AME | 31.88 | 48.81 | 43.42 | 47.51 | 42.90 | 0.19 | 0.26 | 0.26 | 0.31 | 0.25 | 0.72 | 0.38 | 0.32 | 0.18 | 0.40 |
| LDA | 17.63 | **19.57** | **16.07** | **19.87** | **18.28** | **0.10** | **0.13** | **0.15** | **0.17** | **0.14** | 0.93 | **0.89** | **0.89** | **0.94** | **0.91** |
| PCA | 20.00 | 27.74 | 26.79 | 26.65 | 25.29 | 0.14 | 0.20 | 0.23 | 0.26 | 0.21 | 0.88 | 0.84 | 0.78 | 0.83 | 0.83 |
| TSNE | 18.15 | 27.75 | 34.27 | 41.80 | 30.49 | 0.12 | 0.19 | 0.28 | 0.35 | 0.23 | 0.90 | 0.79 | 0.47 | 0.10 | 0.57 |
| UMAP | 19.50 | 32.46 | 37.96 | 36.66 | 31.64 | 0.11 | 0.21 | 0.29 | 0.33 | 0.23 | 0.91 | 0.72 | 0.42 | 0.26 | 0.58 |

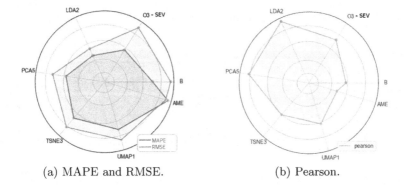

(a) MAPE and RMSE.          (b) Pearson.

**Fig. 3.** Performance indicators for the best model in each solution.

To minimize the weaknesses associated with the increased dimensionality for predicting seasonal influenza, we introduce several dimensionality reduction techniques, such as LDA, PCA, TSNE, UMAP. We observe in Table 1 that the use of the dimensionality reduction techniques shows the lowest errors and the highest Pearson correlation in comparison to the previous models $B$, $SEV$ and $AME$. More specifically, $LDA$ outperforms the other models in all four time horizons across the different performance metrics, MAPE, RMSE, and Pearson correlation, while $PCA$ shows the second best performance. As expected, we also remark that the performance of forecasts deteriorates as the time horizon increases.

Figure 3a and 3b confirm these findings, highlighting the overall performance of the best model of each solution in regards to the metrics. Additionally, they report which one is the best model for each solution. We annotate the best model with its group solution name and number of dimensions, i.e., PCA5 for the PCA solution for a total of 5 dimensions. We notice that the best proxy amongst the $SEV$ alternatives is O3, a major air pollutant. Moreover, the best model for the $LDA$ solution is the LDA2 for a total of 2 dimensions.

Figure 4 displays the predictions of LDA2 against the reported influenza activity level for the four time horizons, 1, 2, 3, and 4 weeks ahead. Overall predictions track the influenza activity level accurately, as shown in the top part of each panel. Close inspection shows that the 1 week ahead predictions from the LDA2 and the actual influenza activity level are very similar, with small errors. For 2, 3, and 4 weeks ahead, LDA2 continues to track the influenza activity level closely, with some undershooting in some cases. In the lower part of each panel, there is a heatmap bar indicating the absolute error between the LDA2 predictions and the influenza activity level.

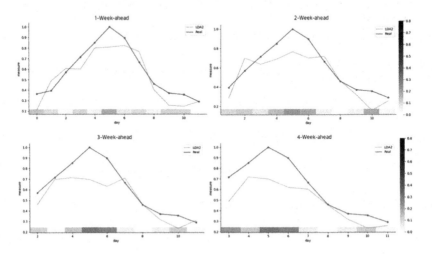

**Fig. 4.** LDA2 predictions against the reported influenza activity level for the four time horizons, 1, 2, 3, and 4 weeks ahead. The time-dependent absolute error is displayed in the lower part of each panel.

## 5   Conclusions

Traditional theoretical approaches highlight the use of the *Single Environmental Factor* concept for predicting seasonal influenza activity. A theoretical swift from *Single Environmental Factor* to the *Multiple Environmental Factors* approach implies an increment of dimensionality, where the application of machine learning techniques transforms the epidemiological field.

In this study, we propose the use of dimensionality reduction techniques to minimize the weaknesses associated with the increased dimensionality when predicting seasonal influenza activity level using multiple environmental factors as external proxies. With dimensionality, we refer to the number of environmental factors included in the predictive model.

Increasing the dimensionality of the model, we achieve a more realistic perspective of the exposure and higher explainability of the multi-causality of influenza. However, that also decreases the performance of the model, i.e., the AME solution. To compensate for this decrease in performance, inspired by the work of Davalos et al. [4], we use supervised and unsupervised dimensionality reduction techniques that achieve higher seasonal influenza forecast accuracy. We use SARIMA and SARIMAX models to produce our seasonal influenza forecasts for 1 to 4 weeks ahead.

Our results show that the best solution to the nowcasting and forecasting task is LDA, which achieves the best performance while considering the multi-causal property of influenza. LDA outperforms the other models in all four time horizons across the different performance metrics, MAPE, RMSE, and Pearson correlation, while PCA shows the second best performance. Thus, the use of dimensionality reduction techniques allows a change in the current understanding of the interaction between environmental variables and their ability to predict seasonal influenza, involving the *MEF* concept, minimizing the impact of increased dimensionality and improving the accuracy of the predictions.

An interesting line of future work lies in the use of more advanced techniques from deep learning to improve the predictive performance, such as autoencoders for dimensionality reduction and LSTM for the nowcasting and forecasting task.

Our nowcasting and forecasting framework could be easily extended to track seasonal influenza activity level in other countries when the environmental factors are available. However, it is important to stress that the influenza seasons are more regular in the Nordic area than in tropical and subtropical regions. Additionally, countries in this area, Norway included, have a strong environmental control policy that regulates particulate matter emissions. Further investigation would be required to verify the effectiveness of our approach in countries with heavier pollution and the interrelation with human health.

**Acknowledgements.** The work of IM and PP has been supported in part by the Digital Futures EXTREMUM project titled "Explainable and Ethical Machine Learning for Knowledge Discovery from Medical Data Sources".

# Appendix

In Table 2 we comparatively present the performance of all models in each solution using the following performance indicators: MAPE, RMSE, and Pearson correlation.

**Table 2.** Performance indicators for all models in each solution.

| Weeks ahead | MAPE | | | | | RMSE | | | | | Pearson correlation | | | | |
|---|---|---|---|---|---|---|---|---|---|---|---|---|---|---|---|
| | 1 | 2 | 3 | 4 | All | 1 | 2 | 3 | 4 | All | 1 | 2 | 3 | 4 | All |
| B | 19.74 | 31.11 | 35.79 | 38.38 | 31.26 | 0.13 | 0.21 | 0.31 | 0.36 | 0.26 | 0.89 | 0.68 | 0.32 | 0.15 | 0.51 |
| temp-SEV | 19.11 | 28.80 | 32.63 | 35.95 | 29.12 | 0.13 | 0.19 | 0.27 | 0.35 | 0.24 | 0.87 | 0.75 | 0.52 | 0.24 | 0.60 |
| relHum-SEV | 23.68 | 39.88 | 47.46 | 44.65 | 38.92 | 0.15 | 0.22 | 0.30 | 0.37 | 0.26 | 0.77 | 0.58 | 0.19 | -0.04 | 0.38 |
| spcHum-SEV | 19.62 | 31.33 | 35.19 | 37.17 | 30.83 | 0.12 | 0.20 | 0.29 | 0.36 | 0.25 | 0.89 | 0.73 | 0.46 | 0.20 | 0.57 |
| airPre-SEV | 17.86 | 27.56 | 31.50 | 34.73 | 27.91 | 0.12 | 0.18 | 0.27 | 0.35 | 0.23 | 0.89 | 0.78 | 0.55 | 0.25 | 0.62 |
| wSpeed-SEV | 24.10 | 32.61 | 39.25 | 38.08 | 33.51 | 0.15 | 0.22 | 0.30 | 0.38 | 0.26 | 0.86 | 0.78 | 0.52 | -0.01 | 0.54 |
| precip-SEV | 22.65 | 28.38 | 32.89 | 36.33 | 30.06 | 0.13 | 0.18 | 0.27 | 0.35 | 0.23 | 0.88 | 0.76 | 0.52 | 0.24 | 0.60 |
| CO-SEV | 19.61 | 28.08 | 32.71 | 34.90 | 28.82 | 0.12 | 0.21 | 0.31 | 0.36 | 0.25 | 0.92 | 0.73 | 0.39 | 0.21 | 0.56 |
| NO-SEV | 20.75 | 28.32 | 34.82 | 36.97 | 30.22 | 0.13 | 0.19 | 0.27 | 0.33 | 0.23 | 0.89 | 0.76 | 0.49 | 0.24 | 0.59 |
| NO2-SEV | 27.07 | 41.92 | 49.26 | 49.68 | 41.99 | 0.16 | 0.25 | 0.32 | 0.35 | 0.27 | 0.78 | 0.44 | 0.11 | -0.14 | 0.30 |
| O3-SEV | 16.71 | 22.11 | 27.90 | 29.27 | 24.00 | 0.11 | 0.17 | 0.26 | 0.34 | 0.25 | **0.94** | **0.89** | 0.64 | 0.28 | 0.69 |
| PM10-SEV | 20.20 | 29.52 | 34.74 | 38.25 | 30.68 | 0.13 | 0.20 | 0.29 | 0.36 | 0.24 | 0.88 | 0.73 | 0.45 | 0.17 | 0.56 |
| PM25-SEV | 13.68 | 27.45 | 36.51 | 33.98 | 27.91 | 0.10 | 0.16 | 0.24 | 0.30 | 0.20 | 0.93 | 0.84 | 0.66 | 0.38 | 0.70 |
| AME | 31.88 | 48.81 | 43.42 | 47.51 | 42.90 | 0.19 | 0.26 | 0.26 | 0.31 | 0.25 | 0.72 | 0.38 | 0.32 | 0.18 | 0.40 |
| LDA1 | 17.83 | 22.10 | 18.89 | 23.68 | 20.62 | 0.11 | 0.15 | 0.17 | 0.21 | 0.16 | 0.92 | 0.88 | 0.86 | 0.84 | 0.88 |
| **LDA2** | **17.63** | **19.57** | **16.07** | **19.87** | **18.28** | **0.10** | **0.13** | **0.15** | **0.17** | **0.14** | 0.93 | **0.89** | **0.89** | **0.94** | **0.91** |
| PCA1 | 18.86 | 28.88 | 37.23 | 40.52 | 31.37 | 0.12 | 0.20 | 0.32 | 0.37 | 0.25 | 0.92 | 0.73 | 0.28 | 0.00 | 0.48 |
| PCA2 | 17.24 | 27.17 | 34.32 | 36.40 | 28.78 | 0.11 | 0.20 | 0.29 | 0.34 | 0.24 | 0.90 | 0.69 | 0.40 | 0.24 | 0.56 |
| PCA3 | 19.86 | 32.84 | 33.72 | 31.39 | 29.45 | 0.14 | 0.23 | 0.31 | 0.33 | 0.25 | 0.90 | 0.78 | 0.49 | 0.34 | 0.63 |
| PCA4 | 17.29 | 25.13 | 27.16 | 27.82 | 24.35 | 0.14 | 0.20 | 0.28 | 0.29 | 0.23 | 0.88 | 0.86 | 0.72 | 0.83 | 0.82 |
| PCA5 | 20.00 | 27.74 | 26.79 | 26.65 | 25.29 | 0.14 | 0.20 | 0.23 | 0.26 | 0.21 | 0.88 | 0.84 | 0.78 | 0.83 | 0.83 |
| PCA6 | 17.36 | 26.05 | 28.28 | 31.58 | 25.82 | 0.13 | 0.19 | 0.23 | 0.28 | 0.21 | 0.89 | 0.87 | 0.85 | 0.86 | 0.87 |
| PCA7 | 20.00 | 27.74 | 26.79 | 26.65 | 25.29 | 0.14 | 0.20 | 0.23 | 0.26 | 0.21 | 0.87 | 0.85 | 0.71 | 0.45 | 0.72 |
| TSNE1 | 85.49 | 91.28 | 157.49 | 74.20 | 102.12 | 0.72 | 0.85 | 2.03 | 1.03 | 1.16 | 0.31 | 0.32 | 0.08 | -0.06 | 0.16 |
| TSNE2 | 67.58 | 90.39 | 72.79 | 59.22 | 72.50 | 0.50 | 0.77 | 0.73 | 0.51 | 0.63 | 0.39 | 0.36 | 0.12 | -0.06 | 0.21 |
| TSNE3 | 18.15 | 27.75 | 34.27 | 41.80 | 30.49 | 0.12 | 0.19 | 0.28 | 0.35 | 0.23 | 0.90 | 0.79 | 0.47 | 0.10 | 0.57 |
| TSNE4 | 26.52 | 31.30 | 38.00 | 45.19 | 35.25 | 0.16 | 0.22 | 0.33 | 0.40 | 0.28 | 0.82 | 0.67 | 0.27 | -0.10 | 0.42 |
| TSNE5 | 22.18 | 31.76 | 36.02 | 44.16 | 33.53 | 0.14 | 0.22 | 0.29 | 0.39 | 0.26 | 0.86 | 0.70 | 0.54 | 0.19 | 0.57 |
| TSNE6 | 22.78 | 29.12 | 33.98 | 39.60 | 31.37 | 0.14 | 0.21 | 0.30 | 0.39 | 0.26 | 0.84 | 0.67 | 0.33 | 0.00 | 0.46 |
| TSNE7 | 24.87 | 35.91 | 41.40 | 50.16 | 38.09 | 0.17 | 0.25 | 0.33 | 0.41 | 0.29 | 0.78 | 0.65 | 0.34 | -0.07 | 0.42 |
| UMAP1 | 19.50 | 32.46 | 37.96 | 36.66 | 31.64 | 0.11 | 0.21 | 0.29 | 0.33 | 0.23 | 0.91 | 0.72 | 0.42 | 0.26 | 0.58 |
| UMAP2 | 25.12 | 46.63 | 56.66 | 60.17 | 47.15 | 0.15 | 0.26 | 0.36 | 0.43 | 0.30 | 0.81 | 0.51 | 0.13 | -0.50 | 0.24 |
| UMAP3 | 20.56 | 33.28 | 35.25 | 42.51 | 32.90 | 0.14 | 0.22 | 0.22 | 0.22 | 0.20 | 0.82 | 0.56 | 0.47 | 0.48 | 0.59 |
| UMAP4 | 28.86 | 41.02 | 50.77 | 62.27 | 45.73 | 0.18 | 0.25 | 0.31 | 0.34 | 0.27 | 0.79 | 0.51 | 0.25 | 0.03 | 0.40 |
| UMAP5 | 28.89 | 44.52 | 55.89 | 57.48 | 46.69 | 0.17 | 0.25 | 0.31 | 0.31 | 0.26 | 0.74 | 0.40 | -0.11 | -0.40 | 0.16 |
| UMAP6 | 32.95 | 51.65 | 56.59 | 65.35 | 51.63 | 0.19 | 0.29 | 0.36 | 0.38 | 0.30 | 0.73 | 0.42 | 0.13 | -0.08 | 0.30 |
| UMAP7 | 35.51 | 50.09 | 60.08 | 68.94 | 53.65 | 0.22 | 0.31 | 0.31 | 0.37 | 0.30 | 0.67 | 0.37 | 0.08 | 0.00 | 0.28 |

# References

1. Austin, E., Coull, B., Thomas, D., Koutrakis, P.: A framework for identifying distinct multipollutant profiles in air pollution data. Environ. Int. **45**, 112–121 (2012)
2. Chadsuthi, S., Iamsirithaworn, S., Triampo, W., Modchang, C.: Modeling seasonal influenza transmission and its association with climate factors in Thailand using time-series and ARIMAX analyses. Comput. Math. Methods Med. **2015** (2015)

3. Chretien, J.P., George, D., Shaman, J., Chitale, R.A., McKenzie, F.E.: Influenza forecasting in human populations: a scoping review. PLoS One **9**(4), e94130 (2014)
4. Davalos, A.D., Luben, T.J., Herring, A.H., Sacks, J.D.: Current approaches used in epidemiologic studies to examine short-term multipollutant air pollution exposures. Ann. Epidemiol. **27**(2), 145–153 (2017)
5. Deng, P., Wang, H., Li, T., Horng, S.J., Zhu, X.: Linear discriminant analysis guided by unsupervised ensemble learning. Inf. Sci. **480**, 211–221 (2019)
6. Dominici, F., Peng, R.D., Barr, C.D., Bell, M.L.: Protecting human health from air pollution: shifting from a single-pollutant to a multi-pollutant approach. Epidemiology (Camb. Mass.) **21**(2), 187 (2010)
7. European Environment Agency: Downloadable data about Europe's environment (2021). https://www.eea.europa.eu/data-and-maps/data#c0=5&c11=&c5=all&b_start=0. Accessed November 2021
8. Ginsberg, J., Mohebbi, M.H., Patel, R.S., Brammer, L., Smolinski, M.S., Brilliant, L.: Detecting influenza epidemics using search engine query data. Nature **457**, 1012–1014 (2009)
9. He, Z., Tao, H.: Epidemiology and ARIMA model of positive-rate of influenza viruses among children in Wuhan, China: a nine-year retrospective study. Int. J. Infect. Dis. **74**, 61–70 (2018)
10. Iuliano, A.D., et al.: Estimates of global seasonal influenza-associated respiratory mortality: a modelling study. The Lancet **391**(10127), 1285–1300 (2018)
11. Johannson, K.A., Balmes, J.R., Collard, H.R.: Air pollution exposure: a novel environmental risk factor for interstitial lung disease? Chest **147**(4), 1161–1167 (2015)
12. Kak, S.: Information theory and dimensionality of space. Sci. Rep. **10**(1), 1–5 (2020)
13. Lin, J., Keogh, E., Wei, L., Lonardi, S.: Experiencing SAX: a novel symbolic representation of time series. Data Min. Knowl. Discov. **15**(2), 107–144 (2007)
14. Van der Maaten, L., Hinton, G.: Visualizing data using t-SNE. J. Mach. Learn. Res. **9**(11) (2008)
15. McInnes, L., Healy, J., Melville, J.: UMAP: uniform manifold approximation and projection for dimension reduction. arXiv preprint arXiv:1802.03426 (2018)
16. Meteorologisk Institutt: Frost API (2021). https://frost.met.no/index.html. Accessed November 2021
17. Miliou, I., et al.: Predicting seasonal influenza using supermarket retail records. PLoS Comput. Biol. **17**(7), e1009087 (2021)
18. Nhung, N.T.T., et al.: Short-term association between ambient air pollution and pneumonia in children: a systematic review and meta-analysis of time-series and case-crossover studies. Environ. Pollut. **230**, 1000–1008 (2017)
19. Nisar, N., et al.: Seasonality of influenza and its association with meteorological parameters in two cities of Pakistan: a time series analysis. PLoS One **14**(7), e0219376 (2019)
20. Park, J.E., Son, W.S., Ryu, Y., Choi, S.B., Kwon, O., Ahn, I.: Effects of temperature, humidity, and diurnal temperature range on influenza incidence in a temperate region. Influenza Other Respir. Viruses **14**(1), 11–18 (2020)
21. Samaras, L., García-Barriocanal, E., Sicilia, M.A.: Comparing social media and google to detect and predict severe epidemics. Sci. Rep. **10**(1), 1–11 (2020)
22. Shafran-Nathan, R., Levy, I., Levin, N., Broday, D.M.: Ecological bias in environmental health studies: the problem of aggregation of multiple data sources. Air Qual. Atmos. Health **10**(4), 411–420 (2016). https://doi.org/10.1007/s11869-016-0436-x

23. Shaman, J., Karspeck, A., Yang, W., Tamerius, J., Lipsitch, M.: Real-time influenza forecasts during the 2012–2013 season. Nat. Commun. **4**, 2837 (2013)
24. Tran, T.Q., Sakuma, J.: Seasonal-adjustment based feature selection method for predicting epidemic with large-scale search engine logs. In: KDD 2019, pp. 2857–2866 (2019)
25. Wen, K.L.: Grey Systems: Modeling and Prediction, Yang's Scientific Research Institute, vol. 4. Yang's Scientific Press (2004)
26. WHO: FluNet (2021). https://www.who.int/tools/flunet. Accessed November 2021
27. WHO: Influenza (seasonal)t (2021). https://www.who.int/news-room/fact-sheets/detail/influenza-(seasonal). Accessed November 2021
28. WHO: Who flumart outputs (2021). https://apps.who.int/flumart/Default?ReportNo=10. Accessed November 2021
29. Yang, W., Lipsitch, M., Shaman, J.: Inference of seasonal and pandemic influenza transmission dynamics. Proc. Natl. Acad. Sci. **112**(9), 2723–2728 (2015)
30. Yu, H.R., et al.: A multifactorial evaluation of the effects of air pollution and meteorological factors on asthma exacerbation. Int. J. Environ. Res. Public Health **17**(11), 4010 (2020)
31. Zheng, Y., Wang, K., Zhang, L., Wang, L.: Study on the relationship between the incidence of influenza and climate indicators and the prediction of influenza incidence. Environ. Sci. Pollut. Res. **28**(1), 473–481 (2020). https://doi.org/10.1007/s11356-020-10523-7

# On Usefulness of Outlier Elimination in Classification Tasks

Dušan Hetlerović[1], Luboš Popelínský[1], Pavel Brazdil[2(✉)], Carlos Soares[3], and Fernando Freitas[4]

[1] KD Lab, FI MU, Brno, Czechia
{445557,popel}@fi.muni.cz
[2] LIAAD - INESC TEC/FEP, University of Porto, Porto, Portugal
pbrazdil@inesctec.pt
[3] Fraunhofer Portugal AICOS and LIACC, Faculdade de Engenharia,
Universidade do Porto, Porto, Portugal
csoares@fe.up.pt
[4] FEUP, University of Porto, Porto, Portugal

**Abstract.** Although outlier detection/elimination has been studied before, few comprehensive studies exist on when exactly this technique would be useful as preprocessing in classification tasks. The objective of our study is to fill in this gap. We have performed experiments with 12 various outlier elimination methods and 10 classification algorithms on 50 different datasets. The results were then processed by the proposed reduction method, whose aim is identify the most useful workflows for a given set of tasks (datasets). The reduction method has identified that just three OEMs that are generally useful for the given set of tasks. We have shown that the inclusion of these OEMs is indeed useful, as it leads to lower loss in accuracy and the difference is quite significant (0.5%) on average.

**Keywords:** Outlier elimination · Metalearning · Average ranking · Reduction of portfolios

## 1 Introduction

One of the common problems machine learning users face is choosing an algorithm for a specific task [23]. The motivation is to either maximize or minimize a quantifiable measure, such as predictive accuracy. Apart from algorithm selection, users may achieve an improvement in performance by incorporating different data preprocessing methods and by selecting appropriate hyperparameter settings for these components. The combination of these three factors constitutes a *workflow (pipeline)* design problem. The search space of alternatives is sometimes referred to as *configuration space*. As this space can be very large, we need tools to help us identify the optimal one for the new task.

Many approaches focus on the issue of how to conduct the search in the given configuration spaces [28]. Other approaches try to redesign this space first

© The Author(s), under exclusive license to Springer Nature Switzerland AG 2022
T. Bouadi et al. (Eds.): IDA 2022, LNCS 13205, pp. 143–156, 2022.
https://doi.org/10.1007/978-3-031-01333-1_12

in order to facilitate the search to be conducted in the future. The work described here falls into the second category. The space considered here includes different machine learning algorithms and outlier elimination methods (OEMs), which can be seen as a particular preprocessing method [25].

Various authors have shown that using outlier elimination as a preprocessing method can improve accuracy [25,26], although this may not always be beneficial. We have decided to investigate this issue. Our first aim was to identify which OEMs are *potentially useful* when taking into account the given classification algorithm and dataset. Our results show that, for some algorithms, such as Naive Bayes, the improvement is quite significant. However, various workflows that include OEMs have the opposite effect, namely they decrease the overall performance. Therefore, we have decided to conduct a more thorough study to determine whether the OEMs are *truly useful* when recommending algorithms for new unseen datasets.

To determine this, we have adapted the approach of [2]. In this work, the authors examined the usefulness of different algorithms (workflows) in a given portfolio, while taking into account a given set of tasks. The algorithms (workflows) that are unlikely to lead to a overall performance improvement are dropped. So, the algorithms (workflows) that remain after the reduction are of interest.

This study has shown that only three OEMs out of the initial set of twelve OEMs are required for solving the given set of tasks. So, these three OEMs that have been identified represent a generally useful knowledge that can be exploited in the design of other, more complex, algorithm recommendation platforms.

## 2   Related Work

**Outlier Detection End Elimination.** One pioneering work in the area of outlier detection and elimination was the work of John and Langley (1995) [16] on the so-called robust decision trees, who studied the effects of label noise. After learning a tree, all misclassified instances were removed from the learning set and a new tree was learned. This was repeated until the learning set was consistent. Although it did not result in accuracy increase, the resulting tree was much smaller. A similar approach for kNN was presented elsewhere [29,33].

Smith and Martinez (2018) [25] explored filtering of misclassified instances. Misclassification was studied both in conjunction with a single classifier or an ensemble of classifiers. In total, 54 datasets were used in conjunction with 9 supervised learning algorithms from Weka [12]. In both cases, misclassified instances were removed. When the same learning algorithm was used to filter misclassified instances and to learn a model, only three algorithms displayed an accuracy increase – LWL lazy learner, Neural net and Ripper. In all cases, using an ensemble of learning algorithms for filtering resulted in a greater increase in classification accuracy than when using a single learning algorithm. However, if compared with majority voting ensemble of the 9 classifiers, the majority voting ensemble reached, on average, the highest accuracy. An extensive and recent discussion of noise filters, as well as a particular solution for elimination of attribute noise can be found in [24].

**Workflow Recommendation with AutoML/Metalearning Systems.** Various approaches exist regarding how to identify the best possible workflow/pipeline (sequence of algorithms) for a given task and for a given configuration space. Some simple ones include, for instance, grid search, random search, and gradient descent method, which is often used in the task of configuring the hyperparameters of neural networks. The approach known as *sequential model-based search/optimization (SMBO)* exploits knowledge of past experiments on the target dataset [14]. The so-called *surrogate model* permits to carry out a relatively fast test to estimate the next best candidate to test. The system AutoWeka [28], for instance, uses this kind of search to identify the potentially best workflow configuration for a given task.

Metalearning approaches gather test results on various datasets and the metaknowledge obtained is used to construct a model estimating the next best candidate to test [5,32]. The metaknowledge gathered represents a set of workflows (pipelines) used in the past, some of which may be useful for the new task. Each workflow (pipeline) can also be seen as a *plan* of different operations to execute. So, one advantage of the metalearning approaches is that one does not need to search for a new plan if a sufficiently rich set already exists. The method called *AR\** [1] exploits an *average ranking* of workflows. It represents a simple method that orders the workflows according to a given performance measure (e.g., accuracy, a combined measure of accuracy and runtime). Hence, this method allows us to evaluate the benefit of adding new workflows to a given portfolio and thus obtain information about its *marginal contribution to performance* [34].

**Analysis and Reformulation of Given Configuration Space.** Various authors have investigated the issue of which parts of the given configuration space are useful for a given set of tasks. Various works exist on the problem of how to establish the relative importance of hyperparameters and their setting (see e.g., [30,34]). Others tried to use the results of prior analysis to reformulate the configuration space. As was mentioned earlier, [2] examined the usefulness of different algorithms (workflows) for a given set of tasks. The results of this analysis was used to reformulate the existing set (portofolio) of algorithms (workflows).

# 3   Research Questions and Methodology

Let us first list the main research questions that we wish to answer in this work:

RQ1: Can we use OEMs in workflows without restrictions?
RQ2: Are some OEMs potentially useful?
RQ3: Can we identify the most useful workflows with OEMs? If so, how?

The research question RQ1 is addressed in a study described in Sect. 5.1. The method used to answer the research question RQ2 is discussed in Sect. 3.2 and the results are presented in Sect. 5.2. The research question RQ3 is addressed in Sect. 3.3 and the results are presented in Sect. 5.3.

### 3.1    Basic Concepts

Let us clarify the meaning of some basic concepts, starting with the notion of *outliers*. Barnett and Lewis [4] define them as observations that deviate so much from the rest of the data that it is likely that they are generated by a different phenomenon than the one being analyzed. If we characterize the points generated by a certain distribution, then outliers can be seen as the points that do not belong to this distribution.

We can distinguish two kinds of noise in a dataset that may even influence each other [35]. *Class noise* appears when instances are incorrectly labelled and may be caused in a process of labelling by a human, while *attribute noise* corresponds to errors in attribute values - caused, for instance, by measurement errors. While class noise may be eliminated by instance filtering, for attribute noise it is not appropriate. The work presented here focuses on attribute noise.

Let us also clarify what we mean by initial and extended of workflows. The *initial workflows* are of the form $CL_k$ represents a particular classification algorithm with default settings. The set of classifiers used in the experiments is shown in Sect. 4. The *initial portfolio* includes the set of these initial workflows.

The *extended workflows* are of the form $OEM_{i,j}, CL_k$, where $OEM_{i,j}$ represents the outlier elimination method $i$ with configuration $j$. The set of outlier elimination methods (OEMs) used in the experiments is shown in Sect. 4. The extended portfolio includes both the initial and the extended workflows.

### 3.2    Determine Whether Some OEMs are Potentially Useful

Informally speaking, the extended workflow $(OEM_{i,j}, CL_k)$ can be considered to be *potentially useful* if it leads to increased performance on many datasets when compared to its initial counterpart $(CL_k)$. The amount of the increase also matters and so we also take this into account. The aim of our experiments are twofold: first, determine whether all, or just some, of the extended workflows with OEMs can be considered as useful. If at least some extended workflows are identified as potentially useful, our aim is to identify the classification algorithm and the datasets involved. The results of this study are presented in Sect. 5.2.

### 3.3    Identify the Most Useful Workflows with OEMs

Our aim is to compare the performance of a chosen algorithm selection method on two different portfolios, the initial and the extended one, which may include some workflows with OEMs. The aim of this comparison is to determine whether it is advantageous to use the extended portfolio. However, we need to be careful, as some workflows that include an OEM may result in a decrease of performance. So, to avoid this, we use a reduction method based on [1] to select the most competitive workflows. This way, the extended set is effectively reduced, by pruning out the non-competitive variants. So one key question is the following: will some of the OEMs "survive" this reduction phase? If so, which ones? Will the final portfolio lead to competitive results? The aim of our experiments discussed in Sect. 5 is to answer these questions and, this way, shed light on the usefulness of outlier elimination methods.

**Method for the Reduction of Portfolios of Workflows.** The reduction method used here is based on the method in [1], but includes various adaptations. This method uses a given portfolio of algorithms (in general workflows) and reduces it by removing non-competitive ones by exploiting the existing performance metadata obtained in prior tests. This is followed by the elimination of workflows that include infrequent OEMs.

Identifying the most competitive algorithm using a given performance measure (A3R, which combines accuracy and runtime) is straightforward. Identifying all algorithms with equivalent performance could be done with recourse to the Wilcoxon signed-ranks test, that exploits *fold* information of the cross-validation procedure. As we do not have this data, we had to use a substitute method instead. This method uses just the $N\%$ of top workflows as the most competitive algorithms for a given dataset. Here we use the top 1% of workflows based on A3R measure (combining accuracy and time) and another top 1% of workflows based on accuracy only. All these workflows are passed to the second phase.

The aim of this phase is to eliminate all workflows which include rather infrequent OEM variants in this portfolio. If a particular OEM variant appears in less than P% of workflows, the corresponding workflows with this variant is marked for elimination. After processing all OEM variants, all corresponding workflows are dropped.

**Algorithm/Workflow Recommendation Method Used.** Here, we have chosen the method *average ranking (AR\*)* [1] as the algorithm/workflow recommendation method. This method was chosen because it is relatively simple and, consequently, it is easy to define different configurations that include all required alternatives (selected classification algorithms with/without OEMs). We have excluded AutoWeka [28], Auto-sklearn [10] or other systems from consideration, as they not include all the OEMs we have considered here.

Method AR* requires that each portfolio of workflows is converted into a ranking on the basis of available performance metadata. Each ranking is then followed to generate recommendations for the dataset left out. This enables to obtain its performance and to calculate how far it is from the best possible performance, i.e., calculate the *loss*. This is repeated as many times as there are datasets, following the leave-one-out (LOO) strategy. Sect. 5.3 shows the median loss obtained across all folds of LOO cycles.

**Evaluation Strategy.** The evaluation strategy adopted here is a leave-one-out (LOO) evaluation strategy. In each cycle, all datasets except one are used to identify the portfolios discussed above. The recommendations of the chosen algorithm selection method are used to calculate the loss on the dataset left out.

## 4    Experimental Setup

Our setup included 50 datasets from the *cc18* benchmark set of OpenML [31] (see Table 5 in the Appendix). We have not used datasets that were deemed to be too easy (the accuracy reported was higher than 95%) or those that had more than 50k instances.

In this study we have used 10 classifiers from the Weka toolkit that were used in one previous study [26] (see Table 1). Obviously, other classifiers could have been chosen (e.g., XGBoost, neural networks), but the choice made is useful for comparisons. All algorithms were used with default parameter settings. Apart from these, we have also used the *default classifier* that simply predicts the most frequent class for each dataset.

**Table 1.** Classifiers used in the experiments

| Classifier | Description |
| --- | --- |
| IBk | 5-Nearest Neighbors classifier [3] |
| J48 | C4.5 Decision Tree classifier [22] |
| JRip | RIPPER propositional rule learner [8] |
| LMT | Classification trees with logistic regression at the leaves [18] |
| Logistic | Logistic regression model with a ridge estimator [19] |
| SimpleLogistic | Linear logistic regression model [27] |
| NaiveBayes | Naive Bayes using estimator classes [17] |
| PART | Generates rules based on partial Decision Tree leaves [11] |
| RandomForest | Random Forest classifier [6] |
| SMO | Sequential minimal optimization for SVM [21] |

Twelve outlier detection and elimination methods (OEMs) have been used, some of which are general (see Table 2), others class-based [20] (see Table 3), representing a richer set than the one used in [25]. Each outlier elimination method (OEM) also has one hyperparameter indicating the percentage of top outliers to be eliminated (top 0.5, 1, 2, 3, 4 or 5%). All five values of this parameter were used in the experiments. Consequently, the total number of OEMs and its variants is 72, if we do not count the null method (12 OEMs, each with 6 hyperparameter settings).

The extended workflows have the format $OEM_{i,j}, CL_k$, where $OEM_{i,j}$ represents a particular outlier detection/elimination method $i$ with a hyperparameter $j$. The total number of extended workflows was 720 (72 OEMs x 10 CLs). As

**Table 2.** General outlier detection methods used

| OD | General outlier detection methods |
|---|---|
| LOF | Local Outlier Factor [7]: Compares the density of instances to its neighbors |
| NN | Nearest Neighbors [26]: Uses distances to the $k$ nearest neighbors |
| IF | Isolation Forest [9]: Using forests, determines the outlyingness of instances based on their path lengths from the root to the isolation node |
| DS | Disjunct Size [26]: Outlyingness based on the size of leaf node of instances in the decision tree |
| TD | Tree Depth [26]: Outlyingness based on the depth of the leaf node using single decision tree |
| TDwP | Tree Depth with Pruning [26]: Same as TD but uses a pruned tree |

each extended workflow was run on 50 datasets, the number of experiments was 36,000. To this, we need to also add the experiments with the initial workflows, which totaled 500 (10 CLs × 50 datasets). Each experiment was performed using 5-fold cross-validation.

## 5 Results

### 5.1 Can We Use OEMs Without Restrictions (RQ1)?

Our results have shown that, on average,[1] the workflows extended with outlier elimination do not exceed the initial counterpart. The only exception is Naive Bayes, whose performance, can, on average be improved by 0.316% by adding OEMs. So, the main conclusion from this experiment is that the OEMs should not be used blindly, without taking into account other aspects.

### 5.2 Determining Whether Some OEMs are Potentially Useful (RQ2)

Following the methodology defined in Sect. 3, we seek extended workflows of the type $OEM_{i,j}, CL_k$ whose performance exceeds the initial workflow $CL_k$ on many datasets. In other words, our aim is to identify outlier methods $OEM_{i,j}$ that are *potentially useful* for a specific $CL_k$.

Some results of these experiments are shown in Table 4. This table shows some potentially useful workflows (*Classifier, OEM*) and the hyperparameter setting of the outlier method indicating how many elements should be left out (column *Out.*). Column *Init.* shows the average accuracy of the initial workflow (a particular classifier) on all datasets. The information in column *Extend.* is similar; it is relative to the workflow extended with the particular *OEM*. Column *Dif.* shows the difference between the two values. Positive values indicate

---

[1] The average is calculated by aggregating the accuracy across different OEMs and datasets.

**Table 3.** Class-based outlier detection methods used

| OD | Class-based outlier detection methods |
|---|---|
| RF-OEX | Random Forest (RF) Outlier Detection and Explanation [20]: Uses $RF$ to calculate the dissimilarity of instances to their own class, the similarity to other classes and general outlyingness |
| CODB | Class Outliers - Distance Based approach [13]: Uses nearest neighbors to calculate the dissimilarity of instances to their own neighborhood, the similarity to other classes and general outlyingness |
| KDN | $K$ Disagreeing Neighbors [26]: Uses class labels of $k$ nearest neighbors to calculate outlyingness |
| CLOF | Class-based Local Outlier Factor: Combines the dissimilarity to its own class, the similarity to other classes and general outlyingness: $LOF(sameclass) + 0.75 * LOF(otherclasses) + 0.25 * LOF(all)$ |
| CL | Class Likelihood [26]: Calculates the probabilities of instances belonging to their own class based on Kernel Densities and the number of occurrences of features |
| CLD | Class Likelihood Difference [26]: CL, but with probabilities of belonging to different class also taken into account |

**Table 4.** Some potentially useful workflows

| Classifier | OEM | Out. | Init. Acc.% | Extend. Acc.% | Dif. Acc.% | # Wins in 50 |
|---|---|---|---|---|---|---|
| NaiveBayes | CODB | 4 | 72.816 | 73.430 | 0.615 | 31 |
| NaiveBayes | LOF | 2 | 72.816 | 73.788 | 0.973 | 30 |
| NaiveBayes | CODB | 3 | 72.816 | 73.389 | 0.573 | 30 |
| NaiveBayes | CODB | 2 | 72.816 | 73.275 | 0.459 | 30 |
| NaiveBayes | KDN | 4 | 72.816 | 73.194 | 0.379 | 30 |
| IBk | DS | 5 | 79.490 | 79.659 | 0.169 | 30 |
| LMT | ClassLikelihood | 1 | 83.475 | 83.579 | 0.104 | 30 |
| LMT | IsolationForest | 0.5 | 83.475 | 83.554 | 0.079 | 30 |
| SMO | RF-OEX | 1 | 79.898 | 79.939 | 0.041 | 30 |
| NaiveBayes | IsolationForest | 2 | 72.816 | 73.793 | 0.978 | 29 |

that the particular $OEM$ had a positive effect on performance. For instance, the use of outlier methods $CODB$ (with Out = 4), together with $NaiveBayes$ classifier, has led to an average increase of accuracy amounting to 0.615%. The improvements were observed on 31 out of 50 datasets (column #$Wins$).

This analysis does not really show how to proceed. That is, if we selected a particular combination of $OEM_{i,j}, CL_k$ this would be a risky guess. As the experiments have shown, it is not guaranteed that this workflow would lead to a better performance. So, the only choice we have is to use the most promising alternatives and conduct tests on a validation set. This topic is discussed in the next section.

### 5.3 Constructing a Portfolio with the Most Useful Workflows with OEMs (RQ3)

In this subsection, we address the question of whether some of the extended workflows that include a particular *OEM* method are useful for algorithm recommendation.

As we explained in Sect. 3, we use the method based on average ranking AR* [1]. This method uses a ranked portfolio of workflows to generate the recommendations to the user. This makes it possible to compare the benefit of having workflows with OEMs in the portfolio. The results are shown in Fig. 1 showing the median curves that aggregate the data of different curves resulting from different cycles of LOO procedure.

All curves start with *default accuracy* for each dataset corresponding to the prediction of the most frequent class. The black loss curve (Baseline 10) includes the 10 base workflows and can be considered as the baseline.

The blue loss curve (Full Ranking 710) includes all 730 workflows. Ten of these are the initial workflows and 720 are the workflows that include OEMs (10 base workflows × 10 OEMs × 6 parameter settings = 720). The advantage of including OEMs is clearly visible. The corresponding curve reaches zero loss, while the black one that uses only classifiers does not. The difference when considering the median curves is rather significant - nearly 0.5%. The downside is that we need to spend more time (around $10^3$ s) testing different alternatives before we encounter a good solution.

The red loss curve (Red Perc 1+1) shows the loss curve relative to the reduced portfolio that includes about 306 workflows on average, i.e., 58% reduction, which is quite significant. This portfolio was obtained by identifying the top performers for each dataset, then joining them without repetitions and constructing a single *A3R* ranking. The top performers include the top 1% of workflows based on A3R measure (it combines accuracy and time) and another top 1% of workflows based on accuracy only. So, this way, we identify 7+7 workflows per dataset. This alternative achieved a somewhat better loss as the total set represented by the blue curve. The advantage of this solution is that the portfolio includes fewer workflows.

The green loss curve (Red Perc 1+1 Subset) uses an even smaller portfolio when compared to the previous case (Red Perc 1+1). The portfolio Red Perc 1+1 is used as a starting point for this operation. The aim is to eliminate all workflows which include rather infrequent OEM variants in this portfolio. If a particular OEM variant appears in less than P% of workflows, the corresponding workflows with this variant is marked for elimination. After processing all OEM variants, all corresponding workflows are dropped. In this study, the threshold of $P = 10\%$ was used. The reduction obtained this way is significant, as it includes just 118 workflows (86% of reduction). Only 3 OEMs appeared in these workflows: RF-OEX, TDWithPrunning and DS.

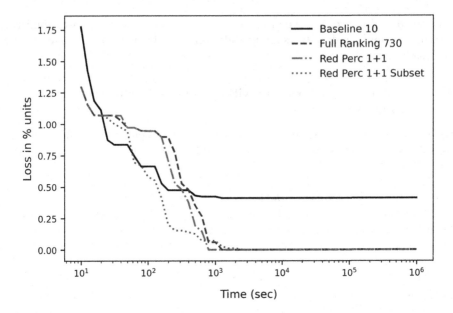

**Fig. 1.** Median loss curves of AR* relative to different portfolios of workflows (Color figure online)

## 6    Future Work and Conclusions

**Future Work.** It would be possible to examine how reliable are the OEMs identified in eliminating certain outliers. This could be done by injecting outliers in a controlled manner and then by examining whether these would be eliminated with the OEMs. Also, we could compare the effect of using OEMs with the noise filters discussed by Saez et al. [24] (see Sect. 2).

We note that outliers are often defined with respect to a particular distribution (see Sect. 3). In this work we have assumed that the distribution is fixed. It would be possible to extend the work presented here to be able to deal with data following a specific distribution. In case of skewed distributions, suitable transformations might help, e.g. Box-Cox, Yeo-Johnson or quantile-based transformations [15].

Although the reduction method used here was applied to a particular setting that includes OEMs, the method is quite general, as it can be applied in other settings. These could include algorithm selection, selection of suitable hyperparameter settings and inclusion of other preprocessing methods. The configuration space obtained with our specific workflow recommendation system can be implanted into other more complex systems. We are planning to conduct other studies in the future to demonstrate this.

**Conclusions.** Our aim was to examine the usefulness of outlier detection/elimination methods (OEMs) in classification. We have considered twelve different OEMs in conjunction with different classifiers and formulated several research questions. We have shown that it is not advisable to use OEMs in workflows without further restrictions. The performance of the workflows extended with OEMs does not usually exceed the performance of the initial counterparts. The workflows with Naive Bayes and OEMs represent an exception, although the gain obtained by including OEMs is not large.

This result lead us to investigate how we could identify the most useful workflows that include some OEMs only, and this way improve the performance. The methodology adopted used a simple algorithm/workflow recommendation system (AR*). We have investigated the effect of selecting different portfolios of workflows in this setting. Our aim was to try to reduce the initial portfolio by eliminating certain elements, without affecting the performance of the workflow recommendation system.

Our results show that if we use OEMs, the results of the workflow recommendation system will improve on average. The gain observed on a study with 50 datasets in a leave-one-out mode was rather significant (0.5%). Our most important result involves the three OEMs identified with our approach, which are RF-OEX, TDwP and DS. Besides, we showed that it is possible to eliminate 86% of the original workflows and still maintain the same loss.

Reducing the number of workflows can be regarded as a reduction of the given configuration space. This topic is relevant to other researcher in AutoML, as it can lead to substantial speed-ups of the search for effective solutions.

**Acknowledgement.** We thank Rita Ribeiro for her comments and suggestions, and Robert Kolcún, Ondrej Kurák and Adam Bajger for the implementation of the testing framework. This work was partially supported by the Faculty of Informatics, Masaryk University, Brno. This work was also partially financed by National Funds through the Portuguese funding agency, FCT - Fundação para a Ciência e a Tecnologia, within project UIDB/50014/2020 and by the project Safe Cities - Inovação para Construir Cidades Seguras, with the reference POCI-01-0247-FEDER-041435, co-funded by the European Regional Development Fund (ERDF), through the Operational Programme for Competitiveness and Internationalization (COMPETE 2020), under the PORTUGAL 2020 Partnership Agreement. We also thank the anonymous referees for their useful comments which enabled us to improve the paper.

# Appendix

**Table 5.** Datasets used in the experiments (total 50)

| Dataset | Inst. | Feat. | Clas. | Dataset | Inst. | Feat. | Clas. |
|---|---|---|---|---|---|---|---|
| dresses-sales | 500 | 13 | 2 | mfeat-fourier | 2000 | 77 | 10 |
| KC2 | 522 | 22 | 2 | mfeat-karhunen | 2000 | 65 | 10 |
| climate-model-simulation-crashes | 540 | 21 | 2 | mfeat-morphological | 2000 | 7 | 10 |
| cylinder-bands | 540 | 40 | 2 | mfeat-pixel | 2000 | 241 | 10 |
| ilpd | 583 | 11 | 2 | mfeat-zernike | 2000 | 48 | 10 |
| balance-scale | 625 | 5 | 3 | KC1 | 2109 | 22 | 2 |
| credit-rating | 690 | 16 | 2 | segment | 2310 | 20 | 7 |
| eucalyptus | 736 | 20 | 5 | ozone-level-8hr | 2534 | 73 | 2 |
| blood-transfusion-service | 748 | 5 | 2 | madelon | 2600 | 501 | 2 |
| pima-diabetes | 768 | 9 | 2 | dna | 3186 | 181 | 3 |
| analcatdata-dmft | 797 | 5 | 6 | splice | 3190 | 61 | 3 |
| vehicle | 846 | 19 | 4 | spambase | 4601 | 58 | 2 |
| tic-tac-toe | 958 | 10 | 2 | churn | 5000 | 21 | 2 |
| vowel | 990 | 13 | 11 | phoneme | 5404 | 6 | 2 |
| credit-g | 1000 | 21 | 2 | wall-robot-navigation | 5456 | 25 | 4 |
| qsar-biodeg | 1055 | 42 | 2 | texture | 5500 | 41 | 11 |
| cnae9 | 1080 | 857 | 9 | optdigits | 5620 | 65 | 10 |
| PC1 | 1109 | 22 | 2 | first-order-theorem | 6118 | 52 | 6 |
| pc4 | 1458 | 38 | 2 | satimage | 6430 | 37 | 6 |
| cmc | 1473 | 10 | 3 | data.va3.gesture | 9873 | 33 | 5 |
| pc3 | 1563 | 38 | 2 | JM1 | 10885 | 22 | 2 |
| semeion | 1593 | 257 | 10 | letter | 20000 | 17 | 26 |
| car | 1728 | 7 | 4 | doushouqi-raw-egtb-2-pieces | 44819 | 7 | 3 |
| spf3 | 1941 | 28 | 7 | bank-marketing-full | 45211 | 17 | 2 |
| mfeat-factors | 2000 | 217 | 10 | electricity | 45312 | 9 | 2 |

# References

1. Abdulrahman, S.M., Brazdil, P., van Rijn, J.N., Vanschoren, J.: Speeding up algorithm selection using average ranking and active testing by introducing runtime. Mach. Learn. **107**(1), 79–108 (2017). https://doi.org/10.1007/s10994-017-5687-8
2. Abdulrahman, S.M., Brazdil, P., Zainon, W.M.N.W., Adamu, A.: Simplifying the algorithm selection using reduction of rankings of classification algorithms. In: ICSCA 2019 Proceedings of the 2019 8th International Conference on Software and Computer Applications, pp. 140–148. ACM, New York (2019)
3. Aha, D., Kibler, D.: Instance-based learning algorithms. Mach. Learn. **6**, 37–66 (1991)
4. Barnett, V., Lewis, T.: Outliers in Statistical Data. Wiley, Hoboken (1978)
5. Brazdil, P., van Rijn, J.N., Soares, C., Vanschoren, J.: Metalearning: Applications to Automated Machine Learning and Data Mining, 2nd edn. Springer, Heidelberg (2022). https://doi.org/10.1007/978-3-030-67024-5
6. Breiman, L.: Random forests. Mach. Learn. **45**(1), 5–32 (2001)

7. Breunig, M.M., Kriegel, H.P., Ng, R.T., Sander, J.: LOF: identifying density-based local outliers. In: ACM SIGMOD Record, vol. 29, pp. 93–104. ACM (2000)
8. Cohen, W.W.: Fast effective rule induction. In: Twelfth International Conference on Machine Learning, pp. 115–123. Morgan Kaufmann (1995)
9. Ding, Z., Fei, M.: An anomaly detection approach based on isolation forest algorithm for streaming data using sliding window. IFAC Proc. Vol. **46**(20), 12–17 (2013)
10. Feurer, M., Klein, A., Eggensperger, K., Springenberg, J.T., Blum, M., Hutter, F.: Auto-sklearn: efficient and robust automated machine learning. In: Hutter, F., Kotthoff, L., Vanschoren, J. (eds.) Automated Machine Learning. TSSCML, pp. 113–134. Springer, Cham (2019). https://doi.org/10.1007/978-3-030-05318-5_6
11. Frank, E., Witten, I.H.: Generating accurate rule sets without global optimization. In: Shavlik, J. (ed.) Fifteenth International Conference on Machine Learning, pp. 144–151. Morgan Kaufmann (1998)
12. Hall, M., Frank, E., Holmes, G., Pfahringer, B., Reutemann, P., Witten, I.H.: The Weka data mining software: an update. SIGKDD Explor. Newsl. **11**(1), 10–18 (2009)
13. Hewahi, N.M., Saad, M.K.: Class outliers mining: distance-based approach. Int. J. Intell. Syst. Technol. **2**, 5 (2007)
14. Hutter, F., Hoos, H.H., Leyton-Brown, K.: Sequential model-based optimization for general algorithm configuration. LION **5**, 507–523 (2011)
15. Hyndman, R.J., Athanasopoulos, G.: Forecasting: Principles and Practice, 3rd edn. OTexts (2021)
16. John, G.H.: Robust decision trees: removing outliers from databases. In: Knowledge Discovery and Data Mining, pp. 174–179. AAAI Press (1995)
17. John, G.H., Langley, P.: Estimating continuous distributions in Bayesian classifiers. In: Eleventh Conference on Uncertainty in Artificial Intelligence, pp. 338–345. Morgan Kaufmann, San Mateo (1995)
18. Landwehr, N., Hall, M., Frank, E.: Logistic model trees. Mach. Learn. **59**(1), 161–205 (2005)
19. le Cessie, S., van Houwelingen, J.C.: Ridge estimators in logistic regression. Appl. Stat. **41**(1), 191–201 (1992)
20. Nezvalová, L., Popelínský, L., Torgo, L., Vaculík, K.: Class-based outlier detection: staying zombies or awaiting for resurrection? In: Fromont, E., De Bie, T., van Leeuwen, M. (eds.) IDA 2015. LNCS, vol. 9385, pp. 193–204. Springer, Cham (2015). https://doi.org/10.1007/978-3-319-24465-5_17
21. Platt, J.: Fast training of support vector machines using sequential minimal optimization. In: Schoelkopf, B., Burges, C., Smola, A. (eds.) Advances in Kernel Methods - Support Vector Learning. MIT Press (1998)
22. Quinlan, R.: C4.5: Programs for Machine Learning. Morgan Kaufmann Publishers, San Mateo (1993)
23. Rice, J.R.: The algorithm selection problem. Adv. Comput. **15**, 65–118 (1976)
24. Sáez, J.A., Corchado, E.: ANCES: a novel method to repair attribute noise in classification problems. Pattern Recogn. **121**, 108–198 (2022)
25. Smith, M.R., Martinez, T.: The robustness of majority voting compared to filtering misclassified instances in supervised classification tasks. Artif. Intell. Rev. **49**(1), 105–130 (2016). https://doi.org/10.1007/s10462-016-9518-2
26. Smith, M.R., Martinez, T., Giraud-Carrier, C.: An instance level analysis of data complexity. Mach. Learn. **95**(2), 225–256 (2013). https://doi.org/10.1007/s10994-013-5422-z

27. Sumner, M., Frank, E., Hall, M.: Speeding up logistic model tree induction. In: Jorge, A.M., Torgo, L., Brazdil, P., Camacho, R., Gama, J. (eds.) PKDD 2005. LNCS (LNAI), vol. 3721, pp. 675–683. Springer, Heidelberg (2005). https://doi.org/10.1007/11564126_72

28. Thornton, C., Hutter, F., Hoos, H.H., Leyton-Brown, K.: Auto-WEKA: combined selection and hyperparameter optimization of classification algorithms. In: Proceedings of the 19th ACM SIGKDD International Conference on Knowledge Discovery and Data Mining, pp. 847–855. ACM (2013)

29. Tomek, I.: An experiment with the edited nearest-neighbor rule. IEEE Trans. Syst. Man Cybern. **6**, 448–452 (1976)

30. van Rijn, J.N., Hutter, F.: Hyperparameter importance across datasets. In: KDD 2018: The 24th ACM SIGKDD International Conference on Knowledge Discovery & Data Mining. ACM (2018)

31. Vanschoren, J., van Rijn, J.N., Bischl, B., Torgo, L.: OpenML: networked science in machine learning. SIGKDD Explor. **15**(2), 49–60 (2013)

32. Vilalta, R., Drissi, Y.: A perspective view and survey of meta-learning. Artif. Intell. Rev. **18**(2), 77–95 (2002)

33. Wilson, D.R., Martinez, T.R.: Reduction techniques for instance-based learning algorithms. Mach. Learn. **38**(3), 257–286 (2000)

34. Xu, L., Hutter, F., Hoos, H., Leyton-Brown, K.: Evaluating component solver contributions to portfolio-based algorithm selectors. In: Cimatti, A., Sebastiani, R. (eds.) SAT 2012. LNCS, vol. 7317, pp. 228–241. Springer, Heidelberg (2012). https://doi.org/10.1007/978-3-642-31612-8_18

35. Zhu, X., Wu, X.: Class noise vs. attribute noise: a quantitative study. Artif. Intell. Rev. **22**, 177–210 (2004)

# Suitability of Different Metric Choices for Concept Drift Detection

Fabian Hinder$^{(\boxtimes)}$, Valerie Vaquet, and Barbara Hammer⊙

CITEC, Bielefeld University, Bielefeld, Germany
{fhinder,vvaquet,bhammer}@techfak.uni-bielefeld.de

**Abstract.** The notion of concept drift refers to the phenomenon that the distribution, which is underlying the observed data, changes over time; as a consequence machine learning models may become inaccurate and need adjustment. Many unsupervised approaches for drift detection rely on measuring the discrepancy between the sample distributions of two time windows. This may be done directly, after some preprocessing (feature extraction, embedding into a latent space, etc.), or with respect to inferred features (mean, variance, conditional probabilities etc.). Most drift detection methods can be distinguished in what metric they use, how this metric is estimated, and how the decision threshold is found. In this paper, we analyze structural properties of the drift induced signals in the context of different metrics. We compare different types of estimators and metrics theoretically and empirically and investigate the relevance of the single metric components. In addition, we propose new choices and demonstrate their suitability in several experiments.

**Keywords:** Concept drift · Concept drift detection · Drift detection metric · Metric adaption

## 1 Introduction

One popular assumption in classical machine learning is that the observed data is generated i.i.d. according to some unknown underlying and stationary probability $\mathbb{P}_X$. Yet, stationarity is often violated for realistic learning tasks such as machine learning based on (streaming) social media entries or measurements of IoT devices, which are subject to continuous change [1,22]. Here, concept drift, i.e. changes of the underlying distribution $\mathbb{P}_X$ occurs, caused e.g. by seasonal changes, changed demands, ageing of sensors, etc. Learning with drift can be dealt with in different ways. Often, data is treated via windowing techniques, and the model is continuously adapted based on the characteristics of the data in an observed time window. Thereby, many approaches deal with supervised scenarios and they aim for a small interleaved train-test error. In recent years, some approaches deal with concept drift in unsupervised settings [6,16]. One

We gratefully acknowledge funding by the BMBF TiM, grant number 05M20PBA.

© The Author(s), under exclusive license to Springer Nature Switzerland AG 2022
T. Bouadi et al. (Eds.): IDA 2022, LNCS 13205, pp. 157–170, 2022.
https://doi.org/10.1007/978-3-031-01333-1_13

fundamental problem, which is part of supervised learning schemes as well as unsupervised drift modelling and which will be in the focus of this publication, is the challenge of drift detection and determination of the time point when drift occurs.

According to [16] most drift detection schemes proceed in four stages: 1) collecting data, 2) building a descriptor of the data in two time windows, 3) computing a dissimilarity based on the obtained the descriptor, 4) normalize the dissimilarity, e.g. by considering an appropriate statistical test. This work focuses on the second and third stage of this scheme, which constitute the most crucial ones. The first stage can be solved in many problem-specific ways without a major effect on the next stages. The decision process in stage four can be bounded independently of the concrete realization: the difference of the output of stage three under the null hypothesis (no drift) and the alternative (drift) constitutes such a bound.

The aim of the present work is to determine the influence of the two major ingredients of stage 2 and 3, namely the used descriptor (stage 2) and the dissimilarity measure applied to the descriptor (stage 3) and to evaluate their influence on the capability to detect drift and localize it in time. We will empirically show that the chosen dissimilarity measure is of minor importance. The descriptor has an impact. In lay terms, it is more important how to estimate rather than what to estimate. This claim will be investigated from a theoretical and an empirical perspective using different estimation schemes.

Beyond this general comparison, we provide new methods to realize stages two and three in an efficient (dataset-specific) way: random projection-based and moment tree-based binning. This is of particular interest since dataset-agnostic dissimilarity measures face the challenge of an inherent trade-off between statistical power or sensitivity and convergence speed.

This work is structured as follows: first (Sect. 2) we recall relevant work from the literature and define the problem setup – in particular, we describe different approaches to tackle the four stages (Sect. 3). We also provide a general argument when an estimator is capable of drift detection (see Theorem 2). In the last section (Sect. 5) we evaluate the metrics and estimators – showing their strengths and weaknesses – and show the suitability of our proposed approaches.

## 2   Problem Setup

In the usual time invariant setup of machine learning, one considers a generative process $\mathbb{P}_X$, i.e. a probability measure, on the data space $\mathcal{X}$. In this context, one views the realizations of $\mathbb{P}_X$-distributed, independent random variables $X_1, ..., X_n$ as samples. Depending on the objective, learning algorithms try to infer the data distribution based on these samples, or, in the supervised setting, the posterior distribution. We will not distinguish between these settings and only consider distributions in general, subsuming supervised and unsupervised modeling [23].

Many processes in real-world applications are time dependent, so it is reasonable to incorporate time into our considerations. One prominent way to do so, is to consider an index set $\mathcal{T}$, representing time, and a collection of probability measures $p_t$ on $\mathcal{X}$, indexed over $\mathcal{T}$, which may change over time [8]. We will usually assume $\mathcal{T} = [0, 1]$. In the following, we investigate the relationship of those $p_t$. Drift refers to the fact that $p_t$ varies for different time points, i.e.

$$\exists t_0, t_1 \in \mathcal{T} : p_{t_0} \neq p_{t_1}.$$

In this context, we consider a sequence of samples $(X_1, T_1), (X_2, T_2), \ldots$, with $X_i \sim p_{T_i}$ and $T_i \leq T_{i+1}$, as a stream. Notice, that we will usually use the shorthand drift instead of concept drift. In this contribution we will mainly focus on the case of one single abrupt drift, i.e. there exist probability measures $P$ and $Q$ and a time point $t_0 \in \mathcal{T}$, such that

$$p_t = \begin{cases} P, & t \leq t_0 \\ Q, & t > t_0 \end{cases}.$$

In this context we can ask two questions, which are referred to as drift detection:

1. *Whether* there is drift, i.e. does $P \neq Q$ hold?
2. If so, *when* does the drift occur, i.e. what is $t_0$?

## 2.1   A General Scheme for Drift Detection

As most drift detection methods are applied in a streaming context, one usually considers time-dependent data samples $S(t)$, observed during a time period $W(t)$. To detect drift, one estimates the dissimilarity of the distributions of a (presumably before drift) *reference time-interval* (or window) $W_-(t)$ and a *current time-interval* $W_+(t)$, which are obtained by splitting $W(t)$. The estimation is done using the sub-samples $S_-(t)$ and $S_+(t)$ called *windows* of $S(t)$ that correspond to $W_-(t)$ and $W_+(t)$, respectively. The way this is done varies depending on the specific algorithm. In this section we discuss some of the most prominent choices for the relevant stages 1–4 of this drift detection scheme as described in [16].

*Stage 1: Acquisition of data:* As stated above most approaches are based on sliding windows, however, the concrete implementation can vary. In particular, the reference window is realized in different ways: as sliding window, stationary, growing window, implicitly within a model, etc. To illustrate the idea we describe the examples of (a variant of) ADWIN and a simple version of an implicit reference window:

*Example 1.* ADWIN [2] uses only one sliding window $S(t_{\text{now}})$. To test for drift this window is split successively into to halves, $S_-(t; t_{\text{now}})$ and $S_+(t; t_{\text{now}})$. Then, these are compared using a suitable distance measure $\hat{d}$, i.e. the statistic of ADWIN is given by $\sup_t \hat{d}(S_-(t; t_{\text{now}}), S_+(t; t_{\text{now}}))$. In the original version

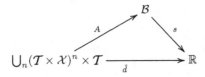

**Fig. 1.** Two stage scheme of estimating distribution dissimilarity from data. Distance of distributions $(\hat{d})$ can be estimated by building a descriptor $(A)$ and then computing a dissimilarity $(s)$.

ADWIN "prepocesses" the data by comparing the result of a fixed classification model against reference labels. However, extensions with other statistical tests are straightforward.

*Example 2.* A simple approach with implicit reference window consists of a reference mean $\hat{\mu}_{\text{ref}} = \mu(S_-(t))$ and a sliding window $S_+(t)$ of fixed size corresponding to $W_+(t)$. If there is no drift, the mean in the current window and the reference should be the same, i.e. $\mu(S_+(t)) \approx \hat{\mu}_{\text{ref}}$. Based in this assumption a drift detection can be performed using a $t$-test. Once a sample drops out of the current window $S_+(t)$ it is used to update $\hat{\mu}_{\text{ref}}$.

Apart from these examples, some approaches use preprocessing such as a deep latent space embedding. We do not explain those possibilities in more detail. Instead, we focus on the case of two windows only and try to evaluate the suitability of different distance measures for the task at hand.

*Stage 2: Building a descriptor:* Comparing two distributions directly based on a sample is usually complicated. Therefore, the process is split into two parts which are visualized in Fig. 1: First a descriptor of the distributions is built (this corresponds to $A$ in Fig. 1), and then the dissimilarity of the distribution is computed based on that descriptor ($s$ in Fig. 1). Possible descriptors are grid- or tree-based binnings, neighbor-, and kernel approaches. We list some of the most popular descriptors together with suitable dissimilarity measures in Sect. 3.

*Stage 3: Computing dissimilarity:* As stated in the last paragraph, computing the dissimilarity of two samples is often reduced to a comparison of descriptors which are based on those samples ($s$ in Fig. 1). Although, several approaches for building descriptors exist, many admit the same or at least comparable dissimilarity measures. For example, if we consider binning descriptors, it does not matter whether the bins are obtained from a grid or a tree, or if the grid or tree is adjusted to the presented data or not.

*Stage 4: Normalization:* As the obtained dissimilarities typically depend on both, the method, i.e. stages 1–3, and also the concrete distribution at hand, it is necessary to normalize the result to obtain a useful scale. One of the most common ways to do this is by a relation of the dissimilarity to the statistic of a statistical test; in this case the $p$-value offers a normalized scale. In the literature a large variety of approaches are considered. However, independently of the concrete normalization, the presence of drift can be observed from the output of stage 3; more formally the post hoc optimal normalization after stage 3 provides an upper bound on the quality of any concrete normalization. Therefore, we will focus on the output after stage 3 in the following.

*Beyond stage 4: Ensemble and hierarchical approaches:* Some authors [16] suggest to combine multiple drift detectors. They are usually arranged in an ensemble, e.g. by combining multiple $p$-values after stage 4 into a single one, or hierarchical, e.g. by combining a computationally inexpensive but imprecise detector with a precise but computationally expensive validation. Although, those approaches differ on a technical level, they do not from a theoretical perspective, as the suggested framework is sufficiently general.

## 2.2   Formal Setup and Research Question

Before we can formally specify question 1 and 2, we first have to define the sampling process:

**Definition 1.** *Let $\mathcal{X}$ be a data space and $\mathcal{T} \subset \mathbb{R}$. Let $(p_t, P_T)$ be a drift process [13] on $\mathcal{X}$ and $\mathcal{T}$, i.e. a distribution $P_T$ on $\mathcal{T}$ and a Markov kernel $p_t$ from $\mathcal{T}$ to $\mathcal{X}$. A window $S$ drawn from $p_t$ during a time interval $W \subset \mathcal{T}$ is a sample $S = \{(x_1, t_1), \cdots, (x_n, t_n)\}$ drawn i.i.d. from $p_t P_T[\,\cdot\,|\,W\,]$, assuming $P_T(W) > 0$.*

We use the following notation: If the choice of $W$ is not specified, we will assume $W = \mathcal{T}$. For the sub-intervals $W_-(t) := (-\infty, t] \cap W$ and $W_+(t) := (t, \infty) \cap W$, we define the sub-windows $S_-(t) := \{(x', t') \in S \mid t' \in W_-(t)\}$ and $S_+(t)$ analogously.

*Question 1: "Whether"* It was shown in [12, Theorem 2] that drift is equivalent to different sub-window distributions, i.e. it exists a $t \in W$ such that $p_{W_-(t)} \neq p_{W_+(t)}$, here $p_W$ denotes the distribution during $W$. Since we do not observe the underlying distributions, but only a window $S$, it is reasonable to quantify this using estimates of the distance of the underlying distributions

$$\hat{d}(S_-(t), S_+(t)) := (s \circ A)(S, t)$$

which should be (significantly) larger than 0 if and only if there is drift. Here we decompose $\hat{d}$ as described before into a descriptor $A$ and a dissimilarity $s$.

Control of the uncertainty of the sampling process when detecting drift can be formalized as follows:

**Definition 2.** *Let $(p_t, P_T)$ be a drift process, and $S$ denote a window drawn from it. An* estimator *$(A, s)$ is a pair of measurable maps, one mapping windows to descriptors, i.e. $A : \cup_n (\mathcal{X} \times \mathcal{T})^n \times \mathcal{T} \to \mathcal{B}$, the other mapping descriptors to dissimilarities, i.e. $s : \mathcal{B} \to \mathbb{R}$. We refer to $\mathcal{B}$ as the* description space.

*An estimator is* drift detecting, *iff it raises correct alarms with a high probability in the following sense: There exists a $0 < \delta < 1/2$ and a number n such that with probability at least $1 - \delta$ over all choices of S, with $|S| > n$, it hold s $\circ A(S,t) > 0$ for some t if and only if there is drift.*

*An estimator is* surely drift detecting, *iff it raises correct alarms with arbitrarily high certainty, that is the above statement holds for all $0 < \delta < 1$.*

Notice, that this definition is applicable for general drift, including gradual, incremental, and periodic. Furthermore, the difference between drift detection and sure drift detection only occurs in the limit of the size of $S$. As long as we are restrained to windows of fixed sample size, both notions are effectively the same.

*Question 2: "When"* We are interested in finding the time point $t_0$ where the drift actually occurs. This is often estimated by the point $\hat{t}_0$ with largest difference of the sub-windows, i.e.

$$\hat{t}_0 = \arg\max_{t \in \mathcal{T}} \hat{d}(S_-(t), S_+(t)).$$

The precision of this estimator can be quantified by mean ratio of samples between the true drift event $t_0$ and its estimate $\hat{t}_0$. This can be formalized as follows:

**Definition 3.** *Let $(p_t, P_T)$ be a drift process with a single abrupt drift event at $t_0$ with $0 < P_T(W_-(t_0)) < 1$. Let $S$ be a window drawn from $p_t$.*

*We define the* precision *of the estimate $\hat{t}_0$ as $1 - P_T( [t_0, \hat{t}_0) \cup (\hat{t}_0, t_0] ).$[1]*

*We say that an estimator $(A, s)$ is* precise, *iff for all $0 < \delta < 1$ and $\epsilon > 0$ there exists a number n, such that with at least probability $1 - \delta$ over all choices of S, with $|S| > n$, the precision is larger than $1 - \epsilon$, assuming drift was detected.*

Notice, that the restriction to a single drift event in the definition of precision is necessary to avoid the ambiguity of which event $\hat{t}_0$ is to be compared to.

As finding the best split $\hat{t}_0$ requires the evaluation of multiple potential split points $t$, an efficient computation is important. As we have to compute the dissimilarity at each time point, efficiency holds if the same descriptor can be used for multiple split points, i.e. $\hat{d}(S_-(t), S_+(t)) = (s \circ A)(S,t) = s(A_0(S),t)$, where $A_0$ is independent of the split point. This gives rise to the following definition:

**Definition 4.** *We say that an estimator $(A, s)$ is* c-complex, *iff $s \in \mathcal{O}(c)$ regarding computational complexity and $A$ factorizes as $A_0 \times id_{\mathcal{T}}$, that means it holds $(s \circ A)(S,t) = s(A_0(S),t)$.*

Notice, that the computational efficiency of $s$ crucially depends on the codomain of $A_0$. For example factorization also holds if we choose the set of all functions from $\mathcal{T}$ to $\mathbb{R}$ and $s$ as the evaluation map.

The notion of complexity restricts how much $A(S,t)$ can be adapted to the split point $t$. Yet, the incorporation of the temporal information contained in $S$

---

[1] Recall that $[a, b) = (a, b] = \emptyset$ for $a \geq b$.

is desirable as it usually leads to better descriptors. We therefore say that an estimator is "arrival time respecting" if the descriptor uses temporal information beyond the split point:

**Definition 5.** *An estimator $(A, s)$ is* arrival time respecting, *iff the obtained descriptor depends on the timing within the sub-windows, i.e. it exists a split of a window $S = S_- \dot{\cup} S_+$, and permutations $\pi_-, \pi_+$, such that $A(S_- \cup S_+, t) \neq A(\tilde{S}_- \cup \tilde{S}_+, t)$, where $\tilde{S}_- = \{(x_i, t_{\pi_-(i)}) \mid i = 1, ..., n_-\}$ is the time-permuted version of $S_- = \{(x_i, t_i) \mid i = 1, ..., n_-\}$ and analogous for $\tilde{S}_+$.*

# 3  Dissimilarity Estimators

We are interested in popular instantiations of stages 2 and 3 and their properties.

Binning can be considered as one of the simplest strategies to estimate a probability distribution. Essentially, the input space is segmented and the number of samples per bin is counted. The ratio of these samples as compared to all provides an estimate for the actual probability. Based thereon, distance measures like total variation [23], Hellinger distance [5], or Kullback-Leibler divergence [4,19] can be computed. We will also consider the Jensen-Shannon metric which is based on the Kullback-Leibler divergence. Binning on a grid was used in the work [23], for example, to estimate the rate of change in data streams.

Since the number of required bins grows exponentially with the number of dimensions, one might consider multiple, separate binnings of low dimensional projections for high dimensional data. Typical choices are projections onto the *coordinate axis/marginals* [5] and onto the *principal components* [19]. While these strategies reduce the complexity of the descriptor, it is not capable of capturing drift that affects the correlation of features or of components with small variance, respectively. As this poses a problem for drift detection in the real world, we propose a new technology: *random projection* binning considers binnings along randomly chosen projection axes.

Instead of using an equally spaced grid structure, one can also consider a recursive splitting of the dataset similar to a decision tree with leaves forming the bins. Depending on the way of splitting, these are *Random Trees*, where the dimension and the split point are chosen completely randomly, or *kdq-Trees* [4], where one successively splits the dimensions along the center. As such splits often lead to slow convergence, we propose to use a comparably new alternative: *Moment Trees* [14], which are designed for conditional density estimation. Here, they are trained to predict the (distribution of) time given data, i.e. $\mathbb{P}_{T|X}$. Notice, that due to the relation to a supervised problem, one can perform a parameter tuning, which is not possible for the other approaches.

Neighborhood-based approaches offer a popular and robust choice in nonparametric methods which have been widely used for various estimators, including Kullback-Leibler divergence [18]. In drift detection the *Local Drift Degree (LDD)* [15] is one method that is explicitly based on $k$-nearest neighbors ($k$-NN).

**Table 1.** Summary of estimators (Drift Detecting: No ✗, Drift detecting (✓), Surely drift detecting ✓, Arrival Time Respecting: No ✗, Yes ✓)

| Descriptor ($\mathcal{B}$) | Metric(s) | DD | ATR | Complexity | |
|---|---|---|---|---|---|
| Marginal Bin. [5] | | ✗ | ✗ | $\mathcal{O}(1)$ | Cumulative histogram |
| Random Proj. Bin. | | (✓) | ✗ | $\mathcal{O}(1)$ | Cumulative histogram |
| Random Tree (Bin.) | Total variation [23], | ✓ | ✗ | $\mathcal{O}(1)$ | Cumulative histogram |
| $kdq$-Tree [4] (Bin.) | Hellinger [5], Jensen- | ✓ | ✗ | $\mathcal{O}(1)$ | Cumulative histogram |
| Moment Tree (Bin.) | Shannon, $D_{\mathrm{KL}}$ [4] | ✓ | ✓ | $\mathcal{O}(1)$ | Cumulative histogram |
| $k$-NN | LDD [15], $D_{\mathrm{KL}}$ [18] | ✓ | ✗ | $\mathcal{O}(k)$ | Neighborhood graph |
| Kernel embedding of distribution [20] | MMD [10] | ✓ | ✗ | $\mathcal{O}(|W|)$ | Cholesky decomposition of kernel matrix |

Another, non-parametric approach are kernels. *Maximum Mean Discrepancy (MMD)* [10] is a kernel-based metric, which was also applied to drift detection [20].

The methods listed above are summarized in Table 1. We investigate their theoretical properties and experimental behavior in the following.

## 4   Theoretical Analysis

We will now discuss some of the properties of the approaches presented in Sect. 3 from a theoretical point of view. We will see that, regarding questions 1 and 2, common estimators are well suited for drift detection. In the following we will always assume a drift process $(p_t, P_T)$ on $\mathcal{X}, \mathcal{T}$, with $\mathcal{T} \subset \mathbb{R}$.

*Linear Projections:* Many, in particular, simple methods use projections as a first step. However, as already discussed by [19] not every possible projection is also suitable. Indeed, most approaches from the literature are not:

*Remark 1.* Linear projections with respect to marginals [5] or principal components [19] are not drift detecting, independent of the further processing. This stays true if $p_t$ is compactly supported.

Conversely, random projections are sufficient for drift detection:

**Theorem 1.** *Let $\mathcal{X} = \mathbb{R}^d$ and assume that $p_t$ is compactly supported, then random projection (with $w \sim \mathcal{N}(0, \mathbb{I})$) with random bins is drift detecting.*

*Proof.* All proofs can be found in the ArXiv version.

However, we will observe that they do not perform well for large dimensionality. We conjecture that this is a consequence of the fact that they are not arrival time respecting, and therefore not adapted to the specific problem at hand.

*Learneable Models:* Many popular machine learning models are also applied to estimate dissimilarities in drift detection. Interestingly, the uniform learnability that qualifies them as valid machine learning models, also assures that the derived estimators are surely drift detecting and precise:

**Theorem 2.** *Let $\mathcal{X}$ be a measurable space and let $\mathcal{H}$ be a hypothesis class of binary classifiers on $\mathcal{X}$. Consider the estimators induced by*

$$\frac{1}{2} - \inf_{h \in \mathcal{H}} \mathbb{E}[\ell_w(h, (X, \mathbf{1}[T \in W_+(t)]))],$$

*where $\ell_w$ denotes the 0-1-loss with class reweighting, i.e. $\ell_w(y', (x,y)) = 1/\mathbb{P}[Y = y]$ if $y \neq y'$ and 0 otherwise. If $\mathcal{H}$ is PAC-learnable, then the estimator is precise. If in addition, for all binary classification tasks on $\mathcal{X}$ there exists a $h \in \mathcal{H}$ that performs better than random, then the estimator is also surely drift detecting.*

To connect this result to the existing literature, observe that (for $\mathcal{X} = \mathbb{R}^d$ and universal $\mathcal{H}$) the estimator is equivalent to the total variation norm.

In particular, if an estimator is based on a uniform learneable model class, it is surely drift detecting and precise, but in general this requires us to retrain the model for each split point $t$. At this point the fact that some models do not need adaptation can increase efficiency. Indeed, for Random Trees and $kdq$-Trees we find the following statements:

**Corollary 1.** *On $\mathcal{X} = [0, 1]^d$ Random Trees and kdq-Trees with total variation norm are surely drift detecting, precise, and $\mathcal{O}(1)$-complex with cumulative histograms as descriptors.*

To obtain a similar result for Moment Trees, we make use of the fact that they can be used for conditional density estimation [14]: The obtained tree is suitable for all classification tasks of the form $\mathbf{1}[T > t]$, which is exactly what is considered by Theorem 2. We therefore conjecture that Moment Trees with total variation norm is drift detecting, precise, arrival time respecting, and $\mathcal{O}(1)$-complex with cumulative histograms as descriptors.

# 5   Empirical Evaluation

Based on the theory provided in Sect. 4, we can derive worst case bounds similar to standard results from classical learning theory for drift detection. Yet, we are also interested in average case bounds obtained from empirical estimations.

We apply the estimators as described in Table 1. For the binning approaches we used different numbers of bins, and equidistant and equilikely bins. In case of Random Projection, we also vary the number of projections. In case of the $k$-NN and tree approaches we vary the number of neighbors and trees. In case of Moment Trees we consider different degrees, ensembles of independently grown Decision Trees and Random Forests. For MMD we use the biased estimator

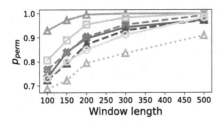

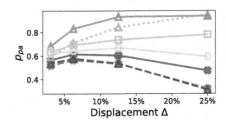

(a) Effect of window length on $p_{\text{perm}}$ on weather dataset.

(b) Effect of displacement ($t = t_0 + \Delta$, $t_0 = 50\%$) on $p_{\text{pa}}(\Delta)$ on weather dataset.

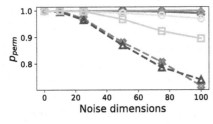

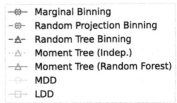

(c) Effect of additional noise dimensions (Gaussian) on $p_{\text{perm}}$ on elec dataset.

**Fig. 2.** Effect of setup parameters on statistical power ($p_{\text{perm}}$) and precision accuracy ($p_{\text{pa}}(\Delta)$) of used estimators.

with Gauss kernel. Notice, that due to the setup no parameter tuning can be performed during a run. In any case we consider all possible combinations of descriptor and dissimilarity measure according to Table 1. For arrival time respecting methods we also consider skipping the last 10% of the reference window during training.

We use the following datasets: "Rotating hyperplane" (RHP) [17], "SEA" [21], "stagger" [9], "RandomRBF" (rbf) [17], "Electricity Market Prices" (elec) [11], "Forest Covertype" (cover) [3] and "Nebraska Weather" (weather) [7]. For labeled datasets, the label is integrated as an additional feature, hence real drift becomes distributional drift. To obtain a sample window with drift we sample two concepts ($S_- \sim p_{W_-} \times U([0, 1/2])$ and $S_+ \sim p_{W_+} \times U([1/2, 1])$) and concatenate them ($S = S_- \cup S_+$); we then permute these samples to obtain a counterpart without drift ($\tilde{S} = \{(x_i, t_{\pi(i)}) \mid i = 1, \cdots, n\}$ where $S = \{(x_i, t_i) \mid i = 1, \cdots, n\}$). In case of real world datasets we obtain two different concepts (before and after drift) by randomly sampling from before and after a given time stamp (we used a two sample test to assure that the obtained batches are indeed different, while the random selection assures no drift within the sub-windows). Analysis of different split points on the same window use the same binning/tree; for other windows (including drift vs. no drift) we create a new binning/tree.

We investigate the effect of windows length, additional noise dimensions, offsets/imbalance (removing oldest 0%, 12.5%, 25% of whole window; drift is at 50%), and displacement of the split point $t = t_0 + \Delta$ (split at $t = 50\%$,

**Table 2.** Empirical upper bounds: $p_{perm}$ (left), $p_{thre}$ (right). Estimators are: Moment Tree (Random Forest), Random Projection Binning, Marginal Binning, Random Tree, MMD, and LDD.

| Dataset | RF | | Rnd Pj | | Marg | | Rnd Tree | | MMD | | LDD | |
|---------|------|------|------|------|------|------|------|------|------|------|------|------|
| SEA     | 0.56 | 0.53 | 0.51 | 0.49 | 0.59 | 0.55 | 0.62 | 0.56 | 0.54 | 0.49 | 0.53 | 0.50 |
| cover   | 1.00 | 0.92 | 0.99 | 0.88 | 1.00 | 0.96 | 0.99 | 0.90 | 1.00 | 0.95 | 0.97 | 0.86 |
| elec    | 1.00 | 1.00 | 1.00 | 1.00 | 1.00 | 1.00 | 1.00 | 1.00 | 1.00 | 0.97 | 1.00 | 1.00 |
| rbf     | 1.00 | 0.99 | 1.00 | 0.99 | 1.00 | 0.93 | 1.00 | 0.96 | 0.98 | 0.90 | 1.00 | 1.00 |
| RHP     | 0.97 | 0.86 | 1.00 | 0.93 | 0.48 | 0.48 | 1.00 | 0.93 | 0.50 | 0.52 | 1.00 | 0.96 |
| stagger | 1.00 | 1.00 | 1.00 | 0.97 | 1.00 | 0.96 | 1.00 | 1.00 | 1.00 | 0.92 | 1.00 | 0.98 |
| Weather | 0.99 | 0.84 | 0.86 | 0.70 | 0.85 | 0.69 | 0.83 | 0.67 | 0.80 | 0.65 | 0.91 | 0.73 |

$53\%, 56\%, 62\%, 75\%$ of the whole window; drift is at $t_0 = 50\%$). We repeat each experiment 1000 times.

*Question 1: "Whether"* We evaluate how well an estimator $\hat{d} = s \circ A$ detects drift. For this purpose, we estimate the probability that the estimation with drift is larger than the one without, i.e. $p_{perm} = \mathbb{P}[\hat{d}(S_-, S_+) > \hat{d}(\tilde{S}_-, \tilde{S}_+)]$, and we evaluate the probability that the estimation with and without drift can be distinguished using a threshold, i.e. $p_{thre} = \sup_b \mathbb{P}[\hat{d}(S_-, S_+) > b \geq \hat{d}(\tilde{S}_-, \tilde{S}_+)]$, where $S_-, S_+$ and $\tilde{S}_-, \tilde{S}_+$ are obtained from $S$ and $\tilde{S}$, respectively, using the same split point $t$. Since $p_{perm}$ is the probability that a random permutation decreases the estimate, it is an upper bound for the statistical power (TP/T) of any normalization. Similarly, $p_{thre}$ is an upper bound for the balanced accuracy ((TP/T + TN/N)/2) of (distribution dependent) threshold-based normalization. Unlike a comparison to 0, this procedure does not suffer from potential biases.

The results for one setup (length 150, split at drift point, no offset, total variation norm and LDD (in case of $k$-NN), where hyper-parameters are selected to optimize $p_{thre}$ in a previous run) are presented in Table 2. An analysis of feature importances shows that the used descriptor has the largest impact on the results, followed by the dataset. Window length and split point displacement are in medium range, the effects of the used dissimilarity, and the offset are marginal.

As can be seen, all methods perform about equally good. Exceptions are Random Trees and Marginal Binning, which are the only methods that are better than random on the SEA dataset (Moment Tree and LDD are also able to solve SEA for larger windows sizes), and Moment Trees (RF) which is the only method that could solve the weather dataset. To show the impact of the window length, we plot the results for different window lengths for the weather dataset (see Fig. 2). As can be seen for most methods, using more samples increases the statistical power. The results on the impact of noise for the Electricity dataset are presented in Fig. 2. Only Moment Trees can handle the noisy version.

**Table 3.** Precision accuracy: $\Delta = 3\%$ (left) and $\Delta = 12\%$ (right). Estimators are: Moment Tree (Random Forest), Random Projection, Marginal Binning, Random Tree, MMD, and LDD.

| Dataset | RF | | Rnd Pj | | Marg | | Rnd Tree | | MMD | | LDD | |
|---------|------|------|------|------|------|------|------|------|------|------|------|------|
| SEA | 0.42 | 0.58 | 0.42 | 0.33 | 0.52 | 0.52 | 0.42 | 0.38 | 0.50 | 0.48 | 0.50 | 0.53 |
| cover | 0.80 | 0.97 | 0.69 | 0.79 | 0.76 | 0.90 | 0.77 | 0.89 | 0.80 | 0.93 | 0.71 | 0.83 |
| elec | 1.00 | 1.00 | 0.94 | 1.00 | 0.94 | 1.00 | 0.95 | 1.00 | 0.80 | 0.90 | 0.95 | 1.00 |
| rbf | 0.96 | 1.00 | 0.93 | 0.99 | 0.81 | 0.91 | 0.89 | 0.97 | 0.81 | 0.90 | 0.94 | 1.00 |
| RHP | 0.73 | 0.93 | 0.75 | 0.90 | 0.48 | 0.48 | 0.76 | 0.90 | 0.50 | 0.47 | 0.75 | 0.92 |
| stagger | 0.93 | 1.00 | 0.84 | 0.94 | 0.71 | 0.82 | 0.94 | 0.99 | 0.82 | 0.91 | 0.78 | 0.94 |
| Weather | 0.68 | 0.93 | 0.52 | 0.53 | 0.56 | 0.60 | 0.54 | 0.54 | 0.62 | 0.67 | 0.64 | 0.74 |

*Question 2: "When"* To evaluate precision of an estimator $\hat{d}$ we empirically evaluate the probability that the estimation at the real split point $t_0$ is larger than the one at the displaced split point $t_0 + \Delta$, i.e. $p_{\mathrm{pa}}(\Delta) = \mathbb{P}[\hat{d}(S_-(t_0), S_+(t_0)) > \hat{d}(S_-(t_0+\Delta), S_+(t_0+\Delta))]$. We refer to this as precision accuracy. Notice, that this corresponds to an ADWIN [2] like split point search. The feature importances provides the same results as before. The results (same setup as Table 2) are shown in Table 3. We also illustrate the behavior for the weather dataset in Fig. 2 for different $\Delta$.

As can be seen the larger the split point displacement ($\Delta$), the higher the precision accuracy. Furthermore, except for two datasets and only with $\Delta = 3\%$, Moment Trees show the best performance. Furthermore, they tend to approach perfect precision accuracy rather quickly.

## 6    Conclusion

In this paper we studied the theoretical and empirical properties of several metrics that are used in drift detection. We also introduced two new metric estimators based on Random Projection Binning and Moment Trees. We found that in most cases the estimation method is more important than the used distance measure, when it comes to drift detection. Also, most datasets can be solved by all methods, when it comes to drift detection. Regarding localizing the drift point, Moment Trees outperform the other methods.

## References

1. Bifet, A., Gama, J.: IoT data stream analytics. Ann. des Télècommun. **75**(9–10) (2020). https://doi.org/10.1007/s12243-020-00811-1
2. Bifet, A., Gavaldà, R.: Learning from time-changing data with adaptive windowing. In: Proceedings of the Seventh SIAM International Conference on Data Mining, April 26–28, 2007, Minneapolis, Minnesota, USA, pp. 443–448 (2007). https://doi.org/10.1137/1.9781611972771.42

3. Blackard, J.A., Dean, D.J., Anderson, C.W.: Covertype data set (1998). https://archive.ics.uci.edu/ml/datasets/Covertype
4. Dasu, T., Krishnan, S., Venkatasubramanian, S., Yi, K.: An information-theoretic approach to detecting changes in multi-dimensional data streams. In: Proceedings of the ACM symposium on the Interface of Statistics, Computing Science, and Applications. Citeseer (2006)
5. Ditzler, G., Polikar, R.: Hellinger distance based drift detection for nonstationary environments. In: 2011 IEEE Symposium on Computational Intelligence in Dynamic and Uncertain Environments, CIDUE 2011, Paris, France, 13 April 2011, pp. 41–48 (2011). https://doi.org/10.1109/CIDUE.2011.5948491
6. Ditzler, G., Roveri, M., Alippi, C., Polikar, R.: Learning in nonstationary environments: a survey. IEEE Comput. Intell. Mag. **10**(4), 12–25 (2015). https://doi.org/10.1109/MCI.2015.2471196
7. Elwell, R., Polikar, R.: Incremental learning of concept drift in nonstationary environments. IEEE Trans. Neural Netw. **22**(10), 1517–1531 (2011)
8. Gama, J.A., Žliobaitė, I., Bifet, A., Pechenizkiy, M., Bouchachia, A.: A survey on concept drift adaptation. ACM Comput. Surv. **46**(4), 44:1–44:37 (2014). https://doi.org/10.1145/2523813
9. Gama, J., Medas, P., Castillo, G., Rodrigues, P.: Learning with drift detection. In: Bazzan, A.L.C., Labidi, S. (eds.) SBIA 2004. LNCS (LNAI), vol. 3171, pp. 286–295. Springer, Heidelberg (2004). https://doi.org/10.1007/978-3-540-28645-5_29
10. Gretton, A., Borgwardt, K., Rasch, M., Schölkopf, B., Smola, A.: A kernel method for the two-sample-problem. Adv. Neural Inf. Process. Syst. **19**, 513–520 (2006)
11. Harries, M., Wales, N.S.: Splice-2 comparative evaluation: electricity pricing (1999)
12. Hinder, F., Artelt, A., Hammer, B.: A probability theoretic approach to drifting data in continuous time domains. CoRR abs/1912.01969 (2019). http://arxiv.org/abs/1912.01969
13. Hinder, F., Artelt, A., Hammer, B.: Towards non-parametric drift detection via dynamic adapting window independence drift detection (DAWIDD). In: International Conference on Machine Learning, pp. 4249–4259. PMLR (2020)
14. Hinder, F., Vaquet, V., Brinkrolf, J., Hammer, B.: Fast non-parametric conditional density estimation using moment trees. In: IEEE Computational Intelligence Magazine. IEEE (2021)
15. Liu, A., Song, Y., Zhang, G., Lu, J.: Regional concept drift detection and density synchronized drift adaptation. In: IJCAI (2017). https://doi.org/10.24963/ijcai.2017/317
16. Lu, J., Liu, A., Dong, F., Gu, F., Gama, J., Zhang, G.: Learning under concept drift: a review. IEEE Trans. Knowl. Data Eng. **31**(12), 2346–2363 (2018)
17. Montiel, J., Read, J., Bifet, A., Abdessalem, T.: Scikit-multiflow: a multi-output streaming framework. J. Mach. Learn. Res. **19**(72), 1–5 (2018). http://jmlr.org/papers/v19/18-251.html
18. Pérez-Cruz, F.: Estimation of information theoretic measures for continuous random variables. In: Koller, D., Schuurmans, D., Bengio, Y., Bottou, L. (eds.) Advances in Neural Information Processing Systems, vol. 21. Curran Associates, Inc. (2009)
19. Qahtan, A.A., Alharbi, B., Wang, S., Zhang, X.: A pca-based change detection framework for multidimensional data streams: change detection in multidimensional data streams. In: Proceedings of the 21th ACM SIGKDD International Conference on Knowledge Discovery and Data Mining, pp. 935–944 (2015). https://doi.org/10.1145/2783258.2783359

20. Rabanser, S., Günnemann, S., Lipton, Z.: Failing loudly: an empirical study of methods for detecting dataset shift. In: Wallach, H., Larochelle, H., Beygelzimer, A., d'Alché-Buc, F., Fox, E., Garnett, R. (eds.) Advances in Neural Information Processing Systems, vol. 32. Curran Associates, Inc. (2019)

21. Street, W.N., Kim, Y.: A streaming ensemble algorithm (SEA) for large-scale classification. In: Proceedings of the Seventh ACM SIGKDD International Conference on Knowledge Discovery and Data Mining, San Francisco, CA, USA, 26–29 August 2001, pp. 377–382 (2001)

22. Tabassum, S., Pereira, F.S.F., Fernandes, S., Gama, J.: Social network analysis: an overview. Wiley interdiscip. Rev. Data Min. Knowl. Discov. 8(5) (2018). https://doi.org/10.1002/widm.1256

23. Webb, G.I., Lee, L.K., Petitjean, F., Goethals, B.: Understanding concept drift. CoRR abs/1704.00362 (2017). http://arxiv.org/abs/1704.00362

# Exploring the Geometry and Topology of Neural Network Loss Landscapes

Stefan Horoi[1,2], Jessie Huang[3], Bastian Rieck[4], Guillaume Lajoie[1,2], Guy Wolf[1,2], and Smita Krishnaswamy[3,5(✉)]

[1] Department of Mathematics and Statistics, Université de Montréal, Montréal, QC, Canada
{stefan.horoi,g.lajoie,guy.wolf}@umontreal.ca
[2] Mila - Quebec Artificial Intelligence Institute, Montréal, QC, Canada
[3] Department of Computer Science, Yale University, New Haven, CT, USA
{jiexi.huang,smita.krishnaswamy}@yale.edu
[4] Institute of AI for Health, Helmholtz Munich, Munich, Germany
bastian.rieck@helmholtz-muenchen.de
[5] Department of Genetics, Yale University, New Haven, CT, USA

**Abstract.** Recent work has established clear links between the generalization performance of trained neural networks and the geometry of their loss landscape near the local minima to which they converge. This suggests that qualitative and quantitative examination of the loss landscape geometry could yield insights about neural network generalization performance during training. To this end, researchers have proposed visualizing the loss landscape through the use of simple dimensionality reduction techniques. However, such visualization methods have been limited by their linear nature and only capture features in one or two dimensions, thus restricting sampling of the loss landscape to lines or planes. Here, we expand and improve upon these in three ways. First, we present a novel "jump and retrain" procedure for sampling relevant portions of the loss landscape. We show that the resulting sampled data holds more meaningful information about the network's ability to generalize. Next, we show that non-linear dimensionality reduction of the jump and retrain trajectories via PHATE, a trajectory and manifold-preserving method, allows us to visualize differences between networks that are generalizing well vs poorly. Finally, we combine PHATE trajectories with a computational homology characterization to quantify trajectory differences.

**Keywords:** Artificial neural network loss landscape · Non-linear dimensionality reduction · Topological data analysis

S. Horoi and J. Huang—Equal contribution.
G. Wolf and S. Krishnaswamy—Equal senior-author contribution.
This work was partially funded by NSERC CGSM & FRQNT B1X scholarships [S.H.]; NSERC Discovery Grant RGPIN-2018-04821, Samsung Research Support [G.L.]; and Canada CIFAR AI Chairs [G.L., G.W.]. The content is solely the responsibility of the authors and does not necessarily represent the views of the funding agencies.

© The Author(s), under exclusive license to Springer Nature Switzerland AG 2022
T. Bouadi et al. (Eds.): IDA 2022, LNCS 13205, pp. 171–184, 2022.
https://doi.org/10.1007/978-3-031-01333-1_14

# 1  Introduction

Artificial neural networks (ANNs) have been successfully used to solve a number of complex tasks in a diverse array of domains. Despite being highly overparameterized for the tasks they solve, and having the capacity to memorize the entire training data, ANNs tend to generalize to unseen data. This is a spectacular feat since their highly non-convex optimization landscape should (theoretically) be a significant obstacle to using these models [2]. Questions such as why ANNs favor generalization over memorization and why they find "good" minima even with intricate loss functions still remain largely unanswered. One promising research direction is to study the geometry of the loss landscape of ANNs. Recent work tried to approach this task by proposing various sampling procedures and linear methods (based on PCA for example) for visualizing loss landscapes and their level curves. In some cases, this approach proved effective in uncovering underlying structures in the loss-landscape and linking them to network characteristics, such as generalization capabilities or structural features [8,15,16,18]. However, these methods have two major drawbacks: (1) they only choose directions that are linear combinations of parameter axes while the loss landscape itself is highly nonlinear, and (2) they choose only one or two among thousands (if not millions) of axes to sample and visualize while ignoring all others.

First, an emerging challenge is how to sample and study such an extremely high dimensional optimization landscape (linear in the number of network parameters) with respect to minimized loss. We posit that one can utilize a manifold structure inherent to relevant connected patches of the loss landscape that are reachable during training processes in order to faithfully visualize the essential characteristics of its "shape". For this, we propose the *jump and retrain* method for sampling trajectories on the low loss manifolds surrounding found minima. The sampled points preserve information pertaining to the generalization capability of the neural network, while maintaining tractability of the visualization.

We then utilize and adapt the PHATE dimensionality reduction method [21], which relies on diffusion-based manifold learning, to visualize these trajectories in low dimensions. In general, visualizations like PHATE are specifically designed to retain and compress as much variability as possible into two dimensions, and thus provide an advantage over previous linear approaches. Our choice of using PHATE over other popular methods, such as tSNE [19] or UMAP [20], is due to its ability to capture both global and local structures of data. In particular, PHATE adequately tracks the continuous training trajectories that are traversed during gradient descent, while other methods tend to shatter them, and thus allows for significantly better visualizations of the manifolds on which these trajectories lie.

Finally, we turn to topological data analysis (TDA) methods to quantify features of the jump and retrain trajectories, and thus characterize the loss-landscape regions surrounding different optima that emerge in networks that generalize well vs poorly. Our approach provides a general view of relevant geometric and topological patterns that emerge in the high-dimensional parameter space, providing insights regarding the properties of ANN training and reflecting on their impact on the loss landscape.

*Contributions:* We present the jump and retrain sampling procedure in Sect. 3.1 and show that the resulting data holds more relevant information about network generalization capabilities than past sampling procedures in Sect. 4.2. We propose a new loss-landscape visualization method based on a variation of PHATE, implemented with cosine distance in Sect. 3.2. Our visualization method is, to our knowledge, different from all other proposed methods for loss-landscape visualization in that it is naturally nonlinear and captures data characteristics from all dimensions. In Sect. 4.3, we show that our method uncovers key geometric patterns characterizing loss-landscape regions surrounding good and bad generalization optima, as well as memorization optima. Finally, we use topological data analysis to characterize the PHATE transformed sampled manifolds and to quantify the differences between them in Sect. 4.4. To our knowledge this is the first time that a combination of data geometry (via PHATE) and topology has been used to analyze the loss landscape of ANNs.

## 2 Preliminaries

### 2.1 PHATE Dimensionality Reduction and Visualization

Given a data matrix $\mathbf{N}$, PHATE first computes the pairwise similarity matrix $\mathbf{A}$ (using a distance function $\phi$ and an $\alpha$-decaying kernel), then row-normalize $\mathbf{A}$ to obtain the diffusion operator $\mathbf{P}$, a row-stochastic Markov transition matrix where $\mathbf{P}_{i,j}$ denotes the probability of moving from the $i$-th to the $j$-th data point in one time step. One of the reasons PHATE excels at capturing global structures in data, especially high-dimensional trajectories and branches, is that it leverages the diffusion operator (also used to construct diffusion maps [5]) by running the implicit Markov chain forward in time. This is accomplished by raising the matrix $\mathbf{P}$ to the power $t$, effectively taking $t$ random walk steps, where $t$ is selected automatically as the knee point of the Von Neumann Entropy of the diffusion operator. To enable dimensionality reduction while retaining diffusion geometry information from the operator, PHATE leverages *information geometry* to define a pairwise *potential distance* as an M-divergence $\mathbf{ID}_{i,j} = \| \log P_{i,:} - \log P_{j,:} \|_2$ between corresponding $t$-step diffusion probability distributions of the two points, which provides a *global context* to each data point. The resulting information distance matrix $\mathbf{ID}$ is finally embedded into a tractable low-dimensional (2D or 3D) space by metric multidimensional scaling (MDS), thereby squeezing the intrinsic geometric information to calculate the final 2D or 3D embeddings of the data. For further details, see Moon et al. [21].

### 2.2 Topological Data Analysis

Topological data analysis (TDA) refers to a set of techniques for understanding complex datasets by means of their topological features, i.e., their connectivity [7]. While TDA is applicable in multiple contexts, seeing increased use in machine learning [10], we focus specifically on the case of graphs. Here, the simplest set of topological features is given by the number of connected components $\beta_0$ and the number of cycles $\beta_1$. Such counts, also known as the *Betti numbers*, are coarse graph descriptors that are invariant under graph isomorphisms. Their expressivity is limited, but can be increased by considering a function $f\colon V \to \mathbb{R}$ on the vertices of a graph $G = (V, E)$ with vertex set $V$ and edge set $E$. Since $V$ has finite cardinality, so does its image $\mathrm{im} f := \{w_1, w_2, \ldots, w_n\}$. Without loss of generality, we assume that $w_1 \leq \cdots \leq w_n$. We write $G_i$ for the subgraph induced by filtering according to $w_i$, such that the vertices of $G_i$ satisfy $V_i := \{v \in V \mid f(v) \leq w_i\}$, and the edges satisfy $E_i := \{(u, v) \in E \mid \max(f(u), f(v)) \leq w_i\}$. The subgraphs $G_i$ satisfy a nesting property, as $G_1 \subseteq G_2 \subseteq \cdots \subseteq G_n$. It is now possible to calculate topological features alongside this *filtration* of graphs, tracking their appearance and disappearance. If a topological feature of dimension $d$ ($d = 0$ for connected components and $d = 1$ for cycles) is created in $G_i$, but destroyed in $G_j$ (for $d = 0$ it might be destroyed because two connected components merge, for instance), we represent this by storing the point $(w_i, w_j)$ in the dimension $d$ *persistence diagram* $\mathcal{D}_{f,d}$ associated to $G$. Persistence diagrams are known to be salient descriptors of graphs and have seen increasing usage in graph classification [12–14,22,26]. Their primary appeal lies in their capability to summarize shape information and the robustness to noise [4] of topological features made them successful shape descriptors in a variety of applications [1,23]. Numerous fixed filtrations have been described for different tasks [13,26], but in our context, a natural choice for $f$ is provided by the *loss function* of the network itself. This will enable us to describe the topology of the loss landscape.

## 3    What Is the "Shape" of the Loss Landscape?

The loss landscape of an ANN can be formulated mathematically as the geometry and topology defined in the high dimensional parameter space $\Theta$ by a loss function $f\colon \Theta \to \mathbb{R}$ that assigns a loss value $f(\theta)$ to every possible parameter vector $\theta$ (e.g., consisting of network weights) based on considered training or validation data. While $f(\theta)$ provides some information for examining and filtering the various configurations of model parameters, the exceedingly high dimensionality of the parameter space (i.e., often in the millions) renders the task of visualizing or analyzing the entire loss-landscape over $\Theta$ virtually impossible. However, since the optimization process considered in this context is guided by the objective of minimizing the loss, we can expect most regions in the high-dimensional $\Theta$ to be of negligible importance, if not unreachable, for the network training dynamics or the viable configurations learned by them. Therefore, the analysis of the loss landscape can focus on regions that are reachable, or reliably traversed, during this optimization process, which we expect would have a much lower intrinsic dimensionality than the ambient dimensions of the entire parameter space.

Our approach to characterizing the "shape" of the loss landscape in such local regions of interest is inspired by the construction of a tangent space of manifolds in intrinsic terms in Riemannian geometry. There, tangent vectors at a given point of interest are defined by aggregating together intrinsic trajectories (on the manifold) traversing through the tangential point. This aggregation, in turn, yields equivalence classes that signify tangential directions, whose span is considered as the tangent space that provides a local intrinsic (typically low-dimensional) coordinate neighborhood in the vicinity of the tangential point. In a similar way, here we propose to leverage trajectories of the network optimization process in order to reveal the intrinsic geometry exposed by them as they flow towards convergence to (local) minima of the loss. The remainder of this section provides a detailed derivation of the three main steps in our approach.

### 3.1    Jump and Retrain Sampling

Gradient-based optimization methods naturally explore low-loss regions in parameter space before finding and settling at a minimum. We hypothesize that keeping track of optimizer trajectories in parameter space is an efficient way of sampling these low-loss manifolds and thus to gather information about the relevant part of the loss regions surrounding minima. This can be seen as an approximation to the Morse–Smale complex [9], a decomposition of $f$ into regions of similar gradient behavior, whose analytical calculation is infeasible given the overall size of $\Theta$. With this in mind we have designed the following "jump and retrain" or J&R sampling procedure. Let $\theta_o$ represent the vector of network parameters at the minimum:

> **for** $seed \in SEEDS$ **do**
> > **for** $step\_size \in STEP\_SIZES$ **do**
> > > Choose a random $v_{seed}$ in $\Theta$ and filter-normalize to obtain $\overline{v}_{seed}$;
> > > Set the ANN parameters to be $\theta_{\text{jump-init}} = \theta_o + step\_size \cdot \overline{v}_{seed}$;
> > > Retrain for $N$ epochs with the original optimizer;
> > > Record parameters $\theta$ and evaluate the loss at each retraining epoch;
> >
> > **end**
>
> **end**

Most of our experiments were conducted with **SEEDS** $= \{0, 1, 2, 3\}$ or $\{0, 1, 2, 3, 4\}$, **STEP_SIZES** $= \{0.25, 0.5, 0.75, 1.0\}$ and $N = 40$ or 50. Given a convolutional neural network with parameters $\theta$ and a random Gaussian direction $v$ with dimensions compatible with $\theta$, $\overline{v}$ is computed as $\overline{v}_{i,j} = \frac{v_{i,j}}{\|v_{i,j}\|}\|\theta_{i,j}\|$, where $v_{i,j}$ represents the $j$th convolutional filter of the $i$th layer of $v$. This filter-wise normalization was presented in [18] as a means to remove the scaling effect present in neural networks using the ReLU non-linearity [6] and allow for meaningful comparisons between the loss landscapes of different ReLU ANNs. Step sizes smaller than 1 were empirically shown to be sufficient to distinguish between smooth regions of the loss landscape surrounding minima that generalize well and regions with dramatic non-convexities surrounding minima that generalize poorly.

## 3.2  PHATE Dimensionality Reduction and Visualization

Since the points sampled with the presented procedure are not simply positioned on a line or a plane, methods that project these points onto a 1D or 2D space are unable to properly visualize all the variation in the data. PHATE has allowed us to bypass the key drawbacks of previously proposed linear visualization methods by (1) Capturing variance in the sampled data from all relevant dimensions and embedding it in a low-dimensional space; and (2) preserving high-dimensional trajectories and global structures of data in ANN parameter space. All modern dimensionality-reduction techniques would have achieved (1) with varying degrees of success. However our proposed cosine-distance PHATE, which uses cosine distance to compute the pairwise similarity matrix $\mathbf{A}$ and to perform MDS, has unique advantages over other state-of the art dimensionality reduction methods to accomplish (2). The use of cosine distance is motivated by the structure of the J&R sampled data and our interest in determining whether or not training trajectories return to the optimum in the same *direction*, as opposed to capturing the *rate* with which they return to the optimum (as would have been measured by the euclidean distance). Training trajectories needing to get around loss-landscape non-convexities would diverge in ANN parameter space, a feature that is captured by the cosine distance even if the size of the training step is the same. In practice, cosine-distance PHATE better preserves the continuity of the training trajectories and the global structure of the data when compared to its euclidean counterpart, resulting in better visualizations. Figure 1 demonstrates the benefits of using cosine PHATE by showing a comparison of multiple such techniques, namely PHATE, PCA, t-SNE [19] and UMAP [20], and how they each embed the data from the J&R sampling (Fig. 1**A**) and an artificial data set having a tree-like structure (Fig. 1**B**) in a 2D space.

While some trajectory-like structure is visible in all low-dimensional embeddings, only PHATE properly captures intra-trajectory variance. PHATE is also the only technique that captures the global relationships between trajectories while t-SNE and UMAP have a tendency to cluster points that are close in parameter space and disregard the global structure of the data. On the artificial data set (Fig. 1**B**), what we observe is that the embeddings of the linear method PCA are highly affected by the noise in the data while t-SNE and UMAP have a tendency of shattering trajectories that should be connected. By accomplishing (1) and (2) PHATE effectively reconstructs the manifold in parameter space from which the jump and retrain data is sampled and allows its embedding in a lower-dimensional space preserving its local and global structure.

## 3.3  Topological Feature Extraction

In order to quantify the shape of the PHATE embeddings, we calculate a set of topological features. To this end, we first compute a kNN graph (with $k = 20$) based on the PHATE diffusion potential distances. Each node of this graph $G$ corresponds to a specific point in parameter space $\theta \in \Theta$ sampled from the loss landscape. We obtain a filtration function from this by assigning each vertex

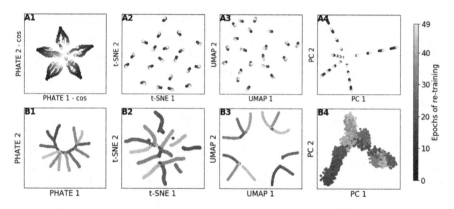

**Fig. 1.** 2D embeddings of the J&R experiment (5 random seeds) results for a WResNet28-2 network using PHATE (**A1**), t-SNE (**A2**), UMAP (**A3**) and the linear method PCA (**A4**). **B:** embeddings of an artificial data set having a fully connected tree-like structure found using the same techniques. We see that PHATE consistently retains continuous trajectory structures while other embeddings (tSNE/UMAP) shatter the structure, or miss important features (PCA) because of uninformative projections to low dimensions.

$\theta$ its corresponding loss value $f(\theta)$. Then we filter over this graph by slowly increasing the loss threshold $t$, which effectively reveals increasingly larger parts of the graph and creates a filtration as described in Sect. 2.2. From this filtration we obtain a set of persistence diagrams $\mathcal{D}_0$, $\mathcal{D}_1$ summarizing the topological features (respectively connected components and cycles) of the respective embedding (we omit the index $f$ for simplicity). As a powerful summary statistic, we calculate the *total persistence* [4] of a persistence diagram $\mathcal{D}$, i.e., $\mathrm{pers}(\mathcal{D}) := \sum_{(c,d) \in \mathcal{D}} |d - c|^2$. $\mathrm{pers}(\cdot)$ serves as a complexity measure that enables us to compare different embeddings. This measure has the advantage that it is invariant with respect to rotations of the embedding. Moreover, it satisfies robustness properties, meaning that it will change continuously under a continuous perturbation of the input filtration. If two loss functions $f$ and $f'$ are *close* (in the Hausdorff sense), their corresponding total persistence values will be close as well [4], making this value a useful summary statistic.

## 4    Geometric and Topological Reflection on ANN Training and Generalization

### 4.1    Experimental Setup

In order to assess the effectiveness of our loss landscape visualizations and characterizations, we trained wide ResNets (WResNets) [24] of varied sizes with depth $\in \{10, 16, 22\}$, width $\in \{1, 2\}$ on the CIFAR10 image classification task [17] from initialization to optimum. The networks were trained with a combination of the following hyperparameters: batch size $\in \{32, 128, 512\}$, weight decay

$\in \{0, 0.0001, 0.001\}$ and either with or without data augmentation (random horizontal flips and crops). Each of the 108 WResNets were initialized identically and trained for 200 epochs using SGD with 0.9 momentum and a learning rate with initial value of 0.1 followed by step decay by a factor of 10 at epochs 100, 150 and 185.

Utilizing data augmentation and weight decay has allowed us to find "good optima" that generalize better, increasing test accuracy from around ~85% (for "bad optima" trained without d.a. and w.d.) to ~95%. We also trained a WResNet28-2 network for memorization by completely randomizing the labels of the training data. This modification was presented in [25] to show that neural networks have the ability to completely memorize the training data sets.

### 4.2   Jump and Retrain Sampling Captures Generalization and Training Characteristics

Past work has shown that networks with different generalization capabilities tend to have optima surrounded by regions of distinct geometrical characteristics [3,11,15,16,18]. Regularization techniques, such as weight decay and data augmentation, are believed to play a role in this difference in geometries [3,15]. Inspired by past results, we formulate the following classification tasks to evaluate loss landscape sampling methods and see if the sampled data holds information about the networks ability to generalize and the geometry of the loss landscape. We used the sampled loss and accuracy values as features and we separated the trained WResNet models into 5 (almost) equally-sized "generalization" classes according to the value of the test loss at optimum. The ~20% of networks with the lowest test losses at optimum were assigned to class 1, and so on. We then trained 11 simple classifiers to predict the generalization class of each network with training losses and accuracy features. All results were obtained from 10-fold cross validation. It is important to note that the classifiers were not tuned to favor any of the sampling procedures. Two similar classification tasks were designed to predict weight decay and whether or not data augmentation was used.

To evaluate the effectiveness of the jump and retrain sampling, we compared it to two other sampling procedures. We refer to the first as *grid sampling*, and it is directly inspired by the 1D or 2D linear interpolations used in past visualization methods [8,15,18]. Here, we randomly choose 3 vectors starting from the optimum ($\theta_o$) and construct a 3D grid using the 3 vectors as basis. The loss and accuracy on the training set is then evaluated at all points on the grid. The second comparison sampling procedure, that we call *naive sampling*, evaluates the loss in random directions ($\theta_i$) centered at the optimum $\theta_0$, and multiple step sizes $c$; i.e. evaluate at $\theta_o + c\theta_i$. This method tests whether using more directions and step sizes when sampling, without the grid-like structure, is more informative since it explores a greater number of directions in parameter

**Table 1.** Mean and standard error (%) of the 11 classifiers accuracies on the 5 class generalization, weight decay and data aug. classification tasks with different features.

| Features | 5 class gen. | Weight decay | Data augmentation |
|---|---|---|---|
| Theoretical random (1/#classes) | 20.0 | 33.3 | 50.0 |
| Randomized J&R retrain loss and accuracy values | 20.7 ± 1.1 | 38.9 ± 1.5 | 52.7 ± 1.9 |
| Grid sampling, train loss and accuracy values | 30.1 ± 2.7 | 51.1 ± 2.9 | 62.3 ± 5.1 |
| Naive sampling, train loss and accuracy values | 31.8 ± 4.0 | 55.7 ± 3.9 | 67.6 ± 5.2 |
| J&R sampling, retrain loss and accuracy values | **39.2** ±4.3 | **58.2** ±3.6 | **72.1** ±5.4 |

space. All methods considered, including J&R, sample 640 points from the loss landscape excluding the optimum itself. We applied the filter-wise normalization presented in [18] when obtaining random directions. As a control experiment, we trained the same classifiers on scrambled versions of the best performing features, making sure classifiers were not overfitting the data and evaluating the impact of feature distributions alone. The results are shown in Table 1.

Using the loss and accuracy values sampled with the J&R procedure as features allows the classifiers to achieve mean accuracies of 39.2%, 58.2% and 72.1% on the generalization, weight decay and data augmentation classifications tasks respectively. This is significantly higher than the mean classification accuracies reached using the data sampled with the other two methods. We confirmed the validity of the classification accuracy with J&R data with permutation tests where the accuracy is essentially the same as random. Indeed, our results indicate that connected patches of the low-loss manifold surrounding the optima, which are found with the jump and retrain procedure, hold more information about the region's geometry and the network's ability to generalize at that optimum than the data sampled with non-dynamical methods. Furthermore, the success of the J&R sampled data on the weight decay and data augmentation classification tasks shows that our sampling method captures information not only about generalization but also about the training procedure. The set of J&R sampled loss and accuracy values seem to have distinct characteristics depending on the training procedure used to reach the minima and whether or not regularization methods were used and to what extent. This helps support the idea that a dynamical sampling of the loss landscape, which mimics the behavior of optimization procedures, is more informative than static sampling methods.

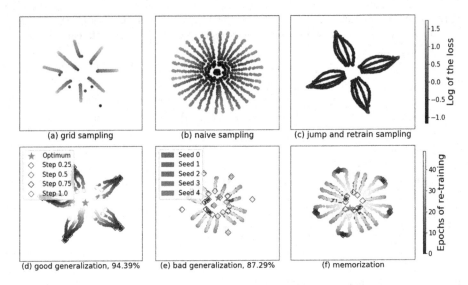

Fig. 2. **Top row:** PHATE embeddings of the data generated with the three sampling procedures colored by loss in log scale. The rigidity of the grid and naive sampling methods makes visualizations less informative. The J&R sampling successfully samples the low-loss manifolds surrounding minima. **Bottom row:** PHATE embeddings comparison between good, bad and memorization minumum. The $\theta_{\mathrm{jump\text{-}init}}$ points are marked by diamonds of colors corresponding to *step_size* and trajectories are colored by *seed* with descending hue, i.e. the color gets whiter as retraining progresses. In contrast to more continuous trajectories returning to near the optimum in the good generalization case, bad generalization and memorization display more random patterns where weights move out before moving back, often switching direction during retraining.

### 4.3    Generalization Indicated by Visual Patterns from Loss Landscape Regions Around Optima

PHATE visualization of the data sampled with the J&R procedure as in Fig. 2(c) clearly demonstrate the trajectories and the low-loss manifold surrounding the found optima that was actually traversed during training. It is more informative that the visualization of data from the other sampling procedures (Fig. 2(a, b)). Also, although all networks achieved ∼0 loss on their respective training sets and only a ∼7% difference in their test set accuracies, Fig. 2(d, f) reveal stark differences between network configurations that memorize (or overfit) versus ones that generalize. The good generalization minimum has a distinctive star shaped pattern. This indicates that even when points are thrown away from the minima they return to it immediately without traveling outward. Thus the minima seems to serve as an effective attractor to which trajectories repeatedly return.

In case of bad minimum, the trajectories start off near the middle of the plot (darker points in the middle of Fig. 2e) but, during the retraining, they diverge toward the edges before occasionally coming back towards the middle of the plot. This outward movement is in stark contrast with the consistent retraining trajectories surrounding the good generalization minimum, which immediately return to the valley. In this sense the minima are not stable and perturbations of the parameters cause networks to escape this minima. The "memorization" minimum plot (Fig. 2f) looks similar to the bad generalization plot, with trajectories that go outward at small step sizes of the jump. However, curiously at larger step sizes, the trajectories seem to return without going outward first, but they do not return immediately, they show some lateral movement, potentially indicating bumpiness in the landscape that they are avoiding.

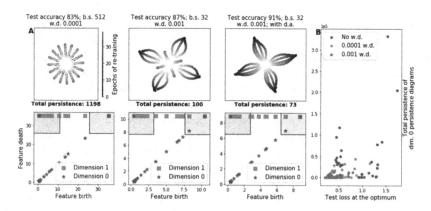

**Fig. 3. A, top row:** 2D PHATE embeddings of the data sampled with the jump and retrain procedure surrounding minima reached by four WResNet16-2 with the same initialization but trained in different ways and thus reaching different accuracies on the test set. **A, bottom row:** Persistence diagrams of the loss-level filtration computed from the respective PHATE diffusion potentials. The total persistence associated with each optima/persistence diagram (dim. 0) is written in bold. Both PHATE and the topological features of the loss landscape seem to differentiate these four networks which have very different generalization capabilities. **B:** Total persistence of dimension 0 computed from the jump & retrain data for each network w.r.t. the test loss at optimum. Colors indicate the value of the weight decay used during training.

### 4.4 Generalization May Be Related to Low Topological Activity in Near-Optimum Regions

PHATE has allowed us to generate low dimensional representations of the low-loss manifolds sampled through the jump and retrain procedure. Here, topological data analysis enables us to quantify the topological features of these manifolds and thus characterize the loss landscape regions surrounding different optima. In Fig. 3A we show the PHATE visualizations of the jump and retrain data sampled around different optima of a WResNet16-2 network and the corresponding dimension 0 and 1 persistence diagrams. From the PHATE visualizations alone it is clear that the sampled manifold have different structures. In fact, the persistence diagrams confirm that these manifolds also have different topological features. In particular, optima that generalize poorly seem to be surrounded by manifolds with more topological activity, the two persistence diagrams on the left having more high-persistence points (higher density of points in the red rectangles of Fig. 3**A**). Conversely, networks that generalize well have both zero and one dimensional topological features emerging later in the loss threshold (green rectangles).

In order to verify this observation in a more general case, we also computed the *total persistence* (see Sect. 3.3) of the persistence diagrams corresponding to each one of the 108 trained WResNets. In Fig. 3**B** we plot these values as functions of the test loss at optimum and color the points according to the value of weight decay used during training to reach those points. The first thing we observe is that optima surrounded by regions of high topological activity tend to have a higher loss value at the optima, while low-loss optima have a lower associated total persistence. This further confirms the idea that good generalization optima are surrounded by relatively flat loss-landscape regions while bad generalization optima tend to be situated in regions with many non-convexities. Furthermore we observe that optima found with the most aggressive weight decay (namely 0.001) are surrounded by regions of relatively low topological activity while optima reached without the use of weight decay are associated with the highest levels of total persistence. These results seem to suggest that the use of weight decay, an efficient regularization method, allows optimizers to find minima on low-loss manifolds with low-persistence topological features. Past results have linked the use of regularization techniques to finding good generalization minima surrounded by flat regions, i.e. regions of low geometrical activity. We have expanded on these results by showing that the topological activity in those regions is also relatively low when compared to regions surrounding optima found without regularization.

## 5    Discussion and Conclusion

We propose a novel approach to dynamically sample the loss landscapes of deep learning models which takes theoretical inspiration from the fields of Riemannian geometry and dynamical systems. Our sampling method efficiently samples points from the low-loss manifolds surrounding minima found through gradient descent. The resulting sampled data holds more information than past loss landscape sampling methods about the geometry of the loss landscape, the network ability to generalize at the optimum and the training procedure and regularization used to reach that optimum. We then present a new loss landscape visualization method based on the state-of-the-art PHATE dimensionality reduction method, which is able to reconstruct the high-dimensional trajectories sampled in two dimensional representations. Our approach enables geometric exploration of the sampled manifolds and regions surrounding generalization and memorization optima, found via ANN training, to provide insight into generalization capabilities and training of the network. Finally, topological data analysis enables us to characterize these regions through the computation of their topological features. We found that weight decay, a powerful regularization technique, allows ANN optimizers to find minima in regions of lower topological activity. An interesting research direction would be to try to apply dimensionality reduction techniques that better take into account the time dependency of the data. We expect in future work our sampling, visualization and topological characterization approaches to enable more methodical paradigms for the development of ANNs that generalize better, train faster, and to provide fundamental understanding of their capabilities.

# References

1. Amézquita, E.J., Quigley, M.Y., Ophelders, T., Munch, E., Chitwood, D.H.: The shape of things to come: topological data analysis and biology, from molecules to organisms. Dev. Dyn. **249**(7), 816–833 (2020)
2. Blum, A.L., Rivest, R.L.: Training a 3-node neural network is NP-complete. In: Hanson, S.J., Remmele, W., Rivest, R.L. (eds.) Machine Learning: From Theory to Applications. LNCS, vol. 661, pp. 9–28. Springer, Heidelberg (1993). https://doi.org/10.1007/3-540-56483-7_20
3. Chaudhari, P., et al.: Entropy-SGD: biasing gradient descent into wide valleys. In: 5th International Conference on Learning Representations (ICLR) (2017)
4. Cohen-Steiner, D., Edelsbrunner, H., Harer, J.: Stability of persistence diagrams. Discrete Comput. Geom. **37**(1), 103–120 (2007)
5. Coifman, R.R., Lafon, S.: Diffusion maps. Appl. Comput. Harmon. Anal. **21**(1), 5–30 (2006)
6. Dinh, L., Pascanu, R., Bengio, S., Bengio, Y.: Sharp minima can generalize for deep nets. In: Precup, D., Teh, Y.W. (eds.) Proceedings of the 34th International Conference on Machine Learning. Proceedings of Machine Learning Research, vol. 70, pp. 1019–1028 (2017)
7. Edelsbrunner, H., Harer, J.: Computational Topology: An Introduction. American Mathematical Society, Providence (2010)
8. Goodfellow, I.J., Vinyals, O., Saxe, A.M.: Qualitatively characterizing neural network optimization problems. arXiv preprint arXiv:1412.6544 (2014)
9. Gyulassy, A., Bremer, P.T., Hamann, B., Pascucci, V.: A practical approach to Morse-Smale complex computation: scalability and generality. IEEE Trans. Vis. Comput. Graph. **14**(6), 1619–1626 (2008)
10. Hensel, F., Moor, M., Rieck, B.: A survey of topological machine learning methods. Front. Artif. Intell. **4**, 52 (2021)
11. Hochreiter, S., Schmidhuber, J.: Flat minima. Neural Comput. **9**(1), 1–42 (1997)
12. Hofer, C., Kwitt, R., Niethammer, M., Uhl, A.: Deep learning with topological signatures. In: Advances in Neural Information Processing Systems (NeurIPS), vol. 30, pp. 1634–1644. Curran Associates, Inc. (2017)
13. Hofer, C.D., Graf, F., Rieck, B., Niethammer, M., Kwitt, R.: Graph filtration learning. In: Proceedings of the 37th International Conference on Machine Learning. Proceedings of Machine Learning Research, vol. 119, pp. 4314–4323 (2020)

14. Horn, M., De Brouwer, E., Moor, M., Moreau, Y., Rieck, B., Borgwardt, K.: Topological graph neural networks. In: 10th International Conference on Learning Representations (ICLR) (2022)

15. Im, D.J., Tao, M., Branson, K.: An empirical analysis of the optimization of deep network loss surfaces. arXiv preprint arXiv:1612.04010 (2016)

16. Keskar, N.S., Mudigere, D., Nocedal, J., Smelyanskiy, M., Tang, P.T.P.: On large-batch training for deep learning: generalization gap and sharp minima. In: 5th International Conference on Learning Representations (ICLR) (2017)

17. Krizhevsky, A., Hinton, G., et al.: Learning multiple layers of features from tiny images. Technical report, MIT & NYU (2009)

18. Li, H., Xu, Z., Taylor, G., Studer, C., Goldstein, T.: Visualizing the loss landscape of neural nets. In: Advances in Neural Information Processing Systems (NeurIPS), vol. 31, pp. 6389–6399. Curran Associates, Inc. (2018)

19. van der Maaten, L., Hinton, G.: Visualizing data using t-SNE. J. Mach. Learn. Res. **9**, 2579–2605 (2008)

20. McInnes, L., Healy, J., Saul, N., Grossberger, L.: UMAP: uniform manifold approximation and projection. J. Open Sour. Softw. **3**(29) (2018)

21. Moon, K.R., et al.: Visualizing structure and transitions in high-dimensional biological data. Nat. Biotechnol. **37**(12), 1482–1492 (2019)

22. Rieck, B., Bock, C., Borgwardt, K.: A persistent Weisfeiler-Lehman procedure for graph classification. In: Proceedings of the 36th International Conference on Machine Learning. Proceedings of Machine Learning Research, vol. 97, pp. 5448–5458 (2019)

23. Rieck, B., et al.: Uncovering the topology of time-varying fMRI data using cubical persistence. In: Advances in Neural Information Processing Systems (NeurIPS), vol. 33, pp. 6900–6912. Curran Associates, Inc. (2020)

24. Zagoruyko, S., Komodakis, N.: Wide residual networks. In: Richard, C. Wilson, E.R.H., Smith, W.A.P. (eds.) Proceedings of the British Machine Vision Conference (BMVC), pp. 87.1-87.12. BMVA Press (2016)

25. Zhang, C., Bengio, S., Hardt, M., Recht, B., Vinyals, O.: Understanding deep learning requires rethinking generalization. In: 5th International Conference on Learning Representations (ICLR) (2017)

26. Zhao, Q., Wang, Y.: Learning metrics for persistence-based summaries and applications for graph classification. In: Advances in Neural Information Processing Systems (NeurIPS), vol. 32, pp. 9855–9866. Curran Associates, Inc. (2019)

# Selecting Outstanding Patterns Based on Their Neighbourhood

Etienne Lehembre[1]([✉])(iD), Ronan Bureau[2](iD), Bruno Cremilleux[1](iD),
Bertrand Cuissart[1](iD), Jean-Luc Lamotte[2,3](iD), Alban Lepailleur[2](iD),
Abdelkader Ouali[1](iD), and Albrecht Zimmermann[1](iD)

[1] GREYC, CNRS UMR 6072, UNICAEN, Normandy Univ. Caen, Caen, France
{etienne.lehembre,bruno.cremilleux,bertrand.cuissart,abdelkader.ouali,
albrecht.zimmermann}@unicaen.fr
[2] CERMN, EA 4258 FR CNRS 3038 INC3M SF 4206 ICORE, UNICAEN,
Normandy Univ. Caen, Caen, France
{ronan.bureau,jean-Luc.lamotte,alban.lepailleur}@unicaen.fr
[3] Sorbonne Université, UFR 919, 4 place Jussieun, 75252 Paris cedex 05, France

**Abstract.** The purpose of pattern mining is to help experts understand
their data. Following the assumption that an analyst expects neighbouring patterns to show similar behavior, we investigate the interestingness
of a pattern given its neighborhood. We define a new way of selecting
*outstanding* patterns, based on an order relation between patterns and
a quality score. An outstanding pattern shows only small syntactic variations compared to its neighbors but deviates strongly in quality. Using
several supervised quality measures, we show experimentally that only
very few patterns turn out to be outstanding. We also illustrate our
approach with patterns mined from molecular data.

**Keywords:** Pattern selection · Structured pattern mining · Local
deviation

## 1 Introduction

The purpose of data mining is to help experts to analyze their data by providing valuable results. When those results come in the form of patterns, whether
conjunctions of attributes or items, sequences, trees, or graphs, a recurring problem is that there are simply too many of them for a human to work through.
Once this problem was recognized, research first focused on reducing the output through the notion of *condensed representations* [11], a plethora of *quality
measures* [13], and *pattern set mining* techniques [7] were designed, all of which
fall short, however. Even when creating condensed representations, there are
typically still hundreds or even thousands of patterns left, as is the case no matter which quality measure one uses. In addition, the latter lead to the question
which measure to use for a given task. Pattern set mining, finally, works well
enough when the goal is to create a set of non-redundant patterns to be used as

© The Author(s), under exclusive license to Springer Nature Switzerland AG 2022
T. Bouadi et al. (Eds.): IDA 2022, LNCS 13205, pp. 185–198, 2022.
https://doi.org/10.1007/978-3-031-01333-1_15

descriptors in downstream tasks such as classification or clustering, but less so when it comes to offering an expert an interpretable result set.

Here, we start from the assumption that an analyst expects that patterns which are neighbors in the pattern space show similar behavior. Hence, a pattern showing different behavior from what one expects given similar patterns deserves a second look. To find these patterns, which we will call *outstanding* going forward, we use a Hasse Diagram (HD), a directed acyclic graph (DAG), as a representation of the pattern space. This DAG encodes a partial order between patterns whose interestingness is quantified by a quality measure. Patterns that are scored very differently than the average of neighboring patterns are considered *outstanding*.

The main contribution of the paper is a new way of selecting outstanding patterns, given an order relation between patterns, and a quality measure on patterns. We formulate our idea in general terms since it can be applied for any pattern language (e.g., items, sequences, graphs). With items, we illustrate our approach by using the lattice of formal concepts derived from data as the encoding HD. We define the notion of a *selector*, a function that outputs the set of outstanding patterns given a HD and a quality measure. Outstanding patterns will then be those that show only small syntactic variations compared to their neighbors but deviate strongly in quality. Notably, this deviation is not necessarily positive: a pattern might be outstanding because it correlates much more weakly with a class label, for instance, than its neighbors. Using several supervised quality measures, we show experimentally that only very few patterns turn out to be outstanding and that the number varies depending on the measure. Our contribution is an outgrowth of the concept of activity cliffs [12] on molecular data, which define a noticeable modification of the biological activity for a small modification of the chemical structure. We therefore also illustrate our method on using patterns mined from molecular data, which are the main focus of our application interest.

The paper is organized as follows. In the next section, we discuss the literature related to our problem setting and proposal. In Sect. 3, we introduce necessary background knowledge. In Sect. 4, we present the selector. In Sect. 5, we report experimental results on transactional data derived from UCI data sets and on molecular data and discuss them. We conclude in Sect. 6.

## 2   Related Work

Since the introduction of constraint-based pattern mining, an on-going theme has been how to help the experts identify the most valuable patterns from result sets containing thousands or even millions of them. A well established solution is to find a condensed representation of the patterns such as closed [11, 17] or free patterns [3], i.e., maximal or minimal patterns from the support-based equivalence classes. Since real data are often noisy, [3] proposed error-tolerant variants.

Another direction is to focus on the best patterns according to quality measures [13]. The survey [15] divides measures in two categories: absolute measures and advanced ones. Advanced measures are based on statistical models (independence model, partition models, MaxEnt models) having different complexities. However, there are numerous measures and it remains difficult to clearly identify the advantages and limitations of each one. The quality of a selected pattern can be assessed via syntactically linked patterns during computation [4], somewhat similar to our proposal.

Recent research has highlighted the benefits of the *unexpectedness* of a pattern when contrasted with given information depending either on the data or on prior knowledge of the analyst [2]. For instance, by sampling patterns fulfilling data-independent constraints under assumptions about the symbol distribution (i.e. null models), the authors of [1] derive a model of background noise, and identify thresholds expected to lead to interesting results, i.e. results that diverge from the expected support derived from super- and sub-patterns. Another approach combines sampling and isotonic regression in order to arrive at pattern frequency spectrum for frequent itemset mining [14]. By comparing those thresholds to ones derived from data where all items are independent, one can identify thresholds or which the result set is expected to contain interesting patterns. Self-sufficient itemsets, finally, are itemsets the support of which cannot be predicted from their sub-sets or super-sets [16]. However, these approach are limited to itemset data. Our method differs in that we do not make assumptions about syntactic relationships between patterns. In addition, we do not make an independence assumption w.r.t. pattern elements.

Also closely related to our work, in the context of web queries modeled according to the setting of the Formal Concept Analysis, [5] uses the siblings of a node to define the interestingness of a new query. However, the method does not take into account the whole set of siblings and it is linked to frequencies observed in the extents and intents of the concepts whereas our approach can use any quality measure defined on patterns.

## 3    Background

As usual in the pattern mining paradigm, let us consider $\mathcal{D}$ a dataset, $\mathcal{L}$ a pattern language and $\preceq$ a partial order relation on the patterns in $\mathcal{L}$. The support of a pattern $p$, $Supp(p)$, is the number of transactions containing $p$. The pattern space can be modelled by its Hasse diagram, a DAG whose set of vertices maps the set of patterns and whose edges depict the order relation: there is an edge $(p, q)$ from a pattern $p$ to a pattern $q$ if $p \preceq q$ and if there is no other pattern $r$ between $p$ and $q$ ($p \preceq r$ and $r \preceq q$). From an edge $(p, q)$, we say that $p$ is a *parent* of $q$, that $q$ is a *child* of $p$. The *siblings* of a pattern is the set of patterns that share a common parent with it. Figure 1 depicts an example of these relationships: the siblings of the pattern $S$ (in red) are $S_i$ (in purple), the parents of $S$ are $P_i$ (in blue).

In the itemset setting, $\mathcal{D}$ is a set of transactions, each transaction containing one or more distinct literals called items $I$. A pattern $X$ is an element of $2^I$. The order relation on the patterns is the usual inclusion relation $\subseteq$ . In the itemset setting and considering closed itemsets [11], the Hasse diagram is then a Galois lattice [6].

Many quality measures have been described in the literature [13,15] and the interestingness of a pattern will be quantified by a measure $f : \mathcal{L} \times \mathcal{D} \mapsto \mathbb{R}$.

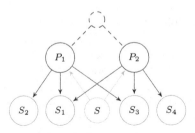

**Fig. 1.** Retrieving siblings (purple/$S_i$ and red/$S$) from a source vertex (red) and its parents (blue/$P_i$). (Color figure online)

## 4   Outstanding Pattern Selector: How to Exploit Siblings

To select outstanding patterns, the method is based on the principle that an analyst expects patterns that are neighbors in the pattern space to show similar behavior. Therefore a pattern showing different behavior from its neighbors according to a quality measure $f$ deserves attention. The sibling patterns being structurally close, their quality should be similar. If a pattern is scored differently from its siblings, it is highly interesting as a outstanding sibling. Thus, we seek for local variations of interestingness. This phenomenon is not captured when $f$ is applied to each pattern individually, as is usual in the frequent or association pattern setting. Concretely, we say that a pattern $X$ is *outstanding* when its quality deviates from the mean quality of its siblings $\mathcal{S}(X)$. The *sibling mean* $\mu(\mathcal{S}(X), \mathcal{D})$ is:

$$\mu(\mathcal{S}(X), \mathcal{D}) = \frac{\sum\limits_{s \in \mathcal{S}(X)} f(s, \mathcal{D})}{|\mathcal{S}(X)|}$$

Then $\mu(\mathcal{S}(X), \mathcal{D})$ is compared to the standard deviation of the siblings:

$$\sigma(\mathcal{S}(X), \mathcal{D}) = \sqrt{\frac{\sum_{s \in \mathcal{S}(X)} (f(s, \mathcal{D}) - \mu(\mathcal{S}(X), \mathcal{D}))^2}{|\mathcal{S}(X)|}}$$

The selector is defined as:

$$OPS(\mathcal{L}, f, \mathcal{D}, \delta) = \{X \in \mathcal{L} : |f(X, \mathcal{D}) - \mu(\mathcal{S}(X), \mathcal{D})| \geq \delta * \sigma(\mathcal{S}(X), \mathcal{D})\}$$

Thus, $X$ is outstanding if its quality deviates at least $\delta$ standard deviations from the mean of the qualities of its siblings, $\delta$ being a user-supplied parameter. We consider the quality measure as a random variable, which distribution varies locally, while staying normally distributed around a local mean. Moreover, the behavior of the quality measure will impact the selection. A homogeneous quality measure will lead the selector to select a few chosen ones while an heterogeneous quality measure will produce more outliers.

One of the appeals of using the standard deviation instead of a classic threshold is that the selector adjusts to its environment: if the siblings of a pattern are all relatively close to a particular support value, a small increase over this value can be interesting. Similarly, take the example of the *growth rate* [8] as the quality measure $f$. Let us assume furthermore that $\mathcal{D}$ is partitioned into two classes, and most of the siblings are *Jumping Emerging Pattern* (JEP) [8,9], i.e. patterns that have a support of zero in the negative class. JEPs have a tendency to overfit; our selector, on the other hand, keeps a JEP only if it indicates a local deviation. Moreover, it can select interesting patterns that are not JEP.

In practice, as shown in the next section, the number of outstanding patterns is small, allowing a human domain expert to manually inspect them.

## 5  Experiments

In this section, we show experimental results illustrating the reduction in patterns, as well as the behavior of four quality measures. In the next section, we provide results on itemset data, and in Sect. 5.3 on graph data representing molecules. We use our experiments to answer several questions:

- Does selecting outstanding patterns reduce the size of the result set significantly?
- Does changing the quality measure change how many patterns are outstanding?
- Can outstanding patterns be easily characterized in terms of the score they receive from an interestingness measure?
- Do outstanding patterns from self-sufficient itemsets, another type of pattern that takes itemsets' neighborhoods into account, albeit syntactic ones?

### 5.1  Itemset Data

The data we used are itemset data derived from UCI data sets, which we downloaded from the CP4IM repository[1]. The data have been binarized by the maintainers of the repository, the majority class named positive class, and minority classes merged into a single negative class.

We performed closed frequent set mining with minimum support thresholds (denoted by $\theta$) of 10%, 15%, and 20%. In the resulting graph $G(\mathcal{V}, \mathcal{E})$ each vertex

---

[1] https://dtai.cs.kuleuven.be/CP4IM/datasets/.

**Table 1.** Characteristics for selected UCI datasets and their number of self-sufficient itemsets.

| Data set | Mushroom | Primary-tumor | Soybean | Splice-1 |
|---|---|---|---|---|
| Transactions | 8124 | 336 | 630 | 3190 |
| Items | 119 | 31 | 50 | 287 |
| Density | 18% | 48% | 32% | 21% |
| Self-sufficient itemsets for $\theta = 10\%/15\%/20\%$ | 69 69/68/53 | 16 13/11/8 | 55 49/33/30 | 38 30/9/3 |
| Data set | tic-tac-toe | vote | zoo-1 | |
| Transactions | 958 | 435 | 101 | |
| Items | 27 | 48 | 36 | |
| Density | 33% | 33% | 44% | |
| Self-sufficient itemsets for $\theta = 10\%/15\%/20\%$ | 24 24/24/0 | 39 39/39/39 | 64 62/60/48 | |

is labeled with a closed itemset. We tested four quality measures: $\chi^2$, confidence, normalized Growth Rate (NGR)[2]:

$$\begin{cases} NGR(X, \mathcal{D}) = \quad 1.0 \quad & if \ GR(X, \mathcal{D}) = \infty \\ NGR(X, \mathcal{D}) = \frac{GR(X,\mathcal{D})}{1+GR(X,\mathcal{D})} \quad & otherwise \end{cases}$$

and Weighted Relative Accuracy (WRAcc). For the latter three, we chose the positive class as target. For the OPS threshold, we chose $\delta = 2$ since 95% of all values of a normal distribution fall into the interval $[\mu - 2 \cdot \sigma, \mu + 2 \cdot \sigma]$.

As Fig. 2 shows, only very few itemsets are outstanding compared to their siblings, with at most 3.052% selected by confidence and NGR on the *splice* data set for the 10% minimum support threshold. Notably, this is in addition to the reduction achieved by mining closed itemsets. We take this as evidence that selecting outstanding patterns results in small enough result sets that domain experts could inspect them (and their neighborhoods) manually to gain deeper insight into the underlying phenomena. We can also compare the behavior under different support thresholds, i.e. the results for a single data set and a single measure, and for different quality measures, i.e. the results in a single line.

While increasing the support threshold mostly reduces the number of outstanding patterns as well, this is not always the case, as can be seen for the *zoo-1* data set, for instance. Using confidence or GR as a quality measure leads to fewer outstanding patterns than using $\chi^2$ and WRAcc does, with the exception of the *splice-1* (10%) and *vote* (10%, 15%) data sets. A particularly remarkable data set is the *tic-tac-toe* one where not a single pattern stands out.

---

[2] We normalize the growth rate because the unnormalized growth rate can have $\infty$ as a value, which prevents the calculation of mean and standard deviation.

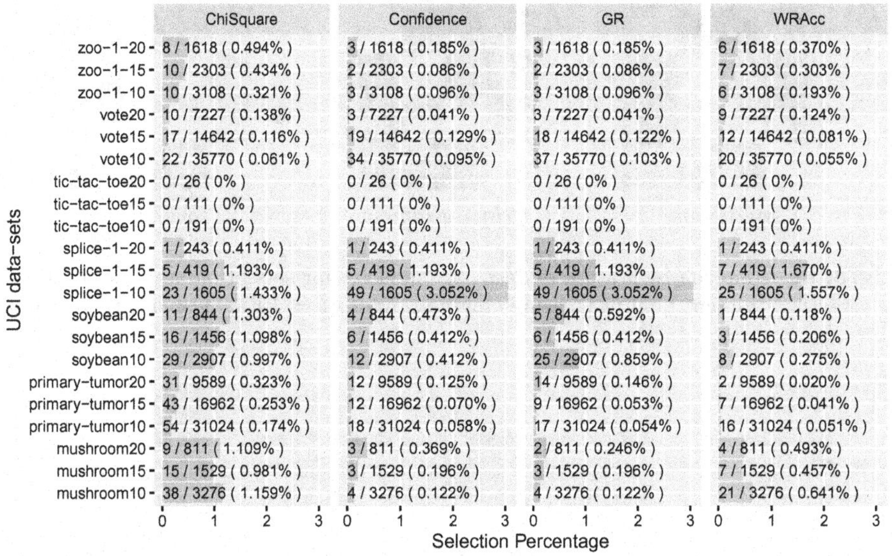

| UCI data-sets | ChiSquare | Confidence | GR | WRAcc |
|---|---|---|---|---|
| zoo-1-20 | 8 / 1618 ( 0.494% ) | 3 / 1618 ( 0.185% ) | 3 / 1618 ( 0.185% ) | 6 / 1618 ( 0.370% ) |
| zoo-1-15 | 10 / 2303 ( 0.434% ) | 2 / 2303 ( 0.086% ) | 2 / 2303 ( 0.086% ) | 7 / 2303 ( 0.303% ) |
| zoo-1-10 | 10 / 3108 ( 0.321% ) | 3 / 3108 ( 0.096% ) | 3 / 3108 ( 0.096% ) | 6 / 3108 ( 0.193% ) |
| vote20 | 10 / 7227 ( 0.138% ) | 3 / 7227 ( 0.041% ) | 3 / 7227 ( 0.041% ) | 9 / 7227 ( 0.124% ) |
| vote15 | 17 / 14642 ( 0.116% ) | 19 / 14642 ( 0.129% ) | 18 / 14642 ( 0.122% ) | 12 / 14642 ( 0.081% ) |
| vote10 | 22 / 35770 ( 0.061% ) | 34 / 35770 ( 0.095% ) | 37 / 35770 ( 0.103% ) | 20 / 35770 ( 0.055% ) |
| tic-tac-toe20 | 0 / 26 ( 0% ) | 0 / 26 ( 0% ) | 0 / 26 ( 0% ) | 0 / 26 ( 0% ) |
| tic-tac-toe15 | 0 / 111 ( 0% ) | 0 / 111 ( 0% ) | 0 / 111 ( 0% ) | 0 / 111 ( 0% ) |
| tic-tac-toe10 | 0 / 191 ( 0% ) | 0 / 191 ( 0% ) | 0 / 191 ( 0% ) | 0 / 191 ( 0% ) |
| splice-1-20 | 1 / 243 ( 0.411% ) | 1 / 243 ( 0.411% ) | 1 / 243 ( 0.411% ) | 1 / 243 ( 0.411% ) |
| splice-1-15 | 5 / 419 ( 1.193% ) | 5 / 419 ( 1.193% ) | 5 / 419 ( 1.193% ) | 7 / 419 ( 1.670% ) |
| splice-1-10 | 23 / 1605 ( 1.433% ) | 49 / 1605 ( 3.052% ) | 49 / 1605 ( 3.052% ) | 25 / 1605 ( 1.557% ) |
| soybean20 | 11 / 844 ( 1.303% ) | 4 / 844 ( 0.473% ) | 5 / 844 ( 0.592% ) | 1 / 844 ( 0.118% ) |
| soybean15 | 16 / 1456 ( 1.098% ) | 6 / 1456 ( 0.412% ) | 6 / 1456 ( 0.412% ) | 3 / 1456 ( 0.206% ) |
| soybean10 | 29 / 2907 ( 0.997% ) | 12 / 2907 ( 0.412% ) | 25 / 2907 ( 0.859% ) | 8 / 2907 ( 0.275% ) |
| primary-tumor20 | 31 / 9589 ( 0.323% ) | 12 / 9589 ( 0.125% ) | 14 / 9589 ( 0.146% ) | 2 / 9589 ( 0.020% ) |
| primary-tumor15 | 43 / 16962 ( 0.253% ) | 12 / 16962 ( 0.070% ) | 9 / 16962 ( 0.053% ) | 7 / 16962 ( 0.041% ) |
| primary-tumor10 | 54 / 31024 ( 0.174% ) | 18 / 31024 ( 0.058% ) | 17 / 31024 ( 0.054% ) | 16 / 31024 ( 0.051% ) |
| mushroom20 | 9 / 811 ( 1.109% ) | 3 / 811 ( 0.369% ) | 2 / 811 ( 0.246% ) | 4 / 811 ( 0.493% ) |
| mushroom15 | 15 / 1529 ( 0.981% ) | 3 / 1529 ( 0.196% ) | 3 / 1529 ( 0.196% ) | 7 / 1529 ( 0.457% ) |
| mushroom10 | 38 / 3276 ( 1.159% ) | 4 / 3276 ( 0.122% ) | 4 / 3276 ( 0.122% ) | 21 / 3276 ( 0.641% ) |

Selection Percentage

**Fig. 2.** Selection statistics (#outstanding patterns/#patterns/%) on UCI data-sets. (Color figure online)

Notably, using different quality measures lead to different sets of outstanding patterns to be selected. Figure 3 shows a heatmap representation of the Jaccard similarity between result sets for three example data sets. For the *primary-tumor* data set (middle), there is little similarity between the different results, for the *soybean* data set (right-most figure), *confidence* and *GR* give very similar results. The full set of figures can be found in the supplementary material.

As we mentioned in the introduction, outstanding patterns are not necessarily among the *best* patterns in terms of class correlation, for instance. This is shown by Fig. 4 on the primary tumor data set with the confidence measure: for all minimum support thresholds, also itemsets with low confidence are selected. Figures for other data sets and quality measures can be found in the supplementary material available at https://github.com/Etienne-Lehembre/Outstanding-Pattern-Selector.git.

## 5.2 Comparison to Self-sufficient Itemsets

A method that is close in spirit to our proposal are the *self-sufficient* itemsets proposed by Webb *et al.* [16]. Self-sufficient itemsets, can be considered independently from each other, as can outstanding patterns, which is not the case for patterns selected by pattern mining techniques. The full definition of self-sufficiency is too involved to reproduce here[3] but self-sufficiency includes the requirement that the probability of itemsets' occurrence cannot be inferred by

---

[3] We direct the interested reader to the original publication.

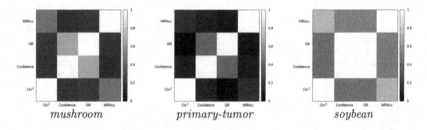

**Fig. 3.** Heatmap representation of Jaccard similarity for sets of outstanding patterns selected for different quality measures for *mushroom* ($\theta = 10\%$), *primary-tumor* ($\theta = 15\%$), *soybean* ($\theta = 15\%$).

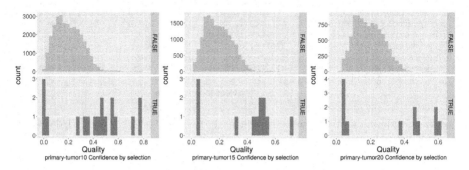

**Fig. 4.** Distribution of confidence values for the *primary tumor* data set, outstanding patterns in the bottom row, non-outstanding patterns on top. Results for minimum support 10% in the left-most column, 15% center, 20% right-most.

the probability of subsets' and supersets' occurrences. This requirement translates into comparing itemsets to their predecessors and successors in a DAG where vertices are labeled with the full set of possible itemsets and edges indicating extension of itemsets with individual items. We therefore want to know how many of the outstanding itemsets we select are self-sufficient and vice versa.

We ran the OPUSMINER implementation available at https://eda.mmci.uni-saarland.de/prj/selfsufs/ on the UCI data sets mentioned above. The lower part of Table 1 reports the number of self-sufficient itemsets and a comparison to Fig. 2 shows that there is no obvious relationship between the number of outstanding and self-sufficient itemsets. Not all self-sufficient itemsets are frequent under the minimum support thresholds we use, and the bottom-most row of Table 1 shows their number for the three different support thresholds.

Self-sufficient itemsets also cannot expected to be closed itemsets. We therefore identified for each self-sufficient itemset the corresponding closed frequent itemset, and compared this set to the set of outstanding itemsets selected. Table 2 shows for each support and each quality measure which proportion of outstanding itemsets are also self-sufficient (left-hand column per quality measure) and which proportion of self-sufficient itemsets are also outstanding (right-hand column). Missing lines correspond to settings where all values are 0.0, which includes in particular the *tic-tac-toe* data set.

**Table 2.** Self-sufficient and outstanding itemsets for different minimum supports $\theta$ and different quality measures. For each measure, left-hand column shows the proportion of outstanding itemsets that are self-sufficient, right-hand column displays the proportion of self-sufficient that are outstanding.

| Data set | $\theta$ | $\chi^2$ | | Confidence | | NGR | | WRAcc | |
|----------|----------|----------|------|------------|------|------|------|-------|------|
| Mushroom | 10 | 0.16 | 0.48 | 0.25 | 0.14 | 0.25 | 0.14 | 0.29 | 0.48 |
| Mushroom | 15 | 0.13 | 0.15 | 0.33 | 0.13 | 0.33 | 0.13 | 0.14 | 0.13 |
| Primary-tumor | 10 | 0.02 | 0.08 | 0.00 | 0.00 | 0.00 | 0.00 | 0.00 | 0.00 |
| Primary-tumor | 15 | 0.02 | 0.09 | 0.00 | 0.00 | 0.00 | 0.00 | 0.00 | 0.00 |
| Primary-tumor | 20 | 0.03 | 0.12 | 0.00 | 0.00 | 0.00 | 0.00 | 0.00 | 0.00 |
| Soybean | 10 | 0.03 | 0.02 | 0.00 | 0.00 | 0.04 | 0.02 | 0.12 | 0.02 |
| Soybean | 15 | 0.12 | 0.06 | 0.00 | 0.00 | 0.17 | 0.03 | 0.00 | 0.00 |
| Soybean | 20 | 0.18 | 0.07 | 0.00 | 0.00 | 0.20 | 0.03 | 0.00 | 0.00 |
| Splice-1 | 10 | 0.13 | 0.10 | 0.06 | 0.10 | 0.06 | 0.10 | 0.12 | 0.10 |
| Vote | 10 | 0.18 | 0.10 | 0.00 | 0.00 | 0.00 | 0.00 | 0.00 | 0.00 |
| Vote | 15 | 0.12 | 0.05 | 0.00 | 0.00 | 0.00 | 0.00 | 0.00 | 0.00 |
| Vote | 20 | 0.10 | 0.03 | 0.00 | 0.00 | 0.00 | 0.00 | 0.00 | 0.00 |
| zoo-1 | 10 | 0.10 | 0.02 | 0.33 | 0.05 | 0.33 | 0.05 | 0.00 | 0.00 |
| zoo-1 | 15 | 0.10 | 0.02 | 0.50 | 0.05 | 0.50 | 0.05 | 0.00 | 0.00 |
| zoo-1 | 20 | 0.12 | 0.02 | 0.33 | 0.06 | 0.33 | 0.06 | 0.00 | 0.00 |

Generally speaking, we can remark that outstanding itemsets stand not to be self-sufficient and vice versa. W.r.t. individual data sets, we can observe some interesting phenomena. For *mushroom* at $\theta = 10\%$ and $\chi^2$/WRAcc, only one of the four outstanding itemsets is self-sufficient but ten of the self-sufficient itemsets are represented by it, i.e. they are subsets that cover the same transactions. Once we increase the minimum support to $20\%$, there is no itemset left that is both self-sufficient and outstanding. For the *vote* data set, there is a certain correspondence between outstanding and self-sufficient itemsets for $\chi^2$ but none whatsoever for the other quality measures.

## 5.3  Structured Pattern Selection

This section gives an experimental illustration of our method on graph-structured data. This experiment is motivated by the study of chemical and biological data *BCR-ABL* from *ChEMBL23*[4]. In the data, every molecule is labeled as active or inactive; their structure represented as graphs. Negative data is denoted by $\mathcal{D}^-$ in the following. From the 1485 graphs of the data set, we extract closed frequent sub-graphs with at most 7 nodes, and $\theta = 10$.

---

[4] https://www.ebi.ac.uk/chembl/.

As in the case of the closed itemsets we considered above, edges in the resulting DAG connect two vertices $u$ and $v$ if $u$ is labeled with a maximal predecessor of the closed graph labeling $v$. As before, we assess the behavior of different quality measures: $\chi^2$, confidence, NGR, WRAcc.

**Table 3.** Selection statistics on graph data.

| Quality measure | $\chi^2$ | Confidence | NGR | WRAcc |
|---|---|---|---|---|
| Selected | 247 | 30 | 32 | 257 |
| Percentage | 1.589% | 0.193% | 0.205% | 1.653% |
| Total # patterns | 15,544 | | | |

As we can see in Table 3, we select at most 1.7% of mined patterns. We also notice different behaviors for different quality measures: whereas NGR and confidence select small sets, WRAcc and $\chi^2$ select more than six times as many, a number of patterns that could be hard to process by a human domain expert.

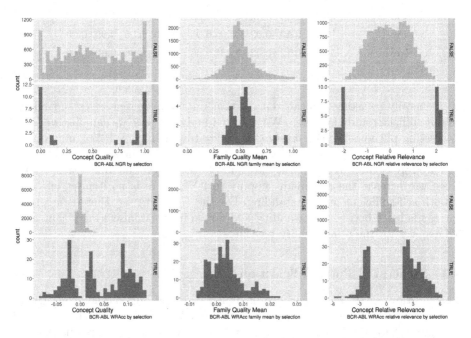

**Fig. 5.** Selection histograms for NGR (top) and WRAcc (bottom).

Figure 5, shows histograms of the scores for GR (top), and WRAcc (bottom). The left-most column shows the distribution of pattern scores, the center column the mean score for neighborhoods, and the right-most one the relative relevance, i.e. deviation of patterns from the mean of their neighborhood, normalized by the standard deviation. Blue histograms are for outstanding patterns, red for non-outstanding ones. As before, we see that outstanding patterns are not necessarily strongly correlated with the active class but might also be those that are unexpectedly weakly correlated (or even negatively correlated). We also see that while the majority of outstanding patterns are two standard deviations off their neighborhood's mean score, there are patterns that deviate even more strongly.

## 5.4    Expert Analysis Upon an Outstanding Pattern and Its Family

The NGR used in the preceding section tends to discount jumping emerging patterns, which are however rather interesting in the context of activity analysis. In the following section we will therefore use another quality measure called $GR_{max}$, which avoids the $\infty$ problem but gives JEPs its due:

$$\begin{cases} GR_{max}(X, \mathcal{D}) = & |\mathcal{D}^-| \quad if \; GR(X, \mathcal{D}) = \infty \\ GR_{max}(X, \mathcal{D}) = GR(X, \mathcal{D)} \quad otherwise \end{cases}$$

We applied $GR_{max}$ to the data-set BCR-ABL extracted from ChEMBL.

**Table 4.** Results on BCR-ABL using $GR_{max}$

|            | Order 1 | Order 2 | Order 3 | Order 4 | Order 5 | Order 6 | Total  |
|------------|---------|---------|---------|---------|---------|---------|--------|
| Total      | 6       | 307     | 5 388   | 8 269   | 1 534   | 40      | 15 544 |
| Selected   | 0       | 6       | 203     | 175     | 12      | 0       | 396    |
| Percentage | 0.00%   | 1.95%   | 3.77%   | 2.12%   | 0.78%   | 0.00%   | 2.55%  |

In Table 4, *order* indicates the number of nodes in the smallest free/generator sub-graph corresponding to closed graphs, allowing us to structure the graph into several layers. A closed graph together with its generator patterns induces an *equivalence class* of graph patterns covering the same data graphs. Each column correspond to a layer, numbered with its order. Rows *Total* indicates the number of equivalence classes in a layer, *Selected* the number of selected equivalence classes, and *Percentage* the percentage of selected equivalence classes. We observe that most of the outstanding patterns are found in the third and fourth layer. This is why the following analysis will be conducted on equivalence classes extracted from the third and fourth layers.

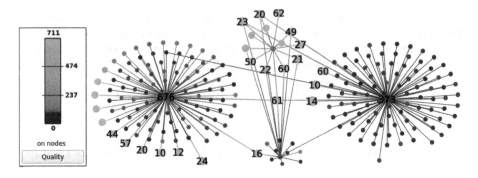

**Fig. 6.** Selected outstanding pattern (centered) along with its parents, and children of the parents. Labeled nodes are selected by OPS or important parent (373 and 676).

Starting from the outstanding pattern, an expert can expect to gain insight into structure-activity relationships (SAR) [10]. As an illustration, consider the center node of Fig. 6. It shows an outstanding pattern appearing in 61 molecules, as well as its parents labelled as 676 and 373, colored according to their $GR_{max}$ value with lighter colors corresponding to higher values. Larger nodes have a higher relative relevance. One of the parents, which differs only by one element syntactically, has significantly higher support values than the others. On both labelled parents, we see a large amount of children that include both patterns that do not correlate with the target class at all, and others that correlate very strongly. Furthermore we see that this family has several selected siblings (labelled nodes which are neither 676, nor 373). It implies that several subsets of molecules are outstanding regarding of each individual families for each pattern. It implies that the molecules' super-sets of our entry point contain cliffs [12] regarding the molecular activity. The outstanding pattern is therefore an entry point to visual analysis by the expert. Therefore, the outstanding pattern is an entry point for a visual analysis by the expert.

## 6   Conclusion

We have proposed a new way of selecting outstanding patterns by comparing them to neighboring patterns: a pattern is outstanding if it deviates clearly from the average of neighboring patterns w.r.t. the value of a quality measure. Our proposal is independent of the pattern language or the quality measure used. As experimentally shown, our selection patterns method leads to a strong reduction in the size of the result set, making the manual exploration by domain experts possible. Results differ significantly between different quality measures, i.e. the choice of quality measure becomes meaningful.

Finally, our selector puts an emphasis on the outstanding pattern's context. The selected pattern is interesting, but its parents, as well as its siblings, are also objects of interest. It can lead us to siblings linked to more than one outstanding pattern. Parents of such siblings become very interesting because outstanding pattern can have either positive or negative qualities, depending on the underlying data. Therefore, our selector offers a new way to study cleaving points inside the pattern language, and thus, the data, putting human in the loop.

**Acknowledgements.** This work was partially funded by the ANR project InvolvD (ANR-20-CE23-0023).

# References

1. Besson, J., Rigotti, C., Mitasiunaite, I., Boulicaut, J.F.: Parameter tuning for differential mining of string patterns. In: ICDM Workshops, pp. 77–86. IEEE Computer Society (2008)
2. Bie, T.D.: Maximum entropy models and subjective interestingness: an application to tiles in binary databases. Data Min. Knowl. Discov. **23**(3), 407–446 (2011)
3. Boulicaut, J.F., Bykowski, A., Rigotti, C.: Free-sets: a condensed representation of boolean data for the approximation of frequency queries. Data Min. Knowl. Disc. **7**(1), 5–22 (2003)
4. Crémilleux, B., Giacometti, A., Soulet, A.: How your supporters and opponents define your interestingness. In: Berlingerio, M., Bonchi, F., Gärtner, T., Hurley, N., Ifrim, G. (eds.) ECML PKDD 2018. LNCS (LNAI), vol. 11051, pp. 373–389. Springer, Cham (2019). https://doi.org/10.1007/978-3-030-10925-7_23
5. Dau, F., Ducrou, J., Eklund, P.: Concept similarity and related categories in search-sleuth. In: Eklund, P., Haemmerlé, O. (eds.) ICCS-ConceptStruct 2008. LNCS (LNAI), vol. 5113, pp. 255–268. Springer, Heidelberg (2008). https://doi.org/10.1007/978-3-540-70596-3_18
6. Davey, B.A., Priestley, H.A.: Introduction to Lattices and Order, Second Edition. Cambridge University Press, Cambridge (2002)
7. De Raedt, L., Zimmermann, A.: Constraint-based pattern set mining. In: Proceedings of the Seventh SIAM International Conference on Data Mining. SIAM (2007)
8. Dong, G., Li, J.: Efficient mining of emerging patterns: discovering trends and differences. In: Proceedings of the Fifth ACM SIGKDD, pp. 43–52 (1999)
9. Kane, B., Cuissart, B., Cremilleux, B.: Minimal jumping emerging patterns: computation and practical assessment. In: PAKDD (2015)
10. Métivier, J.P., Cuissart, B., Bureau, R., Lepailleur, A.: The pharmacophore network: a computational method for exploring structure-activity relationships from a large chemical data set. J. Med. Chem. **61**(8), 3551–3564 (2018)
11. Pasquier, N., Bastide, Y., Taouil, R., Lakhal, L.: Discovering frequent closed itemsets for association rules. In: Beeri, C., Buneman, P. (eds.) ICDT 1999. LNCS, vol. 1540, pp. 398–416. Springer, Heidelberg (1999). https://doi.org/10.1007/3-540-49257-7_25
12. Stumpfe, D., Hu, H., Bajorath, J.: Evolving concept of activity cliffs. ACS Omega **4**(11), 14360–14368 (2019)
13. Tan, P., Kumar, V., Srivastava, J.: Selecting the right objective measure for association analysis. Inf. Syst. **29**(4), 293–313 (2004)

14. Van Leeuwen, M., Ukkonen, A.: Fast estimation of the pattern frequency spectrum. In: ECML PKDD 2014, pp. 114–129 (2014)
15. Vreeken, J., Tatti, N.: Interesting patterns. In: Aggarwal, C.C., Han, J. (eds.) Frequent Pattern Mining, pp. 105–134. Springer, Cham (2014). https://doi.org/10.1007/978-3-319-07821-2_5
16. Webb, G.I.: Self-sufficient itemsets: an approach to screening potentially interesting associations between items. ACM Trans. Knowl. Discov. Data 4(1), 3:1–3:20 (2010)
17. Yan, X., Han, J.: Closegraph: mining closed frequent graph patterns. In: Proceedings of the Ninth ACM SIGKDD, pp. 286–295 (2003)

# Using Explainable Boosting Machine to Compare Idiographic and Nomothetic Approaches for Ecological Momentary Assessment Data

Mandani Ntekouli[1]([✉]), Gerasimos Spanakis[1], Lourens Waldorp[2], and Anne Roefs[3]

[1] Department of Data Science and Knowledge Engineering, Maastricht University, Maastricht, The Netherlands
m.ntekouli@maastrichtuniversity.nl
[2] Department of Psychological Methods, University of Amsterdam, Amsterdam, The Netherlands
[3] Faculty of Psychology and Neuroscience, Maastricht University, Maastricht, The Netherlands

**Abstract.** Previous research on EMA data of mental disorders was mainly focused on multivariate regression-based approaches modeling each individual separately. This paper goes a step further towards exploring the use of non-linear interpretable machine learning (ML) models in classification problems. ML models can enhance the ability to accurately predict the occurrence of different behaviors by recognizing complicated patterns between variables in data. To evaluate this, the performance of various ensembles of trees are compared to linear models using imbalanced synthetic and real-world datasets. After examining the distributions of AUC scores in all cases, non-linear models appear to be superior to baseline linear models. Moreover, apart from personalized approaches, group-level prediction models are also likely to offer an enhanced performance. According to this, two different nomothetic approaches to integrate data of more than one individuals are examined, one using directly all data during training and one based on knowledge distillation. Interestingly, it is observed that in one of the two real-world datasets, knowledge distillation method achieves improved AUC scores (mean relative change of +17% compared to personalized) showing how it can benefit EMA data classification and performance.

**Keywords:** Ecological Momentary Assessment · Machine learning · Explainable Boosting Machine · Knowledge distillation

## 1 Introduction

In the last few years, there has been a renewed research interest in the areas of psychology and psychiatry that has been particularly sparked by recent

© The Author(s), under exclusive license to Springer Nature Switzerland AG 2022
T. Bouadi et al. (Eds.): IDA 2022, LNCS 13205, pp. 199–211, 2022.
https://doi.org/10.1007/978-3-031-01333-1_16

technological and methodological developments for collecting time-intensive, repeated, intra-individual measurements through Ecological Momentary Assessment (EMA) studies [4,11,13,14]. EMA offers the opportunity to capture relevant information about patients' evolution of their mental condition, symptoms and experiences, in real-time and in context of their everyday life. This way, a large amount of personalized data has become available, providing the means for further exploring mental disorders [6]. Consequently, there has been an urgent need for developing statistical methods to model psychological behaviour [18]. Some practical applications of such models could be to predict illness course, determine treatment response or develop tailored psychiatric interventions [3].

Based on literature, EMA time-series data have been mostly studied in a multivariate regression-based approach [8,18]. More specifically, the most popular class of time-series models is the Vector Autoregressive (VAR) model with a goal to estimate the dynamical interactions between all the measured variables (i.e., network structures) [2]. However, the fact that these models can only estimate linear statistical relationships can be a significant issue for mental disorders, where the involved interactions are likely to be quite complex. When many symptoms or variables are involved in the course, these are more prone to interact in a non-linear fashion with each other. Thus, linear models seem insufficient to uncover the possible non-linear interactions and describe precisely the real complex nature of mental disorders.

A promising approach that can learn such complex and higher-order interactions of symptoms is using non-linear machine learning (ML) models [17]. ML models can enhance the ability to accurately predict the occurrence of different behaviors by recognizing complicated patterns or relations between variables in existing data.

This work focuses on two research objectives, examining the idiographic (or personalized) and nomothetic (or group-based) predictive approach, respectively. First, according to the idiographic approach, personalized models are typically applied, as there are possibly different underlying mechanisms that drive a future behavior in each individual. Thus, different non-linear interpretable models are evaluated in terms of performance to test whether they are superior to baseline linear models. Second, we should acknowledge the possibility that shared influences among different individuals may provide a complementary predictive utility. Therefore, prediction models are applied in a nomothetic (group-based) approach showing that integrating data of more than one individual in a single model could also accurately predict future outcomes at a person level [19].

## 2    Methodology

### 2.1    Idiographic (Person-Specific) Approach

Based on the fact that mental disorders can be modeled as a complex system, we assume that illness course and behaviors differ remarkably across individuals. Most individuals suffering from the same disorder are likely to exhibit different symptoms, so different mechanisms possibly influence and drive a future behavior. Therefore, it is proposed that each individual should be examined separately using personalized prediction models [4].

Starting from the widely used linear models, a natural extension of these is the more flexible Generalized Additive Models (GAMs) [9]. The main concept of GAMs remains the same as of the linear ones, expecting for the outcome to be an additive model of feature effects, but relaxing the restriction of the linear relationship. It allows the use of arbitrary functions for representing the features' effects. Subsequently, more flexible, non-linear feature functions can be incorporated. These functions can be based on regression spline models and tree-based models such as single trees or ensembles of bagged trees, boosted trees and boosted-bagged trees.

However, there is still a significant gap between the flexible GAMs and full-complexity models, such as ensembles of trees, regarding accuracy [9]. The main reason of this limitation is that GAMs take into account only univariate terms and not any interaction between features (variables). To deal with this drawback, a more advanced method was developed, called Generalized Additive Models plus Interactions ($GA^2Ms$), which incorporates pairwise interactions between features [10]. The model is described in the following form:

$$g(y) = \sum_i f_i(x_i) + \sum_{i \neq j} f_{ij}(x_i, x_j) \tag{1}$$

where $f$ are the feature functions of features $x$ and $g$ is the link function (e.g. identity or logistic) of the predicted outcome $y$. This model can still be interpretable, using heat maps for representing the pairwise features' interactions, as well as accurate, reaching the performance of the state-of-the-art ML models.

In this work, a fast implementation of the $GA^2Ms$ algorithm was used, called Explainable Boosting Machine models (EBMs), which is part of the Microsoft's open-source Python package InterpretML [12]. The EBMs' learning process makes use of gradient boosting with shallow regression tree ensembles. At each boosting round, a tree is built on a single feature and its residuals are used for training the tree of the following feature. This is repeated for all different features. After several boosting rounds, each feature's trees of all rounds can be combined, leading to tree ensembles as the final features' representation. On top of this, functions for pairwise features' interactions can be additionally incorporated. The FAST method is used to detect and rank features' interactions in order to keep the most significant ones, without the expense of checking all possible combinations [10]. Again, the same training process is performed for the specified pairs.

Because EBMs is a relatively novel method, its performance is evaluated by comparing it to other full-complexity ML models, such as XGBoost, Gradient Boosting Trees (GradBoost) and Random Forest (RF). Afterwards, non-linear models are also compared to linear models, such as Logistic Regression (LogReg) and Support Vector Machines (SVM), using a linear kernel.

## 2.2   Nomothetic (Group-Level) Approaches

Although personalized models are mostly applied, commonalities among different participants may provide complementary predictive utility. Thus, population-level prediction studies are also likely to offer an enhanced performance. Especially, in case of more advanced ML models, incorporating more data could be of more help, compared to the traditional linear models. This approach could have a clear advantage to uncover potential complex hidden relationships between variables.

The most common way of integrating data of more than one individual in a model is to concatenate the data of all individuals together in a single dataset. The augmented dataset is then used to construct a population-based model. Such models produce generalizable predications that can be relevant to a wider range of individuals. For example, a population-based model can be applied to new individuals who have not been included in the training of the model. An additional benefit would be that it can be applied to individuals that cannot be run in a personalized way due to the lack of the necessary amount of training samples (time-points) or samples of the minority class.

The second proposed approach is based on the Knowledge Distillation (also known as teacher-student) method [7]. In this case, information from a larger (teacher) model is used in a smaller (student) model. The original concept of Knowledge Distillation was created with the goal to fill the gap between expressive power and learnability in Neural Networks (NNs). This is achieved by training a small NN after incorporating additional information from a larger and more complex NN. However, the aforementioned gap does not only exist in NNs but also in other machine learning methods like the tree-based models described above [5]. So, the distillation method using information extracted from larger models can be further exploited in non-NN models.

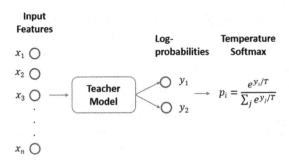

**Fig. 1.** The proposed Knowledge Distillation method: after each sample $(x1, x2, .., xn)$ is input to the teacher model, the extracted log-probabilities $y_i$ are used to the temperature softmax function. The produced $p_1$ or $p_2$ are the labels for the student models.

Inspired by this, the proposed Knowledge Distillation method in our case is illustrated in Fig. 1. First, the teacher model is trained on data from all participants and then information derived from this model is used for training

**Table 1.** Characteristics of the examined datasets. For imbalance ratio and training/test sets, the mean and standard deviation values of all individuals are presented, after pre-processing.

| Dataset | #Participants | #Features | Imbalance ratio | #Training samples | #Test samples |
|---------|---------------|-----------|-----------------|-------------------|---------------|
| Synthetic | 20, 50, 100 | 25, 60 | 2.33 | 35, 70, 210 | 15, 30, 90 |
| Drink | 24 | 15 | 8.45 (5.45) | 72.83 (12.02) | 31.87 (5.24) |
| ThinkSlim2 | 57 | 43 | 5.82 (3.25) | 86 (38.72) | 37.51 (16.68) |

personalized student models for each individual separately. Additional information is gained through the smoothened probabilities $p_i$ (soft labels), which come from the pre-trained teacher model. The log-probabilities $y_i$ of the training samples are softened using a temperature softmax function. The temperature hyperparameter $T$ plays an important role in smoothing the distribution of the outputs, that is necessary to prevent the case of having an one-hot vector as the result of a typical softmax function. Then, the smoothened outputs are used as labels for the personalized student models. Compared to the conventional personalized training that uses hard labels, distillation can provide additional useful information with an aim to improve the personalized models.

## 3    Experimental Setup

### 3.1    EMA Datasets

EMA data is organized in a hierarchical structure for each individual, where observations are collected multiple times a day for a pre-defined period of several weeks. The total number of observations as well as the collection period can be different among individuals because some may experience difficulties in following the schedule of the surveys. All datasets' characteristics used in this paper are briefly reported in Table 1 and more extensively presented as follows.

**Synthetic Datasets.** Due to lack of access to big EMA datasets, we follow a simple method for generating random EMA datasets. These datasets are designed to consist of the feature vectors and labels of each patient, aiming at a 2-class classification problem. It is also commonly noticed that medical-related EMA datasets, as well as the following examined real-world datasets, are characterized as imbalanced. This means that the majority of samples belongs only to one class, whereas much fewer to the other class. Thus, in this case, the ratio of samples assigned to the two classes is 0.7:0.3 in the synthetic datasets as well.

Furthermore, the datasets must be created in a way to be structurally similar to the real EMA data. First, these must incorporate multivariate ordinal and categorical variables. This is a challenging issue, especially in high dimensional datasets. The method of generating our feature vectors is based on sampling from a different random normal distribution for each one. These are afterwards transformed into ordinal features after deriving an equi-width histogram of the distribution, leading to a random number of 6 distinct values, or 2 as categorical variables are typically encoded to binary.

It is also often necessary to impose some flexibility on the data variables, such as noise. Noise can be added to both output labels and feature vectors. Here, a small amount of noise is introduced. More specifically, 20% of the labels are randomly assigned to samples as well as the values of 20% of features are randomly shuffled. Finally, regarding other characteristics of the synthetic datasets, such as the number of individuals, features and samples, a number of choices is evaluated.

**Dataset: Drink.** This first real-world dataset was obtained by a study described in [15]. It was a 2-week collection of data from 33 individuals through 8 daily mobile notifications/surveys. The captured variables included positive and negative emotions, drinking craving and expectancies, self-reported alcohol consumption, impulsivity, as well as social context. All these variables were measured on a scale from 0 to 100. Regarding the output variable, the aim of this prediction was the occurence or not of drinking events at the next time-point. So, a positive label was assigned to each sample when the number of alcoholic drinks at the next time-point was one or higher.

**Dataset: ThinkSlim2.** The second real-world dataset is larger and more challenging. It was obtained by a study described in more detail in [1,16]. This consisted of data collected from 134 overweight individuals multiple times a day (minimum 8) for 7 weeks (excluding the follow-up phase) via a mobile application. From all the measured variables, only some were selected based on the individuals's compliance. The final variables included various positive and negative emotions, location, activity, social context and type of consumed food. The emotion-related variables were measured on a scale from 0 to 10. All other variables were categorical, including a set of predefined choices for each one. Regarding the output variable, the examined scenario was aiming at predicting the next healthy or unhealthy eating event. So, a healthy or unhealthy label was assigned to each sample according to the type of food consumed at the next time-point.

## 3.2   Data Preparation

For each dataset, each participant's EMA data was prepared for analysis separately. These were assessed for the frequency of daily observations as well as the frequency and distribution of the outcome events. First, individuals having very few observations per day or in total were removed. The number of individuals retained was 31 and 76 for the Drink and ThinkSlim2 datasets, respectively.

Additionally, because of the final goal to predict (or classify) the next time-point behavior, consecutive data points had to be collected. For example, for each data point, if the following one (collected within the next 2 h) was absent then we could not retrieve its prediction target and eventually it was also considered as missing. That way, some individuals were found to have so few outcome events of the minority class that subsequent cross-validation steps could not be conducted. So, these participants were also excluded from the final dataset. As a result, the number of retained individuals were 24 for the Drink dataset having an average of 6.18 (std = 0.90) daily points and 57 for ThinkSlim2 with average 3.39 (std = 2.05) points.

As further seen in Table 1, data points of each individual were split sequentially at fixed time intervals into two datasets, a training and a test set, containing the first 70% and last 30% of the data points, respectively.

### 3.3   Data Analysis

**Idiographic Approach.** According to the idiographic approach, separate predictive models were applied to each individual, using various ML algorithms. A necessary step is hyperparameters' tuning, which frequently has a big impact on model's performance. In this paper, a time-series cross-validation method (a variation of KFold, returning first $k$ folds as training set and the $(k+1)$th fold as test set) was used to tune some of the main hyperparameters of the tree-based methods. All these combinations were exhaustively explored for each case using Grid Search and the one resulting to the best cross-validation score was retained for the following analysis. The metric score of interest was $ROC\_AUC$ (or any of the macro average scores), measuring the true-positive rate and false-positive rate for the model's predictions using a set of different probability thresholds. AUC score was chosen for the prediction of both classes to be taken into account equally, regardless the number of samples these classes contained. In other words, the prediction of samples belonging to the majority class should not play a more important role than predicting samples of the minority class.

**Nomothetic Approach.** According to the nomothetic approach, the two methods described in Sect. 2.2 were investigated using Explainable Boosting Machine models (EBMs). EBMs were built using data of all individuals and then compared to the traditional personalized EBMs. In the first method, the training datasets of all individuals were concatenated in a population-level dataset, which was used to train an EBM. The number of interactions was fine-tuned to select the optimal value, as in the personalized models. The performance of this "EBM_all" model was evaluated separately on the testing set of each individual. The testing sets are kept the same as in the personalized approach.

In the second method, information obtained from the first method (teacher model) was further used in personalized EBMs. Each class' log-probabilities of the training samples were extracted and transformed to smoothed probabilities using a temperature softmax function, with the temperature value being selected from a range between 2 and 200. Thus, new datasets were created using the training samples of each individual and the extracted "probabilities" as a target label, instead of the initial hard labels $(0, 1)$. These new datasets created for each individual were used to train the student models, which are EBMs regression models.

**Table 2.** Performance of personalized models (EBM, XGBoost, Gradient Boosting, RF, SVM and Logistic Regression): the mean and standard deviation of the AUC scores are given for all synthetic datasets (each having different number of users, features and samples). Numbers in bold indicate the highest mean AUC score for each dataset, while underlined numbers indicate cases where EBMs' score is close to the highest one.

| #Users | #Feat | #Samples | EBM | XGBoost | Grad | RF | SVM | LogReg |
|---|---|---|---|---|---|---|---|---|
| 20 | 25 | 50 | 0.715 (0.149) | **0.747 (0.145)** | 0.699 (0.179) | 0.734 (0.168) | 0.638 (0.185) | 0.700 (0.149) |
| 20 | 25 | 100 | **0.736 (0.142)** | 0.707 (0.127) | 0.706 (0.132) | 0.735 (0.130) | 0.664 (0.130) | 0.702 (0.087) |
| 20 | 25 | 300 | **0.695 (0.154)** | 0.663 (0.148) | 0.678 (0.133) | 0.691 (0.147) | 0.684 (0.163) | 0.667 (0.157) |
| 20 | 60 | 100 | 0.757 (0.147) | **0.762 (0.181)** | 0.745 (0.153) | 0.760 (0.142) | 0.620 (0.147) | 0.634 (0.143) |
| 20 | 60 | 300 | **0.761 (0.127)** | 0.752 (0.121) | 0.749 (0.107) | 0.747 (0.127) | 0.672 (0.105) | 0.685 (0.113) |
| 50 | 25 | 50 | **0.736 (0.170)** | 0.722 (0.170) | 0.668 (0.157) | 0.711 (0.155) | 0.634 (0.188) | 0.657 (0.173) |
| 50 | 25 | 100 | 0.718 (0.128) | 0.718 (0.133) | 0.706 (0.128) | **0.726 (0.121)** | 0.655 (0.145) | 0.690 (0.132) |
| 50 | 25 | 300 | 0.750 (0.111) | 0.739 (0.108) | 0.741 (0.107) | **0.751 (0.111)** | 0.739 (0.123) | 0.744 (0.121) |
| 50 | 60 | 100 | 0.680 (0.154) | **0.684 (0.148)** | 0.675 (0.136) | 0.667 (0.148) | 0.558 (0.150) | 0.603 (0.136) |
| 50 | 60 | 300 | **0.764 (0.101)** | 0.755 (0.109) | 0.749 (0.103) | 0.757 (0.101) | 0.685 (0.101) | 0.701 (0.102) |
| 100 | 25 | 50 | 0.688 (0.179) | 0.685 (0.158) | 0.670 (0.172) | **0.695 (0.148)** | 0.572 (0.193) | 0.629 (0.177) |
| 100 | 25 | 100 | 0.675 (0.147) | 0.676 (0.144) | 0.671 (0.144) | **0.690 (0.147)** | 0.613 (0.133) | 0.618 (0.131) |
| 100 | 25 | 300 | 0.751 (0.110) | 0.742 (0.101) | 0.744 (0.104) | **0.757 (0.109)** | 0.748 (0.109) | 0.748 (0.110) |
| 100 | 60 | 100 | **0.737 (0.131)** | 0.711 (0.134) | 0.718 (0.122) | 0.696 (0.122) | 0.600 (0.131) | 0.634 (0.122) |
| 100 | 60 | 300 | **0.722 (0.131)** | 0.709 (0.128) | 0.710 (0.117) | 0.710 (0.126) | 0.665 (0.091) | 0.668 (0.112) |

## 4    Experimental Results

### 4.1    Synthetic Dataset

**Idiographic Approach.** The initial step to evaluate the described methods was to create synthetic datasets. Using synthetic data, it is easier to understand the problem we have to solve and develop effective and efficient methods for that. To create the data, different values for the dataset's parameters, such as number of subjects, features and samples, were chosen and investigated independently.

Synthetic datasets are first analyzed using a personalized approach. For each combination of the chosen parameters, personalized non-linear and linear models are applied to each individual of every dataset separately. After applying all personalized models, the mean and standard deviation values of the performance (AUC scores) of all created individuals are presented in Table 2. It is clearly visible that the average AUC scores are greater when applying non-linear models. According to the extracted AUC results, EBMs models produce the best average scores in most of the datasets. However, even when RF or XGBoost show the best scores, their difference to EBMs is quite small. Moreover, EBMs achieved more accurate performance when a large number of samples is used for training, such as 100 or 300.

**Nomothetic Approach.** Subsequently, personalized EBMs are evaluated in comparison to the two nomothetic approaches described in Sect. 2.2, the using all data EBMs (EBM_all) and knowledge distillation (KD) method. In case of knowledge distillation, different values for the temperature parameter are evaluated, ranging from 1 to 100. After applying all examined methods, the mean

**Table 3.** Performance of the two nomothetic methods (EBM_all and KD): the mean and standard deviation of the AUC scores are given for all synthetic datasets (each having different number of users, features and samples). Numbers in bold indicate the highest mean AUC score for each dataset, while underlined numbers indicate cases where distillation outperforms personalized EBMs.

| #User | #Feat | #Samples | EBM | EBM_all | KD ($T = 1$) | KD ($T = 5$) | KD ($T = 100$) |
|---|---|---|---|---|---|---|---|
| 20 | 25 | 50 | 0.715 (0.149) | **0.804 (0.151)** | 0.753 (0.178) | 0.768 (0.185) | 0.776 (0.178) |
| 20 | 25 | 100 | 0.736 (0.142) | **0.758 (0.162)** | 0.739 (0.134) | 0.735 (0.139) | 0.753 (0.148) |
| 20 | 25 | 300 | 0.695 (0.154) | 0.691 (0.172) | **0.698 (0.167)** | 0.694 (0.171) | 0.690 (0.179) |
| 20 | 60 | 100 | 0.757 (0.147) | **0.813 (0.111)** | 0.786 (0.092) | 0.779 (0.096) | 0.795 (0.097) |
| 20 | 60 | 300 | 0.761 (0.127) | **0.762 (0.119)** | 0.757 (0.111) | 0.756 (0.113) | **0.762 (0.119)** |
| 50 | 25 | 50 | 0.736 (0.170) | **0.756 (0.183)** | 0.707 (0.169) | 0.719 (0.170) | 0.731 (0.166) |
| 50 | 25 | 100 | 0.718 (0.128) | **0.747 (0.146)** | 0.713 (0.162) | 0.720 (0.164) | 0.733 (0.160) |
| 50 | 25 | 300 | 0.750 (0.111) | **0.773 (0.133)** | 0.762 (0.134) | 0.769 (0.135) | 0.769 (0.135) |
| 50 | 60 | 100 | 0.680 (0.154) | **0.735 (0.140)** | 0.689 (0.144) | 0.686 (0.147) | 0.700 (0.151) |
| 50 | 60 | 300 | 0.764 (0.101) | **0.783 (0.120)** | 0.751 (0.119) | 0.755 (0.122) | 0.766 (0.123) |
| 100 | 25 | 50 | 0.688 (0.179) | **0.767 (0.175)** | 0.720 (0.167) | 0.725 (0.171) | 0.736 (0.166) |
| 100 | 25 | 100 | 0.675 (0.147) | 0.723 (0.144) | 0.719 (0.138) | 0.720 (0.135) | **0.726 (0.141)** |
| 100 | 25 | 300 | 0.751 (0.110) | **0.769 (0.121)** | 0.767 (0.120) | 0.765 (0.119) | 0.764 (0.121) |
| 100 | 60 | 100 | 0.737 (0.131) | **0.761 (0.140)** | 0.712 (0.150) | 0.721 (0.147) | 0.738 (0.148) |
| 100 | 60 | 300 | 0.722 (0.131) | **0.736 (0.142)** | 0.724 (0.133) | 0.720 (0.132) | 0.729 (0.139) |

and standard deviation values of the produced AUC scores for each synthetic dataset are presented in Table 3.

In the majority of the examined datasets, it is apparent that using personalized EBMs leads to worse performance than when either of the nomothetic methods is applied. More specifically, EBM_all gives the best results compared to the distillation method in all but three datasets, whereas in one of these, both methods achieved the same score. It is also interesting to mention that their difference, in terms of the mean AUC score, is quite big in some datasets. This is the case in datasets with a small number of samples, such as when characteristics ({users, features, samples}) are {20, 25, 50}, {50, 25, 50}, {100, 25, 50}, {50, 60, 100} and {100, 60, 100}. Therefore, it is important to highlight that collecting sufficient data from each user can benefit the knowledge distillation process.

## 4.2   Dataset: Drink

**Idiographic Approach.** First, the total number of 24 individuals is analyzed using a personalized approach. After applying all different ML models, the results of the personalized predictive models on the testing sets indicated that the produced results highly vary across individuals. For instance, some individuals had quite high AUC results, whereas others' results were at chance level.

To compare the different ML models, we show some of the statistical properties of all AUC scores, using the box and whisker plots in Fig. 2a. In this figure, we present the performance of EBMs compared to the full-complexity ML models as well as the performance of non-linear models compared to the traditionally-used linear ones. Regarding the first comparison, AUC's distribution for EBMs is comparable to the ones of the other non-linear models. Apart from RF, which shows a slightly better overall performance, all statistical properties of the EBMs' scores reached higher values than the other three models. The median value of EBM AUC score is around 0.81, only a bit lower than XGBoost (0.83). It can also be noticed that the minimum value of EBM performance was the highest among ML models, indicating a smaller variation among individuals in the case of EBMs.

Regarding the second comparison, a distinction between the linear and non-linear models is clearly visible. All statistical properties of the AUC scores are lower in the case of linear models. These findings highlight the ability of non-linear ML models to enhance the predictive performance of the traditionally-applied linear ones.

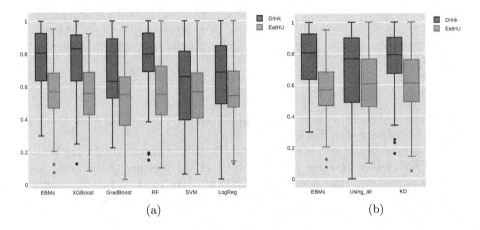

**Fig. 2.** a: AUC performance of all non-linear and linear models b: Comparing the performance of personalized EBMs to the two nomothetic approaches (EBM_all and KD)

**Nomothetic Approach.** In the nomothetic approach, data from all individuals are pooled into one dataset and modeled collectively by one EBM (EBM_all), or further exploited in a personalized way (KD). To facilitate comparison, box and whisker plots are utilized and presented (as before) in Fig. 2b.

Using a nomothetic approach, the AUC distribution of the KD method is improved compared to that of personalized EBMs. This shows more consistent performance scores across individuals, apart from 4 outliers. Regarding the EBM_all method, its AUC distribution is more spread, meaning that the 25th percentile and minimum values are lower compared to personalized EBMs and KD. However, the upper half of its distribution is comparable to the respective part of the distributions obtained through the other cases. Subsequently, by comparing the median values of both approaches, we see that there is a slight distinction between them, where personalized EBMs reach the level of

0.80, whereas around 0.76 and 0.79 for the EBM_all and KD methods, respectively. In contrast to the results on synthetic datasets, we see that in a more realistic dataset, the knowledge distillation method can lead to improved results compared to EBM_all.

### 4.3   Dataset: ThinkSlim2

**Idiographic Approach.** Similar to the previous dataset, the performance of 57 personalized predictive models is first evaluated. As the produced results highly varied across individuals, their performance is also here assessed through box and whisker plots. Figure 2a presents the AUC scores of all different ML methods. According to AUC scores, all models' distributions are comparable to each other, having a quite large range. All methods show similar poor performance, achieving a low median value around 0.57 in the case of non-linear models, whereas around 0.54 for the linear ones. That could be due to the more complex and challenging structure of this dataset, containing a larger number of individuals as well as features, but not more data samples compared to the previous dataset. Another interesting aspect in this experiment is that some AUC values are very close to zero (for all setups). This means that probabilities produced by all models for these individuals lead to a flipped prediction label for almost all testing points.

**Nomothetic Approach.** Finally, personalized EBMs were compared to the two nomothetic approaches, EBM_all and KD. The results of all methods, in terms of AUC scores, are presented in Fig. 2b. The median as well as the 25th and 75th percentile values are similar for both KD and EBM_all, and also increased compared to the respective values of the personalized EBMs. The mean relative AUC increase of KD and EBM_all compared to EBMs are at 17% and 14%, respectively. It is also worth mentioning that there is one individual having an AUC score equal to 0. This means that the probabilities produced by both EBM_all and KD methods for this individual do not map the class labels correctly, maybe because they are different than the rest of the population. In challenging problems, like the one represented by the ThinkSlim2 dataset, where personalized non-linear models do not perform well, both nomothetic approaches are likely to achieve a slightly improved performance.

## 5   Challenges of Modelling EMA Data

Studying the aforementioned two real-world datasets and noticing their varying results across individuals shows the importance of collecting good quality EMA data. Because of the complex nature of psychological behavior, its representation on a dataset can be quite challenging. EMA data collection is a difficult task, trying to capture multiple observations on subjective variables during an intensive period. Thus, it may contain unclear and arbitrary responses as well as missing values.

Missing data is a significant problem of real-world EMA datasets that cannot be controlled during a study. Even though several individuals initially participate in a study, some may not produce enough data for analysis (especially if one needs to take into account the temporal nature of the data). The number of data points that is sufficient depends on the total compliance of each individual during the whole data collection period and also per day. The most common approach to deal with missing data is to delete them while keeping only the complete sets of data. However, this method relies on the assumption that the missing observations are missing at random (MAR) or completely at random (MCAR), which possibly is not always the case.

## 6   Conclusion

This research work highlights the importance of exploiting the wealth of EMA data through more advanced ML models compared to linear ones. Non-linear vs. linear and idiographic vs. nomothetic approaches were investigated for classifying a target variable at a next time-point on different datasets.

The results showed great consistency for the idiographic approach, showing that non-linear models yield an enhanced performance on both synthetic and real-world data. Subsequently, regarding the nomothetic approaches, no clear trends were observed in the results of all datasets. Although the EBM_all method appears to perform best for synthetic datasets, that is not the case for the real-world datasets. Overall, the proposed knowledge distillation method could be recognized as the most beneficial to improve performance of personalized models. However, the differences in both idiographic and nomothetic approaches were not found statistically significant. As a future step, further experiments are needed on more (and larger) datasets for evaluating the examined approaches.

**Acknowledgements.** This study is part of the project "New Science of Mental Disorders" (www.nsmd.eu), supported by the Dutch Research Council and the Dutch Ministry of Education, Culture and Science (NWO gravitation grant number 024.004.016).

## References

1. Boh, B., et al.: An Ecological Momentary Intervention for weight loss and healthy eating via smartphone and Internet: study protocol for a randomised controlled trial. Trials **17**(1), 1–12 (2016)
2. Epskamp, S., et al.: Personalized network modeling in psychopathology: the importance of contemporaneous and temporal connections. Clin. Psychol. Sci. **6**(3), 416–427 (2018)
3. Fried, E.I., van Borkulo, C.D., Cramer, A.O.J., Boschloo, L., Schoevers, R.A., Borsboom, D.: Mental disorders as networks of problems: a review of recent insights. Soc. Psychiatry Psychiatr. Epidemiol. **52**(1), 1–10 (2016). https://doi.org/10.1007/s00127-016-1319-z
4. Fried, E.I., Cramer, A.O.: Moving forward: challenges and directions for psychopathological network theory and methodology. Perspect. Psychol. Sci. **12**(6), 999–1020 (2017)

5. Fukui, S., Yu, J., Hashimoto, M.: Distilling knowledge for non-neural networks. In: 2019 Asia-Pacific Signal and Information Processing Association Annual Summit and Conference (APSIPA ASC), pp. 1411–1416. IEEE (2019)
6. Haslbeck, J.M., Bringmann, L.F., Waldorp, L.J.: A tutorial on estimating time-varying vector autoregressive models. Multivar. Behav. Res. **56**(1), 120–149 (2021)
7. Hinton, G., Vinyals, O., Dean, J.: Distilling the knowledge in a neural network. arXiv preprint arXiv:1503.02531 (2015)
8. van der Krieke, L., et al.: Ecological momentary assessments and automated time series analysis to promote tailored health care: a proof-of-principle study. JMIR Res. Protoc. **4**(3), e100 (2015)
9. Lou, Y., Caruana, R., Gehrke, J.: Intelligible models for classification and regression. In: Proceedings of the 18th ACM SIGKDD International Conference on Knowledge Discovery and Data Mining, pp. 150–158 (2012)
10. Lou, Y., Caruana, R., Gehrke, J., Hooker, G.: Accurate intelligible models with pairwise interactions. In: Proceedings of the 19th ACM SIGKDD International Conference on Knowledge Discovery and Data Mining, pp. 623–631 (2013)
11. Myin-Germeys, I., et al.: Experience sampling methodology in mental health research: new insights and technical developments. World Psychiatry **17**(2), 123–132 (2018)
12. Nori, H., Jenkins, S., Koch, P., Caruana, R.: InterpretML: a unified framework for machine learning interpretability. arXiv preprint arXiv:1909.09223 (2019)
13. Robinaugh, D.J., Hoekstra, R.H., Toner, E.R., Borsboom, D.: The network approach to psychopathology: a review of the literature 2008–2018 and an agenda for future research. Psychol. Med. **50**(3), 353 (2020)
14. Shiffman, S., Stone, A.A., Hufford, M.R.: Ecological momentary assessment. Annu. Rev. Clin. Psychol. **4**, 1–32 (2008)
15. Soyster, P.D., Ashlock, L., Fisher, A.J.: Pooled and person-specific machine learning models for predicting future alcohol consumption, craving, and wanting to drink: a demonstration of parallel utility. Psychol. Addict. Behav. (2021). https://search.ebscohost.com/login.aspx?direct=true&db=pdh&AN=2021-38589-001&site=ehost-live&scope=site
16. Spanakis, G., Weiss, G., Boh, B., Roefs, A.: Network analysis of ecological momentary assessment data for monitoring and understanding eating behavior. In: Zheng, X., Zeng, D.D., Chen, H., Leischow, S.J. (eds.) ICSH 2015. LNCS, vol. 9545, pp. 43–54. Springer, Cham (2016). https://doi.org/10.1007/978-3-319-29175-8_5
17. Stamate, D., et al.: Identifying psychosis spectrum disorder from experience sampling data using machine learning approaches. Schizophr. Res. **209**, 156–163 (2019)
18. Wild, B., Eichler, M., Friederich, H.C., Hartmann, M., Zipfel, S., Herzog, W.: A graphical vector autoregressive modelling approach to the analysis of electronic diary data. BMC Med. Res. Methodol. **10**(1), 1–13 (2010). https://doi.org/10.1186/1471-2288-10-28
19. Wright, A.G., Zimmermann, J.: Applied ambulatory assessment: integrating idiographic and nomothetic principles of measurement. Psychol. Assess. **31**(12), 1467 (2019)

# dunXai: DO-U-Net for Explainable (Multi-label) Image Classification
## Applications to Biomedical Images

Toyah Overton[1,2](✉) [iD], Allan Tucker[1] [iD], Tim James[2] [iD],
and Dimitar Hristozov[2]

[1] Department of Computer Science, Brunel University London, Uxbridge, UK
{toyah.overton,allan.tucker}@brunel.ac.uk
[2] Evotec A.G., Abingdon, UK

**Abstract.** Artificial Intelligence (AI) and Machine Learning (ML) are becoming some of the most dominant tools in scientific research. Despite this, little is often understood about the complex decisions taken by the models in predicting their results. This disproportionately affects biomedical and healthcare research where explainability of AI is one of the requirements for its wide adoption. To help answer the question of what the network is looking at when the labels do not correspond to the presence of objects in the image but the context in which they are found, we propose a novel framework for Explainable AI that combines and simultaneously analyses Class Activation and Segmentation Maps for thousands of images. We apply our approach to two distinct, complex examples of real-world biomedical research, and demonstrate how it can be used to provide a global and concise numerical measurement of how distinct classes of objects affect the final classification. We also show how this can be used to inform model selection, architecture design and aid traditional domain researchers in interpreting the model results.

**Keywords:** Convolutional Neural Networks · Segmentation · Explainability · Class Activation Maps · Blood smear · High-throughput microscopy

## 1 Introduction

Powered by AI, our world is undergoing the next industrial revolution. We are seeing a growing number of sectors utilising AI as a driver for their continued innovation with 'MedTech' - a rapidly growing area of the healthcare industry - seeing an emergence of a paradigm shift in the way that research and development are being carried out. Two particular examples of where AI is becoming rapidly adopted are diagnostics, with some algorithms already outperforming human experts [1], and within drug discovery where AI-created drugs are already being trialled [2].

With the rise in real-world applications of AI, understanding how these algorithms are making their decisions is becoming increasingly important. This is

© The Author(s), under exclusive license to Springer Nature Switzerland AG 2022
T. Bouadi et al. (Eds.): IDA 2022, LNCS 13205, pp. 212–224, 2022.
https://doi.org/10.1007/978-3-031-01333-1_17

even more key in healthcare settings where the lack of explainability of the algorithms could hinder their adoption as useful tools. These requirements are some of the reasons driving the development of the major new interdisciplinary area of research focusing on Explainable AI. Works including Zhou et al. [3] and Ribeiro et al. [4] explore the decisions made by neural networks when classifying objects in images, with these techniques now becoming increasingly popular within the ML community. Conversely, Ghassemi et al. [5] advise caution when considering Explainable AI at the patient-level, suggesting instead that external validation should be the most important requirement for any AI used in a healthcare setting. However, while explainable AI can be used as a tool for validating the model output, it can also be applied to the R&D process in order to identify and correct issues long before clinical approval is sought. Although not in the healthcare setting, Jia et al. [6] pose the question: 'is the model right for the right reasons?' and provide an example in which the Neural Network tested removes contextual information which is not useful to the labelling process - in their case, the model is right for the right reasons.

Convolutional Neural Networks (CNN) are amongst the most widely used types of ML models in the world, thanks to their excellent image classification performance. In recent years, Class Activation Maps (CAMs) have become an increasingly popular method of understanding the complex decision making process of these networks, as is explored in Jia et al. [6]. CAMs are produced by stacking selected convolutional layers of a network, with the degree of their activation used to weight their relative impact of each layer. The resulting maps highlight the areas of the images which contributed most strongly to the final classification.

Whilst very useful in simple classification tasks, on their own these techniques are not immediately applicable in cases where the objects in the image are not directly the target labels for the model. For example, when diagnosing blood disorders, we look at images of blood cells, but we are not interested in determining whether or not the objects in the images are cells. Instead, we aim to label the context in which the cells are present in the image as a whole, using the information about their shape and size, and relative abundance. This could be considered similar to the problem of analysing satellite images showing cars in a urban setting where we are not trying to locate and classify the vehicles themselves but attempt to predict if they are showing a car park, a traffic jam or regular traffic.

In this work, we propose a new framework for summarising the areas of interest of a model when faced with these more complex image classification tasks. Our proposed tool uses segmentation masks for any number of classes of objects found in the images and compares them with the CAMs generated by CNNs to produce a single numerical descriptor, indicating the degree of impact of that class on the overall classification. Our metric can be used by ML experts to improve their network design whilst simultaneously aiding domain experts to interpret the results presented without the need for the them to understand the inner working of the models, as has already been adopted within Evotec.

**Fig. 1.** *Left:* An example image from the ALL-IBD1 dataset from an ALL patient. *Centre:* A sample image for a non-ALL patient. *Right:* An image from the Cell Painting Dataset.

## 1.1 Image Context Classification

In the healthcare applications of ML, we often come across classification problems where the labels we are assigning do not directly correspond to the object found in the image but instead are drawn from the greater context presented in the images. In this work, we focus on just two examples of this: predicting Acute Lymphoblastic Leukemia (ALL) from blood smear images and predicting biological activity from high-throughput microscopy images, however, the methods presented here could be applied to many other areas of research. Both of these classification tasks are well-defined and have been explored in multiple publications using publicly available datasets.

**Predicting ALL - A Single-Task Problem.** ALL is a rare cancer affecting the white blood cells. With the majority of cases being in children, teenagers and young adults, it is the most common form of leukaemia in children. Around 790 people are diagnosed with ALL in the UK each year, and as the cancer is aggressive, the patients' condition can rapidly decline, making early detection and immediate treatment critical. If left untreated, death can occur in just a matter of weeks [8,9]. In diagnosing ALL, one of the first steps includes the analysis of a blood sample by measuring the number of abnormal leukocytes (white blood cells). High numbers of these abnormal cells, referred to as 'blast cells' or lymphoblasts, are indicative of ALL [8]. As the changes to the cell can be detected though their visual inspection, this problem is well suited for the use with CNNs. Figure 1 shows example images used for this analysis. Due to the clear contrast between the healthy leukocytes and lymphoblasts, we could consider this to be a relatively simple example of a visual single-task classification problem [17].

**Predicting Biological Activity - A Multi-label Problem.** The development of new drugs is an expensive process, taking up to 20 years, with cost estimates ranging from 0.5–2.6 billion USD [10]. However, both the development time and cost can be reduced by implementing an early and accurate estimate of the biological effects of drug-like molecules on organisms, referred to as assays. This allows the process to quickly focus on the candidate molecules with the greatest chance of success, ultimately leading to the delivery of much needed medication to patients. ML in general, and in particular deep learning, is an emerging technology in the field of drug discovery, showing great promise and high accuracies in producing such estimates. Several different methodologies have been used to predict the activity for drug-like molecules using a variety of physico-chemical properties and, more recently, data generated using high-throughput imaging assays. Chan et al. [11] published a thorough review on Advancing Drug Discovery via Artificial Intelligence in August 2019, while Zhu [12] published a thorough review of Big Data and Artificial Intelligence Modeling for Drug Discovery in September 2019. Here, we focus on predicting biological assays from high-throughput microscopy images, a subject investigated in depth by Hofmarcher et al. [13]. This is a highly complex classification task, due not only to its multilabel nature but also to the sparsity of the available data. However, despite its importance, no works to date thoroughly explore the problem of explainability in AI for drug discovery.

## 2   The Classification Tasks

### 2.1   Data

**Blood Smear Images.** ALL can be identified by analysing blood smear images, such as those published in the well-curated and high quality Acute Lymphoblastic Leukemia Image Database for Image Processing (ALL-IDB[1]) [9]. This dataset consists of images captured using an optical laboratory microscope, with magnification ranging from 300–500×, and a Canon PowerShot G5 camera. Each image in the database has been classified by expert oncologists to assign accurate labels which can be used for in model training. Whilst two datasets are provided, this work uses the ALL_IDB1 subset, comprised of 108 images taken during September 2005 from both ALL and non-ALL patients. Example blood smear images from both ALL and non-ALL patient are shown in Fig. 1.

**High-Throughput Microscopy Images.** In this work, we also use high-throughput imaging assays - a type of data with growing popularity in the world of AI-driven drug discovery. One such dataset is the Cell Painting Dataset introduced by Bray et al. [14]. Figure 1 shows an example image from their library. In this dataset, cells have been 'painted' with several distinct fluorescent morphological markers simultaneously in order to emphasise the morphological information contained in the images. The dataset consists of 406 multi-well plates, imaged using an ImageXpress Micro XLS automated microscope, with 5 fluorescent channels at ×20 magnification, and 6 fields of view imaged per well. By cross matching the chemicals applied to the cells with their known assays in the

---

[1] Provided by the Department of Information Technology at Universitá degli Studi di Milano, https://homes.di.unimi.it/scotti/all/.

ChEMBL database [15], we were able to produce a set of assay activity labels for our dataset. Assays are only included in the dataset if 10 active and 10 inactive measurements exist, aligning our criteria with these used in other works, including Hofmarcher et al. [13].

## 2.2  Existing Classification Methods

**Predicting ALL.** Given the importance of rapid diagnosis of ALL, it is perhaps not surprising that a large number of publications exist exploring various predictive algorithms. Some of these are traditional ML algorithms, with neural network based approaches becoming more popular in the recent years. Ghadezadeh et al. [17] produce a systematic review of a number of works exploring such applications, summarising the datasets and techniques used. Due to the large pixel resolution of the images in the dataset, as well as the high angular resolution required to observe the small changes in the shape of the cells, a significant proportion of the publications focus on locating the lymphocytes and studying their properties in isolation. This may be achieved through the application of one or more segmentation techniques to sub-sample the images [18] or through feature extraction [19]. Furthermore, a number of publications use the ALL-IDB2 dataset, which is not suitable for our analysis as it consists of expert cropped images focusing only on the areas containing a single lymphocyte.

**Predicting Biological Activity.** The work by Hofmarcher et al. [13] is perhaps the most thorough example of using the Cell Painting Dataset. The authors compare the results of a number of CNNs, including DenseNet [20] and ResNet [21] to their own architecture, GapNet, with these three models obtaining the highest performance. ResNet, DenseNet and GapNet achieved mean AUCs of $0.731 \pm 0.19$, $0.730 \pm 0.19$ and $0.725 \pm 0.19$ respectively, which shows a consistent performance across all three models. The authors however note that GapNet holds an advantage over the other methods as, due to a significantly lower number of convolutional layers and model parameters, it is considerably more efficient to train.

## 2.3  Our Classification Models

We use three classification models for the prediction of labels in both example applications presented in this work. We have selected the ResNet101 and DenseNet121 models, as well as our own modified TensorFlow implementation of the GapNet architecture. We alter GapNet's design, as compared to Hofmarcher et al. [13], to remove some of the constraints that were likely introduced in order to accelerate the training times as opposed to being performance-driven. We marginally increased the number of convolutional layers, as well as the depth of the layers, to bring it closer in line with the VGG architecture on which GapNet is largely based [13]. We also removed all dense layers from the model, with the exception of the final classification layer and directly connected the Global

**Table 1.** Summary of the performance of GapNet, ResNet101 and DenseNet121 on the ALL_IDB1 library and our subset of the Cell Painting dataset. Errors represent the standard deviation of our results across 10 bootstraps.

| Dataset | GapNet average AUC | ResNet101 average AUC | DenseNet121 average AUC |
|---|---|---|---|
| ALL_IDB1 | $98.88 \pm 3.51\%$ | $99.39 \pm 1.41\%$ | $98.53 \pm 1.53\%$ |
| Cell Painting | $82.35 \pm 1.84\%$ | $83.35 \pm 1.71\%$ | $82.39 \pm 1.68\%$ |

Average Pooling (GAP) layers to the final output layer. This brings our model inline with the modern CNN designs, where dense layers are becoming obsolete in favour of Global Pooling layers [20,21]. Whilst this is a considerable departure from the design of the original GapNet, we found this approach to result in nearly identical performance on the same dataset as used by Hofmarcher et al. [13]. Our analysis additionally benefits from this change, as it allows us to treat all three architectures consistently (Table 1).

As the focus of this work is not on the details of the image classification models, the implementations of these models is considered beyond the scope of this paper and is therefore not discussed here. Instead, we are making all of our code publicly available at https://github.com/ToyahJade/dunXai where further details can be found.

**Predicting ALL.** We trained our modified GapNet, ResNet101 and DenseNet121 on 70 images from the ALL-IDB1 dataset, using a further 20 images for the in-training testing. Each model was bootstrapped 10 times and validated using 10 hold-out images. Our training obtained an average AUC of $98.88\pm3.51\%$ for GapNet, $99.39 \pm 1.41\%$ for ResNet101 and $98.53 \pm 1.53\%$ for DenseNet121.

**Predicting Biological Activity.** For the purposes of this work, we simplify the task of predicting biological activity to classifying only the assays originating from the Sanger Institute that are present in our dataset. All of these cells are growth inhibition assays. The reduced dataset, combined with labels for the Cell Painting Images, consists of 27 assays and 21 compounds, found in 942 images. We train our GapNet as well as both ResNet101 and DenseNet121 over 10 bootstraps, each with 615 training images, with a further 262 images being used for the testing. Using a hold-out validation dataset of 330 images, we achieve average AUCs of $82.35 \pm 1.84\%$ for GapNet, $83.35 \pm 1.71\%$ for ResNet101 and $82.39 \pm 1.68\%$ for DenseNet121.

## 3    dunXai

We propose DO-U-Net for Explainable AI, or dunXai, for the analysis of Deep Learning models where their aim is to classify the visual context of the image.

**Table 2.** Summary of the performance of DO-U-Net on the ALL_IDB1 dataset as well as our subset of the Cell Painting dataset for each object type.

| Dataset | Object type | Number in training dataset | Precision | Sensitivity |
|---|---|---|---|---|
| ALL_IDB1 | Erythrocytes | 3,602 | 99.94% | 98.62% |
| | Lymphocytes | 79 | 100.00% | 100.00% |
| Cell Painting | Cell membranes | 145 | 99.31% | 95.83% |
| | Nuclei | 135 | 98.83% | 95.83% |

Our tool can be broken down into three components. First, objects in the images are segmented using DO-U-Net [7], with all distinct instances labeled separately, even when such objects are closely co-located. Secondly, we create CAMs for the models used. Whilst we use GapNet, Densenet and Resnet architectures in this work, any CNN model compatible with the CAM method could be used here. Finally, the segmentation masks and CAMs are compared using our selected algorithm, producing the final numerical descriptions of the relationship between the areas of interest in the images and the final output of the models.

### 3.1   DO-U-Net

We use the Duel-Output U-Net (DO-U-Net), developed in Overton and Tucker [7] as our segmentation model. DO-U-Net is a U-Net [22] based, Encoder-Decoder, Fully Convolutional Network for object segmentation and counting. We chose DO-U-Net over the simpler U-Net in order to improve the quality of the segmentation masks for objects where the edges are not clearly defined in the images. We found this to be a particular issue for lymphoblasts and cell membranes where the extra focus that DO-U-Net puts on detecting the edges allows the network to separate the objects preserving their true area, thus increasing the accuracy of our metrics discussed in Sect. 3.3.

In both of our example applications of dunXai, we are working with data containing two distinct classes of objects. The blood smear images contain erythrocytes and lymphocytes, while the cell painting dataset focuses on cell images where we are able to separate the nuclei of the cell and the membrane that surrounds them. Table 2 highlights the performance of DO-U-Net for each class of objects.

**Application to Blood Smear Images.** We trained two separate DO-U-Net models: one to segment erythrocytes, and a second to segment lymphocytes. Whilst it is possible to use DO-U-Net for multi-label segmentation, we have found that training on each class separately improved our results considerably. When trained using 8 images, divided into smaller 196 × 196 regions, containing 3,602 erythrocytes we achieved a precision of 99.94% and sensitivity of 98.62% on the 4 images used for validation containing 2,035 erythrocytes. Using the

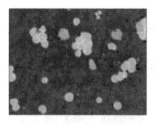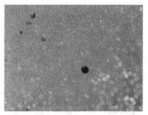

**Fig. 2.** Example CAMs generated for our modified GapNet architecture. *Left:* ALL patient. *Centre:* Non-ALL patient. *Right:* Cell Painting Dataset.

same training images containing 79 lymphocytes, we reached a precision and sensitivity of 100.00% on our validation dataset of 8 images containing 134 lymphocytes.

**Application to High-Throughput Microscopy Images.** Similarly, we trained two separate models to segment the cell membranes and their nuclei. When trained using 105 images containing 6,601 cells, DO-U-Net achieved a precision of 99.31% and a sensitivity of 95.83% for cell membranes, as measured on 8 validation images. For the nuclei, DO-U-Net achieves a precision of 98.83% and a sensitivity of 95.83% using the same data.

## 3.2    Explainable AI: Class Activation Maps

In order to create the CAMs, we follow a methodology similar to that of Zhou et al. [3]. In our case, we use three architectures with GAP as their penultimate layer which allowed us to use the models directly as trained in Sect. 2.3, without the need for modifications. Our implementation of GapNet requires an additional step as the penultimate layer is a concatenation of four GAP layers, taken at different depths of the network. For simplicity we only consider the GAP layer corresponding to the final convolution layer of the model in this work, and use the activation weights for that portion of the concatenated GAP layer. This could be trivially modified to study the impact of the other GAP layers, derived at different depths of the network. Example CAMs for our sample images can be seen in Fig. 2.

## 3.3    dunXai Metrics

By comparing the segmentation masks generated using DO-U-Net and the CAMs produced for each label, we can create a set of numerical descriptors for all images in our dataset. The choice of measurements here depends on the specific research question being investigated. Thanks to the use of DO-U-Net, we could calculate the impact of each instance of the segmented objects or the effects of the background on the classification. However, in the interest of brevity,

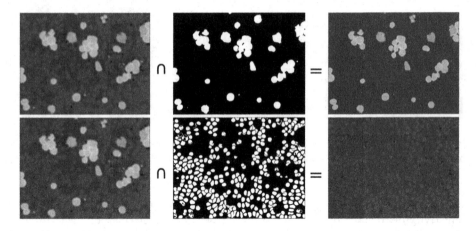

**Fig. 3.** *Left:* CAM generated using our modified GapNet for an ALL patient. *Top Centre:* Lymphocytes segmentation mask. *Bottom Centre:* Erythrocytes segmentation mask. *Right:* Union of the CAMs and the segmentation masks, showing a much stronger activation for lymphocytes.

we cannot demonstrate an exhaustive list of all possible metrics. Instead, we focus on a global property of the image that gives a strong overview of the relationship between the objects it contains and the final classification labels.

Our proposed dunXai score, $d$, measures the mean intensity of the CAM, $\mathbf{C}$, that lies in the region overlapping the objects in question, $\mathbf{S}$ with an area, $\sum S$, normalised to its maximum absolute intensity. Figure 3 shows the union of the segmentation mask and the CAM for two different classes of objects found in our data, which forms the basis of our metric.

$$d = \frac{\sum(\mathbf{C} \cap \mathbf{S})}{\max(|\mathbf{C}|) \times \sum \mathbf{S}} \tag{1}$$

To demonstrate how our proposed dunXai score can be used to analyse the way the models make their complex classification decision, we look at our two examples across the three architectures and all object types present in the data. While calculated for individual images, we can compare the dunXai score across our entire dataset in order to measure the importance of a given class of objects on the final classification.

**Application to Blood Smear Images.** In this simple, single-task classification problem, all of our models produce highly confident predictions, achieving very high AUCs using our validation dataset. To evaluate the importance of each class of objects found in the images, we can take the mean of the dunXai score across all images. For GapNet, we measure a mean score of $0.2738 \pm 0.1736$ for erythrocytes and $0.8969 \pm 0.0948$ for lymphocytes. The much higher score for lymphocytes indicated that the model consistently and strongly relies on these objects to perform the classification. This is consistent with the traditional approach to the classification of ALL. However, both ResNet101 and DenseNet121 achieved a more similar dunXai score for the two classes, with ResNet101 producing a score of $0.2525 \pm 0.1374$ for erythrocytes and $0.2999 \pm 0.1362$ for lymphocytes and DenseNet121 scoring $0.2446 \pm 0.1242$ for erythrocytes and $0.3806 \pm 0.1562$ for lymphocytes. The similarity of the scores suggests that these models do not use the presence of lymphoblasts as the only indicator of ALL. As there is no biological basis for this, our findings could potentially be pointing towards the overfitting of the models.

**Application to High-Throughput Microscopy Images.** This complex, multi-label classification problem often results in less significant predictions, as is also reflected in the overall accuracy of the models. This gives us an opportunity to study the relationship between dunXai scores and the predicted labels as opposed to relying on the mean score. As our dataset spans 27 classes of assays, we propose that a dunXai score should be produced for each class separately. For our dataset, this leads to a lengthy number of results to discuss. We are therefore unable to discuss the analysis for all assays individually in this work, despite the usefulness of the dunXai score on each assay. Instead, we focus on a selected example for one of the assays which demonstrates the approach that could be used to study all remaining assays.

We analyse on one particular cell growth inhibition assay, CHEMBL2363747 with Fig. 4 showing the comparison of the relationships between the predicted labels and dunXai score for both the cell nuclei and membranes across all of the images in our validation sample. Looking at relationship for GapNet, we can see that the cell membranes play a more important part in predicting the assay than the nuclei. The dunXai scores for both classes are broadly consistent for all predictions, showing that the network is likely using a specific level of activation in the region corresponding to these cell types. In this case, the actuations are negative for a large proportion of the nuclei which could mean that the model is looking for the lack of a specific cell behaviour as opposed to its presence - something that could be a feature of this particular assay.

However, if this result is biologically motivated, we would expect to see the same behaviour for both ResNet and DenseNet. Instead, the level of activation in the regions corresponding to both the cell nuclei and their membranes appear to be strongly correlated to the predicted label, with no clear separation between the two classes. This could indicate that the network is not making its decision in the final layers of the model, suggesting that both ResNet and DenseNet are unnecessarily too deep for this task. Our findings could be seen as an independent validation of the conclusion made by Hofmarcher et al. [13] that GapNet is a sufficient architecture for this classification task.

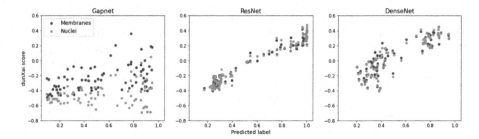

**Fig. 4.** The relationship between our proposed dunXai scores and the classification labels predicted by GapNet, ResNet and DenseNet.

## 4    Conclusion

We have proposed a novel framework for quantitatively evaluating the relationship between the objects found in biomedical images and the predictions of their real-world classification models. We have developed a new metric by simultaneously combining the DO-U-Net generated segmentation masks with CAMs produced for thousands of images using three example architectures. For a simple, single-task classification problem of predicting ALL in blood smear images, we demonstrate that GapNet architecture replicates the manual approach taken to classify these images whilst ResNet and DenseNet take a different route. For a more complex, multi-label problem of predicting assays in high-throughput microscopy images, we use our approach to demonstrate that ResNet and DenseNet have a deeper architecture than is required for this task by comparing the relationship between the predicted scores and our proposed dunXai metric.

**Acknowledgements.** We wish to show our gratitude to Evotec for supporting this research, and specifically thank Michael Bodkin and Daniel Grindrod for providing useful insights and asking the right questions throughout the research, allowing this project to develop. We also thank Karsten Kottig for providing training masks for DO-U-Net for the Cell Painting Dataset, as well as sharing industry insight throughout the project.

We are also immensely grateful to the Department of Information Technology at Universitá degli Studi di Milano for providing the ALL_IDB1 dataset from the Acute Lymphoblastic Leukemia Image Database for Image Processing.

## References

1. McKinney, S.M., Sieniek, M., Godbole, V., et al.: International evaluation of an AI system for breast cancer screening. Nature **577**, 89–94 (2020). https://doi.org/10.1038/s41586-019-1799-6
2. Artificial intelligence-created medicine to be used on humans for the first time. Exscientia. https://www.exscientia.ai/news-insights/artificial-intelligence-created-medicine-to-be-used. Accessed 21 Jan 2021

3. Zhou, B., Khosla, A., Lapedriza, A., Oliva, A., Torralba, A.: Learning deep features for discriminative localization. In: Proceedings of the IEEE Conference on Computer Vision and Pattern Recognition 2016, pp. 2921–2929 (2016). https://doi.org/10.1109/CVPR.2016.319

4. Ribeiro, M.T., Singh, S., Guestrin, C.: Why should i trust you?: Explaining the predictions of any classifier. In: Proceedings of the 22nd ACM SIGKDD International Conference on Knowledge Discovery and Data Mining, pp. 1135–1144 (2016). https://doi.org/10.1145/2939672.2939778

5. Ghassemi, M., Oakden-Rayner, L., Andrew, B.L.: The false hope of current approaches to explainable artificial intelligence in health care. Lancet Digit. Health 3, 745–750 (2021). https://doi.org/10.1016/S2589-7500(21)00208-9

6. Jia, S., Lansdall-Welfare, T., Cristianini, N.: Right for the right reason: training agnostic networks. In: Duivesteijn, W., Siebes, A., Ukkonen, A. (eds.) IDA 2018. LNCS, vol. 11191, pp. 164–174. Springer, Cham (2018). https://doi.org/10.1007/978-3-030-01768-2_14

7. Overton, T., Tucker, A.: DO-U-Net for segmentation and counting. In: Berthold, M.R., Feelders, A., Krempl, G. (eds.) IDA 2020. LNCS, vol. 12080, pp. 391–403. Springer, Cham (2020). https://doi.org/10.1007/978-3-030-44584-3_31

8. Overview: acute lymphoblastic leukaemia. NHS. https://www.nhs.uk/conditions/acute-lymphoblastic-leukaemia/. Accessed 01 Nov 2021

9. Acute Lymphoblastic Leukemia Image Database for Image Processing. Department of Computer Science - Universitá degli Studi di Milano. https://homes.di.unimi.it/scotti/all/#. Accessed 01 Nov 2021

10. Paul, S.M., et al.: How to improve R&D productivity: the pharmaceutical industry's grand challenge. Nat. Rev. Drug Discov. 9(3), 203–214 (2010). https://doi.org/10.1038/nrd3078

11. Chan, S.H.C., Shan, H., Dahoun, T., Vogel, H., Yuan, S.: Advancing drug discovery via artificial intelligence. Trends Pharmacol. Sci. 40, 592–604 (2019). https://doi.org/10.1016/j.tips.2019.06.004

12. Zhu, H.: Big data and artificial intelligence modeling for drug discovery. Ann. Rev. Pharmacol. Toxicol. 60, 573–589 (2020). https://doi.org/10.1146/annurev-pharmtox-010919-023324. First published as a Review in Advance in September 2019

13. Hofmarcher, M., Rumetshofer, E., Clevert, D.-A., Hochreiter, S., Klambauer, G.: Accurate prediction of biological assays with high-throughput microscopy images and convolutional networks. J. Chem. Inf. Model. 59(3), 1163–1171 (2019). https://doi.org/10.1021/acs.jcim.8b00670

14. Bray, M.-A., et al.: A dataset of images and morphological profiles of 30000 small-molecule treatments using the Cell Painting assay. GigaScience 6(12), giw014 (2017). https://doi.org/10.1093/gigascience/giw014

15. The ChEMBL Database. https://www.ebi.ac.uk/chembl/. Accessed 01 Nov 2021

16. ECACC General Cell Collection: U-2 OS, Public Health England. https://www.phe-culturecollections.org.uk/products/celllines/generalcell/detail.jsp?refId=92022711&collection=ecacc_gc. Accessed 20 Jan 2021

17. Ghadezadeh, M., Asadi, F., Hosseini, A., Bashash, D., Abolghasemi, H., Roshanpoor, A.: Machine learning in detection and classification of leukemia using smear blood images: a systematic review. Sci. Program. 2021(06), 1–14 (2021). https://doi.org/10.1155/2021/9933481

18. Sharif, M., et al.: Recognition of different types of leukocytes using YOLOv2 and optimized bag-of-features. IEEE Access 8, 167448–167459 (2020). https://doi.org/10.1109/ACCESS.2020.3021660

19. Vogado, L.H.S., Veras, R.M.S., Araujo, F.H.D., Silva, R.R.V., Aires, K.R.T.: Leukemia diagnosis in blood slides using transfer learning in CNNs and SVM for classification. Eng. Appl. Artif. Intell. **72**, 415–422 (2018). https://doi.org/10.1016/j.engappai.2018.04.024
20. Huang, G., Liu, Z., van der Maaten, L., Weinberger, K.Q.: Densely connected convolutional networks. In: IEEE Conference on Computer Vision and Pattern Recognition, pp. 2261–2269 (2017). https://doi.org/10.1109/CVPR.2017.243
21. He, K., Zhang, X., Ren, S., Sun, J.: Deep residual learning for image recognition. In: IEEE Conference on Computer Vision and Pattern Recognition (2015). https://doi.org/10.1109/CVPR.2016.90
22. Ronneberger, O., Fischer, P., Brox, T.: U-Net: convolutional networks for biomedical image segmentation. In: Navab, N., Hornegger, J., Wells, W.M., Frangi, A.F. (eds.) MICCAI 2015. LNCS, vol. 9351, pp. 234–241. Springer, Cham (2015). https://doi.org/10.1007/978-3-319-24574-4_28

# AGS: Attribution Guided Sharpening as a Defense Against Adversarial Attacks

Javier Perez Tobia[1](✉) [iD], Phillip Braun[2][iD], and Apurva Narayan[1][iD]

[1] The University of British Columbia, Kelowna, Canada
javipt21@mail.ubc.ca, apurva.narayan@ubc.ca
[2] University of Toronto, Toronto, Canada
phillip.braun@mail.utoronto.ca

**Abstract.** Even though deep learning has allowed for significant advances in the last decade, it is still vulnerable to adversarial attacks - inputs that, despite looking similar to clean data, can force neural networks to make incorrect predictions. Moreover, deep learning models usually act as a black box or an oracle that does not provide any explanations behind its outputs. In this paper, we propose Attribution Guided Sharpening (AGS), a defense against adversarial attacks that incorporates explainability techniques as a means to make neural networks robust. AGS uses the saliency maps generated on a non-robust model to guide Choi and Hall's sharpening method to denoise input images before passing them to a classifier. We show that AGS can outperform previous defenses on three benchmark datasets: MNIST, CIFAR-10 and CIFAR-100, and achieve state-of-the-art performance against AutoAttack.

**Keywords:** Adversarial attacks · Computer vision · Machine learning robustness

## 1 Introduction

Thanks to the increase in computing power and storage capacity seen in the last decade, machine learning has gained a lot of popularity. It has shown promising results in a wide range of tasks such as voice recognition [2], resource allocation [34] or autonomous driving [6]; however, its deployment in the real world has been significantly slowed down and, in many cases, opposed. This is due to two of the most important unsolved problems in machine learning: the lack of interpretability of deep learning models and their vulnerability to adversarial attacks.

Most models act as black boxes which, given an input, make a prediction without giving any explanations behind why they generated that output. Taking adversarial attacks into account, this lack of interpretability makes it evident that one cannot blindly trust machine learning models, even more so in safety-critical domains. Many different explainability techniques have been proposed. Generally, they can be grouped in two categories based on their scope [1]: global

© The Author(s), under exclusive license to Springer Nature Switzerland AG 2022
T. Bouadi et al. (Eds.): IDA 2022, LNCS 13205, pp. 225–236, 2022.
https://doi.org/10.1007/978-3-031-01333-1_18

explainability, which is aimed at explaining the behaviour of whole models with techniques like GIRP [38], and local explainability, which is aimed at explaining individual predictions with techniques like LIME [27] or gradient-based attributions (saliency maps) [30]. Despite the successes of these techniques, deep learning is still not fully interpretable and we still cannot explain many of its predictions.

The other roadblock in the widespread deployment of machine learning into the real world is its lack of robustness. Adversarial attacks [32] are carefully crafted small perturbations that can be added to the inputs of a working model to force it to make wrong predictions without changing how the inputs would be interpreted by a human. As can be seen in Fig. 1, these perturbations can alter images in such a way that, even though they look very similar, the network completely misclassifies them. Adversarial examples can be very dangerous and can benefit parties with negative intentions in fields like medicine [13] or autonomous driving [10]. Therefore, building robust models against these attacks is a crucial problem yet to be solved.

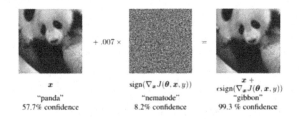

**Fig. 1.** Adversarial example on ImageNet that illustrates how adding a small carefully created perturbation to the image can completely change the prediction [14].

Even though adversarial attacks have been widely studied and many defenses against them have been proposed, there is no universal solution to defend against all of them. Some defenses have solved the problem partially; however, no defense has been found that provides universal robustness against different attack methods and across different architectures and datasets.

The best defense known so far is adversarial training [14], which incorporates adversarial examples into the training set. However, adversarial training tends to overfit models to a specific kind of attack [28] and does not generalize well to new attacks.

Salman et al. have proposed and certified denoised smoothing, a defense against adversarial attacks sampled from a certain $\ell_p$ radius [29]. They propose the combination of randomized smoothing (which smoothes the classifier by adding random noise to the inputs) with a neural network trained to remove the added noise as a means to remove adversarial perturbations. Despite their robust certification, their defense is not as strong against attacks from a different $\ell_p$ norm than what the denoiser has been trained on.

More sophisticated denoising approaches have been proposed such as Deep Denoising Sparse Autoencoder (DDSA) [5], which modifies a denoiser by adding sparsity constraints between the fully connected layers of the encoder and the decoder.

Another relevant denoising approach is high-level representation guided denoiser (HGD) [22]. HGD is composed of a neural network that has been trained to minimize the logit activation difference between clean images and denoised adversarial images. Despite being the winner of the NIPS 2017 competition track, HGD has been shown to be an ineffective defense [4].

As DDSA and HGD, our proposed defense, Attribution Guided Sharpening (AGS), is a denoising approach. Other techniques in the adversarial robustness literature have used attributions but simply as a means to identify adversarial inputs [18,39]. The novelty in AGS comes in using attribution values generated by a non-robust classifier to guide the denoising of adversarial noise. Generally, attacks modify images by increasing the value of pixels that have more weight for the logits of wrong classes. Since attributions give us the ability to analyze the importance of each pixel when making predictions, these same saliency maps can be used to study and correct the influence of individual pixels. In this paper, we do this by using Choi and Hall's sharpening method [7] as the denoising technique.

Our contributions are as follow:

- We introduce the idea of Attribution Guided Denoising (AGD) as a defense against adversarial attacks.
- We propose Attribution Guided Sharpening (AGS): a new defense against adversarial attacks for non-robust models that does not require additional training.
- We evaluate our technique on three benchmark datasets: MNIST [21], CIFAR-10 and CIFAR-100 [20], and show state-of-the-art performance against FGSM, 100-PGD and AutoAttack without the need for adversarial training.

The rest of this paper is divided as follows: Sect. 2 provides an overview of relevant concepts in the fields of adversarial attacks and machine learning explainability; Sect. 3 introduces AGS as a defense and the methodology followed in our implementation; Sect. 4 shows experimental results on MNIST, CIFAR-10 and CIFAR-100; lastly, Sect. 5 summarizes the results of the paper and provides a reflection on the need of more work at the intersection of adversarial defenses and explainable artificial intelligence (XAI).

## 2    Background

### 2.1    Adversarial Attack Generation

Adversarial attacks were introduced as imperceptible non-random perturbations that can change the predictions of a network [32]. This definition has later been extended and adversarial examples need not be imperceptible [12,23] but only require that a human can still interpret the inputs correctly. Unlike noisy data, which is simply perturbed data, whether the perturbation is random or not, adversarial perturbations are generated as the output of an optimization problem targeted to make the network fail.

Adversarial attacks can be classified into two categories: black-box and white-box attacks. Black-box attacks have no knowledge about the model or the defense. They can only query the model and observe its outputs. They usually generate substitute models and generate attacks on these substitute models exploiting the transferability of attacks [26]. On the other side, white-box attacks have full access to the defense, the model architecture and its parameters. They usually generate perturbations by solving an optimization problem that aims to minimize the perturbation ($\delta$) while maximizing a loss function ($\mathcal{L}$), which determines the performance of the network ($\mathcal{F}$), with the goal of changing the outputs of the model $\mathcal{F}(x + \delta) = y' \neq y$ (where $y$ is the real label).

$$\delta = \min_{\delta \in \Delta} \max \mathcal{L}(\mathcal{F}; x + \delta, y) \tag{1}$$

Some relevant attacks in current literature used in this paper are:

*Fast Gradient Sign Method* (FGSM) [14] is a simple but efficient white-box attack that generates adversarial examples by performing the perturbation:

$$x_{adv} = x + \epsilon \, sign(\nabla_x \mathcal{L}(\mathcal{F}; x, y)) \tag{2}$$

where $\nabla_x$ is the gradient of the network ($\mathcal{F}$) with respect to the inputs ($x$) and $\epsilon$ is a parameter that controls the maximum allowed perturbation.

*Projected Gradient Descent* (PGD) [24] is more effective, and perhaps the most commonly used white-box attack. It finds perturbations recursively and projects them onto an $\ell_p$ norm ball of choice after each iteration.

$$x_{adv}^{(i+1)} = x_{adv}^{(i)} + \mathcal{P}_\epsilon(\alpha \nabla_x \mathcal{L}(\mathcal{F}; x_{adv}^{(i)}, y)) \tag{3}$$

where $x_{adv}^{(0)} = x$, $\mathcal{P}_\epsilon$ is the projection onto the $\ell_p$ norm ball designated by $\epsilon$ and $\alpha$ is the stepsize of the applied perturbation. We use $\ell_\infty$ for our experiments.

Despite the successes of these attacks, usually, the evaluation of the robustness of proposed defenses is not done thoroughly, which gives a false sense of robustness.

*AutoAttack* (AA) [8] was proposed to solve this problem. AutoAttack is a parameter-free attack that is both stronger and more reliable than previous attacks used in the adversarial robustness literature. It combines four different attacks: two versions of the parameter-free variant of PGD, Auto-PGD [8], Fast Boundary Adaptive Attack [8], and the black-box attack Square Attack [3].

## 2.2    Attribution Techniques

Since our focus is to find the importance of each pixel of the input image for a specific prediction, we use gradient-based attribution methods to guide the denoising.

Saliency maps [30] are the simplest type of attribution methods. They can be generated by backpropagating the gradient of a class label with respect to an input image on the network. These attribution maps have higher values in the pixels where the images have more relevant features to the class and lower values where the features are not as important.

A more advanced attribution technique, the one used in our defense, is Integrated Gradients (IG) [31]. IG calculates the integral of the saliency maps generated along a straight line from a baseline to the input image. This is more easily understood mathematically as:

$$IG_i(x) = (x_i - b_i) \cdot \int_{\alpha=0}^{1} \frac{\partial \mathcal{F}(b_i + \alpha(x_i - b_i))}{\partial x_i} d\alpha \qquad (4)$$

where $IG_i$ is the attribution of the ith pixel, $b$ is the baseline and $\alpha$ is the parameter for the line from $b$ to $x$. In practice, this is approximated as a Riemann sum by:

$$IG_i^*(x) = (x_i - b_i) \cdot \sum_{k=0}^{m} \frac{\partial \mathcal{F}(b_i + \frac{k}{m} \cdot (x_i - b_i))}{\partial x_i} \cdot \frac{1}{m} \qquad (5)$$

where $m$ is the number of steps in the approximation of the integral.

## 3    Methodology

### 3.1    Choi and Hall Sharpening (CHSharp)

The denoising method used in our defense is Choi and Hall's sharpening [7], which was originally formulated for bias reduction of density estimators. CHSharp was aimed at decreasing the bias near local maxima and local minima, which were often overestimated and underestimated by density estimators. CHSharp uses local constant regression, a form of weighted averaging commonly used in statistics and first proposed by Nadaraya and Watson independently in 1964 [25,35]. CHSharp works as follows: given an evaluation point $x_j$, the estimate for the regression coefficient $\beta_0$ in local constant regression is obtained by minimizing the locally weighted least squares criterion

$$\sum_{i=1}^{n} W_h(x_i, x_j)[y_i - \beta_0]^2. \qquad (6)$$

with respect to $\beta_0$. The solution to 6 is the Nadaraya-Watson estimator,

$$\beta_0 = \frac{\sum_{i=1}^{n} W_h(x_i, x_j) y_i}{\sum_{i=1}^{n} W_h(x_i, x_j)}, \qquad (7)$$

where $W_h(x_i, x_j) = W[(x_i - x_j)/h(x)]$ for some weight function $W$ and bandwidth $h$. The weight function for our purposes is Gaussian $\phi_h$ with standard deviation $h$,

$$\beta_0 = \frac{\sum_{i=1}^{n} \phi_h(x_i - x_j) y_i}{\sum_{i=1}^{n} \phi_h(x_i - x_j)} \qquad (8)$$

Instead of using data pairs $(x_i, y_i)$, which is how regression is normally performed, the sharpening method involves regression of the $x_i$'s against themselves. In other words, we use data pairs $(x_i, x_i)$. In this case, the regression coefficient $\beta_0$ is the sharpened data point $x'_j$, and is given by

$$x'_j = \frac{\sum_{i=1}^{n} \phi_h(x_i - x_j)x_i}{\sum_{i=1}^{n} \phi_h(x_i - x_j)}. \tag{9}$$

which will yield the sharpened data,

$$(x'_1, \ldots, x'_n).$$

This process can then be iterated for further sharpening,

$$x_j^{(m)} = \frac{\sum_{i=1}^{n} \phi_h(x_i^{(m-1)} - x_j^{(m-1)})x_i^{(m-1)}}{\sum_{i=1}^{n} \phi_h(x_i^{(m-1)} - x_j^{(m-1)})} \tag{10}$$

A pixel is therefore only sharpened based on the pixels surrounding it and will be more or less influenced by neighbour pixels depending on the bandwidth used.

## 3.2   Attribution Guided Sharpening (AGS)

Attribution Guided Sharpening (AGS) builds around already existing non-robust classifiers to create a robust defense against attacks. The workflow of AGS is shown in Fig. 2: given a non robust classifier $\mathcal{F}_{nominal}$ that classifies inputs $x \in \mathbb{R}^d$ to classes $y \in \mathcal{C}$, and an input $x$, the non-robust model first predicts the label $y_p^*$. Then AGS calculates the IG attributions, $a$, of the prediction and uses them to guide the CHSharp denoising of $x$. This is done by setting the bandwidth of the CHSharp algorithm equal to some affine function of the attribution $a_i$ of each pixel $x_i$. The transformed image, $\tilde{x}$, then passes through a second classifier, $\mathcal{F}_{sharp}$ to make the robust prediction $\tilde{y}_p$. We refer to this workflow, as shown in Fig. 2, more generally as Attribution Guided Denoising (AGD) because it allows for a lot of different combinations of attribution and denoising techniques.

To understand the intuition behind AGS, consider the classifier $\mathcal{F}_{nominal}$ and an input image $x$ that belongs to class $c$. An adversary will add a perturbation to $x$ to create an image $x_{adv}$ that is classified as $y_p^*$ such that $y_p^* \neq c$. The attribution $a = IG(\mathcal{F}_{nominal}; x_{adv}, y_p^*)$ reveals that pixels that do not represent the class $c$ have high attribution values, which translates into the misclassification of $x_{adv}$. If the attribution of a pixel is high, its bandwidth is high as well in AGS and CHSharp shifts its value closer to that of neighbouring pixels and thus decreases it, which will decrease its attribution for class $y_p^*$ and bring it closer to $c$. If, however, the attribution of a pixel is low, its bandwidth will be correspondingly low, and thus it will not be heavily affected by neighbouring pixels, its value will not change much. In summary, when the processed image $CHSharp(x_{adv})$ gets classified by $\mathcal{F}_{sharp}$, it will be closer to $c$, making the classifier more likely to predict the correct label $\tilde{y}_p$ such that $\tilde{y}_p = c$.

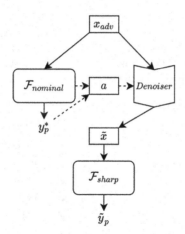

**Fig. 2.** Attribution Guided Denoising workflow. For AGS, the denoiser is Choi and Hall's sharpening method.

## 4    Experiments

In our experiments, we evaluated the performance of AGS on MNIST, CIFAR-10 and CIFAR-100 against FGSM, 100-PGD and AutoAttack. We built our defense using PyTorch and evaluated all attacks using Torchattacks [19]. The architecture used for the MNIST classifier was a Convolutional Neural network (CNN) with 4 convolutional layers as shown in Fig. 3. For CIFAR-10 and CIFAR-100, the architecture of choice was ResNet-18. In our defense procedure, $AGS_{pret}$, we trained $\mathcal{F}_{nominal}$ and used this same network as the $\mathcal{F}_{sharp}$ classifier. All our code is available at https://github.com/Idsl-group/AGS. More details about our training procedure and hyperparameters can be found there.

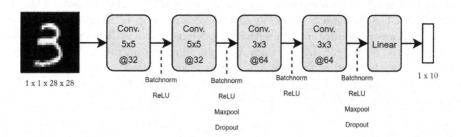

**Fig. 3.** Our CNN architecture.

**Table 1.** Adversarial robustness of AGS and various defenses extracted mainly from [8] against $FGSM$, $\ell_\infty$ $100 - PGD$ and AutoAttack ($AA$). The attack column $None$ refers to the nominal accuracy of the defenses. We use $\epsilon = 0.3$ for MNIST, $\epsilon = \frac{8}{255}$ for CIFAR-10 and CIFAR-100. The column AT refers to whether the model incorporated Adversarial Training as part of the defense or not.

| Model | Dataset | Defense | Params | AT | Attack | | | |
|---|---|---|---|---|---|---|---|---|
| | | | | | $None$ | $FGSM$ | $PGD$ | $AA$ |
| 4-CNN | MNIST | $AGS_{pret}$ | 0.1 M* | ✗ | **99.16** | **98.55** | **98.10** | **96.17** |
| 2-CNN | MNIST | [36] | 0.2 M | ✓ | 98.50 | – | 90.19 | 82.93 |
| 4-CNN | MNIST | [40] | 0.3 M | ✓ | 98.38 | – | 95.25 | 93.96 |
| 2-CNN | MNIST | [24] | 3.3 M | ✓ | 98.53 | 95.60 | 91.97 | 88.50 |
| 2-CNN | MNIST | [11] | 3.3 M | ✓ | 98.95 | – | 95.96 | 91.40 |
| ResNet-18 | CIFAR-10 | $AGS_{pret}$ | 11 M | ✗ | 87.72 | **85.05** | **84.65** | **82.65** |
| WRN-28-10 | CIFAR-10 | [15] | 38 M | ✓ | **89.48** | – | 64.08 | 62.80 |
| WRN-28-10 | CIFAR-10 | [37] | 38 M | ✓ | 88.25 | 67.94 | 63.58 | 60.05 |
| WRN-34-10 | CIFAR-10 | [24] | 48 M | ✓ | 87.14 | 56.1 | 46.46 | 44.04 |
| WRN-106-8 | CIFAR-10 | [33] | 108 M | ✓ | 86.06 | – | 61.87 | 56.03 |
| ResNet-18 | CIFAR-100 | $AGS_{pret}$ | 11 M | ✗ | 62.70 | **61.50** | **59.20** | **59.00** |
| WRN-28-10 | CIFAR-100 | [16] | 38 M | ✗ | 59.23 | – | 33.17 | 28.42 |
| WRN-34-12 | CIFAR-100 | TRADES[a] | 67 M | ✓ | 56.75 | 37.68 | 29.02[a] | 25.23 |
| WRN-34-12 | CIFAR-100 | MART[a] | 67 M | ✓ | 58.27 | 41.24 | 34.12[a] | 28.63 |
| WRN-34-20 | CIFAR-100 | [9] | 192 M | ✓ | **63.55** | – | 35.50[b] | 30.20 |

*M: Millions.
[a]Refers to the implementation of these defenses in [17] where they use a 20-step PGD.
[b]They use ResNet-18 and 20-step PGD for attack evaluation.

Table 1 shows the results of our experiments and demonstrates that AGS provides a significant improvement in robustness on the three datasets studied, even against AutoAttack. While in some cases the drop in clean accuracy due to AGS is more significant than with other defenses, it is still reasonable and is compensated by the remarkable improvements in robust accuracy. This might be alleviated with larger models with a better generalization capability; however, we limit our study to smaller models to make efficient use of our resources and emphasize the potential of this defense.

## 4.1 MNIST

This dataset consists of $28 \times 28$ pixel black and white images of handwritten digits. We trained the $\mathcal{F}_{nominal}$ classifier to 99.39% accuracy and used it to build our $AGS_{pret}$ defense. As Table 1 shows, AGS provides the best robustness on MNIST against all $\epsilon = 0.3$ attacks studied. It achieves a 98.6% accuracy against FGSM, compared to the 95.6% accuracy of [24]. The improvements against PGD are similar with 98.1% robust accuracy versus 95.96% achieved by [11]. More notably, AGS achieves 96.2% robust accuracy against AutoAttack while the second best defense studied achieves only 93.96% [40]. Our architecture is the smallest out of all the architectures studied with only 84,714 parameters while some of the defenses studied, like [11], have over 30 times more parameters. Nevertheless, we also study smaller architectures with a number of parameters closer to 200,000 and 300,000 like [36]. Moreover, AGS is the only defense that does not require adversarial training.

## 4.2  CIFAR-10

This dataset consists of $32 \times 32$ pixel colour images of 10 different categories: airplanes, cars, birds, cats, deer, dogs, frogs, horses, ships, and trucks. We trained the $\mathcal{F}_{nominal}$ classifier to 90.15% accuracy and built our $AGS_{pret}$ defense with it. As Table 1 shows, AGS obtains the best robustness against all $\epsilon = \frac{8}{255}$ attacks studied on CIFAR-10 as well. Again, our model is the only one that does not make use of adversarial training and our architecture is the simplest out of all the studied models with only 11 million parameters compared to 38 million or 108 million used in [15] or [33] respectively. In this case, AGS does not achieve the best nominal accuracy, 87.72%, and is surpassed by [15] with 89.48% nominal accuracy. Nevertheless, AGS still outperforms the other defenses by more than 15% points in robust accuracy against the three studied attacks. We achieve 85.05% against FGSM compared to 67.94% in [37]. Similarly, while [15] only achieves 64.08% and 62.8% robust accuracy against PGS and AutoAttack respectively, AGS provides 84.65% and 82.65% robust accuracies.

## 4.3  CIFAR-100

This dataset is an extended version of CIFAR-10 with 100 classes instead of 10. As with MNIST and CIFAR-10, we first trained the $\mathcal{F}_{nominal}$ classifier that we used for our $AGS_{pret}$ to 67.22% accuracy. The drop in accuracy produced by AGS is more notable in this dataset with only 62.70% clean accuracy compared to 63.55% achieved by [9]. However, AGS still provides the best robustness against all $\epsilon = \frac{8}{255}$ attacks studied despite using a significantly smaller model than the rest of the defenses studied (11 million versus 38 million in [16] or 192 million in [9]). AGS provides a robust accuracy of 61.5% against FGSM compared to 41.24 % provided by [17]. AGS achieves 59.20% and 59% robust accuracy against PGD and Autoattack respectively compared to 35.50% and 30.2% achieved by [9]. All the defenses studied except for AGS and [16] use adversarial training, but AGS still gives the best robust performance with an almost 2-fold improvement in robust accuracy against Auto-Attack.

## 5  Conclusions

In this paper, we have taken a step forward in bridging two of the most important problems with current machine learning: vulnerability to attacks and lack of explainability. We propose a new kind of defense called Attribution Guided Denoising (AGD), which uses the explanations of classification labels of a model to guide the denoising of adversarial noise. Particularly, we introduce Attribution Guided Sharpening (AGS), which uses Integrated Gradient attributions to guide Choi and Hall's sharpening method to successfully remove adversarial perturbations in images. Our experiments on three benchmark datasets (MNIST, CIFAR-10 and CIFAR-100) reveal state-of-the-art performance. We show that AGS provides a better robust accuracy against AutoAttack than other popular defenses in the literature using much smaller models and without the need to retrain the model or use adversarial training.

### 5.1  Looking Ahead

While we have shown that AGS can provide better robust accuracies than most popular defenses and have taken a significant step towards solving the robustness problem, we do not claim to have solved it as others have done before. Evaluating a defense against all existing attacks is not feasible so we limited our evaluation to the two most common attacks in the adversarial literature: FGSM and PGD, and one of the strongest attacks known to date: AutoAttack, which has the advantage of being parameter-free and thus makes evaluations more reliable. Despite the excellent performance of AGS against these attacks, there might be other unexplored attacks that can beat our defense. We encourage the machine learning community to try to craft new attacks that can beat our defense. This is the only possible way to find weaknesses in defenses and make progress towards more reliable machine learning.

We also want to advocate for more work at the intersection of explainability and robustness. We believe that these two fields go hand in hand and that there is a lot of potential at their intersection. It would be interesting to study other possible AGD defenses with different denoising methods or other attribution techniques and to verify the performance of AGD in other domains. We also want to encourage others to find more ways to include explainability in building robust defenses.

# References

1. Adadi, A., Berrada, M.: Peeking inside the black-box: a survey on explainable artificial intelligence (XAI). IEEE Access **6**, 52138–52160 (2018)
2. Amodei, D., et al.: Deep speech 2: end-to-end speech recognition in English and mandarin. In: International Conference on Machine Learning, pp. 173–182. PMLR (2016)
3. Andriushchenko, M., Croce, F., Flammarion, N., Hein, M.: Square attack: a query-efficient black-box adversarial attack via random search. In: Vedaldi, A., Bischof, H., Brox, T., Frahm, J.-M. (eds.) ECCV 2020. LNCS, vol. 12368, pp. 484–501. Springer, Cham (2020). https://doi.org/10.1007/978-3-030-58592-1_29
4. Athalye, A., Carlini, N.: On the robustness of the CVPR 2018 white-box adversarial example defenses. arXiv preprint arXiv:1804.03286 (2018)

5. Bakhti, Y., Fezza, S.A., Hamidouche, W., Déforges, O.: DDSA: a defense against adversarial attacks using deep denoising sparse autoencoder. IEEE Access **7**, 160397–160407 (2019)
6. Bojarski, M., et al.: End to end learning for self-driving cars. arXiv preprint arXiv:1604.07316 (2016)
7. Choi, E., Hall, P.: Miscellanea. Data sharpening as a prelude to density estimation. Biometrika **86**(4), 941–947 (1999)
8. Croce, F., Hein, M.: Reliable evaluation of adversarial robustness with an ensemble of diverse parameter-free attacks. In: International Conference on Machine Learning, pp. 2206–2216. PMLR (2020)
9. Cui, J., Liu, S., Wang, L., Jia, J.: Learnable boundary guided adversarial training. In: Proceedings of the IEEE/CVF International Conference on Computer Vision, pp. 15721–15730 (2021)
10. Deng, Y., Zheng, X., Zhang, T., Chen, C., Lou, G., Kim, M.: An analysis of adversarial attacks and defenses on autonomous driving models. In: 2020 IEEE International Conference on Pervasive Computing and Communications (PerCom), pp. 1–10. IEEE (2020)
11. Ding, G.W., Sharma, Y., Lui, K.Y.C., Huang, R.: MMA training: direct input space margin maximization through adversarial training. arXiv preprint arXiv:1812.02637 (2018)
12. Eykholt, K., et al.: Robust physical-world attacks on deep learning visual classification. In: Proceedings of the IEEE Conference on Computer Vision and Pattern Recognition, pp. 1625–1634 (2018)
13. Finlayson, S.G., Bowers, J.D., Ito, J., Zittrain, J.L., Beam, A.L., Kohane, I.S.: Adversarial attacks on medical machine learning. Science **363**(6433), 1287–1289 (2019)
14. Goodfellow, I.J., Shlens, J., Szegedy, C.: Explaining and harnessing adversarial examples. arXiv preprint arXiv:1412.6572 (2014)
15. Gowal, S., Qin, C., Uesato, J., Mann, T., Kohli, P.: Uncovering the limits of adversarial training against norm-bounded adversarial examples. arXiv preprint arXiv:2010.03593 (2020)
16. Hendrycks, D., Lee, K., Mazeika, M.: Using pre-training can improve model robustness and uncertainty. In: International Conference on Machine Learning, pp. 2712–2721. PMLR (2019)
17. Huang, H., Wang, Y., Erfani, S.M., Gu, Q., Bailey, J., Ma, X.: Exploring architectural ingredients of adversarially robust deep neural networks. arXiv preprint arXiv:2110.03825 (2021)
18. Jha, S., et al.: Attribution-driven causal analysis for detection of adversarial examples. arXiv preprint arXiv:1903.05821 (2019)
19. Kim, H.: Torchattacks: a PyTorch repository for adversarial attacks. arXiv preprint arXiv:2010.01950 (2020)
20. Krizhevsky, A., Hinton, G., et al.: Learning multiple layers of features from tiny images (2009)
21. LeCun, Y., Bottou, L., Bengio, Y., Haffner, P.: Gradient-based learning applied to document recognition. Proc. IEEE **86**(11), 2278–2324 (1998)
22. Liao, F., Liang, M., Dong, Y., Pang, T., Hu, X., Zhu, J.: Defense against adversarial attacks using high-level representation guided denoiser. In: Proceedings of the IEEE Conference on Computer Vision and Pattern Recognition, pp. 1778–1787 (2018)
23. Liu, X., Yang, H., Liu, Z., Song, L., Li, H., Chen, Y.: DPatch: an adversarial patch attack on object detectors. arXiv preprint arXiv:1806.02299 (2018)

24. Madry, A., Makelov, A., Schmidt, L., Tsipras, D., Vladu, A.: Towards deep learning models resistant to adversarial attacks. arXiv preprint arXiv:1706.06083 (2017)
25. Nadaraya, E.A.: On estimating regression. Theory Probab. Appl. **9**, 141–142 (1964)
26. Papernot, N., McDaniel, P., Goodfellow, I.: Transferability in machine learning: from phenomena to black-box attacks using adversarial samples. arXiv preprint arXiv:1605.07277 (2016)
27. Ribeiro, M.T., Singh, S., Guestrin, C.: "Why should i trust you?" Explaining the predictions of any classifier. In: Proceedings of the 22nd ACM SIGKDD International Conference on Knowledge Discovery and Data Mining, pp. 1135–1144 (2016)
28. Rice, L., Wong, E., Kolter, Z.: Overfitting in adversarially robust deep learning. In: International Conference on Machine Learning, pp. 8093–8104. PMLR (2020)
29. Salman, H., Sun, M., Yang, G., Kapoor, A., Kolter, J.Z.: Denoised smoothing: a provable defense for pretrained classifiers. arXiv preprint arXiv:2003.01908 (2020)
30. Simonyan, K., Vedaldi, A., Zisserman, A.: Deep inside convolutional networks: visualising image classification models and saliency maps. arXiv preprint arXiv:1312.6034 (2013)
31. Sundararajan, M., Taly, A., Yan, Q.: Axiomatic attribution for deep networks. In: International Conference on Machine Learning, pp. 3319–3328. PMLR (2017)
32. Szegedy, C., et al.: Intriguing properties of neural networks. arXiv preprint arXiv:1312.6199 (2013)
33. Uesato, J., Alayrac, J.B., Huang, P.S., Stanforth, R., Fawzi, A., Kohli, P.: Are labels required for improving adversarial robustness? arXiv preprint arXiv:1905.13725 (2019)
34. Wang, J.B., et al.: A machine learning framework for resource allocation assisted by cloud computing. IEEE Netw. **32**(2), 144–151 (2018)
35. Watson, G.S.: Smooth regression analysis. Sankhyā Indian J. Stat. **26**, 359–372 (1964)
36. Wong, E., Rice, L., Kolter, J.Z.: Fast is better than free: revisiting adversarial training. arXiv preprint arXiv:2001.03994 (2020)
37. Wu, D., Xia, S.T., Wang, Y.: Adversarial weight perturbation helps robust generalization. arXiv preprint arXiv:2004.05884 (2020)
38. Yang, C., Rangarajan, A., Ranka, S.: Global model interpretation via recursive partitioning. In: 2018 IEEE 20th International Conference on High Performance Computing and Communications; IEEE 16th International Conference on Smart City; IEEE 4th International Conference on Data Science and Systems (HPCC/SmartCity/DSS), pp. 1563–1570. IEEE (2018)
39. Yang, P., Chen, J., Hsieh, C.J., Wang, J.L., Jordan, M.: ML-LOO: detecting adversarial examples with feature attribution. In: Proceedings of the AAAI Conference on Artificial Intelligence, vol. 34, pp. 6639–6647 (2020)
40. Zhang, H., et al.: Towards stable and efficient training of verifiably robust neural networks. arXiv preprint arXiv:1906.06316 (2019)

# VAE-CE: Visual Contrastive Explanation Using Disentangled VAEs

Yoeri Poels$^{(\boxtimes)}$ and Vlado Menkovski

Eindhoven University of Technology, Eindhoven, The Netherlands
{y.r.j.poels,v.menkovski}@tue.nl

**Abstract.** The goal of a classification model is to assign the correct labels to data. In most cases, this data is not fully described by the given set of labels. Often a rich set of meaningful concepts exist in the domain that can describe each datapoint much more precisely. Such concepts can also be highly useful for interpreting the model's classifications. In this paper we propose Variational Autoencoder-based Contrastive Explanation (VAE-CE), a model that represents data with high-level concepts and uses this representation for both classification and explanation. The explanations are contrastive, conveying why a datapoint is assigned to one class rather than an alternative class. An explanation is specified as a set of transformations of the input datapoint, where each step changes a concept towards the contrastive class. We build the model using a disentangled VAE, extended with a new supervised method for disentangling individual dimensions. An analysis on synthetic data and MNIST validates the utility of the approaches to both disentanglement and explanation generation. Code is available at https://github.com/yoeripoels/vce.

**Keywords:** Deep learning · Explanation · Interpretability · VAE

## 1 Introduction

Discriminative models for classification based on deep neural networks achieve outstanding performance given a sufficient amount of training data. They are highly practical as they can be trained in an end-to-end fashion to develop a map $f : X \to Y$ given pairs of datapoints $x \in X$ and labels $y \in Y$. Much of this success is due to their hierarchical nature, which allows them to learn an effective high-level representation of low-level input data. However, this aspect is also the reason for one of their major limitations. Even though the models learn high-level representations, in most cases the model's reasoning is difficult to interpret. The learned representations are often hard to align with existing concepts in the domain. So, these models are commonly considered black boxes that directly map observations to target variables. Such black-box models often lack user trust [22], as we cannot accurately gauge how they make their predictions.

Many approaches have been proposed that focus on developing interpretations of models' decisions and internal representations. When the data consists

© The Author(s), under exclusive license to Springer Nature Switzerland AG 2022
T. Bouadi et al. (Eds.): IDA 2022, LNCS 13205, pp. 237–250, 2022.
https://doi.org/10.1007/978-3-031-01333-1_19

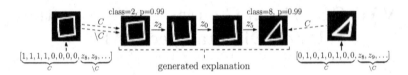

**Fig. 1.** An explanation where lines are concepts, and combinations thereof define classes. The query (left) and exemplar (right) differ in some class-relevant concepts in $C$. This difference is conveyed by transforming in domain $C$, one concept at a time.

of natural images, some of these interpretations rely on the human visual system, by creating visualizations of the model's internal representation of the data (e.g. saliency maps [21,34] or component visualizations [25,30]). In general, such approaches are limited to certain types of data and to the qualitative interpretation by domain experts. In this paper, we propose an approach that includes interpretability as an integral part of the model. Specifically, our model consists of maps $f_c : X \to C$ and $f_y : C \to Y$, where $C$ indicates the domain of high-level human-understandable *concepts*. Map $f_c$ develops an encoding of the datapoint into domain $C$ that we then use to explain the model's decisions, whereas map $f_y$ implements the downstream task of assigning a class to the datapoint.

The explanations that we produce are *contrastive*. Contrastive explanation follows the human tendency of explaining an event by (implicitly) comparing it to an alternative event that did not take place [17,23]. In our case, they convey why a datapoint belongs to one class rather than some other class, by highlighting the differences as a *sequence of transformations* of the datapoint. When considering image data we obtain *visual* explanations; an example is depicted in Fig. 1.

To create suitable explanations we need to be able to represent the data in an interpretable concept space and be able to generate interpretable transformations against a contrastive target. For these purposes we use a generative latent variable model, specifically a Variational Autoencoder (VAE) [15,31]. We employ existing methods to disentangle class-relevant from irrelevant information [3,40], and expand this model with a new method for disentangling individual dimensions. To develop the contrastive explanation, we identify a target datapoint that is associated with the target class, referred to as the exemplar. We then infer a sequence of transformations in concept domain $C$ that interpolates between the query datapoint and the exemplar. The exemplar is selected such that it is representative of its class, and such that the sequence is of minimum length.

We denote our approach as VAE-based Contrastive Explanation (VAE-CE). To be able to validate VAE-CE, we define a method for quantitatively evaluating explanations, using data with a known generating process. We compare VAE-CE to similar VAE-based methods and evaluate the individual components of our method. The two main contributions of this paper can be summarized as follows:

- We propose a method for disentangling a VAE's latent dimensions, which is supervised by data pairs (not) differing in a single semantic concept (Sect. 3.2).

– We propose a method for generating explanations of a datapoints' class assignment. This method considers training a VAE to represent class concepts in individual dimensions in a subpart of the latent space, and using this space to generate interpolations depicting the class-relevant concepts (Sect. 3).

## 2   Related Work

**Image-classification explanations** come in many shapes. Saliency-based methods explain classifications by highlighting the contribution of pixels w.r.t. either the decision itself [21,34] or to an alternative classification [27,29] (i.e. contrastive explanations). To evaluate pixel contributions in a black-box manner, one can perturb the input images, e.g. for classification [32] or for contrasting classes [6].

The use of examples that flip a class decision, counterfactuals, can help explain a model's classification boundaries [39]. Another method for conveying these boundaries considers using a query image and an alternative image, and showing which pieces must be swapped to flip the decision [9]. The use of deep generative models, such as Generative Adversarial Networks (GANs) [8] and VAEs [15,31], has been proposed to explain classification boundaries in a high-level space. Such methods, e.g. [18,26,33,36], involve various approaches to training a generative model and interpolating in its latent space to convey the class boundaries. Alternatively, one can create boundary-crossing translations using datapoints [28].

To interpret decisions one can also work with high-level concepts, e.g. by evaluating learned components [25,30] or by identifying associations between concepts and classifications [14]. More integrated into the model, one can also first detect concepts and use them to classify in an interpretable fashion [1,41]. Other examples of self-explaining methods consider generating textual explanations of classifications [11] and matching image parts to other samples to assign a class [4].

**Disentanglement in VAEs** can be defined as the notion that single latent dimensions are sensitive to changes in single generative factors while being invariant to changes in others [12,19]. It is also used in the context of separating information related to a specific factor from unrelated information [2,40].

Unsupervised approaches generally add regularization with some extra assumptions about the latent space, e.g. [5,12]. Similar to our approach to disentanglement (Sect. 3.2), [42] propose learning a disentangled representation using pairs differing in a single dimension, maximizing mutual information. Regarding unsupervised disentanglement, [19] raised the question whether we can expect well-disentangled representations, showing that strong inductive biases or supervision are a necessity for learning and validating such representations.

Using supervision, one can group datapoints according to a common feature and enforce a part of the latent space to share a representation for this group [2,13]. A weakly-supervised variant of this idea considers heuristically finding common dimensions and sharing them [20]. Alternatively, one can use labels to encourage a disentangled latent space, e.g. by optimizing subspaces to contain or exclude information about a label using classification objectives [3,40].

## 3   Method: VAE-CE

### 3.1   Learning a Data Representation for Class Explanation

To represent the data in a high-level space, we use a VAE [15,31]. A VAE aims to approximate a dataset's distribution under the assumption that its samples $x$ are generated according to latent variable $z$ with known prior $p(z)$; it aims to model $p(x, z) = p(x|z)p(z)$. This relation is approximated using an encoder $q_\phi(z|x)$ and decoder $p_\theta(x|z)$ distribution, parameterized by neural networks, and optimized using a lower bound on the likelihood of the data, the *ELBO*. The reparametrization trick [15] is used to (back)propagate through latent variables.

Since not all information in the data, and consequently in latent variable $z$, is necessarily class related, we wish to *disentangle* class-relevant from irrelevant information. The VAE's *ELBO* objective is extended with classification terms, in line with works such as [3,40]. We split $z$ into subspaces $z_y$ and $z_x$, where the former aims to contain class-relevant information and the latter should contain the remaining information. We use a separate encoder for inferring each latent subspace; the $z_y$ encoder, $q_{\phi_y}(z_y|x)$, serves as the concept encoder, $f_c$.

To achieve this split we introduce categorical distributions $q_{\psi_y}(y|z_y)$ and $q_{\psi_x}(y|z_x)$, parameterized by neural networks, and referred to as the latent spaces' classifiers. The former, $q_{\psi_y}(y|z_y)$, is also used to infer class predictions, serving as $f_y$. For training, we simultaneously optimize both classifiers and both encoders using sample-label pairs $(x, y)$. However, since $z_x$ should contain little information about label $y$, we reverse the loss' gradients for $z_x$'s encoder, $q_{\phi_x}(z_x|x)$, through a Gradient Reversal Layer (GRL) [7]. The full loss terms (including the *ELBO*), where the subscript denotes the optimized parameters, are as follows:

$$\mathcal{L}_{\theta,\phi_y,\phi_x,\psi_y}(x, y) = -\mathbb{E}_{q_{\phi_y}(z_y|x),q_{\phi_x}(z_x|x)}[\log p_\theta(x|z_y, z_x)] \tag{1}$$

$$+ \beta_y KL(q_{\phi_y}(z_y|x)||p_\theta(z)) + \beta_x KL(q_{\phi_x}(z_x|x)||p_\theta(z)) \tag{2}$$

$$- \alpha\mathbb{E}_{q_{\phi_y}(z_y|x)}[\log(q_{\psi_y}(y|z_y))] \tag{3}$$

$$+ \alpha\mathbb{E}_{q_{\phi_x}(z_x|x)}[\log(q_{\psi_x}(y|z_x))], \tag{4}$$

$$\mathcal{L}_{\psi_x}(x, y) = -\mathbb{E}_{q_{\phi_x}(z_x|x)}[\log(q_{\psi_x}(y|z_x))], \tag{5}$$

with hyperparameters $\beta_y$, $\beta_x$ and $\alpha$. All expectations are approximated with single-sample Monte Carlo estimation. We assume $p_\theta(x|z_y, z_x)$ is a factorized Gaussian with fixed variance, letting us approximate (1) as squared error. Prior $p_\theta(z)$ is set to a standard factorized Gaussian, which lets us compute (2) analytically. (3–5) optimize the log-likelihood of the categorical distributions using categorical cross-entropy. Note that (4) is a negation of (5): Both are computed in a single pass using a GRL. Both losses update different components and are minimized simultaneously. Figure 2a shows an overview of the model.

## 3.2   Pair-Based Dimension Conditioning

To produce explanations that convey differences in class concepts, we must manipulate concepts individually. To exercise this control, we aim to learn a representation where individual $z_y$-dimensions control individual concepts. We introduce a new disentanglement method based on two assumptions: (1) a significant change in a latent dimension should correspond to changing a single concept and (2) we can train a model to evaluate such changes. This method acts as additional regularization and is summed to the previously described loss term.

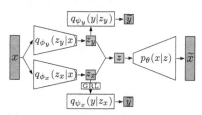 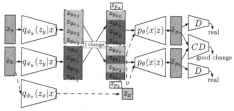

(a) The class-disentangled VAE: $x$ is encoded into $z_x$ and $z_y$, which together reconstruct $\tilde{x}$. Disentanglement is encouraged by auxiliary classifiers.

(b) Individual dimensions are disentangled in an amortized fashion: Randomly constructed latent variables differing in one dimension are optimized to exhibit a single concept change.

**Fig. 2.** The VAE from the viewpoint of class-based and concept-based disentanglement.

Two auxiliary models are used to aid this procedure: A 'Change Discriminator' ($CD$) and a regular 'Discriminator' ($D$), both predicting a value in the range $[0, 1]$. $CD$ is trained beforehand, and infers whether a pair of datapoints exhibits a desirable change. We train $CD$ as a binary classifier with pairs that either indicate a good change (a single concept change) or a bad change (no or multiple concept changes), and use it to optimize latent dimensions to exhibit such changes. $D$ is trained to distinguish between generated and real datapoints, as done in a GAN [8]. It is used to optimize the quality of the samples, avoiding a degenerate solution where non-realistic changes are produced that trick $CD$ (i.e. an adversarial attack [37]). Intuitively, the procedure works by having the VAE decode pairs differing in a single latent dimension and optimizing the model using a 'critic', $CD$, to make this change represent a single concept change. A visualization of the procedure is depicted in Fig. 2b. One step works as follows:

1. Encode two arbitrary datapoints $x_a$ and $x_b$ to their latent representations in $z_y$-space: $z_{y_a}$ and $z_{y_b}$. For the $z_x$-space, only encode datapoint $x_b$ to $z_x$.
2. Construct two latent variables from $z_{y_a}$ and $z_{y_b}$ that share all but one dimension. These variables are denoted as $z_{p_a}$ and $z_{p_b}$. Each dimension is picked from either $z_{y_a}$ or $z_{y_b}$ (equally likely), and all but one dimension are shared.

3. Generate $\widetilde{x}_{p_a}$ and $\widetilde{x}_{p_b}$ by decoding latent representations $(z_{p_a}, z_x)$ and $(z_{p_b}, z_x)$.
4. Optimize the encoders and the decoder such that $CD$ predicts a high-quality change between $\widetilde{x}_{p_a}$ and $\widetilde{x}_{p_b}$ and $D$ predicts that the samples are real.

The corresponding loss term is as follows:

$$\mathcal{L}_{\theta,\phi_y,\phi_x}(\widetilde{x}_{p_a}, \widetilde{x}_{p_b}) = -\alpha_r [\log(D(\widetilde{x}_{p_a})) + \log(D(\widetilde{x}_{p_b}))] \tag{6}$$

$$+ \alpha_p n_y \frac{|z_{p_a} - z_{p_b}|}{|z_{y_a} - z_{y_b}|} \cdot -\log(CD(\widetilde{x}_{p_a}, \widetilde{x}_{p_b})), \tag{7}$$

with hyperparameters $\alpha_r$ and $\alpha_p$, and $n_y$ denoting the number of dimensions in $z_y$. The first component of (7) ensures we do not penalize 'bad' changes when the differing dimension is insignificant. $D$ is trained as a binary classifier (as in a GAN), using generated samples as one class and training samples as the other.

### 3.3  Explanation Generation

Explanations are created by identifying an exemplar, and translating from the query's class concepts to those of the exemplar. The exemplar is chosen from an alternative, e.g. the second most likely, class. When creating explanations we use mean values, rather than samples, of latent variable $z$; we substitute $z$ for $\mu$ in this subsection. We refer to the query and exemplar using subscripts $a$ and $b$.

**Exemplar identification** rests on two principles: (1) how representative a datapoint is of its class and (2) how similar it is to the datapoint we contrast it with. To capture the former we only evaluate datapoints whose class probability is above a given threshold. For the latter, we select the datapoint with the minimum squared difference between the class-specific embeddings $\mu_{y_a}$ and $\mu_{y_b}$.

**Explanation generation** works by transforming the class-relevant embedding from the query $(\mu_{y_a})$ to the exemplar $(\mu_{y_b})$ and showcasing the intermediate steps; the class-irrelevant embedding $(\mu_{x_a})$ is not changed. To highlight one concept per step we change dimension values at once, and allow for multiple switches per step. We allow for the latter as the query and exemplar could share concepts: Switching only the corresponding dimension results in a meaningless step. We aim to find the shortest path of this structure, in line with the Minimum Description Length principle [10]. This path is further optimized w.r.t. two aspects: (1) each step should depict a single concept change and (2) each state should represent a realistic sample. These properties are optimized using $CD$ and $D$.

Not all interpolation paths are explicitly computed, as the quantity of paths changing (groups of) dimensions grows extremely fast.[1] Rather, we build a graph denoting all paths, where each edge denotes the cost of adding this state to the interpolation. For the change of state $\widetilde{x}_i$ to $\widetilde{x}_j$, the cost is computed as follows:

$$w_{ij} = [\alpha(1 - D(\widetilde{x}_j)) + \beta(1 - CD(\widetilde{x}_i, \widetilde{x}_j))] \cdot k^\gamma, \tag{8}$$

---

[1] Equal to the weak orderings of a set: For $n$ dimensions, the $n^{th}$ Fubini number [24].

where $k$ denotes the number of changed dimensions, and $\alpha$, $\beta$, and $\gamma$ are hyper-parameters. While we can find the shortest path in linear time w.r.t. graph size (as the graph is directed and acyclic) [38], the graph itself grows quickly: For $n$ dimensions to change, the explanation graph has $2^n$ nodes and $3^n - 2^n$ edges.

# 4 Experiments

## 4.1 Datasets

**Synthetic data,** used for a controlled evaluation, is structured as follows. The data's underlying concepts are lines (defined by their position and orientation), of which combinations define classes. To then create datapoints, non-trivial noise is added, which seeks to mimic the noise of handwritten shapes (e.g. MNIST). Change pairs (for $CD$) are created by taking a class configuration and hiding some line(s) in both images in the pair, such that only 1 (positive) or 0/2+ lines differ (negative). An overview for the synthetic data is provided in Fig. 3.

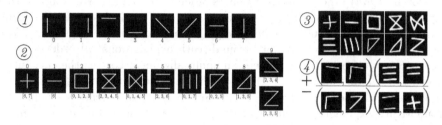

**Fig. 3.** Synthetic data generation. Using lines as concepts ① we form ten classes ②. Noise is added to create datapoints ③. Change pairs are formed using shapes differing in a single line (positive, top row) or in no/multiple lines (negative, bottom row) ④.

**MNIST** [16], used for evaluating a more realistic setting (i.e. with noisy supervision), is augmented as follows. Change pairs are created under the assumption that the underlying concepts are continuous lines. Digits are reduced to individual lines and pixels are clustered according to these lines. Then, pairs are created that exhibit 1 (positive) or 0/2+ (negative) line changes. Examples of MNIST samples and change pairs are depicted in Fig. 4. As creating a full description of each digit is a notably more challenging task than augmenting images to create change pairs, we do not consider methods requiring such supervision.

**Fig. 4.** MNIST samples ① and positive (left)/negative (right) change pairs ②.

## 4.2   Considered Evaluations

**Explanation Alignment Cost (*eac*).** To the best of our knowledge there is no method for quantitatively evaluating explanations of our defined structure. As such, we introduce the explanation alignment cost (*eac*). The *eac* quantifies the quality of a contrastive explanation based on a pair of datapoints $(a, b)$ as input. The explanation consists of an interpolation starting at datapoint $a$, gradually transitioning to the *class-relevant* concepts of $b$. In each step a single concept should change. An explanation for pair $(a, b)$ is evaluated according to the cost of aligning it to a ground-truth explanation. We define a ground-truth explanation as a minimum length sequence starting at $a$, with each subsequent state changing only a single concept from $a$ to $b$. The last state depicts a datapoint with all class-relevant concepts from $b$ and the remaining information from $a$.

The alignments we identify must map every state in the candidate explanation to at least one state in the ground-truth explanation, and vice versa. Additionally, we constrain this mapping such that both aligned sequences are increasing. Such an alignment can be computed using Dynamic Time Warping [35] in $O(nm)$ time (for two sequences of length $n$ and $m$). We compute the cost of each individual state-to-state mapping as the per-pixel squared error and a small constant ($\epsilon = .001$, for discouraging repetitions in the alignment). We compute this cost for all possible ground-truth explanations ($n!$ orders, given $n$ concepts to change) and take the minimum alignment cost as the *eac*. Intuitively, the *eac* measures the quality of individual steps (through the state-to-state error), whether the correct concepts are changed each step (by aligning to ground-truth explanations), and whether the explanation is of minimum length (as redundant steps only increase the alignment cost).

**Representation Quality Metrics.** Additionally, we explore the effects of the conditioning methods on the learned representations. To quantify concept disentanglement, the mutual information gap (*mig*) [5] is used. We estimate the *mig* for the class concepts in $z_y$ following the same procedure as [19]. The *ELBO* components–the reconstruction error and KL divergence–are also evaluated, denoted as *rec*, $kl_y$, and $kl_x$. The classification accuracy, using learned distribution $q_{\psi_y}(y|z_y)$, is denoted as *acc*. Finally, we evaluate the disentanglement of the latent subspaces w.r.t. class labels, by training logistic regression classifiers on the latent space embeddings. Their accuracies are denoted as *l-acc_y* and *l-acc_x*.

**Other Evaluations.** We evaluate whether the exemplar identification process selects variants with more common concepts as follows. Class 9 has 2 variants: Both variants have the same number of concepts in common with classes 1–6, but classes 7 and 8 have more in common with one variant. We query for exemplars and compare the probability of selecting the more common variant using classes 7 and 8 compared to the baseline probability. Also, we visualize explanations using single datapoints to explain, and using input pairs to contrast.

## 4.3   Comparison Overview

**Concept-Disentanglement Approaches.** *DVAE* denotes the baseline (Sect. 3.1). *LVAE* denotes an extension of label-based disentanglement (Sect. 3.1) for individual dimensions: For each $z_y$-dimension a label is provided indicating whether a concept is present, which is used with two auxiliary classifiers (per dimensions) to disentangle the concepts. *GVAE* denotes an adaption of [13] using pairs of datapoints with (at least) one specified matching concept. The inferred values for the $z_y$-dimension corresponding to this concept are averaged out, forcing this information to be shared through optimizing the *ELBO*. To evaluate the effect of the supervision alone, we use an adaptation of *ADA-GVAE* [20] that uses positive change pairs as supervision. While minimizing the *ELBO* on these pairs we average all but one dimension in $z_y$, which is selected as the dimension with the highest KL divergence (between the pair). *VAE-CE* denotes our method (Sect. 3).

**Model Implementations.** All methods share the same encoder and decoder architecture, with 8 latent dimensions for both $z_x$ and $z_y$. Prior distribution $p_\theta(z)$ is set to a standard factorized Gaussian, $\mathcal{N}(0, I)$. Other hyperparameters are optimized using the *eac* on synthetic data. As this cannot be evaluated for MNIST we use the same hyperparameters as chosen for the synthetic data.

**Interpolation Methods.** We denote our method (Sect. 3.3) as *graph*. For comparison, we consider two naive interpolation approaches. First, a smooth interpolation (denoted as *sm*), where we linearly interpolate between the query and exemplar's $z_y$-representation, changing all dimensions at once (using five states). Second, a dimension-wise interpolation (denoted as *dim*), where we change $z_y$-dimensions individually (in random order) if the absolute difference between the values is greater than 1. The leftover dimensions are all changed in the first step.

## 4.4   Results

We train four models for each configuration and report all results as mean $\pm$ standard deviation. For each metric, we mark the best mean value(s) in bold.

**Synthetic Data.** For the *explanation quality*, the *eac* results are provided in Fig. 6a, and explanations are shown in Figs. 6c and 5a. VAE-CE provides the best results, having the lowest *eac* and explanations closely resembling ground-truth explanations. As an ablation study we also used the disentanglement method and the explanation method in isolation (i.e. VAE-CE with other interpolations and *graph* interpolations with other models, see Fig. 6a). While the use of either component shows performance improvements, the scores are dominated by the combination thereof. The *representation-quality* metrics are provided in Table 1 (top). We can observe that the *mig* seems strongly correlated with the explanation quality, whereas other metrics vary, with the baseline performing the best classification-wise. Evidently, extra regularization comes at a cost. For the *exemplar selection experiment*, the baseline probability of picking the selected variant was .790 ± .018, whereas using classes 7 and 8 led to a probability of .938 ± .044, hinting that a variant with more common factors is more likely to be chosen.

**MNIST.** The *explanation quality* evaluations are depicted in Figs. 6b and 5b. Individual line changes are apparent in VAE-CE's explanations but they are noisier than before, likely because of the more complex lines and noisy supervision. However, the explanation steps still resemble line changes, which is less obvious for other methods' explanations. The *representation quality* metrics are provided in Table 1 (bottom). The results paint a similar picture as before, with no method dominating all metrics. We note that DVAE's accuracy is substantially higher than that of other methods, showing the cost of added regularization. As there are no ground-truth concepts available, the *eac* and *mig* are not evaluated.

(a) For synthetic samples.          (b) For MNIST samples.

**Fig. 5.** Explanations generated by VAE-CE. The query datapoints are outlined in red, followed by an explanation transforming the datapoint to the second most likely class. (Color figure online)

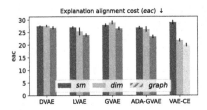

(a) *eac* on synthetic data. Note that *graph* relies on VAE-CE components.

(b) MNIST explanations.

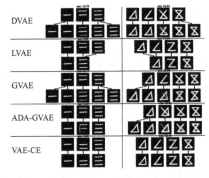

(c) Synthetic data explanations. For each explanation the top row shows the closest ground-truth explanation, whereas the bottom row depicts the created interpolation.

**Fig. 6.** Explanation quality comparisons, using query-exemplar pairs to explain. For the visual comparisons, VAE-CE generates *graph*-based interpolations, whereas other models use the naive interpolation method (*sm* or *dim*) with the lowest *eac*.

**Discussion and Limitations.** The *eac* results and qualitative comparisons indicate that VAE-CE provides benefits over the compared methods w.r.t. explanation quality. All extra regularization comes at a cost however, with each method having lower classification accuracy than the baseline. The remaining representation quality results were mixed, indicating trade-offs between the different regularization approaches in this regard.

We note that the considered datasets align well with our assumptions of the data, i.e. discrete concepts that are shared between classes. This assumption does not necessarily translate to complicated datasets, and extending VAE-CE to handle alternative supervision is non-trivial, highlighting a limitation of our method. Additionally, we compare only to VAE-based explanation methods and consider a limited set of metrics; further evaluations are desirable to strengthen the empirical results.

**Table 1.** Representation quality metrics for synthetic data (top) and MNIST (bottom).

| Model | $mig$ ↑ | $rec$ ↓ | $kl_y$ ↓ | $kl_x$ ↓ | $acc$ ↑ | $l\text{-}acc_y$ ↑ | $l\text{-}acc_x$ ↓ |
|---|---|---|---|---|---|---|---|
| DVAE | .121 ± .03 | 11.9 ± .28 | **4.4 ± .16** | 7.54 ± .22 | **.973 ± .001** | **.975 ± .001** | **.17 ± .02** |
| LVAE | .423 ± .05 | 13.5 ± 1.1 | 11.0 ± 5.4 | 7.05 ± .22 | .954 ± .008 | .962 ± .002 | .208 ± .06 |
| GVAE | .148 ± .07 | **10.2 ± .19** | 7.07 ± .57 | 5.74 ± .76 | .962 ± .001 | .964 ± .001 | .202 ± .02 |
| ADA-GVAE | .34 ± .07 | 10.7 ± .34 | 8.23 ± 1.2 | **4.94 ± 1.1** | .959 ± .001 | .961 ± .001 | .18 ± .04 |
| VAE-CE | **.49 ± .03** | 14.5 ± .6 | 7.81 ± .14 | 7.94 ± .46 | .963 ± .001 | .966 ± .001 | .182 ± .01 |
| DVAE | | 16.0 ± .35 | **4.34 ± .31** | 8.04 ± .25 | **.991 ± .001** | **.994 ± .001** | **.182 ± .01** |
| ADA-GVAE | | **13.6 ± .19** | 10.1 ± 1.1 | **3.6 ± .90** | .965 ± .002 | .97 ± .002 | .20 ± .02 |
| VAE-CE | | 21.7 ± 1.3 | 7.12 ± .29 | 6.65 ± .35 | .98 ± .002 | .983 ± .002 | **.182 ± .01** |

## 5 Conclusions

In this paper, we proposed an interpretability-focused classification model that creates explanations in a concept domain $C$. This method extends a class-disentangled VAE with a new supervised regularization method for disentangling individual concepts. Using this model we generate contrastive explanations, highlighting class concepts using a sequence of transformations. An introductory evaluation shows that the components of our method provide benefits over existing approaches. Ultimately, we believe that the proposed method allows us to learn a more understandable and trustworthy classification model. Topics still of interest consider exploring more complex data, more efficient approaches to explanation generation, and $CD$ implementations using less supervision.

## References

1. Alvarez-Melis, D., Jaakkola, T.S.: Towards robust interpretability with self-explaining neural networks. In: Proceedings of Advances in Neural Information Processing Systems, vol. 31, pp. 7786–7795 (2018)
2. Bouchacourt, D., Tomioka, R., Nowozin, S.: Multi-level variational autoencoder: learning disentangled representations from grouped observations. In: Proceedings of the Thirty-Second AAAI Conference on Artificial Intelligence, pp. 2095–2102 (2018)

3. Cai, R., Li, Z., Wei, P., Qiao, J., Zhang, K., Hao, Z.: Learning disentangled semantic representation for domain adaptation. In: Proceedings of the 28th International Joint Conference on Artificial Intelligence, pp. 2060–2066 (2019)

4. Chen, C., Li, O., Tao, D., Barnett, A., Rudin, C., Su, J.: This looks like that: deep learning for interpretable image recognition. In: Proceedings of Advances in Neural Information Processing Systems, vol. 32, pp. 8928–8939 (2019)

5. Chen, T.Q., Li, X., Grosse, R.B., Duvenaud, D.: Isolating sources of disentanglement in variational autoencoders. In: Proceedings of Advances in Neural Information Processing Systems, vol. 31, pp. 2615–2625 (2018)

6. Dhurandhar, A., et al.: Explanations based on the missing: towards contrastive explanations with pertinent negatives. In: Proceedings of Advances in Neural Information Processing Systems, vol. 31, pp. 590–601 (2018)

7. Ganin, Y., Lempitsky, V.S.: Unsupervised domain adaptation by backpropagation. In: Proceedings of the 32nd International Conference on Machine Learning, pp. 1180–1189 (2015)

8. Goodfellow, I.J., et al.: Generative adversarial nets. In: Proceedings of Advances in Neural Information Processing Systems, vol. 27, pp. 2672–2680 (2014)

9. Goyal, Y., Wu, Z., Ernst, J., Batra, D., Parikh, D., Lee, S.: Counterfactual visual explanations. In: Proceedings of the 36th International Conference on Machine Learning, pp. 2376–2384 (2019)

10. Grünwald, P.D.: The Minimum Description Length Principle. MIT Press, Cambridge (2007)

11. Hendricks, L.A., Hu, R., Darrell, T., Akata, Z.: Grounding visual explanations. In: Ferrari, V., Hebert, M., Sminchisescu, C., Weiss, Y. (eds.) ECCV 2018. LNCS, vol. 11206, pp. 269–286. Springer, Cham (2018). https://doi.org/10.1007/978-3-030-01216-8_17

12. Higgins, I., et al.: beta-VAE: learning basic visual concepts with a constrained variational framework. In: Proceedings of the 5th International Conference on Learning Representations (2017)

13. Hosoya, H.: Group-based learning of disentangled representations with generalizability for novel contents. In: Proceedings of the 28th International Joint Conference on Artificial Intelligence, pp. 2506–2513 (2019)

14. Kim, B., et al.: Interpretability beyond feature attribution: quantitative testing with concept activation vectors (TCAV). In: Proceedings of the 35th International Conference on Machine Learning, pp. 2673–2682 (2018)

15. Kingma, D.P., Welling, M.: Auto-encoding variational bayes. In: Proceedings of the 2nd International Conference on Learning Representations (2014)

16. LeCun, Y., Bottou, L., Bengio, Y., Haffner, P.: Gradient-based learning applied to document recognition. Proc. IEEE **86**(11), 2278–2324 (1998)

17. Lipton, P.: Contrastive explanation. Roy. Inst. Philos. Suppl. **27**, 247–266 (1990)

18. Liu, S., Kailkhura, B., Loveland, D., Han, Y.: Generative counterfactual introspection for explainable deep learning. In: Proceedings of the 2019 IEEE Global Conference on Signal and Information Processing, pp. 1–5 (2019)

19. Locatello, F., et al.: Challenging common assumptions in the unsupervised learning of disentangled representations. In: Proceedings of the 36th International Conference on Machine Learning, pp. 4114–4124 (2019)

20. Locatello, F., Poole, B., Rätsch, G., Schölkopf, B., Bachem, O., Tschannen, M.: Weakly-supervised disentanglement without compromises. In: Proceedings of the 37th International Conference on Machine Learning, pp. 6348–6359 (2020)

21. Lundberg, S.M., Lee, S.: A unified approach to interpreting model predictions. In: Proceedings of Advances in Neural Information Processing Systems, vol. 30, pp. 4768–4777 (2017)
22. Mercado, J.E., Rupp, M.A., Chen, J.Y.C., Barnes, M.J., Barber, D., Procci, K.: Intelligent agent transparency in human-agent teaming for Multi-UxV management. Hum. Factors **58**(3), 401–415 (2016)
23. Miller, T.: Explanation in artificial intelligence: insights from the social sciences. Artif. Intell. **267**, 1–38 (2019)
24. OEIS Foundation Inc.: The on-line encyclopedia of integer sequences (2019). https://oeis.org/A000670
25. Olah, C., Cammarata, N., Schubert, L., Goh, G., Petrov, M., Carter, S.: Zoom in: an introduction to circuits. Distill **5**(3), e00024-001 (2020)
26. O'Shaughnessy, M.R., Canal, G., Connor, M., Rozell, C., Davenport, M.A.: Generative causal explanations of black-box classifiers. In: Proceedings of Advances in Neural Information Processing Systems, vol. 33 (2020)
27. Pazzani, M.J., Feghahati, A., Shelton, C.R., Seitz, A.R.: Explaining contrasting categories. In: Joint Proceedings of the ACM IUI 2018 Workshops Co-Located with the 23rd ACM Conference on Intelligent User Interfaces (2018)
28. Poyiadzi, R., Sokol, K., Santos-Rodriguez, R., De Bie, T., Flach, P.: FACE: feasible and actionable counterfactual explanations. In: Proceedings of the AAAI/ACM Conference on AI, Ethics, and Society, pp. 344–350 (2020)
29. Prabhushankar, M., Kwon, G., Temel, D., AlRegib, G.: Contrastive explanations in neural networks. In: Proceedings of the IEEE International Conference on Image Processing, pp. 3289–3293 (2020)
30. Qin, Z., Yu, F., Liu, C., Chen, X.: How convolutional neural networks see the world - a survey of convolutional neural network visualization methods. Math. Found. Comput. **1**(2), 149–180 (2018)
31. Rezende, D.J., Mohamed, S., Wierstra, D.: Stochastic backpropagation and approximate inference in deep generative models. In: Proceedings of the 31th International Conference on Machine Learning, pp. 1278–1286 (2014)
32. Ribeiro, M.T., Singh, S., Guestrin, C.: "Why should I trust you?" Explaining the predictions of any classifier. In: Proceedings of the 22nd ACM SIGKDD International Conference on Knowledge Discovery and Data Mining, pp. 1135–1144 (2016)
33. Samangouei, P., Saeedi, A., Nakagawa, L., Silberman, N.: ExplainGAN: model explanation via decision boundary crossing transformations. In: Ferrari, V., Hebert, M., Sminchisescu, C., Weiss, Y. (eds.) ECCV 2018. LNCS, vol. 11214, pp. 681–696. Springer, Cham (2018). https://doi.org/10.1007/978-3-030-01249-6_41
34. Selvaraju, R.R., Cogswell, M., Das, A., Vedantam, R., Parikh, D., Batra, D.: Grad-CAM: visual explanations from deep networks via gradient-based localization. In: Proceedings of the IEEE International Conference on Computer Vision, pp. 618–626 (2017)
35. Senin, P.: Dynamic time warping algorithm review (2008)
36. Singla, S., Pollack, B., Chen, J., Batmanghelich, K.: Explanation by progressive exaggeration. In: Proceedings of the 8th International Conference on Learning Representations (2020)
37. Szegedy, C., et al.: Intriguing properties of neural networks. In: Proceedings of the 2nd International Conference on Learning Representations (2014)
38. Cormen, T.H., Leiserson, C.E., Rivest, R.L., Stein, C.: Introduction to Algorithms, 3rd edn. MIT Press, Cambridge (2009)
39. Van Looveren, A., Klaise, J.: Interpretable counterfactual explanations guided by prototypes. arXiv preprint arXiv:1907.02584 (2019)

40. Zheng, Z., Sun, L.: Disentangling latent space for VAE by label relevant/irrelevant dimensions. In: Proceedings of the IEEE/CVF Conference on Computer Vision and Pattern Recognition, pp. 12192–12201 (2019)

41. Zhou, B., Sun, Y., Bau, D., Torralba, A.: Interpretable basis decomposition for visual explanation. In: Ferrari, V., Hebert, M., Sminchisescu, C., Weiss, Y. (eds.) ECCV 2018. LNCS, vol. 11212, pp. 122–138. Springer, Cham (2018). https://doi.org/10.1007/978-3-030-01237-3_8

42. Zhu, X., Xu, C., Tao, D.: Learning disentangled representations with latent variation predictability. In: Vedaldi, A., Bischof, H., Brox, T., Frahm, J.-M. (eds.) ECCV 2020. LNCS, vol. 12355, pp. 684–700. Springer, Cham (2020). https://doi.org/10.1007/978-3-030-58607-2_40

# Evaluation of Uplift Models
# with Non-Random Assignment Bias

Mina Rafla[1,2(✉)], Nicolas Voisine[1], and Bruno Crémilleux[2]

[1] Orange Labs, 22300 Lannion, France
{mina.rafla,nicolas.voisine}@orange.com
[2] UNICAEN, ENSICAEN, CNRS - UMR GREYC, Normandie Univ.,
14000 Caen, France
bruno.cremilleux@unicaen.fr

**Abstract.** Uplift Modeling measures the impact of an action (marketing, medical treatment) on a person's behavior. This allows the selection of the subgroup of persons for which the effect of the action will be most noteworthy. Uplift estimation is based on groups of people who have received different treatments. These groups are assumed to be equivalent. However, in practice, we observe biases between these groups. We propose in this paper a protocol to evaluate and study the impact of the Non-Random Assignment bias (NRA) on the performance of the main uplift methods. Then we present a weighting method to reduce the effect of the NRA bias. Experimental results show that our bias reduction method significantly improves the performance of uplift models under NRA bias.

**Keywords:** Uplift modeling · Machine learning · Non-Random Assignment Bias · Treatment effect estimation · Causal inference

## 1 Introduction

Uplift modeling is a predictive modeling technique that models directly the incremental impact of treatment, such as a marketing campaign or a drug, on an individual's behavior. The applications are multiple: customer relationship management, personalized medicine, advertising, political elections. Uplift models help identify groups of people likely to respond positively to treatment *only because* they received one. A major difficulty in uplift modeling is that data are only partially known: it is impossible to know for an individual whether the chosen treatment is optimal because their responses to alternative treatments cannot be observed. Several works address challenges related to the uplift modeling with single treatment [8] and multiple treatments [24]. The evaluation of uplift models is studied in [18]. State-of-art uplift modeling approaches assume that the groups of individuals are homogeneous. This means that uplift should be modeled on experimental data, i.e., data whose generation is controlled and for which there is no bias between different treatment groups. However, in practice, uplift

© The Author(s), under exclusive license to Springer Nature Switzerland AG 2022
T. Bouadi et al. (Eds.): IDA 2022, LNCS 13205, pp. 251–263, 2022.
https://doi.org/10.1007/978-3-031-01333-1_20

modeling is used with observational data where bias exists. For example, an unanswered commercial call introduces a bias between treated and not treated individuals. Similarly, it is assumed that there is no bias between data used to learn an uplift model and its deployment whereas such a bias may exist. Those biases jeopardize the practical use of uplift modeling methods [15].

This paper aims to study the Non-Random Assignment (NRA) bias, a very common bias in the context of uplift modeling. It occurs when the treatment assignment is dependent on the characteristics of individuals. We address the following research questions: what is the impact of the NRA bias on the main uplift modeling approaches? How can the bias effect be reduced? To answer the first question, we design an experimental protocol that evaluates the impact of the NRA bias on state-of-art uplift methods. Our study allows us to identify several behavioral aspects of uplift methods. Regarding the second question, we propose a weighting method to reduce the effect of the NRA bias on the performance of uplift models. Experimental results show that our bias reduction method significantly improves the performance of uplift models under NRA bias. To the best of our knowledge, this is the first work that focuses on the bias effect in uplift modeling. The remainder of this paper is organized as follows. Section 2 introduces uplift modeling definition and methods, Sect. 3 describes the problem setting and our experimental protocol for evaluating the impact of NRA bias. We present our bias reduction method in Sect. 4 then conclude in Sect. 5.

## 2    Uplift Modeling and Evaluation

### 2.1    Definition

Uplift is a notion introduced by Radcliffe and Surry [17] and defined in Rubin's causal inference models [20] as the *Individual Treatment effect (ITE)*. We now outline the notion of uplift and its modeling.

Let $X$ be a group of $N$ individuals indexed by $i : 1 \ldots N$ where each individual is described by a set of variables $\mathbb{X}$. $X_i$ denotes the set of values of $\mathbb{X}$ for the individual $i$. Let $T$ be a variable indicating whether or not an individual has received a treatment. Uplift modeling is based on two groups: the individuals having received a treatment (denoted $T = 1$) and those without treatment (denoted $T = 0$). Let $Y$ be the outcome variable (for instance, the purchase or not of a product). We note $Y_i(T = 1)$ the outcome of an individual $i$ when he received a treatment and $Y_i(T = 0)$ his outcome without treatment. The uplift of an individual $i$, denoted by $\tau_i$, is defined as: $\tau_i = Y_i(T = 1) - Y_i(T = 0)$.

In practice, we will never observe both $Y_i(T = 1)$ and $Y_i(T = 0)$ for a same individual and thus $\tau_i$ cannot be calculated. However, uplift can be empirically estimated by considering two groups: a treatment group (individual with a treatment) and a control group (without treatment). The estimated uplift of an individual $i$ denoted by $\hat{\tau}_i$ is then computed by using the CATE (Conditional Average Treatment Effect) [20]:

$$CATE : \hat{\tau}_i = \mathbb{E}[Y_i(T = 1)|X_i] - \mathbb{E}[Y_i(T = 0)|X_i] \tag{1}$$

As the real value of $\tau_i$ cannot be observed, it is impossible to directly use machine learning algorithms such as regression to infer a model to predict $\tau_i$. The next section describes how uplift is modeled in the literature.

## 2.2   Uplift Modeling

The uplift modeling literature and a branch of the causal inference literature have recently approached each other [6]. We sketch below the main methods in this field of research.

*Meta-Learners.* Meta-Learners take advantage of usual machine learning algorithms to estimate the CATE. The most classical and intuitive approach is the T-Learner (also known as the **Two-Model** approach in the uplift literature, which is the name that we use in this paper). The T-Learner is made of two independent predictive models, one on the treatment group to estimate $P(Y|X, T = 1)$ and another on the control group to estimate $P(Y|X, T = 0)$. The estimated uplift of an individual $i$ is the difference between those values for the given individual, i.e. $\hat{\tau}_i = P(Y = 1|X_i, T = 1) - P(Y = 1|X_i, T = 0)$. The advantages of this approach are the simplicity and the possibility to use any machine learning algorithm but it has also known limitations [18]. The causal inference community defines other methods such as the S-Learner which includes the variable $T$ in the features with a standard regression, the X-Learner which performs a two-step regression before the estimation of the CATE to deal with the unbalanced size of treatment groups [7], the DR-Learner [9] which combines a two-model approach and the use of the Inverse Propensity Weighting [14].

*Class-Transformation Approach.* The principle of this approach [8] is to map the uplift modeling problem to a usual supervised learning problem. The outcome variable $Y$ is transformed into a variable $Z$ as illustrated in Eq. 2. Then a machine learning algorithm is used to learn a model and to predict $P(Z|X)$. The estimated uplift of an individual $i$ is $\hat{\tau}_i = 2 \times P(Z = 1|X_i) - 1$

$$Z = \begin{cases} 1, & \text{if } T = 1 \text{ and } Y = 1 \\ 1, & \text{if } T = 0 \text{ and } Y = 0 \\ 0, & \text{otherwise.} \end{cases} \tag{2}$$

Several studies [3,8] show that this approach has a better performance than the two-model approach.

*Direct-Approaches.* These methods modify supervised learning algorithms to suit them to fit the uplift modeling problem. Then uplift is directly estimated. Examples include methods based on decision trees [22,24], k nearest neighbors [5], logistic regression [12] or reinforcement learning [11].

## 2.3 Uplift Evaluation

Real values of uplift being not observed, supervised machine learning techniques cannot be used and therefore performance measures of the supervised setting are inoperative. That is why uplift is evaluated through the ranking of the individuals according to their estimated uplift value. The intuition is that a good uplift model estimates higher uplift values to individuals in the treatment group with positive outcomes than those with negative outcomes and vice versa for the control group. The qini measure (also known as Area Under Uplift Curve [2, 16]) is based on this principle to evaluate uplift methods. It is a variant of the Gini coefficient. Qini values are in $[-1, 1]$, the higher the value, the larger the impact of the predicted optimal treatment.

# 3 Evaluation of Uplift with Biased Data

This section presents the NRA bias and the experimental protocol that we designed to assess performance of uplift methods under this bias.

## 3.1 Problem Setting

State-of-art uplift methods assume that data are unbiased and that the treatment group comes from the same distribution as the control group, which is not true for real data. In practice, there are differences between treatment and control groups, also known as Non-Random Assignment bias, a prevalent type of bias in uplift modeling. Formally, this bias occurs when $P(T = 1|X) \neq P(T = 0|X)$ (which also means $P(X|T = 1) \neq P(X|T = 0)$). Usually it is easier to collect control data and the treatment group is the most biased because it is more challenging to apply a treatment to individuals and collect the corresponding data due to ethical, political or economic constraints.

This bias problem has been studied in the literature on clinical studies where the goal is to estimate the "Average Treatment Effect" (ATE) defined as $\mathbb{E}[Y_i(T = 1) - Y_i(T = 0)]$. In order to estimate it, the "Propensity Score Matching" (PSM) [21] is used to extract balanced treatment groups on which ATE is estimated. Similarly, in the uplift literature, since uplift methods assume the homogeneity between treatment groups, PSM is used to extract an unbiased sample from a biased dataset. Uplift modeling is applied subsequently as carried in [15]. However, this procedure clearly suffers from a loss of data.

## 3.2 Designing of the Experimental Protocol

This section describes the experimental protocol that we designed to evaluate the behavior of uplift methods under the NRA bias. The principle, to create a NRA bias and observe its impact, is to introduce imbalances in the data regarding the initial distribution of the variables. We do this by modifying proportions of individuals in a non-random way (for example, decreasing the proportion of specific socio-professional categories or ages till it disappears in the data). Such a protocol must satisfy several conditions to correctly evaluate the impact of NRA in order to avoid introducing a bias due to the protocol itself. (1) The chosen variables to introduce bias have to be correlated with the outcome $Y$ or $Y$ given the treatment $T$, otherwise the bias will not affect the uplift modeling. (2) In contrast, the choice of the values of the variables, according to which the proportions of individuals vary, is random. If not, the construction of the populations $E1$ and $E2$ (which will be explained below) may be biased. (3) The bias must be tunable in order to change its rate and quantify its impact on the uplift methods. (4) The created bias is only in the treatment group in order to imitate the natural phenomena as previously explained in Sect. 3.1. (5) The total size of each of the biased learning samples is always the same in order to avoid any variation in the performance due to different learning data sizes.

More precisely, as shown in Fig. 1, two populations $E1$ and $E2$ are created. This is done by choosing a set of variables $V$ and dividing its values into two groups, $C1$ and $C2$, such that the number of individuals defined by the values of $C1$ is equivalent to the number of individuals defined by $C2$. Let $E1$ (resp. $E2$) be the population whose variables correspond to $C1$ (resp. $C2$) and whose sizes are $N1$ and $N2$ respectively. We use a 10-fold cross-validation. In the first training sample, $E1$ and $E2$ have an equal size (i.e. $N1 = N2$), it is considered unbiased and gives a reference value of the qini. The NRA bias is gradually introduced in the treatment group by increasing the size of $E1$ and decreasing the size of $E2$ while preserving the total size of the treatment group. We identify the bias rate of a sample by the variable $b$ where $b = (N1 - N2) \times 100/N$. $b$ goes from $b = 0$ in the unbiased situation to $b = 100$ the most biased situation according to the NRA bias. An uplift model is then learned on each biased sample defined by $b$. All models are then tested on the same test sample and evaluated using the qini. The evolution of the qini according to $b$ allows studying the behavior of an uplift method towards the NRA bias.

## 3.3   Experiments

We apply our protocol to several real and synthetic datasets using the main uplift approaches[1].

***Datasets.*** We use four datasets from politics and marketing fields as well as four synthetic datasets (cf. Table 1). For all the datasets, the outcome is binary.

1. Criteo [3]: a usual marketing dataset for uplift modeling.
2. Hillstrom[2]: a classical dataset for uplift modeling. It is made up of two treatment groups and a control group. We only use the group of people who received an advertising campaign via mail for women's products as the treatment group.

---

[1] For a reproducible purpose, codes and experiment results are available in the supplementary material [19].

[2] http://blog.minethatdata.com/2008/03/minethatdata-e-mail-analytics-and-data.html/.

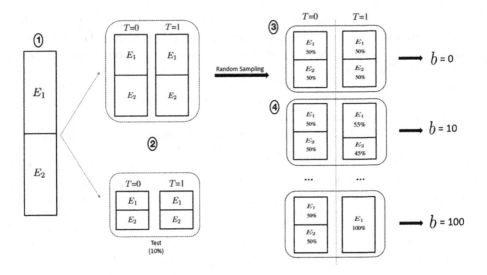

**Fig. 1.** Biased samples generation procedure: (1) Variable(s) $V$ is chosen to create E1 and E2. (2) Creating training and test sets with 10-fold cross validation. (3) Random sampling of treatment and control groups. (4) The sizes of the treatment and control groups are always the same throughout the biasing process.

3. Gerber [4]: a policy-relevant dataset used to study the effect of social pressure on voter turnout.
4. Retail Hero[3]: a dataset of the X5 sales group, the treatment is the action to send SMS to encourage consumers to increase their purchases.
5. Megafon[4]: a synthetic dataset created for uplift modeling. It is generated by telecom companies in order to reproduce the situations encountered by these companies.
6. Zenodo[5]: a synthetic dataset containing trigonometric patterns specifically designed for uplift modeling. We used a subset of 20,000 rows of data (data identified by the variable trial_id = 1 and trial_id = 2).
7. Synth1 and Synth2: two synthetic datasets that we have built as a 2D grid of size $10 \times 10$ in which each cell corresponds to a particular uplift drawn at random. Synth1 is a dataset with a high ATE value and Synth2 has a low response rate.

***Uplift Methods.*** We test 13 uplift methods: two-model approach (2M); class-transformation approach (CT), each with Xgboost and logistic regression (LR); DR-Learner (DR); X-Learner and S-Learner, each with Xgboost and linear regression (LinR). Direct-approaches based on decision trees are tested as well: KL, ED [22] and CTS [24].

---

[3] https://ods.ai/competitions/x5-retailhero-uplift-modeling/data.
[4] https://ods.ai/tracks/df21-megafon/competitions/megafon-df21-comp/data.
[5] https://zenodo.org/record/3653141#.YUCYEufgoW8.

**Table 1.** Dataset characteristics. - Datasets have a balanced size of treatment and control groups. - Independence between treatment and control groups is measured using the C2ST test [13]. A p-value smaller than 0.05 means the null hypothesis is rejected (i.e. treatment independence). - *Value after re-balancing the dataset using PSM [21]

| Datasets | #Rows | #Variables | Response ratio | ATE | Treatment independence |
|---|---|---|---|---|---|
| Criteo | 50000 | 13 | 0.16 | 0.08 | 0.1 |
| Hillstrom | 42693 | 8 | 0.129 | 0.04 | 0.33 |
| Gerber | 76419 | 10 | 0.34 | 0.06 | 0.43 |
| RetailHero | 200039 | 11 | 0.619 | 0.033 | 0.7 |
| Megafon | 600000 | 36 | 0.2 | 0.04 | 0.4375* |
| Synthetic Zenodo | 20000 | 16 | 0.3 | 0.109 | 0.22 |
| Synth1 | 40000 | 2 | 0.32 | 0.241 | 0.197 |
| Synth2 | 40000 | 2 | 0.007 | 0.00125 | 0.33 |

***Implementation Details.*** For each dataset (except Synth1 and Synth2) and for each uplift method, the experimental protocol is applied twice with different contents of $V$: once with the variable the most correlated with $Y$ and once with the variable the most correlated with $Y$ given the treatment group ($T = 1$). For Synth1 and Synth2, $V$ contains the two variables of these datasets. Moreover, given a set $V$, the experiment is repeated twice in order to provide different splittings of $C1$ and $C2$.

## 3.4   Results

***Qini Variability According to $b$.*** Figure 2 illustrates the results (due to space constraints, it is not possible to give all the results). We observe that the NRA bias strongly affects the performance of uplift models[6] (the higher the bias rate, the more significant the decrease of the qini). To provide a global view of the results, we compute for each dataset and each uplift method the *Average Qini*, i.e., the average of qini values according to the bias rates going from $b = 0$ to $b = 100$ (cf. Table 2).

***Overall Ranking.*** To better compare the methods according to their resistance to NRA bias, Fig. 3 shows the average rank obtained by each method based on the Average Qini (all divisions of $V$ are taken into account).

The results of these experiments provide the following messages: (i) the most resistant models to the NRA bias are the ED and X-Learner_LinR, DR_LinR, two-model approach with the logistic regression: the qini strongly decays only

---

[6] When comparison with state of the art is possible, the achieved qini values without bias ($b = 0$) are those usually found in the literature [3].

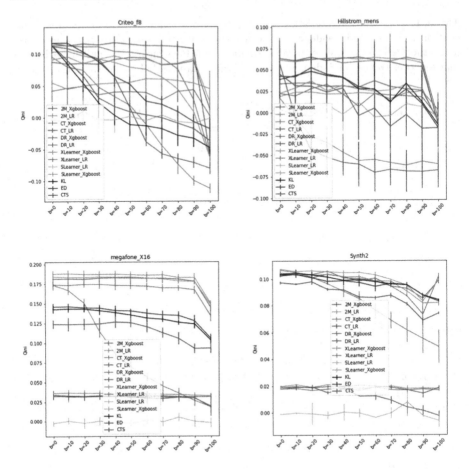

**Fig. 2.** Qini values of uplift methods according to NRA bias rates in the Criteo dataset with the 'f8' variable (top left), Hillstrom dataset with the 'mens' variable (top right), Megafon dataset with the 'X16' variable (bottom left) and Synth2 dataset with its both variables (bottom right). A method name is followed by the learning algorithm used with it.

when the bias rate is high; (ii) the models where the qini gently degrades as the bias rate increases are tree based methods (KL, and CTS) and (iii) the models strongly affected by the bias even with low bias rates are the class-transformation based methods and the S-Learner_LinR.

***Methods Comparison with Statistical Tests.*** We study now the significance of the results regarding the comparison of the uplift methods (cf. Table 2) by using a statistical test. Following the study [1], we choose the Friedman test with the post hoc test of Nemenyi to compare the performance (average qini) of more than two methods across several datasets. Figure 4 depicts the results with a heatmap. The null hypothesis states that there is no significant difference in performance according to the average qini between two methods across the

**Table 2.** Average Qini (multiplied by 100) and its variance (shown in brackets) across datasets and uplift methods (in bold, the best value for each dataset). A dataset name is followed by the names of the $V$ variables used to generate the NRA bias (due to space constraints, the results are given for a single splitting of the $V$ values).

| | TwoModel | | ClassTransformation | | DR | | XLearner | | SLearner | | Trees | | |
|---|---|---|---|---|---|---|---|---|---|---|---|---|---|
| | Xgboost | LR | Xgboost | LR | Xgboost | LinR | Xgboost | LinR | Xgboost | LinR | KL | ED | CTS |
| Criteo_f2 | 6.6 (1.7) | 7.2 (1.6) | 0.2 (1.9) | 1.9 (1.2) | 4.4 (2.8) | **9.9 (0.9)** | 5.5 (2.6) | 8.5 (0.8) | 8.0 (1.9) | −0.2 (1.9) | 0.6 (1.4) | 4.9 (1.3) | 2.1 (1.5) |
| Criteo_f8 | 8.1 (2.6) | 6.3 (2.0) | 0.1 (1.7) | 1.7 (1.0) | 3.7 (2.3) | **9.8 (1.0)** | 5.4 (2.6) | 8.1 (1.1) | 8.4 (1.9) | −0.2 (1.7) | 1.2 (1.6) | 5.2 (1.2) | 2.4 (1.6) |
| Gerber_p2002 | −2.4 (2.0) | 1.1 (1.1) | −2.1 (1.5) | −0.4 (1.2) | −2.0 (1.9) | 0.8 (1.1) | −2.3 (1.9) | **1.4 (1.1)** | −2.0 (2.0) | 0.1 (0.9) | −1.5 (1.8) | −0.9 (1.5) | −0.1 (1.7) |
| Gerber_p2004 | −2.1 (2.0) | 0.8 (1.1) | −1.8 (1.7) | −1.2 (1.3) | −2.1 (1.9) | 0.7 (1.1) | −2.1 (1.8) | **1.2 (1.3)** | −1.8 (2.0) | 0.0 (1.1) | −1.7 (1.8) | −1.5 (1.9) | −0.6 (1.9) |
| Hillstrom_mens | 2.7 (2.1) | **5.5 (2.6)** | −4.1 (2.0) | −4.6 (2.2) | 1.9 (2.4) | 5.4 (2.1) | 2.0 (2.6) | **5.5 (2.2)** | 2.5 (2.7) | 0.2 (2.4) | 2.8 (2.6) | 2.9 (2.5) | 1.0 (2.8) |
| Hillstrom_newbie | 2.8 (2.2) | **6.2 (2.7)** | 0.1 (2.1) | 2.4 (1.9) | 1.0 (2.4) | 5.9 (2.0) | 2.1 (2.3) | 6.0 (2.0) | 3.3 (2.2) | −0.1 (2.4) | 4.2 (2.2) | 4.3 (2.5) | 4.3 (2.5) |
| Megafone_X16 | 17.8 (0.5) | 3.5 (0.4) | 8.6 (0.6) | 3.2 (0.4) | 16.9 (0.5) | 3.0 (0.5) | **18.3 (0.4)** | 3.0 (0.6) | 17.9 (0.4) | −0.0 (0.6) | 13.2 (0.5) | 13.7 (0.5) | 11.6 (0.7) |
| Megafone_X21 | 18.2 (0.4) | 3.5 (0.4) | 12.0 (0.4) | 2.4 (0.5) | 17.4 (0.5) | 3.0 (0.4) | **18.8 (0.4)** | 3.1 (0.4) | 18.4 (0.4) | −0.0 (0.6) | 13.9 (0.5) | 14.0 (0.6) | 10.7 (0.8) |
| Synth1 | 7.0 (0.9) | 0.9 (1.6) | 1.7 (0.9) | −2.9 (1.3) | 9.7 (1.5) | −0.4 (1.5) | **12.6 (1.6)** | −1.6 (2.0) | 12.2 (1.2) | 0.6 (1.6) | 9.7 (1.2) | 8.8 (1.6) | 8.7 (1.2) |
| Synth2 | 9.8 (0.1) | 1.9 (0.1) | 8.1 (0.5) | 1.1 (0.2) | 9.7 (0.2) | 1.9 (0.1) | 9.7 (0.2) | 1.8 (0.1) | **10.1 (0.1)** | −0.1 (0.4) | 9.7 (0.1) | 9.6 (0.2) | 8.7 (0.1) |
| retailHero_age | 0.7 (0.4) | 1.2 (0.3) | 0.3 (0.4) | 0.8 (0.4) | 0.5 (0.4) | **1.3 (0.4)** | 0.5 (0.3) | 1.2 (0.3) | 0.9 (0.3) | −0.0 (0.3) | 0.8 (0.3) | 0.9 (0.3) | 0.9 (0.4) |
| retailHero_trNum | 0.8 (0.4) | 1.2 (0.3) | 0.4 (0.3) | 1.1 (0.4) | 0.4 (0.4) | **1.3 (0.4)** | 0.5 (0.4) | 1.2 (0.4) | 0.9 (0.4) | −0.0 (0.4) | 0.7 (0.4) | 0.7 (0.4) | 0.6 (0.4) |
| zenodoSynth_X10 | 9.7 (1.8) | 12.6 (1.9) | 7.0 (2.2) | 12.1 (1.5) | 7.8 (1.9) | 12.2 (1.9) | 9.4 (1.7) | 12.1 (1.7) | 11.5 (2.0) | 0.0 (2.5) | 12.8 (1.9) | **13.0 (1.9)** | 10.6 (2.6) |
| zenodoSynth_X31 | 9.8 (2.4) | 12.2 (2.0) | 6.6 (2.0) | 12.0 (1.9) | 7.7 (2.1) | 12.3 (1.9) | 9.7 (2.2) | 12.4 (1.7) | 11.7 (2.2) | 0.1 (1.9) | 12.7 (1.9) | **13.2 (2.0)** | 10.2 (2.2) |

datasets. With a value of $p$ (p-value) smaller than 0.05, the null hypothesis is rejected (in green in Fig. 4). Figure 4 and Fig. 3 confirm that the S-Learner and the class-transformation based approaches are the least resistant towards the NRA bias.

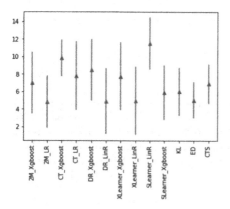

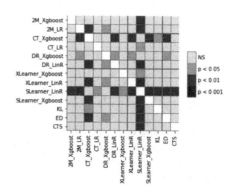

**Fig. 3.** Overall ranking for the different uplift approaches.

**Fig. 4.** Heat map to visualize the comparison between uplift methods. A value of $p$ smaller than 0.05 means that the null hypothesis is rejected. (Color figure online)

## 4 Method to Reduce the NRA Bias Impact

This section presents our weighting method to reduce the effect on the NRA bias on the uplift modeling. Our method is inspired from the *Domain Adaptation* literature where samples of a source dataset are weighted according to their

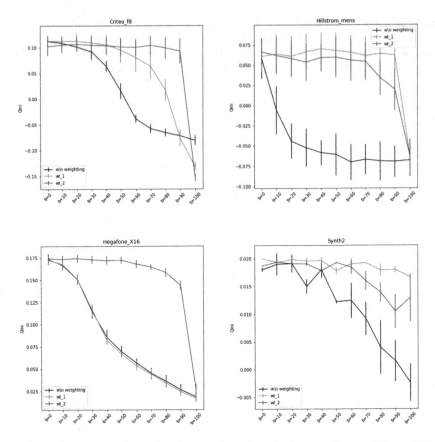

**Fig. 5.** Qini values by class-transformation based methods according to different NRA bias rates with and without reweighting. Top-left: class-transformation approach with Xgboost on Criteo dataset and 'f8' variable. Top-right: class-transformation approach with logistic regression on Hillstrom dataset and 'mens' variable. Bottom-left: class-transformation approach with Xgboost on Megafon dataset with X16 variable. Bottom-right: class-transformation approach with logistic regression on Synth2 dataset with its both variables.

importance to a target dataset [10]. The principle of our method is to weight individuals of the treatment group according to their weight in the control group to make the biased population (the treatment group) similar to the unbiased one (the control group). Our weighting technique is based on the propensity score which is the probability for an individual of being treated ($T = 1$) given his vector of observed variables $X_i$ i.e. $P(T = 1|X_i)$. In observational studies, the propensity scores are not known but they can be learned from the data using a regression algorithm. Our method weights each individual $i$ of the treatment group by $w(X_i)$ s.t.:

$$w(X_i) = P(T = 0|X_i)/P(T = 1|X_i) \tag{3}$$

**Table 3.** Average Qini (multiplied by 100) and its variance (shown in brackets) with the class-transformation based methods (in bold, the best value for each dataset). Dataset name is followed by the names of the $V$ variables used to generate the NRA bias (for space constraints, the results are given for a single splitting of the $V$ values). MAE takes into account all splittings of $V$ into $C1$ and $C2$, as explained previously.

| | Class-transformation with LR | | | | Class-transformation with Xgboost | | | |
|---|---|---|---|---|---|---|---|---|
| | Ref. qini | w/o weights | wt_1 | wt_2 | Ref. qini | w/o weights | wt_1 | wt_2 |
| Criteo_f2 | 11.1 (0.9) | 1.9 (1.2) | 6.1 (1.5) | **8.2 (2.0)** | 9.1 (2.6) | 0.2 (1.9) | 2.6 (1.8) | **4.8 (1.9)** |
| Criteo_f8 | 11.2 (1.0) | 1.7 (1.0) | 5.5 (1.8) | **7.9 (1.7)** | 9.6 (1.2) | 0.1 (1.7) | 3.4 (1.5) | **5.0 (1.8)** |
| Gerber_p2002 | 0.8 (1.6) | −0.4 (1.2) | **0.9 (1.1)** | 0.5 (1.2) | −1.9 (2.0) | −2.1 (1.5) | −1.6 (1.9) | −2.3 (1.8) |
| Gerber_p2004 | 1.1 (1.4) | −1.2 (1.3) | **0.9 (1.3)** | 0.4 (1.1) | −1.6 (2.1) | −1.8 (1.7) | −1.7 (1.8) | −2.3 (1.9) |
| Hillstrom_mens | 5.9 (2.5) | −4.6 (2.2) | **5.3 (2.2)** | 4.2 (2.2) | 1.7 (2.1) | −4.1 (2.0) | −0.2 (2.7) | **0.5 (2.4)** |
| Hillstrom_newbie | 6.3 (1.7) | 2.4 (1.9) | **5.6 (2.0)** | 5.2 (2.1) | 1.7 (1.9) | 0.1 (2.1) | 1.3 (2.0) | **1.4 (2.1)** |
| Megafone_X16 | 3.2 (0.5) | **3.2 (0.4)** | 3.1 (0.4) | **3.2 (0.4)** | 17.3 (0.6) | 8.6 (0.6) | 8.4 (0.5) | **15.5 (0.5)** |
| Megafone_X21 | 3.2 (0.4) | 2.4 (0.5) | **3.1 (0.4)** | 3.0 (0.5) | 17.2 (0.5) | 12.0 (0.4) | 12.0 (0.4) | **16.0 (0.5)** |
| Synth1 | −0.2 (3.4) | −2.9 (1.3) | −1.0 (1.8) | **−0.8 (0.9)** | 2.5 (2.4) | 1.7 (0.9) | 2.5 (0.7) | **8.9 (2.9)** |
| Synth2 | 1.8 (0.0) | 1.1 (0.2) | **1.9 (0.1)** | 1.7 (0.1) | 10.7 (0.0) | 8.1 (0.5) | 8.3 (0.5) | **9.7 (0.2)** |
| retailHero_age | 1.2 (0.4) | 0.8 (0.4) | **1.3 (0.4)** | 1.2 (0.3) | 0.6 (0.4) | 0.3 (0.4) | 0.3 (0.4) | **0.6 (0.4)** |
| retailHero_trNum | 1.2 (0.3) | 1.1 (0.4) | **1.2 (0.4)** | **1.2 (0.4)** | 0.7 (0.4) | 0.4 (0.3) | 0.4 (0.3) | **0.6 (0.3)** |
| zenodoSynth_X10 | 12.3 (1.3) | **12.1 (1.5)** | 11.9 (1.7) | 9.8 (1.8) | 8.0 (3.1) | 7.0 (2.2) | **7.4 (2.0)** | 6.5 (2.1) |
| zenodoSynth_X31 | 11.7 (2.3) | 12.0 (1.9) | **12.1 (1.7)** | 9.9 (2.0) | 6.9 (1.9) | 6.6 (2.0) | **7.2 (2.5)** | 6.5 (2.2) |
| **MAE** | 0 | 2.367 | 0.978 | 1.053 | 0 | 2.803 | 1.953 | 1.592 |

We estimate the probabilities of Eq. 3 by using logistic regression and xgboost. Then the uplift method integrates the weights to amplify the role of the under-represented individuals in the treatment group and estimate $\hat{\tau}_i$. We named wt_1 (resp. wt_2) the use of the logistic regression (resp. xgboost) in the weighting method.

We evaluate our weighting method with the two-model and the class-transformation approaches since these approaches use traditional machine learning algorithms where weights can be given directly at each line (individual). The direct-approaches cannot take into account weights, so we do not use them. Results show a large enhancement in the performance with the class-transformation methods (cf. Fig. 5) and a slight improvement with the two-model approach (the full set of results can be found in the supplementary material [19]). Table 3 details the results with the class-transformation based methods. "Ref. qini" denotes the *reference qini*, that is the qini value of a method without bias (i.e. $b = 0$) and without weighting. The Mean Absolute Error (where $MAE = \frac{1}{n} \sum_{j=1}^{n} |Ref.qini_j - AverageQini_j|$) indicates the gap between the qini obtained by an uplift method and the reference qini. The smaller the gap is, the better the weighting. The gap is much smaller with our weighting methods especially with the logistic regression (LR) than without weighting. Best average qini values are also achieved with weighting except on zenodoSynth_X10.

***Statistical Test.*** Following the study [1], we use Wilcoxon test [23] to determine if our weighting method significantly improves the performance of the uplift methods. This test is used to compare two methods on several datasets. As we perform two tests (on wt_1 and wt_2 methods), in order to control the family-

**Table 4.** p-values obtained with the Wilcoxon test when comparing uplift methods w/o and with weighting.

| Methods | p-value | Methods | p-value |
|---|---|---|---|
| CT_LR w/o weights vs CT_LR with wt_1 | **0.0014** | 2M_LR w/o weights vs 2M_LR with wt_1 | 0.985 |
| CT_LR w/o weights vs CT_LR with wt_2 | 0.106 | 2M_LR w/o weights vs 2M_LR with wt_2 | 0.986 |
| CT_Xgboost w/o weights vs CT_Xgboost with wt_1 | 0.142 | 2M_Xgboost w/o weights vs 2M_Xgboost with wt_1 | 0.356 |
| CT_Xgboost w/o weights vs CT_Xgboost with wt_2 | **0.02** | 2M_Xgboost w/o weights vs 2M_Xgboost with wt_2 | 0.68 |

wise error rate due to multiple tests, the Bonferroni correction is applied and therefore the null hypothesis is rejected when the p-value is smaller than 0.025. Table 4 asserts that our weighting technique improves significantly the class-transformation based methods while there is no significant improvement with the two-model based methods.

***Discussion.*** The weak impact of the weighting method on the two-model approach methods can be explained. The NRA bias does not change in the treatment group the distribution of the outcome $Y$ given populations $E_1$ and $E_2$ (cf. Sect. 3.2). The probability estimations $P(Y|T = 1, X)$ and $P(Y|T = 0, X)$ are then slightly affected, and the performances with and without weighting are similar. This is different with the class-transformation methods which directly estimate $Z$ based on the assumption that the treatment and control groups are equivalent. However, this assumption no longer holds with the NRA bias. Then weighting the treatment group improves the estimation of $Z$ and thus the uplift.

## 5    Conclusion

In this paper, we have studied the effect of the NRA bias when modeling uplift methods. To the best of our knowledge, this is the first work that focuses on the study of bias effect on current uplift models. We have designed an experimental protocol that allows, by varying the bias rate, to study the impact of the NRA bias on uplift methods and to identify classes of behavior for these methods. Inspired by the literature on domain adaptation, we have proposed a method to reduce the effect of the NRA bias by weighting the individuals in the treatment group. Experimental results on eight datasets show that our method significantly improves the uplift estimation performances for the class-transformation based methods.

This work opens several perspectives. As the weighting method reduces the effect of the NRA bias with the class transformation methods, it seems promising to design new methods of this family. On the other hand, it will be fruitful to study other types of bias, such as (i) the deployment bias, which occurs when uplift models are applied to different populations (Covariate Shift situation) or when the behavior of individuals changes with time (Concept Drift situation); (ii) the non-response bias which is a real challenge for uplift modeling with observational data.

# References

1. Demšar, J.: Statistical comparisons of classifiers over multiple data sets. J. Mach. Learn. Res. **7**, 1–30 (2006)
2. Devriendt, F., Guns, T., Verbeke, W.: Learning to rank for uplift modeling (2020)
3. Diemert, E.: A large scale benchmark for uplift modeling (2018)
4. Gerber, A.S., Green, D.P., Larimer, C.W.: Social pressure and voter turnout: evidence from a large-scale field experiment. Am. Polit. Sci. Rev. **102**(1), 33–48 (2008)
5. Guelman, L.A.: Optimal personalized treatment learning models with insurance applications (2015)
6. Gutierrez, P., Gérardy, J.Y.: Causal inference and uplift modelling: a review of the literature. In: PAPIs (2016)
7. Jacob, D.: CATE meets ML - the conditional average treatment effect and machine learning (2021)
8. Jaskowski, M., Jaroszewicz, S.: Uplift modeling for clinical trial data (2012)
9. Kennedy, E.H.: Optimal doubly robust estimation of heterogeneous causal effects (2020)
10. Kouw, W.M., Loog, M.: An introduction to domain adaptation and transfer learning (2019)
11. Li, C., et al.: Reinforcement learning for uplift modeling (2019)
12. Lo, V.S.Y., Pachamanova, D.A.: From predictive uplift modeling to prescriptive uplift analytics: a practical approach to treatment optimization while accounting for estimation risk. J. Mark. Anal. **3**, 79–95 (2015). https://doi.org/10.1057/jma.2015.5
13. Lopez-Paz, D., Oquab, M.: Revisiting classifier two-sample tests (2018)
14. Lunceford, J.K., Davidian, M.: Stratification and weighting via the propensity score in estimation of causal treatment effects: a comparative study. Stat. Med. **23**(19), 2937–2960 (2004)
15. Olaya, D., Coussement, K., Verbeke, W.: A survey and benchmarking study of multitreatment uplift modeling. Data Min. Knowl. Discov. **34**(2), 273–308 (2020). https://doi.org/10.1007/s10618-019-00670-y
16. Radcliffe, N.: Using control groups to target on predicted lift: building and assessing uplift model. Direct Mark. Anal. J. 14–21 (2007)
17. Radcliffe, N.J., Surry, P.D.: Differential response analysis: modeling true responses by isolating the effect of a single action (1999)
18. Radcliffe, N.J., Surry, P.D.: Real-world uplift modelling with significance-based uplift trees (2012)
19. Rafla, M., Voisine, N., Crémilleux, B.: Supplementary material. https://github.com/MinaWagdi/UpliftEvaluation_NRA/
20. Rubin, D.B.: Estimating causal effects of treatments in randomized and nonrandomized studies. J. Educ. Psychol. **66**, 688–701 (1974)
21. Rubin, D.B.: Using propensity scores to help design observational studies: application to the tobacco litigation. Health Serv. Outcomes Res. Methodol. **2**(3), 169–188 (2001). https://doi.org/10.1023/A:1020363010465
22. Rzepakowski, P., Jaroszewicz, S.: Decision trees for uplift modeling with single and multiple treatments. Knowl. Inf. Syst. **32**, 303–327 (2011). https://doi.org/10.1007/s10115-011-0434-0
23. Wilcoxon, F.: Individual comparisons by ranking methods. Biom. Bull. **1**(6), 80–83 (1945). http://www.jstor.org/stable/3001968
24. Zhao, Y., Fang, X., Simchi-Levi, D.: Uplift modeling with multiple treatments and general response types. In: Proceedings of the 2017 SIAM International Conference on Data Mining, pp. 588–596. SIAM (2017)

# A Generic Trace Ordering Framework for Incremental Process Discovery

Daniel Schuster[1,2(✉)] , Emanuel Domnitsch[2], Sebastiaan J. van Zelst[1,2] ,
and Wil M. P. van der Aalst[1,2]

[1] Fraunhofer Institute for Applied Information Technology FIT,
Sankt Augustin, Germany
{daniel.schuster,sebastiaan.van.zelst}@fit.fraunhofer.de
[2] RWTH Aachen University, Aachen, Germany
emanuel.domnitsch@rwth-aachen.de, wvdaalst@pads.rwth-aachen.de

**Abstract.** Executing operational processes generates valuable event data in organizations' information systems. Process discovery describes the learning of process models from such event data. Incremental process discovery algorithms allow learning a process model from event data gradually. In this context, process behavior recorded in event data is incrementally fed into the discovery algorithm that integrates the added behavior to a process model under construction. In this paper, we investigate the open research question of the impact of the ordering of incrementally selected process behavior on the quality, i.e., recall and precision, of the learned process models. We propose a framework for defining ordering strategies for traces, i.e., observed process behavior, for incremental process discovery. Further, we provide concrete instantiations of this framework. We evaluate different trace-ordering strategies on real-life event data. The results show that trace-ordering strategies can significantly improve the quality of the learned process models.

**Keywords:** Process mining · Process discovery · Ordering effects

## 1 Introduction

*Process mining* [17] offers tools and methods to systematically analyze data generated during the execution of operational processes, e.g., business and production processes. These data are referred to as *event data*, which can be extracted from organizations' information systems. Process mining aims to generate valuable insights into the processes under investigation to optimize them ultimately.

*Process discovery*, a key discipline within process mining, comprises algorithms that learn process models from event data. Most process model formalisms focus on describing the control flow of process activities. Note that process model formalisms like BPMN [7] allow modeling, e.g., resource information and data flows, besides the control flow of process activities. In short, process models are an essential artifact within process mining.

© The Author(s), under exclusive license to Springer Nature Switzerland AG 2022
T. Bouadi et al. (Eds.): IDA 2022, LNCS 13205, pp. 264–277, 2022.
https://doi.org/10.1007/978-3-031-01333-1_21

*Conventional* process discovery algorithms [2] are fully automated. Other than configuring parameter settings, they do not provide any form of interaction. Thus, they function as a black box from a user's perspective. Since event data often have quality issues, e.g., wrongly captured, missing, and incomplete process behavior, process discovery can be considered an unsupervised learning task. Many conventional process discovery algorithms yield low-quality models on real-life event data. Automated filtering techniques, such as [4], attempt to solve such data quality problems but often remove too much process behavior. In addition, they cannot add missing process behavior to the event data.

*Domain-knowledge-utilizing* process discovery aims to overcome the limitations of conventional process discovery by using additional knowledge about the process under consideration besides event data and by incorporating user feedback into the discovery, respectively, learning phase [16]. *Incremental* process discovery is a subclass of domain-knowledge-utilizing process discovery where the user gradually selects process behavior that is added to a process model under construction by the discovery algorithm. With incremental process discovery, a user can, for example, examine the process model after each incremental execution and, if necessary, jump back to a previous version of the model and add other observed process behavior. In this way, the user can steer and influence the discovery phase compared to conventional process discovery.

In previous work [14], we introduced an incremental process discovery algorithm that allows to gradually add process instances, i.e., individual process executions, which are also referred to as *traces*, to a process model under construction. An open research question is the influence of the order in which the process behavior is gradually inserted into the process model under construction on the quality of the eventual process model discovered. In this paper, we address this research question by exploring strategies to recommend a trace order. From a practical perspective, these strategies are helpful in situations where, for example, a user selects several traces at once to be added next but does not have any preferences about the exact order in which they are added to the model by the incremental discovery algorithm.

This paper contains two main contributions. First, we define a general framework for trace-ordering strategies within the context of incremental process discovery. The framework can be applied for any incremental process discovery algorithm that gradually adds traces to a process model. Second, we provide instantiations of this framework, i.e., various trace-ordering strategies for an existing incremental process discovery algorithm [14]. Finally, we present an evaluation of the proposed strategies. Our experiments show that using trace-ordering strategies results in significantly better models than random trace selection, cf. [15].

The remainder of this paper is organized as follows. In Sect. 2, we present related work. Section 3 introduces preliminaries. In Sect. 4, we introduce a framework for trace-ordering strategies and provide specific instantiations of this framework. The evaluation by use of real-life event data of these instantiations is presented in Sect. 5. Finally, Sect. 6 concludes this paper.

## 2   Related Work

For a general introduction to process mining, we refer to [17]. In this section, we mainly focus on process discovery. Compared to, e.g., sequential pattern mining [1], process discovery aims to return process models describing the end-to-end control-flow of activities within a process. We refer to [17] to further differentiate process mining from existing data mining techniques. Many conventional process discovery algorithms have been developed; a recent overview can be found in [2]. Regarding the field of domain-knowledge-utilizing process discovery, we refer to [16] for a recent overview. One of the first approaches to interactive process discovery was presented in [6]. The approach involves a user creating a process model gradually in an editor while being supported by the algorithm with suggestions. Regarding incremental process discovery, few approaches exist. In [14] an incremental process discovery algorithm has been introduced that produces process trees. In [10] an incremental approach has been proposed that represents the process as a set of first-order logic formulae. Techniques for *model repair* [8], a research area within process mining, can also be utilized as incremental discovery.

To the best of our knowledge, no related work focuses on trace ordering neither within incremental process discovery nor within process model repair. Outside of process mining, in the context of AI/ML, the influence of ordering data on the learning results has been addressed, for example, in [5,13].

## 3   Preliminaries

For an arbitrary set $X$, we define the set of all sequences over $X$ as $X^*$, e.g., $\langle b, a, b \rangle \in \{a, b, c\}^*$. We denote a totally ordered set by $(X, \preceq)$. Given a base set $X$, we denote the universe of all totally ordered sets by $\mathcal{O}(X)$. A multi-set allows for multiple occurrences of the same element. We denote the set of all possible multi-sets over a base set $X$ as $\mathcal{B}(X)$ and the power set as $\mathcal{P}(X)$.

### 3.1   Event Data

Event data are generated during the execution of operational processes. Table 1 shows an example of an event log. Each row corresponds to an unique event that records the execution of an activity for a specific process instance. Process instances are identified by a case-id. Events that belong to the same process instance, i.e., that have the same case ID, form a trace, i.e., a sequence of events ordered by their timestamp, for example. Consider Table 1, the trace of the process instance "A10000" is $\langle$ "Create Fine", "Send Fine", "Insert Fine Notification", "Add penalty", "Payment"$\rangle$. An event log typically consists of multiple traces. Next, we formally define the concept of a trace and an event log. In the remainder of this paper, we denote the universe of activity labels by $\mathcal{A}$.

**Definition 1 (Trace & Event Log).** *A trace is a sequence of activity labels, i.e., $\sigma \in \mathcal{A}^*$. An event log is a multi-set of traces, i.e., $E \in \mathcal{B}(\mathcal{A}^*)$. We denote the universe of event logs by $\mathcal{E} = \mathcal{B}(\mathcal{A}^*)$.*

**Table 1.** Real-life event log from a road traffic fine management process [12]

| Event-ID | Case-ID | Activity label | Timestamp | ... |
|---|---|---|---|---|
| 1 | A10000 | Create Fine | 09.03.2007 | ... |
| 2 | A10000 | Send Fine | 17.07.2007 | ... |
| 3 | A10000 | Insert Fine Notification | 02.08.2007 | ... |
| 4 | A10000 | Add penalty | 01.10.2007 | ... |
| 5 | A10000 | Payment | 09.09.2008 | ... |
| 6 | A10001 | Create Fine | 19.03.2007 | ... |
| 7 | A10001 | Send Fine | 17.07.2007 | ... |
| 8 | A10001 | Insert Fine Notification | 25.07.2007 | ... |
| 9 | A10001 | Insert Date Appeal to Prefecture | 02.08.2007 | ... |
| 10 | A10001 | Add penalty | 23.09.2007 | ... |
| ... | ... | ... | ... | ... |

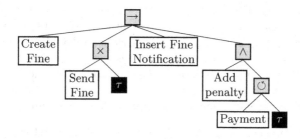

**Fig. 1.** Example of a process model represented as a process tree

Since we are only interested in the various sequences of executed process activities and multiple cases can have the same sequence of executed activities, we define an event log as a multi-set of traces. For an event log $E \in \mathcal{E}$, we write $\overline{E} = \{\sigma \in E\} \subseteq \mathcal{A}^*$ to denote the set of unique traces. For instance, given the event log $E = [\langle a,b,c\rangle^5, \langle a,b,b\rangle^3]$, i.e., an event log containing five times the trace $\langle a,b,c\rangle$ and three times the trace $\langle a,b,b\rangle$, $\overline{E} = \{\langle a,b,c\rangle, \langle a,b,b\rangle\}$.

## 3.2 Process Models

Process models describe process behavior, especially the control flow of process activities. For example, consider Fig. 1, showing a process tree, i.e., an important process model formalism within process mining [17]. The process tree specifies that the activity 'Create Fine' is executed first. Next, 'Send Fine' is optionally executed, followed by 'Insert Fine Notification'. Finally, 'Add Penalty' is executed parallel to potentially multiple executions of 'Payment'. A formal definition of process trees is outside the scope of this paper; we refer to [17].

This paper abstracts from a specific process model formalism, e.g., Petri nets or process trees. Thus, we generally define the universe of process models by $\mathcal{M}$. Each process model $M$ defines a language, i.e., a set of accepted traces. As such, we denote the language of a process model $M \in \mathcal{M}$ by $L(M) \subseteq \mathcal{A}^*$.

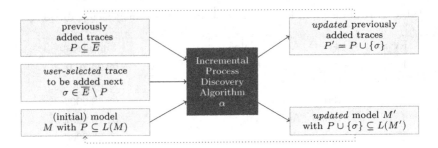

**Fig. 2.** Overview of the procedure of an incremental process discovery algorithm

### 3.3 Incremental Process Discovery

Conventional process discovery algorithms can be seen as a function $d : \mathcal{E} \rightarrow \mathcal{M}$. Incremental process discovery algorithms form a specific class of process discovery algorithms that gradually learn a process model. Figure 2 shows an overview of the procedure used by incremental process discovery algorithms. Given an event log $E \in \mathcal{E}$ and an (initial) process model $M \in \mathcal{M}$, a trace $\sigma \in E$ that is added by the incremental process discovery algorithm to the process model $M$. The resulting process model $M'$, which describes the previously added traces $P$ and the trace $\sigma$, is then used as an input in the next iteration. Next, we formally define an incremental process discovery algorithm.

**Definition 2 (Incremental Process Discovery Algorithm).** *The function* $\alpha : \mathcal{M} \times \mathcal{P}(\mathcal{A}^*) \times \mathcal{A}^* \rightarrow \mathcal{M}$ *is an incremental process discovery algorithm if for any process model* $M \in \mathcal{M}$, *set of previously added traces* $P \in \mathcal{P}(\mathcal{A}^*)$ *with* $P \subseteq L(M)$, *and trace to be added* $\sigma \in \mathcal{A}^*$ *it holds that* $P \cup \{\sigma\} \subseteq L(\alpha(M, P, \sigma))$.

## 4 Dynamic Trace-Ordering Strategies

In this section, we present the proposed approach to order trace candidates. First, we present a general framework on how to define trace-ordering strategies for incremental process discovery. Finally, we present concrete strategies.

### 4.1 General Framework

In this section, we present the proposed framework for defining Dynamic Trace-Ordering Strategies (DTOS) for incremental process discovery. In Fig. 3, we depict the proposed framework. A DTOS consists of $n \geq 1$ sequentially applied *strategy components (sc)*. Each strategy component $sc_i$ orders all input trace candidates $C_{i-1}$ according to some internal logic. The calculated ordering of the trace candidates represents a ranking which trace should be added next to the process model $M$. A 'minimal' trace in $(C_{i-1}, \preceq)$ represents the most suitable candidate to be added next according to the current strategy component $sc_i$. Next, we formally define a strategy component.

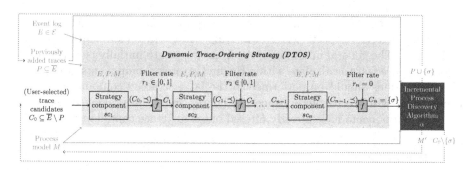

**Fig. 3.** Proposed framework for dynamic trace-ordering strategies that consist of sequentially aligned strategy components, $sc_1$ until $sc_n$, which order the trace candidates from best to worst suitability. After each strategy component, a filter function $f$ removes the worst suited trace candidates. After the last strategy component $sc_n$, the function $f$ filters such that a single trace candidate $\sigma$ remains that is then fed into the incremental process discovery algorithm.

**Definition 3 (Strategy component).** *A strategy component is a function $sc : \mathcal{E} \times \mathcal{P}(\mathcal{A}^*) \times \mathcal{P}(\mathcal{A}^*) \times M \rightarrow \mathcal{O}(\mathcal{A}^*)$ that maps an event log $E \in \mathcal{E}$, a set of previously added traces $P \subseteq \overline{E}$, a set of trace candidates $C \subseteq P \setminus \overline{E}$, and a process model $M \in \mathcal{M}$ to an ordered set of trace candidates $(C, \preceq) \in \mathcal{O}(C)$. We denote the universe of strategy components by $\mathcal{SC}$.*

After each strategy component, a filter function $f$ filters out the worst suited trace candidates. Each call of the filter function $f$ can be configured via a filter rate $r_i \in [0,1]$. A filter rate of 1 results in no trace candidate being filtered. A filter rate of 0 results in only one trace candidate remaining. Thus, $C_n \subseteq C_{n-1} \subseteq ... \subseteq C_1 \subseteq C_0$ holds (cf. Fig. 3). Each strategy component together with the subsequent filtering can be viewed as a knock-out step that reduces the number of trace candidates that are potentially to be added next to the process model $M$. Next, we formally define a filter function and a DTOS.

**Definition 4 (Filter function).** *A filter function $f : \mathcal{O}(A^*) \times [0,1] \rightarrow \mathcal{P}(\mathcal{A}^*)$ maps an ordered set of traces $(C, \preceq) \in \mathcal{O}(A^*)$ and a filter rate $r \in [0,1]$ to a set of traces $C' \in \mathcal{P}(\mathcal{A}^*)$ such that $C' \subseteq C$, $|C'| = max\{1, \lceil r * |C| \rceil\}$, and $\forall c' \in C' \forall c \in C \setminus C'(c' \leq c)$.*

**Definition 5 (Dynamic trace-ordering strategy (DTOS)).** *A DTOS is a non-empty sequence of strategy components and corresponding filter rates, i.e., $\langle (sc_1, r_1), ..., (sc_n, r_n) \rangle \in (\mathcal{SC} \times [0,1])^*$ with $r_n = 0$ for $n \geq 1$.*

We consciously decided to design a DTOS as a sequence of strategy components and filters that work in a knock-out fashion, i.e., every strategy component orders the trace candidates, and subsequently, a function filters out the worst trace candidates. This decision was taken to keep the computational effort low because it is crucial to compute recommendations fast in an interactive process discovery setting. The use of multiple strategy components within a DTOS allows combining different aspects when evaluating which trace candidate should be added next. The general intention of the framework is to initially perform evaluations that are fast to calculate within the first strategy components. More complex evaluations should be performed in the later strategy components. These components will receive fewer trace candidates since the previously executed strategy components have already filtered out some trace candidates.

## 4.2   Instantiations

Here, we present specific strategy components, i.e., instantiations of Definition 3. We provide general applicable strategy components that are independent of a specific incremental process discovery algorithm and strategy components which are specifically tailored for the incremental process discovery algorithm introduced in previous work [14]. Next, we briefly present six strategy components.

**Alignment Costs.** Alignments [18] are a state-of-the-art conformance checking technique that quantifies to which extent a trace can be replayed on a process model. They further provide diagnostic information on missing and unexpected behavior when comparing a trace with a process model. The costs of an optimal alignment reflect the conformance degree of the trace and the closest process model execution. Given a process model, we can assign costs, i.e., alignment costs, to each trace candidate. These costs are then used to rank/sort the trace candidates, i.e., the trace candidate with the lowest costs first and the trace candidate with the highest costs last. The intention is to first add trace candidates to the process model that are close to the specified behavior by the current process model. Note that the computation of alignments has an exponential time complexity, i.e., also called the *state space explosion problem* [3].

**Missing Activities.** When starting to discover a process model incrementally, it is likely that the first process models obtained do not describe all process activities that have been recorded in the event data. This results from the fact that in many real-life event logs not every trace contains all possible executable process activities of a process. The 'missing activities strategy' ranks the trace candidates according to their number of activity labels already present in the process model $M$. Trace candidates that contain process activities present in the current process model $M$ get costs 0. For the other trace candidates, costs correspond to the number of unique activity labels within the trace that are not yet part of the process model $M$.

**Levenshtein Distance.** This strategy compares the trace candidates among each other by calculating the Levenshtein distance, i.e., a metric to compare the distance between two sequences based on edit operations: insertion, deletion, and substitution. The idea behind this strategy is to favor traces that are more similar to all other traces that still need to be potentially added. For example, consider the three trace candidates with corresponding frequency values in Table 2. We compare all traces and weigh the different Levenshtein distances according to the trace frequency. In the example, we would choose the trace $\langle a, b \rangle$ as the best trace candidate to be added next.

**Table 2.** Example of the weighted Levenshtein distance for trace candidates

| Trace candidates | Frequency in $E$ | Weighted Levenshtein distance | Rank |
|---|---|---|---|
| $\langle a, b \rangle$ | 100 | $50 * lev(\langle a, b \rangle, \langle a, b, b \rangle) + 20 * lev(\langle a, b \rangle, \langle a, c \rangle) = 70$ | 1 |
| $\langle a, b, b \rangle$ | 50 | $100 * lev(\langle a, b, b \rangle, \langle a, b \rangle) + 20 * lev(\langle a, b, b \rangle, \langle a, c \rangle) = 140$ | 2 |
| $\langle a, c \rangle$ | 20 | $100 * lev(\langle a, c \rangle, \langle a, b \rangle) + 50 * lev(\langle a, c \rangle, \langle a, b, b \rangle) = 200$ | 3 |

**Brute-Force.** Assume a process model $M$, an event log $E \in \mathcal{E}$, the set of previously added traces $P \subseteq \overline{E}$, and a set of trace candidates $C \subseteq \overline{E} \setminus P$ (cf. Fig. 3). The strategy separately applies the incremental process discovery (cf. Fig. 2) to all trace candidates in $C$ and the model $M$. As a result, $|C|$ different process models are obtained. A quality metric, i.e., the F-measure representing the harmonic mean of recall and precision, is calculated on the given event log $E$ for each obtained model. The trace candidate that yields a process model with the highest F-measure is ranked first.

**LCA Height.** This strategy is tailored to the incremental process discovery algorithm introduced in our earlier work [14]. The incremental process discovery algorithm uses process trees (cf. Fig. 1) as a process model formalism. When incrementally adding a new trace to the model, the central idea of the algorithm is to identify subtrees that need to be modified so that the new trace fits the language of the model. These deviating subtrees are called LCAs in [14]. Depending on which trace is added, the LCAs that must be altered change.

The key idea of this strategy is to avoid changing large parts of the already learned process model upon adding a new trace. Thus, the strategy prefers trace candidates that lead to only minor changes in the process model. Therefore, the strategy computes for each trace candidate in $C \subseteq \overline{E}$ the height of the first LCA, i.e., the first subtree in the process model $M$, that must be altered[1]. The height of an LCA is defined by the path length from the LCA's root node to the root

---

[1] Note that per trace that is incrementally added, various LCAs might be changed. However, without fully executing the incremental process discovery approach for a trace, we only can compute the first LCA that must be changed. Therefore, there is a risk that the first LCA will be rated as good based on the strategy, but that further LCAs will have to be changed, which the strategy would rate as bad.

Table 3. Overview of the strategy components

| Abbreviation | Strategy component (Sect. 4.2) | Algorithmic specific or general |
|---|---|---|
| C | Alignment Costs | General |
| M | Missing Activities | General |
| L | Levenshtein Distance | General |
| B | Brute Force | General |
| D | Duplicates | Specific |
| H | LCA Height | Specific |

node of the entire tree, i.e., the entire process model $M$. Trace candidates are then descending ordered based on the first LCA's height.

**Duplicates.** This strategy is tailored to the incremental process discovery algorithm introduced in our earlier work [14]. These LCAs, i.e., subtrees of the process tree, may have multiple leaf nodes with the same activity label, i.e., *duplicate labels*. In general, duplicate labels can increase the precision of a process model and are therefore desirable. When altering an LCA, the incremental process discovery algorithm [14] rediscovers the LCA using a conventional process discovery algorithm [11]. The downside of this rediscovery is that the used conventional process discovery algorithm [11] is not able to discover process trees with duplicate labels. Thus, the rediscovery would remove the potentially desirable duplicate labels in the LCA that have been learned so far. Thus, this strategy, called *Duplicates*, favors trace candidates whose first LCA does not contain leaf nodes with duplicate labels. Trace candidates are ascending ordered based on the number of duplicate leaf nodes.

## 5    Evaluation

In this section, we present the experimental evaluation. First, we present the experimental setup. Subsequently, we present and discuss the results.

### 5.1    Experimental Setup

To keep the experimental setup independent of a particular user selecting trace candidates to be added next (cf. Sect. 1), we assumed the following: given an event log and an initial process model, all traces are eventually added to the model incrementally. Thus, the set of trace candidates represents in the beginning the entire event log. After one incremental discovery step—a trace selected by an ordering strategy is added to the model by the incremental discovery algorithm—the added trace is removed from the trace candidate set.

  Given the strategy components' abbreviations in Table 3, we created all potential orderings by shuffling the order of C, M, L, D, and H. Finally, strategy

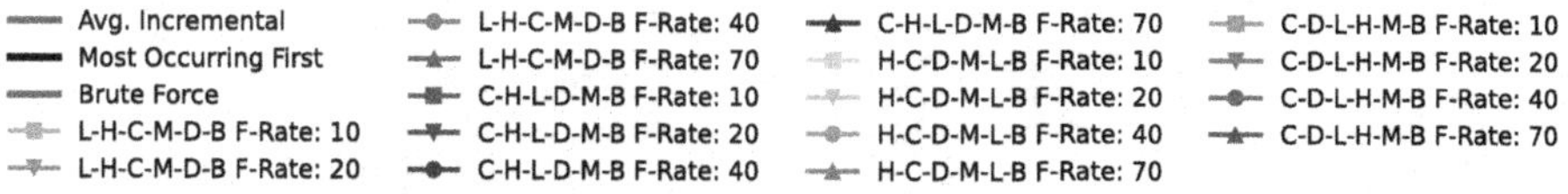

| | | | |
|---|---|---|---|
| ——— Avg. Incremental | —●— L-H-C-M-D-B F-Rate: 40 | —▲— C-H-L-D-M-B F-Rate: 70 | —■— C-D-L-H-M-B F-Rate: 10 |
| ——— Most Occurring First | —▲— L-H-C-M-D-B F-Rate: 70 | —■— H-C-D-M-L-B F-Rate: 10 | —▼— C-D-L-H-M-B F-Rate: 20 |
| ——— Brute Force | —■— C-H-L-D-M-B F-Rate: 10 | —▼— H-C-D-M-L-B F-Rate: 20 | —●— C-D-L-H-M-B F-Rate: 40 |
| —■— L-H-C-M-D-B F-Rate: 10 | —▼— C-H-L-D-M-B F-Rate: 20 | —●— H-C-D-M-L-B F-Rate: 40 | —▲— C-D-L-H-M-B F-Rate: 70 |
| —▼— L-H-C-M-D-B F-Rate: 20 | —●— C-H-L-D-M-B F-Rate: 40 | —▲— H-C-D-M-L-B F-Rate: 70 | |

**Fig. 4.** Legend for the results shown in Fig. 5 and Fig. 6

component B is added to each strategy. Note that the brute force (B) strategy component is computationally expensive, and therefore we decided to always add this strategy component at the end. This procedure leads to 5! = 120 different strategy component orderings. To avoid further expansion of the parameter space, we used one filter rate for each strategy component within a strategy, except the last one (cf. Fig. 3). For instance, the strategy L-H-C-M-D-B F-Rate 10 (cf. Fig. 4) represents the strategy where first the Levenshtein distance component is applied and finally the brute force component. All components within this specific strategy use a filter rate of 0.1≙10%. We applied the different strategies on real-life event logs using the incremental process discovery algorithm presented in [14]. Further, we measured the F-measure, i.e., the harmonic mean of recall and precision, of each incrementally discovered process model using the given event log. We used four publicly available real-life event logs [9,12,19].

### 5.2   Results & Discussion

In Fig. 5, we depict the results of 16 dynamic strategies, a static strategy, i.e., most occurring trace variant first (black line), the brute force component as a stand-alone strategy (gray line), random trace orderings (blue lines), and the average of the random trace orderings (red line). Note that we only show a selection of the strategies evaluated. Per log, we provide two x-axis scales: percentage of processed traces and percentage of uniquely processed trace variants.

We observe that for all four event logs, the trace candidate order has a significant impact on the F-measure, cf. the large area covered by the blue lines in Fig. 5. The solid red line represents the average of the blue lines. Thus, the red line can be seen as a baseline as it represents the quality of the models if a random trace order is applied. We see that *most strategies are clearly above the red line*. Thus, applying a strategy is often better than randomly selecting trace candidates. Note that with incremental process discovery, the goal is often *not* to include all traces from the event log, as event logs often have data quality issues. We observe that the brute force approach as a stand-alone strategy (gray line) often performs better than the other strategies, although the brute force approach can be considered as a *greedy* algorithm. For the *domestic* event log, the brute force as a stand-alone strategy could not be used as the calculation was still not completed after several days. In Fig. 6 we depict the computation time per strategy. In general, we observe that an increasing filter rate per strategy component ordering leads to an increasing computation time. This observation can be explained because each strategy includes the brute force strategy component as the last step. We also find that the brute force approach as a single

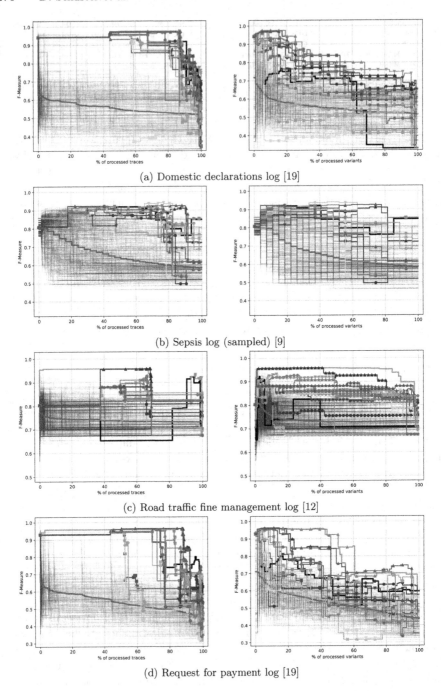

(a) Domestic declarations log [19]

(b) Sepsis log (sampled) [9]

(c) Road traffic fine management log [12]

(d) Request for payment log [19]

**Fig. 5.** F-measure values of the incrementally discovered process models. Most evaluated strategies (cf. Fig. 4) perform better than the baseline (red line). Blue lines indicate the solution space (not complete, as not every possible trace ordering can be evaluated due to a large number of trace variants per event log). (Color figure online)

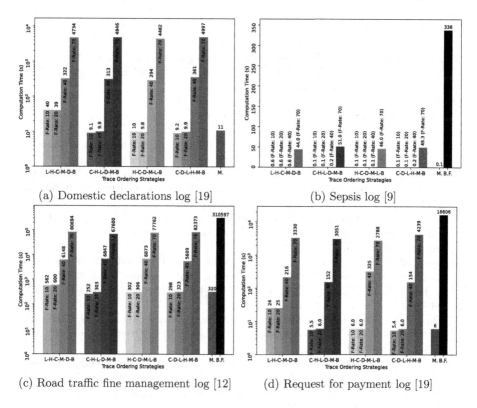

(a) Domestic declarations log [19]

(b) Sepsis log [9]

(c) Road traffic fine management log [12]

(d) Request for payment log [19]

**Fig. 6.** Computation time of the strategies (cf. Fig. 4) per event log

strategy (gray bar) has a significantly longer computation time than the other strategies. In short, it can be stated that many of the presented strategies lead to better process models, i.e., outperforming randomly selecting a trace to be added. Nevertheless, no clear strategy can be identified that always works best on all tested event logs.

# 6    Conclusion

We presented a framework to define trace-ordering strategies for incremental process discovery. We introduced general strategy components and evaluated different strategies on real-life event data based on the framework. The results show that the trace-ordering strategies can improve the quality of the learned process models. For future work, we are interested in non-sequential compositions of strategy components, e.g., each strategy component ranks all trace candidates, and finally, a score is determined. However, this requires more efficient computable strategy components. Finally, we plan to integrate trace-ordering strategies in our incremental process discovery tool Cortado [15].

# References

1. Agrawal, R., Srikant, R.: Mining sequential patterns. In: Proceedings of the Eleventh International Conference on Data Engineering. IEEE Comput. Soc. Press (1995). https://doi.org/10.1109/ICDE.1995.380415

2. Augusto, A., et al.: Automated discovery of process models from event logs: review and benchmark. IEEE Trans. Knowl. Data Eng. **31**(4), 686–705 (2019). https://doi.org/10.1109/TKDE.2018.2841877

3. Carmona, J., van Dongen, B., Solti, A., Weidlich, M.: Conformance Checking. Springer, Berlin (2018). https://doi.org/10.1007/978-3-319-99414-7

4. Conforti, R., La Rosa, M., ter Hofstede, A.H.: Filtering out infrequent behavior from business process event logs. IEEE Trans. Knowl. Data Eng. **29**(2), 300–314 (2017). https://doi.org/10.1109/TKDE.2016.2614680

5. Cornuéjols, A.: Getting order independence in incremental learning. In: Brazdil, P.B. (ed.) ECML 1993. LNCS, vol. 667, pp. 196–212. Springer, Heidelberg (1993). https://doi.org/10.1007/3-540-56602-3_137

6. Dixit, P.M., Buijs, J.C.A.M., van der Aalst, W.M.P.: Prodigy : human-in-the-loop process discovery. In: 12th International Conference on Research Challenges in Information Science (RCIS). IEEE (2018). https://doi.org/10.1109/RCIS.2018.8406657

7. Dumas, M., La Rosa, M., Mendling, J., Reijers, H.A.: Fundamentals of Business Process Management. Springer, Berlin Heidelberg (2018). https://doi.org/10.1007/978-3-662-56509-4

8. Fahland, D., van der Aalst, W.M.: Model repair - aligning process models to reality. Inf. Syst. **47**, 220–243 (2015). https://doi.org/10.1016/j.is.2013.12.007

9. Felix Mannhardt: Sepsis cases - event log. https://doi.org/10.4121/uuid:915d2bfb-7e84-49ad-a286-dc35f063a460

10. Ferilli, S., Esposito, F.: A logic framework for incremental learning of process models. Fundam. Inf. **128**, 413–443 (2013). https://doi.org/10.3233/FI-2013-951

11. Leemans, S.J.J., Fahland, D., van der Aalst, W.M.P.: Discovering block-structured process models from event logs - a constructive approach. In: Colom, J.-M., Desel, J. (eds.) PETRI NETS 2013. LNCS, vol. 7927, pp. 311–329. Springer, Heidelberg (2013). https://doi.org/10.1007/978-3-642-38697-8_17

12. M. (Massimiliano) de Leoni, Felix Mannhardt: Road traffic fine management process. https://doi.org/10.4121/uuid:270fd440-1057-4fb9-89a9-b699b47990f5

13. MacGregor, J.N.: The effects of order on learning classifications by example: heuristics for finding the optimal order. Artif. Intell. **34**(3), 361–370 (1988). https://doi.org/10.1016/0004-3702(88)90065-3

14. Schuster, D., van Zelst, S.J., van der Aalst, W.M.P.: Incremental discovery of hierarchical process models. In: Dalpiaz, F., Zdravkovic, J., Loucopoulos, P. (eds.) RCIS 2020. LNBIP, vol. 385, pp. 417–433. Springer, Cham (2020). https://doi.org/10.1007/978-3-030-50316-1_25

15. Schuster, D., van Zelst, S.J., van der Aalst, W.M.P.: Cortado—an interactive tool for data-driven process discovery and modeling. In: Buchs, D., Carmona, J. (eds.) PETRI NETS 2021. LNCS, vol. 12734, pp. 465–475. Springer, Cham (2021). https://doi.org/10.1007/978-3-030-76983-3_23

16. Schuster, D., van Zelst, S.J., van der Aalst, W.M.: Utilizing domain knowledge in data-driven process discovery: a literature review. Comput. Ind. **137**, 103612 (2022). https://doi.org/10.1016/j.compind.2022.103612

17. van der Aalst, W.M.P.: Process Mining: Data Science in Action. Springer, Berlin Heidelberg (2016). https://doi.org/10.1007/978-3-662-49851-4
18. van der Aalst, W.M.P., Adriansyah, A., van Dongen, B.: Replaying history on process models for conformance checking and performance analysis. WIREs Data Min. Knowl. Disc. **2**(2), 182–192 (2012). https://doi.org/10.1002/widm.1045
19. van Dongen, B.F.: BPI challenge (2020). https://doi.org/10.4121/uuid:52fb97d4-4588-43c9-9d04-3604d4613b51

# Bank Statements to Network Features: Extracting Features Out of Time Series Using Visibility Graph

Nirbhaya Shaji[1,4]([envelope]) [ORCID], João Gama[2,3] [ORCID], Rita P. Ribeiro[1,3] [ORCID], and Pedro Gomes[4]

[1] Faculty of Sciences, University of Porto, Porto, Portugal
nirbhaya@lendigo.ng
[2] Faculty of Economics, University of Porto, Porto, Portugal
[3] INESC TEC, Porto, Portugal
[4] Pelican Rhythms LDA, Porto, Portugal
pedro@quickcheck.ng

**Abstract.** Non-traditional data like the applicant's bank statement is a significant source for decision-making when granting loans. We find that we can use methods from network science on the applicant's bank statements to convert inherent cash flow characteristics to predictors for default prediction in a credit scoring or credit risk assessment model. First, the credit cash flow is extracted from a bank statement and later converted into a visibility graph or network. Afterwards, we use this visibility network to find features that predict the borrowers' repayment behaviour. We see that feature selection methods select all the five extracted features. Finally, SMOTE is used to balance the training data. The model using the features from the network and the standard features together is shown having superior performance compared to the model that uses only the standard features, indicating the network features' predictive power.

**Keywords:** Bank statement · Non traditional data · Time series · Network construction · Visibility graph · Complex networks · Regular network · Network features · Feature selection · Cash flow · SMEs · Micro finances

## 1 Introduction

Microfinance institutions (MFI) provide loans to low-income clients, including micro-companies and the self-employed, who traditionally lack access to mainstream sources of finance from traditional banking institutions. These types of clients are considered too risky by traditional banks since they cannot provide real collateral, and they tend to work in informal sectors of the economy. Therefore, whenever an MFI lends to a client, there is an inherent risk of money not coming back, i.e. the client turning into a defaulter; this is called the credit risk. When it comes to assessing the credit risk involved with each loan application,

© The Author(s), under exclusive license to Springer Nature Switzerland AG 2022
T. Bouadi et al. (Eds.): IDA 2022, LNCS 13205, pp. 278–289, 2022.
https://doi.org/10.1007/978-3-031-01333-1_22

a client's lack of verifiable credit history is the major challenge for MFIs in emerging markets [1]. To determine the creditworthiness of the application, in cases when credit history is not available, MFIs rely mainly on the information provided by the client at the time of loan application. This information primarily consists of the traditional socioeconomic data of the client.

Finding relevant features for predicting defaulters from these traditional data has been studied extensively over time [2,3]. Non-traditional data like bank statements can provide additional information on a client's repayment capacity improving the models focusing only on the traditional socioeconomic data [4]. A bank statement is an official document that summarizes the account holder's activity over a certain period, containing all the transactions records-both incoming (credits) and outgoing (debits). For MFI, this credit and debit flow is vital in knowing what is going on with the client's funds during a period.

This work focuses on using time series and network science tools to extract relevant features from bank statements, providing better predictions of the client's ability to repay the loan. A time series is a collection of observations of well-defined data items obtained through repeated measurements over time. For example, the bank statement from the clients can provide the credit and debit clash flow as a time series. Visibility graph [5] method of constructing networks out of time series have shown to conserve their structure in the graph topology. However, these networks inherit several time-series properties in their design as periodicity and randomness. Different network structure measures could then be used to characterize the time series and hence in our case, the bank statement and the nature of the client's repayment capacity.

The paper is organized as follows. After introducing the problem and focus of work, Sect. 2 briefly reviews the related works in this area. Then, Sect. 3 describes the process and methodology used to develop the visibility graph from the bank statement. It also describes some interesting properties seen in the generated graph. Next, Sect. 4 presents the data set and explains the extracted graph features. It also describes the feature selection methods used and explains the evaluation done to check the extracted features' predictive power. Finally, in Sect. 5, we present our conclusion and future work.

## 2    Related Work

Machine learning models are employed extensively for credit risk analysis and credit scoring. Petropoulos et al. [6] identified that machine learning models demonstrated superior performance and forecasting accuracy compared to traditional methods in credit rating.

Recently more non-traditional methods and use of non-traditional data for credit risk assessment have been explored [7]. Ruiz et al. [1] proposed a method to evaluate the predictive power of the non-traditional approach and showed how the assembling of Weight of Evidence (WoE) with different feature selection criteria could result in more robust credit scoring models in microfinance. In addition, non-traditional data such as contact networks have been used to address the problem of the lack of a verifiable customers' credit history using node embedding features [8]. Provenzano et al. [9] further used other non-traditional data to improve credit ratings, such as historical balance sheets, bankruptcy statutes and macroeconomic variables, to develop machine learning models and observed excellent out-of-sample performance results.

Bunker et al. [4] showed that the bank statement derived features have value in improving the credit scoring model. However, relevant features to extract from the bank statement data were decided on in consultation with senior staff members at the lending company. Our work eliminates this drawback of a need for expert knowledge by using tools from network science to map the intrinsic nature of the bank statement to the structural properties of a network and later extract them through relevant network metrics.

In [10], Silva et al. presented a comprehensive and well-structured review of existing univariate and multivariate time series to networks algorithm mappings, highlighting their similarities and differences, the data characteristics they capture, and the main references and results.

Lacasa et al. [5] proposed visibility mappings from (univariate) time series to complex networks, based on traditional visibility algorithms from computational geometry [11]. Later, following Luque et al.'s work [12] to reduce the computational complexity associated with NVGs by restricting the visibility lines to be only horizontal, Lacasa et al. [13] introduced directed horizontal visibility graphs by defining a horizontal visibility graph.

## 3    From Bank Statements to Network Features

The high-level view of our approach is summarised as a flow chart in Fig. 1. First, each client's raw data, in the form of a bank statement, is converted to corresponding time series. Then using the visibility graph method, a network is constructed out of the time series. In the following stage, features are extracted from the network and mapped back to the client. Afterwards, feature selection methods are used to select the important features from the pool of all available features, including the features extracted from the visibility graph and the base features of the data set containing the client's traditional socioeconomic data. This is followed by applying an oversampling technique, SMOTE [14], to each cross-validation training data set considering the class imbalance issue. Afterwards, evaluation is done on a Random Forest [15] model with 10-fold cross-validation to do a pairwise Wilcoxon signed rank test between a base model that gets only the initial feature selected predictors from the loan providers database and a "NetworkPlus" model that gets all the predictors available, including the extracted network features.

According to [16], almost any discrete structure can be suitably represented as special cases of graphs, whose features may be characterized, analyzed and eventually related to its respective dynamics. The motivation for this work stems from this idea and looks into how a network view can help in getting information out of a bank statement via time series, which can be of importance in

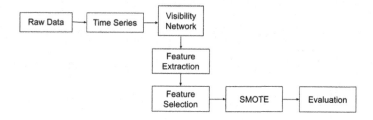

**Fig. 1.** Prediction of defaulters from bank statements: main steps of our approach.

determining the repayment capacity of a loan applicant. Previous works done by Andriana et al. [17] have already shown that time series with different dynamics are mapped into complex networks with different structures. There are several methods currently followed for this mapping. The one that is used here is the Visibility Graphs method.

### 3.1 Visibility Graphs

This method based on the concept of visibility was first proposed in 2008 by Lacasa et al. [5]. Named Natural Visibility Graph (NVG), each node in the graph corresponds, in the same order, to the time series data points and two nodes are connected if there is a line of visibility between the corresponding data points. That is, if it is possible to draw a straight line in the time series that joins the two corresponding data points that intercepts no data "height" between them, then there exists a connection between the data points or an edge between the corresponding nodes.

More formally, we can establish the following visibility criteria: two arbitrary data values $(t_a, y_a)$ and $(t_b, y_b)$ will have visibility, and consequently will become two connected nodes of the associated visibility graph, if any other data $(t_c, y_c)$ placed between them fulfills:

$$y_c < y_b + (y_a - y_b) * \frac{(t_b - t_c)}{(t_b - t_a)} \quad (1)$$

The associated graph extracted from a time series is always:

1. connected - each node sees at least its nearest neighbors (left and right);
2. undirected - the way the algorithm is built up, there is no direction defined in the links;
3. invariant under affine transformations of the series data - the visibility criterion is invariant under re-scaling of both horizontal and vertical axes, and under horizontal and vertical translations.

### 3.2 Daily Time Series to Visibility Graphs

The visibility graph mapping is illustrated in Fig. 2. After outlier removal and normalization, each of the points in the time series become vertices in the visibility network of the credit flow. The days numbered 42, 51, 86 and 87 which had

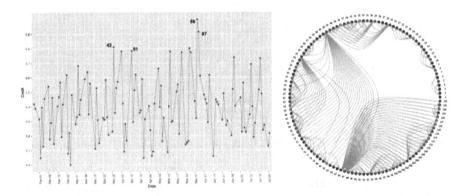

**Fig. 2.** Visibility graph of daily credit time series from a bank statement. The node colour indicates the node degree. Blue indicates a lower degree while red indicates a higher degree. Green indicates a degree value between blue and red. (Color figure online)

high daily credit can be seen as having high degree nodes because of its visibility around the other points in the time series. Mapping of daily credit to visibility graph was implemented by an algorithm where each unique pair of points in the time series were taken and checked for any obstruction by any points that came between them. For example, for checking if there is a possible edge between data points at time 6 and time 23, the algorithm takes all the point in between them one by one and find its magnitude or value of y axis. If one of these points has a magnitude greater than:

$$y_b + (y_a - y_b) * \frac{(t_b - t_c)}{(t_b - t_a)} \tag{2}$$

where $y_a$ and $y_b$ are the credit value for points a $=6$ and b $=23$ and $t_a$ and $t_b$ are the time for those points which in our case is 6 and 23, then there is no edge between point 6 and point 23.

The color of the nodes is an indication of its degree. The color varies from blue to green to red. Lower degree being blue and higher degree being red. In the network in Fig. 2 each nodes corresponds to each of the days numbered from 1 to 122 (length of the time series in display), arranged in anti-clock wise direction starting from outer middle right end of the circular structure. The dome/tent shaped edge grouping inside the networks brings out the periodicity indicating a clear regularity in the graph opposed to a randomness. We can see shorter period repeating patterns and fewer longer ones too. Nodes with green color and its spacing indicate shorter periods.

### 3.3 Properties of the Generated Graphs

Previous works have shown that time series with different dynamics are mapped into complex networks with different structures. Also the associated graph inherits some structure of the time series, and consequently the process that generated the time series can be characterized by using graph theory. The structure of the time series is seen to be conserved in the visibility graph topology by periodic series converted into regular graphs, random series into random graphs, and fractal series into scale-free graphs [5].

Since one of the aim of trying visibility graph method for the problem in hand is to detect any periodicity, or even any indication of the duration of periodicity, initial intention was to look into the degree distribution of network to see if it is formed by a finite number of peaks related to the series period. Generically speaking, all periodic time series are mapped into regular graphs, the discrete degree distribution being the fingerprint of the time series periods. Figures 3 and 4 show the visibility graphs of the daily credit and debit time series and the corresponding degree distribution for each.

Since the outliers have been removed, the chances of finding data points with very high visibility, which corresponds to nodes that are hubs, are lesser than in random networks. This can be seen also from the degree distribution as shown in Fig. 4. And it can be seen that both debit and credit visibility graph have similar short periodic regions.

Analysing Figs. 3 and 5, which are the daily and weekly visibility graph of the same client, and looking at the interval of appearance of high degree nodes, it can be seen that there are monthly cycles with a period of 4 to 5 weeks in between them. At the same time another client's weekly visibility graph (cf. Fig. 6), indicates less periodicity and regularity.

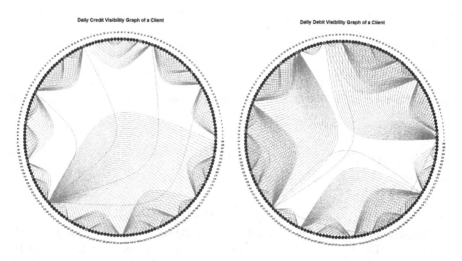

**Fig. 3.** Credit and debit visibility graph of same bank statement of client 1.

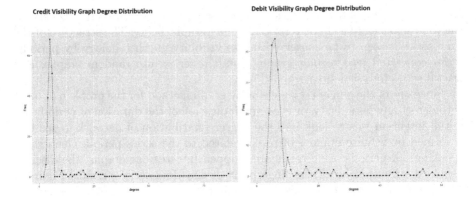

**Fig. 4.** Degree distribution of daily credit and debit visibility graph of client 1

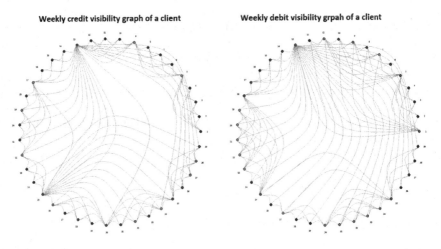

**Fig. 5.** Weekly credit and debit visibility graphs of client 1, depicting some periodicity and regularity.

## 4    Case Study

### 4.1    Data Set

The data used in this work comes from a MFI providing loans to small businesses in several regions in a country in Sub-Saharan Africa. The data includes all the information the MFI gets with a loan application. These include data about the business owner, business details and the details of the loan that they have applied for. The data also contains the digital bank statement linked to the clients business. The duration of the bank statement can be between 6 to 10 months. The bank statement data includes transaction date and the amount of credit or debit that happened for that particular transaction. The data is labeled good or bad based on whether the client was able to repay or not. Total of the daily credit

**Weekly credit visibility graph of another client**     **Weekly debit visibility grpah of another client**

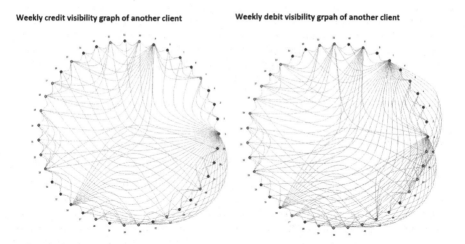

**Fig. 6.** Weekly credit and debit visibility graphs of client 2, depicting less periodicity and regularity.

transactions is calculated for each of the bank statements through the duration of the available data. This daily credit is converted to a time series which is used to construct the network. Even though the submitted bank statements are between 6 and 10 months long, there could be days when no credit happened, making the data size not necessarily of 6 to 10 times 30 days long time series. The presence of public holidays and situations like recent pandemic brings in a lot of noise or empty space in the time series that make traditional method inadequate for the purpose of time series analysis. The inflow and outflow of money to such an account differ vastly from a personal bank account. Detecting the inflow periodicity or at least a presence of periodicity becomes crucial in deciding whether the business will be able to repay the loan successfully with a weekly, bi weekly or monthly repayment periodicity. Matching the repayment plan to the clients' capacity of payment will ensure both the parties benefit from the loan with reduced risk.

## 4.2   Feature Extraction

We extracted five network features from the daily credit network of each client constructed using the visibility graph method:

1. Graph Information Criterion (GIC) [18]: GIC is Kullback-Leibler divergence or L2 distance between our undirected credit visibility graph and an Erdos-Renyi random graph (ER) with the probability to connect a pair of vertices being the same as our undirected credit visibility graph.
2. Number of edges: The number of edges in our network which corresponds to the number of daily credit lower than local peaks.
3. Number of vertices: The number of vertices in our undirected credit visibility graph which corresponds to the length of the bank statements.

4. Number of vertices with degree greater than average degree of the network: This corresponds to the hubs or high peaks in our network which corresponds to days with higher visibility.
5. Mean distance of the network: This is the average path length in a graph, by calculating the shortest paths between all pairs of vertices using a breadth-first search.

## 4.3   Feature Selection

Feature selection is the process of choosing variables that are useful in predicting the response. It is considered a good practice to identify which features are important when building predictive models especially when dealing with high-dimensional data so as to reduce the complexity of the model and to make the model faster. However for our work the role of feature selection is mainly in determining whether the features we choose from the network, based on its structural significance, are actually indicative of the defaulting of the client. Along with the 5 network features extracted from network 78 features from the tradition data source where also tested using the 3 feature selection methods which are:

1. Information Value: Out of the 5 network properties 4, (1,2,3 and 4), where selected with Information value greater than 0.3.
2. Boruta [19]: All 5 where selected under a tentative rough fix condition.
3. Recursive Feature Elimination (RFE): Out of the 5 network properties 4, (2,3,4 and 5) where selected.

Table 1 shows the features that where selected by each of the methods. The union of all the selected features where taken to get the final predictor set for evaluation, which included all the 5 features we took from the network.

**Table 1.** Feature selection methods (Information Value, Boruta and RFE) and network features selected as important.

|  | Graph Information Criterion (GIC) | No. of edges | No. of vertices | No. of vertices (with degree > avg. degree) | Mean distance of the network |
|---|---|---|---|---|---|
| IV | Selected | Selected | Selected | Selected | Not Selected |
| Boruta | Selected | Selected | Selected | Selected | Selected |
| RFE | Not Selected | Selected | Selected | Selected | Selected |

### 4.4    Evaluation

A Random Forest [15] classification model with 10-fold cross validation was used to evaluate the F1 score of the test fold prediction. F1 score was chosen considering the imbalance class ratio of the target and since our aim here is to compare model performance. The size of the data set used in the test is 369 data points. Since the good to bad class ratio was 7:3, a common challenge with predicting credit defaulters, Synthetic Minority Oversampling Technique (SMOTE) [14] was used to balance the train data. Smote was applied only to the train set for each of the 10 folds evaluation set to deal with the class imbalance problem.

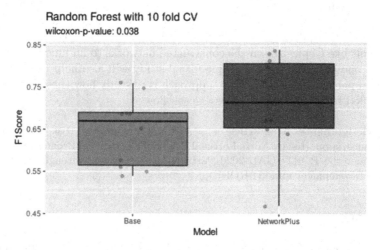

**Fig. 7.** F1 score distribution obtained by Random Forest with 10-fold cross-validation, on Base model with only the predictors from the loan providers database and Net-workPlus model with all available predictors including the extracted network features.

Following that, the pairwise Wilcoxon signed rank test was conducted between a base model, that gets only the initial, feature selected, predictors from the loan providers database and a "NetworkPlus" model that gets all the available predictors including the extracted network features. The Wilcoxon test gave a p-value less than 0.05 (cf. Fig. 7) indicating there is enough evidence to reject the null hypothesis that both the model performed same.

The pair of box plots in Fig. 7 shows the average F1 score over the 10-folds of the evaluation. The median line of NetworkPlus model box lies entirely outside of Base model box, indicating a significant difference between the groups.

## 5    Conclusion and Future Work

In this work, we tried to see if there is any method that can extract the inherent nature of a bank statement into features that can indicate repayment capacity to use in the credit risk prediction model. We found that we can convert the daily credit time series to a daily credit network using the visibility graph method that contains relevant features in its structural complexity. A cash flow times series like bank balance or credit and debit movement of a business are very complex, considering the social nature of the processes causing it. With this work, we found that the network view of the bank statement can provide information on the periodicity in the cash inflow and give insights into short term patterns within the flow. Furthermore, various feature selection methods selected all the features extracted from the visibility network as carrying value to the default prediction problem. Other evaluation results also indicate the predictive power of these network features over traditional predictors.

The immediate future step would be to explore how we can use debit networks in a similar way. Finding more network measures that can give information about both the credit and debit visibility network together can also be considered. Using tools like Gephi [20] on the constructed networks to find more information than the one available from a simple visual study will also help bring out more structural patterns. Another future approach is to study how these networks can be classified based on their businesses cash flow.

**Acknowledgements.** This article is a result of the project Risk Assessment for Microfinance, supported by Norte Portugal Regional Operational Programme (NORTE 2020), under the PORTUGAL 2020 Partnership Agreement, through the European Regional Development Fund (ERDF).

# References

1. Ruiz, S., Gomes, P., Rodrigues, L., Gama, J.: Assembled feature selection for credit scoring in microfinance with non-traditional features. In: Appice, A., Tsoumakas, G., Manolopoulos, Y., Matwin, S. (eds.) DS 2020. LNCS (LNAI), vol. 12323, pp. 207–216. Springer, Cham (2020). https://doi.org/10.1007/978-3-030-61527-7_14
2. Nalić, J., Švraka, A.: Using data mining approaches to build credit scoring model: case study - implementation of credit scoring model in microfinance institution. In: 2018 17th International Symposium INFOTEH-JAHORINA (INFOTEH), pp. 1–5 (2018)
3. Blanco, A., Pino-Mejías, R., Lara, J., Rayo, S.: Credit scoring models for the microfinance industry using neural networks: evidence from peru. Expert Syst. Appl. **40**(1), 356–364 (2013)
4. Bunker, R., Zhang, W., Naeem, M.A.: Improving a credit scoring model by incorporating bank statement derived features. 10 (2016)
5. Lacasa, L., Luque, B., Ballesteros, F., Luque, J., Nuño, J.C.: From time series to complex networks: the visibility graph. 105(13), 4972–4975 (2008)
6. Petropoulos, A., Siakoulis, V., Stavroulakis, E., Klamargias, A.: A robust machine learning approach for credit risk analysis of large loan level datasets using deep learning and extreme gradient boosting, in are post-crisis statistical initiatives completed? (B. for International Settlements, ed.), vol. 49 of IFC Bulletins chapters, Bank for International Settlements (2019)

7. Ruiz, S., Gomes, P., Rodrigues, L., Gama, J.: Credit scoring in microfinance using non-traditional data. In: Oliveira, E., Gama, J., Vale, Z., Lopes Cardoso, H. (eds.) EPIA 2017. LNCS (LNAI), vol. 10423, pp. 447–458. Springer, Cham (2017). https://doi.org/10.1007/978-3-319-65340-2_37

8. Paraíso, P., Gomes, P., Ruiz, S., Rodrigues, L., Gama, J.: Using network features for credit scoring in microfinance: extended abstract. In: 2020 IEEE 7th International Conference on Data Science and Advanced Analytics (DSAA), pp. 783–784 (2020)

9. Provenzano, A.R., et al.: Machine learning approach for credit scoring (2020)

10. Silva, V., Silva, M., Ribeiro, P., Silva, F.: Time series analysis via network science: concepts and algorithms. Wiley Interdisc. Rev. Data Min. Knowl. Discovery 11, 05 (2021)

11. Ghosh, S.K.: Visibility algorithms in the Plane. Cambridge University Press (2007)

12. Luque, B., Lacasa, L., Ballesteros, F., Luque, J.: Horizontal visibility graphs: exact results for random time series. Phys. Rev. E. 80, 046103 (2009)

13. Lacasa, L., Nuñez, A., Roldán, E., Parrondo, J.M.R., Luque, B.: Time series irreversibility: a visibility graph approach. Eur. Phys. J. B 85, 1–11 (2012)

14. Bowyer, K.W., Chawla, N.V., Hall, L.O., Kegelmeyer, W.P.: SMOTE: synthetic minority over-sampling technique. CoRR, vol. abs/1106.1813 (2011)

15. Breiman, L.: Random forests. Mach. Learn. 45, 5–32 (2001)

16. Costa, L.D.F., Rodrigues, A., Travieso, G., Boas, P.R.V.: Characterization of complex networks: a survey of measurements. Adv. Phys. 56(1), 167–242 (2007)

17. Campanharo, A.S.L.O., Sirer, M.I., Malmgren, R.D., Ramos, F.M., Amaral, L.A.N.: Duality between time series and networks. PLOS ONE 6, 1–13 (2011)

18. Takahashi, D.Y., Sato, J.R., Ferreira, C.E., Fujita, A.: Discriminating different classes of biological networks by analyzing the graphs spectra distribution. PLOS ONE 7, 1–12 (2012)

19. Kursa, M.B., Rudnicki, W.R.: Feature selection with the boruta package. J. Stat. Softw. 36, 1–13 (2010)

20. Bastian, M., Heymann, S., Jacomy, M.: Gephi: an open source software for exploring and manipulating networks (2009)

# Modular-Relatedness for Continual Learning

Ammar Shaker[1(✉)], Francesco Alesiani[1], and Shujian Yu[2]

[1] NEC Laboratories Europe GmbH, Kurfuerstenanlage 36, 69115 Heidelberg, Germany
{Ammar.Shaker,Francesco.Alesiani}@neclab.eu
[2] UiT The Arctic University of Norway, Tromsø, Norway
yusj9011@gmail.com

**Abstract.** Deep Neural Network (NN) architectures often achieve super-human performance in many application domains. Recent models are made of up to billions of parameters (e.g. GPT2 and GPT3 for Natural Language Processing) and require massive training resources. How can these models be trained on sequences of tasks without negatively affecting each other? Continual Learning (CL) methods tackle the problem of incrementally updating NN models with new tasks while retaining the performance on previously learned tasks. In this paper, we propose a continual learning (CL) technique that is beneficial to sequential task learners by improving their retained accuracy and reducing catastrophic forgetting. The principal target of our approach is the automatic extraction of modular parts of the neural network (NN) and then estimating the relatedness between the tasks given these modular components. This technique is applicable to the CL family of rehearsal-based (e.g., the Gradient Episodic Memory) approaches where episodic memory is needed. Empirical results demonstrate remarkable performance gain (in terms of robustness to forgetting) for methods such as GEM based on our technique, especially when the memory budget is very limited.

## 1 Introduction

Despite the success in outperforming humans on complex tasks, such as playing Go with and without human guidance [24,25], machine learning methods still lack the human ability to retain learned skills without forgetting [5,12,16,21]. Continual learning is a branch of lifelong learning that tackles task knowledge accumulation, while minimizing the effect of forgetting how to perform on previously trained tasks. In recent years, there have been significant advancements in mitigating catastrophic forgetting through different learning schemes. The regularization-based methods such as EWC [12] and R-EWC [15] penalize model updates that are harmful to previously observed tasks. Rehearsal-based methods such as GEM [16], AGEM [5], and iCaRL [21] aim at weakening the forgetting by replaying real or pseudo examples while learning new tasks.

Despite satisfactory performances achieved by these methods, they usually explicitly model the task-relatedness between the new task and previous ones in the learning objective.

There are only a few exceptions that consider task-relatedness. Dynamically expandable network (DEN) [28] computes the relatedness to decide whether the network's capacity should be increased in a layer-wise manner. The expert gate (EG) [1],

© The Author(s), under exclusive license to Springer Nature Switzerland AG 2022
T. Bouadi et al. (Eds.): IDA 2022, LNCS 13205, pp. 290–301, 2022.
https://doi.org/10.1007/978-3-031-01333-1_23

on the other hand, trains a powerful autoencoder for each task and estimates the relatedness between the new task $\tau$ and the $t$-th old task with the reconstruction error of the $t$-th autoencoder on the data from the task $\tau$, thus, requiring an additional architecture to compute the relatedness. Both methods follow a train-and-evaluate framework to estimate the task relatedness, which is always computationally expensive and sensitive to the selected models. For example, if one resorts to a powerful autoencoder in EG, this autoencoder could likely fit the data from all tasks with just marginal differences. Task rehearsal method (TRM) [26] is one of the early works that measure the relatedness in the task sequential setting. This relatedness is then used to generate rehearsal examples to achieve transfer learning in a functional manner. Despite the explicit relatedness computation in these methods, the absence of the network's modular decomposition causes the modular-relatedness to be ignored. In our work, we model the relatedness not only among tasks, but also with respect to parts of the NN that we group in modules.

Motivated by evidence from neuropsychology and neurobiology that animal and human brains are organized into segregated modules based on their functionality [2], a modular neural network is an aggregation of computationally independent subnetworks.

In this work, we present a general approach to mitigate task forgetting by deriving a technique that integrates task relatedness into the learning of modular networks. The detailed contributions of this paper are twofold:

*(i)* A novel CL framework based on *modularization* and *relatedness* (Sect. 3): It enables the automatic discovering of groups of neurons (in each layer) that are mutually independent or less dependent, and proposes an adaption of the learning process to consider the relevance between tasks given each of these groups.

*(ii)* An example realization of how modular-relatedness could be implemented: As a proof of concept, we propose a modular extension to GEM.

## 2   Background Knowledge

### 2.1   Continual Learning Problem Definition

Sequential task learning: Consider $N$ classification tasks $\mathbb{T} = \{(X_t, Y_t)|t \in \{1, \ldots, N\}\}$, where each task $T_t$ is represented by the set of $N_t$ data samples $T_t = \{X_t, Y_t\} = \{(x_{ti}, y_{ti}) : i \in \{1, \ldots, N_t\}\}$, $x_{ti} \in \mathbb{R}^{p_t}$ is an input instance with $p_t$ dimensionality, while $y_{ti} \in \mathbb{Y}_t = \{c_1, \ldots, c_{m_t}\}$ is a class label taken from $m_t$ unique categories. This formulation is the generic one that multi-task and continual approaches often consider. For simplicity, we target the setting when $p_t = p$, $m_t = m$, and $\mathbb{Y}_t = \mathbb{Y}$ for all $t \in \{1, \ldots, N\}$.

Neural network parametrization: Consider representing the neural network by the function $f(x; \theta) \colon \mathbb{R}^{p_t} \to [0, 1]^{|\mathbb{Y}|}$ that computes the scoring function $f_c(x; \theta)$ for each category $c \in \mathbb{Y}$ being the correct label for the instance $x$ through a multi-layered neural network parameterized by $\theta \in \Theta$. For a $D$-layered network, the set of parameters $\theta = \{\omega_{ij}^d, b_j^{d+1}|d \in 1, \ldots, D-1\}$ contains the weights $\omega_{ij}^d$ of the connections between the units $u_i^d$ in the $d$th layer and the units $u_j^{d+1}$ in the $(d+1)$th layer, and the bias terms $b_j^d$ of the units in the $d$th layer. The scoring function resulting from the forward propagation in the $D$-layered network takes the form:

$$f_j(x; \theta) = \phi \left( \sum_i \omega_{ij}^{D-1} o_i^{D-1} + b_j^D \right) \tag{1}$$

$$o_j^d = \phi \left( \sum_i \omega_{ij}^{d-1} o_i^{d-1} + b_j^d \right), \tag{2}$$

where $o_j^d$ is the $j$th unit's output at the $d$th layer, $o_j^1$ represent the features of the input data, and $\phi$ is an activation function. In this regard, Eq. (2) is indeed the function $o_j^d(x)$ that computes the representation of $x$ given all the units of the previous layers $1, \ldots, d-1$ and the connections from layer $d-1$ to the unit $u_j^d$. For a given loss function $\mathcal{L}$, multi-task learning methods aim at finding a general parametrization $\theta$ that minimizes the objective $\sum_{t \in \mathbb{T}} \mathbb{E}_{(x_t, y_t) \sim T_t} \mathcal{L}(f(x_t; \theta), y_t)$ [7], i.e., observing all tasks at the same time and minimizing their joint loss simultaneously. Generally speaking, after learning on $t-1$ tasks, continual learning aims at finding $\theta_t$ that is the least harmful to the previous tasks:

$$\arg\min_{\theta_t} \mathbb{E}_{(x_t, y_t) \sim T_t} \mathcal{L}(f(x_t; \theta), y_t) \tag{3a}$$

$$\text{s.t. } \mathbb{E}_{(x_k, y_k) \sim T_k} \mathcal{L}(f(x_k; \theta_t), y_k) \leq \mathbb{E}_{(x_k, y_k) \sim T_k} \mathcal{L}(f(x_k; \theta_{t-1}), y_k) : k < t ,$$

even without having the ability to access $\{X_k, Y_k\}$ for $k < t$. Failing to satisfy the conditions in (3) means a deterioration of performance on previous tasks, which is often referred to as catastrophic forgetting.

## 2.2  Modular Networks

Layer-wise modularization methods aim to assign each unit $u_i^d$ (in layer $d$) to a group $g_k$. As a result, the groupings $g_1^d, \ldots, g_{K_d}^d$ of the $d$th layer's units are created, where $K_d$ is the number of groups. From each group $g_i^d$, the function $G_i^d$ can be defined as

$$G_i^d(x; \theta) : \mathbb{R}^{p_t} \to \mathbb{R}^{|g_i^d|}, G_i^d(x; \theta) = [o_j^d(x) | u_j^d \in g_i^d] . \tag{4}$$

## 2.3  Gradient Episodic Memory

GEM [16] is a rehearsal-based continual learning method with an episodic memory $M$ storing a subset of the observed examples. For a total number of $N$ tasks, for each task $T_k$, the set of examples $M_k$ is preserved where $|M_k| = |M|/N$. GEM's main aspect is constraining the loss on the episodic memory to decrease while updating the network's parameters on the new task $T_t$. This is achieved by adding the decrease of the loss, $l(f(; \theta), M_k) = \frac{1}{M_k} \sum_{(x_i, y_i) \in M_k} l(f(x_i; \theta), y_i)$, on $M$ as a constraint in the search for parameters after observing the example $(x, y)$ from the current task $T_t$:

$$\arg\min_{\theta} \quad l(f(x; \theta), y) \tag{5a}$$

$$\text{s.t. } l(f(; \theta), M_k) \leq l(f^{t-1}(; \theta), M_k) : k < t , \tag{5b}$$

where $f^{t-1}(;\theta)$ is the found parameterization after learning the previous $t-1$ tasks. Solving problem (5) can be done efficiently by inferring an increase in the loss from the angle between the gradients of the loss before and after the update, which we refer to as $q_k$ and $q$, respectively. If all these constraints (a constraint for each previous task $T_k$) are satisfied, then the episodic memories' losses should not increase. However, when one of these constraints is violated, the authors propose to project the gradient $q$ to the closest gradient $\tilde{q}$ in squared $l_2$ norm, i.e., solving the following problem:

$$\arg\min_{\tilde{q}} \quad \tfrac{1}{2}\|q - \tilde{q}\|_2^2 \tag{6a}$$

$$\text{subject to } \langle \tilde{q}, q_k \rangle \geq 0 \text{ for } k < t . \tag{6b}$$

Problem (6) has the primal quadratic program:

$$\arg\min_{z} \tfrac{1}{2}z^\top z - q^\top z + \tfrac{1}{2}q^\top q \tag{7a}$$

$$\text{subject to } \quad Rz \geq 0 , \tag{7b}$$

where $R$ is the matrix of the negative gradients on all previous $t-1$ tasks computed on the episodic memories $M_k$, $R = -(q_1; \dots; q_{t-1})$. Instead of solving the primal problem (7) whose number of variables could be in millions (the number of the network's parameters $|\tilde{q}| = |\theta| = |\Theta|$), the following dual problem is defined

$$\arg\min_{V} \tfrac{1}{2}v^\top R R^\top v + q^\top R^\top v \tag{8a}$$

$$\text{subject to } \quad v \geq 0 . \tag{8b}$$

Upon finding $v$, the projected gradient is computed as $\tilde{q} = R^\top v + q$.

## 3  General Approach

In the following, we describe a general method that exploits the relation between two tasks given a subset of parameters (module) of the network. This method lies in the spectrum between looking at every parameter in its singularity (EWC) and taking all parameters at once (GEM). As observed by Ramasesh et al. [20], we hypothesise that tasks' overwriting (leading to forgetting) becomes inevitable between tasks similar in the representation space.

### 3.1  Relatedness Estimation

At first, we introduce a measure of similarity (relatedness) between tasks' representations. Given the $k$th module in the $d$th layer, $g_k^d$, the tasks $T_1$ and $T_t$, and their underlying sampling probability distributions, $P_1$ and $P_t$, the estimate of their divergence conditioned on $g_k^d$ is given by $D(P_1(y|x; g_k^d)\|P_t(y|x; g_k^d)) = D(P_1(y|G_k^d(x))\|P_t(y|G_k^d(x)))$. In this work, we measure the divergence from $P_1(y|G_k^d(x))$ to $P_t(y|G_k^d(x))$ with the recently suggested Bregman-correntropy conditional divergence [29], which avoids the density estimation of the data and is more statistically powerful than the classical KL. For brevity, we give its definition as follows.

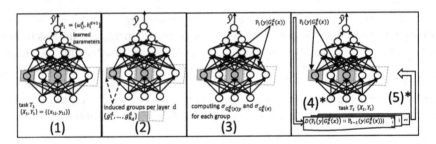

**Fig. 1.** The general approach of modular-relatedness for continual learning. Phase 1: training the initial model parameters $\theta = \{w_{ij}^d, b_j^{d+1} | d \in 1, \ldots, D-1\}$ on the first task, $T_1$. Phase 2: the induction of the modular groups $\{g_1^d, \ldots, g_{K_d}^d\}$ for each layer $d \in \{2, \ldots, D-1\}$. Phase 3: computing the covariance matrices $\sigma_{G_k^d(x)y}$ and $\sigma_{G_k^d(x)}$ characterizing $P_1(G_k^d(x), y)$ and $P_1(G_k^d(x))$, respectively, for each group $g_i^d$. For each forthcoming task $T_t$, Phases 4 and 5 are performed iteratively. Phase 4: for each group, $g_i^d$, computing the discrepancy between the conditional distributions of the current task $T_t$ and the previous tasks $T_k$ ($k < t$). Phase 5: employing the computed discrepancies for the training on the next batches of data.

**Definition 1.** *The asymmetric conditional discrepancy [29] between the two conditional probability distributions $P_A(y|x)$ and $P_B(y|x)$ is defined as the quantity:*

$$D_{\varphi,B}(P_A(y|x)\|P_B(y|x)) = D_{\varphi,B}(\sigma_{xy}\|\rho_{xy}) - D_{\varphi,B}(\sigma_x\|\rho_x), \qquad (9)$$

*where $\sigma_{xy}, \rho_{xy} \in \mathcal{S}_+^{p+1}$ denote positive semidefinite matrices characterizing the joint probability distributions $P_A(x,y)$ and $P_B(x,y)$. Similarly, $\sigma_x, \rho_x \in \mathcal{S}_+^p$ characterize the marginal distributions $P_A(x)$ and $P_B(x)$. $D_{\varphi,B}$ is the Bregman matrix divergence [13] $D_{\varphi,B}(\sigma\|\rho) = \varphi(\sigma) - \varphi(\rho) - \mathrm{tr}((\nabla\varphi(\rho))^T(\sigma - \rho))$ between the two positive semidefinite matrices $\sigma, \rho \in \mathcal{R}^{n \times n}$, where $\varphi : \mathcal{R}^{n \times n} \to \mathcal{R}$ is a strictly convex and differentiable function. The Bregman divergence represents a class of divergence functions where the von Neumann $D_{vN}$ and the LogDet $D_{\ell D}$ divergences can be instantiated based on the choice of $\varphi^1$. One realization of $\sigma$ and $\rho$ could be the covariance matrix or the centered correntropy matrix [6]. The symmetric conditional discrepancy is defined as:*

$$D_{\varphi,B}(P_A(y|x) :: P_B(y|x)) = \frac{1}{2}(D_{\varphi,B}(P_A(y|x)\|P_B(y|x)) \\ + D_{\varphi,B}(P_B(y|x)\|P_A(y|x))). \qquad (10)$$

For simplicity, we omit the subscripts of the Bregman matrix divergence $D_{\varphi,B}$ in the remainder of the paper.

---

[1] Setting $\varphi(\sigma) = (\sigma \log \sigma - \sigma)$ gives the von Neumann divergence [18]: $D_{vN}(\sigma\|\rho) = (\sigma \log \sigma - \sigma \log \rho - \sigma + \rho)$. $\log \sigma$ is the matrix logarithm. Setting $\varphi(\sigma) = -\log \det \sigma$ gives the LogDet divergence: $D_{\ell D}(\sigma\|\rho) = \sum_{i,j} \frac{\lambda_i}{\theta_j}(v_i^T u_j)^2 - \sum_i \log\left(\frac{\lambda_i}{\theta_i}\right) - n$.

### 3.2   Modularization

The measure of relatedness between tasks $T_1$ and $T_t$ given the module $g_k^d$ would be inversely proportional to the symmetric discrepancy $D(P_1(y|G_k^d(x)) :: P_t(y|G_k^d(x)))$, as defined in (10). The general approach, depicted in Fig. 1, starts by learning the model's parameters on the first task $T_1$ and then finding the modular groups for each network's layer. The choice of modularization method, in our approach, is a generic component that where any modularization can be used. Having defined (or induced) modules, we compute for the first task, $T_1$, and for each following task, $T_t$, the covariance matrices $\sigma_{G_k^d(x)y}$ and $\sigma_{G_k^d(x)}$ of $P_t(G_k^d(x), y)$ and $P_1(_k^d(x))$ for each module $g_k^d$, needless to say that this computation can be efficiently performed in one pass.

The computed covariances allow us to estimate $D(P_t(y|G_k^d(x))||P_j(y|G_k^d(x)))$ for each $j < t$ for each $G_k^d$; the estimation can be theoretically re-computed after each sample or each batch (depending on the available computation resource). The estimated divergence is the core element used in each training step, depending on the training procedure and objective. In the next sections, we present a realization of how the technique outlined here can extend state-of-the-art methods to lessen catastrophic forgetting.

## 4   Modular-Relatedness for Rehearsal-Based Continual Learning

### 4.1   Modular GEM

The *Modularization* and *Relatedness* application to GEM consists of two main aspects: *(i)* the modular partitioning of the units of each of the network's layers, and *(ii)* the discrepancy estimation of each task's representation projected in each group. The first aspect concerns the creation of the groups $g_1^d, \ldots, g_{K_d}^d$ for each layer $d \in \{2, \ldots, L - 1\}$, and the second aspect leads to the computation of the discrepancy $(r_i^d)_k = D(P_t(y|G_i^d(x; \theta)) :: P_k(y|G_i^d(x; \theta)))$ between task $T_t$ and each previous task $T_k$ $(k < t)$ given the group $g_i^d$, see the definition of the discrepancy in Eq. (10).

The first part, grouping, allows us to slice the gradients $q$ of problem (6) into $q_1$ the gradient for the first layer's parameters, and $q_i^d$ the gradients for each group $g_i^d$ in each layer $d \in \{2, \ldots, L\}$, since each group $g_i^d$ concerns the set of parameters $\theta_i^d = \{\omega_{ij}^d, b_j^{d+1} | u_i \in g_i^d \wedge \text{ for each } j\}$. Similarly, the gradient projection $\widetilde{q}$, that is searched for, becomes $\widetilde{q}_1$ and $\widetilde{q}_i^d$ for each group $g_i^d$. This formulation allows us to change the constraints such that the inner product is computed on the group-wise gradients and not on all parameters at once. Therefore, we formulate the new problem

$$\underset{\widetilde{q}}{\arg\min} \qquad \frac{1}{2}\|q - \widetilde{q}\|_2^2 \tag{11a}$$

$$\text{subject to } \langle \widetilde{q_i^d}, (q_i^d)_k \rangle \geq (h_i^d)_k \text{ for each } (g_i^d)_k, \ k < t , \tag{11b}$$

$$\text{subject to } \langle \widetilde{q_1}, (q_1)_k \rangle \geq 0 \text{ for } k < t , \tag{11c}$$

where $(h_i^d)_k$ is proportional to the inverse of $exp(-(r_i^d)_k)$ and normalized over the seen tasks $T_k$ $(k < t)$. In other words, for a group that establishes a strong relation between the current and the previous task, the angle between its gradients $\widetilde{q_i^d}$ and $(q_i^d)_k$ should be smaller than that when such a relation is absent. The primal problem of the quadratic program solving (11) becomes: $\arg\min_z \frac{1}{2}z^\top z - q^\top z + \frac{1}{2}q^\top q$ subject to $Rz \geq H$. Finally, we solve the dual problem

$$\arg\min_V \frac{1}{2}v^\top R R^\top v + q^\top R^\top v \tag{12a}$$

$$\text{subject to} \qquad v \geq h \ . \tag{12b}$$

As in (8), the new projected gradient is computed as $\tilde{q} = R^\top v + q$.

### 4.2   Network Modularization

In this work, we suggest to employ log-likelihood modularization at the neuron-level. Log-likelihood modularization: This type of modularization searches for the grouping that maximizes the likelihood of the neurons' group assignment. Watanabe et al. [8] propose a modular decomposition of trained neural networks into a set of independent sub-networks. This decomposition considers each unit's assignment $u_i^d$ (in layer $d$) to a group $g_k$ as a latent variable, and defines the probability for each group to connect to each neuron of the previous and the following layers as a parameter. These parameters and the group assignment are found by maximizing the likelihood of observing the groups given the connections to the previous and following layers, $d - 1$ and $d + 1$, respectively. To this end, the expectation-maximization algorithm is iteratively employed to find the groups.

### 4.3   Complexity Analysis

The complexity for computing the conditional discrepancy $(r_i^d)_k = D(P_t(y|G_i^d(x;\theta)) :: P_k(y|G_i^d(x;\theta)))$ between task $T_t$ and a previous task $T_k$ ($k < t$) given the group $g_i^d$ constitutes the following: (i) computing the covariance matrices $\sigma_{G_i^d(x)y}$ and $\sigma_{G_i^d(x)}$, for each of task $T_t$ and task $T_k$, takes $O(N(|g_i^d| + 1)^2)$ where $|g_i^d|$ is the size of the group $g_i^d$ and $N$ is the batch size. (ii) Computing $J_{vN}$ on two covariance matrices from $\mathcal{R}^{(|g_i^d|+1)\times(|g_i^d|+1)}$ requires the eigenvalue decomposition which is $(O(|g_i^d|+1)^3)$. Hence, the final complexity for a batch is $O((|g_i^d| + 1)^3 + N(|g_i^d| + 1)^2)$. Notice that this complexity is independent of the dimensionality of the data and is only controlled by the dimensionality of the features.

## 5   Related Work

### 5.1   Continual Learning

Regularization-based CL methods add a penalty term to the learning objective such that older knowledge is retained when learning on new tasks. Elastic weight consolidation (EWC) [12] penalizes the change of each parameter by a weight proportional to the diagonal Fisher information matrix (FIM) (the diagonal of the inverse Hessian of the negative log-likelihood). R-EWC [15] suggests rotating the parameter space such that FIM is diagonal. Synaptic intelligence (SI) [30] measures the accumulative contribution of each parameter to the loss change as a measure of importance instead of FIM.

Another important family of methods is the replay-based methods that maintain a small set of examples of previous tasks to be rehearsed during the learning on the new task. Gradient episodic memory (GEM) [16], for example, employs the memory examples to constrain the direction of the model's update to reduce performance deterioration on the memory. Averaged GEM (AGEM) [5] is one of GEM's extensions that suggest an averaging over GEM's constraints to gain computational efficiency. This family also includes pseudo-rehearsal methods [23] that apply random input to previous models to simulate previous tasks. Later, we elaborate more on GEM, as a representative of the family of replay-based methods, and present our extensions using the proposed technique. Other CL families include parameter isolation methods, generative coreset methods; the surveys [14, 19] and [10] offer an extensive overview of the topic.

## 5.2  Modular Neural Networks

Neural networks were developed with inspiration from human brain structures and functions. The human brain itself is modular in a hierarchical manner. The learning process always occurs in a very localized subset of highly inter-connected nodes that are relatively sparsely connected to nodes in other modules [17]. That is to say that the human brain is organized as functional, sparsely connected sub-networks [9]. Many existing works in neural networks can be analyzed and interpreted from the perspective of modularization. In general, there are three levels of modularization: modularization in a sub-network; modularization in a layer-wise manner; and modularization concerning specific neurons or groups of neurons. The majority of methods realize modularization in a layer-wise level. For example, [11] developed a way to greedily learn each layer of a neural network without backpropagation via approximating gradient signals locally at each layer.

In [8], the authors propose a community detection-based method that partitions each layer into maximally independent and mutually exclusive modules. In this work, we focus on the modularization in a neuron-level, such that a set of functionally connected neurons in each layer are automatically identified and grouped.

## 6  Experiments

### 6.1  Setting: Online Continual Learning

In the following, we present the experimental results using the online setting proposed in [22]. In this setting, the samples of each task form a sequence that is observed only once, i.e., single pass. We use a simple neural network architecture, a fully-connected network with two hidden layers (100 units) and single head. The input layer is of size $28 \times 28$, and the single head output layer has 10 neurons. The architecture is comparable to that employed in [16]. The ReLu activation function is used in the hidden layers, and SGD is used to minimize the softmax cross-entropy on the output predictions.

**Datasets and Performance Measures.** We use for the evaluation the following data sets: *(i)* MNIST Permutations (**mnistP**) [12], *(ii)* MNIST Rotations (**mnistR**) [16], *(iii)* Permuted Fashion-MNIST (**fashionP**) [27], and *(iv)* Permuted notMNIST (**notm-nistP**) [3]. Images of all these data sets are of the same size, $28 \times 28$ pixels.

To measure the learning-ability and resistance to forgetting, we compute the often used performance measures: *(i)* Learning accuracy (LA) is the average accuracy on each task after directly learning it. *(ii)* Retained accuracy (RA) is the averaged performance on all tasks after learning on all tasks. *(iii)* Backward transfer (BT) is the difference between LA and RA [4], hence, it measures the loss in performance due to forgetting.

**Comparison Protocol.** In our framework, we claim to improve the performance of continual learning methods by showing how modular-relatedness to previous tasks can be exploited to prevent catastrophic forgetting. To verify this claim, we evaluate our extension, ModGEM, which alters GEM as a representative of rehearsal-based methods. We compare the performance of ModGEM against that of its original method, GEM, and the Meta-Experience Replay (MER) [22]. To ensure a fair comparison, we perform a grid-based hyperparameter search on each data set for each method; the search protocol and the found parameters are reported in Appendix A.

In the following experiment, we observe a sequence of ten tasks with only 1000 samples per task. The evaluation is performed on 10,000 for each task.

As for the modularization method, we implement the community detection-based modularization [8] using ten iterations and then choosing the detected modules with the highest log-likelihood. We also fix the number of groups to be $K_d = 5$ for ModGEM.

**Comparing Mod-GEM Versus GEM.** In this experiment, we compare at first Mod-GEM versus GEM, using the above described online setting while restricting the memory budget to be ten samples per task.

Table 1 shows that ModGEM outperforms GEM on each of notmnistP, mnistP and fashionP with margins of 4%, 4%, and 2% retained accuracy, respectively. The only exception here is mnistR, where GEM is only 1.6% better than ModGEM. Both methods have relatively the same learning accuracy, which results in a better backward performance achieved by ModGEM. The gain in both LA and RA that our modification causes to GEM is accompanied by a better backward transfer (BT) on all data sets except for mnistR. Similarly, ModeGEM outperfroms MER in terms of LA on all data sets, and has a better RA performance on notmnistP and fashionP with a large margin, and has a similar performance on mnistP.

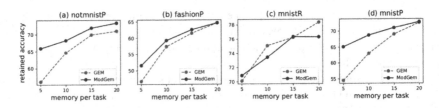

**Fig. 2.** Retained accuracy performance curves for ModGEM, and its original method GEM. The curves are computed when the memory budget is taken from the set $\{5, 10, 15, 20\}$.

**Table 1.** Performance comparison between ModGEM, GEM and MER. The numbers in parentheses are the standard errors (SE) of the means in the former row.

| Data | MER | | | GEM | | | ModGEM | | |
|---|---|---|---|---|---|---|---|---|---|
| | RA | LA | BT | RA | LA | BT | RA | LA | BT |
| notmnistP | 50.6 | 55.1 | −4.6 | 64.2 | 78.6 | −14.36 | **68.41** | **80.51** | −12.1 |
| | (0.7) | (0.8) | (0.7) | (0.4) | (0.1) | (0.4) | (0.2) | (0.1) | (0.2) |
| fashionP | 53.3 | 61.2 | −7.8 | 56.86 | 67.4 | −10.54 | **58.47** | **67.52** | −9.05 |
| | (0.8) | (0.9) | (0.8) | (0.18) | (0.1) | (0.17) | (0.14) | (0.06) | (0.15) |
| mnistR | **81.2** | 81.3 | −0.2 | 75.75 | 85.05 | −9.3 | 74.15 | **85.19** | −11.04 |
| | (0.2) | (0.2) | (0.2) | (0.2) | (0.07) | (0.21) | (0.22) | (0.06) | (0.19) |
| mnistP | **68.9** | 75.9 | −7.0 | 64.4 | **80.38** | −15.97 | 68.57 | **80.37** | −11.8 |
| | (0.3) | (0.2) | (0.3) | (0.25) | (0.07) | (0.26) | (0.14) | (0.11) | (0.12) |

**Modular-Relatedness Under Different Memory Constraints.** In this experiment, we evaluate the effect of different memory budgets on RA of GEM, and our proposed method. The experiments vary the memory size from the set $\{5, 10, 15, 20\}$. Figure 2 depicts the RA curves versus the memory budget (x-axis). The subfigures show how the curves of ModGEM, most of the time, dominate those of GEM and with a large margin. There is, sometimes, the trend for GEM to improve when more memory is granted, and its curve does meet with that of ModGEM on the fashionP data. This result indeed confirms our intuition that the modular-relatedness plays the role of an augmented memory when memory budget is scarce, moreover, ModGEM seems to offer an empirical upper bound of what GEM can achieve, as confirmed on notmnistP, fashionP and mnistP. Interestingly, no clear pattern can be deduced from Fig. 2(c) on mnistR since the difference between the two curves does not exceed 1%.

## 7    Conclusion

In this work, we present a *modularization* and *relatedness* technique that exploits tasks' modular-relatedness based on the discrepancy of their latent representations. The method automatically discovers groups of neurons (modules) in each layer, and, given these modules, adapts the learning process to account for the tasks' relatedness. We apply this technique to GEM and propose Mod-GEM. A significant performance gain is observed on the learning and retained accuracy using Mod-GEM compared to GEM. Future work is twofold. First, we aim at studying the applicability of our technique in a broader spectrum of continual learning families. Second, we are investigating the use of this technique in meta-learning, where task relatedness plays an essential role in choosing the right prior. Here modular-relatedness would help in choosing the right prior over the modular sub-networks.

## A    Hyperparameter Search

To ensure a fair comparison, we start with a grid-based hyperparameter search for each of the methods on each of the datasets using a sample of 5 tasks and 300 samples per task. For GEM, we search for the parameters, the learning rate $lr \in \{0.001, 0.003, 0.01, 0.03, 0.1, 0.3, 1.0\}$ and the margin $mg \in \{0.0, 0.1, 0.5, 1.0\}$. The found parameters are reported in the following:

- GEM found hyperparameters
  - $lr \in \{0.001, 0.003, 0.01$ (notmnistP,mnistR, mnistP, fashionP), $0.03, 0.1, 0.3, 1.0 \}$
  - $mg \in \{0.0$ (notmnistP,mnistR, mnistP, fashionP), $0.1, 0.5, 1.0\}$
- Meta-Experience Replay found hyperparameters:
  - learning rate: $lr \in \{0.001, 0.003, 0.005, 0.01, 0.03, 0.1$ (fashionP, mnistP, mnistR, notmnistP) $\}$
  - across batch meta-learning rate: $\gamma = 1$
  - within batch meta-learning rate: $\beta \in \{0.01$ (fashionP, mnistP, mnistR), $0.03$ (notmnistP), $0.1, 0.3, 1.0\}$

Without any further tuning, we adopt the same found parameter to our proposed modification. As for the relatedness measure, we employ (10) when $D_{\varphi,B}$ is the von Neumann divergence by setting $\varphi(\sigma) = (\sigma \log \sigma - \sigma)$. $\sigma$ is the covariance matrix of each task's latent representation at each group.

## References

1. Aljundi, R., Chakravarty, P., Tuytelaars, T.: Expert gate: lifelong learning with a network of experts. In: Proceedings of the IEEE Conference on Computer Vision and Pattern Recognition, pp. 3366–3375 (2017)
2. Azam, F.: Biologically inspired modular neural networks. Ph.D. thesis, Virginia Tech (2000)
3. Bulatov, Y.: Machine Learning, etc: notMNIST dataset, September 2011
4. Chaudhry, A., Dokania, P.K., Ajanthan, T., Torr, P.H.: Riemannian walk for incremental learning: understanding forgetting and intransigence. In: Proceedings of the European Conference on Computer Vision (ECCV), pp. 532–547 (2018)
5. Chaudhry, A., Ranzato, M., Rohrbach, M., Elhoseiny, M.: Efficient lifelong learning with a-gem. arXiv preprint arXiv:1812.00420 (2018)
6. Chen, B., Xing, L., Xu, B., Zhao, H., Zheng, N., Principe, J.C.: Kernel risk-sensitive loss: definition, properties and application to robust adaptive filtering. IEEE Trans. Signal Process. **65**(11), 2888–2901 (2017)
7. Chen, Z., Liu, B.: Lifelong machine learning. Synth. Lect. Artif. Intell. Mach. Learn. **12**(3), 1–207 (2018)
8. Watanabe, C., Hiramatsu, K., Kashino, K.: Modular representation of layered neural networks. Neural Networks **97**, 62–73 (2018)
9. Clune, J., Mouret, J.-B., Lipson, H.: The evolutionary origins of modularity. Proc. Roy. Soc. B: Biol. Sci. **280**(1755), 20122863 (2013)
10. De Lange, M., et al.: Continual learning: a comparative study on how to defy forgetting in classification tasks. arXiv preprint arXiv:1909.08383 (2019)

11. Jaderberg, M., et al.: Decoupled neural interfaces using synthetic gradients. In: International Conference on Machine Learning, pp. 1627–1635. PMLR (2017)

12. Kirkpatrick, J., et al.: Overcoming catastrophic forgetting in neural networks. Proc. Natl. Acad. Sci. **114**(13), 3521–3526 (2017)

13. Kulis, B., Sustik, M.A., Dhillon, I.S.: Low-rank kernel learning with Bregman matrix divergences. JMLR **10**(2), 341–376 (2009)

14. Li, Z., Hoiem, D.: Learning without forgetting. IEEE Trans. Pattern Anal. Mach. Intell. **40**(12), 2935–2947 (2017)

15. Liu, X., Masana, M., Herranz, L., Van de Weijer, J., Lopez, A.M., Bagdanov, A.D.: Rotate your networks: better weight consolidation and less catastrophic forgetting. In: 2018 24th International Conference on Pattern Recognition (ICPR), pp. 2262–2268. IEEE (2018)

16. Lopez-Paz, D., Ranzato, M.: Gradient episodic memory for continual learning. In: Advances in Neural Information Processing Systems, pp. 6467–6476 (2017)

17. Meunier, D., Lambiotte, R., Bullmore, E.T.: Modular and hierarchically modular organization of brain networks. Front. Neurosci. **4**, 200 (2010)

18. Nielsen, M.A., Chuang, I.L.: Quantum Computation and Quantum Information. Cambridge University Press, 10th (ed.) (2011)

19. Parisi, G.I., Kemker, R., Part, J.L., Kanan, C., Wermter, S.: Continual lifelong learning with neural networks: a review. Neural Networks (2019)

20. Ramasesh, V.V., Dyer, E., Raghu, M.: Anatomy of catastrophic forgetting: Hidden representations and task semantics. arXiv preprint arXiv:2007.07400 (2020)

21. Rebuffi, S.-A., Kolesnikov, A., Sperl, G., Lampert, C.H.: icarl: incremental classifier and representation learning. In: Proceedings of the IEEE conference on Computer Vision and Pattern Recognition, pp. 2001–2010 (2017)

22. Riemer, M., et al.: Learning to learn without forgetting by maximizing transfer and minimizing interference. arXiv preprint arXiv:1810.11910 (2018)

23. Robins, A.: Catastrophic forgetting, rehearsal and pseudorehearsal. Connect. Sci. **7**(2), 123–146 (1995)

24. Silver, D., et al.: Mastering the game of go with deep neural networks and tree search. Nature **529**(7587), 484–489 (2016)

25. Silver, D., et al.: Mastering the game of go without human knowledge. Nature **550**(7676), 354–359 (2017)

26. Silver, D.L., Mercer, R.E.: The task rehearsal method of life-long learning: overcoming impoverished data. In: Cohen, R., Spencer, B. (eds.) AI 2002. LNCS (LNAI), vol. 2338, pp. 90–101. Springer, Heidelberg (2002). https://doi.org/10.1007/3-540-47922-8_8

27. Xiao, H., Rasul, K., Vollgraf, R.: Fashion-mnist: a novel image dataset for benchmarking machine learning algorithms (2017)

28. Yoon, J., Yang, E., Lee, J., Hwang, S.J.: Lifelong learning with dynamically expandable networks. arXiv preprint arXiv:1708.01547 (2017)

29. Yu, S., Shaker, A., Alesiani, F., Principe, J.C.: Measuring the discrepancy between conditional distributions: methods, properties and applications. In: Proceedings of the Twenty-Ninth International Joint Conference on Artificial Intelligence, pp. 2777–2784 (2020)

30. Zenke, F., Poole, B., Ganguli, S.: Continual learning through synaptic intelligence. In: Proceedings of the 34th International Conference on Machine Learning-Volume 70, pp. 3987–3995. JMLR. org (2017)

# Combining Multiple Data Sources to Predict IUCN Conservation Status of Reptiles

Nádia Soares[1], João F. Gonçalves[2,3], Raquel Vasconcelos[2,3], and Rita P. Ribeiro[1,4(✉)]

[1] Faculty of Sciences, University of Porto, Porto, Portugal
rpribeiro@fc.up.pt
[2] CIBIO, Centro de Investigação em Biodiversidade e Recursos Genéticos, InBIO Laboratório Associado, Campus de Vairão, Universidade do Porto, Porto, Portugal
[3] BIOPOLIS Program in Genomics, Biodiversity and Land Planning, CIBIO, Campus de Vairão, Porto, Portugal
[4] LIAAD-INESC TEC, Porto, Portugal

**Abstract.** Biodiversity loss is a hot topic. We are losing species at a high rate, even before their extinction risk is assessed. The International Union for Conservation of Nature (IUCN) Red List is the most complete assessment of all species conservation status, yet it only covers a small part of the species identified so far. Additionally, many of the existing assessments are outdated, either due to the ever-evolving nature of taxonomy, or to the lack of reassessments. The assessment of the conservation status of a species is a long, mostly manual process that needs to be carefully done by experts. The conservation field would gain by having ways of automating this process, for instance, by prioritising the species where experts and financing should focus on. In this paper, we present a pipeline used to derive a conservation dataset out of openly available data and obtain predictions, through machine learning techniques, on which species are most likely to be threatened. We applied this pipeline to the different groups within the Reptilia class as a model of one of the most under-assessed taxonomic groups. Additionally, we compared the performance of models using datasets that include different sets of predictors describing species ecological requirements and geographical distributions such as IUCN's area and extent of occurrence. Our results show that most groups benefit from using ecological variables together with IUCN predictors. Random Forest appeared as the best method for most species groups, and feature selection was shown to improve results.

**Keywords:** Biodiversity conservation · Extinction risk assessment · Data integration · Machine learning

© The Author(s), under exclusive license to Springer Nature Switzerland AG 2022
T. Bouadi et al. (Eds.): IDA 2022, LNCS 13205, pp. 302–314, 2022.
https://doi.org/10.1007/978-3-031-01333-1_24

# 1    Introduction

Biodiversity loss is causing several emerging problems to humankind [5,14]. Health issues, reduced food security, increased contact with diseases and more unpredictable weather events have been related to biodiversity loss and estimated to be worsened by it in the future. Reptiles in particular, play an important role in keeping ecosystems healthy and balanced by serving as predators and preys, pollinators or seed dispersers [17]. In the face of global environmental change, it is vital to understand how much biodiversity is being lost. Knowing which species are most at risk of becoming extinct is vital to guide decision making and to establish priorities for conservation efforts, resource allocation and reevaluation of conservation status.

This study proposed a working pipeline for data preparation, modelling and evaluation. The goal was to create a model of the conservation status of species in the Reptilia class that could be used to make predictions for species not yet evaluated. The modelling task was formulated as a binary classification problem, where species were labelled as either threatened or non-threatened according to IUCN criteria. IUCN assessment relies mainly on two predictors based on the spatial distribution of presences of a given taxon: the Extent Of Occurrence (EOO) and the Area Of Occupancy (AOO). We compared different sets of predictor variables for each group of species to evaluate the impact of using ecological and geographical variables, both by themselves and with other predictors used by IUCN.

The main contributions of our work were: (i) a curated dataset of ecogeographical and conservation data for reptiles, (ii) a processing pipeline applicable to multiple taxa, and, (iii) the first large scale study testing several models to automate the assessment of conservation status of one of the most under-assessed taxonomic groups, the reptiles, (iv) a comparison and comment on predictor importance, including experimental results and discussion on the usage of different groups of variables to augment two traditional predictors used by IUCN.

The paper was organised as follows. In Sect. 2 we reviewed the state of the art of studies conducted in this area. In Sect. 3 we described our proposed pipeline to gather and preprocess the occurrence data from multiple sources, aggregating it into a species dataset, and building and evaluating the model. In Sect. 4 we laid out the experimental setup and presented the results. We concluded in Sect. 5 by discussing the outcomes of our work and its potential future applications. Finally, due to space limits, the complete description of features considered in the species dataset, the subset selected for each group and detailed results obtained in the modelling phase were made available in bit.ly/3coZNC0.

# 2    Related Work

Even though standards and guidelines are still being defined for the application of data science to ecology and conservation, several works in ecology have emerged in recent years. In particular, machine learning techniques have been applied to predict conservation status at a global or continental scale [2,12,15].

In a previous work, the authors focused on the flora of the African continent and created a complementary method, the Preliminary Automated Conservation Assessments (PACA) [15]. It used large numbers of species data from RAINBIO and GBIF and estimates thereof and, based on the IUCN Criteria A (estimation of population reduction) and B (estimation of geographic distribution), automatically categorised species using six preliminary levels. Those levels could then be used to prioritise more extensive and detailed conservation assessments. Other works also devised a workflow to facilitate the process of predicting conservation status of multiple taxa [12]. Like the previous work, this method was applied to land plants (over 150,000 species), but at a global level. It used geographic, environmental and morphological trait data and applied a Random Forests (RF) to predict the conservation status. Comparing the results from two datasets, one with spatial data only and another with spatial and morphological, the authors concluded that the spatial-only performed better, possibly due to the lack of morphological data, which led them to use fewer data points. A comparison between recent studies using machine learning methods can be seen in Table 1.

**Table 1.** Summary of related work applying machine learning to assess the conservation status of species. For each work, the scale, variables, classification type, tested algorithms, and target taxonomic group is given.

| Source | Scale | Variables | Response | Algorithms | Group |
|---|---|---|---|---|---|
| [1] | Global | Geographic<br>Ecological<br>Human impact | Binary | Decision trees, RF, boosted trees, k-NN, SVM, NN, | Mammals (terrestrial) |
| [2] | Global | Physiological<br>Geographic<br>Ecological<br>Human impact | Binary | RF | Reptiles |
| [4] | Global | Taxonomic<br>Geographic<br>Human impact<br>Conservation action | Binary | RF | Plants (bulbous monocot) |
| [8] | Local | Physiological<br>Geographic<br>Ecological | Continuous | Decision trees, regression models | Plants (angiosperms) |
| [10] | Global | Taxonomic<br>Physiological<br>Geographic<br>Ecological | Multi-class | CLMM | Fish (groupers) |
| [11] | Global | Taxonomic<br>Geographic<br>Ecological<br>Human impacts | Binary | RF non-ML methods | Plants (several groups) |
| [12] | Global/<br>Continental | Geographic<br>Ecological<br>Morphological | Binary | RF | Plants (terrestrial) |

# 3 Methodology

## 3.1 Preliminaries

The IUCN Red List of Threatened Species (https://www.iucnredlist.org/) is the most complete source of information on the conservation status of species. The IUCN assessment of conservation status consists of nine categories, seven of which representing different levels of extinction risk. In decreasing levels of concern: Extinct (EX), Extinct in the Wild (EW), Critically Endangered (CR), Endangered (EN), Vulnerable (VU), Near Threatened (NT) and Least Concern (LC). EX and EW represent species that are thought to no longer exist or to exist only *ex situ*. Species under CR, EN or VU categories are considered as Threatened, while NT and LC are considered Non-Threatened species. Data Deficient (DD) includes species that were evaluated, but there was not enough data to place them under a levelled category. DD and Not Evaluated (NE) represent species not assessed. It is not known whether they are threatened or not, so IUCN advises caution not to assume they are safe. Species may be very close to extinction, but due to the lack of data or formal evaluation they fall into one of these two categories.

IUCN Red List uses five criteria (A-E) which are meant to be usable and comparable across different taxa. This comparability ensures proper prioritisation decisions and standardises the process. Criteria take into account many factors, including the number of populations, population trends, fragmentation level, EOO, AOO, number of locations, and probability of becoming EW.

Based on IUCN criteria and labelled data, the classification models developed in this work discriminate between threatened and non-threatened species, and were trained and evaluated using species where the conservation status was known to fall under one of the five levels of threat from CR to LC. Predictions were generated for DD and NE species.

## 3.2 Proposed Pipeline

We propose a five-steps pipeline to gather occurrences, construct a tidy dataset of species, include relevant predictors, build machine learning models and evaluate their performance, as follows.

**Step 1: Occurrence Data.** The first step was to retrieve occurrence data from several sources. Occurrence data conveys the presence/absence of a species in geographic (or cartographic) coordinates for a given point in time. Abundance data may also be available, i.e. the number of observed individuals at a given location and date of sighting. Here, we were only interested in presence records, since one cannot be sure if an absence indicates that a species does not exist in that location or habitat, or if it simply was not detected at observation time. Abundance data with counts higher than zero were also considered as presences. Data was retrieved from four online open databases GBIF (https://doi.org/10.15468/dl.kkfc5m), PREDICTS (https://www.predicts.org.uk/pages/outputs.html), BioTIME (https://biotime.st-andrews.ac.uk/downloadFull.php),

LPI (https://www.livingplanetindex.org). Each dataset was preprocessed and merged into a single occurrence dataset without duplicate entries. These datasets were filtered to contain only species of the class Reptilia and to include only data points with a taxonomic rank of species or subspecies. Species taxonomic classification in the 'Tree of Life' is ever evolving. New findings from biologic and genetic studies may lead species to be splitted or merged, subspecies to be promoted to species or vice-versa. Since our data spans over decades, we needed a way to map older records to the most up to date taxonomy. The Reptile Database (http://www.reptile-database.org) contains taxonomic information of 11,440 reptiles, as of December, 2020, including synonyms of each taxa and it was used to harmonise the species names on our (presence-only) occurrence dataset. Predictor variables used for model development were decided with the help of experts and literature review. These provided information about species habitat describing climate, vegetation, topography and geomorphology linked to presence data. These variables can be grouped into two main categories: (i) geographical and (ii) ecological. Regarding geographical variables, which describe the spatial distribution of species records, we had AOO and EOO along with latitude/longitude-derived features. Regarding ecological variables, these features describe species habitat and requirements linked to climate (temperature and precipitation), topography (e.g., elevation, slope, surface roughness) as well as habitat heterogeneity calculated from satellite-based vegetation indices (e.g., fraction of vegetated cover). In total we used 35 variables. Predictors were represented in raster layers which allowed to extract values from each one using the geographic location of data points. Marine species were excluded from this analysis. Even though many of them spend a part of their time on land, we would need to use a different set of predictors that explains their marine habits and ecosystem better. Without them, our models would not be able to learn from a significant part of their habitats. Additionally, we assumed that occurrences of terrestrial species located on water were due to imprecise coordinates. These points were imputed by looking for the nearer land cell in a radius incremented by 1 up to 10 km. Reptile taxa reside mostly in tropical or temperate climates, so coordinates falling in extreme latitudes (larger than 70°N or 70°S) were removed from the dataset. Moreover, occurrences without the observation year, or before the year 2000 were discarded due to the uncertainty associated with older positioning systems such as GPS or GLONASS. After this filter, our occurrence dataset spanned two decades, from 2000 to 2020. Lastly, only species with at least 20 occurrences as suggested in [13] were kept, to have a minimum amount of information for model training.

**Step 2: Relevant Features.** Occurrences were divided into five groups by their species' clade, namely, amphisbaenians, crocodiles, lizards, snakes and turtles. Tuataras were intentionally left out, since this clade comprises only one species with very unique characteristics and do not fit into any of the other groups. A 6th group contained the data points of all taxa. The original set of ecological variables contained 29 features from the three groups detailed before (19 climatic, 4 topographic and 6 habitat heterogeneity predictors). This was a large number of features for the amount of species present in each group, and many of these variables are known to be highly correlated. Moreover, each reptile group has different characteristics, which may lead to different environmental needs. To better model the conservation status of each group, we selected different sets of variables for each one and ran a Principal Component Analysis (PCA) on the occurrences for each group. From these, we kept the variables that maximise the variance of each of the top PCA dimensions, according to the Pearson criteria by retaining 80% of the variance, keeping the actual original variables. The pipeline can be applied to other taxa by picking an appropriate set of original variables for those species.

**Step 3: Species-Level Dataset.** At this point, presence data was aggregated from spatial occurrences to the species level to match the target variable (i.e., IUCN species threat status). This was done by calculating the mean and the standard deviation of each of the ecological predictors selected by the PCA step, to express how much a species was able to occupy habitats with different range of environmental conditions aiming to describe species realised niche (i.e., a n-dimensional hypervolume). Moreover, the geographical features were created from the occurrence data and added to the species datasets. Note that our goal was to make predictions for the current risk of a species being threatened, and not to predict its future threat level. The labels were extracted from the IUCN threat level, and matched with the corresponding species already manually assessed. IUCN categories CR, EN and VU were classified as **threatened** and, the NT and LC categories as **non-threatened**. Binarization was performed to increase the discriminative power, as some threat categories had a low number of species. DD and NE do not have a risk value, so they were not used for training. The result of this step was a set of six species level datasets, corresponding to the five groups of species, plus the entire species pool aggregating all previous groups. The characteristics of these datasets are presented in Table 2.

**Table 2.** Dataset characterization for each group. The number of examples (species, Nsp) and variables (Nv), the imbalance ratio (IR) and the minority class (threatened, T, or non-threatened, nT) is given for each group.

| Group | Nsp | Nv | IR | Minority class |
|---|---|---|---|---|
| Amphisbaenians | 19 | 21 | 0.73 | nT |
| Crocodiles | 21 | 23 | 0.91 | nT |
| Lizards | 2103 | 21 | 0.52 | T |
| Snakes | 970 | 21 | 0.36 | T |
| Turtles | 147 | 23 | 0.62 | nT |
| All species | 3260 | 24 | 0.50 | T |

None of the datasets had a perfect balance between threatened and non-threatened species, but the imbalance was not too steep. For the most imbalanced groups, there were more non-threatened than threatened species, while the groups where threatened was the majority class tended to be less imbalanced. Also, there was a big difference in the number of examples across the groups of species. Independently of which was the minority class for a given group, threatened was always used as the positive class.

**Step 4: Predictive Modelling.** Over the built datasets, we trained different binary classification models to discriminate between threatened and non-threatened species. An additional feature selection, using recursive feature elimination [6], was tested to try to improve results further. *Lizards, snakes* and *all species* groups, had a higher imbalance ratio and their minority class was the class of interest, i.e., threatened species. In this domain, the cost of a false negative is higher, as it may lead to the lack of conservation efforts being allocated to threatened species. On the other hand, a false positive may mean that the already scarce funding would be distributed to species that do not need it. Thus, we preferred to optimise sensitivity, but without losing too much specificity.

**Step 5: Predict Conservation Status.** In this last step of the pipeline, previously trained models were used to obtain predictions for previously unassessed species (i.e. DD and NE according to IUCN criteria). These species are of particular interest for this application given that the lack of information may imperil them harder. To understand which factors contribute the most to predicting the threat status of species, we also calculated variable importance scores.

The pipeline and feature selection workflow were summarised in Fig. 1.

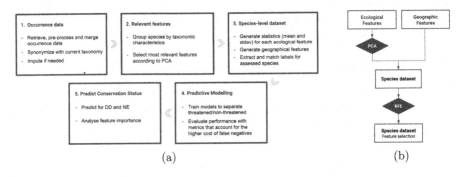

**Fig. 1.** (a) The five steps of the data processing pipeline, and (b) the workflow used for selecting the ecological and geographic variables for each dataset.

## 4   Experimental Results

We designed our experimental setting to answer the following research questions. **RQ1:** Did the usage of ecological and other geographical variables, not typically used in IUCN assessments, have an effect on the classification of species into threatened or non-threatened? **RQ2:** What were the most important features for the classification task? **RQ3:** Which modelling algorithms performed best?

## 4.1  Datasets

The dataset resulting from the data integration contains 3260 reptile taxa (species and subspecies). As previously mentioned, these were split into six datasets representing highly distinct species groups: amphisbaenians, crocodiles, lizards, snakes, turtles and all species.

To evaluate if there was a gain from using features other than AOO and EOO, which are traditionally used by IUCN to generate assessments, we created five distinct datasets for each group. All datasets contain the same set of species, only the features vary. The first dataset—the baseline—only used the values of AOO and EOO. Often, it was not possible to calculate these two values accurately or these depict a shallow representation of the species niche hypervolume and, in those cases, it would be good to rely on a more complete proxy set of features. To assess if environmental predictors would have a satisfying performance and could be used without the presence of AOO and EOO, one other dataset uses only ecological variables. A different dataset contained both AOO and EOO, ecological variables and other geographical variables derived from the occurrences data points: minimum and maximum latitudes, latitude length, median longitude and median distance to the equator. For both the dataset of ecological and of geographical features an extra step of feature selection was run, generating two more datasets. These are summarised as follows: AOO_EOO - dataset containing only AOO and EOO, the two most important variables considered in IUCN assessments; EcoFeatures - dataset containing only ecological variables; EcoFeatures_FS - EcoFeatures dataset post-processed by a feature selection step, using backwards selection; AllFeatures - datasets containing both AOO and EOO, and ecological variables, plus other geographical features derived from the occurrences dataset; AllFeatures_FS - AllFeatures dataset post-processed by a feature selection step, using backwards selection.

At the end, we had 30 different datasets. Regardless of the groups, the first dataset was our baseline, as we wanted to understand how the performance of models using other datasets was comparatively to the one used for IUCN assessment.

## 4.2  Experimental Setup

We used $2 \times 5$-fold cross validation setup to train classification models, for each group: RF, used by other recent studies in prediction conservation status of species [4,11,12]; XGBoost, another ensemble strategy that has performed better than RF in some settings; decision trees, a simple algorithm, which may have better results in smaller datasets due to their smaller natural tendency to overfit; GLM, extensively used in this domain [7], that creates a linear decision boundary, which may be desirable for groups with a low species count; and, finally k-NN, a traditional machine learning model. Each model was run in the entire dataset, and in a subset of features selected by RFE [6], a backwards selection method, keeping the minimum number of features to optimise model accuracy.

Each algorithm used a grid search approach to tune the parameters for each dataset: RF [9] - $mtry = \{2, \ldots, 7\}$, $nodesize = \{1, \ldots, 5\}$, $ntree = \{5, 10, 20, 50, 100, 200, 500\}$; XGBoost [3] - $nrounds = \{5, 10, 20, 50, 75, 100, 200\}$, $eta = \{0.01, 0.1, 0.3, 0.5\}$, $max\_depth = \{2, \ldots, 4\}$, $colsample\_bytree = \{0.5, 1\}$ and $min\_child\_weight = \{1, \ldots, 5\}$; k-NN [6] - $k = \{1, \ldots, 20\}$; and rpart [6] - $max\_depth = \{1, \ldots, 14\}$. The range of values for the tuning of $k$ in k-NN and $max\_depth$ in rpart was chosen to allow a good set of values to be tested without compromising too much on performance. We stopped testing higher values when the performance of the models was not improving for any group, C5.0 [6] and GLM [6] had no parameter tuning. Additionally, the classification threshold was also tuned, for each dataset and method, by testing each value from 0.10 to 1, with increments of 0.05. The tuning process maximised the sensitivity of the models, without letting specificity drop to values lower than 0.7. Over the six algorithms used, a total of 1086 parameter values were tested for the five datasets of each of the six groups of species, leading to a total of 195,480 models trained using this tuning process.

The models were evaluated using sensitivity, specificity, precision, AUC, TSS and F-measure with $\beta = 0.5$. These metrics are common when dealing with imbalanced data. AUC and TSS, in particular, were used by other related studies (e.g., [16]). The used F-measure, a combined metric of precision and recall (sensitivity), is aligned with the domain goals. Furthermore, to assess if the performance of the models using a different dataset was significantly better with respect to the baseline dataset (AOO_EOO), we used the paired one-sided Wilcoxon test. We also applied this test to the pairs of the 'ecological' and the 'all' features datasets, allowing us to test how the ecological variables alone would perform against the all features as a baseline.

### 4.3   Results and Discussion

Figure 2 summarises the comparison between the five datasets using $F_{0.5}$, AUC and TSS, and for each of the six groups. Each dot represents the mean of the results of a model across the 10 folds of our $2 \times 5$-fold cross validation setup. The standard deviation is represented by the vertical line. For a given group, models with an opaque colour performed significantly better when comparing to the results of the same algorithm over the AOO_EOO dataset.

The results showed that most groups of species benefited from using ecological and geographical features, since, for multiple groups, AllFeatures and AllFeatures_FS datasets performed better than AOO_EOO dataset, at least for some of the methods. Overall, models for smaller groups, namely amphisbaenians and crocodiles with only 19 and 21 species, respectively, had a larger performance variation across algorithms. This reflects the importance of gathering more species occurrence (or abundance) data and including a broader set of species for modelling purposes. These results also suggested that when deciding on how to group species for modelling, one should balance between having groups that reflect species with similar taxonomic, phylogenetic and/or functional characteristics (to be represented by the same set of variables), and also, having enough data points for the methods to be able to properly learn and to generalise.

The results of the best models for each of the six groups, according to $F_{0.5}$, AUC and TSS, are shown in Table 3. The full set of results is available on https://bit.ly/3coZNC0 and the code for getting them here https://github.com/nadias/Combining-Multiple-Data-Sources-to-Predict-IUCN-Conservation-Status-of-Reptiles. Overall, RF was the best model for these metrics on four out of six groups. These results were in accordance with conclusions reported in previous conservation studies [4,11,12]. Moreover, in general, the extra step of feature selection yielded better results when compared to its counterpart without feature selection.

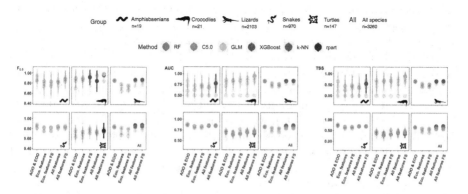

**Fig. 2.** Performance of the models for group, method and dataset, according to $F_{0.5}$, AUC and TSS. Results in opaque colour significantly outperformed the same algorithm over the AOO_EOO dataset. (Color figure online)

**Table 3.** Best model for each group based on $F_{0.5}$, its estimates of $F_{0.5}$, AUC and TSS metrics, method and dataset used to achieve that performance.

| Group | $F_{0.5}$ | AUC | TSS | Method | Dataset |
|---|---|---|---|---|---|
| Amphisbabaenians | 0.97 | 0.88 | 0.75 | GLM | AOO_EOO |
| Crocodiles | 0.99 | 0.98 | 0.95 | RF | AllFeatures_FS |
| Lizards | 0.87 | 0.84 | 0.68 | RF | AllFeatures_FS |
| Snakes | 0.87 | 0.88 | 0.76 | RF | AOO_EOO |
| Turtles | 0.88 | 0.77 | 0.54 | XGBoost | EcoFeatures_FS |
| All species | 0.88 | 0.86 | 0.72 | RF | AllFeatures_FS |

To better understand the role of each feature in the predictions by the different models, we also evaluated the feature importance using caret's varImp function in R [6], a wrapper function with specific methods for calculating feature importance of different types of models. Figure 3 shows the ranking of variables by taking into account the features importance for C5.0, GLM, RF, XGBoost and rpart, over the AllFeatures datasets, using only the top five variables obtained with each method. As it would be expected, both EOO and AOO had an important role in the classification. Nevertheless, other variables contributed to improving the performance of the model, especially, geographic and bioclimatic variables. Results also suggest that statistical dispersion measures (e.g., standard deviation) perform generally better since these portray species ecological tolerance ranges.

As for our research questions, we could see that regarding RQ1, when generating predictions about the conservation status of species, ecological and geographical variables other than AOO and EOO affected the classification of species, since several models performed better when these were included. Regarding the most important features mentioned by RQ2, we have seen that EOO and AOO are the top-important features for most of the models, followed by other geographic features related to the species' latitudinal range, and then by ecological variables that have a non-negligible contribution to the models. Regarding the best modelling technique (RQ3), we have demonstrated that RF generated the best models for most groups, consistent with the fact that many studies on this domain used this algorithm. Additionally, feature selection was an important step included in the proposed pipeline. For most groups, the feature selection step generated the best models.

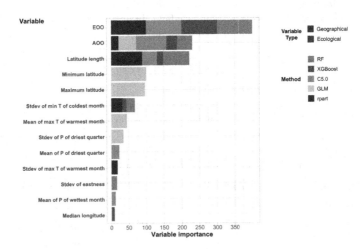

**Fig. 3.** Cumulative variable importance for AllFeatures dataset across models.

# 5    Conclusions

We devised a comprehensive pipeline that may be applied to generate automatic conservation assessments using IUCN's conservation status, which may aid in the mostly manual process of analysing data and can be applied to other taxonomic group. This pipeline included several steps to tackle very relevant issues in the application domain such as data curation and imputation, feature generation and selection, and model tuning and dataset comparison. Overall, our models performed well according to standard metrics used in the ecology and conservation domain and metrics that consider the higher cost of false negatives. Results showed that some models may be improved by using more features besides those traditionally used by IUCN criteria, which reside mostly on the area and extent of occurrence. Those features are, in decreasing order, geographic (mainly the latitudinal range of species but also their longitudinal distribution), bioclimatic indices, habitat, and topographic heterogeneity.

Besides predicting whether a species is threatened or not, experts want to be able to understand what factors contribute to that decision. This would allow us to assess the model's behaviour and ideally, gain new insights into what variables influence threat. With the exception of k-NN, the algorithms tested in this work were either based on trees or linear models, providing a good degree of transparency and explainability.

We think that the large volume of data currently available can be used to perform a general model-assisted assessment across many other under-assessed taxonomic groups, that can be complemented by more focused studies. This can also be used to guide priorities and rank species according to their predicted extinction risk, helping IUCN specialists to better direct their assessments and governmental entities to more efficiently allocate conservation efforts. This framework can be applied to other taxonomic groups by implementing the same steps in data from a different set of species, and given that relevant predictor variables are used at appropriate spatial scales. Moreover, other sets of features could be tested, for instance, variables that depict anthropogenic disturbances on species habitats such as land use change, landscape fragmentation, wildfires, invasive species, which influence the amount, the connectivity and the ability of species finding suitable environments.

Future improvements in the pipeline could also open up the possibility of forecasting species threat status and addressing climate change impacts by feeding models data from climate scenarios provided by UN's Intergovernmental Panel on Climate Change (IPCC). These scenarios are a set of projections of how the climate may evolve in the future, according to different greenhouse gas emission pathways. Such application is deemed critical for domain specialists to anticipate species vulnerabilities in the face of global environmental change.

**Acknowledgements.** This work was financed by National Funds through the Portuguese funding agency, FCT - Fundação para a Ciência e a Tecnologia, within project LA/P/0063/2020 and contracts CEECIND/02331/2017 (J. Gonçalves) and

DL57/2016/CP1440/CT0002 (R. Vasconcelos) under the scope of the Individual Scientific Employment Stimulus Program and 'Norma transitória', respectively.

# References

1. Bland, L., Collen, B., Orme, D., Bielby, J.: Predicting the conservation status of data-deficient species. Conserv. Biol. **29**, 250–259 (2014)
2. Bland, L.M., Böhm, M.: Overcoming data deficiency in reptiles. Biol. Conserv. **204**, 16–22 (2016)
3. Chen, T., et al.: XGBoost: extreme gradient boosting (2021). R package version 1.3.2.1
4. Darrah, S.E., Bland, L.M., Bachman, S.P., Clubbe, C.P., Trias-Blasi, A.: Using coarse-scale species distribution data to predict extinction risk in plants. Divers. Distrib. **23**(4), 435–447 (2017)
5. Keesing, F., et al.: Impacts of biodiversity on the emergence and transmission of infectious diseases. Nature **468**(7324), 647–652 (2010)
6. Kuhn, M.: Caret: classification and regression training (2020). R package version 6.0-86
7. Lehmann, A., Overton, J., Austin, P.: Regression models for spatial prediction: their role for biodiversity and conservation. Biodivers. Conserv. **11**, 2085–2092 (2002)
8. Leão, T.C.C., Fonseca, C.R., Peres, C.A., Tabarelli, M.: Predicting extinction risk of Brazilian Atlantic forest angiosperms. Conserv. Biol. **28**(5), 1349–1359 (2014)
9. Liaw, A., Wiener, M.: Classification and regression by randomForest. R News **2**(3), 18–22 (2002)
10. Luiz, O., Woods, R., Madin, E., Madin, J.: Predicting IUCN extinction risk categories for the world's data deficient groupers (Teleostei: Epinephelidae). Conserv. Lett. **9**, 342–350 (2016)
11. Nic Lughadha, E., et al.: The use and misuse of herbarium specimens in evaluating plant extinction risks. Philos. Trans. R. Soc. Lond. B Biol. Sci. **374**(1763), 20170402 (2019)
12. Pelletier, T.A., Carstens, B.C., Tank, D.C., Sullivan, J., Espíndola, A.: Predicting plant conservation priorities on a global scale. Proc. Natl. Acad. Sci. U.S.A. **115**(51), 13027–13032 (2018)
13. Proosdij, A., Sosef, M., Wieringa, J., Raes, N.: Minimum required number of specimen records to develop accurate species distribution models. Ecography **39**, 542–552 (2016)
14. Romanelli, C., et al.: Connecting global priorities: biodiversity and human health, a state of knowledge review. WHO and Secretariat for the Convention on Biological Diversity, p. 360 (2015)
15. Stévart, T., et al.: A third of the tropical African flora is potentially threatened with extinction. Sci. Adv. **5**(11), eaax9444 (2019)
16. Thuiller, W., Lafourcade, B., Engler, R., Araújo, M.B.: BIOMOD - a platform for ensemble forecasting of species distributions. Ecography **32**(3), 369–373 (2009)
17. Valido, A., Olesen, J.: Frugivory and seed dispersal by lizards: a global review. Front. Ecol. Evol. **7**, 49 (2019)

# LG4AV: Combining Language Models and Graph Neural Networks for Author Verification

Maximilian Stubbemann[1]([envelope]) [ID] and Gerd Stumme[1,2] [ID]

[1] Knowledge and Data Engineering Group, University of Kassel, Kassel, Germany
{stubbemann,stumme}@cs.uni-kassel.de
[2] L3S Research Center, Leibniz University of Hannover, Hannover, Germany
stumme@l3s.de

**Abstract.** The verification of document authorships is important in various settings. Researchers are for example judged and compared by the amount and impact of their publications and public figures are confronted by their posts on social media. Therefore, it is important that authorship information in frequently used data sets is correct. The question whether a given document is written by a given author is commonly referred to as authorship verification (AV). While AV is a widely investigated problem in general, only few works consider settings where the documents are short and written in a rather uniform style. This makes most approaches impractical for bibliometric data. Here, authorships of scientific publications have to be verified, often with just abstracts and titles available. To this point, we present LG4AV which combines language models and graph neural networks for authorship verification. By directly feeding the available texts in a pre-trained transformer architecture, our model does not need any hand-crafted stylometric features that are not meaningful in scenarios where the writing style is, at least to some extent, standardized. By the incorporation of a graph neural network structure, our model can benefit from relations between authors that are meaningful with respect to the verification process.

**Keywords:** Authorship verification · Language models · Graph neural networks · Co-authorships

## 1 Introduction

Evaluation of research strongly depends on bibliometric databases. Today, they are used for the assessment of productivity and impact of researchers, conferences and affiliations. Because of their rising relevance for the evaluation of the scientific output of individual authors, it is crucial that the information which is stored in such databases is correct. However, with the rapid growth of publication output [5], automatic inspections and corrections of information in bibliometric data is needed. A major challenge in this area is authorship verification (AV), which aims to verify if a document is written by a specific author. In general,

© The Author(s), under exclusive license to Springer Nature Switzerland AG 2022
T. Bouadi et al. (Eds.): IDA 2022, LNCS 13205, pp. 315–326, 2022.
https://doi.org/10.1007/978-3-031-01333-1_25

AV is widely investigated [11,12,20], with a majority of existing work handling author verification by capturing writing styles [8,12], assuming that they are unique among different authors. This assumption does not hold in environments where the available texts are short and contain uniform language patterns. An example of this is given by author verification tasks for scientific documents. In such settings, the availability of full texts is rare because bibliometric data sets often contain only abstracts and titles. In such scenarios the variety of writing styles and linguistic usage is rather limited.

Additionally, the focus in AV research is on documents with one author, while verification of multi-author documents is seldom done. Here, the information about known multi-authorships can enhance the verification process because it provides a meaningful graph structure. For example, scientific authors are more likely to write papers that would also fit to their co-authors and twitter users are expected to post about the same topics as the persons they follow. The incorporation of such graph structures is rarely investigated.

Here we step in with LG4AV. Our novel architecture combines language models and graph neural networks (GNNs) to verify whether a document belongs to a potential author. This is done without the explicit recap of the known documents of this author at decision time which can be a computational bottleneck. This is especially true for authors with a large amount of known documents. Additionally, LG4AV does not rely on any hand-crafted stylometric features.

By incorporating a graph neural network structure into our architecture, we use known relations between potential authors. In this way, we are able to account for the fact that authors are more likely to turn to topics that are present in their social neighborhood. We experimentally evaluate the ability of our model to make verification decisions in bibliometric environments and we review the influence of the individual components on the quality of the verification decisions.

LG4AV is available on GitHub[1] and a longer version of this paper which includes experiments on authors not seen at training time is available on arXiv.[2]

## 2    Related Work

Authorship verification is a commonly studied problem. PAN@CLEF[3] provides regular competitions in this realm. However, their past author verification challenges were based on a setting where either small samples of up to ten known documents for each unknown document were provided (2013–2015) or pairs of documents were given where the task was to decide whether they were written by the same person (2020, 2021). Both scenarios are not applicable for bibliometric environments, where the amount of known document can reach up to hundreds.

Many well-established methods for author verification develop specific hand-crafted features that capture stylometric and syntactic patterns of documents. For example, [15] uses features such as sentence-lengths, punctuation marks and

---

[1] https://github.com/mstubbemann/LG4AV.

[2] https://arxiv.org/abs/2109.01479.

[3] https://pan.webis.de/shared-tasks.html.

frequencies of n-grams to make verification decisions. While the use of n-grams was already studied in earlier works such as [17], there are still recent methods that build upon them, such as [24]. Another well established approach is given by [21] where the authors successively remove features and observe how this reduces the distinction between two works. This approach is still known to be the gold standard [4,24]. Despite its advantages, it is known to perform worse on short texts. Therefore, [4] proposes a modification that is also applicable to shorter texts. However, this work experiments with documents of 4,000 words per document, which is still much longer then abstracts of scientific publications.

Recently, methods based on neural network architectures, such as RNNs and transformer models, emerged [2,3]. Note, that both of these approaches need to train head layers for each individual author. This makes them impractical for AV in bibliometric data where thousands of authors has to be considered.

One of the few works that experiments with bibliometric data is [12], which uses full text of a small subset of authors and ignores co-authorship relations. Most other works that deal with bibliometric data tackle the closely related problem of *authorship attribution* (AA), i.e., with questions of the kind "who is the author of $d$" instead of "is $a$ author of $d$" [6,7,14].

One of the few works in the realm of AV that explicitly takes into account that research papers are multi-author documents is [26]. In their work, the authors derive a similarity based graph structure of text fragments for authorship attribution for multi-author documents. In contrast, our aim is to incorporate past co-authorship relations to verify potential authorships.

# 3    Combining Language Models and Graph Neural Networks for Author Verification

We always assume vectors $v \in \mathbb{R}^m$ to be row-vectors. For $M \in \mathbb{R}^{n \times m}$, we denote by $M_i$ the $i$-th row of $M$ and with $M_{i,j}$ the $j$-th entry of the $i$-th row of $M$.

## 3.1    Problem

Let $t$ be a fixed time point and let $G = (A, E)$ be a graph with $A = \{a_1, \ldots, a_n\}$ being a set of authors and $E \subseteq \binom{A}{2}$ a set of edges present before $t$. Additionally, let $D$ be a set of documents. Let, for all authors $a \in A$, be $D(a) \subseteq D$ the set of their known documents until $t$. Let $U$ be a set of documents created after $t$ with unknown authorships. The goal is to verify for a set $P \subseteq A \times U$, whether for each $(a, u) \in P$ $a$ is an author of $u$, i.e., to compute a verification score $f(a, u) \in [0, 1]$. Our formulation differs from the usual setting where the problem is broken down to sequences of pairs $(D_i, d_i)_{i=1}^{l}$ where the task is to determine for each $i \in \{1, \ldots, l\}$ if the *unknown document* $d_i$ is from the same author as the set of *known documents* $D_i$. These settings are closely connected in the sense that each author $a$ can be interpreted as the set of his known documents $D(a)$ at training time. However, approaches adopted to this setting often assume to have already pairs of known document sets and unknown documents [15] at training time or they explicitly use the set of known documents for verification [16,24,27].

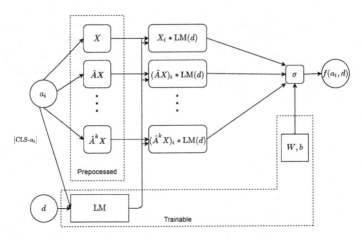

**Fig. 1.** Forward step. LG4AV gets as input an author $a_i$ and a document $d$. The author specific cls-token is added to the front of $d$ which is then feed through the language model (which is BERT in our case). The $i$-th rows of $X, \hat{A}X, \ldots, \hat{A}^k X$ are individually component-wise multiplied with the output of LM, which constitutes the incorporation of the GNN structure. The resulting vectors are concatenated and fed through a fully connected layer with a sigmoid activation. Here, $k$ displays the maximal amount of neighborhood aggregations, i.e., the maximal $j$ for which $\hat{A}^j X$ is incorporated.

### 3.2   Combining Language Models and Graph Neural Networks for Author Verification

We develop an end-to-end model to tackle the author verification problem. For this, we additionally assume to have for each author $a \in A$ a vector representation $x_a \in \mathbb{R}^s$. At training time, our model gets as input pairs $(a, d) \in A \times D$ and is trained on predicting whether $a$ is author of $D$, i.e., $d \in D(a)$. For inference at testing time, the model gets as input pairs $(a, u) \in P$ and decides whether $a$ is author of $u$ by computing a verification score $f(a, u)$. For both training and testing, author-document pairs $(a, d)$ are forwarded through the network in the following manner. We add a special token to represent the current author to the beginning of $d$. The resulting document is then guided through a language model. Additionally, we incorporate a graph neural network structure by 1) computing vector representations of $a$ that depend on its graph neighbors, 2) combining these vector representations with the output of the language model 3) and forwarding through a fully connected layer to get a verification score. In the following, we discuss the individual components and give a detailed explanation of the network inference. A sketch of LG4AV is given by Fig. 1.

*The Language Model.* As language model, we choose the standard BERT [10] model which we assume the reader to be familiar with. Even though there are a multitude of newer models built upon it and outperforming it on NLP tasks,

BERT is considered to be the common basic pre-trained transformer model. We therefore use it here to demonstrate our approach. We feed the full document at once through BERT and extract the output of the [CLS] token. This practice has already been applied to abstracts of scientific documents [9] and social media data [31]. Our language model can be interpreted as a map $LM : D \cup U \to \mathbb{R}^m$.

To combine the output of the language model with the neighborhood aggregated author vector representation, we need to ensure that the output of the language model has the same dimension as the feature vectors of the authors, i.e., $m = s$. Hence, we extend LM by a linear layer on top of the BERT model, if needed.

To give the language model information about the current author $a \in A$, we replace the regular [CLS] token by an author-dependent classification token [CLS-a]. Hence, the information of the current author is encoded into the input of the language model. To nourish from the optimization of the [CLS] token that was done in the pre-training procedure of BERT, we initialize for each author $a \in A$ the token-embedding of [CLS-a] with the token-embedding of [CLS].

*The Graph Neural Network.* The Graph Convolutional Network (GCN) [18] is a base for many modern graph neural network architectures. It is a 2-layer neural network with an additional *neighborhood aggregating* step at the input and hidden layer. This method leads to problems in batch-processing. Since the feature vector of each node is merged with feature vectors of adjacent nodes at the input and hidden layers, the corresponding node vectors have to be in the same batch.

To solve this problem we use a GNN architecture that only aggregates neighborhood information **before** weight matrices are multiplied with feature vectors. Then, the neighborhood-aggregation can be done once in a preprocessing step over the full feature-matrix. Such an approach is for example introduced by [29]. Here, the authors propose a linear model of the form $X \mapsto \sigma(\hat{A}^k X W)$, with $\hat{A}$ being a normalized adjacency matrix and $W$ a trainable weight matrix. In contrast, SIGN [25] proposes to have multiple input layers with different neighborhood aggregations of the form $X \mapsto \hat{A}_k X W$. Here, $\hat{A}_k$ can for example be a power of a normalized adjacency matrix or powers of matrices that are based on triangles in the graph. While the model in [29] is more simple, it has the disadvantage that it only uses $\hat{A}^k X$ and not incorporates X itself. Hence, it only uses the aggregated feature vector of a node without a special emphasis on the features of the node itself. For LG4AV, we use a new model that is strongly inspired by both of the introduced approaches.

*LG4AV.* Let $X \in \mathbb{R}^{n \times s}$ be the feature matrix of all authors, i.e. $X_i = X_{a_i}$. Let $k \in \mathbb{N}$. Let $\tilde{A}$ be the adjacency matrix of $G$ with added self loops. For each $i \in \{1, \ldots, n\}$, let $\deg(i) := \sum_{j=1}^n \tilde{A}_{i,j}$ be the degree of $a_i$ in G and let $D \in \mathbb{R}^{n \times n}$ with $D_{i,i} := \deg(i)$ and $D_{i,j} = 0$ if $i \neq j$. Let then $\hat{A} := D^{-\frac{1}{2}} \tilde{A} D^{-\frac{1}{2}}$ be the normalized adjacency matrix. For a given pair $(a_i, d)$ of an author and a document the network inference is done in the following manner. For all $l \in \{0, \ldots, k\}$, we concatenate the vectors $v_l(a_i, d) := (\hat{A}^l X)_i * LM(d)$ to a vector

$v(a_i, d) := (v_0(a_i, d), \ldots, v_k(a_i, d))$. Hence, $k$ displays the maximum amount of times, neighborhood features are aggregated. Here, $*$ denotes the element-wise product. To derive a verification score from this concatenated vector, we feed $v(a_i, d)$ into a fully connected layer with a weight matrix $W \in \mathbb{R}^{s(k+1) \times 1}$, a bias $b \in \mathbb{R}$ and a sigmoid activation. Hence, the full network inference of LG4AV is given by the equation $f(a_i, d) := \sigma(v(a_i, d))W + b)$.

For training we use all pairs $(a, d) \in A \times D$ with $d \in D(a)$ as positive examples. For each $a \in A$ we sample $|D(a)|$ documents $d \in D \backslash D(a)$ to generate negative examples. We use binary cross entropy as loss function.

## 4   Experiments

We use a data set which contains publication information of the German and international AI research community [19]. It contains titles and abstracts from Semantic Scholar [1] which are needed for LG4AV but are not included in DBLP[4]. The relations between authors and papers are based on DBLP which is, in our experience, comparably accurate with good name disambiguation. This is crucial to prevent wrong authorship information in the data itself.

We use the data set of the German AI researchers as our first data set. As a second data set, we extract all authors with publications at the KDD conference and all their publications from the data set of the international AI researchers. We refer to the first as the *GAI* and to the second as the *KDD* data. Basic statistics of the resulting data can be found in Table 1. We generate training, validation and testing data for both data sets in the following manner.

- We discard all publications without an English abstract.
- For each publication, we use the title and the abstract as input for the language model and concatenate them via a new line char to generate the text that represents this publication.
- We build the co-author graph of all authors until 2015. From this co-author graph, we discard all author nodes that do not belong to the biggest connected component. Let $A$ be the set of authors that are nodes in this graph. We use this graph for the neighborhood aggregation. We denote the set of publications until 2015 of these authors with $D_{\text{train}}$.
- We generate for all authors and each of their publications a positive training example. For all authors, we then sample papers from $D_{\text{train}}$ which they are not an author of. We sample in such a way that we have for each author an equal amount of positive and negative examples.
- We use data from 2016 for validation. More specifically, we use for all authors $a \in A$ all publications that they have (co-) authored in 2016 as positive validation examples. Let $D_{\text{val}}$ be the set of these publications. We sample for all authors papers from $D_{\text{val}}$ that they are not author of as negative validation examples. Again, we sample in such a way that we have for each author an equal amount of positive and negative validation examples.
- We use publications from 2017 and newer to analogously generate test data.

---

[4] https://dblp.org/.

**Table 1.** Basic statistics of the data sets. We display from left to right: 1) The number of authors in $A$, 2) the number of edges in the co-author graph of these authors at training time, 3) the number of training examples, 4) the number of validation examples, 5) the number of test examples.

|     | # Authors | # Edges | # Train | # Validation | # Test |
| --- | --- | --- | --- | --- | --- |
| GAI | 1669 | 4315 | 175118 | 14314 | 41558 |
| KDD | 3056 | 9592 | 254096 | 19976 | 61804 |

### 4.1 Baselines and Configurations of LG4AV

*N-Gram Baseline.* This baseline is strongly inspired by the baseline script of the AV challenge of PAN@CLEF 2020. For all authors we generate a "super-document" by concatenating all their documents that are available for training. For all pairs of authors $a$ and documents $d$ at validation and testing time, we measure the similarity between $d$ and the superdocument of $a$. If the similarity is above a given threshold $t$, we classify the pair as a positive example. To measure similarities, we build a character-based $n$-gram TF-IDF vectorizer upon all papers available at training time, using only the 3000 most frequent $n$-grams across the documents that the vectorizer is built on.

We tune $n$ via grid-search on $\{1 \ldots 10\}$ and choose the value that corresponds to the highest AUC on the validation set. We tune the threshold on the set $\{\frac{1}{999}i - \frac{1}{999} \mid i \in \{1, \ldots, 1000\}\}$. Note, that this means to sample 1000 evenly spaced points in $[0, 1]$. We also test the median of the distances of the validation examples as threshold. Since the AUC is independent of this threshold, we tune on the validation F1 score after the best $n$ is chosen.

*GLAD* [15]. This method is intended for pairs of the form $(D, d)$ where $D$ is a set of documents and $d$ is a single document. Note, that GLAD needs such pairs already for training. Since our data consists of pairs $(a, d)$ with $a$ an author and $d$ a document, we build training examples for GLAD in the following manner. Let $P_{\text{train}}$ be the set of all author-document pairs available at training time and let, for all $(a, d)$, be $l_{(a,d)} \in \{0, 1\}$ the label of that pair. For each author $a$ we collect the set $D_{a,+} := \{d \mid (a, d) \in P_{\text{train}}, l_{(a,d)} = 1\} = \{d_{a,+,0}, \ldots, d_{a,+,m}\}$ of positive and the set $D_{a,-} := \{d \mid (a, d) \in P_{\text{train}}, l_{(a,d)} = 0\} = \{d_{a,-,0}, \ldots, d_{a,-,m}\}$ of negative training examples. For each $i \in \{0, \ldots, m\}$, we train GLAD with $(D_{a,+} \backslash \{d_{a,+,i}\}, d_{a,+,i})$ with a positive label and $(D_{a,+} \backslash \{d_{a,+,i}\}, d_{a,-,i})$ with a negative label. For validation and testing, we replace pairs $(a, d)$ by $(D_{a,+}, d)$.

GLAD works as follows. For each pair $(D, d)$ a vector representation is computed that consists of features that are solely build on $D$ or $d$, such as for example average sentence length and joint features, which are build on $D$ and $d$, such as entropy of concatenations of documents of $D$ and $d$. This vector representations are then fed into a support-vector machine. While the authors of [15] uses a linear support-vector machine with default parameter setting of scikit-learn [23], we enhance GLAD by tuning the $c$-parameter of the support-vector machine and additionally experiment with radial kernels where we tune the $\gamma$-parameter. For both parameters, we grid search over $\{10^{-3}, \ldots, 10^3\}$ on the validation AUC.

*RBI* [24]. The ranking-based impostors method verifies a pair $(D, d)$ with the help of a set $D_e$ of external documents. To use exactly the information available for training and thus have a fair comparison, we use $D_{a,+}$ as the known documents and $D_{a,-}$ as the external documents for each pair $(a, d)$.

By studying for each $d_i \in D$ how many documents of $D_e$ are closer to $d$ than $d_i$ is to $d$, the impostors method computes a verification score where pairs with higher scores are more likely to be positive examples. To compute vector representations for documents, we stick to the procedure in [24]. We choose the following parameters for RBI. We grid search $k \in \{100, 200, 300, 400\}$, choose cosine similarity as the similarity function and select the aggregation function between mean, minimum and maximum function. For the meaning of the parameters, we refer to [24]. We use the AUC score on the validation data to choose the best parameters. To derive binary predictions from the verification scores, we use the median of all verification scores from the validation data.

*Siamese BERT (S-BERT)* [28]. In this method, pairs of documents are feed through BERT and the network is trained to put document pairs close together which are from the same author. To derive examples from a training pair $(a, d)$, we sample from $D_{a,+}\backslash\{d\}$ 3 documents $d_1, d_2, d_3$ to generate the training examples $(d_1, d), (d_2, d), (d_3, d)$. If $(a, d)$ is a validation or test example we set the distance of $(a, d)$ to the mean of the distances of $(d_1, d), (d_2, d), (d_3, d)$.

This model is trained with a linear decreasing learning rate starting at $5 * 10^{-5}$ and weight decay of $0.01$. We use a contrastive loss function with a margin of $0.1$ and cosine distance because this led to the highest AUC score in [28]. To choose the threshold $t$ which separates positive and negative examples at validation and testing time, we grid search over $\{0, 0.02, \ldots, 1.998, 2\}$ on the validation F1 score and classify all pairs as positive which have a distance not higher then $t$. We use a batch-size of 2 and accumulate 4 batches for an effective batch size of 8. As S-BERT tends to lead to unstable results, which is commonly observed for BERT models [22, 30], we do 10 runs for both data sets and report mean values of the runs which lead to a reasonable solution, i.e., an AUC over $0.51$.

*Configurations of LG4AV.* We use three different configurations of LG4AV to evaluate the importance of the individual components. Namely, we work with *LG4AV-2*, a "regular" LG4AV model with $k = 2$ which is a common choice in the realm of GNNs [13, 18] and *LG4AV-0*, with $k = 0$. Hence, the latter model does not use any graph information. We use it to evaluate to which extent the graph information enhances the verification process. Additionally, we experiment with *LG4AV-F*. This model coincides with LG4AV-2 with the difference, that we freeze all BERT parameters and just train the weight matrix $W$. This allows us to understand if the fine-tuning of the BERT parameters is indeed necessary.

**Table 2.** Results. For S-Bert, we report means over runs with an AUC over 0.51. On the GAI data set, LG4AV-2 significantly outperforms LG4AV-0 with $p = 0.05$ with respect to a t-test and a Wilcoxon test. On the KDD data set, LG4AV-2 significantly outperforms LG4AV-0 with $p = 0.01$ with respect to a t-test and a Wilcoxon test. For both data sets, this holds for all three performance indicators.

| | GAI | | | KDD | | |
|---|---|---|---|---|---|---|
| | AUC | ACC | F1 | AUC | ACC | F1 |
| N-Gram | .8624 | .7874 | .7817 | .7592 | .6887 | .7008 |
| GLAD | .8328 | .7500 | .7150 | .7322 | .6698 | .6200 |
| RBI | .8251 | .7478 | .7391 | .7452 | .6823 | .6647 |
| S-BERT | .9196 | .8492 | .8516 | .8207 | .7373 | .7602 |
| LG4AV-2 | **.9247** | **.8541** | **.8569** | **.8522** | **.7675** | **.7808** |
| LG4AV-0 | .9207 | .8492 | .8519 | .8465 | .7619 | .7771 |
| LG4AV-F | .8384 | .7576 | .7767 | .7622 | .6866 | .7110 |

To derive classification decisions for computing F1 and accuracy scores, we grid search a threshold $t$ over $\{0, 0.002, \ldots, 0.998, 1\}$ on the validation F1 score.

### 4.2  Implementation Details

We use the "regular" BERT base uncased model and train for 3 epochs. After the element-wise multiplication of the BERT output and the text features, we dropout with probability of 0.1. We use ADAM with weight decay of 0.01 and a learning rate of $2 * 10^{-5}$ with linear decay and a batch size of 4. We do gradient accumulation of 4 for an effective batch size of 16. To generate features for each author, we feed their known documents through the not fine-tuned BERT model and build the mean point vector of the vector representations of the [CLS] tokens.

Because of the instability of BERT fine-tuning [22,30], we do 10 runs for all configurations of LG4AV and report mean scores. For this runs, we use the same 10 different random seeds for weight initialization and for data shuffling. We do this because early experiments indicated that LG4AV-2 and LG4AV-0 perform better for the same random seeds (and therefore same shuffles of the training data).

### 4.3  Results and Discussion

The results can be found in Table 2. LG4AV outperforms all baselines. We especially point out that LG4AV also lead to slight improvement over S-BERT, which also uses language models and is, because of the sampling procedure that increases the amount of training examples, more time-expensive. As we replace one training example with 3 new samples for S-BERT, an epoch lasts about a factor 3 longer for S-BERT.

Note, that LG4AV uses for all authors their papers until 2015 to both build the positive training examples and for computing their feature vector. Hence, considering the positive examples, the network is trained on verifying author-document pairs where the document is additionally used to build the features of this author. Thus, it is reasonable to expect that the availability to generalize to unseen documents is limited. However, the results on the test set, which contains only documents not used for the features vectors, show that this is not the case.

The above mentioned instability of BERT models is indeed inherited to LG4AV. For some random seeds, LG4AV does not converge to a reasonable solution and results in AUC scores are around 0.5. Hence, we recommend to try different random seeds for training and not rely on one training run. Because of this and since the results of LG4AV-2 and LG4AV-0 are very close, we compare them with statistical significance tests to investigate if the co-author information significantly enhances the verification decisions. Based on the random shuffling and initialization procedure explained above, we decide to use a paired t-test and paired Wilcoxon tests over the 10 runs. To sum up, the results indicate that the incorporation of co-author information lead to significant enhancements. Still, the comparable results for $k = 0$ show that our idea of combining author features with a language model even works without co-author information. In contrast, if the BERT layers are frozen, the performance declines considerably. Hence, fine-tuning is crucial for success.

The performance gap between the data sets is remarkable. Because the GAI data uses data from all domains of AI while the KDD data is limited to authors with connections to topics of the KDD, it stands to reason that the documents of the KDD data set are more topically related. Thus, the worse results on the KDD data support our hypothesis that AV for bibliometric data is not about distinguishing writing styles, but about identifying relevant topics of authors.

## 5    Conclusion and Outlook

In this work, we presented LG4AV, a novel architecture for author verification. By combining a language model with a graph neural network, our model does not depend on any handcrafted features and is able to incorporate relations between authors into the verification process. LG4AV surpasses methods that use handcrafted stylometric and n-gram text features when it comes to verification of short and, to some extent, standardized texts. Hence, LG4AV is especially helpful to correct authorship information in bibliometric data sets, especially when only abstracts and titles are available.

Future work could include applications of LG4AV to different settings, as for example social media posts. Additionally, it is promising to investigate temporal evolution of interests of authors. Does the performance decrease, if the temporal distance between the training and test set is increased? Does the performance increase if only recent texts are considered to verify new potential authorships?

**Acknowledgment.** This work is partially funded by the German Federal Ministry of Education and Research (BMBF) in its program "Quantitative Wissenschafts-forschung" as part of the REGIO project under grant 01PU17012A. We thank Dominik Dürrschnabel and Lena Stubbemann for fruitful discussions and comments on the manuscript.

# References

1. Ammar, W., et al.: Construction of the literature graph in semantic scholar. In: Proceedings of the 2018 Conference of the North American Chapter of the Assoc. for Computational Linguisticss, pp. 84–91. Association for Computational Linguistics (2018)
2. Bagnall, D.: Author identification using multi-headed recurrent neural networks. In: Working Notes of CLEF. CEUR Workshop Proceedings, vol. 1391 (2015)
3. Barlas, G., Stamatatos, E.: Cross-domain authorship attribution using pre-trained language models. In: Maglogiannis, I., Iliadis, L., Pimenidis, E. (eds.) AIAI 2020. IAICT, vol. 583, pp. 255–266. Springer, Cham (2020). https://doi.org/10.1007/978-3-030-49161-1_22
4. Bevendorff, J., Stein, B., Hagen, M., Potthast, M.: Generalizing unmasking for short texts. In: Proceedings of the 2019 Conference of the North American Chapter of the Association for Computational Linguistics, pp. 654–659. Association for Computational Linguistics (2019)
5. Bornmann, L., Mutz, R.: Growth rates of modern science: a bibliometric analysis based on the number of publications and cited references. J. Assoc. Inf. Sci. Technol. **66**(11), 2215–2222 (2015)
6. Bradley, J.K., Kelley, P.G., Roth, A.: Author identification from citations. Department of Computer Science, Carnegie Mellon University, Pittsburgh, PA, USA, Technical report (2008)
7. Caragea, C., Uban, A.S., Dinu, L.P.: The myth of double-blind review revisited: ACL vs. EMNLP. In: Proceedings of the 2019 Conference on Empirical Methods in Natural Language Processing and the 9th International Joint Conference on Natural Language Processing, pp. 2317–2327. Association for Computational Linguistics (2019)
8. Castro-Castro, D., Arcia, Y.A., Brioso, M.P., Guillena, R.M.: Authorship verification, average similarity analysis. In: Recent Advances in Natural Language Processing, pp. 84–90 (2015)
9. Cohan, A., Feldman, S., Beltagy, I., Downey, D., Weld, D.S.: SPECTER: document-level representation learning using citation-informed transformers. In: Proceedings of the 58th Annual Meeting of the Association for Computational Linguistics, pp. 2270–2282. Association for Computational Linguistics (2020)
10. Devlin, J., Chang, M., Lee, K., Toutanova, K.: BERT: pre-training of deep bidirectional transformers for language understanding. In: Proceedings of the 2019 Conference of the North American Chapter of the Association for Computational Linguistics, pp. 4171–4186. Association for Computational Linguistics (2019)
11. van Halteren, H.: Linguistic profiling for authorship recognition and verification. In: Proceedings of the 42nd Annual Meeting of the Association for Computational Linguistics, pp. 199–206. ACL (2004)
12. Halvani, O., Winter, C., Graner, L.: Assessing the applicability of authorship verification methods. In: Proceedings of the 14th International Conference on Availability, Reliability and Security, pp. 38:1–38:10. ACM (2019)
13. Hamilton, W.L., Ying, Z., Leskovec, J.: Inductive representation learning on large graphs. In: Advances in Neural Information Processing Systems, vol. 30, pp. 1024–1034 (2017)
14. Hill, S., Provost, F.J.: The myth of the double-blind review?: author identification using only citations. SIGKDD Explor. **5**(2), 179–184 (2003)

15. Hürlimann, M., Weck, B., van den Berg, E., Suster, S., Nissim, M.: GLAD: groningen lightweight authorship detection. In: Working Notes of CLEF. CEUR Workshop Proeedings, vol. 1391 (2015)

16. Jankowska, M., Milios, E.E., Keselj, V.: Author verification using common n-gram profiles of text documents. In: 25th International Conference on Computational Linguistics, pp. 387–397. ACL (2014)

17. Kešelj, V., Peng, F., Cercone, N., Thomas, C.: N-gram-based author profiles for authorship attribution. In: Proceedings of the Conference Pacific Association for Computational Linguistics, vol. 3, pp. 255–264 (2003)

18. Kipf, T.N., Welling, M.: Semi-supervised classification with graph convolutional networks. In: 5th International Conference on Learning Representations (2017)

19. Koopmann, T., et al.: Proximity dimensions and the emergence of collaboration: a HypTrails study on German AI research. Scientometrics **126**, 1–22 (2021). https://link.springer.com/journal/11192/volumes-and-issues/126-12

20. Koppel, M., Schler, J.: Authorship verification as a one-class classification problem. In: Proceedings of the Twenty-First International Conference on Machine Learning, vol. 69. ACM (2004)

21. Koppel, M., Schler, J., Bonchek-Dokow, E.: Measuring differentiability: unmasking pseudonymous authors. J. Mach. Learn. Res. **8**, 1261–1276 (2007)

22. Mosbach, M., Andriushchenko, M., Klakow, D.: On the stability of fine-tuning BERT: misconceptions, explanations, and strong baselines. In: International Conference on Learning Representations (2021)

23. Pedregosa, F., et al.: Scikit-learn: machine learning in Python. J. Mach. Learn. Res. **12**, 2825–2830 (2011)

24. Potha, N., Stamatatos, E.: Improved algorithms for extrinsic author verification. Knowl. Inf. Syst. **62**(5), 1903–1921 (2019). https://doi.org/10.1007/s10115-019-01408-4

25. Rossi, E., Frasca, F., Chamberlain, B., Eynard, D., Bronstein, M.M., Monti, F.: SIGN: scalable inception graph neural networks. CoRR abs/2004.11198 (2020)

26. Sarwar, R., et al.: CAG: stylometric authorship attribution of multi-author documents using a co-authorship graph. IEEE Access **8**, 18374–18393 (2020)

27. Seidman, S.: Authorship verification using the impostors method. In: Forner, P., Navigli, R., Tufis, D., Ferro, N. (eds.) Working Notes for CLEF. CEUR Workshop Proceedings, vol. 1179 (2013)

28. Tyo, J., Dhingra, B., Lipton, Z.: Siamese BERT for authorship verification. In: Faggioli, G., Ferro, N., Joly, A., Maistro, M., Piroi, F. (eds.) Working Notes of CLEF. CEUR Workshop Proceedings, vol. 2936, pp. 2169–2177. CEUR-WS.org (2021)

29. Wu, F., Jr., A.H.S., Zhang, T., Fifty, C., Yu, T., Weinberger, K.Q.: Simplifying graph convolutional networks. In: Proceedings of the 36th International Conference on Machine Learning. Proceedings of Machine Learning Research, vol. 97, pp. 6861–6871 (2019)

30. Zhang, T., Wu, F., Katiyar, A., Weinberger, K.Q., Artzi, Y.: Revisiting few-sample BERT fine-tuning. In: International Conference on Learning Representations (2021)

31. Zhu, J., Tian, Z., Kübler, S.: Um-iu@ling at semeval-2019 task 6: identifying offensive tweets using BERT and SVMs. In: Proceedings of the 13th International Workshop on Semantic Evaluation, SemEval@NAACL-HLT 2019, pp. 788–795. Association for Computational Linguistics (2019)

# Efficient Subgroup Discovery Through Auto-Encoding

Joost F. van der Haar, Sander C. Nagelkerken, Igor G. Smit,
Kjell van Straaten, Janneke A. Tack, Rianne M. Schouten,
and Wouter Duivesteijn$^{(\boxtimes)}$

Technische Universiteit Eindhoven, Eindhoven, the Netherlands
{j.f.v.d.haar,s.c.nagelkerken,i.g.smit,k.v.straaten,
j.a.tack}@student.tue.nl, {r.m.schouten,w.duivesteijn}@tue.nl

**Abstract.** Current subgroup discovery methods struggle to produce good results for large real-life datasets with high dimensionality. Run times can become high and dependencies between attributes are hard to capture. We propose a method in which auto-encoding is applied for dimensionality reduction before subgroup discovery is performed. In an experimental study, we find that auto-encoding increases both the quality and coverage for our dataset with over 500 attributes. On the dataset with over 250 attributes and the one with the most instances, the coverage improves, while the quality remains similar. For smaller datasets, quality and coverage remain similar or see a minor decrease. Additionally, we greatly improve the run time for each dataset-algorithm combination; for the datasets with over 250 and 500 attributes run times decrease by a factor of on average 150 and 200, respectively. We conclude that dimensionality reduction is a promising method for subgroup discovery in datasets with many attributes and/or a high number of instances.

**Keywords:** Subgroup discovery · Auto-encoding · Dimensionality reduction

## 1  Introduction

Subgroup Discovery (SD) is a data mining method used to discover interesting relationships between objects in a dataset with respect to a specific target variable. The SD outcome is typically represented as a set of rules called subgroups [10]. SD methods are often used on real-world problems, such as the detection and description of Coronary Heart Disease risk groups [8], fraud detection in the healthcare domain [16] and identifying flight delay patterns [23]. Real-life problems often involve datasets with high dimensionality. For many SD methods, handling such large datasets can be an issue. The most commonly used method to address this problem is by applying sampling. However, this method

---

J. F. van der Haar, S. C. Nagelkerken, I. G. Smit, K. van Straaten and J. A. Tack—
These authors contributed equally to this work.

© The Author(s), under exclusive license to Springer Nature Switzerland AG 2022
T. Bouadi et al. (Eds.): IDA 2022, LNCS 13205, pp. 327–340, 2022.
https://doi.org/10.1007/978-3-031-01333-1_26

has the downside of not taking dependencies and relationships between variables into account which can result in important data loss for subgroup discovery. It seems that no research is conducted on reducing the dimensionality of a dataset via auto-encoding prior to applying subgroup discovery methods. Using auto-encoding as a method to reduce the dimensionality of a dataset may solve the issue of important data loss since this method is able to uncover latent low-dimensional non-linear structures in the data [11], which allows it to minimize the dimensionality reduction information loss. Therefore, this paper investigates the effects of auto-encoding on the results of various existing SD methods.

### 1.1   Main Contribution

We propose an alternative method that enables the application of SD on larger datasets. We show that preprocessing datasets by performing dimensionality reduction using auto-encoders can improve the efficiency of SD, while maintaining or improving subgroup quality and coverage of discovered subgroups. Run times can be a few hundred times less for datasets with many attributes. At the same time, we can increase the coverage and explore different regions in the data for any algorithm if datasets are reasonably sized. We can do this while achieving equivalent or even higher subgroup qualities, both on average and for the best subgroup, depending on the dataset.

## 2   Related Work

### 2.1   Subgroup Discovery

Subgroup Discovery methods (see [10] for a survey) can be partitioned into three groups. The first group of methods are extensions of classification algorithms, such as EXPLORA [14], MIDOS [29], SD [8], and CN2-SD [18]. The second group contains extensions of association algorithms, such as APRIORI-SD [13] and Merge-SD [9]. The third group consists of evolutionary algorithms, such as NMEEF-SD [3]. Herrera et al. [10] noticed that many of the above listed subgroup discovery techniques have difficulties with real-world problems due to high dimensionality of the datasets associated with such problems. Usually, there are two solutions for data mining algorithms that do not perform well under high dimensional datasets, namely reducing the data size without changing the outcome radically or redesigning the algorithm so that it can handle huge datasets. The most applied method to reduce the dimensionality of a dataset is sampling, in which particular instances of a dataset are selected according to certain criteria [10]. A downside of this technique is that this could lead to loss of important knowledge for the SD task when not considering dependencies and relationships between variables. Therefore, when reducing the dimensionality of a dataset, it must be ensured that no important data is lost which is necessary for the extraction of important subgroups [10].

## 2.2   Dimensionality Reduction

The goal of dimensionality reduction is to produce a compact low-dimensional encoding of a given high-dimensional dataset. Principal Component Analysis (PCA) [28] aims to find a linear subspace of a dimension lower than the dimension of the original dataset, such that the data points lie mainly on this linear subspace, and thus maintain most of the variability of the data [25,27]. Linear Discriminant Analysis (LDA) [24] is a classifier that is used to find a linear combination of features, which separates a number of classes of data. The main idea is to ensure that the samples after projection have maximum between-cluster-distance and minimum within-cluster-distance in the new subspace [27]. Isomap [25] performs multidimensional scaling in the geodesic space of the non-linear data manifold, rather than in the input space. Lastly, auto-encoders [27] reduce dimensionality very well while maintaining more information than the four aforementioned dimensionality reduction methods for most datasets. Additionally, auto-encoders are better capable of detecting repetitive structures than the alternative methods.

## 3   Preliminaries

A dataset $D$ consists of a set of individuals $I$ and attributes $A$, such that $D = (I, A)$. A subgroup description, also called a complex pattern $P$, is a set of selectors, also called basic patterns [2]. For a nominal attribute, a selector is a Boolean function that is true if $a_i \in A = v_j$ for the individual, and false otherwise. For numeric attributes, the value of the selector is set to true for an individual if the attribute value for that individual is in the interval $[\min_j : \max_j]$, thus if $a_i \in [\min_j : \max_j]$, and false otherwise. The set of all basic patterns in the dataset is denoted by $\Sigma$. The subgroup description $P$ is then defined by a conjunction of basic patterns: $P(i) = \mathrm{sel}_j \wedge ... \wedge \mathrm{sel}_n$, $\mathrm{sel}_m \in \Sigma$, $m = j, ..., n$ for individual $i \in I$. This pattern can then be interpreted as a rule for a subgroup $S_P := \{i \in I | P(i) = true\}$ [2]. A subgroup $S_P$ is thus defined as the set of all individuals $i \in I$ that satisfy the rule based on the conjunction in $P$, consisting of a set of selectors.

Subgroup Discovery is a technique for descriptive and exploratory data mining. The goal of SD is to identify subsets of a given dataset that display interesting behaviour [2]. The interestingness of behaviour is defined as "distributional unusualness with respect to a certain property of interest" [29]. To what extent behaviour is interesting, is evaluated with respect to certain interestingness criteria, which are formalized by a quality function. Using this quality function, a subgroup discovery algorithm identifies a set of interesting subgroups. In this paper, we employ Weighted Relative Accuracy (WRAcc) [17] as quality function. The WRAcc of a subgroup is defined in the following way [20]:

$$\mathrm{WRAcc}(S_P) = \frac{|S_P|}{|I|} * (p_{S_P}(\text{target} = 1) - p_I(\text{target} = 1))$$

The task of Subgroup Discovery in this paper now becomes equivalent to the formal problem definition in [6, Problem Statement 1], with $\Omega = D$, $\mathcal{D}$ is as described earlier in this section, $\varphi = \text{WRAcc}$, $q = 100$, and $\mathcal{C} = \varnothing$.

## 3.1    Auto-Encoding

An auto-encoder is a three-layered neural network, consisting of an encoding layer, an encoded layer, and a decoding layer. The encoding layer takes an individual $i \in \mathbb{R}^d$ as input and reduces it to an item $h \in \mathbb{R}^{d'}$, where typically $d' \ll d$. This layer is subsequently decoded to produce a reconstructed version $i' \in \mathbb{R}^d$ of the individual. The objective of the auto-encoder is then to minimize the reconstruction error $J(i, i') = \frac{1}{2}\|i - i'\|_2^2$ [27], such that this reconstructed version is as close to the original data entry as possible. Given a dataset $D$, such a network can be trained using backpropagation of the so-called mean squared error, which is the average of this loss over the data in $D$. This training occurs for a certain number of epochs, which are passes through the dataset. To prevent overfitting, the training can stop earlier once the test error has not improved for a certain number of steps. Once the auto-encoder has completed training, its encoded layer can be used as a dimension-reduced version of the input data.

The structure of auto-encoders can vary with regard to the number of hidden layers, size of the hidden layers, and activation function used in its neurons. Deep auto-encoders tend to perform better than shallower ones with only a single hidden layer [11], although this advantage disappears if the number of free parameters becomes too big as a result [11]. The neurons in the layers can have several activation functions. Often the Leaky ReLU [21] activation function is used, due to strong performance and immunity to the dying neuron problem. The Leaky ReLU activation function is given by:

$$f(x) = \begin{cases} \alpha x & \text{if } x < 0 \\ x & \text{if } x \geq 0 \end{cases}$$

Here, $\alpha$ is a typically small coefficient that is chosen by the user.

## 4    Methodology

We propose a method of combining auto-encoding with SD. Our original dataset $D$ may contain attributes of any type: binary, nominal, and numeric. Auto-encoding expects input data that is real-valued, and we bridge that gap by one-hot encoding all non-numeric attributes of the original dataset. This results in a new dataset $D'$ whose individuals take value in $\mathbb{R}^d$, and whose dimensionality is larger than the number of attributes in the original dataset: $d \geq |A|$. Subsequently, an auto-encoder neural network is trained on this dataset $D'$ using backpropagation on the mean squared error. This auto-encoder has $d'$ encoded features, where $d'$ is chosen in such a way that it provides a balance between a small number of features and a high representativeness of the features. Once this auto-encoder is developed, every individual $i \in D'$ is transformed to an item $h \in \mathbb{R}^{d'}$. Using this set of transformed items and associated set of attributes, we can perform SD as described in Sect. 3, directly using this new data in existing SD algorithms.

### 4.1 Experimental Setup

To conduct our analysis on the effect of auto-encoding on the performance of SD, we perform multiple experiments[1]. These experiments are conducted using several SD algorithms with various datasets (see Sect. 4.3). We test the algorithms both with and without auto-encoding and compare the results. The employed SD algorithms are beam search [6], APRIORI-SD [13], Best First Search (BFS) [31], and Depth First Search (DFS) [20]. These are implemented in Python, using the adapted code from [5] for the beam search algorithm and a modified version of the Python package pysubgroup [20] for the other algorithms.

For all datasets, the auto-encoder is implemented using TensorFlow 2.0 [1] in Python. The number of encoded features $d'$ of the auto-encoder is selected individually for each dataset. Here, we choose a number that provides a good balance between the number of features and the error function. The intuition here is similar to that of the elbow rule (or critical point rule) in clustering [26]. The selected values for $d'$ are reported in Table 1.

During the tuning of the number of features, the number of epochs and patience for early stopping are set to 100 and 10, respectively. We set the number of hidden layers before and after the encoded layer to 4 and the number of neurons per layer to 512, 256, 128, and 64 (reversed in the decoder). For the neurons, we use the Leaky ReLU activation function with $\alpha = 0.3$, following the findings of [30].

We evaluate the performance of auto-encoder based SD along three axes. Firstly, to represent subgroup quality, we report the mean and maximum WRAcc for the 100 best-found subgroups. Secondly, to represent dataset coverage, we determine the number of items that are present in at least one subgroup, as well as the number of distinctive items[2] between vanilla and auto-encoder based SD: *added items* are those present in at least one subgroup found through auto-encoder based SD but in none of the subgroups found through vanilla SD, and the reverse are *lost items*. Thirdly, to represent subgroup diversity, we check the distribution of the number of subgroups in which each item is present.

---

[1] cf. Github repository at https://github.com/JFvdH/Efficient-SD-through-AE.

[2] Notice that, for making these distinctive comparisons, we must compare presence or absence of individuals in subgroups in the original data space, with presence or absence of encoded items in subgroups in the encoded space. Naively, this may seem nontrivial, but notice that the number of individuals and the number of items is identical: when encoding, the *representation* of each individual is changed and its number of attributes may change, but each individual has *one unique counterpart item* in the encoded space. This enables identification of added and lost items across the divide between original data space and encoded space.

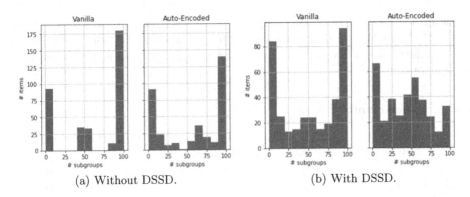

(a) Without DSSD.    (b) With DSSD.

**Fig. 1.** Effect of Diverse Subgroup Set Discovery (DSSD) on distributions of item occurrence in subgroups.

### 4.2 Algorithms and Settings

The SD algorithms that we analyse are beam search [6], APRIORI-SD [13], Best First Search (BFS) [31], and Depth First Search (DFS) [20]. All algorithms are set to find subgroups with a depth of 2, meaning that they have to find subgroups using patterns of at most 2 selectors. All subgroups are parameterized to report the best 100 subgroups found, evaluated by WRAcc. For beam search, additional parameters require configuration: the beam width was set to (a generous) 100, the minimum support for a subgroup to be considered was set to 2% of the dataset, and numeric attributes were treated with the lbca discretization method from [22] with granularity 5.

We adapt the SD algorithms to incorporate the lessons learned from Diverse Subgroup Set Discovery (DSSD) [19]. In beam search, a candidate subgroup is discarded unless its quality differs from the quality of its seed subgroup. For the other algorithms, the same principle is implemented in a slightly different way: a candidate is now discarded if its quality is (approximately) equal to any current candidate's quality and all but 1 selectors are identical. Figure 1 illustrates the effect of this DSSD strategy on the distribution of the number of subgroups encompassing items: variety increases under DSSD.

### 4.3 Data

The six datasets used for this research are extracted from the UCI Machine Learning Repository. Those datasets are selected since they all have different compositions such that a variety of dataset characteristics are tested. An overview of the number of rows, number of attributes, and type of attributes is presented in Table 1.

For the Soybean dataset, all rows with missing data are dropped. This means that $N$ decreases from 307 to 266. In the Arrhythmia dataset, one attribute contained 376 missing values. Instead of removing the majority of our rows, we

**Table 1.** Metadata (before preprocessing) of datasets used for the experiment.

| Dataset | N | #Attributes | | | $d'$ |
|---|---|---|---|---|---|
| | | Discrete | Numerical | Total | |
| Ionosphere | 351 | 0 | 34 | 34 | 5 |
| Soybean(-large) | 307 | 35 | 0 | 35 | 9 |
| Adult | 48842 | 8 | 6 | 14 | 7 |
| Mushroom | 8124 | 22 | 0 | 22 | 5 |
| Arrhythmia | 452 | 73 | 206 | 279 | 8 |
| Indoor | 21048 | 2 | 520 | 522 | 9 |

chose to drop this attribute, resulting in a remaining 205 numerical attributes in this dataset. After this attribute drop, 32 rows contain further missing values. Those rows are dropped resulting in $N = 420$. The datasets Ionosphere, Adult, and Mushroom did not contain any missing values, so $N$ remains 351, 48842, and 8124, respectively. Lastly, in the Indoor dataset, multiple target variables are present. We select BuildingID as the target of our SD run and drop all other target variables. No rows are dropped, so $N$ remains 21048.

WRAcc evaluation requires one target class per dataset to be designated as the positive class. For Ionosphere we select "good", for Mushroom we select poisonous mushrooms, for Adult we select persons making over 50K a year, for Arrhythmia we select having any heart disease, for Soybean we select soybeans having any "spot" classification, and for Indoor dataset we select all objects having BuildingID '2'.

Lastly, to ensure proper training of the auto-encoder, the attributes in the Adult and Arrhythmia datasets are standardized before auto-encoding. These datasets contain attribute values of significantly varying orders of magnitude. If not standardized, training based on the mean square error becomes both very unstable and skewed towards only those attributes with large values. This leads to poor results of the encoder. Hence, all data entries are standardized by subtracting the sample mean and dividing by the sample standard deviation of the specific attribute.

## 5   Results

An overview of the results of the algorithms with and without auto-encoding can be seen in Table 2. All auto-encoders had a small number of encoded features compared to the original numbers of features. With this lower dimensionality, depending on the dataset and algorithm, slightly varying results are obtained.

Firstly, in Table 2a we find that the coverage of the discovered subgroups using beam search is increased for every dataset except for the Mushroom dataset (where it stays approximately the same). This observation will be further discussed in Sect. 6. From the inspection of the added and lost items, we see that,

**Table 2.** Comparative performance of Subgroup Discovery with and without auto-encoding, in terms of runtime, quality, and coverage.

(a)  Beam search, using min_sgsize = 2%, n_chunks = 5, beam_width = 100.

| Dataset | Vanilla | | | Auto-encoded | | | | | Items | |
|---|---|---|---|---|---|---|---|---|---|---|
| | Run time (s) (Algorithm) | WRAcc Max | Mean | Coverage | Run time (s) Tun. | Enc. | Alg. | WRAcc Max | Mean | Coverage |
| Ionosphere | 396 | 0.141 | 0.132 | 0.858 | 50 | 5 | 41 | 0.097 | 0.087 | 0.883 | 33 (0.094) | 24 (0.068) |
| Soybean | 221 | 0.250 | 0.248 | 0.508 | 61 | 4 | 90 | 0.166 | 0.143 | 0.662 | 48 (0.180) | 7 (0.026) |
| Adult | 945 | 0.066 | 0.065 | 0.458 | 4810 | 650 | 180 | 0.064 | 0.062 | 0.565 | 7740 (0.158) | 2528 (0.052) |
| Mushroom | 309 | 0.242 | 0.226 | 0.566 | 1184 | 133 | 46 | 0.163 | 0.153 | 0.553 | 993 (0.122) | 1096 (0.135) |
| Arrhythmia | 7800 | 0.085 | 0.082 | 0.450 | 83 | 6 | 91 | 0.084 | 0.073 | 0.540 | 106 (0.252) | 68 (0.162) |
| Indoor | 47644 | 0.117 | 0.114 | 0.378 | 4980 | 650 | 187 | 0.165 | 0.149 | 0.463 | 2972 (0.141) | 1191 (0.057) |

(b)  Best-first search.

| Dataset | Vanilla | | | Auto-encoded | | | | | Items | |
|---|---|---|---|---|---|---|---|---|---|---|
| | Run time (s) (Algorithm) | WRAcc Max | Mean | Coverage | Run time (s) Tun. | Enc. | Alg. | WRAcc Max | Mean | Coverage | Added | Lost |
| Ionosphere | 0.9 | 0.069 | 0.043 | 0.997 | 50 | 5 | 0.1 | 0.089 | 0.021 | 0.972 | 1 (0.003) | 10 (0.028) |
| Soybean | 0.2 | 0.241 | 0.162 | 0.944 | 61 | 4 | 0.1 | 0.115 | 0.033 | 0.910 | 13 (0.049) | 22 (0.083) |
| Adult | 2.7 | 0.069 | 0.030 | 0.853 | 4810 | 321 | 0.5 | 0.053 | 0.011 | 0.936 | 5463 (0.112) | 1432 (0.029) |
| Mushroom | 0.9 | 0.182 | 0.093 | 1.000 | 1184 | 133 | 0.1 | 0.113 | 0.021 | 0.936 | 0 (0.000) | 522 (0.064) |
| Arrhythmia | 46.9 | 0.066 | 0.058 | 0.705 | 83 | 6 | 0.2 | 0.058 | 0.017 | 0.874 | 91 (0.217) | 20 (0.048) |
| Indoor | 108.7 | 0.107 | 0.106 | 0.400 | 4980 | 650 | 0.4 | 0.109 | 0.032 | 0.900 | 10530 (0.500) | 3 (0.000) |

(c)  Depth-first search.

| Dataset | Vanilla | | | Auto-encoded | | | | | Items | |
|---|---|---|---|---|---|---|---|---|---|---|
| | Run time (s) (Algorithm) | WRAcc Max | Mean | Coverage | Run time (s) Tun. | Enc. | Alg. | WRAcc Max | Mean | Coverage | Added | Lost |
| Ionosphere | 1.0 | 0.069 | 0.043 | 0.989 | 50 | 5 | 0.1 | 0.043 | 0.015 | 0.949 | 15 (0.043) | 1 (0.002) |
| Soybean | 0.3 | 0.241 | 0.162 | 0.944 | 61 | 4 | 0.1 | 0.087 | 0.027 | 0.944 | 15 (0.056) | 15 (0.056) |
| Adult | 5.05 | 0.063 | 0.029 | 0.853 | 4810 | 321 | 0.5 | 0.054 | 0.011 | 0.936 | 5463 (0.112) | 1432 (0.029) |
| Mushroom | 1.4 | 0.182 | 0.120 | 1.000 | 1184 | 133 | 0.1 | 0.120 | 0.022 | 0.936 | 0 (0.000) | 522 (0.064) |
| Arrhythmia | 46.6 | 0.086 | 0.062 | 0.681 | 83 | 6 | 0.2 | 0.083 | 0.022 | 0.855 | 97 (0.231) | 24 (0.057) |
| Indoor | 117.1 | 0.109 | 0.107 | 0.350 | 4980 | 650 | 0.5 | 0.134 | 0.039 | 0.909 | 11752 (0.558) | 0 (0.000) |

(d)  APRIORI-SD.

| Dataset | Vanilla | | | Auto-encoded | | | | | Items | |
|---|---|---|---|---|---|---|---|---|---|---|
| | Run time (s) (Algorithm) | WRAcc Max | Mean | Coverage | Run time (s) Tun. | Enc. | Alg. | WRAcc Max | Mean | Coverage | Added | Lost |
| Ionosphere | 1.1 | 0.074 | 0.046 | 0.997 | 50 | 5 | 0.3 | 0.086 | 0.022 | 0.972 | 1 (0.003) | 10 (0.028) |
| Soybean | 0.2 | 0.241 | 0.162 | 0.944 | 61 | 4 | 0.1 | 0.112 | 0.032 | 0.914 | 13 (0.049) | 21 (0.079) |
| Adult | 2.6 | 0.063 | 0.029 | 0.853 | 4810 | 321 | 0.6 | 0.055 | 0.011 | 0.936 | 5463 (0.112) | 1432 (0.029) |
| Mushroom | 0.4 | 0.182 | 0.093 | 1.000 | 1184 | 133 | 0.1 | 0.106 | 0.021 | 0.936 | 0 (0.000) | 522 (0.064) |
| Arrhythmia | 39.3 | 0.084 | 0.062 | 0.702 | 83 | 6 | 0.8 | 0.078 | 0.022 | 0.855 | 90 (0.214) | 26 (0.061) |
| Indoor | 94.8 | 0.129 | 0.122 | 0.290 | 4980 | 650 | 1.7 | 0.116 | 0.039 | 0.909 | 13016 (0.618) | 0 (0.000) |

besides increasing coverage, beam search with the auto-encoded data covers a different region of the data for most datasets. Some items are newly included in its 100 best subgroups and other items are now excluded. For the Adult dataset, however, very few items are lost while many are added. Thus, here, auto-encoding expands the coverage region.

In Tables 2b, 2c, and 2d, we find consistent effects on the coverage for the other three algorithms. Increased coverage is only achieved for the Adult,

Arrhythmia, and Indoor datasets: the larger ones in terms of items and/or attributes. For the smaller datasets, the vanilla algorithms already achieve such high coverage that auto-encoding can only match the coverage. The coverage of the Adult data (relatively many items) is a few percentage points higher for all three algorithms. Auto-encoding based SD manages to cover 15% points more of the Arrhythmia data (relatively many attributes). Lastly, for the Indoor data (relatively many attributes and items), the coverage is increased by at least 50% points for BFS, DFS, and APRIORI-SD. For these algorithms, the number of items added and lost for the bigger datasets show similarities with the numbers for beam search. Namely, in the Adult and Arrhythmia data, a part of the items is newly included after auto-encoding while another part is excluded. The findings, therefore, cover different regions of the data. For the Indoor data, on the other hand, many items are added to at least one subgroup while few to none are lost for each algorithm. Hence, we find that auto-encoding increases the coverage of all subgroup discovery algorithms significantly for data with a high number of items and/or attributes. It includes different regions of the data or expands the current regions. For smaller datasets, the coverage is approximately equal.

In terms of WRAcc quality of the found subgroups, again, a difference can be seen between the three smaller and three larger datasets. Table 2a displays that the maximum and mean WRAcc after auto-encoding are worse for Ionosphere, Soybean, and Mushroom when performing beam search. Oppositely, the qualities for the bigger Adult and Arrhythmia datasets remained similar after auto-encoding. The subgroups found on the Indoor dataset are substantially better with auto-encoding than without. It is likely that due to the high number of numerical variables, the attributes that are present do not have enough expressive power to form strong groups with a small number of selectors while the encoded attributes do have this expressive power.

For the other algorithms, we find similar results in Tables 2b, 2c, and 2d. An important distinction, however, is that the mean WRAcc scores over the 100 subgroups after auto-encoding are generally lower for all datasets, indicating that the number of high-quality subgroups is lower. From the maxima, though, we can see that the performance with auto-encoding of the three big datasets is good, again. For all three algorithms, the maximum WRAcc scores for the Adult and Arrhythmia data are equivalent with and without auto-encoding. One exception is APRIORI-SD, in which auto-encoding decreases the maximum WRAcc for the Adult data. The maximum WRAcc score for the Indoor dataset is higher with auto-encoding using BFS and DFS and only slightly lower for APRIORI-SD. For the smaller Soybean and Mushroom datasets, again we find that the maximum WRAcc scores decreases with auto-encoding for APRIORI-SD, DFS, and BFS. On the other hand, the subgroups of the Ionosphere dataset, which has a reasonably high number of numerical features, have a higher maximum WRAcc with auto-encoded features for BFS and APRIORI-SD algorithm.

Finally, run times of the algorithms itself on auto-encoded versions of each dataset are improved across all of Table 2. For the Indoor dataset, the time is reduced by a factor of over 250 for multiple algorithms. In Table 2a, we see that the beam search run time for the Arrhythmia data is decreased from more than 2 h to 91 s and for the Indoor dataset it is even decreased from over 13 h to just 3 min. Of course, this neglects tuning and training time of the auto-encoders: for some combinations of dataset and algorithm this time is longer than the gained algorithm run time. For the combination of Arrhythmia and Indoor with beam search, we see that the gained time is bigger than the total model development time.

## 6   Discussion

From the results, we can derive that feature reduction using auto-encoding can help to improve subgroup discovery for datasets with many attributes and/or instances. We found that, depending on the algorithm and dataset, the coverage, quality, and run time can be improved by auto-encoding the data. For smaller datasets with fewer attributes, this improvement is smaller. Here, the coverage is often similar and the run time is shorter, but the quality of the subgroups is generally lower. The method could still be used to explore different regions within the data but, in general, the added value is low.

For the datasets that do benefit from auto-encoding, we saw that for some dataset-algorithm combinations, the model development time is higher than the algorithm run time. However, for the largest two datasets in terms of attributes, we already saw that the model development time is very small compared to the run time of beam search without auto-encoding. This benefit will only become more apparent for larger datasets. On top of that, tuning and training the auto-encoder only has to occur once. Thus, in case multiple algorithms must be run, this can all occur with the same encoded features. Similarly, if one has to investigate a similar dataset with new instances every once in a while (e.g. monthly fraud detection investigation), the auto-encoder does not need to be re-trained and the same model can still be used. Hence, in several scenarios, the model development time is still not a deal-breaker if the initial development time is longer than a one-time run of the model.

Another potential limitation of feature reduction using auto-encoding is the decrease in interpretability. When creating patterns from selectors that include the original attributes of the dataset, all rules can directly be read and interpreted. This allows for clear interpretation of the rules and one can find a logic based on these rules. For encoded features, however, you do not know the meaning of the attributes and therefore the developed rules are hard or impossible to interpret. While this inevitable loss of interpretability will always be present, this does not mean that the subgroups become unusable. In some scenarios, like fraud detection, people will mainly be interested in the instances that are in a subgroup. Then, the interpretation of the rules is less relevant. Besides, if you would want to find an intuition behind the subgroups, you can still trace back the instances in the subgroups and inspect their attribute values compared to the general dataset. For example, Fig. 2 displays that the best subgroup found in the Adult dataset has different proportions of education categories compared to the

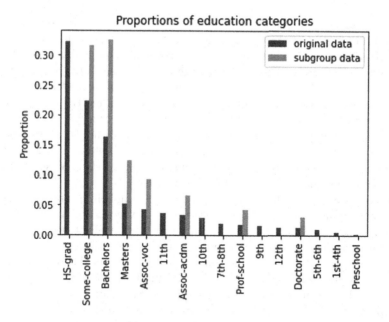

**Fig. 2.** Adult education category histogram for top subgroup and full dataset.

original dataset. From this, we can clearly see that the subgroup only contains persons with higher education levels. This, intuitively, makes sense when looking for people with a high income. Hence, we conclude that dimensionality reduction in subgroup discovery could still prove to be useful for interpretation. In fact, this expands the subgroup language expressibility: without auto-encoding, a subgroup defined on education level will take the form of an equality constraint to a single value or a set of values; with auto-encoding, a subgroup can be expressed by the skewed orange histogram of education level values.

## 7  Conclusions

Dimensionality reduction through auto-encoding can improve subgroup discovery (SD) for large datasets. Multiple SD algorithms find subgroups with higher or equivalent quality and better coverage for datasets with a high number of attributes and/or instances when auto-encoding is performed beforehand. On Indoor, the dataset with the largest number of attributes within our experiments, pre-processing through auto-encoding doubles the coverage reached by the BFS, DFS, and APRIORI-SD algorithms (cf. Table 2). With auto-encoding, the beam search algorithm finds subgroups with improved WRAcc quality.

In addition to improved coverage and subgroup quality, the run times of the algorithms are improved greatly. Across Table 2, run times of the algorithms decreased substantially for each algorithm-dataset combination. For datasets with many attributes, we found a decrease in run time of a factor of more than

100. This can have a great impact when handling real-life datasets. For beam search on the Indoor dataset, which has 21 048 instances, the run time decreased from over 13 h to just 3 min while improving coverage and quality. In practice, the number of instances can become even larger leading to an even bigger difference in run times. To achieve this improved run time, the auto-encoder first has to be trained which also takes time. For larger datasets, we found that the decrease in algorithm run time outweighs the model development time.

The increased performance of auto-encoded subgroup discovery comes at the cost of a decrease in interpretability. As the example of Fig. 2 illustrates, intuition can still be derived from the items that are within the subgroup, and the subgroup language becomes more expressive.

In short, we can conclude that using auto-encoding before subgroup discovery is a promising method that can increase the quality, coverage, and run times for subgroup discovery when datasets are large with many attributes.

Future research naturally emerges along two competing axes. On the one hand, we would want to investigate whether we can recover the lost interpretability of subgroups while achieving similar results, by employing interpretability-preserving dimensionality reduction techniques. Straightforward candidates are Principal Component Analysis with constraints on homogeneity and sparsity [4], and the Interpretable Kernel DR algorithm [12]. On the other hand, we would want to investigate whether the lost interpretability allows for better predictive performance, in a LeGo setting [15]: exploiting found subgroups as extra features for multi-label classifiers [7] and as dummy variables in regression models [6, Sect. 8.1] has proven to work; we would want to investigate whether they could be enhanced through auto-encoding.

**Acknowledgments.** This work is part of the research program Data2People with project EDIC and partly financed by the Dutch Research Council (NWO).

# References

1. Abadi, M., Agarwal, A., Barham, P., et al.: TensorFlow: large-scale machine learning on heterogeneous systems (2015). https://www.tensorflow.org/
2. Atzmueller, M.: Subgroup discovery. Wiley Interdisc. Rev. Data Min. Knowl. Discov. **5**(1), 35–49 (2015)
3. Carmona, C.J., González, P., del Jesus, M.J., Herrera, F.: NMEEF-SD: non-dominated multiobjective evolutionary algorithm for extracting fuzzy rules in subgroup discovery. IEEE Trans. Fuzzy Syst. **18**(5), 958–970 (2010)
4. Chipman, H.A., Gu, H.: Interpretable dimension reduction. J. Appl. Stat. **32**(9), 969–987 (2005)
5. Duivesteijn, W., van Dijk, T.C.: Exceptional gestalt mining: combining magic cards to make complex coalitions thrive. In: Proceedings of MLSA (2021)
6. Duivesteijn, W., Feelders, A.J., Knobbe, A.: Exceptional model mining. Data Min. Knowl. Disc. **30**(1), 47–98 (2015). https://doi.org/10.1007/s10618-015-0403-4
7. Duivesteijn, W., Loza Mencía, E., Fürnkranz, J., Knobbe, A.: Multi-label LeGo—enhancing multi-label classifiers with local patterns. In: Hollmén, J., Klawonn, F., Tucker, A. (eds.) IDA 2012. LNCS, vol. 7619, pp. 114–125. Springer, Heidelberg (2012). https://doi.org/10.1007/978-3-642-34156-4_12

8. Gamberger, D., Lavrač, N.: Expert-guided subgroup discovery: methodology and application. J. Artif. Intell. Res. **17**, 501–527 (2002)
9. Grosskreutz, H., Rüping, S.: On subgroup discovery in numerical domains. Data Min. Knowl. Disc. **19**(2), 210–226 (2009)
10. Herrera, F., Carmona, C.J., González, P., del Jesus, M.J.: An overview on subgroup discovery: foundations and applications. Knowl. Inf. Syst. **29**(3), 495–525 (2011)
11. Hinton, G.E., Salakhutdinov, R.R.: Reducing the dimensionality of data with neural networks. Science **313**(5786), 504–507 (2006)
12. Hosseini, B., Hammer, B.: Interpretable discriminative dimensionality reduction and feature selection on the manifold. In: Brefeld, U., Fromont, E., Hotho, A., Knobbe, A., Maathuis, M., Robardet, C. (eds.) ECML PKDD 2019. LNCS (LNAI), vol. 11906, pp. 310–326. Springer, Cham (2020). https://doi.org/10.1007/978-3-030-46150-8_19
13. Kavšek, B., Lavrač, N.: APRIORI-SD: adapting association rule learning to subgroup discovery. Appl. Artif. Intell. **20**(7), 543–583 (2006)
14. Klösgen, W.: EXPLORA: a multipattern and multistrategy discovery assistant. In: Advances in Knowledge Discovery and Data Mining, pp. 249–271 (1996)
15. Knobbe, A., Crémilleux, B., Fürnkranz, J., Scholz, M.: From local patterns to global models: the LeGo approach to data mining. In: Proceedings of LeGo workshop @ ECMLPKDD, pp. 1–16 (2008)
16. Konijn, R.M., Duivesteijn, W., Kowalczyk, W., Knobbe, A.: Discovering local subgroups, with an application to fraud detection. In: Pei, J., Tseng, V.S., Cao, L., Motoda, H., Xu, G. (eds.) PAKDD 2013. LNCS (LNAI), vol. 7818, pp. 1–12. Springer, Heidelberg (2013). https://doi.org/10.1007/978-3-642-37453-1_1
17. Lavrač, N., Flach, P., Zupan, B.: Rule evaluation measures: a unifying view. In: Džeroski, S., Flach, P. (eds.) ILP 1999. LNCS (LNAI), vol. 1634, pp. 174–185. Springer, Heidelberg (1999). https://doi.org/10.1007/3-540-48751-4_17
18. Lavrač, N., Kavšek, B., Flach, P., Todorovski, L.: Subgroup discovery with CN2-SD. J. Mach. Learn. Res. **5**(2), 153–188 (2004)
19. van Leeuwen, M., Knobbe, A.: Diverse subgroup set discovery. Data Min. Knowl. Discov. **25**, 208–242 (2012)
20. Lemmerich, F., Becker, M.: pysubgroup: easy-to-use subgroup discovery in Python. In: Brefeld, U., et al. (eds.) ECML PKDD 2018. LNCS (LNAI), vol. 11053, pp. 658–662. Springer, Cham (2019). https://doi.org/10.1007/978-3-030-10997-4_46
21. Maas, A.L., Hannun, A.Y., Ng, A.Y.: Rectifier nonlinearities improve neural network acoustic models. In: Proceedings of ICML Workshop on Deep Learning for Audio, Speech and Language Processing (2013)
22. Meeng, M., Knobbe, A.: For real: a thorough look at numeric attributes in subgroup discovery. Data Min. Knowl. Disc. **35**(1), 158–212 (2020). https://doi.org/10.1007/s10618-020-00703-x
23. Proença, H.M., Klijn, R., Bäck, T., van Leeuwen, M.: Identifying flight delay patterns using diverse subgroup discovery. In: Proceedings of SSCI, pp. 60–67 (2018)
24. Riffenburgh, R.H.: Linear discriminant analysis. Ph.D. thesis, Virginia Polytechnic Institute (1957)
25. Tenenbaum, J.B., de Silva, V., Langford, J.C.: A global geometric framework for nonlinear dimensionality reduction. Science **290**(5500), 2319–2323 (2000)
26. Thorndike, R.L.: Who belongs in the family? Psychometrika **18**(4), 267–276 (1953)
27. Wang, Y., Yao, H., Zhao, S.: Auto-encoder based dimensionality reduction. Neurocomputing **184**, 232–242 (2016)
28. Wold, S., Esbensen, K., Geladi, P.: Principal component analysis. Chemom. Intell. Lab. Syst. **2**(1–3), 37–52 (1987)

29. Wrobel, S.: An algorithm for multi-relational discovery of subgroups. In: Komorowski, J., Zytkow, J. (eds.) PKDD 1997. LNCS, vol. 1263, pp. 78–87. Springer, Heidelberg (1997). https://doi.org/10.1007/3-540-63223-9_108
30. Xu, B., Wang, N., Chen, T., Li, M.: Empirical evaluation of rectified activations in convolutional network. arXiv preprint arXiv:1505.00853 (2015)
31. Zimmermann, A., De Raedt, L.: Cluster-grouping: from subgroup discovery to clustering. Mach. Learn. 77(1), 125–159 (2009)

# Simulation of Scientific Experiments with Generative Models

Stepan Veretennikov[1], Koen Minartz[1], Vlado Menkovski[1(✉)] ⓘ,
Burcu Gumuscu[2] ⓘ, and Jan de Boer[2] ⓘ

[1] Department of Mathematics and Computer Science,
Eindhoven University of Technology, Eindhoven, The Netherlands
{k.minartz,v.menkovski}@tue.nl
[2] Department of Biomedical Engineering, Eindhoven University of Technology,
Eindhoven, The Netherlands
{b.gumuscu,j.d.boer}@tue.nl

**Abstract.** Lab experiments are a crucial part of research in natural sciences. High-throughput screening is leveraged to generate hypotheses, by evaluating a wide range of experimental parameter values and accumulating a wealth of data on the corresponding experimental outcomes. The data is subsequently analyzed to design new rounds of experiments. While discriminative models have previously proven useful for screening data analytics, they do not account for randomness inherent to lab experiments, and do not have the capacity to capture the potentially high-dimensional relationship between the experiment input parameters and outcomes. Instead, we take a data-driven simulation perspective on the problem. Inspired by biomaterials research experiments, we consider a case where both the input parameter space and the outcome space have a high-dimensional (image) representation. We propose a deep generative model that serves simultaneously as a simulation model of the experiment, i.e. allows to generate potential outcomes conditioned on the experiment input, and as a tool for inverse design, i.e. generating instances of inputs that could lead to a given experiment outcome. A proof-of-concept evaluation on a synthetic dataset shows that the model is able to learn the embedded relationship between the properties of the input and of the output in a probabilistic manner and allows for experiment simulation and design application scenarios.

**Keywords:** Generative models · Disentangled latent space · Simulation of experiments · Biomaterials engineering

## 1 Introduction

High-throughput screening (HTS) is a technology for automated experiments that has gained traction in various disciplines, for example drug discovery [10] and biomaterial design [6,13]. HTS accelerates scientific discovery and the design process by evaluating a vast set of inputs in parallel. In other words, a high-throughput screening takes samples $p_i$ from the space $P$ of input parameters

© The Author(s), under exclusive license to Springer Nature Switzerland AG 2022
T. Bouadi et al. (Eds.): IDA 2022, LNCS 13205, pp. 341–353, 2022.
https://doi.org/10.1007/978-3-031-01333-1_27

of the experiment in bulk and produces a collection of observations of the bio-chemical outcome $x_i$ from the experiment outcome space $X$. Nevertheless, HTS is limited by the time required to conduct the experiments and by the capacity of the lab in terms of the number of inputs that can be evaluated. One way to address this problem is to develop a model of the relationship between spaces $P$ and $X$. However, since both spaces may be high-dimensional, the task is typically simplified to a classification [1,11,13,14] or regression [6] problem, where a few outcome features of interest $f_i^x$ are predicted based on numerical properties of the input $p = (p_1, p_2, \ldots, p_n)$. As an example, in biomaterials research, this approach has been used to show that the rate of macrophage attachment correlates with the size of texture patterns on the surface [15]. To optimize $f_i^x$ in the next experiment, some properties $p_j$ are adjusted in a way that enhances the desired outcome features according to the model, e.g., by designing textures with larger or smaller patterns in the biomaterials example.

The implications of this approach are that, firstly, such models are point estimate models, that is, they predict a single (expected) value of the outcome feature $f_i^x$ and do not account for randomness inherent to many types of experiments in natural sciences. Secondly, machine learning is used as a tool to learn correlations between engineered features, and the underlying high-dimensional relationship might not be fully captured. Thirdly, the outcome $x$ is predicted in parts ($f_i^x$) by several independent models, which limits the capacity of *inverse design*, where the objective is to find parameters $p \in P$ that are likely to lead to a desired outcome.

**Fig. 1.** Experiment simulation model (left); Inverse design model (right).

To address the outlined limitations of the plain modeling approach to screening data analysis, in this paper we consider the concept of a data-driven *simulation* model of a HTS experiment. Such a model aims to mimic the mapping $P \to X$ based on the available screening data by generating possible outcomes $x \in X$ in response to an input $p \in P$. We further consider the design task as inverse to experiment simulation, which is reflected by the mapping $X \to P$: given an outcome $x \in X$, possibly with desired properties, the task is to generate inputs $p \in P$ that could lead to that outcome. An illustration is provided in Fig. 1.

We argue that an experiment simulation model could be useful for various research fields, since, firstly, it would allow to observe a full outcome $x$ as an output of the model instead of observing a number of predictions for distinct features $f_i^x$. Secondly, whereas only a fraction of the input parameter space $P$ can be covered by lab experiments in reasonable time, a simulation model, once trained, can be queried many times to evaluate an arbitrary number of unseen inputs, hence serving as an augmentation to the HTS framework. Furthermore, such a model accounts for uncertainty of the underlying relationship, i.e. when an input sample can lead to a variety of outcomes, and an observed outcome could originate from a variety of inputs. We further argue that *deep generative models* are a particularly promising tool to develop such simulation models. Firstly, deep generative models are known to be suitable for tasks on high-dimensional datasets. Secondly, generative models allow to incorporate uncertainty with probability distributions: an input $p$ leads to a probability distribution of outcomes $x$, and an outcome originates from a probability distribution of inputs.

To investigate the applicability of generative models to simulation of lab experiments, we consider a specific problem in biomaterials engineering (Sect. 3.1), where HTS is used to study the impact of a material's surface topography on living cell behavior at scale. In this application, both the topography design space $(P)$ and the cell response space $(X)$ have image representation. We propose a deep generative model that is aimed to simultaneously serve as a simulation model of the cell-surface topography experiment, and as a tool for cell response-conditioned topography design. The proposed model is built upon a Variational Autoencoder (VAE) [8] architecture and builds on DIVA [7] to derive a disentangled latent space, which offers control over individual generative factors of the cell response. This control is particularly useful for the design task. The key idea is to model the relationship $P \leftrightarrow X$ in the latent spaces $L_P \leftrightarrow Z_X$ instead of the original spaces, which we implement with shared latent subspaces. The latent subspaces of the cell model, corresponding to independent cell features, are assumed to also be part of the latent space in the topography model, where they represent the factors of variation in topographies that influence the respective cell features. As a result, the model allows for cross-conditional generation: cell images given a topography image and topography images given a cell image or a cell feature value. To summarize, the contributions of the present work are as follows:

- We introduce a generative modeling perspective on the problem of lab experiments simulation, addressing the outlined challenges of 1. high dimensionality of the input and output data spaces and 2. high uncertainty of the underlying relationship, intrinsic to such experiments.
- Inspired by the use-case of biomaterials research, we propose a deep generative simulation model with a disentangled latent space for the case where both the input and output spaces are represented by images, and the outcome features of interest are measurable, independent and reflect visual attributes. The proposed model constitutes a two-sided VAE that connects two different datasets using a shared latent space.

– We provide a proof-of-concept evaluation for the proposed architecture on a synthetic dataset with an embedded relationship. The obtained model disentangles the outcome features of interest and is able to unravel the relationship between topographies and cells.

## 2    Related work

The two most prevalent approaches in deep generative models are VAEs [8] and Generative Adversarial Networks (GANs) [4]; a VAE simultaneously learns a deep latent variable model and an inference model by optimizing a lower bound (ELBO) on the log-likelihood of the observed data, while a GAN consists of a generator $G$ that tries to mislead a discriminator $D$ into classifying a generated sample $x \sim p_G(x)$ as a sample from the real dataset $x \sim D$ and vice versa. Deep generative models have become a popular tool for learning disentangled representations [3]; in particular, the DIVA approach [7] extends the vanilla VAE and disentangles the latent space by partitioning it into independent subspaces. Due to their flexibility, generative models have started to gain traction in scientific experiment and design applications. Examples of successful applications can be found, amongst others, in the domains of molecular science [12] and material microstructure design [16]. Although these works demonstrate the potential of generative models in scientific applications, they generally consider only data from a single domain and try to simulate experiments conditioned on low-dimensional features (e.g. incident particle energy), or generate designs with favourable low-dimensional properties (e.g. stiffness). In contrast, we consider the case where both $P$ and $X$ are high-dimensional, e.g. represented by images, and are related via a non-deterministic relationship. Moreover, rather than searching through the latent space, we explicitly accommodate generating $p \in P$ conditioned on a user-specified $x \in X$.

## 3    Proposed Approach

### 3.1    Use Case: Biomaterials Research

Biomaterials are artificially designed materials that are able to interact with living tissue to fulfill a desired function. Biomaterials are used in various applications as part of medical devices, e.g. in production of stents, sutures, hip implants and artificial heart valves [13]. To design such materials, the field of biomaterials engineering studies cell behavior in response to different materials. Several studies have shown that the topography of the material's surface impacts different aspects of cell phenotype, such as cell morphology [1,2,5,6,13], expression of biomarkers [5,11,13,14], cell proliferation [2,11,13,15] and metabolic activity [1,2]. The task is therefore to find the optimal surface topography with respect to the desired cell response for a particular application. To study the cell-surface topography interaction at scale, HTS is used, in which living cells are exposed to a large collection of algorithmically generated surface topographies produced on a chip [13], after which they are stained with fluorescent dyes and captured in images. The resulting screening data is a collection of observations, where a surface topography, represented by an image (or alternatively, using a numerical parameterization) is paired with the resulting cell response, represented by cell images and by numerical cell features.

## 3.2 Model Concept

In the scope of this work we assume that topographies $p$ may influence cell images $x$ through visually discernible, measurable and independent cell features $f_i$. Accordingly, a cell image can be described by a combination of these properties and residual variation $\varepsilon$, which is not influenced by topographies. We aim to derive a fully factorized latent space $Z_X = Z_{f_1} \times Z_{f_2} \times \ldots \times Z_{f_n} \times Z_\varepsilon$, where $n$ is the number of cell features, such that each latent subspace $Z_{f_i}$ encodes the variation in $X$ explained only by the feature $f_i$. The subspace $Z_\varepsilon$ captures the residual variation in $X$ that is not explained by the features $f_i$. Subsequently, we reuse the latent subspaces $Z_{f_1}, \ldots, Z_{f_n}$ in the latent space $L_P$ of $P$. Each subspace $Z_{f_i}$, being considered as part of $L_P$, represents the influence of topographies on a cell feature $f$. Furthermore, an additional residual subspace $L_\varepsilon$ is introduced to capture the variation in $P$ that is not related to any influence on $X$.

## 3.3 Implementation

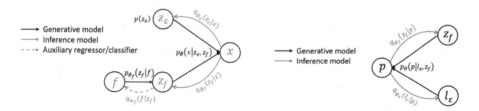

**Fig. 2.** Graphical model for $X$ (cell model).    **Fig. 3.** Graphical model for $P$ (topography model).

The cell model (Fig. 2) is a VAE [8] with a factorized latent space with one or multiple latent variables $z_f$ and a single latent variable $z_\varepsilon$. All latent variables have distinct encoders $q_{\phi_f}(z_f|x)$, $q_{\phi_\varepsilon}(z_\varepsilon|x)$ with unshared parameters, as suggested by [7]. The latent variable $z_f$ has a conditional prior distribution $p_{\theta_f}(z_f|f)$, while $z_\varepsilon$ has an standard normal prior $p(z_\varepsilon)$. A single decoder $p_\theta(x|z_\varepsilon, z_f)$ is used to generate cell images. To achieve a disentangled latent space, an approach similar to DIVA [7] is used: auxiliary regressors $q_{w_f}(f|z_f)$ are included in the training process, which aim to predict the values of the corresponding features $f$ based on latent representations $z_f$ of cell images $x$. We further introduce an auxiliary parameterized normal prior $p_{\theta_{pr}}(z_f)$ (Eq. 1), referred to as the *full prior*, for conditional prior distributions $p_{\theta_f}(z_f|f)$. The full prior has a zero mean, while the parameters representing the variance by dimensions are made trainable with the condition that their sum equals one. The purpose of the full prior is to 1. impose a normal distribution on the marginal distribution $p_{\theta_f}(z_f)$, the shape of which is otherwise uncontrolled, and to 2. approximate the marginal distribution by learning the variance parameters instead of calculating it directly (Eq. 1–2); the full prior with learned variance parameters $p_{\theta_{pr}^*}(z_f)$ is later used as a substitute for the marginal distribution $p_{\theta_f}(z_f)$ in the topography model (Fig. 3).

The topography model is also a VAE with a factorized latent space, which comprises the latent variables $z_f$ from the cell model, as well as an additional latent variable $l_\varepsilon$ for the variation in topographies that is uninformative for cell response prediction. Similarly to the cell model, the topography model has a single decoder $p_\vartheta(p|l_\varepsilon, z_f)$, and its latent variables $z_f$, $l_\varepsilon$ have distinct encoders $q_{\varphi_f}(z_f|p)$, $q_{\varphi_\varepsilon}(l_\varepsilon|p)$ with unshared parameters. The latent variable $l_\varepsilon$ has a standard normal prior $p(l_\varepsilon)$, while for the latent variable $z_f$ the full prior distribution from the cell model $p_{\theta_{pr}^*}(z_f)$ is taken as a prior distribution (Eq. 3). The variance parameters of the full prior are learned during training of the cell model and are fixed in the topography model (denoted by $*$), as will be explained further. The combined model is illustrated in Fig. 4.

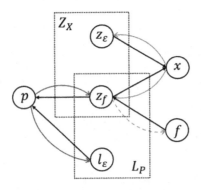

$$p_{\theta_{pr}}(z_f) = N(0, diag(\sigma^2_{\theta_{pr}})),$$
$$\text{such that} \sum_i (\sigma_{\theta_{pr}})_i^2 = 1 \quad (1)$$

$$p_{\theta_f}(z_f) = \int p_{\theta_f}(z_f|f)p(f)df \quad (2)$$

$$p_{top}(z_f) \equiv p_{\theta_{pr}^*}(z_f) \approx p_{\theta_f}(z_f) \quad (3)$$

**Fig. 4.** Combined model with a shared latent variable $z_f$.

Notably, independently training VAE-like objectives for both components would result in two independent models with unrelated latent variables $z_f$, since initially there is no component that binds topographies and cells from the training pairs $(p^i, x^i)$ in the combined architecture. The challenge is therefore to enforce a shared latent subspace, i.e. to ensure that $z_f$ is the *same* latent space in both the cell model and topography models. To address this issue, we propose two likelihood-based auxiliary training objectives, the goal of which is to establish the connection between the datasets through the latent space using the training data. The first (first term in Eq. 5) aims to maximize the likelihood of cell images given a topography image while the second (second term in Eq. 6) aims to maximize the likelihood of topography images given cell images. Furthermore, to train the combined model, a three-step training procedure is proposed. Each of these steps consists of optimizing an objective function until convergence of the validation loss, after which the next step commences.

1. All the components of the cell model are trained in the first step. It is done by maximizing objective $F_1(x, f)$ (Eq. 4) with respect to all involved parameters. The hyperparameters include $\beta_\varepsilon, \beta_f, \beta_{pr}, \alpha_f$. Subsequently, the weights of all the components of the cell model are fixed (denoted by $*$). This step ensures the cell model's ability to (re)construct cell images, possibly conditioned on $f$.

$$
\begin{aligned}
F_1(x, f) = \; & \mathbb{E}_{q_{\phi_\varepsilon}(z_\varepsilon|x)q_{\phi_f}(z_f|x)} \log p_\theta(x|z_\varepsilon, z_f) \\
& - \beta_\varepsilon \, KL\left(q_{\phi_\varepsilon}(z_\varepsilon|x) \,||\, p(z_\varepsilon)\right) \\
& - \beta_f \, KL\left(q_{\phi_f}(z_f|x) \,||\, p_{\theta_f}(z_f|f)\right) \\
& - \beta_{pr} \, KL\left(p_{\theta_f}(z_f|f) \,||\, p_{\theta_{pr}}(z_f)\right) \\
& + \alpha_f \, \mathbb{E}_{q_{\phi_f}(z_f|x)} \log q_{\omega_f}(f|z_f)
\end{aligned}
\tag{4}
$$

2. In the second step, the topography-model encoder(s) $q_{\varphi_f}(z_f|p)$ corresponding to the shared variable $z_f$ is trained by maximizing objective $F_2(x, p)$ (Eq. 5) with respect to parameters $\varphi_f$. Notably, $z_\varepsilon$ is sampled from the posterior $q_{\phi_\varepsilon^*}(z_\varepsilon|x)$. The only hyperparameter in this step is $\beta_{pf}$. Once trained, the weights of the encoder are fixed: $q_{\varphi_f^*}(z_f|p)$. In this step, the simulation functionality of the combined architecture is optimized, i.e. the model learns to encode a given topography such that the already trained cell-model decoder can generate cell images that could have resulted from this topography.

$$
\begin{aligned}
F_2(x, p) = \; & \mathbb{E}_{q_{\phi_\varepsilon^*}(z_\varepsilon|x)q_{\varphi_f}(z_f|p)} \log p_{\theta^*}(x|z_\varepsilon, z_f) \\
& - \beta_{pf} \, KL\left(q_{\varphi_f}(z_f|p) \,||\, p_{\theta_{pr}^*}(z_f)\right)
\end{aligned}
\tag{5}
$$

3. Finally, the remaining components of the topography model, i.e. $q_{\varphi_l}(l_\varepsilon|p)$, $p_\vartheta(p|l_\varepsilon, z_f)$, are trained by maximizing objective $F_3(x, p)$ (Eq. 6) with respect to parameters $\varphi_l, \vartheta$. Intuitively, the final step targets the ability of the model to design new topographies, which includes both reconstruction of a given topography, as well as design of topographies that could result in a given cell image. The hyperparameters include $\eta$, $\beta_l$, where $\eta$ controls the balance between reconstruction error and quality of cell response-conditioned topography design.

$$
\begin{aligned}
F_3(x, p) = \; & \mathbb{E}_{q_{\varphi_l}(l_\varepsilon|p)q_{\varphi_f^*}(z_f|p)} \log p_\vartheta(p|l_\varepsilon, z_f) \\
& + \eta \, \mathbb{E}_{p(l_\varepsilon)q_{\phi_f^*}(z_f|x)} \log p_\vartheta(p|l_\varepsilon, z_f) \\
& - \beta_l \, KL\left(q_{\varphi_l}(l_\varepsilon|p) \,||\, p(l_\varepsilon)\right)
\end{aligned}
\tag{6}
$$

## Application Scenarios

1. Experiment simulation. To generate cell images $x$ for a given topography $p$, the topography is processed with the topography-model encoder $q_{\varphi_f^*}(z_f|p)$, after which samples $z_f \sim q_{\varphi_f^*}(z_f|p)$ and $z_\varepsilon \sim p(z_\varepsilon)$ are passed to the cell-model decoder $p_{\theta^*}(x|z_\varepsilon, z_f)$.
2. Topography design. To generate topography images $p$ for a given cell image $x$, the model is queried in the opposite direction. A given $x$ is mapped to a posterior distribution $q_{\phi_f^*}(z_f|x)$, after which samples $z_f$ from the posterior and $l_\varepsilon$ from $p(l_\varepsilon)$ are passed to the topography-model decoder $p_{\vartheta^*}(p|l_\varepsilon, z_f)$.
3. Topography design based on $f$. The model can also take a value of the cell feature $f$ as an input. In this case, samples $z_f \sim p_{\theta_f^*}(z_f|f)$ from the conditional prior are used by the decoder to generate topographies.

## 4   Evaluation

### 4.1   Dataset

We created a synthetic dataset that comprises 50,000 synthetic images of cells and 50,000 synthetic images of topographies, all 128 by 128 pixels.[1] A cell image is defined by four features: roundness ($f_1$), elongation ($f_2$), nucleus size ($f_3$) and rotation angle ($f_4$); $f_1, f_2, f_3$ are chosen to be the cell features of interest, while $f_4$ is assumed to be an irrelevant noise feature. A topography image contains nine identical shapes in a grid and is defined by two features: roundness ($g_1$) and radius ($g_2$). At creation all features were randomly generated.

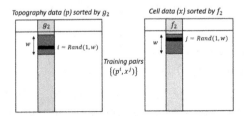

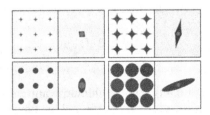

**Fig. 5.** Creating artificial training pairs $\{p^i, x^i\}$.

**Fig. 6.** Artificial relationship: examples of training pairs.

To verify the proposed approach it is necessary to establish some relationship between topography images and cell images and subsequently unravel this relationship using the model. Consequently, it is assumed that the radius of a topography ($g_2$) positively influences the elongation of a cell ($f_2$). In order to

---

[1] The source code and the data are available at https://github.com/stepanveret/biomatsim.

create artificial training pairs (topography image, cell image) with positive relationship between $g_2$ and $f_2$, the topography data table is firstly sorted by $g_2$ and the cell data table is sorted by $f_2$, both in ascending order. Secondly, a sliding window having width[2] $w = 1000$ is propagated through both tables in parallel. At each position, a single row index inside the sliding window is taken at random independently for each of the tables, and the two selected rows form a training pair. An illustration of this procedure is provided in Fig. 5. Examples of training image pairs are shown in Fig. 6.

## 4.2   Results

**Disentangled Latent Representation of Synthetic Cell Images.** After the first step of the training procedure, a qualitative latent space traversal approach is used to evaluate the disentanglement in the latent space (Fig. 7, top). Each feature $f$ is varied, and for each value a sample $z_f \sim p_{\theta_f}(z_f|f)$ is passed to the decoder to generate a cell image, while the other $z_f$ samples are fixed. The leftmost images correspond to zero values of $f_i$. It can be seen that elongation $f_2$ and nucleus size $f_3$ are well captured and disentangled by the model in the $z_f$ subspaces, since only the respective properties of the cell image change. Whereas the space $z_{f_1}$, corresponding to roundness, is moderately correlated with elongation, i.e. not fully disentangled. Further, we qualitatively established that $z_\varepsilon$ encoded the residual variation in cell images (rotation angle $f_4$): we randomly sampled $z_\varepsilon \sim p(z_\varepsilon)$ with all $z_f$ fixed at the means of the posterior distributions $q_{\phi_f}(z_f|x)$ of a given cell image $x$ (Fig. 7, bottom).

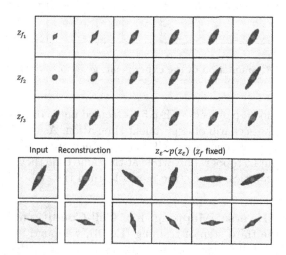

**Fig. 7.** Latent space traversal: $z_{f_1}, z_{f_2}, z_{f_3}$ (top); $z_\varepsilon$ (bottom).

---

[2] The width $w$ of the sliding window regulates the variance of the dependency.

**Modeling the Influence of Topographies on Cells for Experiment Simulation.** In the second step of training (Eq. 5) the goal is to model the possible influence of topographies on cells by training the topography-model encoders for each $z_f$ subspace. The hyperparameters $\beta_{pf,i}$ ($i = 1, 2, 3$) control the penalty on the posteriors $q_{\varphi_f}(z_f|p)$ for diverging from the full prior distributions $p_{\theta_{pr}^*}(z_f)$, learned in the previous step. We searched over several values of $\beta_{pf}$ (identical values for all $f$) in the range between $(100, 1000)$ and trained the second-step objective (Eq. 5) for 5–10 epochs; we observed that the value of $KL_2{}^3$ is significantly larger than $KL_1$, $KL_3$ for all tested values of $\beta_{pf}$. Arguably, this was to be expected, since $z_{f_2}$ corresponds to cell elongation, which is the only feature correlated to the topography design parameters in the data: for $i \neq 2$, there is no utility for posteriors $q_{\varphi_{f_i}}(z_{f_i}|p)$ to deviate from the priors $p_{\theta_{pr,i}^*}(z_{f_i})$, since this yields no reduction in the cell image reconstruction loss. By contrast, using a control-case dataset, in which topography and cell images are paired randomly, we observe that $KL_i$ values are all close to zero, which implies the model learns no relationship, as expected.

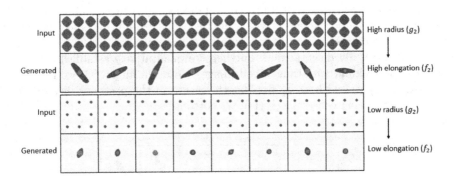

**Fig. 8.** Simulation of the experiment: given $p$, generate $x$.

Once the second-step objective (Eq. 5) is trained until convergence, the model can be tested in the scenario of experiment simulation. As can be seen in Fig. 8, the model is capable of generating cell images, which are elongated according to the radius of the input topography, while at the same time they are diverse in the remaining cell properties. Hence, the model learned the embedded relationship.

**Modeling the Inverse Mapping for Cell-Conditioned Topography Design.** After the third step of training (Eq. 6), we found that, although the architecture successfully generated topographies with radii that were expected based on the input cell's elongation, the diversity of the generated designs was limited. To mitigate this issue, we extend our main approach with the idea of [9],

---

³ $KL_i$ stands for the average $KL\left(q_{\varphi_{f_i}}(z_{f_i}|p) \,\|\, p_{\theta_{pr,i}^*}(z_{f_i})\right)$.

where a VAE architecture is enriched with a discriminator model. The discriminator outputs $D(p)$, the estimated probability that a given topography $p$ originates from the dataset $P$, and is trained to maximize Eq. 7. At the same time, the base model, with all components frozen except for the decoder $p_\vartheta(p|l_\varepsilon, z_f)$, is treated as a generator. Apart from the main objective, it aims to mislead the discriminator and to generate topography samples that resemble true topographies; the maximization objective (Eq. 6) is extended in Eq. 8.

$$F_D(x,p) = \mathbb{E}_{p \sim P} \, log \, D(p) \; - \; \mathbb{E}_{p_G \sim p(l_\varepsilon)q_{\phi_f^*}(z_f|x)p_\vartheta(p|l_\varepsilon,z_f)} \, log \left(1 - D(p_G)\right) \quad (7)$$

$$F_{VAE/GAN}(x,p) = F_3(x,p) \; + \; \xi \, \mathbb{E}_{p_G \sim p(l_\varepsilon)q_{\phi_f^*}(z_f|x)p_\vartheta(p|l_\varepsilon,z_f)} \, log \, D(p_G) \quad (8)$$

As a result, the model learned to generate diverse topography images in the task of cell-conditioned topography design with the radius feature $g_2$ corresponding to elongation $f_2$ of a given cell, as shown in Fig. 9. Finally, the model is tested in the third application scenario: topography design based on a cell feature value $f$. Figure 9 shows different generated topographies for a series of increasing values of cell elongation $f_2$, taken as input to the model. It can be seen that the radius $g_2$ of the generated topographies increases, while the residual feature, roundness $g_1$, varies.

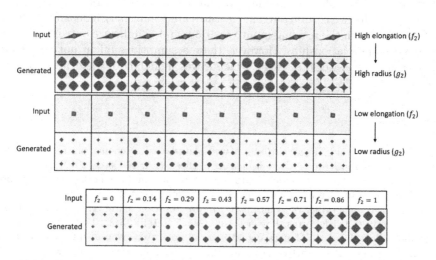

**Fig. 9.** Cell image-conditioned topography design (top). Cell feature value-conditioned topography design (based on cell elongation $f_2$) (bottom).

# 5    Conclusion

Although high-throughput screening and first-principle simulation have advanced scientific experiment and design methods in the past decades, such approaches are still limited by finite lab capacity or long simulation times, especially when both the parameter and outcome spaces are high-dimensional. Therefore, using machine learning to design and simulate experiments can substantially accelerate the iterative experiment and design cycle. We propose to use a deep generative model in which the parameter and outcome space share latent subspaces, allowing for both the holistic simulation of experimental outcomes, conditioned on parameters (in silico experiments), as well as generating parameters that could have led to a user-specified outcome (in silico design). A proof-of-concept evaluation on a synthetic dataset, inspired by biomaterials research, shows that the proposed architecture is able to capture relationships between high-dimensional input and output spaces and allows for both simulation and design use cases.

The proposed approach has a number of limitations, providing grounds for future work. Firstly, the model relies on the assumption that the experiment's outcome is composed of a set of independent and measurable features, while the actual outcome features may be to varying degrees correlated or uncertain. This observation suggests a future research direction aimed to drop the independence assumption and to develop latent representations that allow for correlated outcome features, yet preserve interpretability at the same time. Secondly, the proposed model implies the assumption that the factors of variation in the input space that influence certain outcome features are 1. mutually independent, 2. are independent from the residual input variation, and 3. influence outcome features via one-to-one relationships. However, these assumptions might not necessarily hold in many real-world settings, which leaves modeling of the general case for future work.

# References

1. Beijer, N., et al.: TopoWellPlate: a well-plate-based screening platform to study cell-surface topography interactions. Adv. Biosyst. **1**, 1700002 (2017)
2. Beijer, N.R., et al.: Dynamic adaptation of mesenchymal stem cell physiology upon exposure to surface micropatterns. Sci. Rep. **9**(1), 1–14 (2019)
3. Bengio, Y., Courville, A., Vincent, P.: Representation learning: a review and new perspectives. IEEE Trans. Pattern Anal. Mach. Intell. **35**(8), 1798–1828 (2013)
4. Goodfellow, I., et al.: Generative adversarial nets. Adv. Neural Inf. Process. Syst. **2**, 2672–2680 (2014). https://dl.acm.org/doi/10.5555/2969033.2969125
5. Hulshof, F.F., et al.: Mining for osteogenic surface topographies: in silico design to in vivo osseo-integration. Biomaterials **137**, 49–60 (2017)
6. Hulsman, M., et al.: Analysis of high-throughput screening reveals the effect of surface topographies on cellular morphology. Acta Biomater. **15**, 29–38 (2015)
7. Ilse, M., Tomczak, J.M., Louizos, C., Welling, M.: DIVA: domain invariant variational autoencoders. In: Medical Imaging with Deep Learning, pp. 322–348. PMLR (2020)

8. Kingma, D.P., Welling, M.: Auto-encoding variational bayes. arXiv preprint arXiv:1312.6114 (2013)

9. Larsen, A.B.L., Sønderby, S.K., Larochelle, H., Winther, O.: Autoencoding beyond pixels using a learned similarity metric. In: International Conference on Machine Learning, pp. 1558–1566. PMLR (2016)

10. Mayr, L.M., Bojanic, D.: Novel trends in high-throughput screening. Curr. Opin. Pharmacol. $9(5)$, 580–588 (2009)

11. Reimer, A., et al.: Scalable topographies to support proliferation and oct4 expression by human induced pluripotent stem cells. Sci. Rep. $6$, 18948 (2016)

12. Sanchez-Lengeling, B., Aspuru-Guzik, A.: Inverse molecular design using machine learning: generative models for matter engineering. Science $361(6400)$, 360–365 (2018)

13. Unadkat, H.V., et al.: An algorithm-based topographical biomaterials library to instruct cell fate. Proc. Natl. Acad. Sci. $108(40)$, 16565–16570 (2011)

14. Vasilevich, A.S., et al.: Designed surface topographies control ICAM-1 expression in tonsil-derived human stromal cells. Front. Bioeng. Biotechnol. $6$, 87 (2018)

15. Vassey, M.J., et al.: Immune modulation by design: Using topography to control human monocyte attachment and macrophage differentiation. Adv. Sci. $7(11)$, 1903392 (2020)

16. Wang, L., Chan, Y.C., Ahmed, F., Liu, Z., Zhu, P., Chen, W.: Deep generative modeling for mechanistic-based learning and design of metamaterial systems. Comput. Methods Appl. Mech. Eng. $372$, 113377 (2020)

# A Learning Vector Quantization Architecture for Transfer Learning Based Classification in Case of Multiple Sources by Means of Null-Space Evaluation

Thomas Villmann[1]([✉])(iD), Daniel Staps[1], Jensun Ravichandran[1](iD),
Sascha Saralajew[2](iD), Michael Biehl[3](iD), and Marika Kaden[1](iD)

[1] Saxon Institute for Computational Intelligence and Machine Learning (SICIM),
University of Applied Sciences Mittweida, Mittweida, Germany
`thomas.villmann@hs-mittweida.de`
[2] NEC Laboratories Europe GmbH, Heidelberg, Germany
[3] Bernoulli Institute for Mathematics, Computer Science and Artificial Intelligence,
University of Groningen, Groningen, The Netherlands

**Abstract.** We present a method, which allows to train a Generalized Matrix Learning Vector Quantization (GMLVQ) model for classification using data from several, maybe non-calibrated, sources without explicit transfer learning. This is achieved by using a siamese-like GMLVQ-architecture, which comprises different sets of prototypes for the target classification and for the separation learning of the sources. In this architecture, a linear map is trained by means of GMLVQ for source distinction in the mapping space in parallel to the classification task learning. The respective null-space projection provides a common data representation of the different source data for an all-together classification learning.

**Keywords:** Transfer learning · Learning vector quantization · Multiple source learning · Null-space evaluation

## 1 Introduction

Classification learning from different data sources is challenging because the data frequently are not calibrated appropriately [2,5,35]. Thus learning from such databases requires a careful data handling and merging. Another option is to apply transfer learning for those data using a concept drift assumption [18,33,37–39]. In this setting, the data from one source serve as the basis model training for classification and afterwards the data from the other sources are mapped in such a way that the trained model can be applied for these, too [19,39]. Generally, transfer learning for concept drift processing is well established [7,15,38,39]. The transfer mapping function can be approximated by an affine transformation using a Taylor expansion assumption [26].

ⓒ The Author(s), under exclusive license to Springer Nature Switzerland AG 2022
T. Bouadi et al. (Eds.): IDA 2022, LNCS 13205, pp. 354–364, 2022.
https://doi.org/10.1007/978-3-031-01333-1_28

The standard transfer learning approach fails in our setting of several sources, if not enough data are available from a single source to train the classifier model adequately. In this case, usually all data are calibrated first and subsequently the whole data set can serve for model training, i.e. the firstly mentioned strategy has to be applied as usual in the field of *source domain adaptation* and *multiple source learning* [5]. Accordingly, an adequate calibration of the data requires a careful processing to keep the useful data information [13]. Yet, there is a great variety of preprocessing tools and methods available [34]. Yet, this preprocessing frequently is done independently from the subsequent classification task. Thus, valuable information might be lost such that the subsequent classification learning suffers from insufficient information [6].

To overcome these difficulties the preprocessing should take care of the targeted classification problem. In this contribution we propose a learning vector quantization (LVQ) approach to solve this challenge. LVQ variants for transfer learning constitute a robust alternative to deep learning approaches [10,19,21] with theoretical justifications for learning behavior [4,32]. Moreover, LVQ constitutes a prototype-based approach which establishes an interpretable classifier model [14,22,23,36].

The proposed model is based on the matrix variant of generalized learning vector quantization (GMLVQ) [29]. GMLVQ is a variant of LVQ, which additionally to classification learning adjusts a linear data mapping for optimum class separation. We adapt this model to learn to distinguish the sources, on the one hand side, restricting here the concept drift to consist of linear transformations [17]. On the other hand, projecting the data into the null-space of the learned linear GMLVQ-mapping leads to a leveling of the data differences with respect to the sources. If this linear mapping has limited rank it offers a great variability to do so. Therefore, to tackle the challenge of classification learning from data of several sources, we suggest to apply classification learning in this null-space exploiting the remaining variability of source separation. Thus, the mapping information is shared by both procedures, source separation and classification learning and, hence, can be seen as a siamese-like setting. We denote this kind of transfer learning based on GMLVQ as *null-space transfer classification learning* (T-GMLVQ).

The remainder of the paper is as follows: First, we briefly introduce GMLVQ. Thereafter, we explain the null-space transfer classification learning model based on limited rank GMLVQ. An exemplary application and concluding remarks finalize the contribution.

## 2    Learning Vector Quantization

Learning vector quantization (LVQ) as introduced by T. KOHONEN supposes data vectors $\mathbf{x} \in T = \{\mathbf{x}_k\}_{k=1}^{N} \subseteq \mathbb{R}^n$ together with class labels $c(\mathbf{x}) \in \mathcal{C} = \{1, \ldots, C\}$ for training [12]. Further, the LVQ-model requires prototype vectors $\mathbf{w}_j \in W = \{\mathbf{w}_k\}_{k=1}^{K} \subset \mathbb{R}^n$ with class labels $c(\mathbf{w}_j)$ such that each class is represented by at least one prototype. A new data vector is assigned to a class by means of the nearest prototype principle

$$\mathbf{x} \mapsto c(\mathbf{w}^*) \qquad \text{with} \qquad \mathbf{w}^* = \text{argmin}_{\mathbf{w}_j \in W} \left( d(\mathbf{x}, \mathbf{w}_j) \right)$$

where $\mathbf{w}^*$ is denoted as the winning prototype for the input $\mathbf{x}$ with respect to $W$, and $d$ is a dissimilarity measure in $\mathbb{R}^n$. According to [27], prototype learning in LVQ can be realized as a stochastic gradient descent learning regarding the cost function $E = \sum_{\mathbf{x} \in T} f(\mu(\mathbf{x}))$ approximating the overall classification error, where $f$ is a monotonically increasing function and

$$\mu(\mathbf{x}) = \frac{d(\mathbf{x}, \mathbf{w}^+) - d(\mathbf{x}, \mathbf{w}^-)}{d(\mathbf{x}, \mathbf{w}^+) + d(\mathbf{x}, \mathbf{w}^-)}$$

is the classifier function taking negative values for correct classification. Here, $\mathbf{w}^+$ is the closest prototype to $\mathbf{x}$ with correct label whereas $\mathbf{w}^-$ is the closest prototype with incorrect label. If the dissimilarity $d$ is chosen as

$$d_{\Omega}(\mathbf{x}, \mathbf{w}) = (\Omega(\mathbf{x} - \mathbf{w}))^2 \tag{1}$$

and the *mapping matrix* $\Omega \in \mathbb{R}^{m \times n}$ is also subject of adaptation during learning. This approach is known as the *generalized matrix* LVQ (GMLVQ) [29], which usually requires some regularization of $\Omega$ to ensure the numerical stability [28]. In case of $m < n$, it is the *limited rank* GMLVQ (*LiRaGMLVQ*) [3]. Generally, GMLVQ belongs to the class of interpretable classifier models [1] known to be robust and optimizing classification margins [4,24].

## 3    Null-Space Transfer Classification Learning for GMLVQ Using a Siamese-Like Architecture

In the following we assume that the data are obtained from different sources. Hence, they are equipped with a source label $s(\mathbf{x}) \in \mathscr{S} = \{1, \ldots, S\}$. Additionally, the data are assigned to classes by means of class labels $c(\mathbf{x}) \in \mathcal{C}$. The task is to classify the the data correctly independently from the source domain. Yet, the sources may show considerable variations of the data.

To solve this task, the essential idea of the *Transfer Learning GMLVQ* (T-GMLVQ) is to suppose two kinds of prototypes: the usual set $W$ of *class prototypes* $\mathbf{w}_j$ with class labels $c(\mathbf{w}_j)$ and the set $\mathscr{W}$ of so-called *source prototypes* $\boldsymbol{\omega}_j$ with source labels $s(\boldsymbol{\omega}_j) \in \mathscr{S}$. The prototypes are responsible for the class and the source discrimination, respectively. Further, we assume a *LiRaGMLVQ* framework applying a mapping matrix $\Omega$ for the source separation, i.e. $\Omega \in \mathbb{R}^{m \times n}$ with $m < n$ is valid.

Now the idea is to train a GMLVQ model for the source prototypes $\boldsymbol{\omega}_j \in \mathscr{W}$ using a sub-orthogonal matrix $\Omega \in \mathbb{R}^{m \times n}$ with rank $m < n$ in (1) to calculate $d_{\Omega}(\mathbf{x}, \boldsymbol{\omega}_j)$ whereas

$$\delta_{\Omega}(\mathbf{x}, \mathbf{w}_k) = \left( \left( \mathbf{I}_n - \Omega^T \Omega \right) (\mathbf{x} - \mathbf{w}_k) \right)^2 \tag{2}$$

is used as the dissimilarity for the class prototypes $\mathbf{w}_k \in W$. More precisely, we consider two classifier functions

$$\nu_\Omega (\mathbf{x}) = \frac{d_\Omega (\mathbf{x}, \omega^+) - d_\Omega (\mathbf{x}, \omega^-)}{d_\Omega (\mathbf{x}, \omega^+) + d_\Omega (\mathbf{x}, \omega^-)} \tag{3}$$

and

$$\mu_\Omega (\mathbf{x}) = \frac{\delta_\Omega (\mathbf{x}, \mathbf{w}^+) - \delta_\Omega (\mathbf{x}, \mathbf{w}^-)}{\delta_\Omega (\mathbf{x}, \mathbf{w}^+) + \delta_\Omega (\mathbf{x}, \mathbf{w}^-)} \tag{4}$$

sharing the information contained in the mapping matrix $\Omega$. In (3), $\omega^+$ is the best matching source prototype $\omega_j$ with respect to the dissimilarity $d_\Omega (\mathbf{x}, \omega_j)$ and with correct source label $s (\omega_j) = s (\mathbf{x})$ whereas $\omega^-$ is the best matching source prototype with incorrect source label. In analogy in (4), $\mathbf{w}^+$ is the best matching class prototype $\mathbf{w}_k$ regarding the dissimilarity $\delta_\Omega (\mathbf{x}, \mathbf{w}_k)$ with correct class label $c (\mathbf{w}_k) = c (\mathbf{x})$ and $\mathbf{w}^-$ is the corresponding counterpart.

Hence, the classifier function $\nu_\Omega (\mathbf{x})$ from (3) detects wrongly determined sources by taking positive values. Analogously, $\mu_\Omega (\mathbf{x})$ from (4) yields positive values in case of misclassifications.

The resulting cost function of T-GMLVQ combines both classifier functions and reads as

$$E_{T-GMLVQ} = \sum_{\mathbf{x}} \alpha \cdot f (\mu (\mathbf{x})) + (1 - \alpha) \cdot g (\nu (\mathbf{x})) \tag{5}$$

taking into account the source information as well as the class information of the training data $\mathbf{x}$. It realizes a siamese architecture, which is visualized in Fig. 1. The parameter $\alpha \in [0, 1]$ controls the relative importance of source and class separation, respectively.

As we will show in the next section, the source separation takes place in the projection space $\mathbb{R}^m$ determined by the mapping $\Omega$ using the source prototypes $\omega_j$. The class discrimination is performed in the null-space of $\Omega$ by means of the class prototypes $\mathbf{w}_j$.

The learning can be realized as a stochastic grading descent learning according to the local loss

$$l (\mathbf{x}) = \alpha \cdot f (\mu (\mathbf{x})) + (1 - \alpha) \cdot g (\nu (\mathbf{x}))$$

with respect to the adjustable parameters, which are obviously the class prototypes $\mathbf{w}_k$, the source prototypes $\omega_j$ but additionally also the low-rank mapping matrix $\Omega$.

## 4   Mathematical Justification of the T-GMLVQ

In the following we give a mathematical justification for the setting of the T-GMLVQ approach described above.

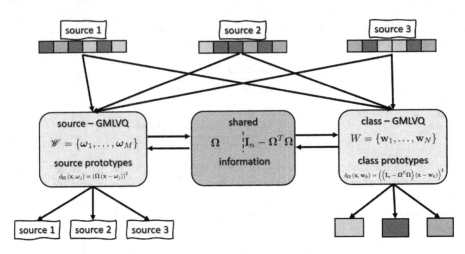

**Fig. 1.** Visualization of the proposed siamese architecture for T-GLVQ. Two types of prototypes are used for source and class separation, respectively. The information is shared by the sub-orthogonal $\Omega$-matrix in the dissimilarities $\delta_\Omega\left(\mathbf{x}, \mathbf{w}_k\right)$ and $d_\Omega\left(\mathbf{x}, \boldsymbol{\omega}_j\right)$.

We suppose a sub-orthogonal matrix $\Omega \in \mathbb{R}^{m \times n}$ with $m < n$. Hence, $\Omega\Omega^T = \mathbf{I}_m$ holds with $\mathbf{I}_m$ being the unity matrix in $\mathbb{R}^m$.[1] Therefore, $\mathbf{P} = \Omega^T\Omega$ is an *orthogonal projection matrix* and $\mathbf{Q} = \mathbf{I}_n - \mathbf{P}$ is the *complementary orthogonal projector* [11]. It maps an arbitrary vector $\mathbf{x} \in \mathbb{R}^n$ into the null space *null* $(\Omega)$ of $\Omega$, i.e. $\hat{\mathbf{x}} = \mathbf{Q} \cdot \mathbf{x} \in null\,(\Omega)$ as well as $\hat{\boldsymbol{\omega}} = \mathbf{Q} \cdot \boldsymbol{\omega} \in null\,(\Omega)$ and $\hat{\mathbf{w}} = \mathbf{Q} \cdot \mathbf{w} \in null\,(\Omega)$ are valid for the source and the class prototypes, respectively [8,11]. Using the decomposition into the orthogonal sum

$$\mathbf{x} - \boldsymbol{\omega} = \mathbf{P}\left(\mathbf{x} - \boldsymbol{\omega}\right) + \mathbf{Q}\left(\mathbf{x} - \boldsymbol{\omega}\right) \tag{6}$$

the similarity

$$d_\Omega\left(\hat{\mathbf{x}}, \hat{\boldsymbol{\omega}}\right) = \left(\Omega\left(\mathbf{P}\left(\mathbf{x} - \boldsymbol{\omega}\right) + \mathbf{Q}\left(\mathbf{x} - \boldsymbol{\omega}\right)\right)\right)^2$$

of the null-space projections $\hat{\mathbf{x}}$ and $\hat{\boldsymbol{\omega}}$ reduces to $d_\Omega\left(\hat{\mathbf{x}}, \hat{\mathbf{w}}\right) = \left(\Omega\mathbf{P}\left(\mathbf{x} - \boldsymbol{\omega}\right)\right)^2$ because $\Omega\mathbf{Q}\left(\mathbf{x} - \boldsymbol{\omega}\right) = \mathbf{0}$. Thus, any optimization of $\mathbf{Q}$ regarding a class prototype $\mathbf{w}_k$ does not contribute to $d_\Omega\left(\hat{\mathbf{x}}, \hat{\mathbf{w}}\right)$. This motivates the use of $\delta_\Omega\left(\mathbf{x}, \mathbf{w}_k\right)$ from (2), where obviously $\mathbf{Q} = \mathbf{I}_n - \Omega^T\Omega$ holds and $\mathbf{Q}$ is subject of matrix learning in GMLVQ for the class prototypes. of course, because both classifier functions, $\nu_\Omega\left(\mathbf{x}\right)$ and $\mu_\Omega\left(\mathbf{x}\right)$, share the dependency on $\Omega$, the class learning and the source learning are not independent although different prototypes are used.

The proposed method allows the following interpretation: The source separation learning optimizes $\Omega$ for best results regarding this source discrimination. Yet, projection of the data into the null-space of $\Omega$ levels (or at least

---

[1] Usually, sub-orthogonal matrices are defined in terms of column zero vectors or equivalently $\Omega \in \mathbb{R}^{n \times m}$. Then, the more common relation $\Omega^T\Omega = \mathbf{I}_m$ is equivalently valid.

reduces) the differences regarding the sources. Hence, class separation learning optimizes the $\boldsymbol{\Omega}$ matrix in such a way that the complementary projection matrix $\mathbf{Q} = \mathbf{I}_n - \boldsymbol{\Omega}^T \boldsymbol{\Omega}$ delivers best class separation.

We remark that if the training set $T$ contains samples with source label but unknown class membership these data can still be taken into account in terms of the source classifier function $\nu_\Omega (\mathbf{x})$.

Further, to impose the sub-orthogonal matrix property of $\mathbf{Q}$ without any renormalization according to a Gram-Schmidt-orthonormalization algorithm, we could introduce a penalty term

$$p(\boldsymbol{\Omega}) = \left(\det \left(\boldsymbol{\Omega}^T \boldsymbol{\Omega}\right)\right)^2 - 1 \qquad (7)$$

in the cost function $E_{T-GMLVQ}$ from (5). It can be seen as an analogue to the regularization term regarding the $\Omega$-learning suggested in [28] for GMLVQ.

Thus, we obtain

$$\hat{E}_{T-GMLVQ} = \sum_{\mathbf{x}} \alpha \cdot f\left(\mu\left(\mathbf{x}\right)\right) + (1 - \alpha - \beta) \cdot g\left(\nu\left(\mathbf{x}\right)\right) + \beta \cdot p\left(\boldsymbol{\Omega}\right)$$

as a new cost function in this case with $\alpha, \beta \geq 0$ and $\alpha + \beta \leq 1$ as adjustable parameters to be chosen in advance. Otherwise, approaches which implicitly guarantee the sub-orthogonality while adapting the matrix $\boldsymbol{\Omega}$ should be considered [16]. Otherwise, if sub-orthogonality is completely dropped, more complicate projections have to be applied [11].

## 5  Exemplary Application – Analysis of Polluted Breathing Air Spectra

We present an application of the method to detect classes of polluted breathing air by means of multicapillary column coupled ion mobility spectrometry (MCC-IMS) measurements [20,31].[2] For each measurement, a total of 240s-retention-time-spectrum was derived with a drift time of 0 to 20.48 ms. The resulting heat maps were preprocessed according to the procedure specified in [20]. Ultimately, each measurement delivers a peak spectrum with respect to a peak list of $n = 230$ peaks regarding the identified regions of interest (ROI).

In this conceptual study, three measurement devices were used (sources – S1: sn180169, S2: sn200157, S3: sn200158). Five air classes have to be discriminated. For each source and each class only 10 measurements are available, respectively. Data samples (heat maps) for each class and source are depicted in Fig. 2.

We applied GMLVQ for each source separately and afterwards the model to the data of the other sources. In comparison we applied T-GMLVQ to the

---

[2] For the measurements a MCC-IMS-device from STEP Sensortechnik und Elektronik, Pockau, Germany (STEP IMS NOO) was used.

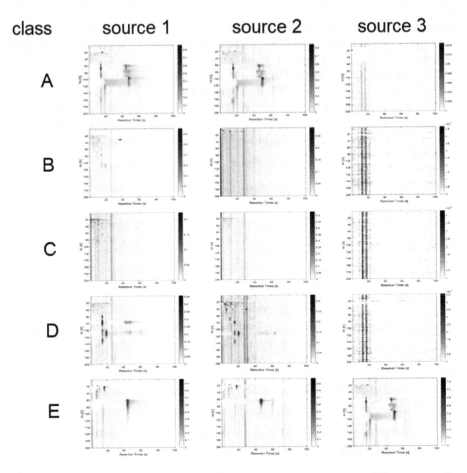

**Fig. 2.** Data samples (heatmaps) for the classes and sources. In each heat map, the horizontal axis is the retention time whereas the vertical axis represents the drift time. According to the processing described in [20], regions of interest are identified according to all samples, the average of which in each heat map deliver together the respective data sample spectrum. These spectra are used in the analysis.

merged data set. For all experiments we used only one class prototype per class. For T-GMLVQ, also only one source prototype was used for each source. The mapping dimension of the mapping matrix $\Omega$ was chosen as $m = 10$ such that the remaining dimensionality of the null-space $null\,(\Omega)$ is 220 giving the flexibility for class separation learning. The results are depicted in Table 1. The results presented here are obtained by five-fold cross validation.

**Table 1.** Accuracy results for MCC-IMS spectra classification regarding the data from three sources (devices) obtained by GMLVQ and T-GMLVQ.

| | GMLVQ | | | T-GMLVQ |
|---|---|---|---|---|
| | $S_1$ | $S_2$ | $S_3$ | $S_1 \& S_2 \& S_3$ |
| $S_1$ | 99.7 $\pm$ 0.6 | 18.5 $\pm$ 4.1 | 17.7 $\pm$ 1.6 | 97.8 $\pm$ 0.04 |
| $S_2$ | 16.0 $\pm$ 0.6 | 100 $\pm$ 0.0 | 92.6 $\pm$ 4.2 | 100 $\pm$ 0.0 |
| $S_3$ | 23.1 $\pm$ 1.9 | 93.0 $\pm$ 1.5 | 99.2 $\pm$ 1.1 | 95.6 $\pm$ 0.08 |

We observe that the separately trained GMLVQ models are not able to transfer the classification ability with respect to the training source to the other sources. Particularly, source S1 seems to be quite different. Yet, T-GMLVQ is able to discriminate the classes very well in all source-specific subsets of the data.

## 6    Conclusion and Future Work

In this paper we introduced null-space transfer classification learning by means of limited rank GMLVQ to classify data from different sources. The approach uses a siamese architecture of coupled GMLVQ models with prototypes for sources and classes, respectively. Both sub-networks share the information regarding the appropriate data transformations realized by linear mappings. This siamese architecture allows to exploit this information in parallel such that classification learning is possible also if only a few data samples are available from each source. Future work will extend this approach to non-linear $\mathbf{\Phi}$ mappings or its affine approximations, i.e. we replace the matrix $\mathbf{\Omega}$ by an affine operator

$$[\mathbf{\Omega} + \mathbf{s}]\,\mathbf{x} \stackrel{def}{=} \mathbf{\Omega}\mathbf{x} + \mathbf{s}$$

containing a *shift vector* $\mathbf{s}$. This will relate the null-space transfer classification learning more closely to tangent metric learning for classification tasks [26]. Particularly, operator can be seen as an affine (Taylor) approximation of a non-linear data transformation [9, 25, 26, 30].

**Acknowledgement.** We thank the colleagues from Digitronic Chemnitz GmbH (Germany) for measuring the data. Further, D.S., M.K., and J.R. acknowledge funding by the European Social Fund (ESF) within a junior researcher group *Maschinelles Lernen und Künstliche Intelligenz in Theorie und Anwnedung* (MaLeKITA) and a PhD grant.

## References

1. Biehl, M., Hammer, B., Villmann, T.: Prototype-based models in machine learning. Wiley Interdisc. Rev.: Cogn. Sci. **7**(2), 92–111 (2016)
2. Bousmalis, K., Trigeorgis, G., Silberman, N., Krishnan, D., Erhan, D.: Domain separation networks. In: Proceedings of the 30th International Conference on Neural Information Processing Systems, pp. 343–351 (2016)

3. Bunte, K., Schneider, P., Hammer, B., Schleif, F.-M., Villmann, T., Biehl, M.: Limited rank matrix learning, discriminative dimension reduction and visualization. Neural Netw. **26**(1), 159–173 (2012)

4. Crammer, K., Gilad-Bachrach, R., Navot, A., Tishby, A.: Margin analysis of the LVQ algorithm. In: Becker, S., Thrun, S., Obermayer, K. (eds.) Proceedings of NIPS 2002. Advances in Neural Information Processing, vol. 15, pp. 462–469. MIT Press, Cambridge (2003)

5. Crammer, K., Kearns, M., Wortman, J.: Learning from multiple sources. J. Mach. Learn. Res. **9**(57), 1757–1774 (2008)

6. Ding, Z., Shao, M., Fu, Y.: Transfer learning for image classification with incomplete multiple sources. In: Proceedings of the International Joint Conference on Neural Networks (IJCNN), pp. 2188–2195. IEEE Press (2016)

7. Gama, J., Žliobaitė, I., Pechenizkiy, M., Bouchachia, A.: A survey on concept drift adaptation. ACM Comput. Surv. **46**(4), 1–37 (2014)

8. Golub, G., Loan, C.V.: Matrix Computations. Johns Hopkins Studies in the Mathematical Sciences, 4th edn. John Hopkins University Press, Baltimore (2013)

9. Hastie, T., Simard, P., Säckinger, E.: Learning prototype models for tangent distance. In: Tesauro, G., Touretzky, D., Leen, T. (eds.) Advances in Neural Information Processing Systems, vol. 7, pp. 999–1006. MIT Press (1995)

10. Heusinger, M., Raab, C., Schleif, F.-M.: Passive concept drift handling via variations of learning vector quantization. Neural Comput. Appl. **253** (2020)

11. Horn, R., Johnson, C.: Matrix Analysis, 2nd edn. Cambridge University Press, Cambridge (2013)

12. Kohonen, T.: Learning vector quantization. Neural Netw. **1**(Supplement 1), 303 (1988)

13. Li, J., Wu, W., Xue, D., Gao, P.: Multi-source deep transfer neural network algorithm. Sensors **19**(18), 3992–4008 (2019)

14. Lisboa, P., Saralajew, S., Vellido, A., Villmann, T.: The coming of age of interpretable and explainable machine learning models. In: Verleysen, M. (ed.) Proceedings of the 29th European Symposium on Artificial Neural Networks, Computational Intelligence and Machine Learning (ESANN 2021), Bruges (Belgium), pp. 547–556, Louvain-La-Neuve, Belgium (2021). i6doc.com

15. Lu, J., Liu, A., Dong, F., Gu, F., Gama, J., Zhang, G.: Learning under concept drift: a review. IEEE Trans. Knowl. Data Eng. **31**(12), 2346–2363 (2019)

16. Mathiasen, A., et al.: What if neural networks had SVDs? In: Larochelle, H., Ranzato, M., Hadsell, R., Balcan, M.F., Lin, H. (eds.) Advances in Neural Information Processing Systems, vol. 33, pp. 18411–18420. Curran Associates Inc. (2020)

17. Paassen, B., Schulz, A., Hammer, B.: Linear supervised transfer learning for generalized matrix LVQ. Mach. Learn. Rep. **10**(MLR-04-2016), 11–19 (2016)

18. Pan, S., Yang, Q.: A survey on transfer learning. IEEE Trans. Knowl. Data Eng. **22**(10), 1345–1359 (2010)

19. Prahm, C., Paassen, B., Schulz, A., Hammer, B., Aszmann, O.: Transfer learning for rapid re-calibration of a myoelectric prosthesis after electrode shift. In: Ibáñez, J., González-Vargas, J., Azorín, J.M., Akay, M., Pons, J.L. (eds.) Converging Clinical and Engineering Research on Neurorehabilitation II. BB, vol. 15, pp. 153–157. Springer, Cham (2017). https://doi.org/10.1007/978-3-319-46669-9_28

20. Purkhart, R., Hillmann, A., Graupner, R., Becher, G.: Detection of characteristic clusters in IMS-spectrograms of exhaled air polluted with environmental contaminants. Int. J. Ion Mob. Spectromet. **15**(15), 63–68 (2012)

21. Raab, C., Schleif, F.-M.: Transfer learning extensions for the probabilistic classification vector machine. Neurocomputing **397**, 320–330 (2020)

22. Rudin, C.: Stop explaining black box machine learning models for high stakes decisions and use interpretable models instead. Nat. Mach. Intell. **1**(5), 206–215 (2019)

23. Rudin, C., Chen, C., Chen, Z., Huang, H., Semenova, L., Zhong, C.: Interpretable machine learning: fundamental principles and 10 grand challenges (2021)

24. Saralajew, S., Holdijk, L., Villmann, T.: Fast adversarial robustness certification of nearest prototype classifiers for arbitrary seminorms. In: Larochelle, H., Ranzato, M., Hadsell, R., Balcan, M., Lin, H. (eds.) Proceedings of the 34th Conference on Neural Information Processing Systems (NeurIPS 2020), vol. 33, pp. 13635–13650. Curran Associates Inc. (2020)

25. Saralajew, S., Nebel, D., Villmann, T.: Adaptive Hausdorff distances and tangent distance adaptation for transformation invariant classification learning. In: Hirose, A., Ozawa, S., Doya, K., Ikeda, K., Lee, M., Liu, D. (eds.) ICONIP 2016. LNCS, vol. 9949, pp. 362–371. Springer, Cham (2016). https://doi.org/10.1007/978-3-319-46675-0_40

26. Saralajew, S., Villmann, T.: Transfer learning in classification based on manifold models and its relation to tangent metric learning. In: Proceedings of the International Joint Conference on Neural Networks (IJCNN), Anchorage, pp. 1756–1765. IEEE Computer Society Press (2017)

27. Sato, A., Yamada, K.: Generalized learning vector quantization. In: Touretzky, D.S., Mozer, M.C., Hasselmo, M.E. (eds.) Advances in Neural Information Processing Systems 8. Proceedings of the 1995 Conference, pp. 423–9. MIT Press, Cambridge (1996)

28. Schneider, P., Bunte, K., Stiekema, H., Hammer, B., Villmann, T., Biehl, M.: Regularization in matrix relevance learning. IEEE Trans. Neural Netw. **21**(5), 831–840 (2010)

29. Schneider, P., Hammer, B., Biehl, M.: Adaptive relevance matrices in learning vector quantization. Neural Comput. **21**, 3532–3561 (2009)

30. Simard, P., LeCun, Y., Denker, J.: Efficient pattern recognition using a new transformation distance. In: Hanson, S., Cowan, J., Giles, C. (eds.) Advances in Neural Information Processing Systems, vol. 5, pp. 50–58. Morgan-Kaufmann (1993)

31. Steppert, C., Steppert, I., Bollinger, T., Sterlacci, W.: Rapid non-invasive detection of influenza-A-infection by multicapillary column coupled ion mobility spectrometry. J. Breath Res. **15**(1), 1–5 (2021)

32. Straat, M., Abadi, F., Göpfert, C., Hammer, B., Biehl, M.: Statistical mechanics of on-line learning under concept drift. Entropy **20**(775), 1–21 (2018)

33. Raab, C., Schleif, F.-M.: Transfer learning extensions for the probabilistic classification vector machine. Neurocomputing **397**, 320–330 (2020)

34. Sun, S., Shi, H., Wu, Y.: A survey of multi-source domain adaptation. Inf. Fusion **24**, 84–92 (2015)

35. Tsai, J.-C., Chien, J.-T.: Adversarial domain separation and adaptation. In: Proceedings of the IEEE 27th International Workshop on Machine Learning for Signal Processing (MLSP), pp. 1–6 (2017)

36. Villmann, T., Saralajew, S., Villmann, A., Kaden, M.: Learning vector quantization methods for interpretable classification learning and multilayer networks. In: Sabourin, C., Merelo, J., Barranco, A., Madani, K., Warwick, K. (eds.) Proceedings of the 10th International Joint Conference on Computational Intelligence (IJCCI), Sevilla, pp. 15–21. SCITEPRESS - Science and Technology Publications, Lda, Lisbon (2018). ISBN 978-989-758-327-8

37. Yan, K., Zhang, D.: Correcting instrumental variation and time-varying drift: a transfer learning approach with autoencoders. IEEE Trans. Instrum. Meas. **65**(9), 2012–2022 (2016)

38. Yang, Q., Zhang, Y., Dai, W., Pan, J.: Transfer Learning. Cambridge University Press, Cambridge (2020)

39. Zhuang, F., et al.: A comprehensive survey on transfer learning. Proc. IEEE **109**(1), 43–76 (2021)

# MuseBar: Alleviating Posterior Collapse in Recurrent VAEs Toward Music Generation

Huiyao Wu and Maryam Tavakol[✉]

Eindhoven University of Technology, Eindhoven, The Netherlands
h.wu1@student.tue.nl, m.tavakol@tue.nl

**Abstract.** Machine learning has shown remarkable artistic values and commercial potentials in the music industry. Recurrent variational autoencoders (RVAEs) have been widely applied to this area due to the condensing, inclusive, and smooth nature of their latent space. However, RNNs are powerful auto-regressive models on their own, where the decoder in a RVAE can be strong enough to work independently from the encoder. When this happens, the model degrades from an autoencoder to a traditional RNN, which is known as *posterior collapse*. In this paper, we propose a cost-effective bar-wise regulation schema called *MuseBar* to alleviate this problem for music generation. We impose a prior on the hidden state of every music bar in the RNN encoder, instead of only on the last hidden state as in the standard RVAEs, such that the latent code is learned under stronger regulations. We further evaluate our proposed method, quantitatively and qualitatively, with extensive experiments on manually scraped musical data. The results demonstrate that the bar-wise regulation significantly improves the quality of the latent space in terms of Mutual Information and Kullback-Leibler divergence.

**Keywords:** Music generation · Variational autoencoder · Recurrent neural networks · Posterior collapse

## 1 Introduction

Recent advances in Artificial Intelligence (AI) have exhibited great values in creative arts such as music composing [18], poem writing [13], painting imitation [5], and so on. Creating arts using AI techniques is efficient, imaginative, inspiring, and for music generation, it can lead to additional commercial benefits. Because of AI, people now have extensive exposure to sophisticated yet user-friendly creation, remixing, and learning tools e.g., Magenta, Flow Machines, MuseNet, etc. Moreover, it can be used for therapeutic purpose as certain types of music have been proven effective in suppressing beta and gamma rhythms in the brain that are correlated with depression and anxiety [9]. Thus, pre-defining various output patterns via AI technologies can undoubtedly save a lot of human labor and produce more effective therapeutic music.

© The Author(s), under exclusive license to Springer Nature Switzerland AG 2022
T. Bouadi et al. (Eds.): IDA 2022, LNCS 13205, pp. 365–377, 2022.
https://doi.org/10.1007/978-3-031-01333-1_29

However, successfully modeling the long sequences of notes in the musical data is very challenging. On the one hand, convolutional neural networks (CNNs) have been adopted to capture the patterns in the musical data [2,11]. CNNs are used to distill the musical features, in which, music data is treated as consecutive images and each image represents a bar in the music notation. These methods are utilized in polyphonic music modeling as they can capture the common patterns among multiple tracks. Nonetheless, they fail to generate the long- and short-term structure of the music, which can not be ignored in long music sequences as the transitions among the bars is what brings the tuneful melodies.

On the other hands, deep generative models [7] have been widely applied for music generation. Recurrent variational autoencoders (RVAEs) are among the most popular frameworks for this purpose due to the representative and continuous nature of their latent space. Nevertheless, RNNs themselves are typically used on their own as powerful auto-regressive models of sequences. The decoder in a recurrent VAE is sufficiently capable of modeling the sequential data and might ignore the latent code from the encoder. With the latent code disregarded, the model degrades from an autoencoder to a traditional RNN. This is known as *posterior collapse*, or *KL vanishing* [1], which could get worse for music generation as music notes are commonly of longer sequences. To alleviate this problem, most of the existing approaches mainly focus on either designing a stronger encoder by stacking LSTM units [16,17] or restricting the power of decoder by introducing additional modules [14]. However, both approaches lead to bulky models with significantly more parameters to learn.

In this paper, we introduce a light-weighted bar-wise regularization technique to address the posterior collapse in RVAEs without incorporating extra parameters and/or additional modules. In a standard RVAE, a prior based on a standard Gaussian distribution is imposed only on the last hidden state of the RNN encoder, which might not be enough for long sequences, and can result in an inaccurate representation of the latent code. Therefore, inspired by the ideas from Li et al. [10], we propose MuseBar, a bar-wise regulation scheme to effectively compress the data into the latent space. Subsequently, the Gaussian prior is applied on multiple hidden states of the RNN-based encoder, and in this way, a stronger regulation is imposed on the model and will theoretically produce a more informative latent space, in particular, during the early phases. Empirical study on manually scraped musical data from different genres shows that Muse-Bar can effectively mitigate posterior collapse and outperforms certain baselines in terms of the quality of the latent space as well as the overall performance.

## 2   Background

### 2.1   MIDI Representation

In order to make music notes accessible to the computer, they have to be encoded according to a certain unified grammar. Musical Instrument Digital Interface (MIDI) is one of the most commonly used formats which we adapt in this paper. MIDI is a technically standard format to describe a protocol, a digital interface,

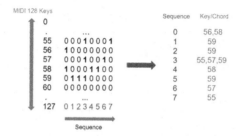

**Fig. 1.** Comparison of piano-roll matrix and MIDI notes.

and connectors, which makes the interaction between various electronic musical instruments, software, and devices possible [15].

Music notes in the MIDI format are often processed to the piano-roll representation, which can be further translated into a matrix indicating which note(s) at a certain pitch is played, at what velocity, and at which time frame. Simply put, a piano-roll matrix is a mathematical representation of a MIDI file that only focuses on musical notes and their key attributes. As depicted in Fig. 1, the pitch value in MIDI files usually ranges from 0 to 127, hence in total, we have 128 different pitches. The 1s in the figure represent the note(s) with particular pitch indicating when the left bar is being played. Although MIDI representation is not able to distinguish whether a key is held for multiple time steps or consecutively pressed during a certain time frame, it is still a practical format for digital composition in music generation due to its adaptability.

### 2.2 Generative Models

**Autoencoders.** An autoencoder (AE) is a neural network that aims at successfully replicating its input $x$ to output $x'$. There are two key parts in an AE, an encoder that compresses the input signal into the latent code $z$, and a decoder that reconstructs the input data from $z$. AEs have been widely used for dimensionality reduction and feature extraction. However, the latent code from an AE is a discrete vector of a fixed length, making it difficult to interpolate. When sampling from such latent vector, we may end up with unrealistic output as the decoder has never encountered some parts of the input before.

**Variational Autoencoders.** Compared to AEs, the latent space of variational autoencoders (VAEs) is designed to be continuous and thus allows for random interpolation and sampling. This is achieved by casting the input data to a distribution instead of a latent code of fixed length. A VAE [8] samples the latent vector $z$ from a prior distribution $p(z)$, which is controlled by parameters $\mu$ and $\sigma$. The encoder is then denoted in conditional probability as $Q_\phi(z \mid x_i)$, where $\phi$ indicates the weights of the encoder network. Correspondingly, a decoder is represented as $P_\theta(x'_i \mid z)$, with $\theta$ being the weights of the decoder.

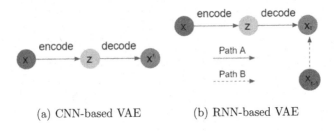

(a) CNN-based VAE    (b) RNN-based VAE

**Fig. 2.** Illustration of information flow in VAEs.

The backbone of both the encoder and decoder in a VAE can be of various neural network structures, while we only focus on recurrent neural networks (RNNs) in this paper, as musical notes are sequential data in essence. More specifically, the encoder $Q_\phi$ is composed of an LSTM module that outputs a series of hidden states $h_1, h_2, \ldots, h_T$ for a given input sequence $\boldsymbol{x} = \{x_1, x_2, \ldots, x_T\}$. The hidden states are used to generate $\mu$ and $\sigma$, which are the parameters of the distribution over the latent code $z$. The latent vector $z$ is sampled from this distribution and is then utilized to initialize the states of the decoder $P_\theta$. The decoder network is also composed of an LSTM module and can auto-regressively reconstruct the input sequence to output $\boldsymbol{x}' = \{x'_1, x'_2, \ldots, x'_T\}$. The overall model is trained to both learn an approximate posterior $Q_\phi(z \mid \mathbf{x})$ which is close to the prior $P(z)$, as in a standard VAE and reconstruct the input sequence (i.e., $x'_i = x_i, i \in \{1, \ldots, T\}$). The loss function is subsequently defined as

$$
\mathcal{L}\left(\boldsymbol{\theta}, \boldsymbol{\phi}; \mathbf{x}_i^{1:t}\right) = \mathbb{E}_{Q_\phi\left(\mathbf{z}^T \mid \mathbf{x}_i^{1:t}\right)}\left[\log P_\theta\left(\mathbf{x}_i^{1:t} \mid \mathbf{z}^T\right)\right] - D_{\mathrm{KL}}\left(Q_\phi\left(\mathbf{z}^T \mid \mathbf{x}_i^{1:t}\right) \| P\left(\mathbf{z}^T\right)\right),
\tag{1}
$$

where $\mathbf{x}_i^{1:t}$ represents the sequential input data and $\mathbf{z}^T$ represents the latent code sampled from the last hidden state of the encoder.

**Posterior Collapse.** Posterior collapse, also known as *KL vanishing*, is a notoriously difficult problem in variational autoencoders, which makes it hard to train an effective model due to the vanish of the KL term in Eq. (1). This phenomenon is particularly obstinate when an RNN is exerted as the backbone of VAE, since the temporal receptive field in RNNs can be unlimited in essence.

An intuitive explanation of such phenomenon is displayed in Fig. 2 [4]. For a standard VAE with a CNN as the backbone, Fig. 2(a) shows that there is only one path moving from encoder $Q_\phi$, to the latent code $z$, and then to the decoder $P_\theta$, when reconstructing the input data $\boldsymbol{x}$. Such a uni-directional flow limits the leak of information along the way and thus makes it easier to collaboratively train the model. However, we will end up with an additional information flow brought by the auto-regressive RNN if the traditional CNN decoder is replaced by an RNN module. For an RNN decoder, the inputs come from two paths, as shown in Fig. 2(b), one is from the latent code $z$ and the other one is from the output of the previous time step. Similar to the standard VAEs, $z$ serves

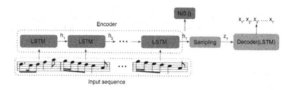

**Fig. 3.** Standard recurrent VAE. (Color figure online)

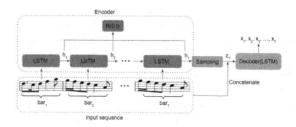

**Fig. 4.** Schematic of the bar-wise regulation on recurrent VAE.

as the global feature vector that supervises the replication of $x$, whereas parts of the ground-truth information of $x$ suffers from leaking at every time step of the sequential decoding. As a result, the decoder becomes powerful enough to generate data on its own and could not utilize stochastic information brought by the trained latent space.

## 3    MuseBar

Effectively compressing the data to the latent space is crucial for the decoder training, as the latent code is later used to initialize and supervise the reconstruction [1,4,6]. Nevertheless, to train an informative latent space especially at the early stages is very challenging, as the encoder has not yet learned to condense the input data. The latent code is hence not strong enough to guide the decoder given its auto-regressive nature. Therefore, the decoder fails to cooperate with the encoder and the latent code becomes meaningless. In order to penalize the decoder from working independently, standard RVAEs, also illustrated in Fig. 3, add one regularizer (red box) into the bottleneck layer to force the latent space to follow the standard Gaussian distribution. However, only a single regulation on the last hidden state of the encoder is insufficient to guarantee an optimal latent space, especially when capturing the long-term dependencies.

Consequentially, following the light of step-wise regulation [10], we propose MuseBar, a bar-wise regularizer, as displayed in Fig. 4, to impose stronger regulations on the hidden states generated from multiple bars in a sequence of music. The resulted Evidence Lower BOund (ELBO) loss is hence

$$\mathcal{L}\left(\boldsymbol{\theta}, \boldsymbol{\phi}; \mathbf{x}_i\right)_{\mathrm{b}} = E_{Q_\phi(\mathbf{z}^\mathrm{T}|\mathbf{x}_i)}\left[\log P_\theta\left(\mathbf{x}_i \mid \mathbf{z}^T\right)\right] - \frac{1}{b}\sum_{t=1}^{b} D_{\mathrm{KL}}\left(Q_\phi\left(\mathbf{z}^t \mid \mathbf{x}_i^{1:t}\right) \| P\left(\mathbf{z}^t\right)\right),$$

(2)

where the final KL term is obtained from the average divergence of each bar in the input sequence.

Given a musical sequence of length $L$ with a number of $b$ bars, a recurrent encoder compresses the input into a low-dimensional latent space where only most representative information is retained. Subsequently, the latent code $z$ of length $l$ is sampled from this space to initialize the decoder, which will be used to reconstruct the input sequence. The entire VAE network is trained under the supervision of a reconstruction loss imposed on the input and output, which in our case, is a binary cross-entropy loss, and a regularizer on the latent space and standard Gaussian distribution, which is quantified as Kullback-Leibler divergence. MuseBar adds a Gaussian distribution prior to every bar of the input sequence as illustrated in Fig. 4. We choose bars as regulation units rather than single beats because musical sequences are usually at least 20 times longer than texts, hence, adding regulation on every beat can lead to a significant increase in the computational costs. Apart from the bar-wise regulation, latent code $z$ is concatenated with the input sequence to form the final input for the decoder instead of solely being used for initialization. This way, more information is passed on to the decoder and theoretically brings richer context.

The main structure of the model consists of a 2-layer LSTM for both encoder and decoder with hidden units of size 512 and input/output dimension of 128, which is the number of pitches in the MIDI representation. Furthermore, the vector $z$ is sampled from the latent space and is both used to initialize the decoder and concatenated with every sequence as the final input for the decoder. In the output layer of the decoder, a sigmoid function is applied in order to convert the output into probabilities. Finally, a binary construction (BCE) loss is used along with the KL divergence to train the model in an end-to-end manner.

## 4   Empirical Study

In this section, we conduct experiments to evaluate the performance of MuseBar compared to several baselines for music generation. The music data is collected from Freepianotutorials[1] and Lakh MIDI Dataset[2], consisting of five major genres which include pop, rock, classical, jazz, and electronic. For each genre, we collect 100–300 songs, depending on the availability of monophonic MIDI files and the productivity of the corresponding musicians. Every song is further preprocessed to be of the same length by either repetition or interruption and then concatenated into a long piece. For simplicity, all musical data is rendered by piano and collected in monophonic MIDI format, with the help of **Music21** library, which is a Python-based toolkit for computer-aided musicology.

---

[1]  https://www.freepianotutorials.net.
[2]  https://colinraffel.com/projects/lmd.

In our setting, the batch size equals to the number of musicians/genres so that we can pick one specific genre/musician based on the batch index later on. Models with different parameter settings are trained for 3k epochs and learning rate is set to 0.001 as an upper limit for the Adam optimizer. During training, we randomly select a snippet of 240 time steps from each musician/genre to feed the model, as 240 is the average time steps needed for a basic structure in a song (intro, verse, pre-chorus, chorus, and bridge) [12], which is approximately 30 s. In addition, we take 80 bars in one snippet on a 4/4 time signature, each contains 4 time steps. To evaluate the performance of our model, we conduct the following experiments.

**Overall Performance.** To verify the effectiveness of the bar-wise regulation, we first compare MuseBar to two baselines: vanilla VAE (**LSTM-VAE**) [3], which is simply composed of an LSTM unit without any special training strategy or regulations, and the one proposed by Bowman et al. [1] (**VAE-BOW**), which is trained under a weight annealing strategy. In the latter, the importance of KL term is progressively raised over time in order to force the model to first learn the latent code and then utilize it. Additionally, we train the bar-wise regularized RVAE combined with the weight annealing method (**MuseBar-BOW**).

**Music Genres.** Monophonic music of different genres vary drastically in terms of the transition intensity and pitch ranges. Classical music tends to have more frequent transitions and wider range of pitch class than pop or rock music, which is the reason why classical music sounds richer in texture and melody. With the aim of exploring the impact of different genres, we train the regularized recurrent VAE with the same network structure on datasets of 5 different genres, respectively pop, rock, classical, jazz and electronic.

**Hyperparameter Exploration.** Autoencoders, or rather the encoder component of them, in general are compression algorithms. Therefore, the size of the latent space greatly impacts the effectiveness and efficiency of the model. A latent code with a small size might not properly capture all the information needed to reconstruct the input, while a larger latent space might end up with too many dead units which consequently become more costly to train. Thus, we tune the model to identify the optimal length of the latent vector $z$ as a hyper-parameter and we vary the length of the latent code from 8 to 128 in a geometric sequence in this experiment. Furthermore, we explore the number of regularizers as another hyper-parameter of the model. To this end, with the input size of 240 time steps consisting of 60 bars under the time signature of 4/4, we experiment different numbers of regularizers from {5, 10, 15, 30, and 60} on both full dataset and separate genres, respectively, corresponding to regulation on every 12, 6, 4, 2, and 1 bar(s).

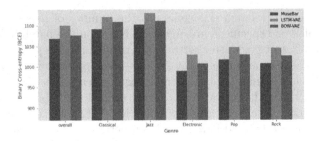

**Fig. 5.** Comparison of Binary Cross-entropy (BCE) in MuseBar and baselines.

### 4.1    Evaluation Metrics

In general, VAEs use the Evidence Lower Bound (ELBO) measure to estimate the negative log likelihood of the data points under the learned distribution to assess the reconstruction loss. Hence, ELBO can be used as the quantitative measure of the overall performance of the model. We further investigate the binary cross-entropy (BCE) and Kullback-Leibler divergence (KL), which are two sub-components of ELBO, in our evaluation.

In addition to the inherent KL term, one of the most commonly used quantitative method for evaluating the quality of encoding is called Mutual Information (MI). In information theory, mutual information is a measure of mutual dependence of two given random variables, which can also be considered as the reduction in the uncertainty about one random variable given the knowledge of another. As such, we compute the MI between the latent space and the sampled latent code to get an idea of how deductive the latent space is from which a latent variable is sampled. The difference between MI and KL is that MI indicates how much information is encoded in the latent code from the latent space, while KL determines how far the latent space is from the standard Gaussian distribution.

### 4.2    Performance Results

**Overall Performance.** The general performance of different methods is evaluated on the joint test set of all genres with the input size of $240 \times 128$ and the latent vector of length 100. The regulation is imposed on every two bars as this leads to the best performance according to the exploration study conducted later on. In order to reduce the effect of randomness, the results are averaged over 10 runs. The performance is further compared with vanilla recurrent VAE (LSTM-VAE) and VAE trained with weight annealing strategy (VAE-BOW), which are shown in Fig. 5. In this figure, only the binary cross-entropy loss is displayed as the Kullback-Leibler divergence and mutual information (MI) are trivial (close to zero) in LSTM-VAEs compared to MuseBar.

In addition, Table 1 summarizes the evaluation results of all methods in terms of three metrics on the entire data as well as each genre. For the entire data (the Overall row), according to binary cross-entropy (BCE), Kullback-Leibler divergence (KL), and Mutual Information (MI), the obtained results illustrate that

**Table 1.** The performance of all methods on the collected dataset.

| | | LSTM-VAE | VAE-BOW | MuseBar | MuseBar-BOW |
|---|---|---|---|---|---|
| Overall | BCE | 1100 | 1076 | 1078 | **1068** |
| | KL | 0.1 | 19 | 22 | **27** |
| | MI | 0.7 | 17 | 20 | **21** |
| Classical | BCE | 1121 | 1109 | 1111 | **1091** |
| | KL | 0.08 | 17 | 20 | **30** |
| | MI | 0.5 | 10 | 11 | **20.3** |
| Jazz | BCE | 1130 | 1111 | 1113 | **1102** |
| | KL | – | 14 | 21 | **32** |
| | MI | – | 15 | 20 | **21.7** |
| Electronic | BCE | 1029 | 1007 | 1001 | **989** |
| | KL | 0.1 | 23 | 29 | **35.7** |
| | MI | 0.9 | 20 | 21 | **24** |
| Pop | BCE | 1047 | 1029 | 1021 | **1017** |
| | KL | 0.09 | 16 | 27 | **32.9** |
| | MI | 0.07 | 15 | 21 | **23.4** |
| Rock | BCE | 1045 | 1026 | 1019 | **1007** |
| | KL | 0.08 | 21 | 27 | **29** |
| | MI | 0.03 | 20 | 23 | **24** |

both VAE-BOW and MuseBar enhance the vanilla recurrent VAE, with MuseBar slightly better than VAE-BOW, but the best performance is achieved when two strategies are combined, i.e., training MuseBar with weight annealing method. Note that the weight annealing strategy balances the two terms in ELBO, which is beneficial when the input size and latent dimension vary drastically. Samples of music generated from our model can be found online[3].

**Music Genres.** In addition to training on the complete dataset, we further investigate the performance of bar-wise regulation and corresponding baselines on each genre used in this paper. The results from both Fig. 5 and Table 1 demonstrate that different genres react differently to the regularization. For classical and jazz, VAE-BOW slightly outperforms MuseBar in terms of BCE, while for other genres MuseBar achieves a better performance. This happens due to both the specialty of the strategy and attributes of the music itself. VAE-BOW is designed to balance the two terms in ELBO, which accordingly focuses on global adjustment, unlike bar-wise regularizer, which is targeted at local bar-wise texture. Therefore, MuseBar is more suitable for genres that are less variant such as electronic and rock. Not Surprisingly, electronic is more sensitive to any form of

---

[3] Link to the sample musics.

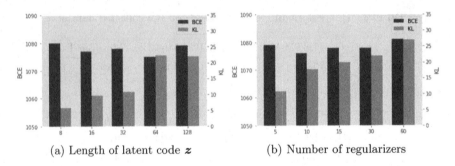

(a) Length of latent code $z$          (b) Number of regularizers

**Fig. 6.** BCE loss and KL-divergence with different parameter settings. (Color figure online)

optimization compared to other genres. We believe this is because of the repetitive property of electronic music, which makes it easier to model and predict. On the other hands, pop and rock music react similarly to either kind of enhancements. We reckon this is because of the indistinct boundary between these two genres. For example, Coldplay can be considered as a rock band and a pop band at the same time. Same applies to the Beatles, Greenday, One Direction, etc. Needless to say that this is also biased toward the collected data.

**Hyperparameter Exploration.** In this experiment, we first explore the impact of different lengths of the latent code. Experiments in this part are conducted on the complete dataset with 30 regularizers. Figure 6(a) plots the performance of MuseBar in terms of varying BCE (orange) and KL (green) measures.

As shown in Fig. 6(a), the size of the latent space does not necessarily have a big influence on BCE as it does on KL. The BCE remains stable with slight fluctuation from 1075 to 1080, while KL varies from 5.7 to 22.3. However, a larger latent space (128) does not outperform a smaller one (64) in terms of both KL and BCE, which means that our model does not require a very large latent space to represent the compression of the input data. In the above experiments, we adapt the size of 100 as the optimal latent dimension for the complete dataset, aiming to effectively and efficiently compress the input sequence.

Additionally, we aim to verify the influence of the number of regularizers on the model. Hence, we evaluate the performance of MuseBar with 5, 10, 15, 30, and 60 regularizers on both full dataset and separate genres, which respectively correspond to regulation on every 12, 6, 4, 2, and 1 bar(s). In this experiment, the latent code is fixed to the length of 100. The results are displayed in Fig. 6(b) for BCE (orange) and KL (green) terms.

Similarly, Fig. 6(b) demonstrates that the number of regularizers does not necessarily have a great influence on BCE as it does on KL divergence. The BCE remains stable with slight fluctuation from 1076 to 1081, while KL term varies from 10.7 to 27.3. The obtained results verify that a stronger regulation leads to a higher KL divergence as the KL reaches its maximum when 60 regularizers

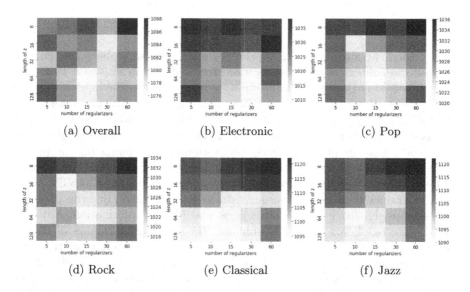

(a) Overall  (b) Electronic  (c) Pop

(d) Rock  (e) Classical  (f) Jazz

**Fig. 7.** Heatmap of BCE with variation of length of $z$ and number of regularizers.

are added to the model. Nevertheless, more regularizers (60) does not surpass less regulations (30) in terms of BCE, which indicates that vigorous supervision is not necessarily beneficial to reconstruction. We believe this is sensitive to the music genre. Genres with more flexible and creative patterns might need more regulations while genres with less variations such as electronic does not require strong regulations.

Consequently, we further investigate the interaction of the number of regularizers and the length of the latent code on each genre. To this end, we conduct extensive exploration experiments, where the achieved results are demonstrated as heatmaps in Fig. 7. We employ BCE as the evaluation metric for this set of experiments as the reconstruction loss is the core measure of interest to evaluate the overall performance of the method.

Overall, Fig. 7 shows that BCE is negatively correlated to the number of regularizers as well as the length of the latent code. When the latent code is of length 8, all music genres reach the largest BCE as the size of the latent space is not sufficient enough to represent the input sequence. However, there is no significant difference regarding BCE when the latent code is above 64. This also testifies the aforementioned assumption that the latent space of a large size might be redundant as it might include inactivated units, which is not utilized by the decoder at all. For various genres, the optimal combination of the number of regularizers and the size of the latent code is also not the same. For example, electronic in general needs more regulations compared to classical or jazz music to reach an optimal BCE. We believe this is due to the repetitive/predictive music notes progression of the electronic genre. Moreover, we conclude that it is easier to reconstruct an electronic piece than a classical one according to the range of the BCE indicated with the side bar.

## 5   Conclusions

In this paper, we aimed to mitigate the posterior collapse problem in recurrent VAEs in the context of music generation. Inspired by the step-wise VAE [10], we proposed MuseBar, which adds stronger regulations to the hidden states of the recurrent encoder during the training process, ensuring a more informative latent space that can be used as a global guidance for the auto-regressive decoder. Extensive experiments are conducted to analyze the impact of the length of the latent code, number of regularizers, and various music genres on the performance. Our model by itself as well as combined with weight annealing strategy (MuseBar-BOW) significantly outperforms vanilla recurrent VAE (LSTM-VAE) and VAE trained with weight annealing strategy (VAE-BOW) in terms of binary cross-entropy, Kullback-Leibler divergence, and Mutual Information. Although the bar-wise regulation effectively enhances the overall performance of RVAEs and mitigates the KL vanishing problem, there are some limitations that hinder the further improvements, such as the MIDI representation and the LSTM architecture. To address the aforementioned issues, we aim to seek for a more fidelitous but also cost-efficient digital representation, and exploit more sophisticated architectures such as bi-directional or pyramid LSTM encoder, that are left for the future work.

## References

1. Bowman, S.R., Vilnis, L., Vinyals, O., Dai, A.M., Jozefowicz, R., Bengio, S.: Generating sentences from a continuous space. In: Proceedings of the Twentieth Conference on Computational Natural Language Learning (2015)
2. Dong, H.W., Hsiao, W.Y., Yang, L.C., Yang, Y.H.: MuseGAN: multi-track sequential generative adversarial networks for symbolic music generation and accompaniment, vol. 32, no. 1 (2018)
3. Fabius, O., Van Amersfoort, J.R.: Variational recurrent auto-encoders. arXiv preprint arXiv:1412.6581 (2014)
4. Fu, H., Li, C., Liu, X., Gao, J., Celikyilmaz, A., Carin, L.: Cyclical annealing schedule: a simple approach to mitigating KL vanishing. In: Proceedings of NAACL (2019)
5. Ha, D., Eck, D.: A neural representation of sketch drawings. arXiv preprint arXiv:1704.03477 (2017)
6. Huang, A., Wu, R.: Deep learning for music. arXiv:1606.04930v1 (2016)
7. Jiang, J., Xia, G.G., Carlton, D.B., Anderson, C.N., Miyakawa, R.H.: Transformer VAE: a hierarchical model for structure-aware and interpretable music representation learning, pp. 516–520 (2020)
8. Kingma, D.P., Welling, M.: Auto-encoding variational Bayes. In: Second International Conference on Learning Representations (2013)
9. Kirk, R., Abbotson, M., Abbotson, R., Hunt, A., Cleaton, A.: Computer music in the service of music therapy: the MIDIGRID and MIDICREATOR systems. Med. Eng. Phys. 16(3), 253–258 (1994)
10. Li, R., Li, X., Chen, G., Lin, C.: Improving variational autoencoder for text modelling with timestep-wise regularisation. arXiv preprint arXiv:2011.01136 (2020)

11. Malekzadeh, S., Samami, M.: Classical music generation in distinct dastgahs with alimnet ACGAN. arXiv preprint arXiv:1901.04696 (2019)
12. McIntyre, P.: Creativity and cultural production: a study of contemporary western popular music songwriting. Creat. Res. J. **20**(1), 40–52 (2008)
13. Oliveira, H.G., Hervás, R., Díaz, A., Gervás, P.: Adapting a generic platform for poetry generation to produce Spanish poems, pp. 63–71 (2014)
14. Roberts, A., Engel, J., Raffel, C., Hawthorne, C., Eck, D.: A hierarchical latent vector model for learning long-term structure in music, pp. 4364–4373 (2018)
15. Rothstein, J.: MIDI: A Comprehensive Introduction, 7th edn. A-R Editions, Middleton (1992)
16. Semeniuta, S., Severyn, A., Barth, E.: A hybrid convolutional variational autoencoder for text generation. In: Proceedings of Empirical Methods in Natural Language Processing (2017)
17. Sønderby, C.K., Raiko, T., Maaløe, L., Sønderby, S.K., Winther, O.: Ladder variational autoencoders. Adv. Neural Inf. Process. Syst. **29**, 3738–3746 (2016)
18. Wu, J., Hu, C., Wang, Y., Hu, X., Zhu, J.: A hierarchical recurrent neural network for symbolic melody generation (2017)

# Parameter Learning in ProbLog
# with Annotated Disjunctions

Wen-Chi Yang[1]([⊠]) [ID], Arcchit Jain[1] [ID], Luc De Raedt[1,2] [ID],
and Wannes Meert[1] [ID]

[1] Department of Computer Science, Leuven.AI, KU Leuven,
Celestijnenlaan 200a - box 2402 3001, Leuven, Belgium
{wenchi.yang,luc.deraedt,wannes.meert}@kuleuven.be,
arcchit.jain.2015@iitkalumni.org
[2] Centre for Applied Autonomous Sensor Systems, Örebro University,
Örebro, Sweden

**Abstract.** In parameter learning, a partial interpretation most often
contains information about only *a subset of* the parameters in the program. However, standard EM-based algorithms use all interpretations to
learn all parameters, which significantly slows down learning. To tackle
this issue, we introduce EMPLiFI, an EM-based parameter learning technique for probabilistic logic programs, that improves the efficiency of
EM by exploiting the rule-based structure of logic programs. In addition, EMPLiFI enables parameter learning of multi-head annotated disjunctions in ProbLog programs, which was not yet possible in previous
methods. Theoretically, we show that EMPLiFI is correct. Empirically,
we compare EMPLiFI to LFI-ProbLog and EMBLEM. The results show
that EMPLiFI is the most efficient in learning single-head annotated
disjunctions. In learning multi-head annotated disjunctions, EMPLiFI is
more accurate than EMBLEM, while LFI-ProbLog cannot handle this
task.

**Keywords:** Learning from interpretations · Probabilistic logic
programming · Expectation maximization

## 1 Introduction

Statistical relational learning [8] and Probabilistic Logic Programming [3,4]
have contributed to various representations and learning schemes that reason about objects and uncertain relational structures among them. Popular
approaches include PRISM [10], Independent Choice Logic [13], Bayesian Logic
Programs [11], Markov Logic Networks [14], Logic Programs with Annotated
Disjunctions [17], CP-Logic [16] and ProbLog [7]. Many of these languages
are based on variants of the distribution semantics [15]. They vary in the
way they define the distribution over logic programs but are equally expressive [2]. In this paper, we use ProbLog's representation. ProbLog has probabilistic facts such as 0.01 :: earthquake, stating that the probability of having

© The Author(s), under exclusive license to Springer Nature Switzerland AG 2022
T. Bouadi et al. (Eds.): IDA 2022, LNCS 13205, pp. 378–391, 2022.
https://doi.org/10.1007/978-3-031-01333-1_30

an earthquake is 0.01, and has clauses such as `alarm :- earthquake`, stating that the alarm goes off if there is an earthquake. In addition, ProbLog supports annotated disjunctions (ADs) such as 0.01 :: `alarm(long)`; 0.19 :: `alarm(short)`; 0.8 :: `alarm(none)`, stating that an alarm has exactly one type of the three types.

ProbLog's parameter learning approach, LFI-ProbLog, is designed only for probabilistic facts, and not for ADs. Hence, LFI-ProbLog cannot learn multi-head AD variables. Even though LFI-ProbLog can learn single-head AD parameters, we will show that it is inefficient and in extreme cases, results in incorrect values. Faria et al. tackled a special case of this efficiency issue for single-head ADs [6]. In contrast, we provide a more general solution that, in addition, also covers multi-head ADs. Although our approach is implemented in ProbLog, it can be applied to other EM-based parameter learning algorithms as what we exploit is the rule-based structure that is shared by all probabilistic logic programs.

The contribution is twofold. First, we introduce EMPLiFI, a new parameter learning approach in ProbLog. EMPLiFI correctly learns multi-head ADs and speeds up learning by exploiting the rule-based structure of logic programs. Second, we prove that EMPLiFI is correct and illustrate how it reduces EM iterations. We compare EMPLiFI with two other EM-based learners, LFI-ProbLog and EMBLEM, and show that EMPLiFI is the most accurate in learning multi-head ADs and takes the fewest EM iterations to converge.

## 2 Preliminaries

**Probabilistic Logic Programming.** A ProbLog theory (or program) $\mathcal{T}$ consists of a finite set of probabilistic facts $\mathcal{F}$, a finite set of clauses $\mathcal{BK}$ and a finite set of annotated disjunctions $\mathcal{AD}$. A *probabilistic fact* is an expression p :: f that states the ground fact f is true with probability p. A *clause* is an expression h :- $b_1, \cdots, b_n$ where h is a literal and $b_1, \cdots, b_n$ is a conjunction of literals, stating h is true if $b_1, \cdots, b_n$ is true. ProbLog defines probability distributions over ground facts in a Herbrand base $L_\mathcal{T}$. The probabilistic facts define a probability distribution over *possible worlds*. All ground facts in a possible world $W$ are *true* and all that are not in $W$ are *false*. The probability of a possible world $W$ is defined as $P(W|\mathcal{T}) = \prod_{f_i \in W} p_i \prod_{f_i \in L_\mathcal{T} \setminus W} (1-p_i)$. The *success probability* of a query $q$ is the sum of the probabilities of the possible worlds that entail $q$, formally, $P_s(q|\mathcal{T}) = \sum_{I \subseteq L_\mathcal{T}, I \models q} P(I|\mathcal{T})$. A *partial interpretation* $I$ is an incomplete possible world that contains truth values of some (but not all) atoms. If an atom a (resp. ¬a) is in $I$, then a is true (resp. false). Otherwise, the truth value of a is unknown. Hence, a partial interpretation $I$ represents a number of possible worlds, and the probability of $I$ is the success probability of the conjunction of the literals in $I$, i.e. $P(I) = P_s(\bigwedge_{l \in I} l)$.

**Annotated Disjunctions in ProbLog.** An *annotated disjunctions* (ADs) is a clause with one or more mutually exclusive heads of the form $p_1 :: h_1; \cdots; p_k :: h_k$ where $\sum_{i=1}^{k} p_i = 1$, stating that if the body is true, exactly one head is made true, where the choice of $h_i$ is governed by $p_i$. Although the ProbLog language and semantics allow for ADs, only probabilistic facts (and a transformation) are used for inference. Hence, most transformations encode ADs as probabilistic facts as the first step [5,7]. For example, a three-head AD $0.2 :: a1; 0.2 :: a2; 0.6 :: a3 :-b$ is encoded as

```
0.2::h1.                 0.25::h2.                1.0::h3.
a1:-b,h1.                a2:-b,\+h1,h2.           a3:-b,\+h1,\+h2,h3.
```

where h1, h2 and h3 are hidden facts. The last fact h3 can be dropped for inference but we keep it in because we will later need it for learning. This encoding is designed to compute the probabilities correctly for the inference task but is insufficient for learning and results in incorrect values (see Sect. 3).

## 3   Learning from Interpretations in ProbLog

In this section, we review LFI-ProbLog and illustrate its two issues. Later, Sect. 4 will introduce a new learning approach that resolves these issues. The parameter learning task in ProbLog is as below.

**Given**

- A ProbLog program $\mathcal{T}(\mathbf{p}) = \mathcal{F} \cup \mathcal{BK} \cup \mathcal{AD}$ where $\mathcal{F}$ is a set of probabilistic facts, $\mathcal{BK}$ is a set of background knowledge and $\mathcal{AD}$ is a set of ADs. $\mathbf{p} = \langle p_1, \cdots, p_N \rangle$ is a set of unknown parameters where each parameter is attached to a probabilistic fact or an AD head.
- A set $\mathcal{I}$ of partial interpretations $\{I_1, ..., I_M\}$.

**Find** maximum likelihood probabilities $\widehat{\mathbf{p}}$ for all interpretations in $\mathcal{I}$. Formally,

$$\widehat{\mathbf{p}} = \arg\max_{\mathbf{p}} P(\mathcal{I}|\mathcal{T}(\mathbf{p})) = \arg\max_{\mathbf{p}} \prod_{m=1}^{M} P_s(I_m|\mathcal{T}(\mathbf{p}))$$

Given initial parameters $\mathbf{p}^0 = \langle p_1^0, \cdots, p_N^0 \rangle$, an Expectation Maximization (EM) algorithm computes $\mathbf{p}^1$, and in this fashion, enumerates a series of estimations $\mathbf{p}^2, ..., \mathbf{p}^T$. The process terminates after $T$ iterations when the log likelihood does not improve more than an arbitrary small value $\epsilon$. LFI-ProbLog, is summarized by Eq. 1 [7,9], which takes $\mathbf{p}^t$ to compute $\mathbf{p}^{t+1}$. Intuitively, based on $\mathbf{p}^t$, a new estimate $p_n^{t+1}$ is the expected count of $\mathbf{f}_n$ being true divided by the total count of $\mathbf{f}_n$, formally,

$$p_n^{t+1} = \frac{\sum_{m=1}^{M} \sum_{k=1}^{K_n^m} P(\mathbf{f}_{n,k}|I_m, \mathcal{T}(\mathbf{p}^t))}{\sum_{m=1}^{M} K_n^m} \tag{1}$$

where $K_n^m$ is the number of ground instances represented by $\mathbf{p}_n :: \mathbf{f}_n$ in $I_m$. We will use the following running examples throughout this paper to illustrate two issues of LFI-ProbLog and our approach to tackle them.

*Running example 1.* Consider the following *Smokers* program with three parameters $\mathbf{p} = \langle \mathtt{p_1}, \mathtt{p_2}, \mathtt{p_3} \rangle$, stating that a person is a smoker with probability $\mathtt{p_1}$, and any smoker (resp. non-smoker) has cancer with probability $\mathtt{p_2}$ (resp. $\mathtt{p_3}$).

```
person(X).                          p1::smokes(X):-person(X).
p2::cancer(X):-smokes(X),person(X). p3::cancer(X):-\+smokes(X),person(X).
```

Consider interpretations $I_1 = \{\mathtt{smokes(a), cancer(a)}\}$, $I_2 = \{\mathtt{smokes(b)}, \neg \mathtt{cancer(b)}\}$, $I_3 = \{\neg\mathtt{smokes(c),cancer(c)}\}$, $I_4 = \cdots = I_{102} = \{\neg\mathtt{smokes(\cdot)}, \neg\mathtt{cancer(\cdot)}\}$. As all interpretations are fully observable, we obtain $\langle \mathtt{p_1}, \mathtt{p_2}, \mathtt{p_3} \rangle = \langle 2/102, 1/2, 1/100 \rangle$ by simply counting.

*Running example 2.* Consider the following *Colors* program with three parameters $\mathbf{p} = \langle \mathtt{p_1}, \mathtt{p_2}, \mathtt{p_3} \rangle$ that jointly denote a probability distribution of the color of a ball.

```
p1::green;p2::red;p3::blue:-ball.            ball.
```

Given interpretations $I_1 = \{\mathtt{green}\}$, $I_2 = \{\mathtt{red}\}$ and $I_3 = \{\mathtt{blue}\}$, we obtain $\mathbf{p} = \langle 1/3, 1/3, 1/3 \rangle$ by counting.

The first issue of LFI-ProbLog is efficiency-related. When learning single-head ADs, LFI-ProbLog takes into account *all* interpretations, including the irrelevant ones that do not contain information about the parameter to be learned. These irrelevant interpretations introduce an undesired inertia in EM learning, as illustrated in Example 1.

*Example 1.* For LFI-ProbLog, the Smokers program must be transformed into the following program with hidden facts $\mathtt{h_1}, \mathtt{h_2}$ and $\mathtt{h_3}$.

```
p1::h1.           p2::h2.            p3::h3.           person(X).
smokes(X):-person(X) h1.
cancer(X):-smokes(X),person(X),h2.   cancer(X):-\+smokes(X),person(X),h3.
```

Given initial parameters $\mathbf{p}^0 = \langle 0.1, 0.1, 0.1 \rangle$, by applying Eq. 1, we obtain $\mathbf{p}^1 = \langle p_1^1, p_2^1, p_3^1 \rangle$ as follows.

$$p_1^1 = \frac{1+1+0+0\times 99}{102} = \frac{2}{102}, p_2^1 = \frac{1+0+.1+.1\times 99}{102} = 0.108, p_3^1 = \frac{.1+.1+1+0\times 99}{102} = 0.012$$

By repeatedly applying Eq. 1, we further obtain a series of estimates $\mathbf{p}^2 = \langle 2/102, 0.116, 0.01 \rangle$, $\cdots$, $\mathbf{p}^{100} = \langle 2/102, 0.445, 0.01 \rangle$. Notice that $\mathtt{p_2}$ does not converge to 0.5 after 100 iterations even though all interpretations are fully observable. This is resulted from the irrelevant interpretations $I_3, \cdots I_{102}$.

The second issue is that LFI-ProbLog does not correctly learn all possible multi-head ADs. This is because how their probabilities are transformed from $\mathbf{p}$ to $\mathbf{\acute{p}}$ [5] (cf. Sect. 2). This transformation is incorrect in learning as the parameters are not known and must be learned, as illustrated in Example 2.

*Example 2.* For LFI-ProbLog, the Colors program must be transformed into the following program with hidden facts gh, rh and bh, and the given initial parameters must be transformed. Say, given $\mathbf{p}^0 = \langle 0.2, 0.2, 0.6 \rangle$, the transformed probabilities are $\acute{\mathbf{p}}^0 = \langle 0.2, 0.25, 1.0 \rangle$.

```
ṕ1::gh.                    ṕ2::rh.                    ṕ3::bh.              ball.
green:-ball,gh.            red:-ball,\+gh,rh.         blue:-ball,\+gh,\+rh,bh.
```

By applying Eq. 1, we obtain $\acute{\mathbf{p}}^1$ as follows.

$$\acute{p}_1^1 = \frac{1+0+0}{3} = 0.333 \qquad \acute{p}_2^1 = \frac{0.25+1+1}{3} = 0.750 \qquad \acute{p}_3^1 = \frac{1+1+1}{3} = 1$$

We future obtain $\acute{\mathbf{p}}^2 = \langle 0.333, 0.917, 1 \rangle, \cdots, \acute{\mathbf{p}}^{10} = \langle 0.333, 1, 1 \rangle$, which corresponds to the incorrect AD parameters $\mathbf{p}^{10} = \langle 1/3, 2/3, 0 \rangle$.

## 4   Learning with Annotated Disjunctions

We propose EMPLiFI, a parameter learning approach in Eq. 2, as a solution to the issues discussed in Sect. 3. This section illustrates EMPLiFI, and Sect. 5 will prove EMPLiFI's correctness.

$$p_n^{t+1} = \frac{\sum_{I_m \in I_{\mathbf{p}_n}} \sum_{j=1}^{J_n^m} P(\mathbf{h}_{n,j}, \mathbf{b}_{n,j} | I_m, \mathcal{T}(\mathbf{p}^t))}{\sum_{I_m \in I_{\mathbf{p}_n}} \sum_{j=1}^{J_n^m} P(\mathbf{b}_{n,j} | I_m, \mathcal{T}(\mathbf{p}^t))} \qquad (2)$$

where

- $\mathbf{h}_{n,j}$ and $\mathbf{b}_{n,j}$ are the j-th possible ground instance represented by $\mathbf{p}_n :: \mathbf{h}_n$ and the corresponding body in $I_m$
- $J_n^m$ is the total number of ground instances represented by $\mathbf{p}_n :: \mathbf{h}_n$ in $I_m$
- $I_{\mathbf{p}_n}$ is the set of all *relevant interpretations* to $\mathbf{p}_n$

If the denominator is zero, then $p_n^{t+1}$ will not be updated. Intuitively, based on $\mathbf{p}^t$, a new estimate $p_n^{t+1}$ is the expected count of the head divided by the expected count of the body. Unlike LFI-ProbLog that assumes all parameters are attached to a fact, EMPLiFI recognizes and exploits AD rule structures, which enables efficient EM and multi-head AD learning.

### 4.1   Relevant Interpretations

At this point, it is important to stress that some interpretations do not contain information about a rule p :: h :-b. An interpretation $I$ is called irrelevant to p if the conditional probability components $P(\mathbf{h}_n, \mathbf{b}_n | \cdot)$ and $P(\mathbf{b}_n | \cdot)$ solely depend on the old probability estimate $\mathbf{p}^t$, formally,

$$P(\mathbf{h}, \mathbf{b} | I, \mathcal{T}(\mathbf{p}^t)) = P(\mathbf{h}, \mathbf{b} | \mathcal{T}(\mathbf{p}^t)) \text{ and } P(\mathbf{b} | I, \mathcal{T}(\mathbf{p}^t)) = P(\mathbf{b} | \mathcal{T}(\mathbf{p}^t)) \qquad (3)$$

As irrelevant interpretations slow down learning (see Example 1), it is our aim to identify them for each parameter.

The *dependency set* of a ground atom a in a ProbLog theory $\mathcal{T}$, denoted by $dep_\mathcal{T}(a)$, is the set of all atoms that occur in some SLD-proof of a [7]. The dependency set of multiple atoms is the union of their dependency sets. A ground fact $f \in \mathcal{T}$ is relevant to an interpretation $I$ if it is in the dependency set of $I$, namely $f \in dep_\mathcal{T}(I)$. Similarly, a ground clause is relevant to $I$ if it is used in the SLD proof of $I$. Then, the *interpretation-restricted theory*, denoted by $\mathcal{T}_r(I)$, is the union of all relevant facts and clauses [9]. A restricted theory is a subset of the original ground program, in fact, it is usually much smaller than the original program. Using the restricted theory, we can define relevant interpretations for learning a parameter.

**Definition 1** *(Relevant Interpretation) For a ProbLog theory $\mathcal{T}$, an interpretation $I$ is relevant to an atom $a_n \in \mathcal{T}$ if and only if $a_n$ is in the interpretation-restricted theory $\mathcal{T}_r(I)$, namely $a_n \in \mathcal{T}_r(I)$.*

Since a parameter $p_n$ always corresponds a unique atom $a_n$ in $\mathcal{T}$, we define $p_n$-relevant interpretations using $a_n$, formally, $\mathcal{I}_{p_n} = \{I \in \mathcal{I} | a_n \in \mathcal{T}_r(I)\}$. We have defined relevant interpretations for single-head ADs and probabilistic facts.

*Example 3.* Consider the Smokers program and $I_2 = \{\text{smokers(b)},$ $\neg\text{cancer(b)}\}$, the dependency set of $I_2$ is $dep_\mathcal{T}(I_2) = \{\text{h1, h2, smokes(b)},$ $\text{cancer(b)}\}$ and the corresponding restricted theory $\mathcal{T}_r(I_2)$ is

```
p1::h1.                      p2::h2.                        person(b).
smokes(b):-person(b),h1.     cancer(b):-smokes(b),person(b),h2.
```

Therefore, $I_2$ is relevant to $p_1$ and $p_2$ according to Definition 1. We obtain the relevant interpretation sets for all three parameters as $\mathcal{I}_{p_1} = \{I_1, \cdots, I_{102}\}$, $\mathcal{I}_{p_2} = \{I_1, I_2\}$, and $\mathcal{I}_{p_3} = \{I_3, \cdots, I_{102}\}$. Given initial parameters $\mathbf{p}^0 = \langle 0.1, 0.1, 0.1 \rangle$, we obtain $\mathbf{p}^1 = \langle 2/102, 1/2, 1/100 \rangle$ after one EM iteration by applying Eq. 2, as opposed to Example 1.

## 4.2 Directly Learning Multi-head ADs

Recall that ProbLog's transformations result in incorrect learning of multi-head ADs (see Sect. 3). To gain correctness, it is required to maintain mutual exclusivity in the interpretation-restricted theory. To do so, we define the *AD dependency set*, $dep_\mathcal{T}^{AD}(I) \supseteq dep_\mathcal{T}(I)$ to include also mutually exclusive atoms. Intuitively, if $dep_\mathcal{T}^{AD}(I)$ contains an AD head, it must also contain all mutually exclusive heads and their dependency sets. Then, an AD dependency set defines an *AD interpretation-restricted theory* as in Sect. 4.1.

**Definition 2** *(Relevant Interpretation with AD). For a ProbLog theory $\mathcal{T}$, an interpretation $I$ is relevant to an atom $a_n \in \mathcal{T}$ if and only if $a_n$ is in the AD interpretation-restricted theory $\mathcal{T}_r^{AD}(I)$, namely $a_n \in \mathcal{T}_r^{AD}(I)$.*

After defining relevant interpretations for ADs, we can now learn multi-head ADs using Eq. 2.

*Example 4.* Consider the Colors program and $I_1 = \{\text{green}\}$, the AD dependency set $dep_{\mathcal{T}}^{AD}(I_1)$ is $\{\text{ball}, \text{green}, \text{red}, \text{blue}, \text{gh}, \text{rh}, \text{bh}\}$ and the AD restricted theory $\mathcal{T}_r^{AD}(I_1)$ is

| | | | |
|---|---|---|---|
| ṕ1::gh. | ṕ2::rh. | ṕ3::bh. | ball. |
| green:-ball,gh. | red:-ball,\+gh,rh. | blue:-ball,\+gh,\+rh,bh. | |

$I_1$ is relevant to $p_1$, $p_2$ and $p_3$ according to Definition 2. Similarly, $I_2$ and $I_3$ are also relevant to all three parameters. Given initial parameters $\mathbf{p}^0 = \langle 0.2, 0.2, 0.6 \rangle$, we obtain $\mathbf{p}^1 = \langle 1/3, 1/3, 1/3 \rangle$ after one EM iteration by applying Eq. 2.

## 5   Proofs

Section 5.1 will prove EMPLiFI's correctness and Sect. 5.2 will provide insight into how EMPLiFI improves efficiency of EM parameter learning.

### 5.1   Correctness

We start from the EM algorithm for Bayesian Networks [12], i.e. Eq. 4, that differs from EMPLiFI by learning from all interpretations. Since Eq. 4 is correct [12], we can prove the correctness of EMPLiFI, i.e. Eq. 2, by showing they converge to the same values, i.e. Proposition 1.

$$p_n^{t+1} = \frac{\sum_{m=1}^{M} \sum_{j=1}^{J_n^m} P(\mathbf{h}_{\mathbf{n,j}}, \mathbf{b}_{\mathbf{n,j}} | \mathbf{I}_{\mathbf{m}}, \mathcal{T}(\mathbf{p^t}))}{\sum_{m=1}^{M} \sum_{j=1}^{J_n^m} P(\mathbf{b}_{\mathbf{n,j}} | \mathbf{I}_{\mathbf{m}}, \mathcal{T}(\mathbf{p^t}))} \tag{4}$$

**Proposition 1.** *Given a program $\mathcal{T}$, a set of partial interpretations $\mathcal{I}$, and initial parameters $\mathbf{p}^0$. Let $\mathbf{p}^{t,1}$ and $\mathbf{p}^{t,2}$ be the parameter estimates generated by Eqs. 2 and 4, respectively. It is true then $\lim_{t \to \infty} p_n^{t,1} = p_n^{t,2}$*

*Proof.* We prove by induction. When $t = 0$, $\mathbf{p}^{0,1} = \mathbf{p}^{0,2} = \mathbf{p}^0$ holds. Assume that when $t = k$, $\mathbf{p}^{k,1} = \mathbf{p}^{k,2}$ holds. Then, for $t = k+1$, by applying Eq. 2, we obtain $p_n^{k+1,1}$, which we rewrite using $A$ and $B$ to save space.

$$p_n^{k+1,1} = \frac{\sum_{I \in \mathcal{I}_{P_n}} \sum_{j=1}^{J_n^m} P(\mathbf{h}_{\mathbf{n,j}}, \mathbf{b}_{\mathbf{n,j}} | I, \mathcal{T}(\mathbf{p}^{k,1}))}{\sum_{I \in \mathcal{I}_{P_n}} \sum_{j=1}^{J_n^m} P(\mathbf{b}_{\mathbf{n,j}} | I, \mathcal{T}(\mathbf{p}^{k,1}))} = \frac{A}{B} \tag{5}$$

We finish the proof by showing that $p_n^{k+1,2}$ also converges to $\frac{A}{B}$.

$$
\begin{aligned}
p_n^{k+1,2} &= \frac{\sum_{m=1}^{M} \sum_{j=1}^{J_n^m} P(\mathbf{h_{n,j}}, \mathbf{b_{n,j}} | I_m, \mathcal{T}(\mathbf{p}^{k,2}))}{\sum_{m=1}^{M} \sum_{j=1}^{J_n^m} P(\mathbf{b_{n,j}} | I_m, \mathcal{T}(\mathbf{p}^{k,2}))} \quad (\because \text{Equation 4}) \\[4pt]
&= \frac{\sum_{m=1}^{M} \sum_{j=1}^{J_n^m} P(\mathbf{h_{n,j}}, \mathbf{b_{n,j}} | I_m, \mathcal{T}(\mathbf{p}^{k,1}))}{\sum_{m=1}^{M} \sum_{j=1}^{J_n^m} P(\mathbf{b_{n,j}} | I_m, \mathcal{T}(\mathbf{p}^{k,1}))} \quad (\because \mathbf{p}^{k,1} = \mathbf{p}^{k,2}) \\[4pt]
&= \frac{A + \sum_{I \notin \mathcal{I}_{\mathbf{P_n}}} \sum_{j=1}^{J_n^m} P(\mathbf{h_{n,j}}, \mathbf{b_{n,j}} | I, \mathcal{T}(\mathbf{p}^{k,1}))}{B + \sum_{I \notin \mathcal{I}_{\mathbf{P_n}}} \sum_{j=1}^{J_n^m} P(\mathbf{b_{n,j}} | I, \mathcal{T}(\mathbf{p}^{k,1}))} \quad (\because \text{Equation 5}) \\[4pt]
&= \frac{A + \sum_{I \notin \mathcal{I}_{\mathbf{P_n}}} \sum_{j=1}^{J_n^m} P(\mathbf{h_{n,j}}, \mathbf{b_{n,j}} | \mathcal{T}(\mathbf{p}^{k,1}))}{B + \sum_{I \notin \mathcal{I}_{\mathbf{P_n}}} \sum_{j=1}^{J_n^m} P(\mathbf{b_{n,j}} | \mathcal{T}(\mathbf{p}^{k,1}))} \quad (\because \text{Equation 3}) \\[4pt]
&= \frac{A + M_2 \times P(\mathbf{h_n}, \mathbf{b_n} | \mathcal{T}(\mathbf{p}^{k,2}))}{B + M_2 \times P(\mathbf{b_n} | \mathcal{T}(\mathbf{p}^{k,2}))} \quad (\text{Let} M_2 = \sum_{I \notin \mathcal{I}_{\mathbf{P_n}}} J_n^m \text{ and } \because \mathbf{p}^{k,1} = \mathbf{p}^{k,2}) \\[4pt]
&= \frac{A + M_2 \times P(\mathbf{h_n}, \mathbf{b_n} | \mathcal{T}(\mathbf{p}^{k+1,2}))}{B + M_2 \times P(\mathbf{b_n} | \mathcal{T}(\mathbf{p}^{k+1,2}))} \quad (\because \mathbf{p}^{k,2} = \mathbf{p}^{k+1,2})
\end{aligned}
\tag{6}
$$

By definition,

$$
p_n^{k+1,2} = \frac{P(\mathbf{h_n}, \mathbf{b_n} | \mathcal{T}(\mathbf{p}^{k+1,2}))}{P(\mathbf{b_n} | \mathcal{T}(\mathbf{p}^{k+1,2}))}
\tag{7}
$$

By combining Eqs. 6 and 7, we obtain $p_n^{k+1,2} = \frac{A}{B}$.

## 5.2   Convergence Rate

We will prove that EMPLiFI always updates the parameters by a larger margin by considering only relevant interpretations, namely Proposition 2.

**Proposition 2.** *Given a program $\mathcal{T}$, a set of interpretations $\mathcal{I}$, and parameter estimates $\mathbf{p}^t$. Let $\mathbf{p}^{t+1,1}$ and $\mathbf{p}^{t+1,2}$ be the next parameter estimates generated by Eqs. 2 and 4, respectively. It is true that either $p_n^{t+1,1} \leq p_n^{t+1,2} \leq p_n^t$ or $p_n^{t+1,1} \geq p_n^{t+1,2} \geq p_n^t$ holds.*

*Proof.* Following the same reasoning as in Proposition 1, we have

$$
p_n^{t+1,1} = \frac{A}{B} \quad \text{and} \quad p_n^{t+1,2} = \frac{A + M_2 \times P(\mathbf{h_n}, \mathbf{b_n} | \mathcal{T}(\mathbf{p}^t))}{B + M_2 \times P(\mathbf{b_n} | \mathcal{T}(\mathbf{p}^t))}
$$

We also have $P(\mathbf{h_n}, \mathbf{b_n} | \mathcal{T}(\mathbf{p}^t)) = p_n^t \times P(\mathbf{b_n} | \mathcal{T}(\mathbf{p}^t))$ by definition. Hence,

$$
p_n^{t+1,2} = \frac{p_n^{t+1,1} \times B + M_2 \times p_n^t \times P(\mathbf{b_n} | \mathcal{T}(\mathbf{p}^t))}{B + M_2 \times P(\mathbf{b_n} | \mathcal{T}(\mathbf{p}^t))} = \frac{p_n^{t+1,1} \times B + p_n^t \times C}{B + C}
\tag{8}
$$

where $C = M_2 \times P(\mathbf{b_n} | \mathcal{T}(\mathbf{p}^t))$. As $B, C \geq 0$, we have proven Proposition 2.

Equation 8 illustrates that irrelevant interpretations create an inertia, namely $p_n^t \times C$, where $p_n^t$ is the old estimate and $C$ is proportional to the number of irrelevant instances. This inertia not only slows down learning, but also causes numerical instability and results in incorrect values when $C \gg B$ as standard EM terminates before reaching the true probabilities (cf. Example 1).

## 6   Experiments

There are two well-known parameter learning algorithms and implementations for probabilistic logic programming: EMBLEM [1] and LFI-ProbLog [7,9]. We compare EMPLiFI to these two learners to answer the following questions.

**Q1** How much does EMPLiFI speed up EM learning?
**Q2** How well does EMPLiFI handle multi-head ADs?
**Q3** How well does EMPLiFI handle missing data?
**Q4** Does EMPLiFI require more computational resources?

**Programs**

*Emergency Power Supply (EPS)* [18] is propositional, acyclic and contains 24 probabilities[1]. It can be handled by all learner as it has no multi-head ADs.

```
0.95::lowSupply:-a1.                    0.95::highSupply:-a2,a3.
1.0::lowSupply:-highSupply.             0.95::highSupply:-a2,a4.
0.95::failure:-highLoad,\+highSupply.   0.95::highSupply:-a3,a4.
0.95::failure:-lowLoad,\+lowSupply.     0.75::a2:-a3.
0.98::emergency:-\+a3,\+a4.             0.75::a2:-a4.
0.7::l11:-emergency.                    0.85::a1.
0.7::pl1:-emergency.                    0.95::a3.
0.6::highLoad:-l12,l13,pl2,pl3.         0.95::a4.
0.95::lowLoad:-highLoad.                0.8::l12.
0.8::lowLoad:-l11, pl1.                 0.8::pl2.
0.8::lowLoad:-l12, pl2.                 0.8::l13.
0.8::lowLoad:-l13, pl3.                 0.8::pl3.
```

*Smokers* [7] contains 4 probabilities. It has no multi-head ADs but is relational and cyclic. We omit ground facts person/1 and friend/2 to save space.

```
0.2::smokes(X):-person(X).
0.3::smokes(X):-friend(X,Y),smokes(Y),person(X),person(Y),X\=Y.
0.3::cancer(X):-smokes(X),person(X).
0.1::cancer(X):-\+smokes(X),person(X).
```

*Dice* is an AD with 6 heads. The dice has a higher change of throwing a six.

```
0.15::one;0.15::two;0.15::three;0.15::four;0.15::five;0.25::six.
```

---

[1] http://www.machineryspaces.com/emergency-power-supply.html.

*Colors* consists of a single-head AD and two multi-head ADs. To learn this program, one must perform EM, even in the fully observable case because the AD bodies are not mutually exclusive.

```
ball.          0.8::green:-ball.          0.8::large;0.1::medium;0.1::small.
0.3::large; 0.6::medium; 0.1::small:- green.
```

### Experimental Setup and Results

Experiments were run on a 2.4 GHz Intel i5 processor. Learning terminates with $\epsilon = 1e-6$. All interpretations are sampled from the above programs. Partial interpretations are generated by randomly discarding literals in the interpretation, given a missing rate $m \in [0, 1]$. When $m = 0$, interpretations are fully observable. We obtain average measurements by executing all tasks using 5 random seeds. EMPLiFI and LFI-ProbLog programs are compiled as SDDs. Tables 1, 2 and 3 list parameter errors and EM iteration counts. Table 4 lists compilation, evaluation, total times and circuit sizes, which refer to node counts.

**Q1 How Much Does EMPLiFI Speed up EM Learning?** We run all three learners on Smokers and 100 fully observable interpretations. Table 1a shows that EMPLiFI and LFI-ProbLog converge to the same values, but EMPLiFI takes fewer EM iterations. This is consistent with Propositions 1 and 2. EMBLEM is not accurate in Table 1a. Since EMBLEM is not designed to learn all parameters at the same time [1], we split this task into four sub-tasks where each task learns one parameter and all other parameters are set to ground truth values. Results are in Table 1b, where EMBLEM is still the least accurate.

**Table 1.** Smokers. EMPLiFI is the most accurate and takes the fewest EM cycles.

| param | empl | lfip | embl |
|---|---|---|---|
| name | err | err | err |
| smo[.2] | **-.015** | -.015 | -.200 |
| smo[.3] | .046 | .046 | .092 |
| can[.3] | **-.025** | -.025 | -.142 |
| can[.1] | -.055 | -.055 | **-.049** |
| #iters | **19.6** | 51.2 | 108.0 |

(1a) Learning all parameters

| param | empl | | lfip | | embl | |
|---|---|---|---|---|---|---|
| name | err | iters | err | iters | err | iters |
| smo[.2] | **-.007** | **12.4** | -.007 | 12.4 | -.200 | 171.0 |
| smo[.3] | **.039** | **20.0** | .039 | 56.4 | -.083 | 38.0 |
| can[.3] | **-.025** | **3.0** | -.025 | 41.6 | -.178 | 21.0 |
| can[.1] | **-.055** | **3.0** | -.055 | 14.6 | -.100 | 61.0 |

(1b) Learning one parameter

**Q2 How Well Does EMPLiFI Handle Multi-head ADs?** This experiment shows that EMPLiFI is more accurate than EMBLEM and LFI-ProbLog in learning multi-head ADs. We run all three learners on Dice (Table 2) and Colors (Table 3) with 1k sampled interpretations under two settings. The first setting

**Table 2.** Dice. LFI-ProbLog fails when only positive literals are given.

| Param name | Fully observable | | | Only positive | | |
|---|---|---|---|---|---|---|
| | empl | lfip | embl | empl | lfip | embl |
| on[.15] | −.012 | −.012 | −.012 | −.012 | .85 | −.012 |
| tw[.15] | −.017 | −.017 | −.017 | −.017 | .85 | −.017 |
| th[.15] | .010 | .010 | .010 | .010 | .85 | .010 |
| fo[.15] | .000 | .000 | -.000 | .000 | .85 | .000 |
| fi[.15] | −.003 | −.003 | −.003 | −.003 | .85 | −.003 |
| si[.25] | .022 | .022 | .021 | .022 | .75 | .022 |
| #iters | 3.0 | 3.0 | 6.99k | 2.0 | 2.0 | 58.0 |

**Table 3.** Colors. EMPLiFI is the most accurate.

| Param name | Fully observable | | | Only positive | | |
|---|---|---|---|---|---|---|
| | empl | lfip | embl | empl | lfip | embl |
| gr[.8] | −.013 | −.013 | −.048 | .072 | .072 | .200 |
| la[.3] | −.012 | −.078 | −.064 | −.127 | −.148 | −.300 |
| me[.6] | .015 | .017 | −.026 | .100 | .170 | .146 |
| sm[.1] | −.003 | −.005 | .088 | .028 | .210 | .154 |
| la[.8] | −.008 | .002 | −.009 | .046 | .077 | .200 |
| me[.1] | −.008 | −.015 | −.100 | −.045 | −.047 | −.100 |
| sm[.1] | .015 | .012 | −.099 | −.001 | .146 | −.100 |
| #iters | 25.4 | 14.4 | 25.6k | 25.0 | 14.4 | 171.0 |

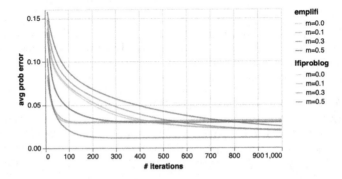

**Fig. 1.** The average error of EPS parameters decreases over EM iterations under all settings. EMPLiFI generally takes fewer iterations to converge compared to LFI-ProbLog.

learns from full interpretations (e.g. {one,¬two, ⋯, ¬six}), and the second setting learns from only positive literals (e.g. {one}). The second setting is fully observable as the truth values of all missing literals can be derived. Table 2 shows that when given all literals, all learners can learn multi-head ADs. However, when given only positive literals, LFI-ProbLog cannot learn. Table 3 shows an example that EMBLEM also fails at learning multi-head ADs.

**Q3 How Well Does EMPLiFI Handle Missing Data?** This experiment shows that EMPLiFI reduces EM iterations in the partially observable setting. We run EMPLiFI and LFI-ProbLog on EPS and 10k interpretations for a series of missingness values in [0, 1]. EMBLEM cannot handle this task with the limit of 3.5 GB memory. Figure 1 shows that EMPLiFI converges much sooner than LFI-ProbLog given either full or partial interpretations.

**Q4 Does EMPLiFI Require More Computational Resources?** We run EMPLiFI and LFI-ProbLog on EPS with 10k interpretations for a series of missingness values. Table 4 shows that EMPLiFI has larger circuits thus longer compilation and evaluation time. This is because EMPLiFI includes information of mutually exclusive AD heads. However, EMPLiFI achieves shorter total execution time compared to LFI-ProbLog as it reduces EM iterations.

**Table 4.** EPS. The total runtime is the sum of compilation and evaluation time.

| missing rate | emplifi | | | | | | lfiproblog | | | | | |
|---|---|---|---|---|---|---|---|---|---|---|---|---|
| | Size | Comp | Eval | Iters | Eval/Iter | Total | Size | Comp | Eval | Iters | Eval/Iter | Total |
| 0.0 | 75.0 | 16.6 | **91.1** | **199.4** | 5.0 | **107.6** | 58.0 | **6.1** | 106.3 | 406.6 | **0.3** | 112.4 |
| 0.1 | 75.9 | 233.6 | **986.2** | **114.0** | 8.7 | **1219.8** | 57.1 | **92.6** | 6865.40 | 1447.6 | **4.7** | 6957.9 |
| 0.3 | 74.9 | 455.1 | **5338.4** | **245.6** | 21.7 | **5793.4** | 53.7 | **165.3** | 15320.8 | 1765.2 | **8.7** | 15486.2 |
| 0.5 | 67.6 | 438.3 | **9133.7** | **418.6** | 21.8 | **9571.9** | 47.0 | **140.8** | 15651.8 | 1920.8 | **8.2** | 15792.6 |
| 0.7 | 50.5 | 265.54 | **6399.1** | **551.8** | 11.6 | **6664.6** | 35.3 | **94.3** | 12029.1 | 2229.8 | **5.4** | 12123.4 |
| 0.9 | 24.5 | 45.4 | **473.4** | **243.6** | 1.9 | **518.8** | 18.2 | **20.1** | 502.7 | 579.4 | **0.9** | 522.8 |

# 7  Related Work

We review EM-based parameter learners. PRISM [10] is one of the first EM learning algorithms, however, it imposes strong restrictions on the allowed programs. LFI-ProbLog [7,9] performs parameter learning of probabilistic logic programs. Before learning AD parameters, it must transform the program, which introduces latent variables that slow down learning. In extreme cases, it can converge to incorrect values. Asteroidea [6,18] tackles this issue by avoiding EM iterations for probabilistic rules, which is a specialization of EMPLiFI that supports single-head ADs, but not multi-head ADs. EMBLEM [1] is another EM-based parameter learner. It can naturally express and learn AD parameters as it is based on the language of Logic Programs with Annotated Disjunctions [17]. Similar to the aforementioned work, EMBLEM uses knowledge compilation techniques. However, it differs in the construction of BDDs as it focuses on learning a single target predicate. When multiple target predicates are present, EMBLEM can converge to incorrect values.

# 8  Conclusion

We have introduced EMPLiFI, an EM-based algorithm for probabilistic logic programs. EMPLiFI supports multi-head ADs and improves efficiency by learning from only relevant interpretations. Theoretically, we have proven that EMPLiFI is correct. Empirically, we have shown that EMPLiFI, compared to LFI-ProbLog and EMBLEM, is more accurate in learning multi-head ADs, and takes fewer iterations to converge. EMPLiFI is available in the ProbLog[2] repository.

---

[2] https://github.com/ML-KULeuven/problog.

**Acknowledgments.** This work was supported by the FNRS-FWO joint programme under EOS No. 30992574. It has also received funding from the Flemish Government under the "Onderzoeksprogramma Artificiële Intelligentie (AI) Vlaanderen" programme, the EU H2020 ICT48 project "TAILOR" under contract #952215, the Wallenberg AI, Autonomous Systems and Software Program (WASP) funded by the Knut and Alice Wallenberg Foundation, and the KU Leuven Research fund.

# References

1. Bellodi, E., Riguzzi, F.: Expectation maximization over binary decision diagrams for probabilistic logic programs. Intell. Data Anal. **17**(2), 343–363 (2013). https://doi.org/10.3233/IDA-130582

2. De Raedt, L., et al.: Towards digesting the alphabet-soup of statistical relational learning. In: Roy, D., Winn, J., McAllester, D., Mansinghka, V., Tenenbaum, J. (eds.) Proceedings of the 1st Workshop on Probabilistic Programming: Universal Languages, Systems and Applications, Whistler, Canada, December 2008

3. De Raedt, L.: Logical and relational learning. In: Zaverucha, G., da Costa, A.L. (eds.) Advances in Artificial Intelligence - SBIA 2008, p. 1. Springer, Heidelberg (2008). https://doi.org/10.1007/978-3-540-68856-3

4. De Raedt, L., Kersting, K.: Probabilistic inductive logic programming. In: De Raedt, L., Frasconi, P., Kersting, K., Muggleton, S. (eds.) Probabilistic Inductive Logic Programming. LNCS (LNAI), vol. 4911, pp. 1–27. Springer, Heidelberg (2008). https://doi.org/10.1007/978-3-540-78652-8_1

5. De Raedt, L., Kimmig, A.: Probabilistic (logic) programming concepts. Mach. Learn. **100**(1), 5–47 (2015). https://doi.org/10.1007/s10994-015-5494-z

6. Faria, F.H.O.V.D., Gusmão, A., Cozman, F.G., Mauá, D.: Speeding-up problog's parameter learning. arXiv:1707.08151 (2017)

7. Fierens, D., et al.: Inference and learning in probabilistic logic programs using weighted Boolean formulas. Theory Pract. Logic Program. **15**(3), 358–401 (2015). https://doi.org/10.1017/S1471068414000076

8. Getoor, L., Taskar, B.: Introduction to Statistical Relational Learning (Adaptive Computation and Machine Learning). MIT Press, Cambridge (2007)

9. Gutmann, B., Thon, I., De Raedt, L.: Learning the parameters of probabilistic logic programs from interpretations. In: Gunopulos, D., Hofmann, T., Malerba, D., Vazirgiannis, M. (eds.) ECML PKDD 2011. LNCS (LNAI), vol. 6911, pp. 581–596. Springer, Heidelberg (2011). https://doi.org/10.1007/978-3-642-23780-5_47

10. Kameya, Y., Sato, T.: Parameter learning of logic programs for symbolic-statistical modeling. arXiv:1106.1797 (2011)

11. Kersting, K., Raedt, L.D.: Bayesian Logic Programming: Theory and Tool. MIT Press, Cambridge (2007)

12. Neapolitan, R.E.: Learning Bayesian Networks. Prentice-Hall Inc., Hoboken (2003)

13. Poole, D.: The independent choice logic for modelling multiple agents under uncertainty. Artif. Intell. **94**(1), 7–56 (1997). https://doi.org/10.1016/S0004-3702(97)00027-1, Economic Principles of Multi-Agent Systems

14. Richardson, M., Domingos, P.: Markov logic networks. Mach. Learn. **62**(1–2), 107–136 (2006). https://doi.org/10.1007/s10994-006-5833-1

15. Sato, T.: A statistical learning method for logic programs with distribution semantics. In: Proceedings of the 12th International Conference on Logic Programming, ICLP 1995, pp. 715–729. MIT Press (1995)

16. Vennekens, J., Denecker, M., Bruynooghe, M.: CP-logic: a language of causal probabilistic events and its relation to logic programming. Theory Pract. Logic Program. **9**(3), 245–308 (2009). https://doi.org/10.1017/S1471068409003767
17. Vennekens, J., Verbaeten, S., Bruynooghe, M.: Logic programs with annotated disjunctions. In: Demoen, B., Lifschitz, V. (eds.) ICLP 2004. LNCS, vol. 3132, pp. 431–445. Springer, Heidelberg (2004). https://doi.org/10.1007/978-3-540-27775-0_30
18. Vieira de Faria, F.H.O., Gusmão, A.C., De Bona, G., Mauá, D.D., Cozman, F.G.: Speeding up parameter and rule learning for acyclic probabilistic logic programs. Int. J. Approx. Reason. **106**, 32–50 (2019). https://doi.org/10.1016/j.ijar.2018.12.012. ISSN 0888613X. Elsevier Inc.

# Semantic-Based Few-Shot Classification by Psychometric Learning

Lu Yin[✉], Vlado Menkovski, Yulong Pei, and Mykola Pechenizkiy

Eindhoven University of Technology, 5600 MB Eindhoven, The Netherlands
{l.yin,V.Menkovski,y.pei.1,m.pechenizkiy}@tue.nl

**Abstract.** Few-shot classification tasks aim to classify images in query sets based on only a few labeled examples in support sets. Most studies usually assume that each image in a task has a single and unique class association. Under these assumptions, these algorithms may not be able to identify the proper class assignment when there is no exact matching between support and query classes. For example, given a few images of lions, bikes, and apples to classify a tiger. However, in a more general setting, we could consider the higher-level concept, the large carnivores, to match the tiger to the lion for semantic classification. Existing studies rarely considered this situation due to the incompatibility of label-based supervision with complex conception relationships. In this work, we advance the few-shot learning towards this more challenging scenario, the semantic-based few-shot learning, and propose a method to address the paradigm by capturing the inner semantic relationships using psychometric learning. The experiment results on the CIFAR-100 dataset show the superiority of our method for the semantic-based few-shot learning compared to the baseline.

**Keywords:** Psychometric testing · Self-supervised learning · Few-shot learning

## 1 Introduction

With enormous amounts of labeled data, deep learning methods have achieved impressive breakthroughs in various tasks. However, the need for large quantities of labeled samples is still a bottleneck in many real-world problems. For this reason, few-shot learning [18,33] is proposed to emulate this by learning the transferable knowledge from the "base" dataset where ample labeled samples are available to generalize to another "novel" dataset which has very few labeled training examples. A popular approach for this problem is meta-learning based phase [7,28] which follows the episodic training procedure to mimic the few-shot tasks. In each few-shot task, a few labeled examples (the support set) are given to predict classes for the unlabeled samples (the query set).

While these formulations have made significant progress, the underlying assumption is that each data point from the support set and query set has a

© The Author(s), under exclusive license to Springer Nature Switzerland AG 2022
T. Bouadi et al. (Eds.): IDA 2022, LNCS 13205, pp. 392–403, 2022.
https://doi.org/10.1007/978-3-031-01333-1_31

single and uniquely identified class association, and the query image must precisely match one of the support set classes. However, as illustrated in the last two rows in Fig. 1, the few-shot learning models that are capable of dealing with classification based on the predefined classes may not be able to identify the right class assignment when there is no exact class matching.

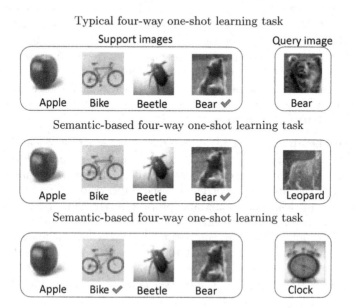

**Fig. 1.** Different settings of few-shot learning tasks. The first row follows a typical four-way one-shot learning setting. The class of the query image matches one of the support set labels. In the second task, the typical few-shot learning model might fail to identify the query image when there is no exact class matching. However, if we could consider the higher-level semantic concept of the carnivores, a correct assignment could still be made by matching bear to leopard. A similar prediction could also be made if we consider the concept of non-living things in the last task.

In a more general setting, if considering the concept at a higher level, e.g., whether they are large carnivores or living things in Fig. 1, one could determine the right class association. Humans are very capable of inferring these concepts on a higher level, while typical few-shot learning algorithms are not specifically designed for this under single discriminating class descriptions. They treat each class equally without considering their intra hierarchical semantic relationships. One possible reason for this limitation might be the supervision approach: the traditional label-based supervision is incompatible with the complex conception hierarchy. Fortunately, much progress has been made in learning from other types of supervision, such as psychometric testing [9]. While label-based supervision reduces the comprehensive semantic relationships to given discrete labels, these psychometric testing based methods could elicit the relative conception similarities and full-depth of knowledge by transmitting the annotations progress to pair or triplet comparisons. Then the elicited knowledge could be used for other downstream tasks such as clustering or segmentation [35,36]. Enabled with such techniques, our work aims to extend the capabilities of few-shot learning models towards a more challenging setting, the semantic-based few-shot learning.

To be specific, we assume there is a shared concept hierarchy covering both base and novel classes. Self-supervised learning (SSL) is applied for feature learning at the first stage. Psychometric testing is then followed to capture the similarities of the semantic concepts from base dataset. We use these semantic similarities to fine-tune the learned features from SSL, and map them to a semantic embedding space where we transfer the learned hierarchical knowledge from base classes to novel classes for semantic few-shot prediction.

Our contributions could be summarized as follows.

* We define a new problem setting, the semantic-based few-shot learning. It aims to identify the correct assignment to query image by higher-level concepts when there is no class matching between query and support images.
* We analyze the limitations of label-based supervision under the semantic-based few-shot learning setting and propose a psychometric learning based approach to tackle this problem.
* We evaluate our method by comparing it with a typical few-shot baseline (prototype network [28]) on CIFAR-100 dataset [17]. The results demonstrate that our method could significantly outperform this baseline in semantic-based few-shot learning even using fewer annotations from base data.

## 2   Related Work

There are three lines of research closely related to our work: psychometric testing, few-shot learning, and self-supervised learning.

**Psychometric Testing.** Psychometric testing [9] aims to study the perceptual processes under measurable psychical stimuli such as tones with different intensity or lights with various brightness. In general, two types of psychometric experiments could be carried. Firstly, the absolute threshold based method tries to detect the point of stimulus intensity that could be noticed by a participant. For example, how many hairs are touched to the back of hand before a participant could notice. Secondly, the discriminative based experiments aim to find the slightest difference between two stimuli that a participant could perceive. Participants might be asked to describe the difference in direction or magnitude between these two stimuli or forced to choose between the stimuli concerning a specific parameter of interest (also known as two-alternative-force choice (2AFC) test [5]). Some scholars extend the 2AFC to M-AFC methods [4] by comparing $M$ stimuli in one test to elicit the subjects' perception of more complex multimedia such as videos or images [6,29,35,36]. In our work, we take advantage of the 3-AFC method to align with our loss function. Three samples are presented in one test to elicit the annotator's perception regarding the conception similarity.

**Few-Shot Learning.** Meta-learning (learning to learn) has gained increasing attention in the machine learning community, and one of its well-known applications is few-shot learning. Three main approaches have emerged to solve this problem. Metric learning based methods aim to learn a shared metric in feature space for few-shot prediction, such as prototypical network [28], relation networks [30] and matching networks [33]. Optimization based methods follow the idea of modifying the gradient-based optimization to adapt to novel tasks [7,10,23]. Memory based approaches [7,12,21,27] adopt extra memory components for novel concepts learning, and new samples could be compared to historical information in the memories.

While these frameworks lead to significant progress, little attention has been paid to leveraging the knowledge hierarchy and dealing with the situation when there is no precise label matching between query images and support images, i.e., the semantic-based few-shot learning scenario.

**Self-supervised Learning.** When human supervision is expensive to obtain, self-supervised learning could be a general framework to learn features without human annotations by solving pretext tasks. Various pretexts have been studied for learning useful image representation. For example, predicting missing parts of the input image [19,26,31,37,38], the image angle under rotation transformation [11], the patch location, or the number of objects [24]. Recently, another line of researches follows the paradigm of contrastive learning [1,3,13,15,16,22,25,34] and get the state of the art performance. The learned image features could be utilized for downstream tasks such as image retrieval or fine-tuning for classification. In our work, we take advantage of the SimCLR [3] framework and fine-tune the learned features with psychometric testing for semantic image representations.

## 3    Semantic-Based Few-Shot Learning

Our proposed framework contains three parts. First, as we aim to tackle the limitation caused by label-based supervision, we assume no label information is provided in advance. Self-supervised learning (SSL) is applied for representation learning in the first stage. Next, we adopt a psychometric testing procedure [9] that relies on discriminative testing to obtain transferable semantic conception relationships. The elicited conception similarities are then used to fine-tune the features learned by SSL using a multi-layer perceptron (MLP) [8] in a semantic representation network. In the last stage, with the fine-tuned network, we could search for each query's most semantically similar image in support set by Euclidean distances, even when the target and query images are not sharing the same class. We illustrate our whole framework in Fig. 2.

### 3.1    Problem Formulation

Consider the situation we are given a base dataset contains classes $C_{base}$ with adequate labeled images, and a novel dataset contains classes $C_{novel}$ where only

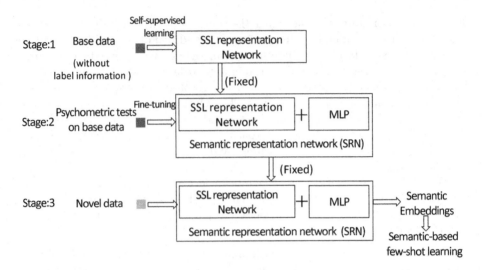

**Fig. 2.** Overview of the proposed method.

a few labeled samples are available per class. There is no overlapping with these two datasets, i.e., $C_{base} \cap C_{novel} = \emptyset$. The general idea of the few-shot problem is taking advantage of the sufficient labeled samples in $C_{base}$ to obtain a good classifier for the novel class $C_{novel}$. In a standard $N$-way $K$-shot classification task, we random sample $N$ classes from novel class $C_{novel}$ with $K$ samples per class to form the support set, and sample query images from the same $N$ classes to create the query set. We aim to classify the query images into these $N$ classes based on the support set.

Then we extend the problem to the semantic-based few-shot learning scenario. Assume we have a conception tree $G = (V, E)$ where $V$ means the nodes and $E$ are edges. The bottom layer class $C = c_1, ..., c_n \in V$ denotes the lowest level of concepts that we concern, and could merge to more general concepts (superclass nodes) if they are conceptually similar. An example for such a structure is given in Fig. 3. The base class $C_{base}$ and novel class $C_{novel}$ are represented as the leaf nodes and share the same superclasses nodes. As we aim to solve this problem without label-based supervision, we are not able to specify a few-shot task using the label information as the typical few-shot learning setting, i.e., sampling multiple images with the same labels to create a class in support set. Therefore, we random sample $N$ image without specifying their classes from the $C_{novel}$ to build the support set and sample one image as a query to form a **N-way 1-shot** semantic-based few-shot learning task. Our goal is to find the most semantically similar image from support set to a query.

The semantic distance between two samples $(x, y)$ is defined by the height of the lowest common subsumer (LCS) of these samples divided by the height of the hierarchy [2,32]:

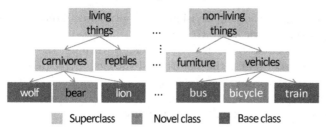

**Fig. 3.** CIFAR-100 with knowledge hierarchy.

$$D_s(x, y) = \frac{height(lcs(x, y))}{max_{w \in V} height(w)} \tag{1}$$

As $D_s(x, y)$ ranges from 0 to 1, we could define the semantic similarity by:

$$S_s(x, y) = 1 - D_s(x, y) \tag{2}$$

An example could be seen in Fig. 3. The LCS of $wolf$ and $lion$ are $carnivores$, and the height of the hierarchical tree is 3. Therefore $D_s(wolf, lion) = \frac{1}{3}$, and $S_s(wolf, lion) = \frac{2}{3}$. Note that the typical few-shot learning is a special case when $S_s(x, y) = 1$, in which $x$ is the query image, $y$ is from support set, and $x, y$ belong to a same leaf node.

### 3.2   Self-supervised Feature Learning

We use self-supervised learning to learn the image features from $C_{base}$ before using psychometric testing for fine-tuning. SimCLR [3] framework is applied in our work for its conciseness and good performance. It learns representation by maximizing the similarity between two views (augmentations) of the same image.

From $C_{base}$, we randomly sample $N$ images each batch and create two random augmentation views for each image to form $2N$ data points. Each data pair generated from the same image is considered a positive pair, or a negative pair if it's from different images. The contrastive loss function for a mini-batch could be written as:

$$L_{self} = -\sum_{i=1}^{2N} log \frac{exp(sim(z_i, z_{j(i)}/\tau))}{\sum_{a \in A(i)} exp(sim(z_i, z_a)/\tau)} \tag{3}$$

where $z_i = g(f(x_i))$, $f(\cdot)$ a neural network called encoder to extract features from augmented images, $g(\cdot)$ is the projection head that maps features to a space where contrastive loss is applied. Cosine similarity $sim(u, v)$ is adopted to measure the similarity of $u$ and $v$ by the dot product between their $L_2$ normalized features. $\tau$ denotes a scalar temperature parameter. $i$ is the index or all the $2N$ augmented views of images. $j(i)$ is the index of positive view to image $i$ and $A(i)$ is the set of all indices except $i$.

### 3.3    Psychometric Testing

Different from label-based supervision, we apply three-alternative-force choice (3AFC) [4] psychometric tests to elicit the semantic perceptions from $C_{base}$. These perceptions could be transferred to $C_{novel}$ through the shared high-level conceptions (superclasses) in the hierarchical knowledge tree (as shown in Fig. 3).

To be specific, we sample three images from $C_{base}$ and ask the annotators to choose the most dissimilar one (see Fig. 4). By carrying this simple task, perceptions of conception similarities are obtained.

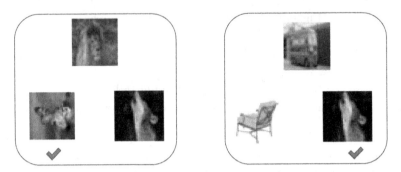

Which Image is the most dissimilar to the other two?

**Fig. 4.** Examples of two 3AFC psychometric testings. In the first test, annotators tend to choose the butterfly as the most dissimilar one since other two are large carnivores. In the second test, annotators are more likely to choose the wolf because it is the only living things.

Next, a semantic representation network (SRN) is built to map these perceived conception similarities to embedding distances. Specifically, we add a multi-layer perceptron (MLP) with a single hidden layer on top of the representations learned from SSL, freeze the SSL network, and fine-tune the MLP by the following dual-triplet loss function [35,36] :

$$L = \sum_{i=1}^{N} \left[ d(x_{p1}^i, x_{p2}^i) - d(x_n^i, x_{p1}^i), +m \right]_+ \tag{4}$$
$$+ \left[ d(x_{p1}^i, x_{p2}^i) - d(x_n^i, x_{p2}^i), +m \right]_+$$

where $x_n$ is the negative image chosen by annotator, $x_{p1}, x_{p2}$ are two unpicked positive images that have closer concept similarity at the 3AFC tests (see Fig. 4). $d(x, y)$ denotes the these two points' Euclidean distance between the normalized features extracted by our semantic representation network. $N$ is the number of psychometric tests in a mini-batch.

This loss function encourages images that the annotator perceives similar to be close to each other and enforces a distance margin $m$ between positive pairs and negative pairs.

### 3.4   Semantic-Based Few-Shot Prediction

After fine-tuning our proposed network with 3-AFC tests from $C_{base}$, we could extract visual features for image samples from $C_{novel}$ using this network and apply the nearest neighbor search method for semantic-based few-shot learning prediction. Specifically, for a query image in a task, we compute its normalized Euclidean distance to each support sample and find the nearest one, which is the predicted most semantically similar image to the query when considering a higher-level concept.

## 4   Experiments and Discussion

Since the label-based supervision is a bottleneck that limits the models' potential in the semantic-based few-shot learning setting, we assume no label information and no conception structure are preprovided for both $C_{base}$ and $C_{novel}$. However, we are then not able to assess whether the semantic assignment to query is correct using the defined semantic similarity metric (see Eq. 2). Therefore, we simulate a virtual annotator who always precisely responds to the 3AFC tests based on a given knowledge hierarchy, so that the accuracy could be measured in an objective manner by this semantic similarity.

We evaluate our model on CIFAR-100 dataset under three metrics: the typical few-shot learning accuracy, the semantic-based few-shot learning accuracy, and the required annotation numbers. Then we investigate how the number of psychometric test responses impacts the model's performance. Besides, a TSNE visualization [20] of the learned features is plotted for an intuitive understanding.

**Dataset.** We use the CIFAR-100 in our experiment and build an inner conception hierarchy tree based on the preprovided coarse and finer labels. Besides, we build another layer on top of the coarse level labels by distinguishing living from non-living things. A three-layer conception tree is then created, which includes 2, 10, 100 nodes from top to bottom layers, as illustrated in Fig. 3. 60 classes are randomly sampled from the bottom layer as base classes, and the rest 40 classes are used for novel classes.

**Few-Shot Learning Accuracy.** Note when there is a label matching between the query image and support images, i.e., the semantic similarity is equal to 1, the semantic-based few-shot learning problem is then transmitted to a typical few-shot learning problem. We choose the prototypical network [28] as a baseline and compared it with our proposed method in both typical few-shot learning accuracy and semantic-based few-shot learning accuracy.

In our work, we use the SGD optimizer with momentum 0.9, and set the decay factor to 0.1. When extracting image features in SSL, ResNet50 [14] is applied as backbone and are trained for 1000 epochs with 128 batch-size. The learning rate decays from 0.5 at epoch 700, 800 and 900. When fine-tuning by psychometric responses, margin value, learning rate, training epochs are set to 0.4, 0.001, 15 respectively. During prototypical network training, we use the same backbone of SSL for a fair comparison, train the model 100 epochs with 10000 tasks each epoch, and set the learning rate to 0.1 that decays every 20 epochs.

The results are reported in Table 1. It could be seen without losing too much accuracy of typical one-shot learning (decreasing by 4.95% in 5-way, and 2.43% in 20-way). We could boost the ability of semantic-based one-shot learning significantly (increasing by 9.98% in 5-way, and 7.35% in 20-way). Furthermore, the annotation burdens on base data are dramatically released from 36000 times label-based annotations to 1000 times psychometric testings.

Table 1. Comparison with the baseline.

| Model | Annotation type | Number of annotations ($C_{base}$) | 5-way 1-shot Acc (%) | | 20-way 1-shot Acc (%) | |
|---|---|---|---|---|---|---|
| | | | Typical | Semantic | Typical | Semantic |
| PN [28] | Label based | 36000 | **57.52** | 42.37 | **31.18** | 19.81 |
| SRN (Ours) | Psychometric testing | **1000** | 52.57 | **52.35** | 28.75 | **27.16** |

**Impact of the Number of Psychometric Test Responses.** We train our model using 500 psychometric tests in the first iteration and add 500 more tests to retrain the model in each of the following iterations. The model is evaluated under the 5-way 1-shot scenario and we plot the results in Fig. 5. It could be noticed that the accuracy of typical few-shot learning remains steady with different numbers of psychometric tests. That is because our psychometric tests only aim to provide semantic constrain rather than learning discriminative features. We also find that the ability of semantic few-shot learning gets a noticeable improvement when increasing training samples from 500 to 1000 tests but keeps stuck after that. The possible reason might be that with the help of pre-trained SSL features, we could easily get a high accuracy using only a few psychometric tests. However, as we only fine-tune on MLP without training the whole network, the semantic few-shot accuracy would quickly reach a bottleneck even with more psychometric responses.

**TSNE Visualization.** We visualize the embedding features of five categories randomly chosen from $C_{novel}$ (See Fig. 6). It could be seen that with our proposed method, categories that are similar in concepts tend to be closer to each other. For example, all the non-living things (mountain, forest, streetcar) are located in the top area while living things (bee, tiger) are placed bottom. Mountain and forest are the nearest two clusters since they are "all outdoor scenes" and their semantic distance is the closest among the five categories. On the other hand, the prototypical network could successfully separate the five categories apart from each other, but they are located randomly in the graph without considering the semantic relationships.

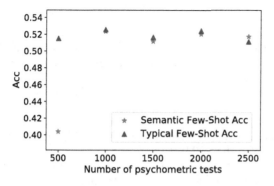

**Fig. 5.** 5-way 1-shot learning accuracy under different number of psychometric tests.

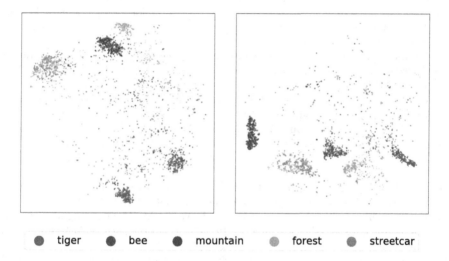

●　tiger　　●　bee　　●　mountain　　●　forest　　●　streetcar

**Fig. 6.** Embedding visualization after TSNE with our proposed method (left), and prototypical network (right).

## 5    Conclusion

Few-shot learning is typically under label-based supervision, which discards the semantic relationships and fails to make a class association when there is no label matching between support and query set. However, humans could easily identify the right association by considering a higher-level concept. Inspired by this, we present a psychometric testing based method that could capture images' high-level conception relationships to address the challenge. We evaluate our method on CIFAR-100 dataset. The results indicate that our method is capable of achieving higher semantic-based few-shot learning accuracy even with fewer annotating burdens than the baseline.

# References

1. Bachman, P., Hjelm, R.D., Buchwalter, W.: Learning representations by maximizing mutual information across views. arXiv preprint arXiv:1906.00910 (2019)
2. Barz, B., Denzler, J.: Hierarchy-based image embeddings for semantic image retrieval. In: 2019 IEEE Winter Conference on Applications of Computer Vision (WACV), pp. 638–647. IEEE (2019)
3. Chen, T., Kornblith, S., Norouzi, M., Hinton, G.: A simple framework for contrastive learning of visual representations. In: International Conference on Machine Learning, pp. 1597–1607. PMLR (2020)
4. DeCarlo, L.T.: On a signal detection approach to m-alternative forced choice with bias, with maximum likelihood and Bayesian approaches to estimation. J. Math. Psychol. **56**(3), 196–207 (2012)
5. Fechner, G.T.: Elemente der psychophysik, vol. 2. Breitkopf u, Härtel (1860)
6. Feng, H.C., Marcellin, M.W., Bilgin, A.: A methodology for visually lossless JPEG2000 compression of monochrome stereo images. IEEE Trans. Image Process. **24**(2), 560–572 (2014)
7. Finn, C., Abbeel, P., Levine, S.: Model-agnostic meta-learning for fast adaptation of deep networks. In: International Conference on Machine Learning, pp. 1126–1135. PMLR (2017)
8. Friedman, J.H.: The Elements of Statistical Learning: Data Mining, Inference, and Prediction. Springer, Heidelberg (2017)
9. Gescheider, G.A.: Psychophysics: The Fundamentals. Psychology Press (2013)
10. Gidaris, S., Komodakis, N.: Dynamic few-shot visual learning without forgetting. In: Proceedings of the IEEE Conference on Computer Vision and Pattern Recognition, pp. 4367–4375 (2018)
11. Gidaris, S., Singh, P., Komodakis, N.: Unsupervised representation learning by predicting image rotations. arXiv preprint arXiv:1803.07728 (2018)
12. He, J., Hong, R., Liu, X., Xu, M., Zha, Z.J., Wang, M.: Memory-augmented relation network for few-shot learning. In: Proceedings of the 28th ACM International Conference on Multimedia, pp. 1236–1244 (2020)
13. He, K., Fan, H., Wu, Y., Xie, S., Girshick, R.: Momentum contrast for unsupervised visual representation learning. In: Proceedings of the IEEE/CVF Conference on Computer Vision and Pattern Recognition, pp. 9729–9738 (2020)
14. He, K., Zhang, X., Ren, S., Sun, J.: Deep residual learning for image recognition. In: Proceedings of the IEEE Conference on Computer Vision and Pattern Recognition, pp. 770–778 (2016)
15. Henaff, O.: Data-efficient image recognition with contrastive predictive coding. In: International Conference on Machine Learning, pp. 4182–4192. PMLR (2020)
16. Hjelm, R.D., et al.: Learning deep representations by mutual information estimation and maximization. arXiv preprint arXiv:1808.06670 (2018)
17. Krizhevsky, A., Hinton, G., et al.: Learning multiple layers of features from tiny images (2009)
18. Lake, B., Salakhutdinov, R., Gross, J., Tenenbaum, J.: One shot learning of simple visual concepts. In: Proceedings of the Annual Meeting of the Cognitive Science Society, vol. 33 (2011)
19. Larsson, G., Maire, M., Shakhnarovich, G.: Learning representations for automatic colorization. In: Leibe, B., Matas, J., Sebe, N., Welling, M. (eds.) ECCV 2016. LNCS, vol. 9908, pp. 577–593. Springer, Cham (2016). https://doi.org/10.1007/978-3-319-46493-0_35

20. Van der Maaten, L., Hinton, G.: Visualizing data using t-SNE. J. Mach. Learn. Res. 9(11) (2008)
21. Mishra, N., Rohaninejad, M., Chen, X., Abbeel, P.: A simple neural attentive meta-learner. arXiv preprint arXiv:1707.03141 (2017)
22. Misra, I., Maaten, L.V.D.: Self-supervised learning of pretext-invariant representations. In: Proceedings of the IEEE/CVF Conference on Computer Vision and Pattern Recognition, pp. 6707–6717 (2020)
23. Nichol, A., Schulman, J.: Reptile: a scalable metalearning algorithm. arXiv preprint arXiv:1803.02999 **2**(3), 4 (2018)
24. Noroozi, M., Pirsiavash, H., Favaro, P.: Representation learning by learning to count. In: Proceedings of the IEEE International Conference on Computer Vision, pp. 5898–5906 (2017)
25. Oord, A.v.d., Li, Y., Vinyals, O.: Representation learning with contrastive predictive coding. arXiv preprint arXiv:1807.03748 (2018)
26. Pathak, D., Krahenbuhl, P., Donahue, J., Darrell, T., Efros, A.A.: Context encoders: feature learning by inpainting. In: Proceedings of the IEEE Conference on Computer Vision and Pattern Recognition, pp. 2536–2544 (2016)
27. Santoro, A., Bartunov, S., Botvinick, M., Wierstra, D., Lillicrap, T.: Meta-learning with memory-augmented neural networks. In: International Conference on Machine Learning, pp. 1842–1850. PMLR (2016)
28. Snell, J., Swersky, K., Zemel, R.S.: Prototypical networks for few-shot learning. arXiv preprint arXiv:1703.05175 (2017)
29. Son, I., Winslow, M., Yazici, B., Xu, X.: X-ray imaging optimization using virtual phantoms and computerized observer modelling. Phys. Med. Biol. **51**(17), 4289 (2006)
30. Sung, F., Yang, Y., Zhang, L., Xiang, T., Torr, P.H., Hospedales, T.M.: Learning to compare: relation network for few-shot learning. In: Proceedings of the IEEE Conference on Computer Vision and Pattern Recognition, pp. 1199–1208 (2018)
31. Trinh, T.H., Luong, M.T., Le, Q.V.: Selfie: self-supervised pretraining for image embedding. arXiv preprint arXiv:1906.02940 (2019)
32. Verma, N., Mahajan, D., Sellamanickam, S., Nair, V.: Learning hierarchical similarity metrics. In: 2012 IEEE Conference on Computer Vision and Pattern Recognition, pp. 2280–2287. IEEE (2012)
33. Vinyals, O., Blundell, C., Lillicrap, T., Wierstra, D., et al.: Matching networks for one shot learning. Adv. Neural. Inf. Process. Syst. **29**, 3630–3638 (2016)
34. Wu, Z., Xiong, Y., Yu, S.X., Lin, D.: Unsupervised feature learning via nonparametric instance discrimination. In: Proceedings of the IEEE Conference on Computer Vision and Pattern Recognition, pp. 3733–3742 (2018)
35. Yin, L., Menkovski, V., Liu, S., Pechenizkiy, M.: Hierarchical semantic segmentation using psychometric learning. arXiv preprint arXiv:2107.03212 (2021)
36. Yin, L., Menkovski, V., Pechenizkiy, M.: Knowledge elicitation using deep metric learning and psychometric testing. arXiv preprint arXiv:2004.06353 (2020)
37. Zhang, R., Isola, P., Efros, A.A.: Colorful image colorization. In: Leibe, B., Matas, J., Sebe, N., Welling, M. (eds.) ECCV 2016. LNCS, vol. 9907, pp. 649–666. Springer, Cham (2016). https://doi.org/10.1007/978-3-319-46487-9_40
38. Zhang, R., Isola, P., Efros, A.A.: Split-brain autoencoders: unsupervised learning by cross-channel prediction. In: Proceedings of the IEEE Conference on Computer Vision and Pattern Recognition, pp. 1058–1067 (2017)

# Author Index

Printed in the United States
by Baker & Taylor Publisher Services